THE GREATER PHILADELPHIA REGION

A NEW HISTORY FOR THE TWENTY-FIRST CENTURY

VOLUME 1

THE GREATER PHILADELPHIA REGION

Edited by

Howard Gillette, Jr. and Carolyn T. Adams

PENN

University of Pennsylvania Press

Philadelphia

The University of Pennsylvania Press gratefully acknowledges funding support for the print version of *The Encyclopedia of Greater Philadelphia* from the Philadelphia Funder Collaborative for the Semiquincentennial, a philanthropic partnership of the Connelly Foundation, the William Penn Foundation, the Neubauer Family Foundation, the Pew Charitable Trusts, the Hamilton Family Charitable Trust, and Comcast; and from the members of the External Board of Advisors of the University of Pennsylvania Press.

Published by
University of Pennsylvania Press
Philadelphia, Pennsylvania 19104-4112, USA

www.pennpress.org

EU Authorized Representative: Easy Access System Europe
Mustamäe tee 50, 10621 Tallinn, Estonia, gpsr.requests@easproject.com

Printed in the United States of America on acid-free paper

10 9 8 7 6 5 4 3 2 1

Hardcover ISBN: 978-1-5128-2604-3

A catalogue record for this book is available from the Library of Congress.

Cover and Book Design by Shubhani Sarkar, sarkardesignstudio.com

Front cover—*Top: Philly Rising* virtual mural. Design © 2020 Nilé Livingston. Commissioned by the City of Philadelphia Mural Arts Program. All rights reserved. Reprinted by permission. *Bottom:* Charles Wellford Leavitt's design for a grand approach to the new Delaware River Bridge to Philadelphia, *Camden First*, 1924, Camden County Historical Society.

Back cover—*Top:* Undated aerial view of early construction at the King of Prussia Mall. Special Collections Research Center, Temple University Libraries. *Middle:* Two children in Southwest Philadelphia's Eastwick section, 1976, Special Collections Research Center, Temple University Libraries. *Bottom: Manayunk*, by Augustus Kollner, 1879, Free Library of Philadelphia.

PUBLISHED IN ASSOCIATION WITH
The Encyclopedia of Greater Philadelphia

EDITOR-IN-CHIEF
Charlene Mires

Mid-Atlantic Regional Center for the Humanities
(MARCH)
at Rutgers University—Camden

The Greater Philadelphia Region
EDITED BY
Howard Gillette, Jr. AND Carolyn Adams

Greater Philadelphia and the Nation
EDITED BY
Charlene Mires AND Jean R. Soderlund

Greater Philadelphia and the World
EDITED BY
Andrew Heath

R I V E R
STREET
SOMERSETT
STREET
LEHIGH
HUNTINGTON
COLUMBIA
READING
RAIL ROAD
AVENUE
STREET
STREET
STREET
STREET
ROAD
STREET
ROAD

Contents

CHAPTER 6

NETWORKS

TRAILS, CANALS, RAILS, AND ROADS

CHAPTER 7

CORE AND PERIPHERY

Chapter 8

COUNTIES

Chapter 9

REGIONAL GOVERNANCE AND STEWARDSHIP

Preface

We all exist in place and time. Place may seem easy enough to visualize, starting with the room where you are reading this book, your home, street, and neighborhood. Beyond that immediate view, though, you might need a map to see your town, county, or the route you travel to and from work—and a more extensive map or even a satellite view to find your place within a wider region, the nation, and the world. While existing in those many dimensions, you also inhabit a place in time, marked by a date within the narrative of your personal experience. But this, too, extends and entwines with multiple layers of time, from family lineage and cultural heritage to flows of social, political, and economic history. Compounding matters, none of us stands still. We constantly move in place and time, interacting with multiple communities as visible as a stadium filled with fans or as virtual as a network of users in a data stream.

How are we to fathom this complex web of existence and history, to see not only ourselves but our neighbors and common interests? How can we know what has gone before and prepare for what may come next? How can we sort through and assess the avalanche of information produced moment by moment in a digital age? These are some of the needs that the editors seek to address with this book, one of a set of three published simultaneously by the University of Pennsylvania Press: *The Greater Philadelphia Region*; *Greater Philadelphia and the Nation*; and *Greater Philadelphia and the World*. This book and its companions derive from more than a decade of collaboration among hundreds of writers, editors, research assistants, and civic partners who took up the challenge of advancing knowledge of Philadelphia and the surrounding region. Their findings first appeared digitally, one topic at a time, in *The Encyclopedia of Greater Philadelphia*. However, these books are not a print replica of the *Encyclopedia*, which at the time of the books' publication exists online at https://philadelphiaencyclopedia.org/ as a project of the Mid-Atlantic Regional Center for the Humanities (MARCH) at Rutgers University—Camden. The books are, instead, curated and updated collections of selected topics. They are arranged thematically, highlighting connections that may not become apparent from casual Internet searching, and framed with new essays that illuminate the rich patterns of the region's experience. The goal is to draw insights from the encyclopedia's many parts, to create a different reading experience and deeper understanding of the region's reach and history.

By happy coincidence, the digital *Encyclopedia of Greater Philadelphia* grew at a pace that enabled publication of these thematic books for 2026, the nation's 250th anniversary. It is a fitting time to reflect on Philadelphia's impact and reach across the region, the nation, and the world. Drawing upon recent generations of scholarship, and often advancing new knowledge, these books convey to the general reading public an up-to-date, diverse history of Philadelphia in its many dimensions. They are milestones that offer starting points for the next generations who take up the challenge of understanding this dynamic region, whether they are pursuing personal knowledge, insights for news reporting or tourism, local information for teaching, foundations for new research, or background for developing public policy.

Philadelphians have not often paused to assess the deep history of their city and the surrounding region. The first attempt came in the 1820s, while memories of the colonial and revolutionary eras remained. To preserve those memories, John Fanning Watson, a banker, collected oral histories for his *Annals of Philadelphia*, published in multiple editions beginning in 1830. Decades passed before the three-volume *History of Philadelphia, 1690–1884* appeared as one of many such massive histories published in the years following the nation's centennial. Its lead author, J. Thomas Scharf, a Baltimore-based author of similar histories of his home city and St. Louis, teamed with Philadelphia journalist Thompson Westcott to produce the work. A generation later, in 1912, the prolific biographer and history writer Ellis Paxson Oberholtzer published *Philadelphia: A History of the City and Its People, a Record of 225 Years*. Journalist Joseph Jackson compiled a four-volume *Encyclopedia of Greater Philadelphia* during the 1930s, but the next deep dive into the city's history did not come until the multiple-authored *Philadelphia: A 300-Year History*, which finally appeared in 1982 after many years of effort, shepherded to conclusion by historian Russell F. Weigley.

In contrast to these earlier works, this book and its companions encompass not only the city but also a "Greater Philadelphia" extending across eastern Pennsylvania, southern New Jersey, and northern Delaware. "Greater Philadelphia" is a phrase with resonance for Philadelphia dating at least to the 1890s, an era of growth, annexation, and aspiration for cities in the United States. Philadelphia accomplished its greatest leap of annexation earlier, in 1854, when the city's limits extended to the boundaries of Philadelphia County. But in the last decade of the nineteenth century, as electric streetcars brought outlying towns into urban orbits, Philadelphia joined other cities in imagining a "greater" region of cities and suburbs. The phrase "Greater Philadelphia" (or uncapitalized "greater Philadelphia") became common during the period bookended by Chicago's 1889 vote to annex 126 square miles, which allowed it to surpass Philadelphia in population, and the consolidation of the five boroughs into "The City of Greater New York" in 1898. During the 1890s, the reach of the streetcar lines also inspired boosters of "Greater Camden" and "Greater Wilmington" to imagine orbits of influence centered on their cities and converging with more populous Philadelphia. As the Wilmington *Evening Journal* editorialized in 1895, "In a few years the great metropoli of Pennsylvania and Delaware will be connected by a chain of residences, and then may come a greater Philadelphia."

More than a geographic term, "Greater Philadelphia" at the turn of the twentieth century signaled superiority and aspiration. Philadelphia politicians invoked the phrase as early as 1894, when Samuel H. Ashbridge campaigned for mayor on the platform "A Greater Philadelphia." By this he meant that an already "great" city could be made greater through improvements such as better port facilities on the Delaware River. Subsequent mayoral candidates, both Democrats and Republicans, championed Greater Philadelphia as a shorthand for their commitment to progress. By the time John E. Reyburn served as mayor, between 1907 and 1911, the Greater Philadelphia envisioned by his comprehensive planning committees included projects such as the diagonal parkway between City Hall and Fairmount Park, a convention hall, and modern subways.

Philadelphia businesses also adopted and propelled "Greater Philadelphia" into common usage. In the wake of the economic panic of 1893, for example, the Wanamaker & Brown and William H. Wanamaker stores celebrated their survival in business with ads published in three states, proclaiming "Greater Philadelphia recognized our courage and sound judgment by flocking into our stores." Newspaper ads for the larger Wanamaker's department store regularly described its scope of business as "Greater Philadelphia," and Gimbel Brothers ran "Greater Philadelphia Sales." Reaching out to the wider region, the J. B. Van Sciver Co. of Camden proclaimed itself "The Furniture Center of Greater Philadelphia." During the First World War, shipbuilding on the Delaware River helped to define a "Greater Philadelphia" industrial region uniting the three states of Pennsylvania, New Jersey, and Delaware.

By the 1920s, organizations and businesses ranging from sports clubs to real estate firms adopted names starting with "Greater Philadelphia" to associate their activities not only with the city but also its suburbs. The phrase reached greatest prominence in the middle of the twentieth century, when business leaders formed a Greater Philadelphia Movement to reform the city's corrupt politics and redevelop Center City, but it echoed through organizational names into the twenty-first century. While indicating scopes of interest connecting the city and its suburbs, the phrase continued to infer aspirations to greatness.

This book adopts "Greater Philadelphia" in its geographic sense to indicate a regional scope. Like earlier uses, the term as used here is not limited by a fixed geographic boundary but rather refers to the interdependence between the city and its periphery across parts of three states: southeastern Pennsylvania, southern New Jersey, and northern Delaware. Embedded in this region are flows of people, cultures, ideas, and products that connect the Philadelphia area with the nation and the world. Each topic developed for *The Encyclopedia of Greater Philadelphia*, the source for many of the essays in this book, represents a focused investigation into the region's scope and impact. The extent of the region emerges differently by topic and across time, but patterns are evident and revealing.

To highlight connections among topics, section introductions and conclusions in this book were written in collaboration by the editors, Howard Gillette, Jr. and Carolyn T. Adams. Numerous editors of *The Encyclopedia of Greater Philadelphia* had a hand in developing the selected essays, and they are listed in the acknowledgments that follow the text. Also important to production of this manuscript were managing editor Hillary Kativa, who coordinated the illustrations; copy editors Tamara Gaskell and Donald D. Groff (who also served as website managing editor); editorial assistants Hannah Lee and Luke Hoheisel; and our editor Robert Lockhart of the University of Pennsylvania Press. In keeping with the goals of *The Encyclopedia of Greater Philadelphia*, we hope that the collective effort to create this book serves to connect the past with the present, to build community, and to create a legacy that benefits the Philadelphia region.

CHARLENE MIRES

Editor-in-Chief,
The Encyclopedia of Greater Philadelphia

PENNSYLVANIA
DELAWARE
REGIONAL PLANNING FEDERAT
OF THE
PHILADELPHIA TRI-STATE DIST
REGIONAI
FOR THE
PHILADELPHIA TRI-S
PREPARED BY
THE REGIONAL PLANNIN
1931
GALLOWAY
ABSECON
GREAT BAY
LITTLE EGG HARBOR

Chapter 1

Why Regions Matter

Howard Gillette, Jr.

Philadelphia-area residents, going back centuries, have lived and played a part in a wider regional environment. The ebb and flow of life experience was never contained by a single location or jurisdiction. Over time regional interrelationships became ever more important in the exchange of goods and services, the pursuit of opportunity, and the realization of the promise of a good life. Yet regions—even as they became accepted as critical elements in the national economy—have been poorly demarcated and understood on a personal level. Who is to say what a region's boundaries are or to whom they matter? Does census designation as part of a standard metropolitan statistical area make a region, or are regions more the product of specific kinds of kinship and allegiance?

Leading regionalists assure us that regions matter. As Bruce Katz and Jennifer Bradley declare in their 2013 book, *The Metropolitan Revolution*, "Cities and metros aggregate people and places in a geography that is large enough to make a difference but small enough to impart a sense of community and purpose."[1] Quite good, you might say on a theoretical level, but what about lived experience? Does one really know or care about the places our travels take us through and to for work or for recreation? In a specialized and increasingly fragmented world, are we not entitled to remain ignorant of the whole while we take advantage of the parts?

This book, derived from the larger *Encyclopedia of Greater Philadelphia* project, animates the importance of regional institutions, norms, and experience to help readers find themselves not only in time but in place. Through images, maps, and references for further reading, research, and places to visit, this volume helps users answer immediate questions while also pointing to their larger context. Far from static, such forms of information are intended to draw readers into journeys of discovery, which may open more questions than they answer. Such journeys have added value by informing not just individuals but the collective body of those living in proximity to one another, whose common good depends to a considerable degree on having common knowledge of the larger environment they inhabit.

This kind of community of shared knowledge—what Manuel Pastor and Chris Brenner at the University of Southern California's Center for Environmental and Regional Equity call an epistemic community—is essential to realizing the full potential of a region's human and monetary resources. They are not ones to minimize the hurdles to achieving anything close to common information, let alone the will to act on it. "Knowing together," they admit, "will not always produce growing together, but it can help."[2] Part of the secret to reaching a point where individual learning becomes civic in character, they contend, is compiling the stories regions tell about themselves. In Philadelphia, that starts with our history. What this compilation represents, then, is a set of stories fundamental to the Philadelphia area's evolution over time and space.

The central city has shaped and been shaped over time by a shifting geographic area covering

FIGURE 1. Regional Plan for the Philadelphia Tri-State District, 1931. ATHENAEUM OF PHILADELPHIA.

much of southern New Jersey, eastern Pennsylvania, and northern Delaware. As transportation networks extended beyond trails Native Americans laid out to turnpikes, canals, rails, and roads, area residents shifted their places of work and residence. They nonetheless carried with them lasting values and experience. William Penn's legacy of religious tolerance, for instance, nourished religious practice, even as different denominations scattered. Ethnic concentrations in Philadelphia also scattered, carrying with them not just distinct religious attachments but social traditions that left their mark on new communities.

So great has been this metropolitan diaspora over the years, it is hard to see the whole at any one time. Suburban communities that once were predominantly white have become more diverse and their politics more reflective of the city proper than they were even a few years ago. Traffic that once flowed into the city in the morning and returned at night subsequently proceeded both ways as commuters pursued employment outside as well as inside the city. Theater, university education, and the arts, once found largely in the city, became accessible throughout Greater Philadelphia. As Carolyn Adams and her colleagues argue in their 2008 book *Restructuring the Philadelphia Region*, "distinguishing between only two traditional categories of city versus suburbs no longer makes sense because of the increasing differentiation in the character of both." The postmodern metropolitan region, geographer Stephen M. Wheeler adds, "is fragmented politically, and most often highly diverse demographically, a veritable mosaic in terms of both physical form and social structure."[3] Such change does not add up to a singular experience so much as challenge any prospect that what once was common practice will always be so.

Regional awareness and governance have had a rich, though limited, history in the Philadelphia area. As early as 1931, the Regional Planning Federation of the Philadelphia Tri-State District, formed in 1928, laid out a grand vision for the area. Other regional compact organizations formed over the years, as detailed in Chapter 9 of this volume. Mandated to address specific sectoral issues, such as transportation or the environment, they tended to operate in narrowly functional ways, no matter how important their work. Where they assumed broader importance in areas affecting the economy of the larger region, in the formation of the Delaware River Port Authority, for instance, they still operated more according to narrow state interests. In the years before the Great Recession of 2008, when a portion of bridge tolls were directed at redevelopment, funds were divided strictly according to the priorities of the respective Pennsylvania and New Jersey representatives. Broader interests, such as building a magnet for tourism along the Delaware River, floundered once public opinion forced the authority to abandon goals beyond facilitating transportation across the river. Yet, even when a relatively obscure agency—to the public at least—makes decisions of consequence, it can cause an uproar. This happened in 2021 when the Delaware River Basin Commission banned fracking in the basin area while approving at the same time a site for processing liquified gas in Gloucester County, New Jersey, across from Philadelphia International Airport. While the first decision pleased environmentalists, the second raised widespread fears about the prospect of accidents in transporting the liquified gas by trucks and trains.[4] Building opposition to the proposal across multiple jurisdictions across two states proved daunting.

Regional stakeholders took a rare step in acknowledging their importance to one another in 1995 when two thousand of them participated in a summit aimed at identifying and acting upon their common concerns. Organized by University of Pennsylvania history professor Theodore Hershberg on the basis of years of research and teaching about the Philadelphia region, the meeting at the Pennsylvania Convention Center was asked to embrace Benjamin Franklin's advice at the time of the American Revolution, that we must "all hang together or assuredly we shall all hang separately." Hershberg gained the support of the Chamber of Commerce of Greater Philadelphia and the *Philadelphia Inquirer*, which ran a special supplement assessing the region's assets by way of previewing the convention. Written by a team headed by Neal Peirce, who helped launch a new regionalism movement a decade earlier with his landmark book *Citistates* and associated website, the supplement opened with the declaration, "Philadelphia and its sister counties could become one of the world's greatest citistate regions in the twenty-first century." While such a result was anything but assumed, the authors took a positive tone toward the modern transformation of the city and region as industry departed, writing, "Clearly the painful shutdowns of the 1970s, with factory lights flickering out from Chester to Camden to Fairless Hills to Frankford, did not signal the economic death many feared. They were more like the shedding of an old industrial skin, a molting process from which the region is emerging with a new, promising economic pattern."[5]

The conference's reach extended only to southeast Pennsylvania, a practical matter, as Hershberg explained the decision to me later, of wanting to deal with only one state government. As a consequence, its effect was not comprehensive, even though the *Inquirer* supplement did address southern New Jersey. It did result, however, in the formation of the Metropolitan Philadelphia Policy Center under the direction of David Thornburgh, son of the former Pennsylvania governor and, at the time, director of the Economy League of Greater Philadelphia. The center drew immediate funding from the William Penn Foundation and support from the Reinvestment Fund and 10,000 Friends of Pennsylvania as well as the Economy League. Within a year, it issued a dire report, "Fight (or) Flight," warning that as a result of policy failures the entire region was at risk of being overwhelmed by farm-devouring sprawl, without attendant gains in population or jobs. Writing in the center's glossy periodical, *Greater Philadelphia Regional Review* in 2002, Margaret Pugh O'Mara, having recently completed her doctoral degree in history at the University of Pennsylvania, blamed area failures on social and political fragmentation, writing: "While localism has strengthened community identity in the region, it has weakened Greater Philadelphia's regional identity. This has, in turn, diminished the region's ability to remain competitive as it prevents the region from joining its many assets together and jointly deciding its future." Notably, O'Mara traced an identical concern back to the work of the Regional Planning Federation in the 1930s.[6]

In the early years of the twenty-first century the Economy League laid out competing scenarios for the future. Following the lead of Peirce and others, the league stressed that the better the level of regional cooperation, the better the results. To codify its findings, the organization initiated the World Class Greater Philadelphia initiative with the goal of making the region a top place to live, work, and play by 2026, the 250th anniversary of the signing of the Declaration of Independence.[7] Regional cooperation remained tenuous, however, in ensuing years. Writing for the influential *Philadelphia Citizen* newsletter in 2021, for instance, editor Larry Platt decried the lack of cooperation between Philadelphia mayor Jim Kenney and surrounding suburban jurisdictions, citing Kenney's admission that he rarely talked with suburban leaders in any substantive manner. "What Hershberg recognized in the '90s," Platt contended, "might be even more true today. In an increasingly globalized marketplace, it is regions—not states or cities—that are best positioned to compete economically."[8]

Platt's criticism may have been overstated. Coincidentally, two civic leaders associated with Drexel University's Lindy Institute for Urban Innovation saw quite a different situation. Recounting Philadelphia's near miss in being selected to host Amazon's second world headquarters in 2018, they cited the city's proposal "as the playbook for Philadelphia's post-COVID-19 renaissance." The pitch to Amazon, they argued, "demonstrated the power of collective action in lifting Philadelphia up in the eyes of the world as a city with dynamism, energy, and a sound future."[9] Coincidentally, authors Alan Greenberger and Harris Steinberg were joined at Lindy by Bruce Katz, who in leaving his position at Washington's Brookings Institution set to work on devising ways metropolitan areas could more effectively capitalize on the regional applications of COVID relief funds. Meanwhile, the Economy League, under new leadership, had been building a cadre of regional leaders of different backgrounds and perspectives by bringing them together to examine the experiences of other city-regions, keeping an eye at the same time on potentially building a more formal regional compact of Philadelphia-area municipalities over time.[10]

Formal organizational efforts, no doubt, remain critical to the economic prosperity of Greater Philadelphia and, by extension, the well-being of its inhabitants. But at a time when governance is fragmented and people are dangerously at odds in social experience and outlook, finding common ground is more important than ever. No body of scholarship can do that alone, but we can hope here to stimulate interest in our shared heritage beyond allegiance to a favorite sports team or place to visit. Whether our readers' interest grows from the stories of people or place, greater knowledge of the heritage of 250 years and more should provide common points of reference and a clearer sense of collective identity.

NOTES

1. Bruce Katz and Jennifer Bradley, *The Metropolitan Revolution: How Cities and Metros Are Fixing Our Broken Politics and Fragile Economy* (Washington, D.C.: Brookings Institution Press, 2013), 6.
2. Chris Brenner and Manuel Pastor, *Equity, Growth, and Community: What the Nation Can Learn from America's Metro Areas* (Oakland: University of California Press, 2015), 11–17.
3. Carolyn Adams et al., *Restructuring the Philadelphia Region: Metropolitan Divisions and Inequality* (Philadelphia: Temple University Press, 2008), 5; Stephen M. Wheeler, "The New Regionalism: Key Characteristics of an Emerging Movement," *Journal of the American Planning Association* 68 (2002): 271.
4. "Looking Downstream," editorial, *Philadelphia Inquirer*, March 7, 2021; Zoya Teirstein, "The Delaware River Paradox: Why Fracking Is So Hard to Quit," *Grist*, April 15, 2021.https://grist.org/politics/the-delaware-river-basin-paradox-why-fracking-is-so-hard-to-quit/.
5. Neal R. Peirce, *Citistates: How Urban America Can Prosper in a Competitive World* (Washington, D.C.: Seven Locks Press, 1993); "Reinventing the Region," special report, *Philadelphia Inquirer*, March 26, 1995. See also, Theodore Hershberg, "The Case for Regional Cooperation," *Regionalist* 1 (Fall 1995): 13–32.
6. Bob Fernandez, "Report's Bleak Assessment of Region Is a Call to Action," *Philadelphia Inquirer*, October 21, 2001; Margaret Pugh O'Mara, "Learning from History: How State and Local Policy Choices Have Shaped Metropolitan Philadelphia's Growth," *Greater Philadelphia Regional Review*, Spring 2002, 16–21.
7. Economy League of Greater Philadelphia, *2026: Future Histories of Greater Philadelphia* (April 2011).
8. Larry Platt, "Revisiting Regionalism," *Philadelphia Citizen*, April 2, 2021.
9. Alan Greenberger and Harris Steinberg, "Amazon HQ2 Pitch Can Be the Playbook for Post-COVID Renaissance," *Philadelphia Inquirer*, May 26, 2021. Prepared in cooperation with the Chamber of Commerce of Greater Philadelphia, the proposal pointed to regional resources, yet remained highly city-centric. Notably Philadelphia rejected overtures to submit a proposal in conjunction with Camden, which would have offered a more integrated regional approach.
10. The Economy League describes what it calls its GPLEX360 program as "an effort to move the needle. By traveling and learning together, this group of decision-makers gets an infusion of exposure to other cities' best ideas, and a concentrated dose of high-level networking. GPLEXers have connected on many occasions to generate real change that benefits our region. 'There's nothing more powerful than a close network of movers and shakers who can solve problems on the fly with real cross-sector collaboration.'" The league spells out its philosophy for nurturing regional stewardship in "The Practice of Stewardship: Developing Leadership for Regional Action," *Greater Philadelphia Regional Review*, Winter 2003–4, 8–13.

To William Penn Esq
Proprietor & Governer of
PENN-SYLVANIA
This Mapp is humbly Dedicated
and Presented.
by Jno. Harris.
THE COUNTY OF PHILADELPHIA
THE COUNTY OF BUCK
The Dutch Township
The Proprietaryes Mannor of Gilberts
Perquaminck Cr.
Society Land
Wm Penn Junr: Man^r. of Williamstadt
Letitia Penns Man^r. of Mountjoy
Plymouth Township
Ma^r: Jasper Farmer
Gulielma Maria Penns Man^r. of Springfeild
German Township
The Mannor of Moreland
The Liberty Lands of Philadelphia City
Fairmount
Mannor of Springetsberry
Philadelphia
Wicaco
Society
Francford Cr.
Dublin
Whitpane Creek
Hollanders Creek

Chapter 2

GREATER PHILADELPHIA EXAMINED

Carolyn T. Adams

Variously defined as key elements of its identity have shifted over time, the Greater Philadelphia region has been an especially dynamic and unusually fragmented entity compared to other U.S. metropolitan areas. The region not only crosses multiple state lines; it is further divided into hundreds of extremely small communities, many of which date back to the colonial era. Although that formal fragmentation barely changed across the centuries, informal connections among residents reached across town boundaries, gradually building webs of regional relationships based on economic and transportation connections that linked producers to markets, workers to jobs, and households to churches, stores, and taverns. As those everyday connections multiplied across county and township lines, the fragmentation of governmental authority posed substantial obstacles to coordinated planning for the region, leading citizens to rely on nongovernmental organizations to span the governmental boundaries that subdivide the region.

Natural features shaped the territory's historical development. A range within the Appalachian Mountains separated the Atlantic coastline from the interior woodlands, stretching from northeast to southwest. The mountains' long, even ridges, with deep valleys in between, presented an important obstacle to east–west land travel. This meant that the region's early residents were better connected to other East Coast communities than to the interior, because of the difficulty of traveling across mountainous barriers.

The river system also exerted strong influences on human settlement. That system centered on the Delaware River flowing south from the Catskill Mountains. Primary tributaries from the north and west fed into the Delaware River: the Lehigh River originating between ridges of the Appalachian Mountains, the Schuylkill River flowing from what later became the city of Reading, and the Brandywine River flowing from the Welsh Mountains in northern Chester County southeast into the Delaware River at the location where Europeans built the city of Wilmington.

The historic homeland of the indigenous Lenape people crisscrossed the entire Delaware River system, creating a complex pattern of overland paths leading to commonly used locations to ford the rivers and streams. The Delaware River symbolized the regional unity among the Lenape, who explained to the European newcomers that "we reckon ourselves all one, because we drink one water."[1]

Europeans shattered that regional unity by subdividing the Lenape homeland into separate provinces, counties, and townships and establishing patterns of government that descended to the twenty-first century. Dutch and Swedish trappers and timber merchants initially visited the territory on the eastern bank of the Delaware River in the 1600s, but they were displaced by British settlers in the 1660s when Britain's King Charles II granted the proprietorship of the colony to his brother James. James attracted Quakers to settle in Salem and Burlington and named the area after the isle of Jersey in Britain. In 1674 New Jersey was divided into East Jersey and West Jersey, two distinct provinces of the proprietary colony (a division that was soon reversed in 1702).

William Penn's Grant

To develop the territory on the western bank of the Delaware River, Britain's King Charles II in 1681 granted the province of Pennsylvania to William Penn, who attracted Quakers and other religious nonconformists to the New World. Penn's land grant from the British Crown encompassed what eventually became the state of Pennsylvania. In addition, Penn acquired land farther south on the Delaware, but his rule there was only short-lived, ending in 1704 when the settlers broke away from Penn to form the Lower Counties of Delaware.

Using the river as the boundary dividing western New Jersey from Pennsylvania and Delaware, European settlers began creating county boundary lines, and in some instances subdividing those original counties as, for example, when Lancaster County was carved out of Chester County in 1729, and when Berks County was created from parts of Philadelphia, Chester, and Lancaster Counties in 1752. Well after the American Revolution had formally established state boundaries, citizens continued subdividing territory to create new county units like Montgomery County, Pennsylvania (carved out of Philadelphia County in 1784); Delaware County, Pennsylvania (carved out of Chester County in 1789); Mercer County, New Jersey (carved out of Somerset and Middlesex Counties in 1838); and Camden County, New Jersey (carved out of Gloucester County in 1844).

Below the county level, William Penn fervently supported the formation of small towns that could practice direct democracy to conduct local affairs. For example, most of the townships in Delaware County were originally incorporated before 1700. Already-small townships became even smaller wherever residents successfully petitioned the state to carve boroughs out of existing townships. Some settlers favored boroughs because, unlike townships, boroughs provided some public and commercial facilities like docks and weighing stations, as well as constables who could settle disputes and keep the peace in the area. Many of the townships in Montgomery County were incorporated in the eighteenth century, with boroughs carved out in the nineteenth century. That pattern was repeated in Bucks and Chester Counties.

New Jersey also adopted small townships, measured by both land area and population. By 1776, the entire state of New Jersey had been divided into thirteen counties, eight of which were ultimately subdivided into smaller counties, which in turn were split into townships. Many of those early townships were further subdivided, sometimes reflecting political disputes, but most often to ensure that local farmers and merchants controlled road development and maintenance in their vicinity. From the 1840s through the 1920s, New Jersey incorporated a handful of new municipalities every year, often due to complaints that an existing local government was not responding to specific concerns. In some cases, residents in one part of town simply resisted spending for streets and sewers in other parts of town, which led to separation and creation of new municipalities.

Early Settlement Patterns

Early settlers immigrated mainly as farmers, turning both sides of the Delaware River into landscapes of scattered farmsteads producing agricultural products and livestock. The main cultural groups populating Pennsylvania during the colonial period were the English (who predominated in the city of Philadelphia and townships closest to its borders); Germans (in the northern section of Bucks County and what became Montgomery County, as well as Lancaster County); the Scots Irish in Chester County; and the Welsh on the northern border of Delaware County. In colonial West Jersey, William Penn's influence assured the dominance of English Quakers among early colonists. The lower colonies on the Delaware—later the state of Delaware—first settled by Scandinavian Lutherans and Dutch Reformed, subsequently attracted English Quakers and Welsh Baptists. In the eighteenth century, Delaware became increasingly British, with the Church of England gaining adherents before the American Revolution. In all parts of the tri-state region, religious dissenters like Quakers and Mennonites settled in sizable numbers, lured by Penn's promise of religious freedom.

FIGURE 2. Thomas Holme map showing townships, counties, and lots surrounding the planned city of Philadelphia at the core, 1687. LIBRARY OF CONGRESS.

People of African descent arrived with the region's earliest European settlers as enslaved laborers as early as 1639, although they were few in number.[2] The first slave ship to arrive in Philadelphia, in 1684, brought 150 enslaved Africans into a population of about two thousand. Often arriving from previous bondage in the Caribbean, the enslaved filled many labor needs in the region's diverse economy. Pennsylvania settlers' preference for growing wheat on small farms meant they had a limited need for enslaved labor, but Delaware growers cultivated more labor-intensive crops like tobacco and corn. Philadelphia, never as reliant on the institution as New York City, fostered slavery along with indentured servitude for most of a century until the enslaved population reached a peak of about one thousand on the eve of the Revolution. By 1783, however, the enslaved population had dropped to under 450 people, while the number of free Black people had increased tenfold to about one thousand. Increasing moral doubts about slavery as well as the Revolution's rhetoric of liberty contributed to gradual abolition, although unevenly across the region.[3] Local free Black people and migrants entering the region formed communities around new African American churches in Philadelphia and whole new settlements, especially in southern New Jersey, including Timbuctoo in Burlington County, Free Haven (later renamed Lawnside) in Camden County, and Gouldtown in Cumberland County. A number of these free African settlements sat along New Jersey's so-called "Greenwich Line" of the

Underground Railroad. In Philadelphia, the number of African Americans continued to climb in the first part of the nineteenth century, comprising more than 10 percent of the population by 1810 and climbing to 14,500 in 1830.

The settlement pattern in this agricultural economy centered on family farms operating as self-contained units and producing most of what families needed. Itinerant craftsmen traveled from farm to farm, selling wares that families could not produce for themselves. The Irish traveler Isaac Weld reported in the 1790s that between Philadelphia and Lancaster he found "not any two dwellings standing together" except in Downingtown. Towns were simply not necessary to rural life. The network of thriving agricultural towns that William Penn had envisioned failed to materialize in most parts of the region. Some taverns standing at important crossroads offered travelers food, drink, and beds, spawning small settlements around them. Even the county seats that sat within thirty miles of Philadelphia (the distance of one day's ride with a loaded wagon) remained small despite their important functions like holding courts, recording deeds, and registering wills.

Riverside Industrial Outposts

Early industrial outposts sprang up along the rivers because early mills were powered by waterwheels. Already by the American Revolution, the riverbanks of the region were dotted with paper mills, flour mills, textile mills, and ironworks. With advanced mechanization, the Delaware River spawned factory towns like Trenton and Bristol upriver from Philadelphia, along with Camden and Wilmington on the lower Delaware, as well as the city of Chester, which by the mid-nineteenth century grew into a diversified manufacturing center of ships, steel, iron, and brass. Other manufacturing centers grew on the banks of the Schuylkill, for example Conshohocken, which was spawned in the 1830s by iron foundries that manufactured sheet-iron, saws, shovels, and spades. Also along the Schuylkill River, a major manufacturing district rose in Manayunk, whose massive cotton and woolen mills led it to be labeled "the Manchester of America" in the 1830s.

In the Pine Barrens of southern New Jersey, sizable iron deposits gave rise to eighteenth- and nineteenth-century ironworks, while abundant sand enabled the production of glassware well into the twentieth century. Rather than functioning as rivals, those secondary industrial centers along the two rivers and in southern New Jersey tended to reinforce Philadelphia's regional dominance because they shipped their products through the port of Philadelphia.

Camden became the largest of Philadelphia's manufacturing satellites, growing during the nineteenth century into a major industrial hub, particularly after the Civil War.[4] By 1870 the city boasted factories that produced iron, nickel, oil cloth, and chemicals. By 1880, woolen mills also operated there, and at the turn of the twentieth century, Camden attracted the gigantic New York Shipbuilding Company, which expanded rapidly with the coming of World War I. The Victor Talking Machine Company also employed thousands of workers. Camden became the undisputed industrial center of South Jersey, although it never rivaled Philadelphia's dominance in the region.

Philadelphia's business and civic leaders cemented their preeminent position in 1854 when they successfully pressured the Pennsylvania legislature to adopt the Act of Consolidation merging more than two dozen towns clustered near the Philadelphia port. After two decades of social disorder and rioting in the 1830s and 1840s, civic leaders demanded more effective services and security, which they hoped could be provided by a large-scale professionalized government. The state legislature responded to their plea by consolidating twenty-nine separate districts, townships, and boroughs into a single large city, declaring that Philadelphia would henceforth function as both a county and city government.

Economic and Transportation Linkages

While county and township lines gained legitimacy as legal and political boundaries, they did not constrain economic activity. Settlers across the Delaware Valley established cross-boundary transportation links to help them succeed economically. Early in the colonial era, successful farmers began carting their surplus crops to Philadelphia to sell in the region's central marketplace or to export by ship. The river separating Pennsylvania from New Jersey posed no great obstacle to New Jersey growers because as early as 1688 a commercial ferry crossed the river between Philadelphia and Camden.

William Penn had declared Pennsylvania county governments to be responsible for building and maintaining roads—a function that county officials often fulfilled simply by connecting short stretches of roadbed that had been built earlier by settlers. Such jerry-rigged roadways rarely provided the shortest route to Philadelphia, where most farmers wanted to cart their produce. The roadbeds were treacherous, clogged by tree stumps and other debris. To improve the situation, the legislatures of Pennsylvania, New Jersey, and Delaware began chartering private investment groups to build and maintain toll roads, the first of which was the Lancaster Turnpike built between 1793 and 1795. Dozens of toll roads followed until the advent of railroads. Along with those turnpikes, early mill owners and craftsmen used the rivers to ship their surplus to other parts of the colonies through the Philadelphia port.

Nineteenth-century railroad builders seized opportunities to deploy the new rail technology not only to tie local industries to distant markets, but also to transport local residents quickly and conveniently around the region. Among the first railroads in the nation, the Camden and Amboy Railroad was chartered in 1830 to provide passenger and freight service between New York City and Philadelphia via Camden, where passengers would shuttle between train and ferryboat to cross the Delaware River. In 1831, the Delaware Railroad built a line from Philadelphia to Wilmington. It was intended primarily for passenger service but served as a secondary freight route. Then in 1832 the Philadelphia, Germantown, and Norristown Railroad (PGN) began operating within Philadelphia County. Two great railroad companies—the Pennsylvania Railroad and the Reading Railroad—gradually built and bought out other rail companies in the region to create networks of passenger service to virtually every community within thirty miles of Philadelphia and to recreational locations like the Jersey Shore.[5]

Across the second half of the nineteenth century, railroad companies shaped development patterns that persisted for a century or more. Nineteenth-century homebuilders created suburban developments in Pennsylvania and New Jersey that relied on railroad transportation to carry office workers daily into and out of Philadelphia. Mostly these new developments sold housing to middle- and upper-income families. For example, in the late 1850s the Pennsylvania Railroad began serving the early residents of the Main Line communities built in the Pennsylvania suburbs of Montgomery and Chester Counties. Also in the 1850s, the Camden and Atlantic Railroad offered New Jersey suburban residents daily service between Philadelphia and suburbs like Haddon Township. The viability of such desirable suburbs depended upon the thirteen rail branches that ultimately were consolidated into Conrail in 1976.

The Highway Transportation Boom

The internal combustion engine brought massive change to the region, the most obvious sign of which was the highway network built from the 1950s onward, giving individual households and businesses convenient door-to-door access to virtually any location in the region. For the first time since its founding, Philadelphia was threatened by competition from surrounding communities. Both families and companies used their new freedom to move away from the region's urban centers—not just Philadelphia, but also the region's other industrial centers: Trenton, Camden, Chester, and Wilmington. After 1950 all those cities, including Philadelphia, suffered dramatic population losses, which they never regained in the twentieth century.

Instead, population gains after 1950 concentrated in the region's suburbs. The mid-distance suburbs attracted the most affluent households. Early in the history of suburban development, these communities proved to be appealing to well-to-do families who sought to escape the city yet wanted to remain within easy traveling distance of Philadelphia. Even at the turn of the twenty-first century, the majority of the region's affluent households still tended to prefer locations far enough from the city to offer a suburban lifestyle, yet close enough to offer a reasonable commute to jobs, entertainment, and other downtown attractions. A smaller yet significant number of affluent residents gained access to those amenities by moving into row houses and condominiums within walking distance of downtown.

Many of the suburbs closest to the edge of the city developed as working-class communities with older housing stocks built at higher densities. The most challenged communities in the region tended to be older boroughs attracting residents with modest incomes. Some older suburbs sat along the banks of the Delaware River, reflecting the early geographic influence of the main commercial waterway and the ongoing decline of manufacturing firms that lined it. Since these older communities tended to be completely built out, with little room for new investment, they experienced the greatest difficulty maintaining public services on a restricted property tax base.

Towns at the outer edge of the region proved to be attractive to middle-income households who wanted a suburban lifestyle but could not afford to buy homes in the pricey mid-distance suburbs. They were willing to trade longer commutes in order to gain suburban amenities. Springfield Township, for example, sits on the northern edge of Bucks County, bordering Northampton and Lehigh Counties. As late as the mid-1960s, over 90 percent of that township's acreage was in agriculture, woods, and water. Yet by the turn of the twenty-first century, the town's population had exploded to five thousand people. A New Jersey example was Southampton Township in Burlington County, originally settled by Quakers and slow to develop in the twentieth century. In the 1980s almost three-quarters of its land was declared to be part of the Pinelands Preserve, off-limits to suburban development. The small village of Vincentown served as a town center for other parts of the township that came to be dotted with housing developments and retirement communities.

The Cities Assert Themselves

Leaders in the region's urban centers responded to the threatening tide of post–World War II suburbanization by undertaking massive redevelopment projects to reassert the centrality of cities in the region's growth. The largest of those urban renewal efforts in the 1960s occurred in Philadelphia with the redevelopment of Society Hill and the construction of the Penn Center office complex near city hall.[6] Then in the 1970s, planners launched a downtown project that would link the region's two great railroads, the Reading and the Pennsylvania, into a single transit network. With funding that came largely from the federal government, SEPTA broke ground in 1978 on a massive underground project to connect the two downtown rail hubs. When completed in 1984, the Commuter Tunnel created a unified rail system anchored in downtown Philadelphia that spanned the Pennsylvania side of the region. It also provided access to Camden and the New Jersey suburbs by intersecting with the PATCO High Speed Line at the transit station at Eighth and Market Streets.

Other regional cities also responded to the exodus to the suburbs by launching revitalization plans, many of them designed to accommodate automobiles, a priority regarded as vital to reviving downtowns. In 1957 Trenton unveiled plans to demolish a declining downtown district known as Coalport in order to replace it with a gleaming new industrial and residential complex. Trenton leaders also supported the state's proposal to build the New Jersey Route 29 highway through downtown Trenton along the banks of the Delaware River (a decision later criticized for separating the waterfront from the heart of the city). Also in 1957, Wilmington's city council approved routing Interstate 95 through several of the city's stable neighborhoods and, in the 1960s, favored urban renewal projects that cleared an African American neighborhood to make way for what would eventually become government buildings. Camden's pro-growth coalition, which styled itself the Greater Camden Movement, backed a 1962 renewal plan that based its optimistic vision on the assumption that the urban core could be revitalized by making central parcels of land available and assuring easy automobile access to jobs in the city.

As they pursued downtown revival, few urban planners in the 1960s foresaw that suburbanites would use highway networks not just to gain access to the city, but also to move easily from suburb to suburb, creating new patterns of commuting that bypassed central cities altogether. For example, the U.S. Route 202 corridor spanning Philadelphia's northern suburbs became a particularly important path for suburb-to-suburb trips. Nor did planners foresee the rapid rise in the last decades of the twentieth century of reverse commuting from city residences to suburban jobs. In 1980, almost 15 percent of Philadelphia workers held jobs in the suburbs; by 2000 that percentage had climbed to almost 25 percent, and it continued increasing in the twenty-first century. Reverse commuters were virtually forced to use increasingly congested highways because the region's rail system did not easily accommodate reverse commuting.

Some observers speculated that Philadelphia faced unusual difficulty defining its regional footprint because it competed for regional dominance against New York City to the north and Washington, D.C., to the south, the two powerful centers of the U.S. economy and government. Although long regarded as a drawback, this geographic midpoint appeared by the turn of the twenty-first century to confer advantages in attracting residents and businesses that sought a location in the Northeast Corridor but wanted to avoid the congestion and cost of New York and Washington.

Greater Philadelphia's Competitive Advantage

Toward the end of the twentieth century, urban planners across the United States shifted their gaze from renewal at the neighborhood level to broader concerns about regional development patterns. The urban analyst Anthony Downs lamented that "for half a century America has had one dominant vision of how its metropolitan areas ought to grow and develop. It is best described as unlimited low-density sprawl."[7]

Rejecting that twentieth-century pattern, regional planners in Philadelphia as elsewhere adopted plans that would concentrate future growth in existing cities and towns while preserving the region's open spaces. The Delaware Valley Regional Planning Commission devised an elaborate guide for future build-out of Greater Philadelphia that recognized that "the region's public transit network is a tremendous asset and provides a significant advantage for the region amid rising energy costs and concerns about climate change"[8] and launched an initiative promoting "First Generation Suburbs" to promote older suburbs' main street business districts in combination with transit upgrades. Many suburban towns along SEPTA's regional rail system could serve as exactly the kind of nodes for future development that other metropolitan regions lack. They feature walkable town centers that became so popular in the twenty-first century that the U.S. Environmental Protection Agency created and published a National Walkability Index to score communities across the nation.

Who Defines the Region?

Since 1950 the federal government's Office of Management and Budget (OMB) has defined metropolitan regions for purposes of the U.S. Census. OMB's original definition of the Philadelphia region in 1950 included the central city plus Bucks, Chester, Delaware, and Montgomery Counties in Pennsylvania and Burlington, Camden, and Gloucester Counties in New Jersey. OMB based that definition on the adjacent counties having a high degree of economic and social integration with the central city, measured by commuting and employment. Over the half century that followed, the federal definition of the region changed multiple times, as the commuting shed of Philadelphia expanded to incorporate more suburban territory. By the 2010 census, the OMB had added three counties to its original definition: Salem County, New Jersey; New Castle County, Delaware; and Cecil County, Maryland.

Nongovernmental groups, however, have drawn the region's boundaries in different ways depending on the specific goals they pursued. Across the twentieth century, a variety of quasi- and nongovernmental commissions, special-purpose authorities, and nonprofit associations emerged to pursue particular projects and goals, each of them defining the region to fit its own objectives. Whereas voters expected county and township officials to act for the benefit of their own citizens, nongovernmental organizations had wider latitude to pursue regional goals. Starting in the twentieth century, the region benefited from the work of such nonelected bodies.

In the mid-1960s, when it was established as a metropolitan planning agency to receive and expend federal transportation dollars, the Delaware Valley Regional Planning Commission (DVRPC) defined the metropolitan area as including five Pennsylvania counties (Philadelphia, Bucks, Delaware, Chester, and Montgomery) and four New Jersey counties (Burlington, Camden, Gloucester, and Mercer) because these counties shared a transportation network of roads, rails, and airports. "Delaware Valley" was a term in vogue in the mid-twentieth century. But civic leaders in Philadelphia

FIGURE 3. Super Bowl celebration, 2018. Fans of the Philadelphia Eagles football team line both sides of Broad Street to celebrate the team's victory in Super Bowl LII against the Minnesota Vikings. The team's floats made their way to the Benjamin Franklin Parkway for a victory rally on the steps of the Philadelphia Museum of Art. PHOTOGRAPH BY DONALD D. GROFF.

who were determined to emphasize the city's primacy as the critical heart of a rapidly growing region favored the label "Greater Philadelphia."

A good example was the regional chamber of commerce, which until the mid-twentieth century had been known as the Trades League of Philadelphia. As an increasingly regional body, it changed its name to the Chamber of Commerce of Greater Philadelphia in 1952. The chamber's regional footprint duplicated the set of counties in the DVRPC but added Salem County in New Jersey and New Castle County in Delaware.

A different boundary line was drawn in 1996 with the creation of the region's top tourism promoter, the Greater Philadelphia Tourism Marketing Corporation, which became VisitPhilly.com in 2010. Its definition of "Philadelphia and the Countryside" included only the central city and the four suburban counties of eastern Pennsylvania. It omitted the New Jersey counties because the agency was heavily financed by the Pennsylvania state government.

As is obvious from the examples above, no fixed definition of the region's boundaries attained universal acceptance. Each organization pursued its objectives by constructing its own definition of the region. Lacking a standard definition of what constitutes "the region," area inhabitants have rarely identified themselves as residents of Greater Philadelphia, with the possible exception of sports fans throughout the city and suburbs who have historically identified with the city's major teams.

Philadelphia became one of only a handful of cities that built as many as three stadiums within a single sports complex. The chosen site in South

Philadelphia had been developed in the 1920s to house Sesquicentennial Stadium for the 1926 Sesquicentennial Exposition. In 1967 the Flyers hockey team and the 76ers basketball team moved into the Spectrum Arena in that area. Then in 1971 nearby Veterans Stadium became home to the Phillies baseball team and Eagles football team. Both facilities served their resident teams until the opening decade of the twenty-first century, when new facilities replaced the older venues. Although other locations were considered, the teams chose to remain in the sports complex in South Philadelphia where they could be easily reached from the suburbs by car because of the location near exits off both Interstate 95 and Interstate 76. The fact that thousands of avid sports fans from the suburbs poured into South Philadelphia for every home game fostered their identification with the rest of the region as perhaps no other activity could.

NOTES

1. Jean R. Soderlund, *Lenape Country: Delaware Valley Society Before William Penn* (Philadelphia: University of Pennsylvania Press, 2014), 168.
2. Darold D. Wax, "Quaker Merchants and the Slave Trade in Colonial Pennsylvania," *Pennsylvania Magazine of History and Biography* 86 (1962): 143–159.
3. Andrew K. Diemer, *The Politics of Black Citizenship: Free African Americans in the Atlantic Borderland, 1817–1863* (Athens: University of Georgia Press, 2016).
4. Howard Gillette, Jr., *Camden After the Fall: Decline and Renewal in a Post-Industrial City* (Philadelphia: University of Pennsylvania Press, 2005), 17–38.
5. Gillette, *Camden After the Fall*, 17–38.
6. Gregory L. Heller, *Ed Bacon: Planning, Politics, and the Building of Modern Philadelphia* (Philadelphia: University of Pennsylvania Press, 2013).
7. Anthony Downs, *New Visions for Metropolitan America* (Washington, D.C.: Brookings Institution, 1994), 3.
8. Delaware Valley Regional Planning Commission, *Connections: The Regional Plan for a Sustainable Future* (Philadelphia: DVRPC, 2009), 85.

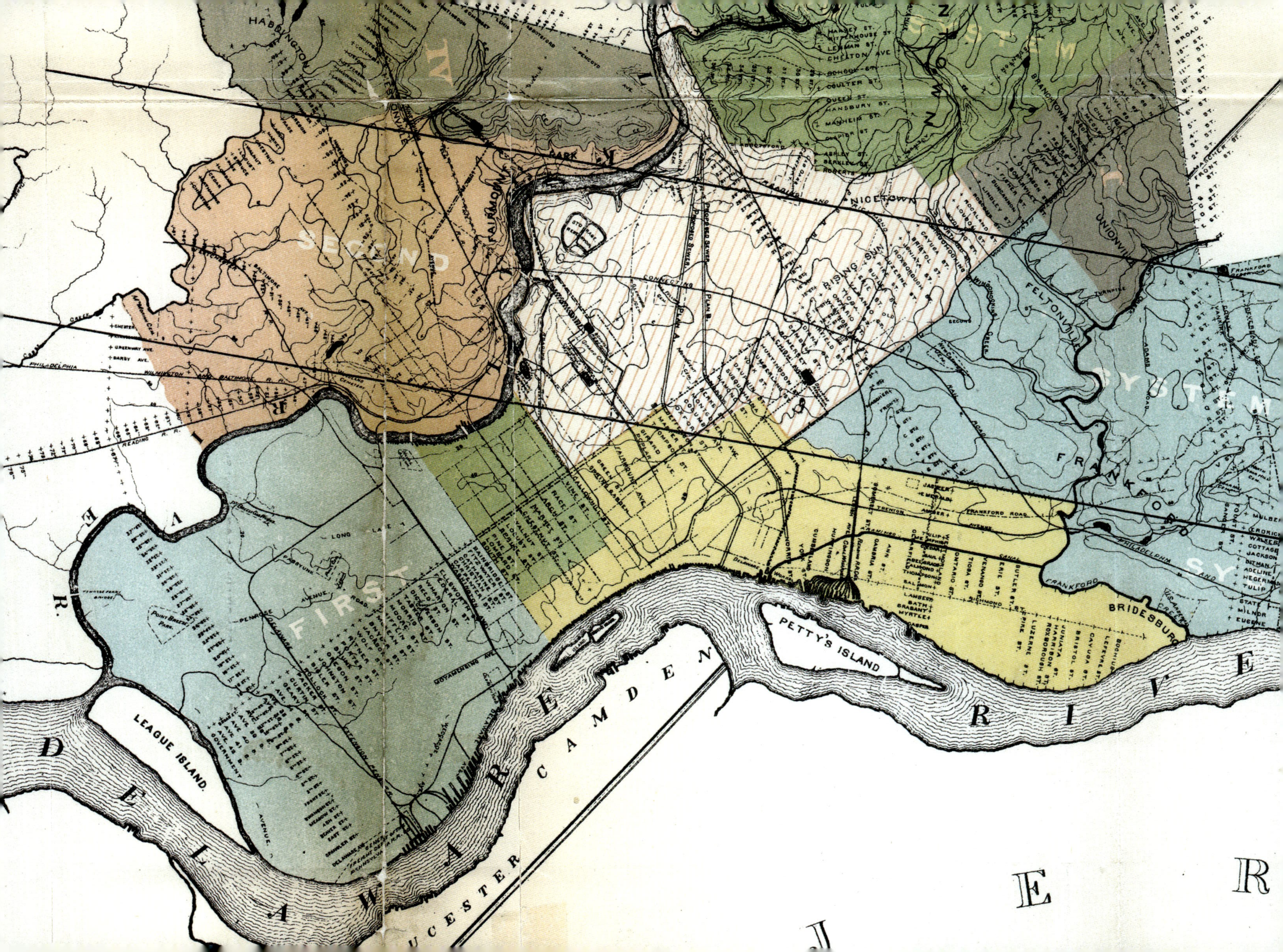

DELAWARE RIVER
CAMDEN
LEAGUE ISLAND.
PETTY'S ISLAND
BRIDESBURG
FIRST
SECOND
FAIRMOUNT
PARK
NICETOWN
RISING SUN
FELTONVILLE
UNIONVILLE
FRANKFORD
HABBINGTON
SYSTEM

Chapter 3

NATURAL FEATURES

Introduction

Geography may not be destiny but it nonetheless has had much to do with the location, nature, and extent of human settlement and, in turn, its effect on natural resources. William Penn's decision to locate the infant city of Philadelphia at the confluence of two rivers on a flat plain ideal for building was both fortuitous and consequential. As European settlement grew, it spread, not randomly but in accordance with nature's bounty: rivers and creeks that extended the reach of trade, forests once turned to lumber that offered shelter, and coal once extracted from the earth that fueled homes as well as the machines that spurred the Industrial Revolution.

Indigenous peoples had navigated the land for centuries, establishing pathways to opportunity, which the Europeans who followed them learned to utilize themselves. As these new settlers built roads and turnpikes, bridges and ferries, canals and railroads, they extended and deepened regional connections. The land, however, remained a primary factor in their decisions. The mountainous plain to the west provided obstacles to horse-drawn canal barges, forcing the Pennsylvania legislature to introduce rail links to what became a mixed system designed to move newly extracted coal and deliver it to emerging cities along the route, including Reading and Norristown, Phoenixville and Conshohocken, as well as Philadelphia.

Over time, as natural resources were turned to production, rival centers of gravity emerged to challenge Philadelphia's centrality. These outlying locations attained their own identity, such as the Lehigh Valley in Pennsylvania and the Brandywine Valley in Delaware, both appropriately deriving their name from bodies of water that did so much to shape the built environment and economic development. The New Jersey Pine Barrens created its own distinctive set of opportunities, thus affording its own identity. Sandy soil limited opportunity for traditional farming but offered just the right ingredients for growing berries and producing glass. Wood for charcoal and iron bog enabled mills and factories over time. The more than 780 square miles constituting the Delaware Bay nurtured vast maritime resources, from oysters to salt hay, to form the backbone of a distinctive economy over the four centuries following European contact.

Modernization broke the hold of geography on settlement, as an ever-growing network of roads and highways freed settlers from earlier physical restraints on the location of work and residence. As the region's reach expanded as a consequence, so did the phenomenon of sprawl. As the built environment pushed back nature, what appeared as a single entity from the air became increasingly fragmented in lived experience. While critics called for greater regional cooperation, they did so in the face of intensifying loyalties to particular places rather than the whole. Nature remained an asset, allowing area residents to take advantage of natural resources, including some areas that had once been given over to industry, such as rails-to-trails or historic byways. These helped form people's attachments to the area's natural assets, but it remained to be seen whether such loyalties and an expanding environmental movement would lead to greater regional understanding and cooperation.

Topography

Michael Nairn

Landforms and the processes that have shaped them—processes of the earth, time, climate, and humankind—are key to understanding the configuration and evolution of the Greater Philadelphia region. Knowledge about these features derives from topography, the description of landforms that includes, among many other things, mountain ranges, hills, valleys, watercourses, and bodies of water.

If there is one adjective to describe the topography of the Delaware Valley, that adjective is gentle. There are neither tall mountains nor deep valleys like those found in northeastern Pennsylvania. The land has always been rich and productive, contributing to the region's wealth. The Lenape understood its advantages as did successive waves of settlers. The future, however, is never predictable, and that same gentle topography characterized by large expanses of tidal areas may be threatened with inundation if current predictions of relative sea level rise come to pass.

The Greater Philadelphia region straddles two physiographic provinces: the Coastal Plain that borders the Atlantic Ocean stretching south from Long Island to the Gulf Coast and Mexico and the Piedmont, a one-thousand-mile-long plateau that extends from the Coastal Plain westward to the Appalachian Mountains. The region's topography includes both the relatively flat landscapes of the Coastal Plain and the rolling ridgetops with steeply incised stream valleys that mark the Piedmont. This transition from the Piedmont to the Coastal Plain explains why the Schuylkill River has cut a steep valley as it flows through the Piedmont from Valley Forge to Fairmount in Philadelphia, while in contrast the topography of Center City Philadelphia and southern New Jersey is relatively flat. Wilmington, Delaware, founded on Brandywine Creek just upstream from the Delaware River, is similarly located on this transition.

Signs of topography's central role in shaping the development of the Greater Philadelphia area are readily found in historic place names. The Lenape named the location just upstream from the confluence of the Schuylkill River and Wissahickon Creek "Manayunk," literally the "place where we drink." There, in the deeply incised Piedmont river valley that the Schuylkill River had cut through some of the oldest rock in North America, the river slowed as it approached the confluence with the Wissahickon Creek, depositing sediment and creating an accessible floodplain where the Lenape could gather, drink water, and fish. Down through the centuries, the power of water has been among the most important influences shaping the metropolitan region.

European settlers lent equally descriptive names to the landscape. In southern New Jersey, the townships on high ground like Mount Laurel, Mount Holly, and Pine Hill were named to distinguish them from the surrounding lower-lying terrain of the Inner Coastal Plain. Dutch settlers named the Schuylkill ("hidden river") for the way the ever-changing mosaic of deposited sediment at its mouth hid the river's channel. Also named for characteristics of the land, Ridge Pike travels the length of one of the Piedmont's rolling ridgetops, separating the Schuylkill and Wissahickon valleys. Fairmount, which became the site of the Philadelphia Museum of Art, looks down on the narrow floodplain of the Schuylkill and Delaware Rivers where in 1682 Thomas Holme laid out Philadelphia.

Within the Coastal Plain lies approximately two-thirds of New Jersey (including all of southern New Jersey) and all of Delaware south of Wilmington. In Pennsylvania, the Coastal Plain is only a small band, up to five miles wide bordering the Delaware River. The distinguishing topographical feature of the Coastal Plain is its relative flatness, with average slopes of less than 1 percent and in many places even shallower. Consequently, surface drainage is relatively poor throughout much of the Coastal Plain. Localized flooding is widespread. In some places surface water collects in shallow lakes, particularly in places like the

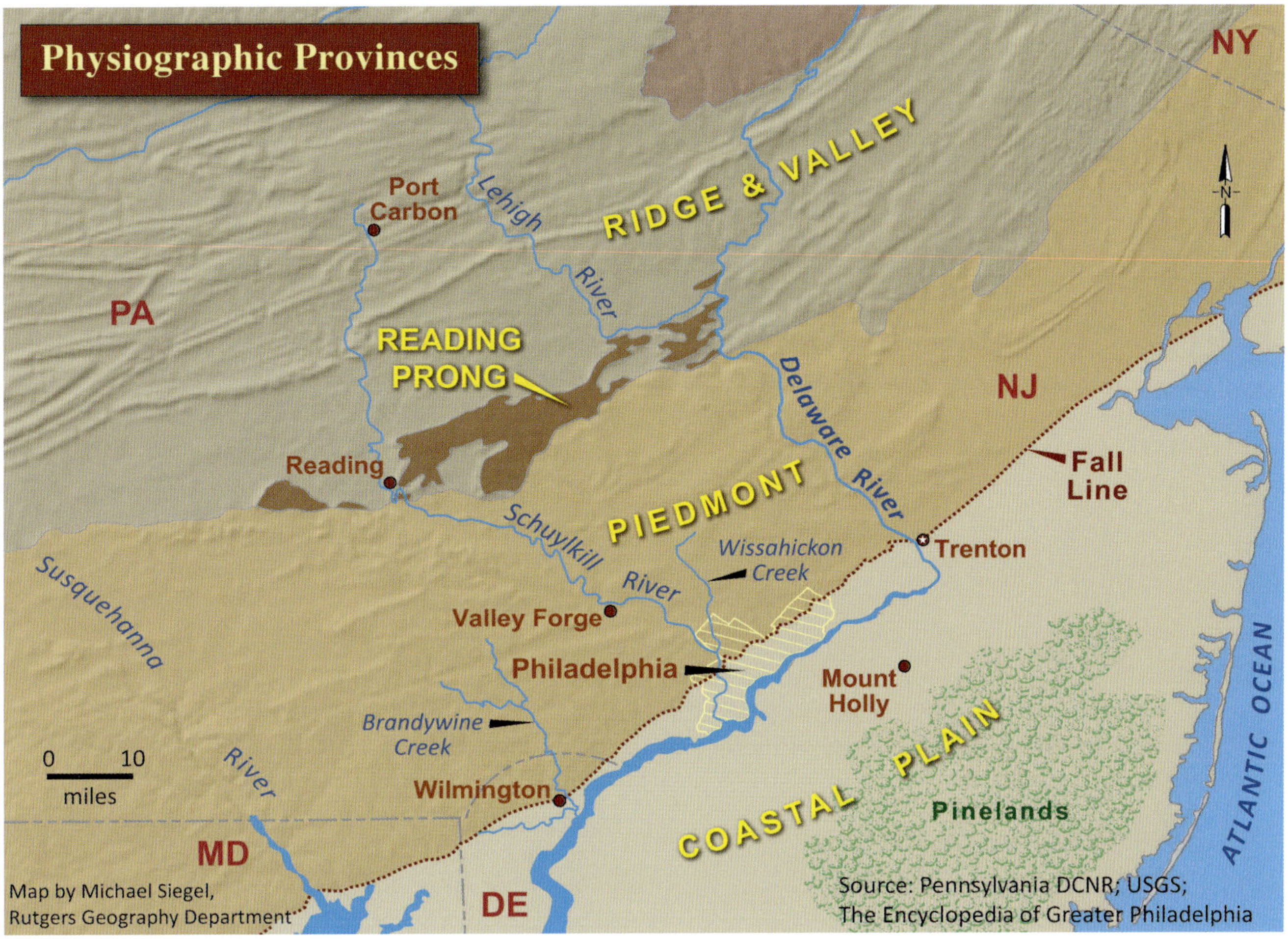

MAP 1. Philadelphia: where the Piedmont meets the Coastal Plain. MAP BY MICHAEL SIEGEL.

Pine Barrens where most of New Jersey's cranberry crop is harvested.

The Coastal Plain, however, is not entirely flat. Sporadically along the entire Coastal Plain, places of higher elevation rise seventy-five to one hundred feet above the surrounding landscape. These formations are categorized as "cuestas," where a cap of consolidated rock sits atop the unconsolidated sands and gravels of the surrounding Coastal Plain, making them more resistant to erosion. In southern New Jersey, these higher elevations form an elongated, northeast-southwest trending, discontinuous belt of higher land. Included in it are Mount Holly (elevation 154 feet), Mount Laurel (elevation 148), Pine Hill (elevation 203), and Camden County's unnamed high point just east of Berlin (elevation 219). The belt forms a ridgeline dividing the Inner and Outer Coastal Plains. Rivers and creeks on the east side flow across the Outer Coastal Plain and drain to the Atlantic Ocean, while those on its west side flow across the Inner Coastal Plain, draining into the Delaware River.

Topographically, the Delaware River formed the Inner Coastal Plain, where the river has cut a rather broad but shallow valley. At Philadelphia, the valley ranges from six to ten miles wide while at its mouth around Dover, Delaware, it is about forty miles wide. At Philadelphia, the river channel was lined by sandy banks about twenty feet high into which English settlers at the time of William Penn's arrival dug caves for protection from the harsh winter.

West of Philadelphia, the Piedmont's defining feature is its rolling, gently sloping ridgetops with moderately deep soils dissected by streams and rivers. The Piedmont runs from the New Jersey Palisades along the Hudson River south to Georgia. It varies in width from about 40 miles in Pennsylvania to 125 miles in North Carolina. Named for the Italian Piedmont, the foothills of the Alps, it is a plateau sandwiched between the lower Atlantic Coastal Plain and the higher elevations of the New England province and the Ridge and Valley province that includes the Appalachians, the Blue Ridge Mountains, and the Great Smokies.

This geologically complex area has experienced repeated episodes of tectonic plates crashing into each other and then pulling apart over millions of years. Between 500 million years ago until 250 million years ago, the North American and African plates crashed together, ultimately forming a high mountain range. During these events, igneous rocks were deformed under great pressure to produce the highly metamorphic schists and gneisses that are found on the Piedmont today. Wissahickon schist, the sparkly, micaceous rock commonly used in buildings in the nineteenth and early twentieth centuries, resulted from these events.

The Schuylkill River originates in the Ridge and Valley province flowing through the Piedmont and onto the Coastal Plain. Flowing south through the soft rock of a limestone valley at Valley Forge, the Schuylkill encounters a hard ridge of Chickies Quartzite, some of the hardest rock known, where it makes a ninety-degree turn, until it finds a seam or fracture in the ridge and makes another ninety-degree turn, heading southeast. Drivers in this area came to know it through traffic reports as the "Conshohocken Curve." The water flow then encounters an area of softer, more erodible schists and gneisses around the Manayunk area, through which the river has cut a steep, narrow, three-hundred-foot-deep canyon.

Given its topography, Manayunk was particularly important to the region's early industrial development. To facilitate shipping along the Schuylkill River, the Schuylkill Navigation Company built Flat Rock Dam in 1818 upstream from Manayunk, dug a two-mile canal on the wide floodplain, and installed locks along the canal to mitigate the twelve-foot fall from Flat Rock Dam to the river's downstream path into Philadelphia. To help finance the venture, the company sold access to waterpower that allowed a significant number of mills to be built and subsequently thrive. Past its confluence with Wissahickon Creek, the canyon widens and the river slows as it approaches Fairmount, where it drops to the Coastal Plain.

Like Manayunk, many other settlements sprang up at a "fall line," where a river's sudden, steep descent produced rapids and waterfalls that stopped ships from moving farther. Cities formed at such locations because transportation to seaports was easiest from there, and because waterpower was available to operate mills and factories.

Many of the East Coast's major cities are located on the fall line between the Piedmont and the Inner Coastal Plain, including Wilmington, Delaware, on Brandywine Creek; Philadelphia on the Schuylkill River; and Trenton, New Jersey, on the Delaware River. As geographer Peirce Lewis explained, early settlements prospered along the fall line as they gained advantage over their competitors by controlling their situation, access to trade routes into the adjacent hinterlands, and the ability to ship goods downstream. These places often became iconic, as illustrated by the gold dome of the New Jersey State Capitol in Trenton sitting upon the higher ground at the fall line, and the lofty classical architecture of the Philadelphia Museum of Art atop Fairmount, with its steps made famous by the movie *Rocky* (1976).

Below the fall line, the rivers and creeks are tidal, and the topography approaches dead flat. As the rivers and creeks fall from the Piedmont to the Inner Coastal Plain, they deposit sediment as their velocities slow, and they spread out over the plain, separating into multiple channels called distributaries. Twice a day, tides flow up the Delaware River from Delaware Bay and back out again. The river has no perceptible gradient or slope throughout its tidal reach from Trenton to Delaware Bay, and because of this the course of the Delaware River has remained relatively stable.

Sediment deposited when the river floods its banks has been the main source of land building on its floodplain for the last six thousand years. In Philadelphia the Schuylkill River—the Delaware River's largest tributary—has flowed into it, depositing its sediment and forming a large delta that covered most of the land south of Snyder Avenue in South Philadelphia as well as the land upon which the stadiums, the Navy

Yard, the former Sunoco Refinery, and the Philadelphia International Airport were built.

The sediment formed large areas of tidal freshwater wetlands, which were neither land nor water but instead an "aqueous terrain" that was constantly shifting. These areas were some of the first to be modified by European settlers who diked and drained them for agriculture. In the eighteenth and nineteenth centuries, they were thought to harbor miasmas, unhealthy airs and vapors that caused yellow fever, prompting efforts to drain and fill them to meet demand for urban expansion. In an ironic twist, draining these wetlands *did* reduce yellow fever, not because they produced vapors, but because they provided habitat for the *Aedes aegypti*, the mosquito that transmitted the disease. Tidal freshwater wetlands subsequently came to be recognized as some of the most productive landscapes on the planet. Of the approximately 6,000–10,000 acres (some measurements estimate the top end of the range to be as high as 12,800 acres) that once covered the Schuylkill River delta area, only 286 acres remain.

In the Delaware Valley region, the most severe impacts from climate destabilization and sea level rise can be expected in the filled tidal wetland areas. Because the mid-Atlantic coastline is subsiding while mean sea level is rising, relative sea level rise in the region is estimated to be twice the global average.

Much of the region's vital infrastructure has been built in the Schuylkill River delta area. Because of the importance to the region's economy, along the Delaware riverfront in both Pennsylvania and New Jersey, the impacts of sea level rise in the early twenty-first century created potential for widespread reverberations. Relative sea level rise, coupled with storms of increasing frequency and severity, created increasing risk of severe flooding for areas within the tidal zone. Critical infrastructure such as the Philadelphia International Airport, the innovation and technology hub of the Philadelphia Naval Yard, and the Southwest Sewage Treatment Plant that processes sanitary and storm sewage from Philadelphia, Montgomery, and Delaware Counties, confronted the need to adapt or be relocated. Transportation infrastructure such as the Interstate 95 corridor and Admiral Wilson Boulevard also faced future reconstruction or relocation. Entire neighborhoods built over filled tidal wetlands such as Tinicum Township and Eastwick, the largest urban renewal project in the country, were projected to be partially inundated within thirty years and completely inundated by the end of the twenty-first century. The salt line—that is, the extent to which saltwater reaches upriver—was projected to move farther toward Philadelphia, potentially imperiling the intakes for Philadelphia's drinking water supply.

Low-lying tidal areas have always been attractive to build upon because it required less labor to build dikes and drainage canals to transform them from tidal freshwater wetlands to agricultural lands than it

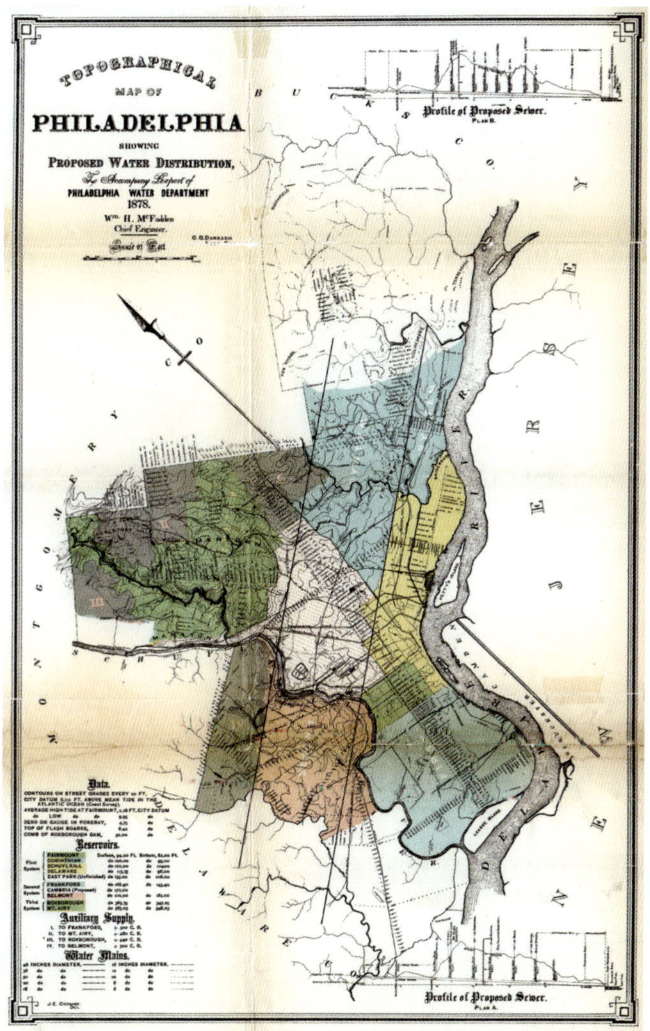

FIGURE 4. Topographical map of proposed water distribution to the city of Philadelphia, 1878, showing the physical challenges to its distribution. PHILADELPHIA WATER DEPARTMENT.

did to transform the Piedmont, where it was necessary to cut down large, mature trees, changing forested to agricultural lands. As technology advanced, these lowland areas became even more attractive for development and the land modifications more extensive. Yet, these same areas proved to be most vulnerable as climate changed and sea levels rose. Planners in the 2020s proposed that these areas be redesigned to make room for the river, mimicking their original drainage patterns to help alleviate flooding caused by anticipated sea level rise. On the other hand, higher elevations in the Piedmont likely faced far fewer challenges from many of these same issues.

Delaware Bay

Michael J. Chiarappa

The Delaware Bay does not often get the historical acknowledgment received by its estuarine neighbor, the Delaware River, but it exerted equal weight in shaping the Philadelphia region's cultural and economic development. Over seven hundred square miles in size and bordered by New Jersey and Delaware, the Delaware Bay is one of America's premier maritime gateways, connecting the Philadelphia region to both international and domestic trade. While the bay's extensive salt marshes, along with limited sheltered harbors, prevented certain economic and military uses, its natural resources duly compensated for these environmental obstacles. The bay's waters fostered an array of navigational skills among shoreline residents, a tradition that would later pay dividends when sail and steam transport expanded in the nineteenth century. Stands of timber lining the bay's shoreline and tributaries facilitated the growth of shipbuilding, an industry that flourished until almost the end of the twentieth century. Most notably the use of the bay's marine resources—from its well-known oysters to salt hay—formed the backbone of its economic fortunes for the four centuries following European contact.

Taking note of what was already apparent to local Native American populations, colonial observers envisioned the bay's far-reaching potential. Referring to the Delaware Bay as part of a "Terrestrial Canaan," a 1676 promotional broadside for West New Jersey singled out the bay's "great numbers of Sturgions, Lobsters, Oysters, and many other Sea-Fish," as well as its capacity to serve as a gateway for natural resource use "a hundred Miles into the Country." William Penn cast the Delaware Bay and its resources as an organizing agent of Philadelphia's regional dynamics and the city's rise as an international entrepôt.

Following the pattern of the Dutch and Swedes who preceded them, English settlers continued the practice of harvesting the Delaware Bay's rich stores of fur-bearing animals and coordinated these activities with trade among the Lenape Indians. But being intent on permanent settlement, the British instituted the commercial use of the bay's waterborne and terrestrial resources. Wider consumption of shellfish (oysters, clams) and finfish (shad, sturgeon, rockfish) raised concern over the sustainability of these stocks enough to prompt New Jersey to enact in 1719 one of the first laws in America regulating the use of natural oyster beds.

Soils along the bay's shore were not as fertile as those along the Delaware River, but some areas did produce profitable yields of grain crops and corn, and farmers working along the Delaware Bay and its tributaries during the colonial and early national periods availed themselves of vessel transport afforded by this estuarine system. The environs around Greenwich, New Jersey—which straddled the colony/state's Inner and Outer Coastal Plains—were most notable in this regard, and Greenwich emerged as the Delaware Bay's most prominent eighteenth-century port and supplier to Philadelphia.

Amid these agricultural developments, construction of earthen dikes and banks enabled farmers to reclaim tidal marshes and meadows, transforming the bay's shoreline. Once drained, these banked meadows allowed efficient harvesting of cordgrass, provided grazing for livestock and sheep, and, when sufficiently relieved of prior saltwater content, could be used to raise a variety of crops. The bay's moderate climate allowed colonial settlers—particularly those who arrived from New

FIGURE 5. Map by English cartographer William Faden depicting the primary inlets and outlets of Delaware Bay, 1778. The numerical values indicate depth in feet at the time of recording. COLLECTION OF MICHAEL J. CHIARAPPA.

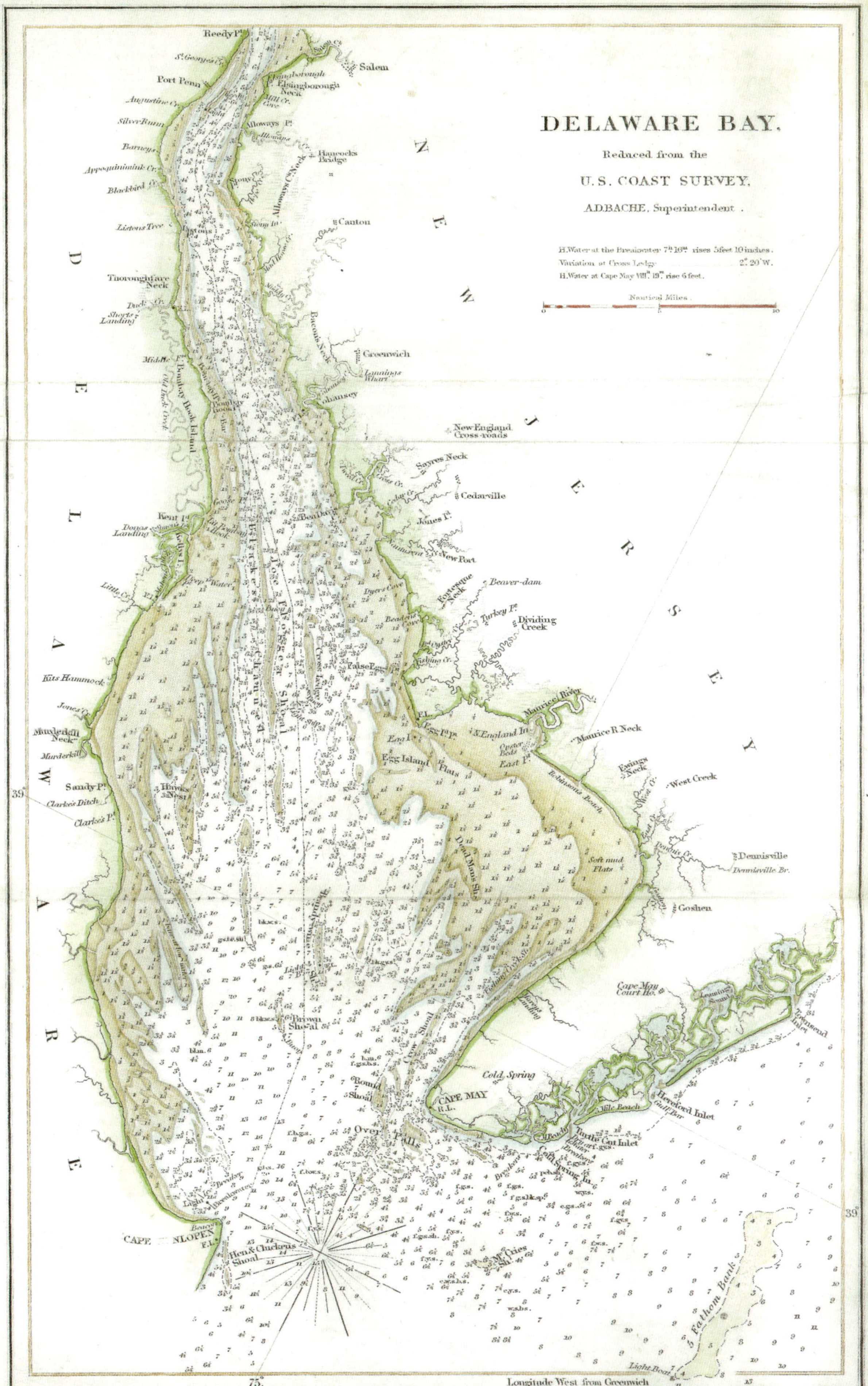

E. & G.W. BLUNT, N. YORK.

Drawn & Engraved by C. Copley.

England's colder temperatures—to pasture animals at longer intervals in salt meadows and reclaimed tidal lands.

Shallops and flatboats brought agricultural commodities from the bay shore to Philadelphia, as well as a variety of products derived from the region's timber supply. Eighteenth-century newspaper accounts and wills from the Delaware Valley highlight the importance of woodlots, particularly important in bay shore areas where soil conditions hindered profitable agriculture. Among those who prepared timber for market were the area's Swedish and Finnish settlers. Having brought their well-known woodman's skills to the New World, they were conspicuous participants in the Delaware Bay region's wood economy. Delaware Bay residents harvested merchantable cordwood for export to Philadelphia and provided other wood products such as barrel staves, ship planking, naval stores (tar, pitch), and charcoal. The bay region's impressive stands of Atlantic white cedar provided valuable roof shingles and house sheathing as well as material for boatbuilding, a regional tradition that endured until the end of the twentieth century.

While agriculture and wood harvesting carried forward into the nineteenth century, joined by an increasing emphasis on truck farming that continued into the twentieth century, the economic ambitions gripping the Philadelphia region transformed the use of the bay's waters. Central to these commercial and industrial goals was the need to move commodities, particularly in bulk, to and from Philadelphia through the Delaware Bay to points all along the East Coast of the United States. The Navigation Act of 1817 limited such shipping, known as the coastwise trade, to American-flagged vessels. Duly incentivized by shipping demand and legal protections, bay shore residents from New Jersey and Delaware built, crewed, and owned coastal schooners (principally two- and three-masted). Experienced in working the water, they seized on the opportunities presented by this emerging maritime economy.

Arguably the Delaware Bay's most significant tributary, New Jersey's Maurice River sported a robust schedule of coastal schooner and barkentine construction between the 1830s and 1880s. An important 1882 survey of U.S. shipbuilding by Henry Hall showed the Maurice River towns of Mauricetown, Dorchester, and Leesburg were the beneficiaries of these activities and singled out Mauricetown as "being dependent on building [vessels] and navigation [coastwise trade]" with "50 to 60 sea captains living in the place, [where] almost everybody owns shares in vessels."

These same economic ambitions ultimately impacted the Delaware Bay's most valuable marine resource—the oyster—which became a culinary staple throughout the Delaware Bay/River corridor, from Philadelphia's finest dining rooms to an array of oyster bars and cellars serving ordinary citizens. New Jersey stood ready to exploit the market potential of its rich oyster beds. Legislation in the mid-nineteenth century authorized the transplanting of seed oysters from natural spawning areas to barren bay bottoms privately leased from the state. Oystermen found that transplanting oysters to the higher salinity levels of Maurice River Cove improved growth, enhanced the quality of their meats, and offered greater control in cultivating their product for market. When ready for market, schooners and sloops transported oysters to Philadelphia.

The arrival and improvement of rail connections along New Jersey's Delaware Bay shoreline, from the 1870s through the early 1900s, dramatically transformed the oyster industry and attracted unprecedented levels of investment from throughout the region. The West Jersey and Seashore Railroad (WJSR), a subsidiary of the Pennsylvania Railroad, and the Central Railroad of New Jersey (CRRNJ) financed the construction of modern shipping facilities at, respectively, "Maurice River" on the eastern side of the Maurice River and at "Bivalve" on the river's western side. Servicing far-flung markets from rail connections in Philadelphia and New York City, these facilities helped drive an ever-increasing volume of oyster harvests. Each of these multiunit facilities teemed with activity as workers bagged, barreled, and shipped oysters and, eventually, removed them from their shells and canned them in new shucking houses. This work linked Philadelphia's commission merchants and restaurateurs—many of whom operated from the city's Dock Street Market—to vessel captains, policymakers, and scientists, as well as to African Americans who arrived from the Chesapeake to work on oyster boats and as shuckers. All this activity reflected the oyster industry's onetime status as the economic bedrock of the Delaware Bay region with its inextricable ties to Philadelphia.

New transportation methods also transformed the Delaware Bay's shad and sturgeon fisheries. Each species returned to its natal grounds to spawn in the spring, a ritual that energized a number of small communities on the New Jersey and Delaware sides of the bay. Of all these fishing sites, Bayside—outside of Greenwich—was arguably the most prominent due to CRRNJ rail connections linking it to Philadelphia and New York markets. The combination of shad and sturgeon skiffs, floating cabins, and shoreside processing buildings defined this amphibious extension of Philadelphia's economic sphere. But neither fishery was immune from overfishing and pollution. When sturgeon fishermen met in Philadelphia around 1900 to organize the Sturgeon Fishermen's Protective Society, it was too late to stem the tide of depletion. The combined effect of pollution and fishermen unwilling to curb their catch meant that the sturgeon fishery—once plentiful enough to allow people to affordably purchase caviar sandwiches—was in the midst of its final days.

Rail and steamship service operating from Philadelphia opened the Delaware Bay to recreational activity during the second half of the nineteenth century, and this trend continued in the twentieth as automobiles further democratized leisure pursuits. Hotels, such as the Warner House at the confluence of the Delaware Bay and New Jersey's Cohansey River, were emblematic of this enthusiasm and accommodated visitors from throughout the mid-Atlantic region and beyond. But smaller guesthouses and cottages were more the norm. By the late nineteenth century, Fortescue, New Jersey—centrally located on the Delaware Bay—epitomized the modest accommodations that typified vacation life along the bay. Some visitors swam, others engaged in recreational fishing and crabbing, while others simply sat on the beach and gazed at the bay's glistening waters. The bay shore's plentiful waterfowl and shore birds attracted hunters from Philadelphia's most prominent social circles, and they frequented plush accommodations such as the Sora Gun Club on the Cohansey River. Thomas Eakins's paintings of hunting scenes on the bay brought national attention to these activities and, in turn, fostered interest from the Philadelphia Sketch Club, the Philadelphia Watercolor Society, and a host of documentary photographers and writers motivated by the region's local color. The Delaware Bay inspired participants in the nature study movement, including writer Dallas Lore Sharp, a Delaware Bay native whose rise to national prominence was grounded in experiencing the bay's natural endowments. The cumulative effect of cultural and environmental commentary laid the foundation for conservation of the bay's tidal marshes throughout the twentieth century, as well as promoted the roots of ecotourism at birding sites whose reputation garnered international fame.

When, in the early nineteenth century, federal and state authorities began planning the implementation of modern navigational aids in the Delaware Bay and along its shorelines, they unabashedly signaled this estuarine system's critical role in advancing the fortunes of the Greater Philadelphia area. The city's status as America's largest freshwater port underscored the urgency of these measures, and the Delaware Bay became a crucible for some of the nation's most important developments in lighthouse technology and a focal point of work conducted by the U.S. Army Corps of Engineers. Anchored to the bay's floor, channel lights at Brandywine Shoals (1850), Fourteen Foot Bank (1885), Cross Ledge (1877–78), Miah Maull Shoal (1909), and Ship John Shoal (1877) epitomized the environmental dominion and economic ambition that drove these engineering measures. Joining these channel lights was a collection of shoreline lighthouses whose appearance conformed to regional vernacular building idioms in New Jersey and Delaware. These navigational aids form a technological backdrop of longstanding challenges that have confronted the Delaware Bay, such as biological invasions—most notably oyster diseases MSX (*Haplosporidium nelsni*) and dermo (*Perkinsus marinus*).

This technological context has been central to historical debates over the effects of water diversion farther up the Delaware estuary and ecological concerns surrounding the dredging of a deeper ship channel and barge traffic on the bay's tributaries. Passage of federal legislation in the 1880s made dredging a focal point of efforts to improve the navigability of the Delaware Bay and River. While deepening the channel allowed larger vessels greater access to Philadelphia, it also heightened the potential environmental cost of accidents (oil spillage,

FIGURE 6. The Delaware River, stretching from Wilmington to Philadelphia. An industrial spine to the region, the waterway sustained prosperity, even as it generated multiple environmental issues. U.S. Department of Commerce, 1940. ATHENAEUM OF PHILADELPHIA.

fires) involved in such shipping. Deepening the bay and river channel also increased the possibility of elevated salinity levels farther up the estuary and the potential ecological toll of changes in its water chemistry.

Starting in the 1950s, modern environmentalism reframed the utopic vision of the Delaware Bay cast by European settlers four centuries earlier. By the dawn of the twenty-first century, the Delaware Bay was still an ever-present backdrop of economic ambitions driving redevelopment of the port of Philadelphia, along with similar initiatives at ports in Salem, Paulsboro, Gloucester, and Camden, New Jersey, and Wilmington, Delaware. With intermodal shipping now firmly ensconced in Philadelphia's economy, the Delaware Bay's shipping lanes assumed renewed importance in regional planning. But greater environmental consciousness contributed to revised perspectives on the bay's future. Operation of the Salem and Hope Creek Nuclear Generating Station (construction started in 1968) in Lower Alloways Creek, New Jersey, did not go unchallenged. Studies in the 1980s documented the generating station's role in Delaware Bay fish mortality. Environmentalism's most conspicuous impact led to unprecedented emphasis on recreational uses of the Delaware Bay and the rise of ecotourism in the region. These priorities led to renewed interest in the Bombay Hook National Wildlife Refuge (1937) in Delaware and the creation of the Cape May National Wildlife Refuge

(1989) in New Jersey. Complementing these federal measures was the active acquisition of shoreline areas by the states of New Jersey and Delaware for public use. In the twenty-first century, the bay's present and future remained immersed in contested perspectives over how its human use and ecological health could best be sustained.

Delaware River

Carolyn T. Adams

For centuries the Delaware River supplied its region with water, food, transportation, and waterpower to run mills to saw timber and produce grain, paper, and textiles. As the largest undammed river in the United States east of the Mississippi, its bounty seemed limitless. William Penn recognized its value when he located his port city of Philadelphia on its banks in a place that would give European settlers access to the Atlantic Ocean and enable trade with Europe and the Caribbean. Unfortunately, like many environmental assets held in common, the river's resources eventually suffered from overuse by the population along its banks. So great was the strain on this natural resource that in the mid-twentieth century political leaders launched new regional institutions to clean the river and coordinate water usage by the many jurisdictions along its banks.

Issuing from two neighboring locations in the Catskills region of New York State, the Delaware flows for 330 miles to the Atlantic Ocean. The West Branch of the river starts in the town of Jefferson southwest of Albany, New York, while the East Branch springs from a small pond nearby in the village of Grand Gorge. Those two headwaters join together to flow southward, picking up additional water from tributaries, including the Lehigh River, the Schuylkill River, and the Brandywine Creek, before finally emptying into the Delaware Bay.

The river's massive watershed—covering 13,539 square miles of territory within the states of New York, Pennsylvania, New Jersey, and Delaware—was once the homeland of the Lenape, who based their collective identity as a people on the fact that they all fished in its waters, drank from its feeder streams, and relied on its currents to transport their canoes over long distances. They called it "Lenape Wihittuck," meaning the rapid stream of the Lenape. So closely did the early Europeans identify the Indigenous people with the great river that, once they had renamed the river for the Englishman Thomas West, also known as Lord De La Warr in the mid-1600s, the newcomers began referring to the Native inhabitants as the Delaware people.

Among the first Europeans to encounter the Lenape, the English navigator Henry Hudson arrived at Delaware Bay while sailing up the coast of North America for the Dutch. In 1640 the Dutch established their first trading post at Fort Nassau (near present-day Gloucester City, New Jersey), exchanging Dutch cloth and goods for beaver pelts. When in 1682 the English Quaker William Penn arrived with his charter from Charles II, making him sole proprietor of the colonial territory, he deliberately sited his commercial center of Philadelphia where it could serve the needs of settlements up and down the river, but also connect the colony to more distant markets. Early settlers quickly began to produce commodities, not just to support their own needs, but also for export.

They built ferries across the river to enable easy travel over large stretches of the province. The Quaker village of Bristol was established in 1697 as a market town for Bucks County farmers. The ferry there took passengers from the Pennsylvania side to Burlington, New Jersey. Eventually, Bristol grew into an important commercial and shipbuilding center. Farther north on the New Jersey side of the river, the town of Lambertville began as the site where in 1733 Coryell's Ferry connected New Jersey travelers to the Pennsylvania village of New Hope. Lambertville gradually developed across the centuries into a manufacturing center for paper, rubber, spokes, and wheels. Undoubtedly, the most famous crossing was George Washington's daring decision to transport his troops across the river at McConkey's Ferry on Christmas night 1776 and lead them to a successful surprise attack against the Hessian troops quartered at Trenton, New Jersey, the morning of December 26.

The creeks that fed into the Delaware River spawned some of the earliest water-powered mills in the area. A gristmill built in 1679 where Trenton now stands processed the grain produced by local farmers. Once it was milled, they sent the grain downriver to Philadelphia for export. In the eighteenth century, iron mills and forges sprang up along the river, and by 1760 there was a thriving colonial iron industry that exploited the ore, wood, and waterpower found there. By the 1840s, sawmills located at most of the major tributaries in the upper Delaware River valley rafted their lumber down the river.

To transport other commodities from the upper Delaware, however, producers needed more than the swift flow of the river. Riverboats, barges, and rafts carrying lumber, produce, and other commodities to market had to make their way through a succession of rapids, falls, and shallows impassable during large parts of the year. The steep waterfall located at Trenton discouraged large boats from traveling from the upper Delaware all the way south to Philadelphia.

The pressure to overcome these obstructions increased dramatically with the discovery of valuable anthracite coal in northeastern Pennsylvania. That motivated the Pennsylvania legislature to build a canal alongside the Delaware River. By 1830 anthracite coal mined in northeastern Pennsylvania was gaining a growing market in Philadelphia because it burned hotter than other coals in factory furnaces. To connect the coalfields of northern Pennsylvania to urban manufacturers, builders completed the Delaware Division of the Pennsylvania Canal in 1832. That sixty-mile-long Delaware Canal ran from Bristol in lower Bucks County all the way north to Easton, along the bank of the Delaware River, connecting at its north end to the Lehigh Canal and opening the anthracite coalfields to markets in Philadelphia. In fact, anthracite made up more than 90 ercent of the Delaware Canal's cargo.

Early mills and lumberyards coexisted with abundant fish populations. During the colonial period, the river and bay boasted more than three hundred species of fish including catfish, lamprey, eel, trout, smelt, perch, and pike. Sturgeon and shad figured especially prominently in the diets of the colonists. For example, the shad was said to have saved George Washington's troops from starvation. At the river's southern extreme, Delaware Bay spawned a legendary oyster industry, which prospered until the end of the nineteenth century when harvests started shrinking. None of these aquatic populations remained as plentiful once the river became industrialized.

Railroads gained popularity in the mid-1800s, reducing the waterway's value for transporting goods and travelers. But at the same time, railroads enlarged the market area for the manufacturing plants that lined its banks. Gradually the stretch of river from Trenton south to the Delaware Bay became one of the most highly industrialized regions of the United States, producing textiles, rubber and leather goods, ships, railroad equipment, and steel. Early manufacturers clustered along the shore in industrial villages like Frankford, Kensington, and Bridesburg. In the 1870s Henry Disston developed the entire Tacony neighborhood surrounding his northeast Philadelphia saw works. In Camden, prior to the Civil War, factory owners built housing for workers close to their waterfront mills, sawmills, lumberyards, and railroad companies.

The industrial neighborhood of Frankford in Philadelphia offered a good example of the river's role in Philadelphia's industrial development. In the 1660s, Swedes built a gristmill on the northeast bank of Frankford Creek. Then in the early nineteenth century larger factories began to appear in Frankford, attracting more workers, which in turn led to the building of more housing, shops, and services. Like the majority of the factories in the rest of the city, many of those plants produced textiles. In the period just before World War I, Frankford boasted over 150 mills.

Many locations along the river developed industrial specialties. In 1848 German immigrant John Roebling built a plant in Trenton that became one of New Jersey's famed factories, making the wire rope essential to building suspension bridges, including, most famously, the Brooklyn Bridge. By 1904, when the business needed a larger site with access to the water, it built a new facility on the river at Kinkora, some ten miles from the Trenton plant. Bridesburg spawned a concentration of chemical companies during the Civil War that later became serious polluters.

Major shipyards along the Delaware River included the Cramp Yard in Kensington, the New York Shipbuilding Yard in Camden, and the Sun Shipyard in Chester. Other manufacturers on its banks included oil refineries, food-processing companies, and sugar refineries. In Wilmington, the DuPont Company chose to locate its heavily polluting Chambers Works in New Jersey across the Delaware River from Wilmington.

There they produced dyes, petroleum chemicals, Freon, and other substances. Many of these companies chose the river location because it could supply large quantities of water used in production or to dispose of effluents easily and cheaply.

The coming of railroads served not only to transport goods, but also passengers, including some who rode the rails to enjoy the scenic beauty of the Delaware Water Gap, a notch that the Delaware River cut into the Kittatinny mountain ridge about seventy-five miles west of New York City. Starting in the mid-nineteenth century, the Delaware Water Gap became one of the most popular summer resorts in the eastern United States. In 1856 the Delaware, Lackawanna, and Western Railways opened a line from New York City when only one hotel served the Water Gap. Soon a dozen more hotels served visitors who came to enjoy the scenery, hiking, rafting, and boating.

Closer to Philadelphia the river spawned an entirely different kind of recreation at the turn of the twentieth century when trolley companies invested in amusement parks as a way to increase their weekend traffic. The Delaware River became a favored spot for the popular new pastime, attracting many city dwellers. In Gloucester County, New Jersey, Lincoln Park opened in 1890, followed by Washington Park in 1895. For several decades, both attracted thousands of visitors. In Salem County, Riverview Beach Park opened in 1891 with picnic tables, a dance hall, carousel, and eventually a Ferris wheel; here, most visitors from Philadelphia and Wilmington came by river. In Burlington County, the owner of land on Burlington Island built a pier, pavilion, bathhouse for swimmers, and ice cream stand in 1900. This became the Island Beach Amusement Park whose roller coaster, "the Greyhound," proved to be its most popular attraction.

From colonial days, runoff from tanneries and slaughterhouses contaminated the river. Down through several centuries, increasing numbers of people and enterprises along the river used it as a public sewer to carry untreated waste from their properties. With the growth of manufacturing, the danger to the river increased markedly. Sewers that mixed together stormwater and sewage in a single pipe emptied directly into the river, dumping industrial wastes. Waterborne diseases, particularly cholera and typhoid fever, sickened thousands of Philadelphians during the years between the Civil War and the beginning of the twentieth century. Especially deadly outbreaks of those diseases during the 1890s forced the city to open the Torresdale sand filtration plant in 1908 as a way to clean water taken from the Delaware. By 1912 the city was chlorinating all city water.

Despite such measures to treat the water taken out of the Delaware, the river itself remained an open sewer, filled with industrial and human wastes. In the early 1900s, Philadelphia's sewers were dumping more than two hundred thousand tons of solids into the Delaware each year. A 1934 article in the *Philadelphia Inquirer* complained that the few remaining shad found in the river tasted like petroleum.

In 1948, Congress passed the federal Water Pollution Control Act making federal dollars available for river cleanup. That helped Philadelphia to construct three primary sewage treatment plants, the last of which was completed by 1953. Those plants removed solids from the city's sewage going into the river but did not eliminate the waterborne bacteria that continued to consume all the available oxygen, depriving fish of the oxygen they needed to thrive in the Delaware. Suburban growth during the 1950s and 1960s in popular riverside locations like the Levittown housing development and the nearby U.S. Steel plant at Fairless Hills added to the load carried by the Delaware.

The largest water users were power plants. Other large water-using industries were steel, petroleum, chemicals, and paper. More water was used for cooling than for all other industrial purposes. And since warm water contains less dissolved oxygen than cooler water, fish and other aquatic life suffered from rising water temperatures in addition to contaminants in the river water. Although the river's defenders tried to mount clean-water campaigns in the early 1920s and late 1930s, industrial lobbyists resisted those efforts.

Disputes arose when the actions taken in one state affected the citizens and enterprises located in other states. As the population of the basin increased over time, some of the most bitter disagreements involved droughts and floods. For example, in 1928 New York City started to draw water from several tributaries of the Delaware River, putting New York in direct conflict with villages and towns of New Jersey and Pennsylvania

FIGURE 7. View of the Delaware River working waterfront, extending to the Center City skyline, 1930. LIBRARY COMPANY OF PHILADELPHIA.

that were using the Delaware for their water supply. In 1929 New Jersey initiated (and Pennsylvania joined) a bill of complaint asking the U.S. Supreme Court to stop New York City from diverting water from the Delaware River basin. In 1931, the court ruled that the interests of each of the four river-basin states—Delaware, New Jersey, New York, and Pennsylvania—should be given equal consideration in the management of the shared waterway. The court allowed New York City to draw 440 million gallons of water a day from the Delaware and its upstream. That decision, however, did not resolve the competition for river water.

To resolve such disputes over the river's shared resources, in 1936 the states of Pennsylvania, New Jersey, Delaware, and New York formed the Interstate Commission on the Delaware River Basin (Incodel) to control and prevent water pollution, plan the conservation of water supply for the use of the cities, and plan development along the banks of the entire river.

Incodel proceeded aggressively to press all four state legislatures to pass pollution-control measures. To support its campaign, it prevailed on the U.S. Army Corps of Engineers to conduct scientific water-pollution studies and to work with regional companies on a new voluntary plan to reduce oil and refuse dumping. However, industrial production during World War II reversed the modest improvements achieved during the 1930s. During the war years companies were allowed to dump more waste than at any other time in history. Regulators were unwilling to restrain producers supporting the war effort. The port of Philadelphia became so vile that a number of ships simply refused to dock at their scheduled destination. Tests indicated that the river water entering the city's water treatment plants was the most polluted of any major U.S. city.

Seeking a new approach to shared management of this critical resource, the four states in 1961 joined with the federal government to create a successor organization. In that year President John Kennedy signed the Delaware River Basin Compact creating the Delaware River Basin Commission (DRBC), which absorbed the staff and assets of Incodel. In addition to the basin's four state governors, the compact also included the regional U.S. Army Corps of Engineers—becoming the first equal partnership between federal and state governments in river-basin management. The DRBC was not intended to coerce participating jurisdictions to comply with the majority preference, but to serve as a framework for negotiating tensions and conflicts in the management of the river.

As the first federal-state watershed compact, the DRBC became the first agency to specify the maximum volume of pollution that can be discharged daily into the river by polluters in 1968, holding them to standards more stringent than the U.S. Environmental Protection Agency (EPA) issued years later. The DRBC's efforts were strengthened in 1972 when Congress passed the Clean Water Act, making it illegal to dump pollutants into the nation's rivers without a permit from EPA and required wastewater treatment plants to improve their standards. The key to that law's success in the Delaware watershed, as elsewhere in the United States, was that Congress supplied 75 percent of the money needed to upgrade local plants. Between 1972 and 1990, over $1.5 billion was spent on wastewater treatment plants along the Delaware between Wilmington, Philadelphia, and Trenton, noticeably improving levels of dissolved oxygen.

In the 1960s and again in the early 1980s, the DRBC focused much of its effort on mediating among the states during a series of punishing droughts. Then in the first decade of the twenty-first century, the river experienced three major floods in three years (2004–6) that severely damaged homes and land along the riverbanks. Enraged residents of towns along the Delaware, mainly from the Water Gap south to the Lambertville/New Hope area, blamed the floods on New York City leaders who insisted on keeping the water levels too high in the reservoirs that served their city, as a hedge against shortages. In response to the standoff the DRBC crafted a Flexible Flow Management Program in 2007. The plan allowed a seasonal drawdown of a specific volume of water from the reservoirs, based on forecasts of likely snowpack buildup during the winter. Although this approach to meeting the conflicting goals of the state governments did not satisfy all parties equally, local governments along the river worked in association with DRBC and the Federal Emergency Management Agency to implement the plan.

Like the river's shared hazards, its infrastructure also called for coordinated management. Among the most important installations have been the bridges that connect Pennsylvania with New Jersey. In 1919 the two states created the Delaware River Bridge Joint Commission to build a bridge connecting central Philadelphia with downtown Camden and to collect tolls to maintain that bridge. To great fanfare, the Delaware River Bridge (later renamed the Benjamin Franklin Bridge) opened in 1926 just days before Philadelphia celebrated the 150th anniversary of the signing of the Declaration of Independence. Over the decades, the agency renamed itself the Delaware River Port Authority (DRPA) and constructed three more bridges across the river—the Walt Whitman, Commodore Barry, and Betsy Ross—along with a bistate rail line (PATCO) to carry riders from the New Jersey suburbs into and out of Philadelphia.

The mainly constructive relations between the two states within the DRPA hit a snag in the mid-1990s over a controversial plan to deepen the Delaware to forty-five feet by dredging the river bottom. Since 1941, the river's main channel from Philadelphia and Camden southward to the mouth of the Delaware Bay had been maintained at a depth of forty feet. But in the final decade of the twentieth century, port planners recognized the ship channel needed to be deeper if Philadelphia's port wanted to compete against other East Coast ports like Baltimore and Norfolk, Virginia, that could accommodate larger ships coming from Asia through the Panama Canal.

Political leaders in both Delaware and New Jersey strenuously opposed digging up the riverbed for fear that toxic dredge materials from the river bottom would be disposed of in their states. Prominent environmental groups including the Sierra Club also worked to block the project. To meet those objections, Pennsylvania governor Ed Rendell, a champion of the project, agreed to allow those dredge spoils to be deposited in abandoned coal mines in Pennsylvania. Ultimately, the federal government made the decision, based on the principle of federal supremacy over navigable waterways. In October 2009 the Army Corps of Engineers decided to allow the project, and dredging began in March 2010. The project to deepen the Delaware River main channel to forty-five feet was completed in February 2020.

Despite periodic disagreements about how the river's assets should be preserved, examples of regional cooperation like the Delaware River Basin Commission and the Delaware River Port Authority showed that broad consensus existed about the river's value to all parts of the region. However, government alone, even when working across jurisdictional boundaries, could not carry the entire burden of protecting the river. In 2014 the William Penn Foundation launched a Delaware River Watershed Initiative committing $100 million to coordinate the work of over sixty community associations and nonprofit organizations. All these nongovernmental groups agreed to work on land preservation and restoration projects on the river's banks as a way to reduce runoff from farm fields, stem the loss of forests, and prevent the depletion of groundwater. The partners agreed to monitor water quality at five hundred sites in the watershed and share information.

In the Supreme Court decision of 1931 allocating rights to the waters of the great Delaware River to the four states comprising its watershed, Justice Oliver Wendell Holmes remarked, "A river is more than an amenity, it is a treasure." As a treasure held in common, the Delaware River provided those living on its banks with countless opportunities to make use of its bounty. In so doing, this treasure that crosses local, county, and state boundaries, tested the region's capacity to cooperate in preserving its waters from overuse and even destruction. Through a combination of local initiative and federal resources, the region's inhabitants largely proved themselves capable of meeting that challenge.

Schuylkill River

Howard Gillette, Jr.

Extending some 130 miles in a generally southeasterly direction from its source at Tuscarora Springs in the anthracite coal region of Schuylkill County to its point of confluence with the Delaware River in Philadelphia, the Schuylkill River has played a central role in shaping the character and aspirations of Philadelphia and the regional hinterland through which it flows. The river's watershed of about two thousand square miles lies entirely within the state of Pennsylvania. Its upper portions originate in the alternating ridge-and-valley formations of the Appalachian Mountains. While historically a prime source of sustenance in its fish and fresh water, the river, as it drew industry to its banks, found its natural benefits diminished by pollution and waste products. In the latter part of the twentieth century, new generations of environmentally conscious citizens acted to restore its natural qualities with multiple benefits for improved health and recreation for the three million people living within its watershed.

Native inhabitants had been camping and fishing on the banks of the Schuylkill for as much as fourteen thousand years before the first Europeans arrived in the seventeenth century. The area was first settled by the Unalachtigo subtribe of the Lenape or "original people" who settled in bands along the rivers and creeks of southeastern Pennsylvania. They referred to the river as *Ganshowahanna*, meaning "falling water," or *Manayunk*, which meant "where we drink." A navigator, Arendt Corrsen of the Dutch West India Company, gave the river its modern name in 1628, when he became the first European to navigate it. Translated as "hidden river," the name is thought to refer to the location of its mouth, obscured from the Delaware River by League Island, later the site of the Philadelphia Naval Shipyard. In 1633, Corrsen was appointed commissary and instructed by the company to acquire land on the river for a plantation and trading post. He purchased a tract known as "Armenveruis" from the Lenape, and in the same year the Dutch erected Fort Beversrede on the site. This fortification stood until about 1651 near the confluence of the Schuylkill and Delaware Rivers near where the Platt Bridge was later erected.

Even as European settlement proliferated, the Lenape maintained settlements along the river, including Nittabakonck ("place which is easy to get to"), a village located where the Schuylkill meets the Delaware River. It was this area where William Penn chose to lay out Philadelphia. Granted a charter to settle the area from Charles II of England as partial repayment of a debt, Penn nonetheless chose to buy the area from the Lenape to ensure peace for the colony. Selected with an eye to tapping the rich agricultural hinterland to assure the city's growth, the site relied on its rivers for supplies of food and lumber that could be floated to the city when water was high enough—usually the spring.

Many streams flowed into the Schuylkill, including the Wissahickon, Plymouth, Sandy Run, Skippack, Pennypack, and Perkiomen Creeks, prompting the construction of dams and mills to produce grain, lumber, oil, paper, and powder and enhance trade. The presence of natural rapids, however, presented obstacles to boats. After several failed attempts in the 1780s and 1790s to fund improvements that would make the rapid-

FIGURE 8. *Manayunk*, by Augustus Kollner, 1879. Although an industrial intrusion to the Schuylkill, the mills of Manayunk were never far from the balm of a natural environment offering a respite from city life. FREE LIBRARY OF PHILADELPHIA.

filled Schuylkill navigable, Philadelphia businessmen finally convinced the Pennsylvania legislature in 1815 to approve the charter of the Schuylkill Navigation Company to construct a slack-water navigation system of canals, dams, and pools between Philadelphia and Pottsville to the northwest in Schuylkill County. Despite setbacks in funding and the death of the chief engineer, the system opened to navigation in 1824, and with an extension to Port Carbon four years later it handled the shipment of newly discovered riches of anthracite coal. Although supporters of the new system envisioned it primarily as a means of securing the flow of natural products to Philadelphia, especially grain (which local businessmen feared might otherwise be sent to Baltimore by way of the Susquehanna River), coal quickly dominated the business.

By the 1840s, the transport of coal had shifted to rail, further enhancing development throughout the Schuylkill River valley. The shift could be seen in Reading, the county seat of Berks County. Boosted not just by the Schuylkill Canal but also the completion in 1828 of the east-west Union Canal connecting the Schuylkill and Susquehanna Rivers, the town of Reading continued to grow following incorporation of the Philadelphia & Reading Railroad in 1833. Farther south, Phoenixville, located at the junction of the Schuylkill and French Creek, utilized the Chester County Canal, completed in 1828, and the Philadelphia & Reading Railroad to gain easier access to raw materials and more efficient transportation of finished products from ironworks established at the onset of the nineteenth century. More generally, from 1820 to the 1860s ironworks, foundries, manufacturing mills, blast furnaces, rolling mills, railroads, warehouses, and train stations sprang up throughout the Schuylkill Valley. Tiny farm villages grew into vibrant company towns, then transitioned into small cities as major industry and supporting businesses transformed local economies and populations swelled. By 1857 more than a million tons of freight moved each year through the valley's diversified transportation system.

Within Philadelphia County industry concentrated along the river's east bank. The effect of shifting energy regimes could be seen most notably in Manayunk—originally called Flat Rock Bridge—where by 1828 there were as many as ten textile mills powered by water backed up by a dam at the Schuylkill and directed through a two-mile canal constructed by the

Schuylkill Navigation Company. The introduction of industrial capitalism undercut the dominance of flour milling as it had flourished for almost a century along the nearby Wissahickon Creek and prompted such popular designations of Manayunk as the "Lowell of Pennsylvania" and the "Manchester of America."

Even in the early years of Philadelphia's commercial growth, officials grew concerned about assuring pure water for its residents. In 1799, the city established a watering committee and selected the Schuylkill as the city's primary water source. As the city quickly outgrew a pumping station located in Centre Square at the heart of the old city, it directed city engineer Frederick Graff to supervise construction of a waterworks at Fairmount, the prominent hill located on the Schuylkill's east bank just north of the original city boundary. There engines would pump water from the river to a reservoir at the top of the hill, where it was distributed by a system of pipes to city subscribers. When steam engines proved costly and dangerous to operate, the watering committee converted the system to waterpower, assisted by construction of a dam at the Falls of the Schuylkill. Located where the river descends from the elevation of the Pennsylvania Piedmont to the low-lying Atlantic Coastal Plain, the area had long been the most famous natural attraction in the vicinity of Philadelphia. Not surprisingly, the area attracted the interest of Philadelphia's wealthiest residents, who built country retreats free of the crowds, heat, and disease associated with the city. Construction of the dam at that location created a quiet pool upstream, ideal for rowing and skating. For the villas on the east bank of the river, however, the change brought swamp conditions and flooded meadowlands that reduced the attractiveness of country living. As conditions worsened, the city, in a further effort to protect the purity of the water, began buying up those estates, turning their properties into parkland. Boosted by state legislation in the 1860s, Philadelphia's expansive Fairmount Park took form on both sides of the Schuylkill in the following years.

Most of the commercial traffic on the Schuylkill River plied the portion between Center City and its mouth because navigation farther north was impeded by the dam at the falls. Following the Civil War a series of wharves and docks went up on the river west of Center City to accommodate ships and barges transporting cargo including coal, ice, lumber, and stone. This increased commercial traffic prompted the United States Army Corps of Engineers to plan river improvements near the Schuylkill's mouth. In 1875 and 1876 dredging took place in the channel near Girard Point, adjacent to what became known as the Penrose Ferry Bridge and near Gibson's Point. This portion of the river was used to ship over 10.8 million bushels of grain to foreign ports.

The Pennsylvania Railroad recognized the economic advantages of Philadelphia's wharves for the import and export of grains including wheat, oats, and corn. Among the elevators constructed to sustain this trade, the largest was the International Navigation Company's Philadelphia-based 650,000-bushel Girard Point elevator erected in 1874 near the junction of the Schuylkill and Delaware Rivers. Other industrial facilities taking advantage of a Schuylkill River location included the Atlantic Refining Company, established at the end of Passyunk Avenue in Point Breeze in 1860. It marked the advent of an influx of petroleum refineries into South Philadelphia. Initially established as a storage facility, by the 1880s Atlantic had become one of the largest refineries in the United States.

The transformation of land on both sides of the Schuylkill River from rural estates and farms to industrial and intensive residential use had direct consequences for the health of the river. As the Philadelphia region grew and its industries expanded, the Schuylkill's pollution increased. The headwaters contributed the effluent from mine drainage and coal silt, and the lower sections were plagued with the waste of a large and growing population. According to the city engineer's report for 1866, "Below Manayunk, the river assumes a dark, dirty, milky appearance, and is covered with soiled waste and shreds from shoddy mills. . . . There is no doubt that a constant deterioration in quality is going on, which, if not arrested, will ultimately force the city to abandon the Schuylkill as a source of supply, if the time to do so has not already arrived."

Problems worsened in the early twentieth century. As anthracite coal production peaked, large amounts of coal-washing wastewater and coal silt discharged into nearby streams. To this were added sewer deposits described in a study by the Philadelphia Bureau of Engineers in 1913 as polluting the entire length through the city, to the point of preventing development along its banks either for pleasure or business. By 1927 the Army Corps of Engineers estimated that the Schuylkill River and its tributaries contained thirty-eight million tons of coal waste.

Civic leader John Frederick Lewis captured the sense of dismay shared by many residents in a 1924 illustrated address presented at the Historical Society of Pennsylvania published the same year. "Scores of cities with but a fraction of Philadelphia population, a tithe of her wealth, and a vastly larger per capita debt," he charged, "might be cited as having recognized the wisdom of waterfront reclamation [and] sewage disposal by other means than by fouling their most valuable asset. Why should Philadelphia not do likewise?" The situation began to change when the Pennsylvania legislature unanimously passed the Clean Streams Act in 1937. A decade later Governor James H. Duff directed a massive cleanup effort resulting in the excavation of twenty-three impounding basins along the river to receive dredged silt. In 1978 the Pennsylvania legislature responded to appeals from the Schuylkill River Greenway Association, founded four years earlier, by designating the Schuylkill the state's first Scenic River.

Restoration of the river accelerated at the turn of the twenty-first century. Building on the state's designation of the Schuylkill as a Scenic River, advocates along the river corridor succeeded in 2000 in securing formation of the Schuylkill Greenways National Heritage Area and associated Greenways River Trail along the 128-mile corridor of the Schuylkill Valley with a commitment to repair environmental damage to the river and its surroundings. A 2003 report to the Schuylkill River Development Corporation on the state of the Schuylkill watershed brought together twenty-five nonprofit organizations with state and local agencies to pledge cooperation in addressing needs for clean water impacted by both population gains and losses along the Schuylkill's tributaries. As a signature project, the organization launched Schuylkill Banks Park, a strip of parkland along the east bank of the river extending from the foot of Fairmount below the waterworks and south into the central city with an eventual destination of the Delaware River. Other organizations devoted to environmental stewardship of the river included the Delaware Riverkeepers Network, the Schuylkill River Greenway Association, the Schuylkill Highlands Conservation Landscape Initiative, the Middle Schuylkill River Conservation Landscape Initiative, the Lower Schuylkill River Conservation Landscape Initiative, the Schuylkill Action Network, the Phoenixville Iron Canal and Trails Association, and the Headwaters Association.

As much as was accomplished to boost the Schuylkill as a recreational asset, its industrial character, and the hazards it represented, were manifest in 2019 when a devastating explosion erupted at the former Atlantic Refinery site. While government and civic leaders sought to secure new environmentally safe uses for the property as the company entered bankruptcy, the costs of remediation and repurposing land under private ownership remained an obstacle, even as nearby residents struggled to secure compensation for damage to their health.

Over many years river-area residents sought balance between beauty and production, serenity and empire. A longtime source of recreation, the Schuylkill had a mixed legacy that was well captured by artist Thomas Eakins. A rower himself, Eakins depicted the serene presence of rowers on the river, never distant, however, from the emblems of industry located nearby. The modern effort to balance industry with nature was the reclamation of tidewater gardens at Southwest Philadelphia's Schuylkill border. There, at the oldest surviving botanical garden in North America, Bartram's Garden, founded in 1728 by botanist John Bartram, modern programs introduced area residents to the natural features of the river and the importance of their conservation. With industrial activity never far away from this spot, it served in the twenty-first century as a prime vantage point for encountering the river's mixed heritage. Coincidentally the City Parks Association revisited John Frederick Lewis's *Redemption of the Lower Schuylkill* with a similarly named exhibit. Clearly, conservationists still had work to do. Yet even after centuries of development along the river's banks, forests regrew to cover about 41 percent of the basin, representing important areas for recreation and wildlife. Agriculture still occupied 40 percent of the acreage, while developed lands represented about 13 percent. Surface and groundwater resources in the basin continued to provide drinking water for more than three million people.

FIGURE 9. *The Champion Single Sculls*, by Thomas Eakins, 1871. The first in a major series by Eakins concerned with sculling (the sport of rowing with two oars), this painting shows the Schuylkill River as the site of an important race in October 1870. On the rail bridge in the background, a whisp of smoke indicates an approaching train. METROPOLITAN MUSEUM OF ART.

Lehigh Valley

Robert F. Smith

Over the centuries, strong ties of transport, investment, and culture grew between the Greater Philadelphia region and the Lehigh Valley. The valley was carved by retreating glaciers twenty thousand years ago and maintained by its namesake river running from the Pocono Mountains, through Blue Mountain, south and east into the Delaware River. Only in recent memory was the region defined as the three counties of Carbon, Lehigh, and Northampton, and the metropolitan areas of Allentown, Bethlehem, and Easton.

The Minsi Trail pathway linked elements of the Lenni Lenape tribe of Native Americans living in the Delaware, Lehigh, and Lackawanna River valleys. This trail, used for trade, communication, and tribal war, led the first Europeans to the valley in the early eighteenth century. The Lenape were forced from the valley after it was granted to the colony of Pennsylvania by the 1737 Walking Purchase. Evangelist George Whitefield, Chief Justice William Allen, and several wealthy Philadelphia investors purchased large tracts of the land in order to build country estates. Whitefield and Allen eventually sold their lands to settlers who developed communities in the region. Moravian missionaries settled Nazareth in 1740, and sect leader Count Nicolaus Zinzendorf founded Bethlehem in 1741. Allen, himself, planned Allentown (originally Northampton Town) in 1762.

Minsi Trail became known as the King's Road and was maintained at the colony's insistence by local communities. It spurred trade, making the valley a major supplier of furs, timber, iron, and agricultural products to Philadelphia. Pennsylvania recognized the region's importance in 1752 by organizing it as Northampton County and naming Easton as the county seat. German immigrants followed the Moravian and Pennsylvania settlement efforts and filled out much of the valley's land by the time of the American Revolution.

In the War for Independence the valley was the site of a Continental Army hospital and a state armory, and provided foodstuffs and supplies to the war effort. Durham Iron Furnace, owned by Irishman George Taylor, produced artillery and ammunition, and Taylor served in the Continental Congress and signed the Declaration of Independence. When the British occupied Philadelphia in the winter of 1777–78, the state moved several manufacturing operations to Bethlehem, and Allentown was used to warehouse Philadelphia's many church bells. Most famously, the Pennsylvania State House bell, later known as the Liberty Bell, was stored in Allentown's Zion German Reformed Church.

After the war, the valley's connections to Philadelphia increased. The beginning of regular stagecoach service in 1796 and the chartering of a turnpike company to manage the route in 1804 transformed the King's Road into Bethlehem Pike. The 1791 discovery of coal in the region drew investment from Philadelphia, whose entrepreneurs Josiah White and Erskine Hazard chartered the Lehigh Coal and Navigation Company to develop the coal field and build the Lehigh Canal between 1818 and 1829. The canal remained in operation until the 1940s, moving coal and iron to Philadelphia's extensive factories and workshops.

Lehigh County was founded in 1812 and Carbon County in 1843 as development in the region strained communications with Easton. Many local residents, however, considered federal, state, and Philadelphia city involvement in the valley even more detrimental to local morality and culture. The Fries Rebellion erupted in 1799 after a federal house tax was zealously enforced. Arrests for nonpayment provoked John Fries to lead his fellow Lehigh Valley citizens in an armed attack on the Bethlehem jail holding the tax dodgers. Fries and others were tried and sentenced to death but pardoned by President John Adams. Political conflict replaced armed uprisings in the nineteenth century as the valley fought against state laws mandating public schools, missionary Methodist expansion, and outside investment in natural resources. But the valley could not stop Philadelphians' investment and interest in the region.

In 1852, the North Pennsylvania Railroad further linked the valley with Philadelphia. The Philadelphia and Reading Railroad then leased that line and built the Perkiomen Railroad and East Penn Railroad to connect various segments of the valley to the Greater Philadelphia region. Asa Packer, however, controlled valley rail traffic by creating the Lehigh Valley Railroad in 1853 from rights-of-way he purchased from Philadelphia investor Nicholas Biddle. These rail routes served to develop various valley industries including cement making, slate mining, and iron and zinc smelting. Crayola, founded in 1885, and Just Born Quality Confections, founded in 1923, used the valley's rail networks and access to resources to provide creative color toys and candies, respectively, to the Philadelphia region and outward to national markets. In 1857, Philadelphian Joseph Wharton founded the Saucon Iron Company, which became Bethlehem Iron in 1861 and Bethlehem Steel in 1899. The steel company, until its 1995 closure, provided for Philadelphia's manufacturing enterprises and for the Delaware River (later Benjamin Franklin) Bridge, built in 1926.

Philadelphia, however, was not the valley's only customer. Bethlehem Steel provided beams and cable for buildings and bridges around the country, including the Golden Gate Bridge, the George Washington Bridge, the Chrysler Building, and Hoover Dam. Crayola Crayons were marketed around the world and were inducted into the National Toy Hall of Fame in 1998. Similarly, Just Born candy company, headquartered in Bethlehem, was given the key to the city of San Francisco for the innovativeness of its products.

Passenger transport in the valley was developed by numerous trolley companies, one of which, the Lehigh Valley Traction Company, began service to Philadelphia, known as the Liberty Bell Line, in 1903. Two years later the company purchased and united all local routes as the Lehigh Valley Transit Company, making it possible to travel from Philadelphia to any part of the valley. Trolley service lasted until 1956

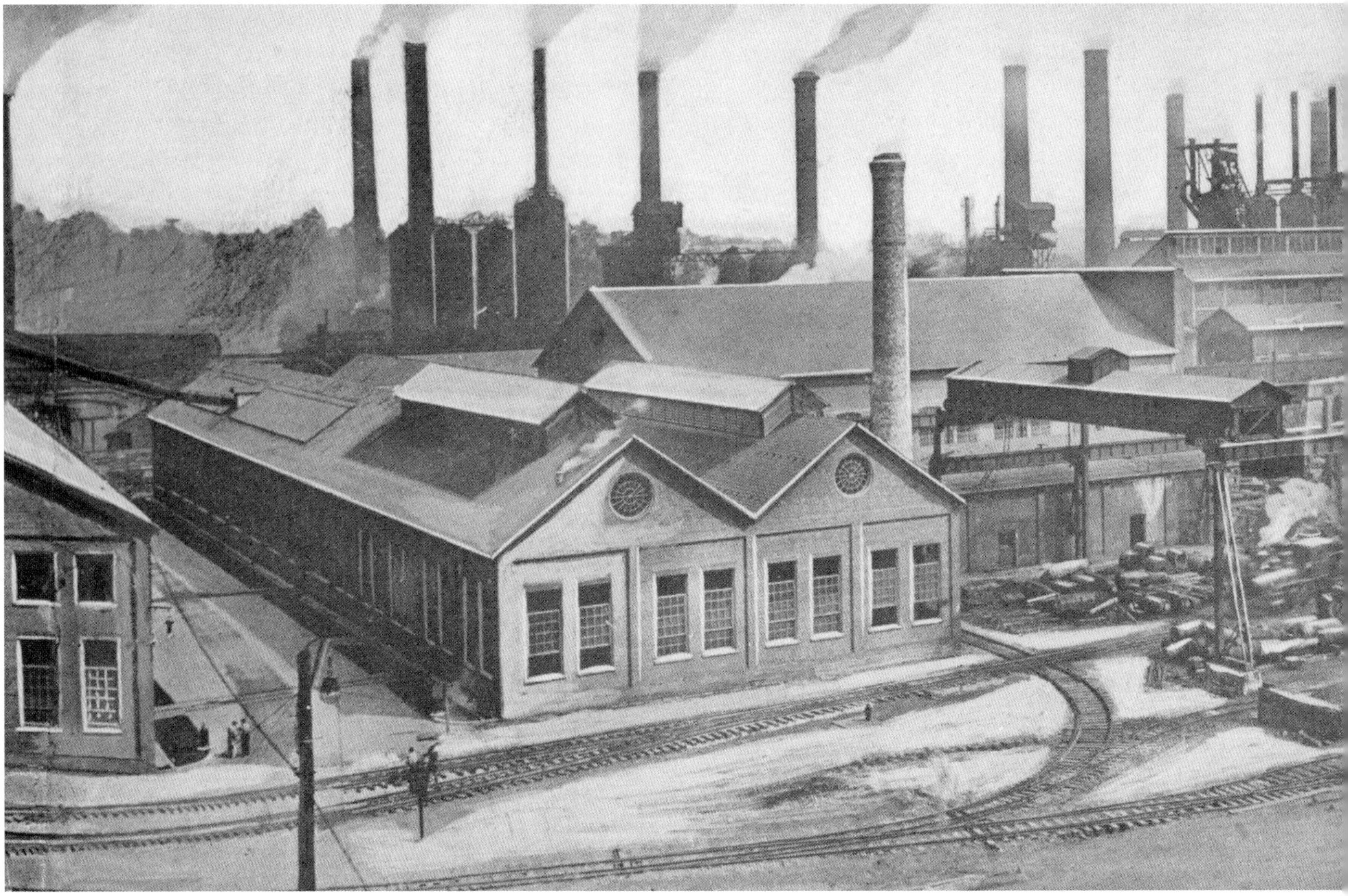

FIGURE 10. Bethlehem Steel Works postcard, ca. 1912. LIBRARY OF CONGRESS.

when post–World War II developments in bus service and personal cars made the rails unprofitable. Many of the transit company's rights-of-way in the valley were transferred in 1970 to Philadelphia's transport company, the Southeastern Pennsylvania Transportation Authority (SEPTA). In 1926, Bethlehem Pike was redesignated as Pennsylvania Route 309 and upgrades began, with segments transformed into highways. Some parts were left to local use and named Old Bethlehem Pike. In 1955, an extension was added to the Pennsylvania Turnpike providing a second road link between the Philadelphia region and the valley.

The construction of Pennsylvania Routes 22 and 78 from the 1950s to the 1970s remade the valley into a New York City bedroom community. Commuters followed the highways west to avoid high costs of living, and bus service developed to transport workers into New York. Likewise, by the 1990s numerous New York firms relocated to the valley or built transport hubs to make use of the workforce and road network. In 2010, the U.S. Census Bureau recognized the importance of this economic and cultural connection by including the valley as part of the New York Metropolitan Statistical Area. Built in 1929, the Lehigh Valley International Airport connected the region to further non-Philadelphia markets and investors. The airport's location and local intermodal service attracted Amazon, FedEx, and Air Transport International to make the valley a shipping hub for their enterprises.

Nevertheless, the valley retained strong cultural and economic ties to Philadelphia as well. Pennsylvania Power and Light (PPL), founded in the Lehigh River valley in 1920, provided electricity to several communities in the outlying Philadelphia region and

was a major founding sponsor of the city's professional soccer team, the Philadelphia Union, which played in Talen Energy Stadium, named after a PPL subsidiary. The Lehigh Valley Phantoms minor league hockey team, farm team to the Philadelphia Flyers, began playing in Philadelphia before moving to Allentown in 2014. Minor league baseball's Ironpigs arrived in the valley in 2008 after becoming a farm team for the Philadelphia Phillies.

The valley was also served by Philadelphia's major media outlets, and numerous health insurance, banking, and engineering firms had shared offices between the valley and Philadelphia. St. Luke's Health Network of Bethlehem and Good Shepherd Rehabilitation Hospital of Allentown both invested in serving the Philadelphia region. The federal government stressed the connection between the two areas by creating the Delaware and Lehigh National Heritage Corridor in 1988, building a park and bike trail system over the unused canal and rail paths that previously linked the areas.

Investors saw the valley as a location to build hubs of transport, communication, and entertainment. In 2007, Sands Casino Resort purchased a large portion of the former Bethlehem Steel site and developed it into a $400 million gaming, live entertainment, hotel, and shopping destination. Opening in 2009, the site drew visitors to the valley from both Philadelphia and New York. Sands became a major sponsor of Musikfest, an annual ten-day summer celebration of all music types. Started in 1984, in 2016 it hosted over nine hundred thousand people. It was created by ArtsQuest, a valley creative arts nonprofit that worked with Sands to develop the Steel Stacks Event Center on the old Bethlehem Steel site for both Musikfest and year-round programming. Wind

Creek Hospitality, an entity of the Porch Bank of Creek Indians, purchased the casino hotel in 2019. Remaining Bethlehem Steel properties as well as former industrial sites around the valley were purchased by the Lehigh Valley Industrial Park (LVIP), an organization created in 1959 to revitalize the valley's economic prospects as traditional enterprises declined. LVIP developed its section of the Bethlehem Steel site into office space, intermodal service, and storage. This investment drew companies like Norfolk Southern, Cigars International, WHEMCO (Lehigh Heavy Forge), and United States Cold Storage to the valley. Philadelphia shoppers were further drawn to the region by the opening in 2006 of the Promenade Shops at Saucon Valley, which featured fifty-eight premium outlet stores.

Much of the valley's redevelopment was also due to its institutions of higher learning and health care. Moravian University, founded as a women's seminary in 1742, played a major role in strengthening Bethlehem's historic core. Lafayette College was founded in 1826, and in 1832 Easton's town fathers convinced Reverend George Junkin to relocate his Manual Labor Academy from Germantown to become part of the college. Lafayette subsequently became the city's cultural heart. Muhlenberg College, founded 1848, and Cedar Crest, founded 1867, promoted Allentown as an undergraduate destination. Asa Packer joined the development of education in the valley by opening Lehigh University in 1865 to provide engineers for his railroad.

Lehigh picked up the research mantle left by Bethlehem Steel, taking over its innovation center and promoting cultural events on Bethlehem's South Side. Among the largest educational institutions in the valley, however, were Northampton Community College (NCC) and Lehigh Carbon Community College (LCCC), with roughly ten thousand and six thousand students respectively as of 2022. They took leading roles in redeveloping the downtowns of Bethlehem and Allentown, respectively. NCC rehabilitated an old Bethlehem Steel structure as an educational and community space. What began as Allentown Hospital in 1899 and a small St. Luke's Hospital for Bethlehem's South Side community in 1872 had by 2014 become the two largest employers in the valley. Lehigh Valley Health Network and St. Luke's Health Network built dozens of facilities throughout the valley and beyond, expanding opportunity and infrastructure. Together they employed 4 percent of the valley's population.

Throughout its development, the valley was an immigrant community. Following settlement by Moravians and Germans in the colonial period, Irish came to the region to work in the canals, railroads, and mines. Irish mine workers famously became known as the Molly Maguires, namesake of labor agitators whose leaders were hanged at the Carbon County prison in Jim Thorpe. Irish immigration was quickly overwhelmed, however, by large numbers of Eastern Europeans, who came to work in the coal mines, iron furnaces, and steel mills. Churches and fraternal organizations located throughout the valley signaled the presence of two dozen different nationalities. Although African American workers were recruited to the valley during the world wars, more recently Latino immigration from Puerto Rico and the Dominican Republic primarily surged, giving the region one of the largest Latino populations in Pennsylvania.

The Lehigh River valley witnessed a great deal of development and change through the centuries. Lenni Lenape, Germans, Slavs, and Latinos each added distinctive marks to the land in terms of transport routes, educational institutions, industrial concerns, and entertainment options. The majority of this development tied the region to Philadelphia, but that did not keep the valley from becoming an economic and cultural hub in its own right.

Brandywine Valley

W. Barksdale Maynard

Less than an hour west of the Quaker City lies the Brandywine Valley, for centuries a green and pleasant counterpoint to the dense urbanism that has defined America's first great metropolis. A region synonymous with gracious living and cultural tourism, the Brandywine Valley has drawn visitors from around the world to enjoy its many public gardens, house museums, and historical attractions. Such tourism has been a longstanding tradition, going back to the nineteenth century, when improved railroad connections made this bucolic area an attractive getaway from crowded Philadelphia, just twenty-three miles away. In the twenty-first century the fame of the Brandywine Valley continued to grow: a national park, First State National Historical Park, was established there in 2013, preserving 1,100 acres of verdant countryside through which George Washington's army marched on its way to the Battle of the Brandywine in September 1777, one of the two largest land battles of the American Revolution.

Although a relatively small place geographically, the Brandywine Valley enjoyed an outsized reputation, having often been celebrated by writers and artists, many of them based in Philadelphia (once called "The Athens of America"), who spread its fame widely. Brandywine Creek is only about sixty miles long, less than half the length of Philadelphia's Schuylkill River, and its watershed of 330 square miles is dwarfed by the Schuylkill's two thousand square miles. Eighty-five percent of the Brandywine watershed is confined to a single county in Pennsylvania, Chester County. Flowing south, it briefly skirts Delaware County at historic Chadds Ford before reaching its terminus in New Castle County, Delaware.

Only in its last few yards does the Brandywine reach the coastal plain; otherwise, it is the quintessential piedmont stream, rapidly falling over boulders of Wissahickon schist or Brandywine blue rock, at times twisting through rolling agricultural landscapes but then slipping into steep-sided valleys thickly wooded with some of the largest hardwood trees in the northeastern United States. Ecologically, the valley abounds with flora and fauna. This owes to a surprising variety of habitats, from freshwater marshes to old-growth forests, and to the region's felicitous location at the junction of North and South (surveyors Charles Mason and Jeremiah Dixon wintered on the Brandywine during the years they surveyed their famous regional borderline, 1763–67). For example, northeastern plants such as hemlock trees mingle here with southeastern species such as umbrella magnolia.

Before European settlement, abundant ecological riches made the Brandywine a congenial place for Lenni Lenape Indians, who hunted game in the hardwood forests or caught shad in the creek, long before dam building interrupted the migration of fish upriver. Natives watched in dismay as Swedes arrived in 1638 and built Fort Christina—the first Swedish settlement in the New World—on a gentle rocky outcrop where it could guard the lower reaches of both the Christina River and Brandywine Creek. A successful Dutch campaign to seize the fort in 1655 was one of the first military encounters by rival European armies on American soil. The name "Brandywine Creek" is Dutch, of uncertain origin; perhaps it refers to the honey-brown color, similar to brandy, of the stream during one of its frequent floods, in visual contrast to the gray and placid Christina. Other theories abound. Nor is there agreement about whether the Brandywine is a "creek" (the typical usage for centuries) or the more recent "river."

When William Penn's Quakers arrived in 1682, Brandywine Creek formed the western boundary of the settled parts of Pennsylvania, with the junction of civilization and wilderness sharply demarcated at "Brumadgam" on the Thomas Holme map of 1687, subsequently Birmingham Township, Chester County. Wilmington, Delaware, was located on a hilltop between the Christina and the Brandywine in 1731, virtually a miniature replica of Philadelphia in layout, and it thrived because of the exceptionally prosperous milling that the Brandywine afforded. With its rapid drop in elevation, this piedmont river was ideally configured for the construction of water-powered mills, as the Swedes had been the first to recognize, establishing a mill seat in what would become Wilmington's Brandywine Park, where traces of the ancient dam survived into the twenty-first century.

By the late eighteenth century, the Brandywine Valley had become a crucible of the Industrial Revolution, with a proliferation of mills (more than one hundred on just the Delaware section of the creek by 1793) that used increasingly advanced technology. The main north-south road in early America, linking Philadelphia and Washington, D.C., crossed the Brandywine at Wilmington, where tourists and travelers (among them George Washington) marveled at the fully automated milling technology on display by Market Street Bridge in Brandywine Village, an enclave of expensive Quaker millers' homes.

The Brandywine witnessed the American debut of the mechanical production of paper just upstream from Wilmington at Gilpin's Mill in 1817, triggering a revolution in the production of books, magazines, and newspapers in the young republic. The ability of

FIGURE 11. *Mill on the Brandywine, Delaware*, by John Rubens Smith, ca. 1828. Depicted in watercolor, a mill complex on Brandywine Creek suggests the fragile harmony between nature and technology achieved during the early decades of the Industrial Revolution. LIBRARY OF CONGRESS.

the fledgling nation to defend itself against menacing European powers was dependent upon the production of gunpowder on the Brandywine by the Du Pont family, which arrived in Delaware from France in 1802 in time to supply powder to fight the Barbary pirates at Tripoli (1801–5) and the British in the War of 1812. On the eve of the Civil War, half of the national output of gunpowder came from Du Pont mills on the Brandywine, including the sturdy stone facilities preserved at Hagley Museum and Library. If industry faded long ago from the Brandywine in Delaware, it continued to thrive upstream at Coatesville, Pennsylvania, where the successor firm to Brandywine Iron Works (1810) remains the oldest steel mill in America. In the twenty-first century, countless local families of Italian and Irish descent could trace their ancestry to the early Brandywine mill workers, some of whose memories were preserved in an ambitious campaign to collect oral histories undertaken in the 1950s by the Hagley Museum. Mill worker housing in dense rows remained a defining characteristic of many neighborhoods in Wilmington.

With nineteenth-century industry came wealth, as the Brandywine became nationally synonymous with technological revolutions in milling. Just outside Wilmington, handsome estates were built overlooking the stream, and poets and writers sang the praises of the valley, with its appealing mix of water-powered industry, picturesque riparian scenery, and tales of lore from Indian days and the Battle of the Brandywine, where the romantic young Marquis de Lafayette had been wounded. The culmination of these literary efforts was eventually *The Brandywine*, a book in the popular Rivers of America series (1941) by Wilmington-born critic Henry Seidel Canby, with illustrations by Andrew Wyeth.

But industry also brought pollution of the creek, and by the 1860s there were calls to preserve land along its banks to safeguard the health of Wilmingtonians, who drank the foul-smelling water. Brandywine Park was established in the 1880s, laced with curving roadways that followed, rather imperfectly, a plan provided by the leading landscape architect of the day, Frederick Law Olmsted. The park was the beginning of a conservation tradition that made the valley a recognized role model in watershed preservation nationwide. Headquartered at Chadds Ford, the Brandywine Conservancy, begun in 1967, expanded to hold more than five hundred conservation easements over 12 percent of the watershed.

As the Du Pont family amassed extraordinary wealth—as late as the 1980s, they were one of the richest families in America—they played the key role in preserving the scenic Brandywine Valley against the looming threat of heavy industry, such as that which engulfed the lower Schuylkill, or the piecemeal suburban sprawl that jostled against Darby Creek, fifteen miles north. The Brandywine Conservancy, for example, was the brainchild of a boisterously enthusiastic Du Pont descendant, George A. "Frolic" Weymouth. The unspoiled flavor of the region—as seen, for example, from the twelve-mile Brandywine Valley National Scenic Byway designated in 2005—owed much to the Du Pont family's traditional concern with large-scale estate agriculture, their cultivation of a pleasing landscape aesthetic, and the cherishing of historic sites.

Their special passion was gardening. America's premier French-style formal garden flourished at the Nemours estate (1910) of Alfred I. Du Pont, an elaborate homage to his French ancestors. A woodland garden underplanted with colorful azaleas flowed over the hillsides at Winterthur ("March Bank" garden, 1902), home of Henry Francis Du Pont, whose collection of American antiques remains unparalleled. Under the creative eye of Pierre S. Du Pont, the nation's largest-ever display garden took shape at Longwood (Main Conservatory, 1921) and later became the flagship cultural attraction of the Brandywine Valley, with more than 1.5 million visitors annually. All these gardens (and associated estates of sprawling size and sumptuous elegance) were funded by industry in places far distant and especially benefited from the windfall profits that the DuPont Company enjoyed from providing gunpowder to the western front in World War I.

As the estates of what contemporaries have nicknamed "Chateau Country" were being laid out and embellished, there simultaneously flourished the Brandywine School of Art, a movement centered on Howard Pyle, the Wilmington-born artist who revolutionized American illustration starting in the 1880s. Pyle moved to Philadelphia to be near the leading publishing houses of the day but eventually returned to the Brandywine Valley, which he regarded as the wellspring of his art, inspiring him deeply with its historical relics, from crumbling colonial houses and mills, to rustic "worm" fences lining dirt roads through the cornfields of the unspoiled countryside, to venerable Old Swedes Church (1698–99) near the Brandywine's mouth. A teacher at Drexel Institute in Philadelphia, Pyle brought his best students to the Brandywine Valley, founding a summer art school on the Brandywine Battlefield at Chadds Ford. His star student arrived in 1902, N. C. Wyeth, who shared Pyle's near-religious devotion to the relics of America's colonial past and settled permanently in Chadds Ford when he began his own, legendary career as the dean of American illustration.

N. C. Wyeth and other former students of Pyle became known as proponents of the "Brandywine school" of illustration, with a strong emphasis on rural life, the colonial heritage, and meticulously researched historical themes. His son Andrew extended the tradition right up to the twenty-first century, living and painting exclusively on the Brandywine all his life, except for summers in Maine, and developing a brooding, rather bleak style deliberately different from his father's. The immense fame of Andrew Wyeth continued to draw tourists and plein-air painters to "Wyeth country" in the Brandywine Valley, where the Brandywine River Museum of Art amassed the world's largest collection of Wyeth paintings, from N. C. right down to Jamie Wyeth, who lived and painted in the area into the twenty-first century.

First State National Historical Park promised to bring ever-more attention to the Brandywine, as an area hailed as "the Most Famous Small River in America." But the modern Brandywine Valley's widespread popularity also fed a surge in population growth, with upscale suburban developments peppering the hilltops and threatening to change the rural character of this historic place forever. The warnings of urbanist William H. "Holly" Whyte about the costs of sprawl came to pass in his native valley: traffic clogged twisty colonial roads, scenic viewsheds were violated, and invasive plants proliferated. As Chester County transformed rapidly, one encouraging sign was its open-space program, launched in 1989 and ultimately responsible for setting aside 28 percent of the county's land. Nonetheless, a worrying symptom of overdevelopment was the markedly increased flooding of the Brandywine, culminating in a record-shattering rise of twenty feet at Chadds Ford following Hurricane Ida in September 2021. The village was inundated beneath brown water, and the Brandywine River Museum of Art suffered damage. The future brings new challenges to this famous valley that has long been loved and celebrated but has proved to be ecologically fragile in the face of modern development pressures.

New Jersey Pine Barrens

Skylar Harris

New Jersey's Pine Barrens, the forest and wetlands area also known as the Pinelands or the Pines, has played a varied but vital role in its region's cultural and economic history. The Pine Barrens have, over time, been a home to Native American populations, a center of early American industry, a hub of military activity, and a focus of ecological and recreational interest. Although inhospitable to most forms of intensive agriculture, the Pinelands have been a crucial site for the commercial farming of blueberries and cranberries, two of New Jersey's most valuable fruit crops.

The Pine Barrens are characterized by high water tables and acidic, nutrient-poor, sandy soil, which supports a broad range of plant and animal life, including rare insectivorous plants, dwarf pine species, and the Pine Barrens tree frog. Much of this habitat is contained within the New Jersey Pinelands National Reserve, a 1.1 million–acre area that spans seven counties and occupies about 22 percent of the state's land mass. Notable residents of this region include Deborah Leeds, who, according to folklore, gave birth to the Jersey Devil, a legendary winged monster with cloven hooves and a forked tail. The area was also home to James Still, the self-taught "Black Doctor of the Pines."

Archaeological evidence indicates that humans began inhabiting the region around 10,000 BCE. While the land proved unable to support intensive agriculture, these early residents created small settlements sustained through hunting and fishing. The best-known native inhabitants were the Lenape, who used controlled fires to remove underbrush that discouraged hunting and agriculture. Because of the environs' poor soil, the region did not attract significant European settlement until the late seventeenth century, when colonists began establishing whaling and shipbuilding settlements on coastal perimeters of the woodlands. These industries made the Pine Barrens a valuable source of lumber and other materials needed to manufacture pitch, tar, and turpentine, leading to the growth of sawmills and early Pinelands towns such as Browns Mills, Dennisville, Tuckahoe, and Port Elizabeth. The area's unique plant life also attracted early botanists.

As colonial settlement intensified, the Pine Barrens also proved to be a valuable source of bog iron deposits, wood for charcoal, peat, and sand for glass production. Beginning in the early eighteenth century, sawmills and gristmills were established in the Pines. The Lenape also continued to reside in the Pinelands until treaties negotiated in the aftermath of the Seven Years' War enacted significant resettlement efforts. In 1758, Brotherton, the first Indian reservation in the colonies, was established in present-day Indian Mills. By 1800, the majority of the Lenape had been forced to migrate out of the region. The Pinelands' non-Native population also began to significantly increase around this time, in large part due to the establishment of iron furnaces and glass factories.

The iron industry thrived in the Pine Barrens throughout the late eighteenth and early nineteenth centuries. Beginning in 1755, Charles Read, a former Philadelphia merchant who had moved to Burlington, New Jersey, to pursue a political career, purchased property in the Pinelands in the hopes of establishing a chain of ironworks and forges in Batsto, Taunton, Etna, and Atsion. After its construction in 1766, Batsto Iron Works became one of the region's first and most prominent sites of iron production, though financial troubles soon forced Read to gradually split up and sell

FIGURE 12. Gathering cranberries from the surface of a flooded bog, Burlington County, N.J. Arthur Rothstein, Farm Security Administration, 1938. LIBRARY OF CONGRESS.

these properties to investors from Philadelphia and the surrounding New Jersey region. These investors and other early iron-making industrialists oversaw iron production at more than thirty forges and furnaces throughout the Pines, such as the Atsion Iron Works, Cohansie Iron Works, Etna Furnace, Martha Furnace, and Speedwell Furnace. These sites played a pivotal role in supplying military forces during the American Revolution and the War of 1812.

Forges and furnaces were joined by other industries, such as the great glassmaking factory of the Pennsylvania landowner and glassmaker Caspar Wistar, who began operating the Wistarburgh Glass Manufactory in violation of colonial laws in 1739 near Alloway, New Jersey. In 1779, the Wistarburgh Glass Manufactory was joined by the Stanger Glass Works, founded by Solomon Stanger, a former employee of Wistar, in what later became Glassboro. By the nineteenth century, more than twenty glass manufactories had been established in Pinelands manufacturing towns like Atco, Barnegat, Clementon, Egg Harbor, Estellville, and Green Bank. The region also developed cotton mills after 1810 and paper mills after 1832. Between 1830 and 1840, residents began cultivating cranberries, a water-intensive crop well suited to the wetlands of the Pines.

Iron production in the Pine Barrens declined precipitously in the mid-nineteenth century as a result of competition from nearby producers in Pennsylvania, collapsing entirely by 1869. Efforts in 1876 by the wealthy Philadelphia industrialist Joseph Wharton to establish agricultural production of sugar, sugar beets, and cotton also ended in failure, as did his 1891 attempt to export water from his Pine Barrens property to Philadelphia (the New Jersey legislature quickly prohibited the practice). As the region's industries declined and many of the former hubs of industry were abandoned, the forests instead became a pathway to more enticing locations. Early railroads crossed through the Pine Barrens as they radiated from the transportation hubs of Philadelphia and New York to South Jersey's early suburbs and the emerging resorts such as Atlantic City and Cape May.

By the early twentieth century, the inhabitants who remained in the Pine Barrens lived in a rural economy based at least partially on hunting and gathering, even as surrounding localities became increasingly densely settled and industrialized. As a result of this cultural and demographic divide, populations surrounding the Pinelands began using the derogatory term "Pineys" to refer to the region's residents. In 1912, this reputation led the eugenicist Henry H. Goddard to publish *The Kallikak Family*, which presented the pseudonymous Pinelands family as a case study in genetic inferiority.

The Pinelands were soon put to new economic uses, however. In 1916, Elizabeth White, a native of the Pine Barrens from a cranberry-farming family, successfully collaborated with botanist Dr. Frank Coville to develop a hybrid blueberry plant for commercial cultivation. This scientific breakthrough led to commercial blueberry farms on White's property at Whitesbog and elsewhere. Along with cranberries, blueberries became a staple commercial crop of the region. In 1917, following the outbreak of World War I, the Pinelands area also became the site of the military installations of Fort Dix and Lakehurst Naval Air Station. A third military base, the Millville Army Air Field, was established in 1943, during World War II.

Despite these developments, the Pine Barrens continued to be largely rural and sparsely populated in comparison to neighboring regions. This made it a point of interest for scientists and environmentalists seeking to study or call attention to its unique ecosystem and its endangered plant and animal life. In 1954, the state of New Jersey purchased Joseph Wharton's old 156-square-mile estate, which had lain vacant since Wharton's death in 1909. The purchase, which gave the state claim to the vast water resources of the tract, also more than doubled the acreage of state parkland. In 1978, Congress designated the federal Pinelands National Reserve (the first such reserve to be created under the National Parks and Recreation Act of 1978), and state and federal agencies were established to control development in the reserve area. The ecosystem was also declared to be a U.S. Biosphere Reserve in 1983 and an International Biosphere Reserve in 1988 by the United Nations Educational, Scientific and Cultural Organization (UNESCO). Featuring local, state, and federal public parks, wildlife management areas, and the historic industrial villages of Batsto and Double Trouble, the Pinelands continued to be a significant tourism and recreational resource for the region.

Trees

Laura Turner Igoe

Trees have been culturally, environmentally, and symbolically significant to the Philadelphia region since the city's founding. They were believed to improve public health, they beautified and refined city streets, parks, and other green spaces, and several were revered as living memorials to past historical events. Trees also faced their fair share of destruction during the nineteenth and early twentieth centuries, as unregulated agricultural clear-cutting, competitive markets for fuel and timber, growing industry, and expanding population eliminated many of the region's forests. Beginning in the late nineteenth century and continuing into the twenty-first century, local, regional, and state organizations have collaborated to increase the tree canopy cover in the Greater Philadelphia area.

Pennsylvania—Latin for "Penn's Woods"—is uniquely positioned as a space where northern and southern tree species overlap, although Appalachian oak forest covers the majority of the state, including around Philadelphia, southern New Jersey, and Delaware. This forest type consists primarily of oaks with black birch, black gum, red maple, hickories, tulip tree, and white pine. William Penn boasted of the arboreal production of the region—which included present-day New Jersey and Delaware—a few years after King Charles II presented him with the Pennsylvania colony in 1681: "The trees of most note are the black walnut, cedar, cypress, chestnut, poplar, gumwood, hickory, sassafras, ash, beech; and oak of divers sorts, as red, white, and black, Spanish, chestnut, and swamp."

By the time Penn arrived in North America, however, Native Americans had already dramatically altered the region's forests. The Lenni Lenape used fire to manage forests, clear land for agriculture, and burn underbrush to encourage the growth of young plants that attracted deer and other small game. Native Americans depended heavily on wood, bark, and vegetable fibers to construct houses and other material goods. When villages exhausted forests after a few decades, communities settled in new sites a few miles away and the process began all over again. By the late seventeenth century, however, European disease had decimated the Native population and many of their cultivated spaces may have become overgrown.

In 1682, when William Penn and surveyor Thomas Holme laid out Philadelphia's streets in a symmetrical grid, they envisioned trees and green space as important components of the city plan. Penn reserved land for five public squares in different sections of the city and he intended for every house to be surrounded by gardens, orchards, or fields, "that [Philadelphia] may be a greene Country Towne which will never be burnt and always be wholesome." Inspired by the many types of trees that grew in the region, Penn named the east-west streets of Philadelphia after local varieties: Cedar (later South), Pine, Spruce, Walnut, Chestnut, Mulberry (later Arch), and Sassafras (later Race).

Even though most Philadelphians did not set aside large portions of their land for trees and plants as Penn envisioned, a 1796 map of Philadelphia by John Hills showed trees to be a defining feature of the city after the Revolutionary War. Trees shaded the grounds behind the Pennsylvania State House (Independence Hall), and wealthy citizens planted them in front of their homes, inspired by the tree-lined promenades of European cities like Paris and Antwerp. Art historian Therese O'Malley has argued that a desire to ornament the new republic motivated an increased interest in landscaping after the Revolution; city trees provided a way to project an aura of refinement and gentility.

In the 1820s, Philadelphia began rehabilitating Penn's five original squares, most of which had fallen into disrepair; several were used as trash dumps, potter's fields, and sites for public hangings. The city attempted to reclaim these spaces through the assignment of commemorative names—Franklin, Washington, Logan, and Rittenhouse—and landscaping. Only the plan for Franklin Square, submitted by the sculptor and city councilman William Rush and painter Thomas Birch, survived as a record of these projects. The design for this northeastern square depicts an ordered, picturesque view of nature. The numerous, evenly spaced trees and symmetrical copses of evergreens and willows reflect a desire to order and beautify public space and underscore the close association between trees and health in early nineteenth-century medical philosophy. Physician Benjamin Rush attributed declining health and yellow fever outbreaks in Pennsylvania to "the cutting down of wood, [which] tends to render a country sickly." He recommended planting trees at unhealthy sites to absorb and purify unwholesome air.

Several squares in Philadelphia became defined by their distinctive trees. Tall Lombardy poplars lined the pathways of Centre Square, the location of a neoclassical engine house powering the city's first waterworks, later, the site of city hall. First brought to the United States from Europe in the 1780s by William Hamilton, the proprietor of the Woodlands estate outside the city, Lombardy poplars became extremely popular throughout the Northeast because they quickly grew to great heights and were easily transplanted. Many American cities planted Lombardy poplars after 1799, the year of George Washington's death, because they were believed to be the first president's favorite tree. Washington Square served as an arboretum to educate the public about horticulture. By 1831, the square contained fifty varieties of North American and European trees, two of which were introduced by Meriwether Lewis and William Clark from their 1804–6 expedition in the Rocky Mountains.

Select trees in the Philadelphia region were venerated as silent witnesses to a historical and environmental past in the nineteenth century. Paintings, prints, textiles, and fine china celebrated the "Treaty Elm," under which it was believed William Penn purchased land for Philadelphia from the Lenape in 1683. Images of the respected tree referenced Philadelphia's creation narrative while also reminding the viewer of the sylvan heritage that contributed to the region's economic success. A blow to that hallowed heritage occurred when the elm fell down in an 1810 storm. The elm's wood was converted into various artifacts—including trinket boxes and portrait busts of Penn—disseminated throughout the nation and even across the Atlantic Ocean to England. The Treaty Elm, through its destruction,

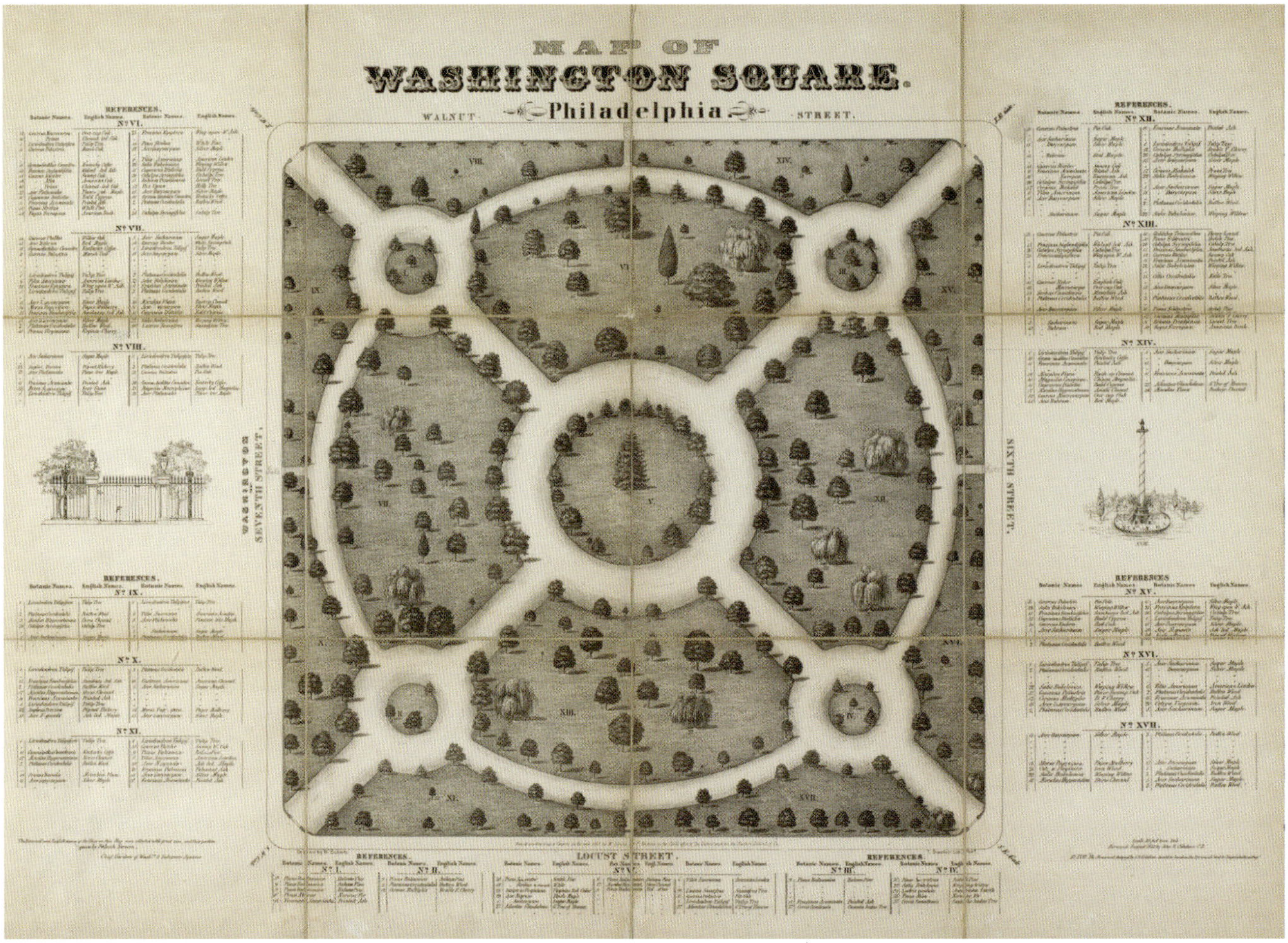

FIGURE 13. Washington Square, 1842. Functioning as an arboretum, the square educated the public about horticulture with its diversity of more than fifty varieties of trees. HISTORICAL SOCIETY OF PENNSYLVANIA.

commemoration, and veneration, served as a tangible symbol of the state's sylvan past, saturated with mythic historical meaning.

While trees were cultivated in city streets and parks and revered as historical eyewitnesses, they were aggressively harvested in the region's hinterlands from the eighteenth until the early twentieth century. Wood served as a primary resource for the region. By 1810, approximately two thousand sawmills in Pennsylvania produced nearly seventy-five million feet of sawed lumber. Philadelphia exported or utilized huge quantities of this wood in shipbuilding, housing, construction, tanning, and fuel.

As a result of rapid wood consumption, timber in easy proximity to transportable waterways became scarce by the beginning of the nineteenth century. Large forests of oak, chestnut, pine, and cedar in southwestern New Jersey, directly across the Delaware River from Philadelphia, almost completely disappeared due to agricultural clear-cutting and fuel consumption. One sawmill operator reported in 1821 that the large rafts of sawed lumber floated downstream to the Delaware River wharves north of Vine Street "have decreased [and] they must decrease more & more . . . the Timber in most places is nearly all cut away." This deforestation increased by the end of the nineteenth century with the advent of the railroad logging era. Geared logging locomotives allowed the lumber industry to harvest vast, previously inaccessible acres of forest, and advances in chemistry permitted all types of wood to be treated and distilled into acetate of lime, wood alcohol, wood tar, charcoal, and gases.

This widespread deforestation alarmed residents of the Greater Philadelphia region who understood the importance of trees within their urban, suburban, or rural environments. Throughout the nineteenth century, artists and writers like Thomas Cole, Frederick Church, Ralph Waldo Emerson, and Henry Thoreau promoted a romantic view of forests as spaces of sublime power and mysticism. In the 1860s, George Perkins Marsh's text, *Man and Nature; or, Physical Geography as Modified by Human Action*, alerted North Americans to the interconnectedness of nature, demonstrating that trees controlled erosion, mediated flooding, and filtered water. As Philadelphia and its surrounding counties developed and industrialized during the nineteenth century, the city began taking steps to preserve wilderness areas in order to protect the upstream sources of its water supply. Philadelphia's city government purchased land along the Schuylkill River and established Fairmount Park in 1855 to prevent industry from accumulating along the riverbanks and polluting the city's drinking water. Fairmount Park commissioners preserved the park's original terrain, with the minor additions of carriage roads and walking paths, noting that "the diversified character of the grounds, and the abundance of noble trees and groves give us, at many points, a Park made to our hands."

By the late nineteenth century, forest education and advocacy campaigns organized by concerned citizens culminated in the establishment of forestry departments and policies at the state and national level. The French botanist François André Michaux, author of the foundational treatise of American forestry, *North American Sylva* (1819), left a legacy of $12,000 to the American Philosophical Society in Philadelphia to fund a lecture series in silviculture (the science-based management of forests). The resulting Michaux Forestry Lectures, presented from 1877 to 1892, represent an early attempt to educate the general public on forestry concerns. The Pennsylvania Forest Association, founded in Philadelphia in 1886, developed from discussions of forest issues at a local women's club. Joseph T. Rothrock, a professor of botany at University of Pennsylvania and frequent Michaux Forestry lecturer, was elected the association's first president and later became the state's first commissioner of forestry.

Over the next century, local, state, and national governments assumed responsibility for the planting, cultivation, and preservation of trees in Pennsylvania, Delaware, and New Jersey. In 1895, the Pennsylvania Forestry Commission appointed by the Pennsylvania State Board of Agriculture reported that forested land in the state had decreased from more than 90 percent to 36 percent of the state's land area, threatening timber supply, water quality, and public health. The commission began purchasing marginal or cutover land abandoned by farmers and timber industries in 1898 in order to encourage forest regrowth and the State Department of Forestry continued these activities after its establishment in 1901. New Jersey established a Forest, Park, and Reservation Commission in 1905, and Delaware introduced a State Board of Forestry in 1909 to monitor and preserve their forests. By 1936, nearly 179 million seedlings raised in state-funded nurseries had been planted in state forests, along streets and highways, and on private land in Pennsylvania. The early twentieth century also saw the establishment of several local, publicly accessible arboretums—including Morris Arboretum of the University of Pennsylvania and Tyler Arboretum in Media—to preserve and study local trees and species from all over the world.

In 2011, the Pennsylvania Horticultural Society partnered with thirteen counties in southeastern Pennsylvania, New Jersey, and Delaware in a "Plant One Million" campaign to restore the tree canopy cover of the region to 30 percent, replacing trees lost to development. The Philadelphia Parks and Recreation Department introduced the TreePhilly initiative in 2012 to provide free yard and street trees and facilitate maintenance workshops for urban communities. Tree canopy covered 20 percent of total land in Philadelphia in 2012, a 4 percent increase from 2008, according to a study by the University of Vermont Spatial Analysis in partnership with the United States Forest Service. Valued for their role in improving air and water quality, blocking noise pollution, providing shade, and reducing the "urban heat island effect," trees became more and more visible within the diverse landscape of the Greater Philadelphia region.

EXPLORE MORE

To learn more about how landscape features established the footprint of the region, see the first volume of *The History of Philadelphia, 1609–1884* (L. H. Everts & Co., 1884) by J. Thomas Scharf and Thompson Westcott, which opens with a thorough description of Philadelphia's topography. Adam Levine puts the city's relationship with its topography in modern perspective in his essay "The Grid versus Nature: The History and Legacy of Topographical Change in Philadelphia," chapter 7 of Brian C. Black and Michael J. Chiarappa's edited book, *Nature's Entrepôt: Philadelphia's Urban Sphere and Its Environmental Thresholds* (University of Pittsburgh Press, 2012). David J. Cuff, William J. Young, Edward K. Muller, and Wilbur Zelinsky provide a regional assessment in *The Atlas of Pennsylvania* (Temple University Press, 1989). See also, Michael Godfrey, *Field Guide to the Piedmont: The Natural Habitats of America's Most Lived-in Region, from New York City to Montgomery, Alabama* (University of North Carolina Press, 1997) and Beryl Robichaud and Murray F. Buell, *Vegetation of New Jersey: A Study of Landscape Diversity* (Rutgers University Press, 1973). Related information can be found in Peter O. Wacker and Paul G. E. Clemens, *Land Use in Early New Jersey: A Historical Geography* (New Jersey Historical Society, 1995).

The Bayshore Center at Bivalve, 2800 High Street, Port Norris, N.J., operates the Delaware Bay Museum, offers educational programs on the aquatic environment, and hosts New Jersey's official tall ship, a restored 1928 oyster schooner, *A. J. Meerwald.* The John DuBois Maritime Museum at 949 Ye Greate Street, Greenwich, N.J., houses a large collection of southern New Jersey maritime-related items from the nineteenth and early twentieth centuries. The Museum of Cape May County, 504 N. Route 9, Cape May Court House, N.J., also has relevant maritime materials. For historical background, see David Budlong Tyler, *The Bay and River Delaware: A Pictorial History* (Cornell Maritime Press, 1955) and Bonnie J. McCay, *Oyster Wars and the Public Trust: Property, Law, and Ecology in New Jersey History* (University of Arizona Press, 1998). Michael Chiarappa describes the fish industry in the Delaware River and Bay areas in chapter 8 of Black and Chiarappa, eds., *Nature's Entrepôt.*

Much of the upper Delaware River's history can be traced through the Delaware and Lehigh National Heritage Corridor running some 165 miles between Wilkes-Barre and Bristol, Pennsylvania. Among the cultural institutions along the route are the National Canal Museum at 2750 Hugh Moore Park Road, Easton, Pennsylvania. Steven Conn's book *Metropolitan Philadelphia: Living with the Presence of the Past* (University of Pennsylvania Press, 2006) focuses on the many forms of interdependence between Philadelphia and its suburbs, with special attention to the region's two great rivers—the Delaware and the Schuylkill—and how they helped shape the region. See also Bruce Stutz's *Natural Lives, Modern Times: People and Places of the Delaware River* (Crown Publishers, 1992), which analyzes the impact of the river on the lives and land holdings of the people who share it, from the Poconos to the marshlands at its lower end. Stutz's book also focuses on how humans have impacted the river, particularly through the industries based in Philadelphia and Trenton. Philadelphia's Science History Institute, at 315 Chestnut Street, maintains a permanent exhibit on the Delaware and Schuylkill River ecologies, engineering systems, and water usage.

Any exploration of the Schuylkill River starts with the Schuylkill River Trail, a multiuse path that will extend 120 miles from Frackville in Schuylkill County through Montgomery, Chester, and Berks Counties to Philadelphia. With much of it over abandoned rail lines, the trail introduces users to evidence of several centuries of industrial development, canal navigation, railroad transportation, quarrying of limestone and iron ore, and the production of iron and steel. Bartram's Garden, at 5400 Lindbergh Boulevard, at the Philadelphia terminus of the river, offers a broad array of environmental programs as well as tours of the naturalist John Bartram's eighteenth-century home. For background on Bartram, see Judith Magee, *The Art and Science of William Bartram* (Pennsylvania State University Press, 2007). Visitors to the nearby John H. Heinz National Wildlife Refuge (8601 Lindbergh Boulevard), originally known as the Tinicum Marsh and spanning the boundary between Philadelphia and Tinicum Township in Delaware County, may observe hundreds of species of plants, trees, birds, insects, and mammals. To learn more about the migratory paths of birds, see Scott Weidensal, *A World on the Wing: The Global Odyssey of Migratory Birds* (W. W. Norton, 2021). The iconic Fairmount Water Works, 640 Waterworks Drive, adjacent to the Philadelphia Museum of Art, offers on-site and off-site tours that explore Philadelphia's waterways and watersheds. The Schuylkill's early artistic influences are explored in the Pennsylvania Academy of the Fine Arts 2019 catalogue, *From the Schuylkill to the Hudson: Landscapes of the Early American Republic*. The Schuylkill River Development Corporation's study *Rediscovering Philadelphia's Hidden River: The Tidal Schuylkill Master Plan*, published in March 2003, offers an updated view of the river and the challenges facing it.

If rivers have shaped human settlement, so too have valleys. Though tied to New York as well as to Philadelphia, much of the Lehigh Valley's settlement patterns as well as economic development owe more to the latter city. The Lehigh River, a tributary of the Delaware, flows southward through the Lehigh Valley before joining the Delaware River in Easton. It helped power the region's steel industry. Much of Bethlehem's rich history can be traced through Historic Bethlehem Museums and Sites, 74 W. Broad Street, Bethlehem. The consolidation of several museums and historic sites, the organization became a founding member of the International Moravian Heritage Network, one of three key eighteenth-century historic Moravian settlements in the world. Much of the city of Bethlehem's steel plant remains extant for visitors to see and admire. The National Museum of Industrial History at 602 E. Second Street in Bethlehem tells much of that story. Chloe E. Taft's *From Steel to Slots: Casino Capitalism in the Postindustrial City* (Harvard University Press, 2016) examines the complicated story of the area's transition from a site of production to one of cultural consumption. More broadly, Karyl Lee Kibler Hall and Peter Dobkin Hall recount area history in *The Lehigh Valley: An Illustrated History* (Windsor Publications, 1982).

A trip to the New Jersey Pinelands should include visits to Batsto Village, 31 Batsto Road, Hammonton, and Whitesbog, 120 W. Whites Bogs Road #34, Browns Mills. For the history and ecology of the area, see John McPhee, *The Pine Barrens* (Farrar, Straus & Giroux, 1968); Richard T. T. Forman, *Pine Barrens: Ecosystem and Landscape* (Academic Press, 1979); and Robert J. Mason, *Contested Lands: Conflict and Compromise in New Jersey's Pine Barrens* (Temple University Press, 1992).

For a far-reaching account of the Brandywine Valley, see W. Barksdale Maynard, *The Brandywine: An Intimate Portrait* (University of Pennsylvania Press, 2015). Maynard connects the area's rich artistic legacy to the land in *Artists of Wyeth Country: Howard Pyle, N. C. Wyeth, and Andrew Wyeth* (Temple University Press, 2021). Further resources can be found at the Brandywine Museum of Art, 1 Hoffman's Mill Road, Chadds Ford, Pa., and the Delaware Art Museum, 2301 Kentmere Parkway, Wilmington, Del.

For further information about the historical context of trees in the region, see Lester A. DeCoster, *The Legacy of Penn's Woods: A History of the Pennsylvania Bureau of Forestry* (Pennsylvania Historical and Museum Commission, 1995) and Donna J. Rilling, "Sylvan Enterprise and the Philadelphia Hinterland, 1790–1860," *Pennsylvania History* (Spring 2000). As a guidebook to help identify and appreciate all the species of trees encountered across the region, consult Paul Meyer, Catriona Briger, and Edward Barnard, *Philadelphia Trees: A Field Guide to the City and the Surrounding Delaware Valley* (University of Pennsylvania Press, 2023). Michael Weilbacher provides suggestions for exploring the natural features in and around Philadelphia in *Wild Philly* (Timber Press, 2023).

Printed for R. Baldwin at the Rose Pate

Chapter 4

Regional Foundations

Introduction

The first peoples to occupy the area that came to be identified as the Greater Philadelphia region were themselves regionalists, although their region was not organized around a dominant population center of the kind that followed the period of their dominance. Making the most of accessible land and streams to nourish their families and build communities in what came to be known as the Delaware Valley, the Lenapes remained apart from other tribes beyond the mountains that divided them from the West. Because they valued peace and inclusion, they managed to accommodate the first European explorers when they arrived in the early seventeenth century, forging trade agreements with them and encouraging limited settlements. The arrival of rival European groups complicated social dynamics as Swedes, succeeding the Dutch, then the English, jockeyed for control of strategic locations from which to enhance trade. Such competition prompted conflict—some of it violent—not just with Native peoples but between Europeans. Europeans erected fortifications that became emblems of a new dynamic involving commitments not just to specific locations but to the surrounding territory they sought to control. Directives from the home countries sought to stabilize and defend settlements, but the situation remained fluid into the eighteenth century.

The fate of European settlements fluctuated as succeeding groups competed for control. The first to suffer from competing European ambitions were Native peoples, as English in West Jersey and Pennsylvania took up Lenape land, pushing them to the margins. The Walking Purchase of 1737, which stripped the Lenape of control over thousands of acres, proved one such dramatic example. As both Native and European resistance against English dominance dissipated, the English declared new lines. Settlers, however, largely ignored the English Proclamation Line of 1763, which Parliament intended to concentrate colonists' settlement east of the Allegheny Mountains. The subsequent line drawn by surveyors Charles Mason and Jeremiah Dixon similarly failed to impose a precise boundary between sections. Nonetheless, such politically sanctioned efforts fostered a perception over time of boundaries between regions, in the latter case one perceived to be free, the other slave.

Clearly, regional fluidity diminished as territorial boundaries solidified and separate jurisdictions formed. Still, the city of Philadelphia, even in its infancy, exerted wide influence, anchoring peoples living now in different states as well as townships and boroughs.

Native Peoples Before 1680

Jean R. Soderlund

Native Americans lived in what became southeastern Pennsylvania, southern New Jersey, and northern Delaware for more than ten thousand years before the arrival of Europeans in the early seventeenth century. By emphasizing peace and trade, the Lenapes retained their sovereignty and power through 1680, unlike Native peoples in New England and Virginia who suffered disastrous conflicts with the colonists. Before William Penn founded Pennsylvania, the Lenapes and their allies among the Swedish, Finnish, and Dutch settlers created a society based on the ideals of peace, individual freedom, and inclusion of people of different beliefs and backgrounds.

The first Americans settled in the region as glaciers gradually receded in North America at the end of the last ice age. Because of the accumulation of ice, the Atlantic seashore was located more than sixty miles to the east of its present location. As the glaciers melted, the ocean level rose, submerging evidence of early communities along the coast. Archaeological data about the people inhabiting the lower Delaware Valley from this early era through the Woodland Period (ca. 1000 BCE to 1600 CE) indicate significant continuity over thousands of years. The Lenapes, like their ancestors, relied upon hunting, fishing, gathering, and—in the later years—small-scale agriculture. They lived in small autonomous towns without palisades, suggesting they kept mostly at peace with their neighbors and more distant nations.

For centuries the Native people of the lower Delaware Valley remained isolated from other parts of the Americas, including the peoples of the Ohio and Mississippi valleys who built agricultural civilizations based on the "three sisters": corn, beans, and squash. These crops complemented one another in cultivation and provided humans a nutritious diet. The geography of Pennsylvania, particularly the north-south orientation of the Susquehanna and Delaware Rivers, limited interaction of Native people of the Delaware Valley with the Mississippians who built cities, tall burial mounds, and stratified societies in the interior of the continent. Though the Lenapes raised corn, beans, and squash by the seventeenth century, they took advantage of the abundance of game animals, fish, shellfish, berries, wild rice, and other foods rather than engage in large-scale agriculture.

The Lenape people included groups such as the Armewamese, Cohanzicks, Mantes, and Sickoneysincks, who built towns along tributaries of the Delaware River and on the Atlantic seacoast near Delaware Bay. They spoke Unami, an Algonquian language similar to the dialects of their allies the Munsees, who controlled the region to the north up into southern New York, and the Nanticokes of Maryland's Eastern Shore. The Lenapes' neighbors to the west were the Susquehannocks, an Iroquoian people of the Susquehanna Valley.

The size of the precontact Delaware Valley population is unknown because European sailors and fishermen brought pathogens even before the Dutch arrived. Colonization by Europeans in North America had a devastating impact on the Lenapes and other Indigenous people because they lacked immunity to smallpox, influenza, measles, and other diseases. In 1600 the Lenapes numbered an estimated 7,500; by the 1650s their population decreased to about 4,000, and to about 3,000 by 1670. The Lenapes' population decline was not as severe in the 1600s as among some other groups whose numbers dropped by 90 percent or more. The Lenapes' success in avoiding war during most of the seventeenth century contributed to their strength and continued sovereignty over their land.

The Lenapes divided work on the basis of gender: women raised crops, gathered nuts and fruit, built houses, made clothing and furniture, took care of the children, and prepared meals, while men cleared land, hunted, fished, and protected the town from enemies. Native women held an equivalent status with men in their families and society; parents extended freedom to their children as well, practicing flexible, affectionate child-rearing.

During the seventeenth century, the Lenapes' sociopolitical structure appears to have been democratic, egalitarian, and based on matrilineal kinship groups, with descent through the mother's line. The heads of kinship groups chose the group's leader, or *sakima*, who held authority by following the people's will. With advice, the *sakima* assigned fields for planting and made decisions on hunting, trade, diplomacy, and war.

FIGURE 14. Some of the Lenape groups who lived along the Delaware River were labeled on this 1639 map of the area that became southern New Jersey. Written in Dutch, the map also explained some of the groups' languages. LIBRARY OF CONGRESS.

In religion, existing evidence suggests that the Lenapes believed the earth and sky formed a spiritual realm of which they were a part, not the masters. Spirits inhabited the natural world and could be found in plants, animals, rocks, or clouds. People could obtain a personal relationship with a spirit, or *manitou*, who would provide help and counsel to the individual throughout his or her life. Lenapes also believed in a Master Spirit or Creator, who was all-powerful and all-knowing, but whose presence was rarely felt.

When Dutch explorers entered the Delaware River about 1615, the Lenapes welcomed their trade. In 1624, they granted permission for a short-lived settlement on Burlington Island and in 1626 allowed construction of Fort Nassau across the river from the future site of Philadelphia. The Lenapes and colonists developed a trade jargon based on Unami that became standard trade language throughout the region.

The Lenapes retained their autonomy and traditional ways of life while selectively adopting new technology from the Europeans. Native women and men appreciated the convenience of woolen cloth, firearms, and metal tools, incorporating them into their culture but not abandoning their traditional economic cycle of hunting, fishing, gathering, and agriculture.

The Dutch trade precipitated war between the Lenapes and Susquehannocks from 1626 to 1636 because the Susquehannocks sought to control the Delaware River. They killed many Lenapes and pushed them from the west to east bank, burning towns and crops. The Lenapes fought back, eager to trade for European cloth, guns, and metal goods in exchange for beaver, otter, and other furs. While these local pelts were thinner because of milder mid-Atlantic winters than those the Susquehannocks obtained from central Canada through the continental fur trade, the Lenapes had a successful market with the Dutch. The war ended by about 1636 when a truce, which developed into an alliance, permitted both the Lenapes and Susquehannocks to trade in the region.

In 1631, violence flared when wealthy Dutch investors started a plantation called Swanendael near present-day Lewes, Delaware, at the mouth of Delaware Bay. It seemed to Lenapes that the Dutch were shifting their priorities from trade to plantation agriculture similar to the English colonists in Virginia who murdered Indigenous people and expropriated land. The Sickoneysincks, the Lenape group near Cape Henlopen, destroyed Swanendael, killing its thirty-two residents. When Dutch captain David de Vries arrived in late 1632, he made peace and reestablished trade with the Sickoneysincks.

Over the next half century, Lenapes controlled the lower Delaware Valley, accepting European trade goods in exchange for rights to small parcels of land for forts and farms, but not plantation colonies. With the attack on Swanendael and its memory, the Lenapes restricted European settlement. In 1670, just 850 Europeans lived in the lower Delaware Valley compared with 52,000 in New England, 38,000 in Virginia and Maryland, and 6,700 in New York and eastern New Jersey. With an estimated population of 3,000 in 1670, the Lenapes remained more numerous and powerful than the Europeans.

Seven years after Swanendael, in 1638, the Lenapes permitted a small group of Swedish, Finnish, and Dutch colonists to establish New Sweden at the location of current Wilmington, Delaware. Lenapes and Susquehannocks traded with New Sweden and the Dutch mariners who continued to frequent the river. While the Europeans fought each other over trade and land, the Lenapes dominated the region. In the mid-1640s they nearly evicted the Swedes because of their lack of trade goods and the bellicose posturing of their governor, Johan Printz. Relations improved by 1654 when Naaman and other Lenape leaders concluded a treaty with the new Swedish governor, Johan Risingh, in which each side promised to warn the other if they heard of impending attack by another nation. They also pledged to discuss problems such as assaults and murders, stray livestock, and land theft before going to war.

By the 1650s, many of the Armewamese group of Lenapes lived adjacent to the Swedes and Finns in the area that became Philadelphia, a locale the Swedish engineer Peter Lindeström praised for its beauty, freshwater springs, multitude of fruit trees, and many kinds of animals. Lindeström identified six towns from the Delaware to the falls of the Schuylkill that the Armewamese built to be near the terminus of the Susquehannock trade. The Lenapes also sold corn as a cash crop to New Sweden when its supplies ran short.

After the Dutch conquered New Sweden in 1655, the Lenapes, Swedes, and Finns solidified their alliance to resist heavy-handed Dutch authority. The Lenapes warned the Swedes of the Dutch assault; their Susquehannock and Munsee allies attacked Manhattan, forcing Director Peter Stuyvesant and his troops to withdraw from the Delaware Valley. While the Dutch claimed the region, the Lenapes ruled their country in alliance with the Munsees, Susquehannocks, Swedes, and Finns.

With the English conquest of the Dutch colony in 1664, the alliance of Lenapes, Swedes, and Finns remained firm as together they resisted English efforts, under the Duke of York, to impose their power and expropriate land. In the late 1660s, the Armewamese left their towns where Philadelphia now stands, migrating to join the Mantes and Cohanzick communities in New Jersey. Although it is unclear whether settlers forced out the Armewamese or they left voluntarily, their relocation moved the center of Lenape population and power across the river.

In 1675–76, the alliance of Lenapes, Swedes, and Finns helped Lenape country escape the horrors of wars like Bacon's Rebellion in Virginia and King Philip's War in New England. Through shared economic goals and common values of peace, individual freedom, and openness to people of different cultures, the Lenapes and their European allies established the ideals of Delaware Valley society before William Penn received his land grant for Pennsylvania in 1681.

New Sweden

Mark L. Thompson

Founded in 1638, the colony of New Sweden survived less than twenty years and at its peak numbered only about four hundred people, most of whom lived along the western bank of the Delaware River between what became Philadelphia and New Castle, Delaware. As small and short-lived as it proved to be, New Sweden had important effects that persisted long after its conquest by Dutch forces in 1655. It was the first lasting European settlement in the Delaware Valley and transformed relationships between Native peoples and Europeans. It also affected the process of European colonization in North America and had a decisive influence on the cultural development of the Greater Philadelphia region.

The idea of planting a Swedish colony in the Delaware Valley came from Peter Minuit, a native of the German city of Wesel on the Lower Rhine. Before becoming involved in the New Sweden venture, Minuit had served six years as the director of New Netherland, a colony established by the Dutch West India Company (WIC) in 1624. After being recalled for squabbling with New Netherland's Reformed minister, Minuit sought out the patronage of Samuel Blommaert, a high official in the WIC who had entered the service of the Swedish government. Soon afterward Blommaert began pushing Minuit's idea for a colony called Nova Sweediae. Eager to demonstrate its status as a great power in Europe, the Swedish government granted its approval and by early 1637 plans for the first voyage began to take shape.

New Sweden was designed to be a miniature copy of New Netherland, the Dutch colony centered on the Hudson River (later English New York). Like New Netherland, it would be a company-owned colony whose main goal was to make a profit by exchanging European-manufactured goods such as cloth, beads, tools, and weapons for furs and skins provided by Native suppliers. The colony's merchants would also purchase tobacco and other commodities from neighboring colonies for resale in Europe. New Sweden would have a small but significant agricultural base so that it could sustain itself and produce its own goods (including tobacco) for trade or sale.

From the start, New Sweden depended for its success upon its relationships with neighboring Native peoples. When Minuit and his small Swedish and Dutch crew sailed up the Delaware River for the first time in the spring of 1638, they made important agreements with several sachems belonging to the Lenapes and the Susquehannocks (or "Minquas"). The Lenapes, who numbered several thousand people at the time, occupied a string of independent communities along the river and were considered by all to be the owners of the lands adjoining it. The Susquehannocks lived farther west in the Susquehanna Valley, where they were just as populous. They were the region's main fur suppliers and had staged destructive attacks on Lenape communities just a few years before. Both sets of peoples welcomed the Swedish colony as a new source of trade goods and a new source of power in their own relations with other Natives in northeastern North America.

With the permission of the Lenape and Susquehannock sachems, Minuit's men erected a small fort (Fort Christina) at the mouth of the "Minquas Kill" (Christina River in modern-day Wilmington, Delaware). Over the next decade, especially under its longest-serving governor, Johan Printz, the colony extended its reach by establishing small, fortified trading posts and farming settlements on both sides of the lower Delaware Valley. The main purpose of New Sweden's forts was to deter trade and settlement by its European rivals, especially the WIC, which asserted that New Netherland's limits extended from the Delaware Bay to New England. However, it was only after Peter Stuyvesant became director-general of New Netherland in 1647 that WIC officials began to press their claims more strongly. Although occasional groups of English colonizers also attempted to trade and plant along the river, arguing that the territory belonged to the English Crown, none was able to secure a permanent foothold.

During the 1640s New Sweden's population grew to about 200 people. Seven ships arrived from Sweden during that decade, bringing soldiers, company servants, a few dozen free settlers, and a handful of Lutheran priests. Most of the servants and freemen were single men but a few families came over as well. Nearly all were Swedish or Finnish, although in the early years

FIGURE 15. This 1940 photograph of a Swedish log cabin interior, dating from the mid-seventeenth century and located on Darby Creek in the Drexel Hill section of Upper Darby, Pa., was one of the few of its kind to survive. Historic Buildings Survey. LIBRARY OF CONGRESS.

the colony included a small number of English and Dutch settlers too. Recruiting free settlers proved to be very difficult for the Swedish government, and many of the colony's inhabitants were sent there as a form of punishment. The flow of settlers stopped abruptly in 1648 and did not restart until six years later. After putting down a mutiny in 1653, Printz left for Sweden, joined by a group of settlers. A mass desertion seems to have followed once they departed. By the time a ship bearing new colonists and a new governor finally arrived in 1654, New Sweden's population had dwindled to about 130 people. Supplemented by the new arrivals, the colony's population rose to about 400. This sudden growth caused its own problems, especially in securing enough food for the newcomers.

During the early years of his governorship, Printz had overseen the construction of several new forts, the expansion of agricultural settlement, and successful participation in the fur trade. By the time he left, the colony had abandoned many of the peripheral forts and could no longer protect itself. Indeed, Printz had been powerless to prevent Stuyvesant from establishing a new fort (Fort Casimir, in contemporary New Castle, Delaware) just downriver from Fort Christina. The colony seemed to revive when Printz's replacement, Johan Risingh, arrived in 1654. His soldiers captured

Fort Casimir (renaming it Fort Trefaldighet), and he and his officers confirmed the colony's alliances with its Lenape and Susquehannock partners. New Sweden's officers also promised the numerous freemen in the colony that they would finally be able to gain title to the company lands that they worked. These promises were not fulfilled. When WIC officials in Amsterdam learned Fort Casimir had been captured, they dispatched a heavily armed warship and two hundred men to New Netherland expressly to conquer the Swedish colony. Within a year, Stuyvesant led a fleet to the Delaware River and forced New Sweden's officers to surrender.

Risingh and thirty-six settlers, soldiers, and officials departed for Europe shortly after the fall of the colony, but most of New Sweden's inhabitants stayed behind in the Delaware Valley, now under Dutch rule. They remained the majority of the European population along the river for the next quarter century. During this era they strengthened their close relationship with the Lenapes, whose population had been reduced by disease but still numbered in the thousands. After the English takeover of New Netherland in 1664 Swedes and Finns often served as mediators between English officials and the Lenapes. Other Europeans also came to rely on the Swedes and Finns for their knowledge of the land. Some scholars believe the iconic American log cabin may have been introduced to North America by so-called "Forest Finns" who had settled in New Sweden.

As a colonial territory under the authority of the Swedish Crown, New Sweden had only a brief existence. But the influence of Swedish and Finnish settlers in the Delaware Valley lasted much longer. Indeed, in the years after conquest, their community seemed to gain greater coherence as new arrivals and old settlers worked out a new form of collective identity under Dutch and then English rule. Even after English colonists began arriving by the thousands in the 1670s and 1680s, Swedes and Finns retained a distinctive place in the diverse Delaware Valley. Supported from afar by the Church of Sweden, their local Lutheran churches ensured that their linguistic and religious attachments survived well into the eighteenth century. A visible reminder of the colony's original influence and lasting impact is the Gloria Dei Church, or Old Swedes' Church, in South Philadelphia. Constructed during the last years of the seventeenth century, its religious services continued more than three hundred years later.

West New Jersey

Jean R. Soderlund

Between 1674 and 1702, New Jersey was divided in half: the proprietary West Jersey colony faced the Delaware River while East Jersey looked toward the Hudson. Although this political division lasted less than three decades, it represented long-standing geographical orientations of the Lenape and Munsee Native inhabitants and European colonists. Benjamin Franklin reputedly called New Jersey "a barrel tapped at both ends," a productive countryside exploited by Philadelphia and New York. While West New Jersey quickly came within Philadelphia's economic orbit, the region nonetheless retained a distinct political and social identity.

Native Americans lived in the Delaware Valley at least ten thousand years before the Dutch, Swedes, Finns, and English arrived in the seventeenth century. The Lenapes, who controlled southern and western New Jersey, lived in autonomous towns along creeks leading to the Delaware River and along the Atlantic coast near Delaware Bay. Some Lenape peoples, such as the Armewamese and Cohanzicks, possessed land on both sides of the river in what are now Pennsylvania, Delaware, and New Jersey. Because Lenapes traveled frequently by canoe, they viewed rivers and streams as highways rather than obstacles.

Prior to the founding of West New Jersey in 1674, European population in the region remained sparse. A small Dutch settlement on Matinicum (now Burlington) Island lasted only from 1624 until 1626 when, on a site across the river from current Philadelphia, Dutch traders established Fort Nassau. A group of New Englanders in 1641 obtained the Lenapes' permission to colonize several Delaware Valley locations, one at Varkens Kill (now Salem River). Dutch opposition and disease destroyed the colony; a small remnant of English settlers became part of the population of New Sweden, which existed from 1638 to 1655 primarily on the west bank of the Delaware. The Dutch conquered New Sweden in 1655 and held the Delaware colony until 1664, when English forces of James, Duke of York took control. A few Dutch and French colonists moved to southwestern New Jersey in the late 1660s, purchasing land from the Lenapes. A few years later, Swedish and Finnish settlers followed suit, departing from the west bank of the Delaware River in rebellion against English land policies, including assessment of quitrents and expropriation of common lands.

The English king Charles II initiated the proprietary colony of New Jersey in 1664 when he granted his brother James, Duke of York the rights of proprietorship, including the power to govern and ability to own and sell land. The duke in turn granted New Jersey to Sir John Berkeley and Sir George Carteret. In 1674, the proprietorship of New Jersey was divided in half, with Berkeley taking West New Jersey, which he promptly sold to John Fenwick in trust for Edward Byllynge. When the English Quakers Fenwick and Byllynge quarreled, three Quaker trustees, including William Penn, mediated the dispute. Adding to these difficulties, the Duke of York refused to transfer the power to govern West New Jersey to the Quaker proprietors.

Complicated financial deals and lawsuits arising from the dispute between Fenwick and Byllynge resulted in two initial Quaker settlements in West New Jersey: Salem founded in 1675 and Burlington in 1677. Fenwick demanded one-tenth of the West New Jersey proprietorship to launch his own settlement, which conflicted with the intentions of Byllynge and the trustees for a unified colony. Byllynge wanted to give Fenwick his tenth in scattered places across West New Jersey, but instead, without Byllynge's assent, Fenwick took his one-tenth in a single location, which he called Salem, and sold 148,000 acres to about fifty purchasers. The Quaker colonists arrived in southern New Jersey in 1675, entering a country dominated by Lenapes where some Europeans, mostly Swedes, Finns, and Dutch, had settled during the previous decade. Fenwick promptly purchased land from the Lenapes of the region—the Cohanzicks—with whom he maintained good relations. Land conveyances of 1675 and 1676 specified that Fenwick would receive territory, "excepted always . . . the plantations in which [the Natives] now inhabit," in return for cloth, rum, guns, and other items.

Despite these conveyances, Salem's status remained insecure because Fenwick, as a result of financial difficulties and legal challenges, lacked English title, deeds, and the right to govern. Governor Edmund Andros of New York, who for the Duke of York until 1680 claimed authority over both banks of the Delaware, jailed Fenwick in New York for two extended periods, leaving the land claims of the Salem colonists unclear.

In 1676, the Quaker trustees and Edward Byllynge implemented plans for settling the other 90 percent of West New Jersey. Byllynge probably drafted the innovative West Jersey Concessions (1676) that described the process for distributing land, granted religious freedom and trial by jury, and set out a plan for mediation of disputes between Lenapes and Europeans. Male property owners residing in West New Jersey would annually elect a general assembly by putting balls into ballot boxes rather than by "the confused way of cries and voices" that was common in other places. The Duke of York delayed implementation of the Concessions by not transferring the right of government to Byllynge until 1680. Byllynge then renounced the Concessions by becoming governor, an office not included in the document. Nevertheless, though the Concessions failed to become the official West Jersey constitution, the document suggests the ideals of the colonists who signed it. Many provisions of the Concessions, including the elected assembly, religious freedom, and trial by jury, became West New Jersey law.

In 1677, Byllynge and the trustees sent the ship *Kent* with 230 Friends to establish the Burlington colony, appointing nine commissioners to govern until an assembly could be elected. When the *Kent* stopped first to inform Andros of their plans to settle, he denied liberty to the Quakers to establish their own government but agreed to appoint the trustees' commissioners as magistrates to report to him. Andros also charged the passengers duties on their cargo, creating considerable ill will. In response to appeals from Byllynge and the trustees, in 1680 the Duke of York transferred the right of government to him, ending the customs fees and meddling of the New York government. An estimated 1,760 Friends settled in West New Jersey by 1682, but after that date most Quaker immigrants accepted

FIGURE 16. *The Province of New Jersey,* by William Fadden, 1877, depicting topography in the northern part of the state and the boundary lines made in 1743 demarcating "West Jersey" and "East Jersey." LIBRARY OF CONGRESS.

THE
PROVINCE of NEW JERSEY,
Divided into
EAST and WEST,
commonly called
THE JERSEYS.
Engraved & Published by Wm. Faden, Charing Cross, December 1st 1777.
This Map has been drawn from the Survey made in 1769 by order of the Commissioners appointed to settle the partition Line between the Provinces of New York & New Jersey by Bernard Ratzer, Lieut. in the 60th Regt. and from another large Survey of the Northern Parts in the possession of the Earl of Dunmore by Gerard Banker. The whole regulated and ascertained by Astronomical observations.
NEW YORK
PROVINCE OF PENNSYLVANIA
BERGEN COUNTY
ESSEX COUNTY
SOMERSET COUNTY
MIDDLESEX COUNTY
MONMOUTH COUNTY
BURLINGTON COUNTY
GLOUCESTER COUNTY
SALEM COUNTY
CUMBERLAND COUNTY
CAPE MAY COUNTY
LONG ISLAND
THE SOUND
STATEN ISLAND
RARITON BAY
THE ATLANTIC
DELAWARE BAY
THE THREE LOWER COUNTIES
NEWCASTLE COUNTY
KENT COUNTY
SUSSEX COUNTY
MARYLAND
Philadelphia
Burlington
Trenton
Princetown
Brunswick
Amboy
Elizabeth Town
Newark
Salem
Wilmington
Great Egg Harbour
Little Egg harbour
Cape May
Cape James
Lewes
ASTRONOMICAL OBSERVATIONS.
Longitude from London / from Philadelphia — Latitude — Observers
Philadelphia 75. 10. 0 — 39. 56. 55 — Ervin Prior Logan 1769
Lewes 75. 3. 0 — 0. 7. 0 — 38. 47. 20 — Biddle 1769
New York Fort 73. 55. 20 — 1. 15. 40 — 40. 42. 50 — Gov. Burnet Ervin Prior 1769
Sandy Hook Light house — 40. 27. 40 — the King's Commissioners
Machacamack Fork — 41. 21. 37 — the King's Surveyors 1769
British Miles about 69½ to a Degree.
Longitude West from Philadelphia
Longitude East from Philadelphia

William Penn's invitation to settle his new Quaker colony of Pennsylvania.

The Swedes, Finns, and Lenapes offered the Burlington colonists assistance despite worry about their increasing numbers. The Swedes and Finns provided shelter soon after the *Kent* arrived and helped the West Jersey commissioners acquire land from the Lenapes. The winter of 1677–78 came before the new settlers could begin constructing Burlington, so they built wigwams like the Lenapes' and depended upon the Natives for corn, vegetables, venison, fish, and fowl. The Burlington colonists brought smallpox and other diseases that, like earlier epidemics, killed many Lenapes. The English settlers took advantage of the devastated Native population to appropriate prime agricultural lands.

During the proprietary period from 1674 to 1702, the West New Jersey colonists organized themselves much like their Lenape neighbors—in autonomous communities governed by local officials, loosely affiliated with neighboring colonial and Native settlements. Byllynge and the trustees founded Burlington as the seat of West New Jersey government. Centralized government from Burlington was impossible because of the distance between small, dispersed settlements and because contested land claims, power struggles, and the English government's efforts to repeal the proprietorship created a power vacuum at the top. County courts in Burlington, Salem, Gloucester, and Cape May provided stability during the proprietary years, however, by punishing crime, hearing disputes, and collecting taxes for roads, bridges, and public buildings.

Although Quakers, including William Penn, founded both West New Jersey and Pennsylvania, the colonies evolved differently in their initial years. In West New Jersey, the continuing power of the Lenapes, smaller European population, and lack of unified leadership in Burlington created more room for local autonomy and intercultural alliances between Natives and colonists than in Pennsylvania, where larger numbers of immigrants and a more hierarchical government held sway. Even so, the two provinces developed close economic ties, as Philadelphia's growth quickly attracted business with West Jersey merchants and farmers, thus continuing a partnership between both sides of the Delaware River.

The proprietary colony of West New Jersey dissolved in 1702 when the proprietors of both East and West New Jersey surrendered their right of government to the English Crown. The proprietors were under numerous pressures, including charges that the colonies were ungovernable, factionalized, and defiant against imperial rule. Though English administrator Edward Randolph suggested that "the country is too large, and the inhabitants too few to be continued a separate government, therefore East Jersey ought to be annexed to New York and West Jersey to Pennsylvania and the three lower counties," the Crown decided on the unified province of New Jersey. The assembly of twenty-four members, equally divided by section, would rotate meetings between Perth Amboy and Burlington. The governor of New York, Edward Hyde, Lord Cornbury, assumed office as the first New Jersey royal governor in 1703.

Pennsylvania Founding

Stephanie Grauman Wolf

In March of 1681, King Charles II of England granted William Penn, gentleman and Quaker, the charter for a proprietary colony on the North American continent. Although both English colonial policy and the organization of the Society of Friends, known as Quakers, were works in progress between the years 1682 and 1701, their combined influence strongly shaped the pattern of scattered farms and religious tolerance that Pennsylvania developed in those early years.

Penn's grant settled an old debt owed by the king to Penn's father, Admiral William Penn. The king's charter to Penn set the northern border of Pennsylvania at 42 degrees north latitude (the border of New York) and the eastern limit at the Delaware River (the boundary with New Jersey), while the western limit was undefined. Named for the admiral as well as for the woodland it encompassed (Penn's woods), the new grant differed in form and substance from those offered to proprietors of other colonies. Under the proprietary system, the grantee obtained a charter from the king and established the colony at his own risk. The Crown looked on it as a feudal estate, a grant equivalent to independent sovereignty limited only by loyalty to the king. Proprietors could grant titles, and they had sole authority to initiate laws, levy taxes, coin money, regulate commerce, appoint provincial officials, administer justice, grant pardons, make war, erect manors, and control the land and waterways.

By the time Penn received his "true and absolute proprietary of Pennsylvania," the powers given to proprietors had become much more limited. He still had complete control of granting land: in the common parlance of the time under one hundred acres constituted a farm, between one hundred and one thousand acres a plantation, and over one thousand acres a manor. Those holding larger parcels could, in turn, sell or rent them as smaller holdings. The proprietor no longer had the right to grant titles of nobility, however, and he had to submit provincial laws to the king for approval, acknowledge the right of Parliament to tax the colony, maintain a provincial agent in London, and present all Pennsylvania laws to the "freemen" or to "their delegates" for approval. Most disappointing to Penn was an added clause that gave the established Church of England's Bishop of London the right to appoint an Anglican minister in Pennsylvania. Penn had recruited settlers, largely Quakers, but also Mennonites and other pietists from widely dispersed parts of Britain and Europe and saw this clause as making them "dissenters in [their] own Countrey." However, since his first law code guaranteed religious freedom from the legal penalties and punishments that inhibited the practice of Quakerism and other dissenting Christian groups in England, it was still possible to promote Pennsylvania as a religious refuge for the persecuted.

In July 1681, Penn issued his first conditions or "concessions" to "adventurers and purchasers" that laid out specifications for a great city on a river, provided for road surveys, related grants of city land to country manors, and set up townships. Penn's blueprint for Pennsylvania was unique among colonial frames of government by containing several provisions requiring that "natives" be treated equally with settlers both economically and legally and that "no man shall . . . in word, or deed, affront, or wrong any Indian."

Penn followed up the Concessions document in May 1682 with the first Frame of Government, which laid out the form and shape of governance in the new colony. The government itself was to consist of the governor, a provincial council, and a general assembly chosen by the freemen, who were defined as those who were resident in the province, were free of servitude, owned and cultivated part of their land, and paid a tax to the government.

Twenty-three ships bearing settlers arrived in the new colony between December 1681 and December 1682. The *Welcome*, William Penn aboard, landed on October 28, 1682. Within two years, fifty ships had arrived in Pennsylvania carrying 600 investors and 4,000 settlers. Penn and his colonists entered a land that was populated by Native Americans and European settlers who provided food and shelter to the newcomers, allowing the new colony to avoid the "starving time" that had been the fate of other earlier colonies to the north and south. Including the Europeans who settled West New Jersey in the 1670s, there were about 2,500 Lenape and 3,000 Europeans on both sides of the Delaware River when Penn's colonists arrived.

The inhabitants were diverse, including the Lenapes from whom Penn purchased land on the west bank of the river. The European inhabitants included the Dutch, who had established a trading post in the area in 1624, and the Swedes and Finns who created the first permanent settlement of New Sweden in 1638. Most of these settlers lived in the area from what was later Philadelphia to New Castle, Delaware. The Dutch conquered New Sweden in 1655 and then, following England's victory over the Dutch in 1664, King Charles's brother, James, Duke of York, took ownership of the west bank of the Delaware River.

In 1682, Penn divided the land along the Delaware River into the counties of Chester, Philadelphia, and Bucks, appointing colonists to serve on each county court and administer local government. To allow Pennsylvania an outlet to the sea, in the same year Penn leased from the Duke of York the land south of Chester County on the western shore of the Delaware Bay, setting the border of the "three lower counties" (later the state of Delaware) twelve miles north of New Castle. The charter for Pennsylvania and the lease for the three lower counties remained separate entities, however, requiring agreement to laws by a single assembly that met alternately at Philadelphia and New Castle. By 1704, the inconvenience of this arrangement led to a mutual agreement to set up distinct assemblies and pass laws separately, although they continued to share a governor. The border between Pennsylvania and Delaware was not actually established until the mid-eighteenth century, with the drawing of the Mason-Dixon Line, which also settled the boundary with Maryland.

Penn's hope for a "Holy Experiment"—where Pennsylvanians did well economically while doing good morally and religiously—failed to materialize. Landed gentleman investors did not, in general, emigrate, and their investments went badly. The Society of Free Traders was bankrupt within a few years. Penn, himself, never achieved the profits he expected. Although he lived until 1718, he only spent four years in Pennsylvania (1682–84 and 1699–1701). He was bedeviled by personal and financial problems and, to resolve them, had to remain in England, where he spent time in debtor's prison.

Early arrivals who prospered were largely farmers from northwestern England, an area of scattered farms, along with urban artisans and workmen, many of them from Germany and Holland. Settlers also came from Ireland, Scotland, Wales, and London and its environs. By 1690 the population of the colony numbered about 11,500, that of the principal city, Philadelphia, about 2,000. Ten years later, the colony had close to 18,000 inhabitants, and Philadelphia over 3,000. The Society of Friends was never established as the official religion of the colony and Quakers were always a minority, although their influence was predominant in both the government and the early society.

While religion continued to motivate many settlers, many more were drawn by the availability of rich farmland. The desire for wealth prompted importation of bound European servants and enslaved Africans. Penn had envisioned a colony of townships, where farms would produce the crops and livestock needed to fuel local centers of government, religion, industry, and trade. Instead, the Thomas Holme 1687 map of Pennsylvania indicates that almost from the beginning scattered farmsteads became the pattern of settlement for the three counties. Lumbering, grist mills to produce flour, and iron-mining operations as well as small manufactories for textiles, paper, and printing dotted the countryside from the 1690s. By 1701, however, Philadelphia had become the focus of trade, manufacture, and civic life, exhibiting most of the attributes of an urban complex and draining the vitality out of potential township centers.

Welsh and German settlers, receiving large grants just outside Philadelphia, made the most determined efforts to maintain their identity. The Welsh Quakers in the Welsh Tract (1684) stood out for their attempts to maintain their own communities with the rights to hold contiguous property, limit the activities of anyone within their boundaries, and govern themselves in their old ways. Within the year, however, assimilation with English Quaker and Anglican settlers overwhelmed the Welsh and the tract survived mainly in Welsh names such as Bala Cynwyd and Bryn Mawr.

The situation of Germantown was unique in the founding years of Pennsylvania. Through some confusion, Penn granted the same territory to both a group of Dutch Quakers and the German-based Frankfort Land Company, whose legal agent was Francis Daniel Pastorius. They arrived at the same time in 1683. As Pastorius was the only member of the company to immigrate, he became, de facto, the leader of the Dutch group, apportioning the land and heading the government. By 1684 the territory acquired its name as it was flooded with German immigrants of many religious sects. The craft occupations of the inhabitants and the distribution of Germantown's land in small lots strung along a highway leading from Philadelphia to the hinterlands, created a miniature urban center. It was chartered as a borough, but failure of the settlers to perform its governmental functions led to loss of that status in 1707. The Quaker meeting retained many of its German beliefs, leading to a protest against slavery in 1688 and a split within the meeting itself over the Keithian controversy in the 1690s about the relationship between Quakerism and Christianity.

Ever since the first "Frame of Government and Laws Agreed Upon in England" in 1682, factions of settlers were dissatisfied with its terms, and it was superseded or amended several times—in 1683, 1684, and 1691. The colony was taken away from Penn in 1693 on suspicion of treasonable association with James II, but returned to him in 1695, initiating yet another charter in 1696.

The final Charter of Privileges was granted in 1701, since the older frames had all been found "not so suitable to the Present circumstances of the Inhabitants," and remained in force until the American Revolution. Each frame had gradually increased the powers of the colony's elected assembly and it now received more privileges than any other legislative body in the English colonies, undoubtedly more than Penn, himself, had originally intended. A unicameral legislature with its assembly elected annually, could initiate legislation and conduct its own affairs, but the proprietor or his governor retained the right to veto legislation.

Most significantly, the first clause of the Charter of Privileges reiterated Pennsylvania's commitment to religious liberty—freedom of worship to all who "acknowledge one almighty God" without attending or belonging to a religious body, and the ability to serve in office by all who believed in Jesus Christ and were willing to affirm, if not swear, allegiance to the government. The affirmation was important to Quakers who refused to swear oaths. Along with Rhode Island and several other colonies, Pennsylvania was a pioneer of the separation of religion and government in the American colonies.

Lower Delaware Counties

Lu Ann De Cunzo

The colonies that became the state of Delaware lay in the middle of the North American Atlantic coast, extending about 120 miles north from the Atlantic Ocean along the southwestern shore of the Delaware (South) Bay and River to within 10 miles of Philadelphia. Between 1609 and 1704, the area was a contested borderland between North and South, as a dozen Native and colonial political and commercial regimes sought to assert authority over the region. William Penn ultimately gained control of the area as an addition to his land grant for Pennsylvania.

The bay and river—named in 1610 by English explorer Samuel Argall in honor of Virginia's governor, Thomas West, Lord De La Warr—provided a rich, diverse estuarine environment for Natives and colonists. A network of natural harbors and navigable rivers enabled trade along the coast and access into the interior. Early historic maps show extensive oyster-laden shoals in the shallow southern reaches of the bay. Shad, sturgeon, and other fish migrated annually up the river. An extensive marsh system lined the bay and river, broken by broad meadows and savannahs. Waterfowl, small mammals, fish, and salt hay abounded, and these lands proved amenable to grazing cattle. The forested coastal plain provided wild game and timber for structures, fencing, and shipbuilding, as did the Great Cypress Swamp in southern Sussex County. The northern Piedmont hills yielded flint for Native people's stone toolmaking, and Europeans exploited the iron ore at Iron Hill, near Newark, New Castle County.

For most of the seventeenth century, Lenape Algonquian people exerted the greatest political and economic control over the country from central New Jersey through eastern Pennsylvania and along the Delaware Bay to its mouth at Cape Henlopen (Sussex County). Led by sachems and councils of elders, they lived in unpalisaded towns and spoke Unami. Over the course of the century, these Lenape Natives created with European settlers a distinctive society that valued peace over conflict, religious freedom, collaboration, respect for diverse people, and local authority. Nonetheless, desire for profits led to contention, and Native traders shifted among European nations to obtain the quantity and quality of goods they sought. Exchange provided the source of the Lenapes' power, which they used to provoke colonial rivalries.

Inland, Susquehannock (Minquas) peoples living in fortified villages along the Susquehanna River proved especially determined to maintain independence in the fur trade and played Swedes, Dutch, and English against each other. A decade of intermittent war with Lenapes between 1626 and 1636 typified the larger contest for control over furs in the North Atlantic world. The outcome earned Susquehannock traders the right to do business in Lenape areas along Delaware Bay and instigated a trade alliance among the groups.

While the Lenapes defended their homeland against the Susquehannocks and northern Haudenosaunee (Iroquois), Europeans from the Dutch Republic's West India Company, the City of Amsterdam, and Sweden established small trading colonies. Lenapes welcomed trade with Dutch sailors, who entered the bay and river by about 1615. The Dutch West India Company established Fort Nassau on the eastern side of the Delaware River in 1626 as part of its colony of New Netherland, an outpost of the Dutch commercial empire and potential source of furs for the expanding European market. Dutch activity expanded in 1629, when officials bargained with a southernmost Lenape community,

Sickoneysincks, for a tract of land reaching from Cape Henlopen to the mouth of the Delaware River. By 1631 the resulting colony, Zwaanendael, consisted of about thirty colonists housed in a palisaded fort. Within a year, however, the venture ended in violence. After the Sickoneysincks determined that the Dutch intended to build an agricultural settlement, not merely a trading fort, they destroyed the fort and its occupants. Though the colony failed, its brief existence prevented the future area of Delaware, or at least southern Delaware, from being adjudged part of Maryland.

In the mid-1630s, Peter Minuit, former director of New Netherland, negotiated with the Swedish government to establish the New Sweden colony under Swedish protection. He understood the strategic geographical importance of the lower Delaware Valley and that the Dutch West India Company had insufficient resources to devote to its development and defense. The New Sweden Company, under leadership of Minuit and other investors, benefited from Dutch colonial experience and funding while enjoying the added advantage of patronage and the protection of the Swedish monarch. For the Crown, New Sweden promised to strengthen the nation's new position as a European power, naval experience, and imperial growth.

The New Sweden Company built Fort Christina, the first permanent European settlement in Delaware, in 1638. The fort, which became the base of one of two primary European settlements along the west side of the river in the seventeenth century, stood at the confluence of the Brandywine and Christina Creeks, later Wilmington, northern New Castle County. At its peak, the colony claimed territory along both sides of the Delaware from the mouth of the bay to the falls (later Trenton, New Jersey), and the settlers traded with Lenapes and Susquehannocks. New Sweden officials established fortifications along the river in an effort to control trade with Indian fur suppliers. Most New Sweden settlers lived along the tributaries of the Delaware River between what later became Wilmington and Philadelphia.

Despite their nations' alliance in Europe, Dutch West India Company and New Sweden Company settlers believed the lower Delaware Valley could not accommodate them both. They maneuvered for trade advantages, particularly after Peter Stuyvesant became director-general of New Netherland in 1647. By 1650, the Dutch administration on Manhattan Island and directors in Amsterdam had realized the importance of settling the lower Delaware. Stuyvesant provocatively replaced Fort Nassau in 1651 with Fort Casimir, a second principal European settlement just south of the Swedish Fort Christina. Stuyvesant was concerned not only with Swedes but with English efforts to colonize the river.

After Stuyvesant invaded New Sweden in 1655, Sweden lost its tenuous foothold in this middling borderland. The Dutch then divided the settlements on the Delaware into two colonies. The City of Amsterdam created its "City Colony" in the region surrounding Fort Casimir below the Christina River, centered on New Amstel (later New Castle). Two rows of house and garden plots extended south from the fort along the river. Purportedly 110 houses were completed within a year for Dutch administrators, soldiers, traders, and a mix of settlers from across northern Europe. Within a few years, however, political infighting and economic turmoil led to outmigration, and the population plummeted. Settlers arriving from Maryland and Virginia caused concern because Charles Calvert, Lord Baltimore considered the lands between the Chesapeake Bay and Delaware River part of his proprietorship. Plans to profit from the tobacco trade with Maryland were stymied by epidemic and the inability of farmers to support the population.

The second Dutch colony, the "Company Colony" north of the Christina River, remained under the administration of Dutch West India Company with a predominantly Swedish and Finnish population. Dutch administrators remained suspicious and distrustful of these settlers. The Dutch renamed the Swedes' Fort Christina as Fort Altena, but the "Swedish nation" remained strong in other settlements upriver. The Dutch depended on the Swedes' skills as farmers, interpreters, messengers, diplomats, and soldiers.

The unstable, contested relationships among the multinational, multicultural population of the lower Delaware Valley paved the way for conquest by the English in 1664, after Charles II granted his brother James, Duke of York proprietary rights to land extending from New England to the east side of Delaware Bay.

A bloodless invasion of the west shore at Fort Casimir extended the English claim, and the duke created New Castle County (1664). Over the next four decades the region experienced a series of English invasions. Beginning in the late 1660s, Swedes, Finns, and Dutch from the Christina valley and New Castle moved west and south, while English settlers, including some from Maryland, moved to the west bank of the Delaware in small but increasing numbers. Often they brought enslaved Africans with them. In 1670 Governor Francis Lovelace established the first local court in southern Delaware, at Whorekill (later Sussex County). By the mid-1670s, distinct communities of Finns, a wealthy elite, and multiethnic peasants had emerged along the lower Delaware. The "Swedish nation" remained autonomous and resilient through alliances with Lenapes and Susquehannocks.

Under the Duke of York, the tobacco economy in Delaware flourished. By 1680, pork and corn joined tobacco as the principal agricultural exports to England, Scotland, and the West Indies. Sufficient population growth and economic development had occurred along the central Delaware coast to warrant the division of Kent County from Whorekill in that year. In some areas these new colonists and descendants of earlier settlers expanded into grain farming and milling and established commercial orchards and animal husbandry operations.

In 1681 William Penn convinced the English Crown to grant him a charter to forty-five thousand square miles on the western side of the Delaware River, with a southern boundary on the river twelve miles north of New Castle. Two years later, just before Penn sailed for Pennsylvania, the Duke of York deeded him possession of the three Delaware counties of New Castle, Kent, and Sussex (the Lower Counties). At the time, only about four hundred non-Native inhabitants—Swedish, Finnish, Dutch, and English settlers, and approximately one hundred enslaved Africans—shared with Lenape peoples the entire settled area from Cape Henlopen to New Castle.

In the 1690s, many Lenapes sold claims along the Delaware and moved west into former lands of Minquas-Susquehannock peoples. The borderland region remained torn by religious schism and political rivalry. An extended dispute with Lord Baltimore over the Maryland-Three Lower Counties of Delaware boundary also plagued Penn's administration.

Penn sought to establish a predominantly Quaker colony. The ethnically, religiously diverse Lower Counties resisted efforts to incorporate them under one proprietary government for Pennsylvania based in Philadelphia. Conflicts arose over autonomy, representation, divergent economic interests, and military defense. Although the region remained Penn's domain, beginning in 1704 a separate assembly governed the Lower Counties of Delaware.

By the early eighteenth century, the increasingly European-American landscape of Delaware's three counties consisted of a few small port towns like New Castle in New Castle County and Lewes in Sussex County and dispersed farmsteads where the land possessed good agricultural qualities. Farmers located their farmsteads near waterways or roads and cleared small areas for buildings and tobacco, rye, barley, and wheat fields, orchards, and livestock grazing lands. As Philadelphia rapidly grew to be the second-largest city in English North America, Delaware became part of the city's agricultural and commercial hinterland.

Walking Purchase

Tim Hayburn

With the Walking Purchase of 1737, Pennsylvania officials defrauded the Delaware (Lenape) out of a vast amount of land, perhaps over one million acres, in the Delaware and Lehigh Valleys. John Penn and Thomas Penn, the sons of William Penn, with James Logan, the provincial secretary of Pennsylvania, devised the land grab by using an unsigned draft of a 1686 deed, obtaining support from the Iroquois and using trickery to take much more land than specified in the draft deed. The Walking Purchase represented a shift from earlier land transactions between William Penn's government and the Delawares and paved the way for tensions that contributed to the Seven Years' War.

After receiving a charter for Pennsylvania in 1681, William Penn sought to purchase the land in southeastern Pennsylvania from the Delawares, obtaining much of the territory before leaving the colony in 1684. His agents negotiated the purchase of

FIGURE 17. Lenape chief Lapowinsa, one of several chiefs who signed the infamous 1737 Walking Treaty, spent the next twenty years trying unsuccessfully to have the treaty voided. Gustavus Hesselius, 1735. WIKIMEDIA COMMONS.

land in central Bucks County in 1686, but the deed was unsigned because Penn failed to send enough trade goods to complete the sale. Penn had left the colony in part to address his financial problems, and the purchase was never fully consummated.

By the 1730s, the increasing population of Pennsylvania coupled with the growing debt of Penn's heirs led the Penns and Logan to defraud the Delawares. Speculators, including Logan, had already purchased tracts of land in northern Bucks County and the Lehigh Valley, but needed an agreement with the Delawares before allowing settlement. Logan produced the unsigned copy of the 1686 deed, claiming that the Delawares had agreed to sell territory that a man could walk in a day and a half north from the boundary at Wrightstown. While the Delawares believed the new boundary would be Tohickon Creek in central Bucks County, Logan and the Penns aimed to obtain territory well beyond the Lehigh River. The alleged deed lacked any signatures or evidence of payment, which weakened the proprietors' claims to the land. Nevertheless, Logan met with Delaware sachems at Pennsbury and continued to press the proprietors' claims.

Logan worked for a rapid resolution to this situation at a series of meetings with Delaware sachems, including Nutimus, Manawkyhickon, Lapowinsa, and Tishcohan, at Stenton, Logan's country estate outside of Philadelphia, in August 1737. Manawkyhickon expressed a willingness to agree to the transaction if the sachems could learn how much land had been ceded to the proprietor in the draft deed. Andrew Hamilton, an agent for the provincial government, produced a map, which misled the sachems into thinking that the purchase involved only territory south of Tohickon Creek. The sachems finally agreed to the transaction after being assured that the Delawares would not be removed from their settlements.

Unbeknownst to the Delawares, colonial agents had already performed a reconnaissance of the territory and cleared a path for the walkers. On September 19, 1737, three colonial walkers set off at a rapid pace; after one and one-half days one man covered over sixty miles. Surveyors acquired even more territory by angling the boundary to the confluence of the Delaware and Lackawaxen Rivers.

When the Delaware Indians protested the amount of land they lost in the Walking Purchase and refused to leave the region north of Tohickon Creek, the Pennsylvania government appealed to the Iroquois to help justify the transaction. Canassatego, an Iroquois spokesman, rebuked the Delawares for not complying with the purchase at a conference in Philadelphia in 1742. Over subsequent years, most Delawares in eastern Pennsylvania moved west to the Ohio River valley and developed trade relations with the French. With the onset of hostilities in the Seven Years' War, many Delawares sided with the French after General Edward Braddock rejected their attempt to forge an alliance with the British. Consequently, the Walking Purchase reflected a shift from William Penn's early diplomacy with the Delawares and alienated them from the British colonists by the mid-eighteenth century.

Proclamation Line

Austin Stewart

The Royal Proclamation of 1763 created an imaginary line along the Appalachian Mountains that prohibited European settlement beyond the crest of the mountains, approximately two hundred miles west of Philadelphia. It thus established the region from the eastern seaboard to the mountains as the extent of British North America. In Pennsylvania the proclamation heightened racial, economic, and political tensions in the 1760s and early 1770s, thus contributing to the colonists' discontent with ineffective British policies. Moreover, between its promulgation on October 7, 1763, and the start of the Revolutionary War, colonists and Native Americans disregarded the Proclamation Line, thus exposing the limitations of British imperial control.

When Britain obtained lands west of the Appalachians from France as a result of the Treaty of Paris (1763), which ended the Seven Years' War (1754–63), British officials needed to reestablish imperial authority over existing British subjects and bring the peoples who resided within these lands—both French and Native—under imperial control. Administrators in England thus devised the Proclamation Line, which essentially cut off eastern Pennsylvania from the western part of the colony and reinforced politically the Appalachian Mountains as a natural barrier to colonial expansion into the Ohio River valley. King George III issued the proclamation, written by members of the British Board of Trade, that aimed to dictate the pace and locations of colonial expansion, endorsed the separation of Natives and colonists, and sought to reap economic benefits from the territories east of the Mississippi River.

In Pennsylvania, the proclamation indirectly intensified racial hatred and cultural conflicts when Native Americans rejected British pretensions to rule in the trans-Appalachian west. In a series of spiritually charged battles known as Pontiac's War (beginning in 1763 after the Treaty of Paris), Native Americans attacked British forts in the region from what later became Michigan through western Pennsylvania. Delaware and Shawnee raided colonial settlements between the Proclamation Line and Susquehanna River valley. In response, frontier colonists, blaming the provincial government for lack of military assistance, indiscriminately attacked local Natives. The so-called Paxton Boys murdered peaceful groups of Conestogas at Conestoga Manor and Lancaster in December 1763, then marched on Philadelphia in the attempt to attack Christian Moravian Indians who came under the provincial government's protection. These events set aggrieved Scots-Irish and German frontiersmen against the government and pacifist Quakers, challenging their political power in Pennsylvania.

The imaginary line also frustrated Pennsylvania land speculators. In the mid-1760s, traders such as George Croghan insisted that economic losses sustained during the Seven Years' War and Pontiac's War entitled them to western lands. In the early 1770s, Benjamin Franklin and associates sent a petition to the Board of Trade that provided rationalization for opening of lands beyond the Appalachian Mountains for Pennsylvanian settlement through the erection of new colonies. Speculators argued that colonists from Virginia, Maryland, and Pennsylvania had already ignored the boundary line and that the lack of political, social, and economic connections between Pennsylvania and its frontier limited the commercial value of the Native trade and the extension of British authority.

For Revolutionary Americans, the Proclamation of 1763 was a highly contentious document that pitted colonists against Indians, frontiersmen against the Pennsylvania government, and merchants, traders, and speculators against the imperial government. While the proclamation was meant to increase imperial authority over the colonies, it actually increased colonial discontent with British policies and demonstrated to both colonists and Native Americans the lack of imperial control over eastern North America.

Mason-Dixon Line

Cameron B. Strang

The Mason-Dixon Line, which settled a border dispute dating back to the founding of Philadelphia, is the southern boundary of Pennsylvania. Originally surveyed by Englishmen Charles Mason and Jeremiah Dixon, the

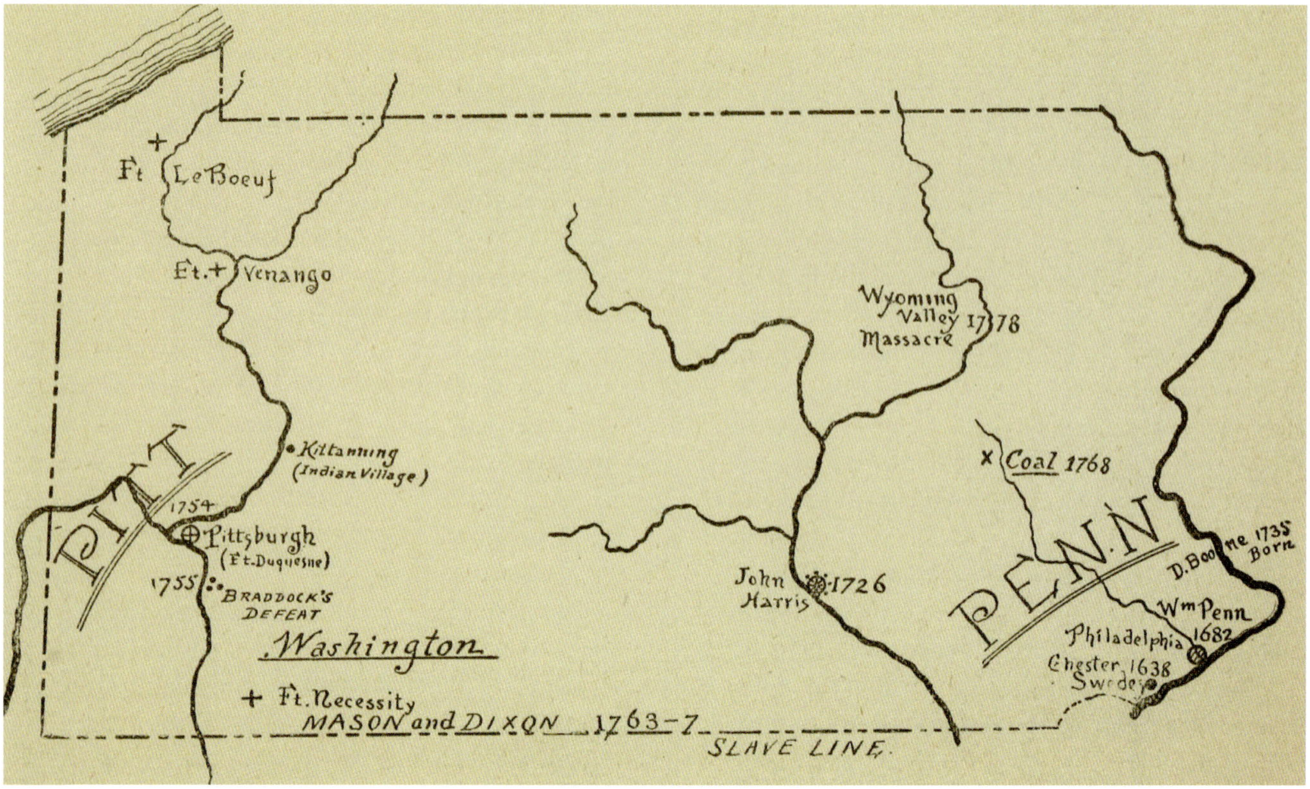

FIGURE 18. Map of the Mason-Dixon Line from an 1894 geography textbook, reflecting the popular misperception that it marked the line between slave and free territories. WIKIMEDIA COMMONS.

line separates Pennsylvania from Maryland and West Virginia along the 39°43′ north parallel and bounds Delaware along an arc that extends from Maryland to the Delaware River. During the nineteenth century the line became a symbolic boundary between the southern and northern United States.

The territorial dispute between Maryland and Pennsylvania began immediately after King Charles II gave William Penn a charter to settle the lands between New York and Maryland in 1681. The charter set Pennsylvania's southern boundary at the fortieth parallel, but the proprietors of both Maryland and Pennsylvania hoped to take advantage of the charter's ambiguities. Pennsylvanians tried to push the boundary farther south and gain a port on the headwaters of the Chesapeake Bay. Marylanders contended that because Philadelphia is below the fortieth parallel, the city should actually be in Maryland.

In 1732 the British Board of Trade set the boundary about fifteen miles south of Philadelphia, though attempts to survey this line were abortive. Colonists on both sides forced the issue by settling on disputed lands and these perceived incursions, many of which were instigated by Marylander Thomas Cresap, led to violence. In 1750, commissioners from both colonies agreed to run a border according to the 1732 agreement and, after struggling to conduct an accurate survey in the early 1760s, asked England's Astronomer Royal for help. He sent Mason and Dixon.

Mason and Dixon arrived in Philadelphia in November 1763 while Pennsylvania was caught up in a cycle of increasingly racialized atrocities between whites and Natives, including the Paxton Boys' massacre. Using state-of-the-art astronomical apparatus, Mason and Dixon surveyed borders between Delaware, Maryland, and Pennsylvania. In 1767, with the help of Iroquois guides, Mason and Dixon tried to extend their line west of the Royal Proclamation Line, which British officials had created in 1763 to regulate the expansion of white colonists into Native lands across the Appalachian

Mountains. But the threat of violence from Delaware Indians, who were then disputing Pennsylvanians' and Iroquois claims to their territory, forced the expedition to turn back. In 1784, astronomers Andrew Ellicott and David Rittenhouse ran the boundary to its intended endpoint—five degrees west of the Delaware River.

During the antebellum era, Americans began to identify the Mason-Dixon Line as delineating the northern and southern sections of the United States. But the line was never a clear boundary between a world where slavery ruled and one where freedom rang. Various forms of free and coerced labor existed along both sides of the line and southern slave owners maintained the legal right to recover enslaved Black people who fled north of the 39°43′ parallel. Although many whites in Maryland, Delaware, and even Philadelphia sought to preserve racial slavery, the proximity of the line and the freedom it promised to runaway slaves forced planters in Maryland and Delaware to experiment with a wide variety of labor regimes. By 1860, large landowners in Maryland and Delaware had become far less dependent on slave labor than those in the Lower South and, ultimately, unwilling to join the confederacy, a crucial factor in the North's eventual victory. For many Americans, the line has remained the iconic boundary between northern and southern cultures.

Hinterlands

Jordan AP Fansler

Since its founding, Philadelphia has acted as a commercial hub for the surrounding region, its hinterlands. Although New Jersey and Delaware had European settlers before Philadelphia's establishment in 1682, Pennsylvania and its founding city quickly became the focus of economic activity in the region extending both east and west of the Delaware River. With an advantageous location, Philadelphia acted as the region's principal port, allowing goods from Britain, the West Indies, and elsewhere to flow in and serving as a gathering point for produce to be exported. From the late seventeenth through the eighteenth century, Philadelphia's hinterlands grew in size and diversification of products, but as the region advanced, other commercial hubs developed to support and rival Philadelphia.

The Delaware River valley was originally populated by the Lenape, or Delaware, people, who shaped the region's initial economic activity. Throughout the seventeenth century, Lenape retained a strong presence in the river valley, and the various Native and European groups generally worked with each other through trade and negotiated rights and privileges. Native American trails became the earliest paths for the colonists, aiding travel, communication, and commerce into the densely forested hinterland. During this early period, Europeans tapped into the preexisting fur trade before developing their own settlements inland. The territory that later became the state of Delaware was first colonized in 1638 by the Swedish, who adopted a plantation pattern in an attempt to emulate Virginia's success with tobacco. However, these settlements were underpopulated, of limited profitability, and experienced conflicts with the local Lenape groups. From 1676 through 1702, New Jersey was divided by a line running from the northwest to the southeast, creating the distinct provinces of East and West New Jersey. West New Jersey was administered by a group of wealthy Quakers, including William Penn, but it was sparsely populated and had no major cities of its own.

After the founding of Philadelphia in 1682, the region's producers saw the new city as a natural commercial center for the Delaware River. William Penn, founder and first proprietor of Pennsylvania, selected a site near the confluence of the Schuylkill and Delaware Rivers to better facilitate shipping. Pennsylvania grew quickly during the five decades before the American Revolution, adding eight inland counties to the original counties huddled by the river (Bucks, Philadelphia, Chester, and the Lower Counties that later became the state of Delaware). Immigrants—free, indentured, or enslaved—strengthened the hinterlands' connection to the burgeoning urban center as they spread through the countryside. In addition to Quakers and other English colonists, Pennsylvania attracted Scots Irish, Germans (including the "Pennsylvania Dutch"), and dissenting religious groups.

At first, in the late seventeenth and early eighteenth centuries, Philadelphia primarily exported raw farm products and timber from these homesteads of the fertile Delaware River valley lands, and the numerous creeks

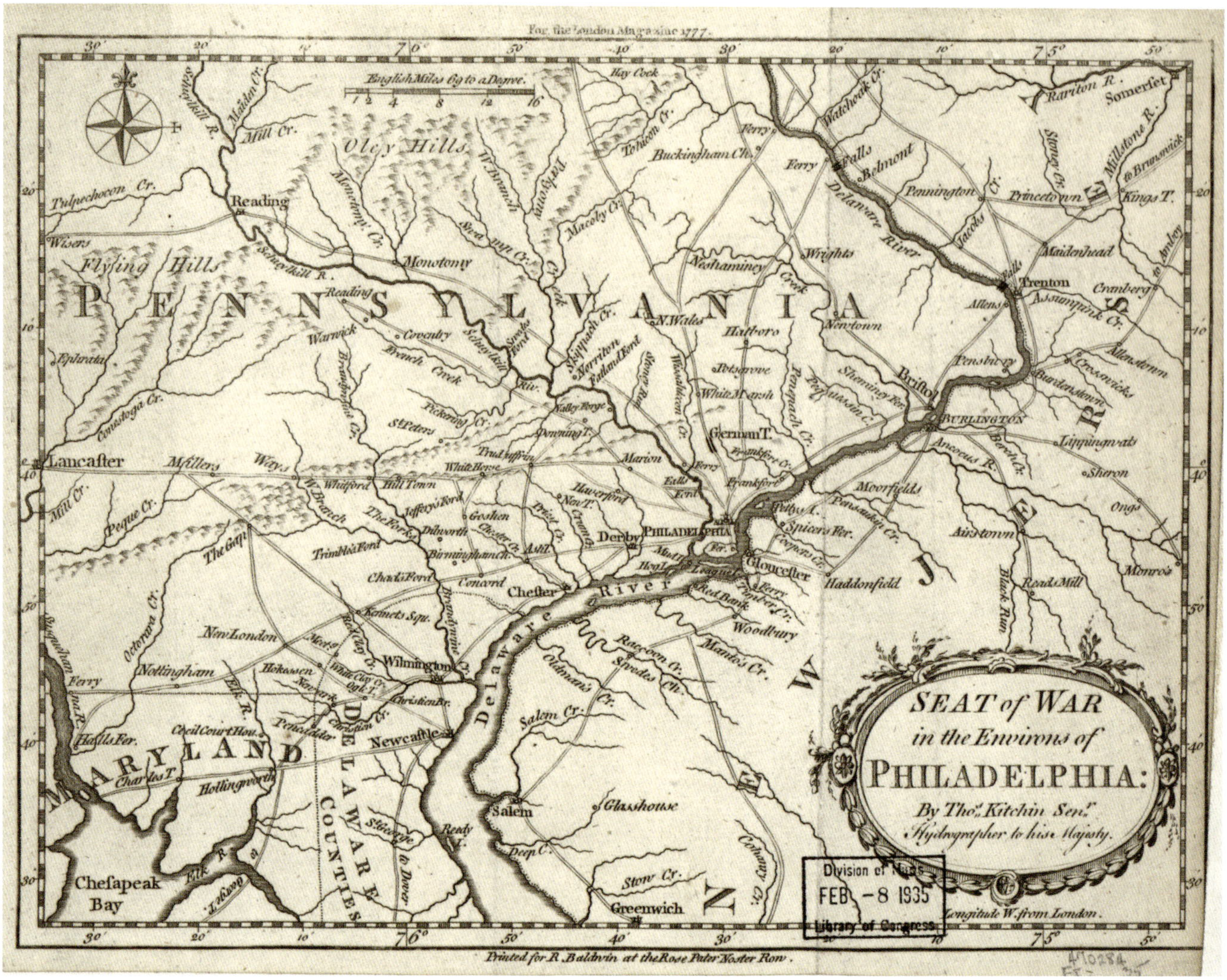

FIGURE 19. This 1777 map, charted by a British cartographer during the American War for Independence, illustrates the extent of the economic region Philadelphia commanded. By the middle of the nineteenth century, Philadelphia served as a commercial hub for a region that spanned parts of Pennsylvania, Delaware, and New Jersey. LIBRARY OF CONGRESS.

and rivers served as transportation routes for the goods. In the eighteenth century, European colonists developed their own settlements in the hinterland areas. Timber resources allowed for a vigorous shipbuilding enterprise. The plantations on the Delaware Bay moved away from tobacco to more diversified farm products such as meat, grain, and timber. The population boomed from migration from the Chesapeake Bay region and immigration abroad, though the towns and cities that grew remained satellites of Philadelphia.

By 1750, increasing grain production made Philadelphia's hinterland the breadbasket of the British Empire. The new emphasis led to an increase in flour mills for processing the grain. Mills of various kinds operated throughout the hinterland but had the highest concentration and outputs in Pennsylvania and northern Delaware, where fertile lands combined with strong streams for waterpower to facilitate the milling of grain. Likewise, iron production and its attendant forges and foundries grew during the same period, primarily in Berks and Lancaster Counties in Pennsylvania and in western New Jersey.

Supplies of timber, flour, iron, and similar stores made Philadelphia an important provider of war materials during the colonial wars. However, the Seven Years' War (1754–63), which erupted from conflicts in far western Pennsylvania, interfered with trade. In Pennsylvania specifically, it created conflicts over the extent of protection the colonial assembly would provide for the hinterlands as the area suffered from destructive raids. During the War for Independence, Philadelphia and its Pennsylvania hinterlands experienced disruption but not for extended periods of time, allowing economic activity to largely continue and cement the hinterlands' role as a producer. By the end of the eighteenth century, they led the new nation in production of textiles and leather goods, as well as metalworking and carpentry.

In the late eighteenth century, the creation and improvement of roads from Philadelphia deep into the hinterlands eased travel, improving freight transportation but also pushing the frontiers beyond the city's reach. Benjamin Franklin advocated for improving road networks, emphasizing the communication benefits as postmaster general. Improving communication and mail helped information from centrally located Philadelphia reach its hinterlands and other colonies (later states) faster than ever, further increasing Philadelphia's economic and political influence. In 1794, Pennsylvania completed a paved turnpike connecting Philadelphia with Lancaster, which lowered transportation costs by as much as two-thirds and was the first of its kind in the nation. This simultaneously drew Lancaster more into Philadelphia's orbit and made it a commercial center in its own right, as a gathering point for central Pennsylvania's goods.

By the turn of the nineteenth century, Philadelphia's hinterlands reached as far west as Lancaster and Reading on the Schuylkill River, and the city's influence extended to the edge of the Appalachian Mountains and the Susquehanna River watershed. The city commanded the Delaware River valley as far north as Trenton at the falls of the Delaware. Ships going in and out of Delaware Bay called on Delaware's smaller ports, such as Wilmington and New Castle, creating a connection for Philadelphia at those locations as well. During the same period, however, New York City to the north and Baltimore to the south grew and rivaled Philadelphia as leading international ports for the mid-Atlantic states, especially from north of Trenton and the Susquehanna valley, respectively.

From the time of its founding, Philadelphia's location and natural resources made it a commercial hub for the surrounding region. As the eighteenth century progressed, manufacturing capabilities increased and Philadelphia's exports became more diversified while the city grew as a commercial and political center through the periods of the American Revolution and early republic.

EXPLORE MORE

The region's history starts with Native peoples, and the Lenape Cultural Center and Trading Post, 169 Northampton Street, Easton, Pa., provides a starting point through exhibits and a website at https://www.lenape-nation.org/ See also the Native American Voices section of the Penn Museum, 3260 South Street, Philadelphia, and the Museum of Indian Culture, 2825 Fish Hatchery Road, Allentown, Pa. Additionally, Native history is explored at the Cumberland County, N.J., Alan E. Carman Museum of Prehistory, 1461 Bridgeton Road, Greenwich, which recounts the world Indians inhabited in the lower Delaware Valley. Nearby, one can find a vast collection of relics displayed under the auspices of the Woodruff Museum of Indian Artifacts in the lower level of the Bridgeton Free Public Library, at 150 E. Commerce Street. Many area artifacts have been recovered from the endangered Indian Head site in Deerfield Township, Cumberland County. For scholarship on the subject, see Jean R. Soderlund, *Lenape Country: Delaware Valley Society Before William Penn* (University of Pennsylvania Press, 2015). Related is Amy C. Schutt's *Peoples of the River Valleys: The Odyssey of the Delaware Indians* (University of Pennsylvania Press, 2007) and Jane T. Merritt, *At the Crossroads: Indians and Empires on a Mid-Atlantic Frontier, 1700–1763* (University of North Carolina Press, 2003). Michael Goode's chapter, "'Rancontyn Marenit': Lenape Peacemaking Before William Penn," in Andrew R. Murphy and John Smolenski's edited book, *The Worlds of William Penn* (Rutgers University Press, 2019), depicts the strategic nature of Lenape relations with Europeans. Richard Veit provides an overview of the long arc of Native settlement in the first chapter of Maxine N. Lurie and Veit's edited book, *New Jersey: A History of the Garden State* (Rutgers University Press, 2012).

Mark L. Thompson provides an overview of early European settlement in the region in *The Contest for the Delaware Valley: Allegiance, Identity, and Empire in the Seventeenth Century* (Louisiana State University Press, 2013). John B. Frantz and William Pencak's edited book, *Beyond Philadelphia: The American Revolution in the Pennsylvania Hinterland* (Pennsylvania State University Press, 1998) explores the regional dimensions of the emerging Greater Philadelphia region.

A sample of modern scholarship on Swedish settlement in American can be found in *New Sweden in America* (University of Delaware Press, 1995), edited by Carol E. Hoffecker and others. The American Swedish Historical Museum in Franklin D. Roosevelt Park, 1900 Pattison Avenue in South Philadelphia, provides a range of exhibits and experiences exploring Swedish settlement in the region. A primary landmark is Gloria Dei (Old Swede's) Church, at 916 S. Swanson Street, Philadelphia, administered by the National Park Service. One can visit the site of the original New Sweden settlement on the Delaware River at the Governor Prinz Park in Essington, Pa. The New Sweden Center, a museum without walls based in Wilmington, Del., promotes the Delaware Valley's history from 1638 to the American Revolution, with a focus on Swedish, Finnish, and Lenape cultures. Among the projects it has supported has been the re-creation of a Swedish farmstead museum in Essington. The structure was originally constructed in Bridgeton, N.J., where it opened in 1988 as part of celebrations of the 350th anniversary of the founding of New Sweden. One of the few surviving examples of New Sweden's log homes is on Darby Creek in Drexel Hill, Pa. It is open to the public on weekends.

For the history of West Jersey, see John E. Pomfret, *The Province of West New Jersey 1609–1702: A History of the Origins of an American Colony* (Princeton University Press, 1956); Thomas L. Purvis, *Proprietors, Patronage, and Paper Money: Legislative Politics in New Jersey, 1703–1776* (Rutgers University Press, 1986); Peter O. Wacker, *Land and People: A Cultural Geography of Preindustrial New Jersey: Origins and Settlement Patterns* (Rutgers University Press, 1975); and Jean R. Soderlund, *Separate Paths: Lenapes and Colonists in West New Jersey* (Rutgers University Press, 2022).

Richard S. Dunn and Mary Maples Dunn's edited book, *The World of William Penn* (University of Pennsylvania Press, 1986), addresses Pennsylvania's founding. Pennsbury Manor, a reconstruction of William Penn's country estate set on the Delaware River in Morrisville, Pa., is a primary site preserving the historical significance of William Penn. Stephanie Grauman Wolf examines early Pennsylvania settlement in *Urban Village: Population, Community, and Family Structure in Germantown, Pennsylvania, 1683–1800* (Princeton University Press, 1976). For a history of Delaware's origins, see John Munroe, *Colonial Delaware: A History* (KTO Press, 1978). The Zwaanendael Museum, 102 Kings Highway, Lewes, Del., was built in commemoration of the first European colony. It serves as a showcase for the Lewes area's maritime, military, and social history. The National Park Service administers six Delaware sites, including several in the Brandywine Valley, under the umbrella of the First State National Historic Park. Among other topics, they examine the settlement of the Delaware Valley, the founding of the nation, the testing of the U.S. Constitution, and the conservation of natural resources. The Delaware Historical Society operates nine historic buildings, including the Delaware History Museum, at 505 N. Market Street, Wilmington.

For the history of the Walking Purchase, see Steven Craig Harper, *Promised Land: Penn's Holy Experiment, The Walking Purchase and the Dispossession of Delawares, 1600–1763* (Lehigh University Press, 2006) and Francis Jennings, "The Scandalous Indian Policy of William Penn's Sons: Deeds and Documents of the Walking Purchase," *Pennsylvania History* (January 1970).

Books examining the history of the Mason-Dixon Line in depth include Edwin Danson, *Drawing the Line: How Mason and Dixon Surveyed the Most Famous Border in America* (Wiley, 2001) and Sally M. Walker, *Boundaries: How the Mason-Dixon Line Settled a Family Feud and Divided a Nation* (Candlewick Press, 2014). Thomas Pynchon provides an imaginative account of Mason and Dixon in his 1997 book of the same name.

Chapter 5

The City and Its Peoples

Introduction

The city Thomas Holme plotted out for William Penn in 1682 was limited in size but large in scope and ambition. From the first lots laid out on the Delaware River where proprietors built homes and businesses, the settlement expanded to not only support the city but also to draw in an ever-widening hinterland. As the approximately two-square-mile city grew, goods and services proliferated, bringing many producers and consumers together in face-to-face exchanges, all the while drawing in a wider array of participants from across the region and ultimately the nation and the world.

The realization of Penn's vision did not happen overnight, however, and as forest gave way to building construction, settlement extended, pulled not just by the lure of open lands, but ultimately by the realization of a mix of diverse peoples of varying wealth and standing. For some time, the boundaries of Penn's green country town remained relatively tight, but with the influx of new residents in the early years of the nineteenth century urban activity extended not just to the city's western boundary at the Schuylkill River but also north and south where adjacent communities formed. Closely attached to the central city economically but maintaining their independence politically as well as establishing their own distinct character, these neighboring communities came into tension with the mother city over time. As immigrant workers concentrated to the south, for instance, social disturbances spilled over to the city proper, causing dismay among propertied Philadelphians but leaving them helpless to act because public authority failed to extend beyond city boundaries. Rioting in 1844 sparked by clashes between Protestants and Catholics left the city unable to maintain the peace.

The desire to maintain order prompted city authorities to seek the consolidation of all the communities within Philadelphia County's 130 square miles into a single city subject to the discipline of a modernized police force. In this way, the city might better instill the values of its founders, of high morality and community responsibility. But city leaders had an even grander vision in mind, of capturing the full human and monetary resources of its immediate neighbors in the cause of dominating the contest for control of western territories, a race for empire made possible only through political discipline equal to economic ambition.

The path to empire was full of obstacles, however. Incorporation into a single urban entity in 1854 did not assure uniform behavior let alone ambition. While the names of some communities survived as identifiable neighborhoods, over time once competing urban villages came to be known more broadly as sections of the consolidated city: North, South, West, Southwest, and Northeast Philadelphia. Such broad designations did not assure, or even reflect, homogenization. Instead, residents, shored up by distinct ethnic, racial, and religious identities and interests, sought to maintain old traditions and affiliations, even as their communities changed over time.

With new ambition came further growth, and the pattern of movement away from the core—known now as Center City—assumed new character. Settlement to the west, aided by the opening of the area's first permanent bridge in 1805 and rail connections downtown, offered the prospect of more space for grander homes still within easy reach of employment. And even as West Philadelphia became a classic streetcar suburb in the second half of the nineteenth century, Northeast Philadelphia became a classic automobile suburb in the mid-twentieth century, more modest in its housing stock, perhaps, but affording residents access to a backyard and commercial outlets while they retained employment ties downtown. Older working communities, at the same time, remained congested as industry intensified north and south of the original city, and housing built close to factories offered few frills to the city's growing working class.

The decline of industrial production in the second half of the twentieth century affected every section of the city, none more than the working-class districts north of Center City. As manufacturing jobs disappeared, many white ethnic workers left their homes for suburban locations, and they, in turn, were replaced by Black residents, many of them part of the Great Migration from the South that began during the 1910s and continued into the 1970s. Without the same industrial jobs to anchor these neighborhoods, poverty and crime grew and living conditions worsened, bringing a new set of tensions with the nearby Center City, now very much part of a postindustrial economy. Those working-class residents who had the means moved to the outer fringe of the city, to South Jersey and to Northeast Philadelphia, especially the area north of Frankford Creek, which remained sparsely populated until after World War II. It was in this late-blooming part of the city that suburban building practices and values took hold, likely spurred by the white backlash to a growing Black presence at the city's core that Mayor Frank Rizzo exploited to gain office in the 1970s.

Urban decline at the core was not irreversible. Generous tax breaks to builders and homeowners in the central city helped slow outmigration and pushed rents up in other core areas, including parts of South, West, and North Philadelphia. Gentrification, where it existed, was not uncontested, however, and as a result revitalization was uneven and its extent and direction unpredictable in the early decades of the twenty-first century.

Consolidation

Andrew Heath

The Consolidation Act of 1854 extended Philadelphia's territory from the two-square-mile "city proper" founded by William Penn to nearly 130 square miles, making the municipal borders coterminous with Philadelphia County and turning the metropolis into the largest in extent in the nation, a position it held until Chicago leaped ahead in 1889. Consolidation's supporters believed the measure would enable municipal authorities to deal with the epidemics of riot and disease that ravaged the city in the 1830s and 1840s, while giving them the power and dignity to contest for metropolitan supremacy. Although the bid to overtake New York as the first city failed, the 1854 act led to some impressive civic achievements. Since its passage, the city's boundaries have barely changed, and despite charter revisions in 1887 and 1951, contemporary Philadelphia still bears the imprint of the mid-nineteenth-century measure.

Until 1854, Philadelphia's population concentrated within the original city boundaries set by William Penn, between the Delaware and Schuylkill Rivers and from what is now South Street to Vine. By 1820, however, inhabitants in the independent boroughs, districts, and townships that made up the rest of the county already outnumbered those in the city proper. Some of these suburbs were places of significance in their own right, with Spring Garden, the Northern Liberties, and Kensington, all north of the city center, ranking as the ninth, eleventh, and twelfth biggest urban settlements in the nation in the 1850 census. These districts, in common with their neighbors, had won

FIGURE 20. The City of Philadelphia as consolidated in 1854. HISTORICAL SOCIETY OF PENNSYLVANIA.

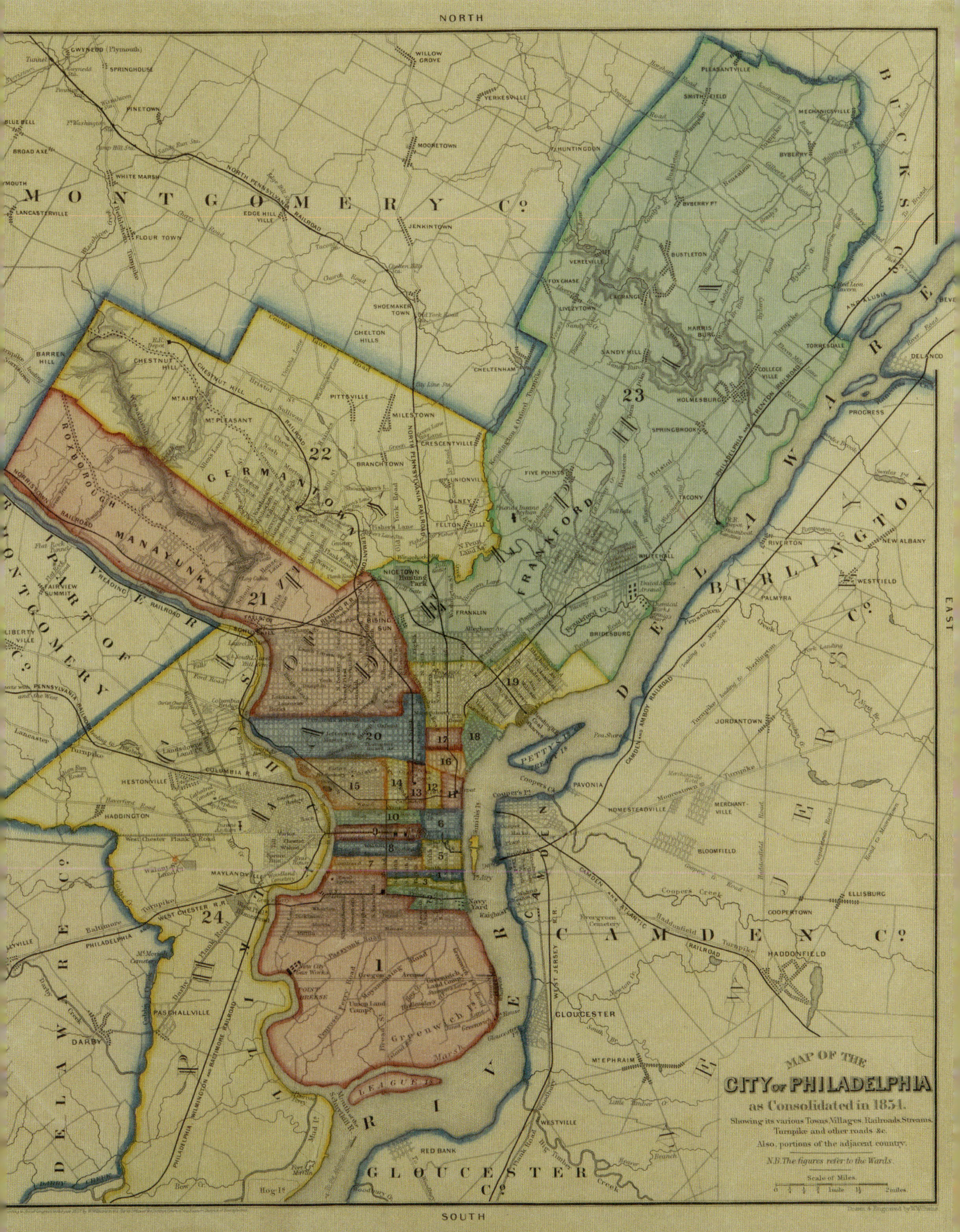
NORTH
MAP OF THE
CITY of PHILADELPHIA
as Consolidated in 1854.
Showing its various Towns Villages, Railroads, Streams, Turnpike and other roads &c.
Also, portions of the adjacent country.
N.B. The figures refer to the Wards.
Scale of Miles.
MONTGOMERY Co.
BUCKS Co.
BURLINGTON Co.
CAMDEN Co.
GLOUCESTER Co.
DELAWARE Co.
DELAWARE RIVER
SCHUYLKILL
GERMANTOWN
MANAYUNK
ROXBOROUGH
FRANKFORD
CAMDEN
NEW JERSEY
LEAGUE IS.
EAST
SOUTH

from the Commonwealth of Pennsylvania the right to establish their own local governments, with powers to tax, borrow, and spend, and thus remained independent of Philadelphia City's control. While they varied in their social and political character, they tended to be poorer and more Democratic than the historic center, which their residents sometimes referred to as the "Whig Gibraltar."

The first organized calls for uniting the built-up portions of the county under one municipal authority came in response to two major riots in 1844. The anti-Catholic violence, which broke out in the northern suburb of Kensington and the southern district of Southwark—both neighborhoods in which Irish immigrants and native-born Protestants lived in close proximity—exposed the inadequacy of the prevailing system of law enforcement. With no uniformed officers in the county, and every jurisdiction responsible for its own policing, there was little to prevent violence from escalating. It took state militia armed with cannons to suppress the Southwark disturbance. Soon after the riots, the *Public Ledger* called for annexing the built-up outlying districts, and in November, citizens gathered at the Philadelphia County Courthouse (Congress Hall) to make the case for enlarging the city boundaries.

The move for a new charter over the winter of 1844–45, however, came to very little. A bill was drawn up for consideration by the Commonwealth—which then, as now, held the power to create, alter, and destroy local government—but influential owners of property and city debt like Horace Binney organized to oppose the proposal. Critics feared that consolidation would hand the keys of the Whig city to suburban Democrats, and that real estate owners in the prosperous city proper would be taxed to pay the interest on loans taken out by indebted outlying districts, which needed to borrow to maintain their rapid growth. The opponents of consolidation lobbied for legislation that would maintain the districts' independence yet still address the issue of civil disorder by requiring that all built-up portions of Philadelphia retain one policeman for every 150 taxable inhabitants.

This measure failed to prevent another major riot in 1849, which sparked renewed calls for annexation. While this time the proposal enjoyed more support from the city's merchants, manufacturers, and professionals, it failed once again in the state capital. Instead of consolidation, Harrisburg legislators established a police force under an elected marshal to deal with disorder across the built-up sections of the metropolis. The Marshal's Police proved relatively successful in maintaining the peace, and despite endemic fighting among rival companies of volunteer firemen and street gangs, there were no major riots from 1850 to the eventual passage of the Consolidation Act in 1854.

Calls for metropolitan union nevertheless grew louder, despite the relative calm of the early 1850s. By then, municipal reformers hoped to do more than inoculate the city against the violence of the preceding decades. Many saw the district system as unnecessarily costly, as dozens of jurisdictions duplicated services that could have been provided more efficiently by a single government. Others feared that the city proper might become "an appendage to her own colonies," as growth in industrial districts like Spring Garden and Kensington outpaced the historic center. Some no longer saw those suburbs as a financial burden, but rather as a potential source of tax revenue, because heavy investment in the Pennsylvania Railroad after its chartering in 1846 had left the city proper far more heavily indebted than its neighbors. Real estate owners in central Philadelphia complained that suburban property holders benefited from the trade that resulted from the rail link to Pittsburgh but had contributed little in the way of public funds to the railroad's construction.

Perhaps most importantly, though, supporters of consolidation believed that only a united Philadelphia would have the power and status to overtake New York in the struggle for metropolitan supremacy, a race the city had languished in for at least three decades as the completion of the Erie Canal (1825) and Chestnut Street's decline as a financial center after Andrew Jackson's attack on the Second National Bank enabled Manhattan to pull ahead. As North and South clashed over the question of slavery extension, advocates of annexation for Philadelphia readily adopted the rallying cry "In Union There Is Strength" for their own cause.

In the early 1850s both of the dominant political parties, the Whigs and the Democrats, promised to back annexation, but in Harrisburg, proposals for charter revision went nowhere. To break the impasse, supporters of the measure—prodded by their erstwhile opponent Binney—decided in 1853 to nominate their own slate of candidates for the Pennsylvania assembly and senate. In alliance with advocates of a professional fire department, they put forward a mixture of independents and regular Whig and Democratic party nominees. At the head of the ticket was Eli Kirk Price, a progressive real estate attorney, while the wealthy locomotive builder Matthias W. Baldwin was among the candidates for the lower house. Most of the consolidation slate triumphed, and before Price went off to take his seat in the senate, an Executive Consolidation Committee met in Philadelphia to draft a bill.

The Executive Consolidation Committee that convened in the Board of Trade rooms at the Merchants Exchange over the winter of 1853–54 represented a cross section of Philadelphia's economic elite. Many owned substantial real estate beyond the historic corporate boundaries, and by proposing to annex the entire county rather than just the much smaller built-up areas adjacent to the city proper, they went much further than their predecessors. Despite murmurs of protest from rural districts, the charter passed both houses and was signed into law in February. The new metropolis, encompassing industrial suburbs, romantic rural retreats, and vast stretches of farmland, came into being four months later.

Architects of the 1854 charter saw it as a victory over the self-interested politicians of the district system and the triumph of a rational, modern government over an antiquated predecessor. Executive power was invested in a mayor elected at-large for a two-year term, and voters chose the nativist playwright Robert T. Conrad as the first to hold the office. In place of the old boundaries on the county map, meanwhile, twenty-four wards sent representatives to the Common and Select Councils. Ward representation preserved an element of localism in the councils—something party politicians quickly learned to exploit—but the financial muscle and territorial reach of the enlarged city enabled urban planning on a far greater scale than previously had been possible.

The Consolidation Act resulted in other important changes for newly expanded Philadelphia. Among them, the legislation gave municipal authorities the duty to preserve open spaces, and before and after the Civil War steps were taken toward creating Fairmount Park, which lay entirely beyond the boundaries of the old city proper. Standardized street names and numbers (1857), a professionalized fire department (1871), and a new city hall at Broad and Market Streets (1871–1901) demonstrated civic authorities' readiness to raise the city's metropolitan status, as did the suburban expansion fueled by horse-drawn streetcar lines and other infrastructure improvements that opened up cheap land in the consolidated city for builders. When Philadelphians in the second half of the nineteenth century contrasted their city of row houses with the tenements of New York, they credited the city's expansion with eliminating the need for "vertical slums."

Perhaps most importantly, though, consolidation gave the municipal government the power to maintain the peace. While violence did occasionally break out—in 1871, for instance, the African American civil rights campaigner Octavius Catto was shot dead on a turbulent election day—the mayor, with his control of a large, uniformed police force, always had the resources at his disposal to prevent the kind of conflagrations that threatened to engulf the city in 1844. Under Republican stewardship, Philadelphia avoided the draft riots that occurred in New York in 1863 and the worst of the conflict between railroads and workers in the Great Strike of 1877. Citizens credited the Consolidation Act for the relative peace in a city once notorious for disorder.

Some of these developments, however, owed more to legislation in Harrisburg than they did to actions by the city government, and by the late 1860s, the habit of state officials overriding the municipal authorities in matters pertaining to the metropolis caused frequent complaints. So too did the tendency of councilmen to claim executive power for themselves, thus weakening the powers of the mayor's office, which consolidators had sought to strengthen. As party bosses—usually Democratic in the immigrant enclaves of South Philadelphia, but Republican in the growing suburbs—established ward strongholds, centralized city and statewide Republican machines distributed jobs and contracts to supporters. After the Civil War a generation of affluent reformers began to see the 1854 act more as a giant source of patronage than a measure designed to bring peace, prosperity, and fiscally responsible government. They hoped another new charter, eventually passed in 1887, would improve matters, but under Republican leadership, Philadelphia's municipal government remained, in Lincoln Steffens's memorable phrase, "the most corrupt and the most contented." This was consolidation's unanticipated legacy, but the act's limitations should not mask its real achievements in laying the foundations of modern Philadelphia.

Center City

Catharine Dann Roeber and Charlene Mires

Forming a core of civic, commercial, and residential life since Philadelphia's seventeenth-century founding, Center City has been a continually evolving experiment in urban living and management. The roughly rectangular area of about 2.3 square miles between the Delaware and Schuylkill Rivers, from Vine Street to South Street, occupies the territory of the original 1682 city plan for Philadelphia. Once a forested expanse with hills, ponds, and streams, the land between the rivers transformed over time into a populated grid where residential and commercial interests jostled, shifted, and spread from east to west to fill in the footprint of "the city proper." Rivers, roads, and later railroads, public transit, and highways linked the city with the wider region, making the urban core a hub for people, culture, and commerce—but also making it possible for residents and businesses to move to outlying neighborhoods and suburbs. In the latter part of the twentieth century, new generations of city planners mobilized to combat the effects of suburbanization and revitalize Center City as a place where residents and visitors could live, work, and play.

Surveyor Thomas Holme and founder William Penn conceived the idea for a gridded city punctuated by garden squares in the 1680s. They drew inspiration from baroque town planning, post–Great Fire of London (1666) concerns for city health, desires to compensate initial investors in Pennsylvania with land, and personal preferences of Penn and early interest groups such as the Free Society of Traders. The plan drawn by Holme intended settlement to occur on both the Schuylkill and Delaware waterfronts and along the main streets of High (later Market) and Broad. After the first printing of the plan in 1683, the river-to-river grid appeared prominently on maps of Pennsylvania, but creating a city in the image of Penn and Holme's plan required nearly two centuries of clearing trees, leveling land, extending streets, and building upon the grid.

Early settlement focused on the Delaware waterfront, which became the main site of commercial and residential building and growth during the colonial era. While property at the city plan's western edge, on the Schuylkill, remained relatively open with scattered farms and industrial workshops, the Delaware riverfront grew with wharves, warehouses, churches, taverns, and houses. Settlement hugged the Delaware shore in a semi-crescent shape, most densely along High Street and thinning to the north and south. More and more residents clustered into the area by subdividing lots. Residences of the most prosperous Philadelphians faced the main streets while smaller houses on back alleys and courts filled with laborers and the poor. Instead of civic buildings on a center square, as Penn and Holme had planned, by the 1720s a town hall and Quaker meetinghouse anchored the city at Second and High Streets. Construction of the Pennsylvania State House (Independence Hall) in the 1730s pulled the city westward to around Fifth Street, but as late as the 1790s Thomas Jefferson received advice to rent quarters east of Seventh Street because "so few houses" stood farther west.

The port on the Delaware, ferries from New Jersey, and roads radiating outward into Pennsylvania, Delaware, and Maryland enabled people and goods to move in and out of the compact city. Throughout the colonial era English, Irish, Scots Irish, Welsh, German, and free and enslaved people of African heritage came through the port of Philadelphia to build and settle the city and surrounding region, which had been occupied earlier by Native American camps and Swedish settlements. From nearby hinterlands and across the Delaware River from New Jersey, agricultural products came to the High Street market and shipped out to other colonies and the world. The presence of the market, which extended to the west as the city grew, gave High Street of the original city plan a new name: Market Street (informally at first, made official in 1858).

The settled area of the city extended to Seventh Street by 1790, and by 1800 the forest had been cleared from river to river. In the decades following the American Revolution, as property values closest to commercial High Street increased, the settled area of Philadelphia became more segregated by economic status. The laboring class and the poor migrated in greater concentrations to low-rent districts at the southern and northern fringe, including a notoriously bawdy area known as "Helltown" north of Arch Street between Third Street and the Delaware River. Beginning in the 1790s and continuing into the early nineteenth century, a significant free African American neighborhood grew at Sixth and Lombard Streets, around Mother Bethel AME Church. African Americans also clustered in the area north of Arch Street and west of Fourth. A German neighborhood formed on the city's northern border, and French immigrants who arrived during the French and Haitian revolutions opened businesses in the vicinity of Second and Walnut.

Philadelphians of the late eighteenth and early nineteenth centuries made choices that imposed order and shaped the look and feel of the city proper for years to come. In 1795, city officials banned wood-frame buildings from inside the city limits, which assured that the fine rows of new homes built in the early decades of the nineteenth century would be made of red brick, often with marble-front raised basements and steps. The city government also looked back to the original city plan to guide improvements of the neglected public squares. Between 1801 and 1829 the center square, which Penn and Holme had intended for public buildings, became home to a neoclassical pump house that architect Benjamin Latrobe designed to supply water to the city via a gravity-fed system from the Schuylkill. In 1825 the city councils gave the squares new names that imprinted history in the landscape: Washington (for the southeast square), Franklin (northeast), Rittenhouse (southwest), Logan (northwest), and Penn (in the center). Washington and Franklin Squares transformed during the 1820s and 1830s from neglected plots and sometime burial grounds into landscaped parks. Rittenhouse and Logan Squares similarly improved during the 1840s and 1850s, as the population spread west. Rittenhouse Square became an especially prime address as lands west of Broad Street began to fill with row houses, new houses of worship, schools, and businesses during the 1850s and 1860s.

While residents and businesses planted new structures across the width of the grid, earlier settled blocks churned with changing purposes and redevelopment. The Merchants Exchange completed in 1834 at Third and Walnut Streets signaled the continuing importance of maritime commerce, as did the 1830s rebuilding of a warehouse district on Front Street north of Market Street and the creation of the waterfront Delaware Avenue, funded by a bequest of merchant Stephen Girard. However, businesses also moved inland from the waterfront and formed specialized clusters for banking, insurance, and publishing. In the oldest sections of the city proper, many colonial-era homes survived but deteriorated into subdivided multiple-family dwellings or industrial workshops. Homes associated with the nation's founders gave way to commercial buildings on High Street, and factories replaced brick houses on Arch and Cherry Streets. Philadelphians built over cemeteries and turned streams into underground sewers.

The relationship of the city proper with outlying areas changed fundamentally from the 1830s through the 1850s, first with the expansion of public transportation networks and then with the Consolidation Act of 1854. Railroads, omnibuses, and horse-drawn streetcars allowed increasing numbers of Philadelphians to move beyond the boundaries of the original "walking city." The Consolidation Act extended the city's boundaries to encompass all of Philadelphia County, but in doing so it reduced the old city proper into a nameless section of a larger whole. "Old city proper" lingered as a name for the central city, remaining in use as late as the 1920s. However, by the late nineteenth and early twentieth centuries "center city" (or "centre city") appeared frequently in newspaper advertisements for real estate and employment, suggesting a widespread understanding of the phrase as a designation for Philadelphia's downtown. During the 1920s and 1930s, Center City (sometimes capitalized and sometimes not) became more common as a place name in advertising, in the names of buildings, and in city government communication. Thereafter, embraced by city planners as well as organizations such as the Center City Residents Association (formed in 1947), Center City dominated as the name for the old city proper.

Following consolidation, Philadelphians made another pivotal decision for the future shape and functions of the central city when they selected Penn (or Center) Square, the site Penn and Holme had intended

FIGURE 21. Depicted from above in 1857, with the Schuylkill River in the foreground, central Philadelphia's industrial expansion is apparent from smokestacks on both riverfronts and dispersed across the city. Population and commercial districts remained largely concentrated east of Broad Street. HISTORICAL SOCIETY OF PENNSYLVANIA.

for public buildings, as the location for a new city hall. The site at Broad and Market Streets, determined by referendum in 1870 after years of debate, followed the westward trend of the city away from the traditional home of municipal government on Independence Square. By the time voters chose Penn Square over Washington Square, substantial development had occurred on Broad Street, including construction of the Academy of Music (opened in 1857) and fine hotels on S. Broad and development of business and industry to the north. Anticipation of the new city hall, which took form between 1871 and 1901, spurred additional nearby development. The Pennsylvania Railroad and Philadelphia & Reading Railroad opened massive new stations on Market Street flanking Penn Square (Broad Street Station, built 1880–82 and expanded 1892–94 at Fifteenth Street, and the Reading Terminal, built 1891–93 at Twelfth Street). Adding to Broad Street's status as a cultural corridor, the Pennsylvania Academy of the Fine Arts moved to its new building designed by Frank Furness in 1876. The same year, as Philadelphia celebrated the nation's centennial, John Wanamaker opened his "Grand Depot" store in the former Pennsylvania Railroad Freight Depot at Thirteenth and Market Street, heralding an era when large department stores drew crowds of shoppers from the city and surrounding areas to an increasingly bustling and diverse downtown.

Older blocks continued to lose their cachet but served as points of entry for immigrants and other new arrivals to Philadelphia. Beginning in the 1870s, a Chinatown began to form in the 900 block of Race Street as Chinese merchants and laundrymen migrated to Philadelphia from the West Coast. With few options, the Chinese created their community in the midst of a vice district known as the Tenderloin, north of Race Street between Sixth and Thirteenth Streets. In the remnants of the colonial city near the Delaware River, refugees from pogroms in Russia created a Jewish Quarter beginning in the 1880s. African Americans migrating from the South to escape repressive Jim Crow conditions extended the historically Black neighborhood around Mother Bethel AME Church westward toward Broad Street and beyond.

In the northwest quadrant of Center City, meanwhile, the new city hall helped to fuel imagination of a grand new boulevard extending northwest to link the center of the city with Fairmount Park. Plans formed slowly but came to fruition with the opening of the Benjamin Franklin Parkway in 1918. The civic improvement gave Philadelphia an expansive new avenue in the style of Paris and spurred development of a new cultural district around Logan Square (which became a traffic circle). In the process, the city demolished 1,300 residential and industrial properties but spared the Cathedral Basilica of Saints Peter and Paul, which had faced Logan Square since 1846.

Although the urban core remained in part residential, by the early twentieth century commerce and culture firmly dominated the landscape and the skyline. The central city reached new heights not only with the 548-foot tower of city hall but also with the advent of skyscrapers, starting with the Land Title Building at Broad and Chestnut Streets (fifteen stories built 1897–98; twenty-two-story addition built 1902). The combination of railroad stations, cultural institutions, department stores, and other businesses anchored Center City as a hub for commercial and cultural life, including conventions that filled Broad Street hotels. At the same time, a greater variety of residents gained the option of commuting from outlying areas on electrified streetcars (introduced in the 1890s), the Market-Frankford Subway–Elevated Line (built 1903–8, extended to Frankford in 1922), and the Broad Street Subway (1928–32). Motor vehicles added flexibility of travel and the option of driving to New Jersey over Philadelphia's first bridge over the Delaware River, the Delaware River Bridge (opened in 1926 and renamed the Benjamin Franklin Bridge in 1955).

As the region became more suburban from the late nineteenth into the twentieth century, Center City felt the impact. By the 1950s and 1960s, urban reformers focused their attention on areas of poverty and "blight" along the Delaware waterfront and in nearby neighborhoods. Pointing to areas that had "changed over the years from aesthetic assets to

FIGURE 22. Philadelphia City Hall, ca. 1900. Decorated throughout with sculptures by Alexander Milne Calder, the structure's 491-foot tower is capped by Calder's twenty-seven-ton cast iron statue of William Penn. LIBRARY OF CONGRESS.

eyesores," the Philadelphia Planning Commission led by Edmund Bacon, the Philadelphia Redevelopment Authority (established 1945), and the Olde Philadelphia Development Corporation (1956) spearheaded massive restructuring plans for Center City that involved redeveloping areas perceived as slums and adding infrastructure. Catering to car culture, highways created new boundaries and connections for Center City. Construction of Interstate 95 along the Delaware waterfront in the 1960s linked Philadelphia to the Northeast Corridor but largely cut off the city from its formerly bustling harbor. On the other side of town, the Schuylkill Expressway reached completion in 1958. Planners also sought to improve movement of automobile traffic across the city with new expressways along the northern and southern boundaries of the old city proper. They succeeded in implementing the Vine Street Expressway, over strong opposition from residents of Chinatown, but could not overcome neighborhood resistance to a planned Crosstown Expressway along South Street.

In Center City, redevelopment sought to compete with the appeal of suburbia with a new mix of residential, recreational, and commercial space, including high-rise apartment buildings and the suburban-style Gallery shopping mall on Market Street. West of city hall, the Penn Center complex of office buildings rose in the corridor where an aging viaduct known as the "Chinese Wall" had carried trains into the old Broad Street Station. Around Independence Hall, historical parks managed by the state and federal governments replaced blocks of commercial buildings. South of Independence Hall, by removing and resettling predominantly ethnic and poor residents, then preserving and restoring the best of their colonial-era homes, urban renewal transformed the old Jewish Quarter into upscale Society Hill. In addition to the urban pioneers who bought and rehabilitated the houses of Society Hill, residents added new vitality to other Center City neighborhoods, for example creating a "Gayborhood" in the vicinity of Thirteenth and Locust Street and an arts community in the abandoned factory lofts east of Third Street and north of Market.

The continuing revitalization of Center City as a mix of residential and commercial historic ambiance and new development built upon these twentieth-century projects. Beginning in 1976, federal tax credits for historic preservation spurred creation of a new supply of luxury apartments through adaptive reuse of old hotels, factories, and office buildings. A boom in skyscraper construction west of Broad Street occurred after 1987, when One Liberty Place broke a longstanding but unofficial practice of respecting the William Penn statue atop city hall as the highest point in the city. Other skyscrapers followed, with Comcast surpassing all others for height with its fifty-seven-story headquarters built in 2008 and again with its sixty-story Technology and Innovation Center built between 2014 and 2018. East of Market Street, after retailing suffered the failures and consolidations of department stores, the onetime showcase urban shopping mall, the Gallery, itself became the site of redevelopment into a retail-entertainment complex called Fashion District Philadelphia.

In an era of industrial decline, Center City anchored a tourism industry that became increasingly important to the region's economy. Promoters showcased the birthplace of a nation with museums and historic sites like Independence National Historical Park as well as yearly attractions such as the Mummers Parade, an abundance of public art, and a thriving dining and entertainment scene. To compete for conventions as well as recreational travelers, the Pennsylvania Convention Center opened in 1993, taking up the whole of four city blocks between Arch and Race Streets from Eleventh Street to Thirteenth (then more than doubling in square footage with an extension to Broad Street in the 2010s). Redevelopment in service to tourism also occurred in Independence National Historical Park, which gained a block-long visitor center, an expanded exhibit hall for the Liberty Bell, the National Constitution Center, and nearby a Museum of the American Revolution.

Stewards of Philadelphia's Center City, like those in other American cities, grappled with the challenge of preserving the past while ensuring a secure future for the city and its residents. Beginning in 1991, the Center City District—a business improvement district—supplemented city services to improve quality of life with initiatives ranging from street cleaning to development of Dilworth Park adjacent to city hall and Sister Cities Park on the Benjamin Franklin Parkway. By the early decades of the twenty-first century, new attention turned toward reintegrating the Delaware River waterfront into the urban grid, and the Schuylkill River Trail opened on the western edge of the original city plan. By 2020, more than 200,000 of Philadelphia's 1.6 million residents lived in Center City and adjacent blocks north to Girard Avenue and south to Tasker Street, including a high concentration of young professionals and increasing numbers of older residents relocating from the suburbs. Although hit hard when the COVID-19 pandemic shut down businesses, tourism, and cultural institutions, Center City steadily regained its footing. In a city of many neighborhoods, Center City remained the heart of political and cultural activity and a visible expression of Philadelphia's growth and change—not only a geographic location, but a signpost of urban vitality.

North Philadelphia

David Amott

Where exactly North Philadelphia begins and ends is a matter of debate. Even native Philadelphians have difficulty identifying the boundaries of this area of their city with precision. This is likely because so many of the neighborhoods located north, northeast, or northwest of Philadelphia's center enjoy common histories and developmental patterns and consequently look a great deal alike. Before the 1682 arrival of William Penn in North America, what is now North Philadelphia was covered with thick woods inhabited by Native Americans. Philadelphia's establishment that same year began the area's gradual transformation from acres of forests to blocks of homes, factories, churches, universities, and other institutions built to serve the area's diverse inhabitants. These inhabitants included Native Americans, English colonists, and enslaved Africans in the seventeenth and eighteenth centuries and waves of immigrants hailing from places as varied as America's southern states; northern, southern, and eastern Europe; the Caribbean; and Latin America in the nineteenth, twentieth, and twenty-first centuries.

The Lenni Lenape Indians were the earliest documented inhabitants of the area that later became North Philadelphia. For thousands of years, the Lenapes occupied the banks of the Delaware and Schuylkill Rivers, establishing several large settlements in and around the area that became North Philadelphia. These settlements included the Coaquannock or "Grove of Tall Pines" camp in the area that later became Laurel Hill Cemetery. Another camp called Nittabakonck, meaning "place that is easy to get to," was situated near where the Wissahickon Creek empties into the Schuylkill River. Today, most of the remnants of these Native peoples are deep underground, accessible only to archaeologists. However, a handful of North Philadelphia roads, including Frankford Avenue and Old York Road, roughly follow trails established by the Lenape and other Native American tribes centuries ago.

After William Penn founded Philadelphia as the capital of his New World colony, the forests that had sustained the Lenape slowly gave way to farms and estates. Hoping to attract people to his new "greene Country Towne" and to encourage development in and around the city, Penn granted the initial investors in Philadelphia lots within the city but also "liberty lands" or "free lots" in areas north of the original city limits where farms could be established. Reminders of North Philadelphia's seventeenth- and eighteenth-century agricultural history exist in the form of landmarks like Judge William Lewis's 1789 Strawberry Mansion (originally called Summerville), Fox Chase Farm (one of Philadelphia's two working farms), and in place names such as "Northern Liberties." Many property lines in North Philadelphia have origins in the farmsteads that were gradually developed as this area urbanized over the nineteenth and twentieth centuries.

When the British occupied Philadelphia during the War for Independence, King George III's soldiers ran their fortifications unhindered through the open ground along present-day Spring Garden Street. After the war, however, development pressure on the northern side of the city increased with the population boom that accompanied Philadelphia's postwar position as the political, financial, and social capital of the United States. One of the first major developments in North Philadelphia following the Revolutionary War was an initiative to build a canal to link the Delaware and Schuylkill Rivers. If completed, the canal would have run along the present route of Pennsylvania Avenue to Broad Street on Philadelphia's west side and would have bordered Spring Garden Street on the city's east side. Due to lack of funds, however, this project floundered and the Philadelphia and Columbia Railroad, the Baldwin Locomotive Works, and various other industries filled in the canal's right of way and the acres of open space along Philadelphia's northern fringes. Not only did this part of the city offer industries convenient access to the Schuylkill and Delaware Rivers and abundant space for growth, but the area was far enough removed from the city center to ensure that industrial smells and toxic chemicals would not interfere with central Philadelphia's more genteel atmosphere.

The initial industrialization that took hold in North Philadelphia at the beginning of the nineteenth century laid the foundation for rapid changes later in the same century. Nineteenth-century maps of Philadelphia offer a compelling visual record documenting how urban expansion gradually eliminated the farms north of the city, replacing them with homes, factories, warehouses, workshops, and other institutions. An 1824 map of Philadelphia published by William Allen shows heavily developed Northern Liberties and Kensington neighborhoods bordering the Delaware River, but sparsely populated blocks immediately north of the central city. Later maps of Philadelphia, such as W. H. Gamble's 1887 *Plan of the City of Philadelphia and Camden*, show blocks of homes and factories stretching beyond Allegheny Avenue. The industrialization that overtook large swaths of open land in North Philadelphia quickly attracted residential development as workers drawn to factory jobs came to settle in the region. Companies such as Nicetown's Midvale Steel, founded in 1867 as Butcher Steel; the large textile mills and tanneries of Kensington; Port Richmond's Cramp Shipbuilders; and hundreds of other manufactories and cottage industries scattered throughout North Philadelphia created the vast array of goods and supported the mercantile culture that earned Philadelphia the nickname "Workshop of the World."

By the 1880s, North Philadelphia's Broad Street neighborhoods competed with Rittenhouse Square and other fashionable districts for urban prestige. Along N. Broad, the nouveau riche who were responsible for much of the industrial development of the surrounding neighborhoods constructed performance halls, social clubs, beautiful churches and synagogues, and proud, turreted homes of brick and brownstone. One of the most ostentatious of these North Philadelphia mansions, belonging to Peter A. B. Widener, stood on the corner of N. Broad and Girard Avenue. This Germanic-style mansion represented the fortune that Widener acquired developing trolley lines, urban rail lines, and other public utilities that opened up great swaths of undeveloped land for urbanization. Wherever Widener's car tracks or railroads were constructed, speculative row, twin, and detached houses quickly followed as trolleys made it possible for workers employed in Center City to commute from neighborhoods located outside of Philadelphia proper.

Philadelphia's rapid development following the 1854 Act of Consolidation gained the city the moniker "city of homes" as blocks of North Philadelphia filled with row houses built to accommodate a growing workforce that included thousands of immigrants, beginning with German and Irish families in the first half of the nineteenth century, followed by Russian, eastern, and southern Europeans in the second half. Amid its factories, mansions, and row houses, North Philadelphia acquired Maennerchor halls and German beer gardens, Irish Catholic churches, Ashkenazi synagogues, Latvian social clubs, and various other religious, ethnic, and cultural institutions. These institutions served as community centers for the many immigrants whose Old World traditions helped them navigate the harsh realities they faced as they established new lives in Philadelphia.

Philadelphia natives also invested in North Philadelphia to create other types of community centers with the intent of helping the area's poorer residents better establish themselves. One of the most notable of these institutions was Girard College, founded by the banker and philanthropist Stephen Girard, who provided millions of dollars upon his death in 1831 to establish a school for "poor, white, male" orphans. Several decades later in 1884, the Baptist preacher Russell Conwell began to give lessons to working-class parishioners in the basement of Grace Temple Baptist Church located on N. Broad Street. Temple University eventually grew from these efforts. In similar fashion, the Catholic bishop James Fredric Wood commissioned Brother Bernard Teliow, the principal of a local Catholic academy, to establish a school for Philadelphia's often-persecuted Catholics. La Salle University was established in Philadelphia's Kensington neighborhood in 1863 but moved several times thereafter, eventually arriving at Olney Avenue in 1930.

FIGURES 23, 24. Historically home to a white ethnic population (including Julius and Miroslawa Palewicz, pictured in front of their home on N. Woodstock Street In 1973), North Philadelphia changed after World War II as a Black population moved in. These homes behind the children playing, though rehabilitated in the 1960s, were subsequently labeled by city planners as blighted and slated for demolition when photographed in 1975. SPECIAL COLLECTIONS RESEARCH CENTER, TEMPLE UNIVERSITY LIBRARY.

North Philadelphia retained a European immigrant flavor until the turn of the twentieth century, when African Americans from southern states began to migrate en masse to Philadelphia and other northern industrial centers, establishing many of North Philadelphia's neighborhoods as important centers of Black culture. Black social groups formed throughout North Philadelphia, and theaters like the Uptown and later the Freedom, both located on N. Broad Street, promoted musical shows featuring gospel, jazz, and other types of performances aimed at African American audiences. North Philadelphia also became a center of Black activism as the area's African American residents fought for better representation and working conditions and against redlining practices that had the effect of barring housing loans to individuals who lived in areas deemed to be "high risk." Nevertheless, white flight from North Philadelphia led to increased segregation in the area during the 1950s and the 1960s, decades that also saw the shuttering of many of the factories that North Philadelphia's residents had long depended upon for work. Each factory closing increased stress on neighborhoods already marred by poverty and growing racial tensions. A low point for North Philadelphia came in 1964 with the Columbia Avenue Riot, which arose out of conflicts between police and North Philadelphia's African American community. The disturbance resulted in hundreds of injuries, arrests, and looted businesses, many of which never reopened.

During the last half of the twentieth century, blocks of decaying buildings and nearly deserted streets registered the impact of the social and economic fraying suffered by many of North Philadelphia's neighborhoods. The general disregard shown North Philadelphia by private investors from the 1950s into the 1990s delivered a devastating blow to this sector of the city. Attempts at renewing North Philadelphia did come in the form of federally funded public housing projects like the Richard Allen Homes, built in 1941, Cambridge Plaza, built in 1957, and the 1967 high-rise Norman Blumberg Projects—projects which, at the time they were built, were hailed as progressive solutions to urban problems. Nevertheless, by the 1980s many had fallen into disrepair and become centers of crime and drug activity. Starting in the 1990s, several were refurbished or, in the case of the Richard Allen Homes, completely torn down and replaced with detached suburban-style town houses. These homes improved neighborhood conditions in sections of North Philadelphia but have also been criticized for not accommodating the city's poorest residents and for being architecturally incongruent with the row houses that dominate much of the area.

In the twenty-first century, North Philadelphia's long history of change continued unabated. Neighborhoods nearest to Center City, including Spring Garden, Northern Liberties, and Fishtown, experienced rapid gentrification as urban professionals occupied newly built town house complexes and patronized the bars, restaurants, and galleries that replaced decaying factory buildings or abandoned lots. Conversely, several neighborhoods further from Center City, including Northwestern Philadelphia and Germantown, largely continued to decline in population. Despite these losses, less-central Northern Philadelphia neighborhoods still attracted job-seeking Puerto Ricans and Dominican and South American immigrants. Latin restaurants, bodegas, cultural institutions, and street murals in Spring Garden, Fairhill, Kensington, Frankford, Olney, and most especially in the North Philadelphia "Centro de Oro" area (located around the intersection of Fifth Street and Lehigh Avenue) reflected the strong Latino presence rooted in North Philadelphia.

Some North Philadelphians openly bemoaned the waves of change that beset their neighborhoods, fearing that familiar characteristics would be lost in the process. Many others recognized, however, that North Philadelphia's history revolves more around transformation than around constancy. Indeed, it is this constant transformation that has made North Philadelphia into one of Philadelphia's most textured and fascinating areas—an area whose built environment not only registers Philadelphia's own poignant story but also many of the historical trends that have informed centuries of broader American history.

Northwest Philadelphia

Abigail Perkiss

Northwest Philadelphia, bound loosely by the Roosevelt Expressway to the south, Broad Street to the east, and the suburbs of Montgomery County to the north and west, has origins as old as the city itself. Developing around the Schuylkill and Wissahickon Creek waterways, and later Fairmount Park, the Northwest expanded and changed with the advent of new technologies and the larger legal, political, and cultural trends of Philadelphia.

In the late seventeenth century, as William Penn worked to establish his "greene Country Towne," the German Township along the Wissahickon came together as a small community of Dutch Mennonite and German Pietist immigrants, bound at first by religious and cultural identity. On August 12, 1689, Penn granted the group its own charter, creating a distinct Germantown borough with a mayor, council, court, and marketplace.

The community prospered in the cloth trade, as townspeople worked as linen weavers, also gaining a reputation as a seedbed of antislavery agitation. In 1688, German Quakers published a resolution condemning the "traffick of men-Body." In 1775, the French-born Anthony Benezet, a longtime resident of Germantown, founded the first abolitionist society in the United States, the Society for the Relief of Free Negroes Unlawfully Held in Bondage, later the Pennsylvania Abolition Society, and by 1800, sixty free Black people (and seven enslaved people) were recorded as living in Germantown.

This legacy of activism persisted in parts of the region, even as it maintained an identity as a largely white and wealthy enclave. For many of Philadelphia's elite, Germantown—with its relatively high elevation at 336 feet, offering scenic views and lazy breezes—became a popular respite from the frenzy of the city. In 1750, loyalist William Allen, later chief justice of the Supreme Court of Pennsylvania, built a country estate at what is now Germantown Avenue and Allens Lane and called the home Mount Airy, bestowing the name for the neighborhood that two centuries later earned a national reputation for racial tolerance.

In the early nineteenth century, as Philadelphia entered the age of industrialization, the Northwest region grew precipitously. In 1815, the city granted a charter to the Schuylkill Navigation Company, charged with improving the navigational system of the Schuylkill River. Less than a decade later, the 108-mile waterway linked Philadelphia with the coalfields of Port Carbon and Pottsville. These advancements brought new life to the communities along the river.

Across the Wissahickon Gorge from Germantown, the borough of Manayunk, part of the larger Roxborough Township and ideally positioned in the river valley, experienced massive development, largely due to local textile manufacturing. From 1817 to 1824 the population expanded from sixty to nearly eight hundred people, and by the late 1820s the community, which just a few years earlier contained little more than a toll house, had become known alternately as the "Lowell of Pennsylvania" and the "Manchester of America." In 1840, the town was incorporated as its own separate borough. The owners of the Manayunk mills resided above the town on the ridge between the river and the Wissahickon, which along with Germantown became one of the wealthiest communities in Philadelphia County.

The consolidation of city and county in 1854 brought the region under the auspices of city institutions and services. Coincidentally, the expansion of the railways opened up the city and made the area more accessible. In the early 1830s, a group of Germantown entrepreneurs set out to create the Philadelphia, Germantown, and Norristown Railroad. The earliest trains arrived in Germantown in 1832, and the community soon developed into the first railroad suburb in Philadelphia and one of the first in the nation. Within a year, the wealthy residents of Chestnut Hill, occupying the northernmost section of Germantown, clamored for a regular stagecoach service to connect their large pastoral plots on the Hill to the Germantown Depot at Germantown Avenue and Price Street. Two decades later, more reliable horsecar and steam rail service came to Germantown, carrying multipassenger vehicles along iron rails. In Chestnut Hill, local commuters raised funds for a permanent railroad connecting the southern and northern ends of Germantown. The new terminal at Chestnut Hill Avenue and Bethlehem Pike opened on July 3, 1854.

With these political and technological changes, the region rapidly expanded. The influx of city residents prompted new housing development throughout Northwest Philadelphia, but even as population surged, residents held strong to each community's independent roots.

It was, in part, the green space around these northwest neighborhoods that allowed homeowners to maintain their autonomy from the rest of the city. Fairmount Park (officially incorporated in 1855) and its forested Wissahickon Gorge acted as a buffer between Germantown and Roxborough and the rest of Philadelphia County. But even the Wissahickon, which had served as the stage for the Battle of Germantown in 1777, felt the effects of the city's industrial growth. At the turn of the eighteenth century, the region had become home to the first two paper mills in North America—the first built by William Rittenhouse at the south end of the gorge in 1690, the second by William Dewees at the northern end in 1708. By 1850, the dense woods and deep valley were home to more than fifty water-powered mills. Mining and blasting broke through the steep cliffs along the southern end of the creek, giving way to the development of the Rittenhousetown mills, and by 1856, the Wissahickon Turnpike, a private toll road, ran through the valley south to north. In the latter half of the 1800s, though, efforts to protect and preserve the water source prompted the Fairmount Park Commission to take over the land, demolishing the mills and in their place erecting several inns and lodges where visitors could enjoy the natural splendor that remained.

By the turn of the century, the population of Northwest Philadelphia was beginning to change. From 1910 to 1930, more than 140,000 African Americans arrived in the city in the first wave of the Great Migration from the South to northern cities. As

FIGURE 25. Northwest Philadelphia row homes in Germantown, E. Walnut Lane, ca. 1910.
UNIVERSITY OF PENNSYLVANIA DIGITAL ARCHIVES.

they settled in South, West, and North Philadelphia, long-established residents began to move outward, creating greater ethnic diversification in the Northwest. Many Italian Americans left South Philadelphia for the Roxborough area. German, Scots Irish, and Irish families moved to Germantown.

As the population shifted, the economy also prompted vast changes. First, road construction along the Schuylkill River connected Northwest Philadelphia to the city center, making automobile travel a reality for the first time. Then, the Great Depression of the 1930s brought the closing of most of the mills along the Schuylkill River corridor, and such neighborhoods as Manayunk and East Falls saw their industrial prowess begin to wane. Many of the large mansions of Chestnut Hill—by the late nineteenth century one of the most elite neighborhoods in the United States—were demolished as the most affluent residents lost fortunes in the stock market. This also led to job losses for the large service economy that existed in the area.

With World War II, the city once again experienced new growth with a second mass migration of African Americans. Philadelphia's Black population increased from nearly 251,000 in 1940 to 376,000 in 1950. At first, most upwardly mobile Black newcomers concentrated in North Philadelphia. After World War II, though, as these increasingly all-Black neighborhoods experienced an acute housing shortage, middle-class African Americans also began to move outward to the Northwest.

When the war ended, communities on the outer edges of the city saw their underdeveloped green space quickly fill with new housing. Although Northwest Philadelphia saw less physical development than other areas of the city, the area still underwent widespread growth. Upper Roxborough experienced development much like the surrounding Montgomery County suburbs, with new houses, green front lawns, and strip malls spreading along Henry and Ridge Avenues. New neighborhoods sprung up along the northwest city borders, including the westernmost pocket of Andorra and West Oak Lane to the east.

In southern Germantown, the Philadelphia Redevelopment Authority allocated $10.6 million for public housing to contend with the growing numbers of Black families moving into the area. West Mount Airy, the community in the central section of historic German Township named for Justice Allen's 1750 home, began to develop its own identity as an economically viable, racially integrated community. Unlike other areas of the region and city, where white residents responded to the arrival of Black families with "fight or flight," community leaders in the upper-middle-class neighborhood created a proactive plan toward interracial living. By the early 1960s, the community was touted across the nation as a site of racial progress. Its counterpart across Germantown Avenue, East Mount Airy, experienced a brief period of integration before transitioning to a predominantly Black middle-class population. Throughout the next decade, similar patterns of white flight and African American settlement took hold in West Oak Lane and Germantown. Across Northwest Philadelphia, churches, schools, and neighborhood organizations offered critical institutional support during these postwar years, helping residents navigate these periods of transition to preserve a sense of community identity.

By the last decades of the twentieth century, as the Northwest section became more enmeshed in the Philadelphia economy and as individual communities responded to the larger political, economic, and cultural forces of the city, the regional identity of the area began to wane. Even as efforts toward local preservation, restoration, and oral history collection highlighted the living history of the region, Northwest Philadelphia became less a cohesive entity than a loosely connected group of neighborhoods, still bound by the common heritage of the natural woodlands of the Wissahickon, the industrial might of the Schuylkill Canal, and the desire for independence as well as strong community ties. Perhaps more than any other section of the city, Northwest Philadelphia retained William Penn's historic mission to create a green country town in an urban center.

South Philadelphia

Mary Rizzo

From the film *Rocky* (1976) to the Italian Market, South Philadelphia's image as an urban village has been entwined with Italian immigration. While South Philadelphia's large Italian immigrant community marked the neighborhood in many ways, an array of ethnic, racial, and religious groups have resided in South Philadelphia since the seventeenth century, making its history the history of immigration and working-class striving in Philadelphia. Drawn here due to the availability of work, each group fought to carve out a space for itself by establishing homes, families, and social institutions in this neighborhood that stretches from South Street to Interstate 76 and from the Delaware River to the Schuylkill River.

South Philadelphia's roots lie with Lenni Lenape Indians who utilized the Delaware shoreline as a source of food. European settlement began with the New Sweden colony, centered in Delaware. The second oldest Swedish church in the United States, Gloria Dei, now known as Old Swedes' Church, was built between 1698 and 1700. After a brief period of Dutch habitation, the English settled here, with King Charles II granting William Penn a charter for Pennsylvania in 1681. When Penn began planning Philadelphia, South Philadelphia was rural farmland outside the city center. It remained that way through the eighteenth century, made up of several separate districts including Southwark, Moyamensing, and Gray's Ferry, names that still describe areas within the neighborhood.

As the nineteenth century progressed, the ethnic composition of South Philadelphia changed. Irish immigrants, who had been among the first settlers of Philadelphia, began to move south in the late eighteenth century, drawn by jobs like coal heaving along the banks of the Schuylkill, and they settled especially in Southwark and Moyamensing. Sharing cramped, dilapidated quarters with the Irish were free African Americans who accounted for 24 percent of Moyamensing's residents in 1830. As nativism swept the nation, both African Americans and the Irish were targets of violence in Philadelphia, spurring the Black community to fight for civil rights in the mid-nineteenth century, with South Philadelphia as an important node. Octavius Catto, one of Philadelphia's first African American civil rights activists, migrated from the South and became a teacher at the Institute for Colored Youth. In addition to raising regiments of Black soldiers for the Union Army in the Civil War, he, along with other activists, battled for the desegregation of the streetcar lines. Catto's murder in 1871 on the day of the first desegregated mayoral election made this victory bittersweet. His funeral, the largest for a Black person in Philadelphia to that time, helped accelerate the rise of the Republican Party, which ruled Philadelphia until the mid-twentieth century.

Even after South Philadelphia joined the larger city under the Consolidation Act of 1854, its image as an impoverished and dangerous area remained. The *New York Tribune* sensationally reported that the districts of Southwark and Moyamensing "swarm with these loafers, who, brave only in gangs, herd together." Moyamensing Prison, which opened on S. Tenth Street in 1835, was another sign of the neighborhood's poverty and social and literal distance from the city center. In operation until 1963, it housed everyone from a drunken Edgar Allan Poe to serial killer H. H. Holmes and Samuel Roth, a smut publisher whose later obscenity conviction ascended to the U.S. Supreme Court.

With the turn of the twentieth century, new immigration added even more complexity to South Philadelphia. Jewish people, for example, represented the largest foreign-born group by 1910. By 1930, they had organized several labor union headquarters and over 140 synagogues. By creating these institutions, immigrants laid claim to the neighborhood. While race, ethnicity, and religion distinguished these groups from each other, one thing they shared was class. The working class dominated South Philadelphia, though, as in all immigrant neighborhoods, some individuals rose in status to become merchants who owned stores and other operations that catered to local needs. While ethnic enclaves dotted the landscape with pockets of homogeneity, competition among ethnic and racial groups for housing and work led to racial conflict. In July 1918, a race riot in South Philadelphia resulted in four days of white violence against Black people, leaving three dead and hundreds seriously injured.

Although Italian immigration to Philadelphia began in the eighteenth century, it was only in the 1880s that large numbers of Italians settled in the area, often through the intercession of employment brokers—*padrones*—who brought them to the United States to help build the Philadelphia subway system and to work as stone cutters, masons, and fruit and vegetable sellers. Not made to feel welcome at the Irish Catholic churches, in 1852 the community established the first Italian national parish in the United States, St. Mary Magdalen de Pazzi Roman Catholic Church. This helped cement an Italian national identity out of the regional identities held by most Italian immigrants, who at the time of their arrival considered themselves as Abruzzese or Pugliese, rather than Italian. They forged strong social ties in South Philadelphia as they founded churches, gathered in bars, and spoke their native tongues.

While the Italian community of South Philadelphia boasted a number of famous figures, like opera singer Mario Lanza, perhaps the most politically influential was a police commissioner and two-term mayor, Frank Rizzo. Growing up on South Rosewood Street, Rizzo capitalized on the law-and-order response that followed the urban uprisings of the late 1960s to assert community control for Philadelphia. Criticized by people of color, gays and lesbians, and progressives, Rizzo built a base of white support that included South Philadelphia but expanded beyond it by fanning fears of racial integration. For example, in 1967–68, Rizzo supported white South Philadelphians, many identifying as Italian, who pressed for closing the predominantly Black Edward Bok Vocational School on S. Ninth Street because of supposed Black violence against whites. However, in their response, the white group used racist language and attacked Black students who attended the school, suggesting that the real goal was maintaining the whiteness of the neighborhood. Black students rallied in protest, but changes increased the percentage of white students attending Bok and helped set Rizzo on his political trajectory.

During the 1970s and afterward, many Italians left South Philadelphia for the southern New Jersey suburbs. Deeply felt ties to South Philadelphia remained, nurtured through visits to family, friends, and churches for festivals and trips to restaurants and specialty stores. Looked at in this way, South Philadelphia's effective

FIGURE 26. Mural of former Philadelphia mayor Frank Rizzo in the Italian Market section of South Philadelphia, 2020. The black splotches on the mural resulted from paint-balloon vandalism intended to protest the controversial tribute to Rizzo. After the widespread Black Lives Matter protests of May–June 2020, the mural was removed and fully painted over by the city on June 7, 2020. PHOTOGRAPH BY DONALD D. GROFF.

borders extend far past the river. Demographic change accelerated in the late twentieth and early twenty-first centuries, continuing the neighborhood's tradition of being an ethnic and racial patchwork. The Italian Market reflected these changes. Originally, Irish immigrants sold produce along this stretch of Ninth Street (between Wharton and Fitzwater Streets). Italian grocers displaced them, taking ownership of the area as seen in its name and marketing. By the late twentieth century, though, the Italian Market shifted again, with Hispanic- and Latino-owned businesses, like taquerias and a tortilleria, abutting Italian specialty groceries and butchers.

While South Philadelphia retained a distinct identity, it also forged deep ties to the region. In the early twentieth century, Italian immigrants worked as migrant laborers in the Vineland, New Jersey, fields that produced tomatoes for Campbell Soup, located in Camden, New Jersey. By the twenty-first century, their descendants owned the farms, which employed Mexican and Vietnamese workers to pick the produce that is sent to the large Food Distribution Center on Pattison Avenue in South Philadelphia, completing the circle. Transportation also joined South Philadelphia to the rest of the world, though the work opportunities this afforded were accompanied by serious upheaval for some. The Walt Whitman Bridge, named for Camden's famed poet, connected South Philadelphia to New Jersey in 1957, but its construction demolished one of the poorest areas of South Philadelphia, known as "The Neck" (below Oregon Avenue, near Third Street), where residents lived a nearly rural lifestyle even though they were just

FIGURE 27. The Italian Market, South Philadelphia, view from Ninth Street toward Esposito's Meats, in business since 1911, ca. 1980. ATWATER KENT COLLECTION, DREXEL UNIVERSITY.

a few miles from Center City. Similarly, Hog Island, once a shipbuilding facility, became the Philadelphia International Airport. Located between two rivers, residents have long counted the ports and waterways as a source of employment, and large tankers and ships—some in service and some rusted to hulks—can be seen from Columbus Boulevard. The Philadelphia Navy Yard on S. Broad Street converted to office space, anchors the southern end of the neighborhood.

South Philadelphians play as well as work. From the construction of Sesquicentennial Stadium in 1926 to the Spectrum in 1967, Veterans Stadium in 1971, and Xfinity Live! in 2012, when residents of the region have wanted to see a baseball or football game or go to a concert, they have come to South Philadelphia. This tradition dates back to the city's founding, as Philadelphia's first theater, the Southwark Theater, opened outside the city limits in South Philadelphia to evade Quaker disapproval. In a neighborhood that has enjoyed rowdy public celebrations since the nineteenth century, the best known is the Mummers Parade on New Year's Day, when comically costumed social clubs accompanied by ornate floats, march from South Philadelphia to the heart of Center City and back. Designated an official city celebration in 1901, the Mummers Parade has been controversial and only in the 1970s did the parade allow women to participate, while blackface continued to be worn until 2020.

In the first decades of the twenty-first century, South Philadelphia continued to be a neighborhood of change. According to the 2010 census, more than half of the neighborhood was white, with African Americans totaling about one-quarter of the population. Asians made up another 12 percent, with a growing Hispanic/Latino population of 8 percent. While Southeast Asian immigration began in the 1970s as the Delaware Valley welcomed refugees, it rose dramatically beginning in the 1990s. Like earlier immigrants, Southeast Asians created their own social worlds, including a vibrant commercial and cultural infrastructure along Washington Avenue that included large supermarkets, restaurants, and music and video stores. However, in a repetition of earlier examples of racially motivated conflict, in 2009 Southeast Asian students were attacked at South Philadelphia High School, bringing to public attention tensions that had been simmering barely below the surface for years. This time, the conflict was primarily between Black and Asian students. Student and community groups rallied through this incident to advocate for better services for immigrants, much in the way that earlier settlers fought for their civil rights.

A mural by the Mural Arts Project acknowledges that immigration is the connective fiber of South Philadelphia. Called *Aqui y Alla* ("Here and There," at 1515 S. Sixth Street), the mural tells the story of the neighborhood's growing Mexican immigrant population. Indigenous youth in Mexico created pieces of the mural, which were sent to Philadelphia and completed by Mexican immigrant youth in South Philadelphia. The continued importance of the homeland pictured in this mural helps put a visual face on the activities of generations of South Philadelphians as they built businesses, created houses of worship, founded civic organizations, and celebrated together. In this city of neighborhoods, the ties that bind South Philadelphians have as often been to faraway places as they have been to the city.

Southwest Philadelphia

Anne E. Krulikowski

Southwest Philadelphia, which along with adjacent Tinicum Township, Delaware County, is the location of the Philadelphia International Airport, greets many visitors to the city. Yet, Southwest Philadelphia, often described as "far" Southwest, is quite possibly the least-known area of the city, even to Philadelphians. Kingsessing, as this vicinity was originally named, was the first section of Philadelphia settled by Europeans and in the twentieth century came to national attention as the Eastwick Urban Renewal Project. Since the early twentieth century, when this seemingly remote location in the city became useful for an airport and other industrial activities, the possible contributions of Southwest Philadelphia to the metropolitan economy have often overshadowed the needs of neighborhood residents.

Southwest Philadelphia is the southern portion of the city lying west of the Schuylkill River. The northern boundary is roughly marked by Baltimore Avenue and Fiftieth and Forty-Ninth Streets; on the west by Cobbs and Darby Creeks, which separate Philadelphia and Delaware Counties; on the south by the Philadelphia International Airport; and on the east by the Schuylkill River. Southwest Philadelphia encompasses the city's Fifty-First and Fortieth Wards and includes the neighborhoods of Kingsessing, Elmwood, Paschall, and Eastwick; below Seventy-Fourth Street, Eastwick is known to residents as "the Meadows." Large nonresidential tracts are occupied by the Heinz Wildlife Preserve, the Philadelphia International Airport, industrial parks, the Southwest Sewage Treatment Plant, and, adjacent to the Schuylkill River, tank farms and oil refineries.

This landscape includes the lowest-lying land within the city, some of it below sea level. The southernmost portion was at one time crisscrossed by a network of creeks. Mud, Hog, Carpenter's, Minquas (Mingo), Province (later State), and Boon's Islands were some of the largest of the Schuylkill River delta islands indicated on early maps. These well-watered meadowlands produced luxuriant grass and weeds for grazing livestock and fertile soil for plowing without the arduous task of removing trees, explaining their attraction for early European farmers.

Kingsessing, from a Delaware Native word most frequently translated as "a place where there is a bog meadow," became the center of Swedish occupation in 1643 when Governor Johan Printz moved the Swedish headquarters to big Tinicum Island. The Swedes built two forts in lower Kingsessing to control the final leg of the Great Minquas Trail (Island Avenue), used by the Susquahannock (Minquas) beaver traders traveling from the Susquehanna Valley to the Schuylkill River. The Dutch and then the English claimed this vicinity—and the valuable beaver trade. William Penn created the township of Kingsessing, corresponding approximately with the later Fortieth and Fifty-First Wards.

Upper Kingsessing provided a convenient link between Philadelphia and points south, while lower Kingsessing seemed more remote. In 1696, the King's Highway (then Darby Road) was laid out from Gray's Ferry (the Lower Ferry), becoming the main artery from Philadelphia to Baltimore and the southern colonies. During the Revolution, an extension through William Hamilton's estate, the Woodlands, linked the road (renamed Woodland Avenue) with the Market Street Ferry. Penrose's Ferry from lower Kingsessing to South Philadelphia was not established until 1742, when a pest house (quarantine hospital) was constructed on Fisher's Island (renamed Province, then State Island) to isolate contagious diseases. This ferry was finally replaced with a bridge in 1853; the fourth bridge, begun in 1949, was renamed the George C. Platt Bridge.

During the War for Independence, Mud Island, adjacent to Province Island, became the site of a significant battle in the Philadelphia Campaign. In November 1777, the British wrested control of the island's Fort Mifflin from American defenders. The victory helped the British to secure the Delaware River, allowing supply ships to reach Philadelphia.

The imperial struggles punctuating the early history of Kingsessing gave way to a peaceful agricultural landscape of farms and country estates for the next century. Limited industrial development occurred in isolated pockets adjacent to throughways and the larger creeks. Cobbs Creek provided water power for the Passmore Textile Mill on Woodland Avenue. Paschalville, laid out in 1810, was inhabited by the mainly British immigrant mill workers. At midcentury, the entire township contained only about 1,800 residents. Just after the Civil War, the Angora Woolen Mill and a small village were established just below Baltimore Pike.

The 1854 Act of Consolidation incorporated Kingsessing Township as the Twenty-Seventh Ward of Philadelphia but made little difference: Kingsessing, as it was still called, remained the slowest-developing section of the city for several more decades. Even the Philadelphia, Wilmington and Baltimore Railroad linking Philadelphia to Baltimore through Kingsessing prior to consolidation did little to foster growth. The rural landscape made accessible by the railroad did encourage sporting activities, though. During the 1960s, the *New York Times* reported on the races at the popular Suffolk Park Race Track and Hotel, established in 1859 adjacent to Bell Road Station, the sole station in southern Kingsessing. In the next decade, the Belmont Cricket Club was located in the northern part of the ward. The Pennsylvania Railroad had closed the Bell Road Station by the time investors began subdividing tracts below Seventy-Second Street in the 1880s.

Perhaps Kingsessing is most important in American history for its famous garden nurseries and seed farms, which also benefited from the combination of a rural landscape and a railroad. Street names such as Botanic, Bartram, Dick's, Lyon's, and Buist commemorate this important local economy. In the eighteenth century, John Bartram created what became the oldest surviving botanic garden in the United States. Railroad industrialist Andrew McCalla Eastwick purchased the house and garden as a private park for his own country house, designed by Samuel Sloan.

In the mid-nineteenth century, the Helendale Nurseries established by John Dick included thirty greenhouses with more than one hundred thousand square feet of glass. The most famous Kingsessing nurseryman, Robert Buist, created one of the first great nurseries in the United States at Rosedale. Buist was the center of a transatlantic horticultural exchange and is also credited with introducing the poinsettia to the United States from Mexico. One of his books, *The Rose Manual* (1844), was the first American gardening book devoted to roses.

This horticultural economy was made possible by the growing numbers of wealthy Americans who established country estates, as well as the rural cemetery and urban park movements. Mt. Moriah, located in Kingsessing and Yeadon, Delaware County, became the third of Philadelphia's great cemeteries, along with Laurel Hill and the Woodlands.

Southwest Philadelphia saw sustained residential and industrial development from the 1880s through the 1920s. Consequently, Ward Forty was made a separate ward before the turn of the century. In the 1890s, several important industries moved to Southwest. Joseph Fels built the Fels Naptha (laundry soap) factory on the site of the old Passmore mill. The J. G. Brill Company in Kingsessing and Baldwin Locomotive, which relocated from Spring Garden to adjacent Delaware County, both employed thousands of local residents.

Immigrant and native-born workers followed the opportunity for industrial employment. Irish, German, Lithuanian, Polish, Italian, and Jewish immigrants built detached and semidetached dwellings, often purchasing extra lots for large gardens. Once families located in the area, they tended to stay for generations. Below Seventy-Fourth Street, some truck and pig farms survived into the mid-twentieth century. The northern area just below Baltimore Pike developed in the first two decades of the twentieth century as home to native-born and northern European immigrants who worked in West Philadelphia or commuted to Center City. This more densely developed residential area was eventually separated from Ward Forty as the city's Fifty-First Ward. As neighborhoods developed, trolley-served Woodland Avenue became an important retail district.

More dramatic changes were wrought by World War I, when the federal government authorized the American International Shipping Corporation to build Hog Island, the world's largest shipyard. The site virtually became a town, with barracks to house almost fifteen thousand male workers. New railroad and trolley tracks transported an additional twenty thousand workers and materials to and from the shipyard. The war initiated a significant demographic change: white and Black southern families found wartime an opportunity to move out of the South. In 1920, Black residents accounted for about 25 percent of the population of about ten thousand (excluding Hog Island dormitories) living below Seventy-Fourth Street at a time when Black residents accounted for about 7 percent of the total population of Philadelphia.

The shipyard, closed in 1921, brought Southwest Philadelphia to the attention of city hall in the competition for funding of transportation and municipal services. Real estate developer David E. Triester named the Fortieth Ward Eastwick and created the Greater Eastwick Improvement Association (GEIA) to obtain more comprehensive municipal services. Seeing the lesson of Hog Island, GEIA leaders, supported by the *Southwest Globe Times*, tied their future to the city when they successfully lobbied for a Southwest airport rather than a Northeast or Camden facility. Charles Lindbergh dedicated the new Southwest airport in 1927, but the muddy landscape proved challenging. The airport moved to Camden, where it resided for a decade. In the 1930s, Mayor S. Davis Wilson negotiated with the federal government for the Hog Island Shipyard site to bring the airport back to Southwest. Works Progress Administration workers filled in the area and built runways as part of Philadelphia's share in the New Deal.

In the 1920s and 1930s, the GEIA less successfully and more controversially publicized the need for modern sewage systems and additional diking along the surviving network of creeks after several hurricanes seriously flooded homes and businesses. Some residents contended the association's publicity created negative views of the area and discouraged investment in modern sewage facilities. Despite this, more residential development occurred in the 1920s than in the three previous decades. The 1920s building boom was so extensive that by the early 1930s sociologist William Weaver predicted the Tinicum Marsh would disappear. By that time, though, Philadelphia residents evicted from houses and apartments in other areas of the city erected shacks in the still largely undeveloped lower marshy areas.

After World War II, the Fortieth Ward once again gained public attention, some of which resulted in improved infrastructure—but not for longtime residents. In 1954, Philadelphia's Mother of the Year, Jennie Harley, was a homemaker from the Meadows (below Seventy-Fourth Street). One year later, though, Harley and her family along with thousands of other Southwest families were evicted when Eastwick was condemned as a slum. Lack of modern sewage services and Depression-era shanties were featured in official city publications and city newspapers. The Philadelphia City Planning Commission had envisioned a "New Eastwick" to support the developing postindustrial service economy. In 1950, the Eastwick Urban Renewal Project began when much of Ward Forty, about three thousand acres, was declared "blighted." Plans to reduce residential and farm use included creating space for an East Coast highway (Interstate 95, which crosses the Schuylkill over the two-tiered Girard Point Bridge) and a hub of transportation and light industry centered on an enlarged international airport. The long-projected Southwest sewage treatment plant was finally constructed as, despite residents' protests, neighborhood demolition began in 1960.

FIGURE 28. Photographed in 1976, two children play in their row house community in Southwest Philadelphia's Eastwick section, showing integration to be a fact of life before the difficult racial transition that followed. SPECIAL COLLECTIONS RESEARCH CENTER, TEMPLE UNIVERSITY LIBRARIES.

Following the demolition, light industrial parks, shopping centers, and some replacement housing were built, but large tracts remained vacant. In 2002, the Philadelphia City Planning Commission certified a forty-block area of Kingsessing as "blighted." Squatting and gap-tooth syndrome (empty lots between dwellings) had become common, and environmental problems continued to plague many residents, especially in the lower area. Despite the 1997 opening of the Southeast Pennsylvania Transportation Authority (SEPTA) Eastwick Station and the relocation of Philadelphia's main post office to Eastwick, in 2006 the entire Eastwick Urban Renewal Area was recertified as a blighted district. The city finally terminated the Eastwick Urban Renewal Project in 2015 though several hundred acres remained undeveloped. Four years later, the city released a feasibility study for that area, conceived with the input of current residents as a "village in the city" anchored by a Main Street. Officials additionally promised to address the flooding Eastwick residents complained had never been adequately addressed by the renewal plan.

In the decades at the turn of the twenty-first century, Southwest Philadelphia faced serious challenges to neighborhood stability, leaving high crime and vacancy rates in an area formerly characterized by high levels of home ownership and middle-class apartment houses. Most Southwest neighborhoods experienced an overall decline in population after 1990, but they developed greater diversity—and racial tension—with an influx of new immigrant groups, primarily West African with some new Vietnamese and Hispanic residents.

The Elmwood neighborhood subsequently experienced some of the most serious racial tensions in the city. This area was predominantly home to Polish and Irish American families centered on Roman Catholic parishes, but the disintegration of the manufacturing economy left many men unemployed. In 1985, when two houses were sold to an African American family and an interracial couple, some white neighbors reacted violently, destroying property with axes and arson. Mayor Wilson Goode declared a state of emergency. Between 1990 and 2000 the white population of Elmwood decreased by almost 70 percent, while the African American population increased. Vietnamese and West African immigrants added to the racial picture. In 2008, John Bartram High School was placed in lockdown when a fight between African American and African students turned into a school riot.

Eastwick, with a longer history of diversity, has not seen the dramatic population shifts of other neighborhoods, although by 2014 African American residents accounted for 76 percent of the residents. Eastwick residents have higher average education levels and homeownership rates than many other neighborhoods in Southwest, perhaps providing more economic and social stability for residents.

Eastwick residents, however, contend with worsening environmental justice issues compounded by episodic flooding, the consequences of incomplete redevelopment, and controversial plans for the future development of vacant areas. Environmental problems, always a challenge in this low-lying vicinity, have worsened with changing land use. Tinicum Marsh, once reduced to about two hundred acres, was preserved by a 1972 act of Congress because it contained the last remaining freshwater tidal marsh in the state. Renamed the John Heinz National Wildlife Refuge at Tinicum, it encompasses one thousand acres. But periodic flooding has increased since much of the vicinity was rezoned for industrial use. Large vacant tracts have attracted illegal dumping of hazardous substances that seep into the ground. Cleanup of former industrial sites has not always been conscientious. In the 1990s, environmental problems caused by nearby oil refineries led to a partly successful lawsuit for improvements to protect local residents. The airport expanded and became the cornerstone for planning development. Thus, the struggles of Southwest Philadelphians to achieve livable family neighborhoods continued in the early twenty-first century.

West Philadelphia

Jake Blumgart

One of the single largest sectors of the city of Philadelphia at almost fifteen square miles between the Schuylkill River to the east and Delaware County to the west, West Philadelphia at its peak, in the early twentieth century, attracted an influx of new residents to its verdant, suburban-feeling neighborhoods. But over the course of the twentieth century, as the area became majority African American, it was hobbled by racist lending and employment practices. As a consequence, large swaths of the area became deteriorated and underpopulated, despite a vibrant Black political and cultural scene and, in the twenty-first century, a resurgent higher education and medical cluster.

West Philadelphia did not exist until the middle of the nineteenth century. Although this part of the region witnessed small settlements of Lenape and Swedes who established Lutheran churches and log cabins on the west side of the Schuylkill, it was not included in the original plan of Philadelphia. William Penn wrote that the area "is likely to be a great part of the settlement of this age" and intended to expand settlement across the river. But he abandoned the idea by 1684, two years after his arrival.

Throughout the eighteenth century much of what would become West Philadelphia remained sparsely populated farmland. But on the far bank of the Schuylkill, port and mercantile infrastructure began to build up at this westward point of entry to the city. A major wagon route, Lancaster Pike, ran through it too, and in 1805 the first permanent bridge was built over the Schuylkill at Market Street. The Darby Road also ran up to this point, granting access to communities like Chester farther down the Delaware River. A few large estates were built during this time as well, most notably the Hamilton family's Woodlands with its iconic Georgian mansion and that of John Bartram, the renowned botanist and Quaker who cultivated extensive gardens along the banks of the Schuylkill.

The new bridge in 1805 spurred growth, prompting a network of industries, including stockyards, lumber mills, slaughterhouses, coal yards, foundries, and glass factories to serve the city across the river. Small communities began to spring up to support these businesses, like Hamiltonville in 1804. The then-scion of the family, William Hamilton, established the estate's Georgian mansion and laid out Hamiltonville as a continuation of Penn's grid in Philadelphia proper. Other settlements followed like Mantua Village, laid out in 1809, carved from the holdings of a local landowner, Judge Richard Peters. Neither area sold well at first, but as the city began to become more highly developed the lots began to sell. By the 1840s developers in Philadelphia, which was the second-largest city in the United States at the time, were already looking beyond the Schuylkill for fresh land, and Abraham Brower's innovative omnibus service, introduced to Philadelphia in 1831, allowed new settlers speedy access into the central city. At the time, the majority of residents were working class—about half immigrants from Ireland, Germany, and England—and settlements of any density tapered off at what would become the boundaries of

Fortieth Street, with the wealthy clustered along Walnut and Chestnut near this westward extremis.

To accommodate the bourgeoning population, in 1844 Hamiltonville, Mantua, and Powelton incorporated together as the borough of West Philadelphia, before being brought into the city proper with the consolidation of 1854. Then the population exploded from eleven thousand in 1850 to twenty-three thousand in 1860. For the next half century at least, West Philadelphia largely became a suburb in the city—abetted by a series of advances in transportation technology, starting with the horsecars of the 1850s.

A bustling light industrial sector continued to grow south of Market Street on land adjacent to the river, relying on the Pennsylvania Railroad's infrastructure to convey goods efficiently. Some of the largest concerns included the metal workings at Job T. Pugh's Auger Works, the Otto Gas Engine Manufacturing Company, and the Allison & Sons Car & Tube Works, one of the biggest wagon manufacturers in the nation until its destruction by fire in 1872. Like the rest of the city's manufacturing sector, West Philadelphia's industry enjoyed great diversity. Everything from printers and bakeries to slaughterhouses and mirror manufacturers dotted this slice of the landscape.

Despite the industry clustered along the area's shores, development in this period remained largely residential in the rest of West Philadelphia. This set its living pattern apart from its counterparts in North and South Philadelphia, where row homes were interspersed with factories and warehouses. On the far side of the Schuylkill, the new housing developments were mostly marketed for the middle and upper classes, whose westward movement was further enabled by the replacement of the omnibus by horsecars in 1858. New routes into the city aided this movement too, like the Chestnut Street bridge completed in 1866.

Then in the 1870s the University of Pennsylvania left its cramped Center City location for West Philadelphia, a move with enormous effect on the development of its surrounding neighborhoods, especially during the second half of the twentieth century. After 1880 the larger houses closer to the river and the university constructed earlier in the century began to be carved into smaller units. Apartment buildings—unusual in this row-house dominated city—began to spring up as well. At the same time, new development moved beyond Forty-Fifth Street out to Cobbs Creek, the border with Delaware County.

The introduction of electric streetcars in the 1890s further altered the area, as those with more resources moved farther out, leaving behind a more broadly based middle class. This process accelerated with the full extension of the Market-Frankford Line in 1907, which further boosted settlement, including that of immigrant and Black laborers living close to the line. By the twentieth century many of the wealthy residents who remained in West Philadelphia located away from the Market-Frankford elevated line or the multiplicity of trolley lines, further accelerating the growth of the Main Line suburbs in the process.

The district still had fewer than 100,000 people in 1890, but every new census revealed meteoric growth. In 1900 West Philadelphia had 148,548 residents, in 1910 the number grew to 247,928, and by 1920 there were 359,601. In 1923 the *Philadelphia Bulletin* estimated that at least half the population of the district commuted to Center City every day. Housing was at a premium, and due to the desirability of the area, the newspaper of record noted that, more than any other section of the city, West Philadelphia encouraged the construction of apartment buildings and the subdivision of old mansions to accommodate the boom. Multiple business corridors sprouted on Fifty-Second Street and Baltimore, Lancaster, Woodland, and Girard Avenues.

By the 1930s one of the more notable developments in West Philadelphia was the growing number of Black residents and the discriminatory pressures that boxed them into an intensely segregated area stretching south to Market Street, west to Fifty-Ninth Street, and bounded to the north and east by the Main Line of the Pennsylvania Railroad and the river beyond it.

The process began during World War I, as Black migrants arrived in the city in increasing numbers. By the end of the 1920s, 220,000 African Americans lived in Philadelphia, and they desperately needed housing beyond the older Black ghetto in North Philadelphia. By the 1940s, the new area of settlement stretched from the river out to Fifty-Ninth Street to house about 44,000 African Americans, from poor and working class by the water to the Black elite in the northwest closest to the Main Line.

FIGURE 29. The West Philadelphia Manufacturing Company, part of the manufacturing sector that emerged west of the Schuylkill River with improved service from the Pennsylvania Railroad, 1858. LIBRARY OF CONGRESS.

The Black population swelled again during World War II, breaking West Philadelphia's racial boundaries by spreading south of Market Street and east of Fifty-Ninth Street. As African Americans began moving across the area, the white population fled to the expanding suburbs. By 1950, West Philadelphia had lost a quarter of its Irish American and 11 percent of its Italian American population, while the African American population increased by 72 percent. As the century wore on, the trend became so total that the only corners of West Philadelphia not overwhelmingly Black were immediately around Drexel and the University of Pennsylvania and in a band of neighborhoods to the west of the higher education cluster that remained racially mixed from 1960 onward.

The Black residents of West Philadelphia were forced to contend with redlining and other discriminatory practices that limited access to capital and higher-paid employment for many residents. They were also discouraged, by legal means or by violence, from immediately following the white population into the growing suburbs. But during the early decades of majority-Black West Philadelphia, these challenges were attenuated by the growth of African American political power and the slowly declining, but still available, unionized industrial jobs.

Public sector employment in city government and the school district offered a wide range of employment opportunities for Black workers, from professional positions as managers and teachers to jobs that required less formal education, like sanitation and transportation. Many public sector unions became majority African American, or at least enjoyed large minorities of Black members, giving their neighborhoods further political and economic anchors.

As West Philadelphia became majority African American, the University of Pennsylvania began an ambitious expansion framed by its 1948 master plan (the university's first update in almost half a century). A few African American neighborhoods close to campus were largely destroyed by eminent domain as a result, most famously the area known as Black Bottom that stood between the university and Powelton Village. The Black neighborhoods closest to the river, and therefore closest to Penn, tended to be those with the lowest income and the least political power. Farther west, African American neighborhoods tended to be more stable, with larger populations of public sector workers and private sector white collar workers, but that was little comfort to the displaced residents of Black Bottom.

The impetus for Penn's expansion came from the infusion of government research funding and the urban renewal dollars made available by the national Housing Act of 1949. During this period the university adopted the moniker "University City" for the surrounding neighborhoods. Penn took full advantage of both instances of postwar federal largesse, competing successfully with its counterparts in higher education for research and development grants—especially after the flood of funding following the Soviet Union's Sputnik success in 1957. Penn also competed with other parts of the city for urban renewal funds (most of the money allocated within West Philadelphia went to the university's ends). The upgrades to campus were impressive. They were also necessary to create a more walkable environment and more housing for a growing student body. But the expansion into surrounding residential neighborhoods embittered many area residents.

In the latter decades of the twentieth century West Philadelphia kept changing as the white population continued to drain out of the city. The remaining African American neighborhoods continued to suffer discrimination in access to jobs and capital while many of the jobs that previously fostered economic stability were lost or undercut by the flight of manufacturing firms. This postindustrial economic vise resulted in the kind of divestment and shadow-economy dealings that blighted many inner-city neighborhoods. In the 1980s some immigrants began to move into the area, chiefly African and Cambodian, although the latter population would almost entirely decamp for other parts of the city by the beginning of the twenty-first century.

In the mid-1980s, crack cocaine reached West Philadelphia and wreaked havoc in many neighborhoods, resulting in a crime wave that scared off many middle-class African Americans and some of the remaining white families as well. The police department made matters worse by earning the distinction of becoming the first U.S. law enforcement institution to bomb its own city. During a confrontation at the fortified compound of the anarcho-primitivist group MOVE in 1985, the police dropped a high explosive on a bunker atop the radicals' home. The resulting explosion sparked a conflagration that consumed much of the block and killed eleven people. In the following decade, farther to the east, general violence continued to rise, as it did in the rest of the country. After several high-profile murders of Penn graduate students living in the mixed-race neighborhoods beyond the campus borders, which had lost much of their white population during the 1990s, the university began to again be active in the community.

Under the guidance of university president Judith Rodin, who was born and raised in West Philadelphia, the school promised not to repeat the aggressive steps taken in the 1950s and 1960s. Instead, it provided unarmed security services to patrol the area and exercised soft power to provide incentives to staff, from professors to janitors, to buy and repair homes in a catchment area around the university. Penn also invested in local public schools, founding the Sadie Alexander School for pre-K through eighth grade. With other anchor institutions in the area, it supported development of the University City District to provide further amenities.

This activity resulted in the rejuvenation of the neighborhoods surrounding the university and the historically mixed-race neighborhood to its immediate west, which in 2010 became majority white for the first time since 1970. The university was not the only force at work; its efforts were aided by a nationwide decline in crime and marginal increase in the desire for urban living among a segment of the professional classes. Meanwhile, in many neighborhoods on the border of Delaware County, conditions worsened during the Great Recession of 2008 and the subsequent decimation of the public sector workforce.

By the early twenty-first century West Philadelphia was about as populous as it had been in 1910, having lost over a hundred thousand residents after 1950. It stood divided, like much of the city and the country, between the haves and the have nots. Its western majority African American neighborhoods were declining in population and median income. Much of the vacancy and crime that blighted West Philadelphia could be found in these areas, which were still cut off from legitimate employment and capital markets. This was counterpoised by the rise of University City, which was quickly becoming a rival for Center City in terms of jobs and investment. It remained to be seen whether the ascendancy of the eastern section of West Philadelphia, where the old industries and worker housing were giving way to new investment, would be enough to buoy the fortunes of the outlying, formerly middle-class areas.

Northeast Philadelphia

Matthew Smalarz

From its initial, colonial foundations as a sparsely populated farming hinterland to its dramatic postwar housing development after World War II, Northeast Philadelphia developed into a desirable destination for those seeking to improve their economic, social, and cultural standing within Philadelphia's city boundaries. Even as Northeast Philadelphia came to symbolize a middle-class environment rooted around homeownership, commercial development, and growing consumer affluence following World War II, it witnessed acrimonious racial tensions between white and Black residents and fostered confrontations with city politicians and policymakers over local concerns related to zoning, commercial, and municipal services. Stretching from Frankford in the Lower Northeast to Somerton in the Far Northeast, its vast geographic expanse underwent dramatic spatial, economic, and racial transformations throughout its complex and still unfolding history.

Northeast Philadelphia's earliest enclave, Frankford, had been inhabited by Lenni Lenape Natives and Swedish settlers prior to the founding of the Pennsylvania colony. Immediately following Pennsylvania's establishment in 1681, Quaker settlers constructed a meetinghouse, built in 1684, and post office, at William Penn's request, in what was initially designated the Manor of Frank during the mid-1680s. Situated to the northeast of the city of Philadelphia, Frankford's importance as a center of commerce and trade grew principally because of its geographic location along the King's Highway (present-day Frankford Avenue). It developed into a manufacturing village in the eighteenth and early nineteenth centuries, drawing in German and English settlers, who opened numerous mills along the Frankford Creek. In addition to European settlers, free Black people established fraternal, religious, and antislavery institutions in the village to counter the creeping signs of residential segregation and employment discrimination surrounding them. Located within the boundaries of Philadelphia County, Frankford's commercial dominance attracted nearby farmers, who principally resided in Northeast townships such as Lower Dublin and Moreland, to process their raw materials and farm products in Frankford's bustling mills. The village also became a vital munitions site for the U.S. Army after the War of 1812, when the federal government began the construction of an arsenal, completed in the mid-1820s, along the banks of the Frankford Creek.

Other settlements, primarily centered on farming and mill activity, dotted Northeast Philadelphia's rural terrain and creek beds prior to and following the Consolidation Act of 1854, with pockets of gilded affluence appearing sporadically along the Delaware River in the late nineteenth century. Multiple townships throughout the Northeast possessed small farming enclaves and communities, especially Bustleton, Somerton, and Fox Chase. In the early 1850s, residents from the Northeast decried the city's plan to annex their communities into a newly consolidated city-county governance authority, which aimed to provide municipal services and policing functions to outlying

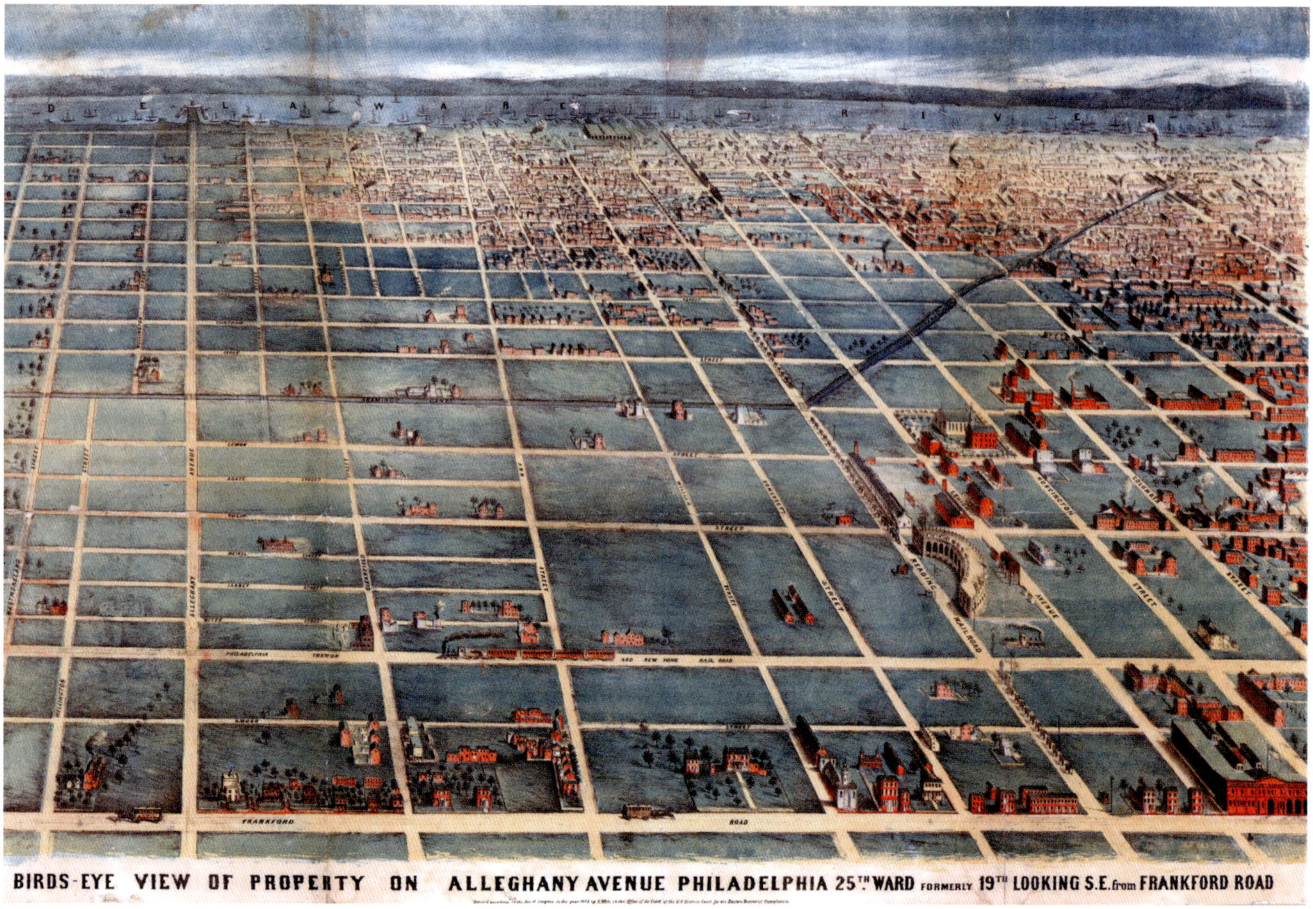

FIGURE 30. Bird's-eye view looking southeast from Frankford Road, Northeast Philadelphia, toward the Delaware River, showing the city between Westmoreland Street and a few blocks south of Columbia Street. Lithograph, William Boell, 1863. FREE LIBRARY OF PHILADELPHIA.

suburbs in exchange for jurisdictional control over their neighborhoods. Some Bustleton residents, afraid of losing their independence, resisted the city's annexation plan by initiating legislation, which ultimately failed, to thwart the proposal. While the Northeast remained predominantly rural following the Act of Consolidation's passage, some of Philadelphia's well-heeled elite erected palatial mansions and estates in Holmesburg and Torresdale, with the most notable Victorian structure being the opulent Glen Foerd mansion, which still overlooks the Delaware River, in Torresdale.

Additional industrial enterprises and communities emerged and flourished immediately north of Frankford along the Delaware River in the mid- to late nineteenth century, as some industrialists sought additional space to accommodate their expanding companies. Henry Disston, an English industrial entrepreneur, moved his burgeoning saw works enterprise from the congested confines of Northern Liberties to Tacony in 1872. Upon relocating his saw works, he gradually constructed a self-sufficient company town to house his workers. Disston's company town attracted both existing and newly arrived ethnic, European immigrant communities, namely Irish, Italian, Polish, and German, and offered them generous benefits and homeownership opportunities, melding them into a productive and loyal working-class community.

In the early twentieth century, Philadelphia's elected officials embraced the City Beautiful movement with the intention of improving the city's infrastructure and attracting affluent suburbanites to downtown Philadelphia. One of these projects, the Northeast

Boulevard, which was renamed the Roosevelt Boulevard in 1918, opened in 1914 to much fanfare, as builders and private developers soon capitalized on the city's investment in the roadway to construct single- and twin-family dwellings along its expansive corridor, especially in the Northwood section of Frankford in the Lower Northeast. As the Roaring Twenties progressed, commercial development also coincided with residential expansion in the Lower Northeast. Local booster organizations, especially the establishment of the Northeast Philadelphia Chamber of Commerce and Sears, Roebuck and Company's new merchandising facility, which opened in 1920, symbolized the Northeast's flourishing commercial identity.

The Great Depression's onset, however, soon dampened the homebuilding spirits of Northeast boosters and exacerbated economic tensions between middle-class WASPs, who inhabited bungalows and mansions along the Boulevard, and ethnic whites and working-class Black people, who remained consigned to industrial enclaves closer to the Delaware River. In the mid-1930s, the Home Owners' Loan Corporation, which created detailed, color-coded residential security maps to demarcate desirable from dilapidated housing throughout the city of Philadelphia, documented and widened, through its discriminatory redlining policies, the emerging residential and class disparities in the Lower Northeast.

The oldest, residential precincts, especially in Tacony and Wissinoming, primarily housed skilled workers laboring in the Disston Saw Works and other industrial facilities east of Torresdale Avenue. Meanwhile, Mayfair, Lawndale, and the Northwood section of Frankford, home to a mixture of white- and blue-collar workers, had experienced significant construction and residential upgrades immediately south of Cottman Avenue and along Roosevelt Boulevard during the 1920s and early 1930s.

The growing demand for adequate housing during World War II, in fact, led to increased racial segregation in, and civic resistance to, public housing projects in Northeast Philadelphia. The 1941 Lanham Defense Housing Act established the funding provisions that facilitated the construction of Pennypack Woods and Oxford Village I in 1942, with both housing complexes only accepting applications from white war workers and their families. Speaking on behalf of anxious, middle-class homeowners in the area, the Northeast Philadelphia Chamber of Commerce resented what it regarded as the federal government's intrusive wartime housing schemes, openly assailing the government's intention to provide affordable housing to war workers in the Northeast, albeit on racially segregated terms.

Generous government benefits, namely the Servicemen's Readjustment Act of 1944 (GI Bill) and Federal Housing Administration (FHA) home lending policies, assisted returning veterans, the majority of whom were white, in their quest to move from Philadelphia's densely packed industrial neighborhoods to the quasi-suburban atmosphere of Northeast Philadelphia following World War II. Prominent builders, most notably Hyman Korman and A. P. Orleans, capitalized on these circumstances to expand home construction west of Roosevelt Boulevard in the Near Northeast, especially in Rhawnhurst, Lawndale, and Oxford Circle, in the late 1940s and 1950s. The Far Northeast, on the other hand, remained largely undeveloped until the late 1950s and 1960s, at which point large contingents of affluent, white households, many of whom were Jewish, were drawn to Cape Cod and ranch dwellings designed with a suburban feel nestled in Bustleton and Somerton. Residential development of a mixed, aesthetic character, containing both row house and single-family dwellings, also unfolded east of Roosevelt Boulevard in the Far Northeast, especially in Torresdale, Holme Circle, and Academy Gardens, throughout the 1950s and 1960s, where an assemblage of white, ethnic Catholics with strong community affiliations to nearby parishes bought homes.

Commercial development, especially shopping centers, also molded the spatial alignment of Northeast Philadelphia's neighborhoods in the postwar period. Just as mini-strip shopping centers began to dot the Northeast's still developing landscape during the 1950s and early 1960s, some Northeast residents, outraged about commercial overexpansion in their neighborhoods, requested the construction of a major shopping facility to counteract the sometimes unwieldy dimensions of commercial growth in the Northeast. In 1961, for instance, civic boosters, city officials, and residents congregated at the Bustleton-Cottman shopping center—a newly erected major regional shopping facility that openly competed for Northeast customers with Philadelphia's central business district—to mark its opening, with Gimbels serving as its principal anchor department store.

Amid the rising tide of middle-class prosperity coursing through Northeast Philadelphia in the postwar period, there also developed a backlash among white homeowners toward proposed zoning changes to accommodate public housing in residential neighborhoods and fair housing proposals offered by civil rights advocates. In July 1959, Harold Stassen, the Republican mayoral candidate, sought the support of Northeast voters by claiming that he would disassemble "City Hall's bungling socialistic experiments" aimed at providing public housing for low-income families and racial minorities in Northeast neighborhoods. While popular defiance toward public housing in the Northeast persisted over the next two decades, Northeast realtors and residents also resisted antidiscriminatory overtures in the private housing market, as calls for fair-housing legislation mounted among Philadelphia city officials and state legislators in the late 1950s and early 1960s. Although the Pennsylvania state legislature passed a fair-housing law in 1961 to end discriminatory practices in the private marketplace, Cecil B. Moore, a prominent African American civil rights advocate who grew dissatisfied with the pace and trajectory of residential desegregation, still accused the Northeast of being a "lily-white island" within the city's limits in 1964.

Racial animosities between white and Black people in Northeast Philadelphia intensified further around busing and school-desegregation proposals during the late 1960s and 1970s. As president of the School Board of Philadelphia, Richardson Dilworth faced staunch opposition from white residents in both the Near and Far Northeast after the school board, working in conjunction with the Philadelphia Commission on Human Relations, released its 1968 desegregation plan for the city's public schools. In their effort to achieve racial equilibrium and enhance educational standards across Philadelphia's public school system, Dilworth and the school board encountered massive resistance to the busing of Black students into the Northeast's overwhelmingly white schools and "reverse" busing, which entailed busing white children into predominantly Black city schools.

Attempts to implement full-blown school desegregation waned during the mayoral tenure of Frank Rizzo, as he appeased many white residents' anxieties, especially after receiving an electoral mandate from Northeast whites in 1971, by curtailing liberal demands for racial parity within Philadelphia's public schools. Public support for mandatory school desegregation in the city's public schools eventually faded in the mid-1970s, at which point city officials and residents agreed to institute a voluntary school-desegregation plan commencing in 1979, which prompted less popular resistance in the Northeast.

As deindustrialization and white flight threatened Philadelphia's already shaky fiscal foundations and deteriorating municipal services during the 1970s and early 1980s, some Northeast residents, including Republican state senator Hank Salvatore, questioned the logic of remaining wedded to the "City of Brotherly Love." After W. Wilson Goode, the first African American elected mayor of Philadelphia, made repeated calls in the 1983 mayoral election to erect a "mini-City Hall" in Northeast Philadelphia in order to offset Northeast residents' fears about declining city services, Senator Salvatore, unmoved by Goode's proposal, declared his intention to introduce legislation in the state legislature that would permit Northeast Philadelphia to secede from the city and become formally known as "Liberty County." Goode, living up to his promise, opened the mini-city hall in the Northeast Center Shopping Center along Roosevelt Boulevard in 1985, severely undercutting the legitimacy of Salvatore's secession agenda, which lost its popular appeal by the late 1980s.

Over the subsequent two decades, Northeast Philadelphia underwent significant demographic and racial changes to become an increasingly diverse, urban community. Starting in the 1990s, white families and individuals began relocating to the surrounding suburban counties and outside the Philadelphia metropolitan region in increasing numbers. In 2011, the Pew Charitable Trusts released a citywide population study that documented the dramatic racial and ethnic transformations that had occurred throughout Philadelphia during the previous twenty years. It found that Northeast Philadelphia's white population had fallen precipitously, from 92 percent in 1990 to 58.3

percent in 2010. The trend continued over the ensuing decade, as the white population in Lower Northeast fell to 21 percent. As middle-class whites migrated outside the city's limits, racial minorities began the process of inhabiting the once predominantly white corridors of Northeast Philadelphia and relied on affordable mass transportation links, such as the Frankford El, for their daily work commutes into the city. Indian families and ethnic Russians moved into the Far Northeast neighborhoods of Bustleton and Somerton, respectively, while African Americans, various Asian groups, and Hispanics relocated from North Philadelphia into the Lower Northeast neighborhoods of Mayfair, Frankford, and Oxford Circle. Once a bastion of racial defiance and material affluence, Northeast Philadelphia evolved into a dynamic, cosmopolitan atmosphere in the early twenty-first century to embrace economic, cultural, and racial diversity in its private and public spaces.

EXPLORE MORE

Philadelphia's history is so closely related to the founding of the nation that exploration of the city's rich history too often starts and stops at Independence National Historical Park and associated sites, notably Independence Hall, the Liberty Bell, and the Constitution Center. There is no reason to downplay the importance of these sites, and the best preparation for exploring their meaning is Charlene Mires's *Independence Hall in American Memory* (University of Pennsylvania Press, 2002). The national story is further elaborated nearby in the exhibits and archives at the Betsy Ross House, Christ Church, the American Philosophical Society, the Museum of the American Revolution, and Elfreth's Alley, between Second and N. Front Streets. But even national stories have local origins of lasting impact. The story of the President's House once occupied by George Washington, now represented directly adjacent to the Liberty Bell exhibit, unveils the harsh reality of enslavement at the site of liberty and the connections between those held in bondage by Washington and their relationship to Philadelphia's vital free Black community. That story, and how it came to be commemorated, is told in Roger C. Aden's *Upon the Ruins of Liberty: Slavery, the President's House at Independence National Historical Park, and Public Memory* (Temple University Press, 2014).

Philadelphia no longer has a museum devoted exclusively to its own history, but much of the research behind this experience can be accessed at the Historical Society of Pennsylvania and the Library Company of Philadelphia at 1300 and 1314 Locust Street, respectively. The African American Museum in Philadelphia at 701 Arch Street includes Philadelphia's Black history within the larger scope of its mission. A key Black site downtown is Mother Bethel A.M.E. Church, at the heart of what was the early Black community, at 419 S. Sixth Street. That community is described in Gary Nash, *Forging Freedom: The Formation of Philadelphia's Black Community, 1720–1840* (Harvard University Press, 1988). Robert Gregg, *Sparks from the Anvil of Oppression: Philadelphia's African Methodists and Southern Migrants, 1840–1940* (Temple University Press, 1993) and Matthew J. Countryman, *Up South: Civil Rights and Black Power in Philadelphia* (University of Pennsylvania Press, 2006) provide accounts of the more recent Black experience.

Andrew Heath examines the motives behind consolidation and its effect in *In Union There Is Strength: Philadelphia in the Age of Urban Consolidation* (University of Pennsylvania Press, 2019). See also Howard Gillette, Jr.'s chapter "The Emergence of the Modern Metropolis: Philadelphia in the Age of Its Consolidation," in *The Divided Metropolis: Social and Spatial Dimensions of Philadelphia, 1800–1975* (Greenwood Press, 1980), edited by William W. Cutler and Gillette. Philadelphia's grand Second Empire city hall, at Broad and Market, which stands in many ways as a physical embodiment of Philadelphia's nineteenth-century aspirations, is available for tours. Gillette examines the origins of its location and the politics behind it in "Philadelphia City Hall: Monument to a New Political Machine," *Pennsylvania Magazine of History and Biography* (April 1973). Zachary M. Schrag, *The Fires of Philadelphia: Citizen-Soldiers, Nativists, and the 1844 Riots over the Soul of a Nation* (Pegasus, 2021) recounts the volatile social conditions that helped spur the consolidation movement. David R. Biddle and Murray Dubin tell the story of Octavius Catto's murder in *Tasting Freedom: Octavius Catto and the Battle for Equality in Civil War America* (Temple University Press, 2010).

Historical organizations representing communities whose name and identity survived beyond consolidation include those in Germantown, Tacony, and Frankford. Studies of individual sections of the city include David R. Contosta, *Suburb in the City: Chestnut Hill, Philadelphia, 1850–1990* (Ohio State University Press, 1992). Abigail Perkiss's *Making Good Neighbors: Civil Rights, Liberalism, and Integration in Postwar Philadelphia* (Cornell University Press, 2014) draws on the experience of West Mount Airy. Timothy J. Lombardo, *Blue-Collar Conservatism: Frank Rizzo's Philadelphia and Populist Politics* (University of Pennsylvania Press, 2018), recounts Rizzo's roots in South Philadelphia and his appeal to residents in the outer wards of Philadelphia, not the least the Northeast sector. Murray Dubin's *South Philadelphia: Mummers, Memories, and the Melrose Diner* (Temple University Press, 1996) provides a strong sense of South Philadelphia as place.

Any exploration of South Philadelphia should include a trip to the Italian Market on Ninth Street between Fitzwater and Wharton Streets. The area has diversified in recent times with the influx of Mexican and Vietnamese businesses. For the origins of the Italian presence, however, see Richard N. Juliani, *Building Little Italy: Philadelphia's Italians Before Mass Migration* (Pennsylvania State University Press, 1998).

North of Center City, Girard College at 2101 College Avenue, which remains a boarding school for academically gifted students of limited means, retains an extensive archive of its long history. El Centro de Oro ("The Golden Block") at the heart of the city's Fairhill neighborhood concentrates a number of institutions showcasing the talents of Latinos nearby, including Taller Puertorriqueno, a showcase for Puerto Rican and other Latin American artwork and cultural objects. Victor Vázquez-Hernández traces the origins of Philadelphia's Puerto Rican community in *Before the Wave: Puerto Ricans in Philadelphia 1910–1945* (Centro Press, 2017).

For West Philadelphia's suburban emergence, see Margaret Marsh, *Suburban Lives* (Rutgers University Press, 1990) and Robert Miller and Joseph Siry, "The Emerging Suburb: West Philadelphia, 1850–1880," *Pennsylvania History* (April 1980). The Woodlands' fifty-four-acre property at 4000 Woodland Avenue is at once an eighteenth-century English pleasure garden, nineteenth century rural cemetery, and a contemporary oasis for its neighbors in West Philadelphia. The extensive university presence in West Philadelphia is addressed in Richardson Dilworth and Scott Gabriel Knowles, eds., *Building Drexel: The University and Its City 1891–2016* (Temple University Press, 2017) and John L. Puckett and Mark Frazier Lloyd, *Becoming Penn: The Pragmatic American University, 1950–2000* (University of Pennsylvania Press, 2015). For a history of the rise of University City, including the Black Bottom neighborhood that was cleared to make way for its emergence, see Laura Wolf-Powers, *University City: History, Race, and Community in the Era of the Innovation District* (University of Pennsylvania Press, 2022).

With much of its land wetlands, the Eastwick neighborhood, as it was named in the 1950s, and the battle it fought against being reconstructed through the urban renewal plans of the late 1950s and 1960s, see Guian A. McKee, "Liberal Ends Through Illiberal Means: Race, Urban Renewal, and Community in the Eastwick Section of Philadelphia, 1949–1990," *Journal of Urban History* (July 2001).

Constructed in 1768, the Johnson House at 6306 Germantown Avenue in Germantown is one of the few Underground Railroad sites open to visitors. Owned by Quakers who supported the antislavery cause, the property is operated as a historic house museum, part of a consortium of eighteen preserved historical sites along the road that connected the early settlement of Germantown to the port of Philadelphia. David W. Young, *The Battles of Germantown: Effective Public History in America* (Temple University Press, 2019), provides a sensitive analysis of the ways the history of the area has been preserved and recounted.

In the Northeast, the once massive Disston Saw Works established in the 1870s survives in much smaller form as Disston Precision, but the legacy of Henry Disston, industrialist and developer of the area, survives in the form of multiple examples of stunning Victorian architecture and Disston Park at the heart of the Tacony community. For a visual historical record of industrial sites, see Philip Scranton and Walter Licht, *Work Sights: Industrial Philadelphia, 1890–1950* (Temple University Press, 1986).

5-1-193

Chapter 6

NETWORKS

TRAILS, CANALS, RAILS, AND ROADS

Introduction

REGIONS ARE NOT CREATED: THEY evolve. As the original two-square-mile city of Philadelphia matured, its reach extended outward, casting its influence as a center for commerce and settlement over more and more territory, even as peoples moving through and out of the city formed the constituent communities. That dynamic intensified and deepened with transportation improvements that fostered new relationships and patterns of exchange. As such networks extended and fragmented over time, the pattern became more complex, their influences more subtle and unpredictable. The "regional" dynamic became harder to identify, but its presence could not be denied.

Before there was a city, serving as a magnet for settlement and industry between the banks of the Delaware and Schuylkill Rivers, there were Native inhabitants, forming communities and establishing networks. The historic homeland of the indigenous Lenape people encompassed the entire Delaware River system marked by a complex pattern of overland paths connecting commonly used locations where travelers forded rivers and streams. Even as European settlement disrupted Native communities, the purposeful network of trails along waterways and bridging mountains survived, guiding subsequent users along these pathways and river crossings. The Pennsylvania portion of the Great Wagon Road, for instance, roughly followed the Great Minquas Trail used by Lenni Lenape, Susquehannocks (Minquas), and European traders. To advance their ambitions, Europeans turned trails into roads and river crossings into sites of business activity by introducing ferries and ultimately bridges. Improvements aimed at boosting trade and communication followed, as legislatures in the new republic authorized private companies to convert rough roads into turnpikes, through which they could realize return on investment by charging tolls. To further extend the city's reach to the rich agricultural hinterland to the west, Philadelphia businessmen sought additional public investment to assist trade. Spurred especially by construction of the Erie Canal, which boosted the fortunes of their New York City rival to the north, and by the flow of interior Pennsylvania goods down the Susquehanna to Baltimore, Philadelphians promoted their own system intended to improve on the use of natural streams and waterways to transport goods into and out of the city. When the rugged mountain terrain to the west proved too great an obstacle for horse-drawn canal boats, they introduced newly tried steam engines to create a mixed canal-rail system known as the Main Line of Public Works. In this way, however cumbersomely, Philadelphia embraced the thirst for trade.

The construction of bridges connecting the central city to West Philadelphia boosted development that took the form of a suburb within the city. Ties extended east as well as west, as both steamboats and ferry crossings to New Jersey facilitated exchange and ultimately travel to New York City. With the development of New Jersey's mixed rail and canal system in the 1830s, travelers from Philadelphia could take a ferry to Camden, board the Camden and Amboy Railroad to Burlington City, and from there travel to Perth Amboy, finally taking a ferry to New York City. If such complicated arrangements did little to extend Philadelphia's dominance as an engine of regional identity, such connections proved nonetheless vital to the widening of vistas, as well as providing a pathway for immigrants entering New York's port on their way to destinations farther south and west.

Growth internal to the city continued with further innovation, most notably electric streetcars and subsequently subways and elevated rail lines. With the introduction of the automobile in the twentieth century, settlement further diversified, helping fill in underdeveloped parts of the city where public transportation between home and work did not exist, while also extending growth beyond the city limits. This step had the contradictory effect of broadening the consciously regional influence exerted by the city, but also weakening its centrality as taxes paid by homeowners accrued to jurisdictions beyond Philadelphia's reach. Suburbanites continued to commute downtown, as they had in the late nineteenth century on the Main Line of the Pennsylvania Railroad, but their civic allegiances to say nothing of their consumer spending went elsewhere, and new forms of regional shopping emerged to compete with downtown department stores. Foundations of daily travel between city and suburb laid through electrification of trolleys in the nineteenth century were largely supplanted by buses as well as by specialized rail routes such as the Red Arrow Lines from the Pennsylvania suburbs or the Port Authority Transit Corporation (PATCO) line to New Jersey.

Just as Europeans had utilized the transportation networks established by Native Americans, contemporary area residents have been able to capitalize on once vital transportation corridors for the very different purposes of walking and biking. Rail and canal paths converted to leisure and tourist activity remind users of the ties that once bound their livelihoods together but now serve recreational purposes instead.

Trails (Native)

Matthew A. Zimmerman

In the Philadelphia region prior to European settlement and during the colonial period, the Lenapes and other Native peoples used their knowledge of the landscape to engineer the most efficient routes through forests, mountains, and often shallow, treacherous waterways. Their complex system of overland paths crisscrossed the region to reach east to the shell fisheries on the Atlantic coast and west into the Wyoming Valley. While Euro-Americans later developed some of these trails into wagon and automobile routes centered on Philadelphia, the Native trails promoted trade and communication with people in many directions within and outside the region.

The Native peoples who engineered trails took full advantage of the mid-Atlantic landscape to overcome difficult travel conditions. By locating trails above flood levels and along mountain ridges, Lenapes and other Natives ensured the routes remained accessible and dry. To avoid excessive ascents through higher elevations, travelers followed trails through mountain gaps or along ridges, such as the stretch of the Great Warriors Path through Greene County, Pennsylvania.

Native travelers often trekked single file along relatively narrow paths. Lenape leaders, with a political system based upon autonomous communities, could not command the labor needed to undertake monumental road construction and public works projects like those of the Incas of Peru. The Tulpehocken Path, from Shamokin to Philadelphia, extended only about eighteen inches across in places. Other trails permitted two travelers to walk side by side. The European introduction of horses gradually led to widening of many routes.

Along the network of paths, travelers frequently encountered other people, stopped to converse, and shared news of recent events or the fruits of a recent hunt. In wartime, trails could be crowded with warriors, both Native and European, intent on violence. In peacetime, however, hunters, traders, messengers, diplomats, and those visiting relatives and friends used the paths. Hospitality and fellowship governed life on the trail during such times. Food could be easily

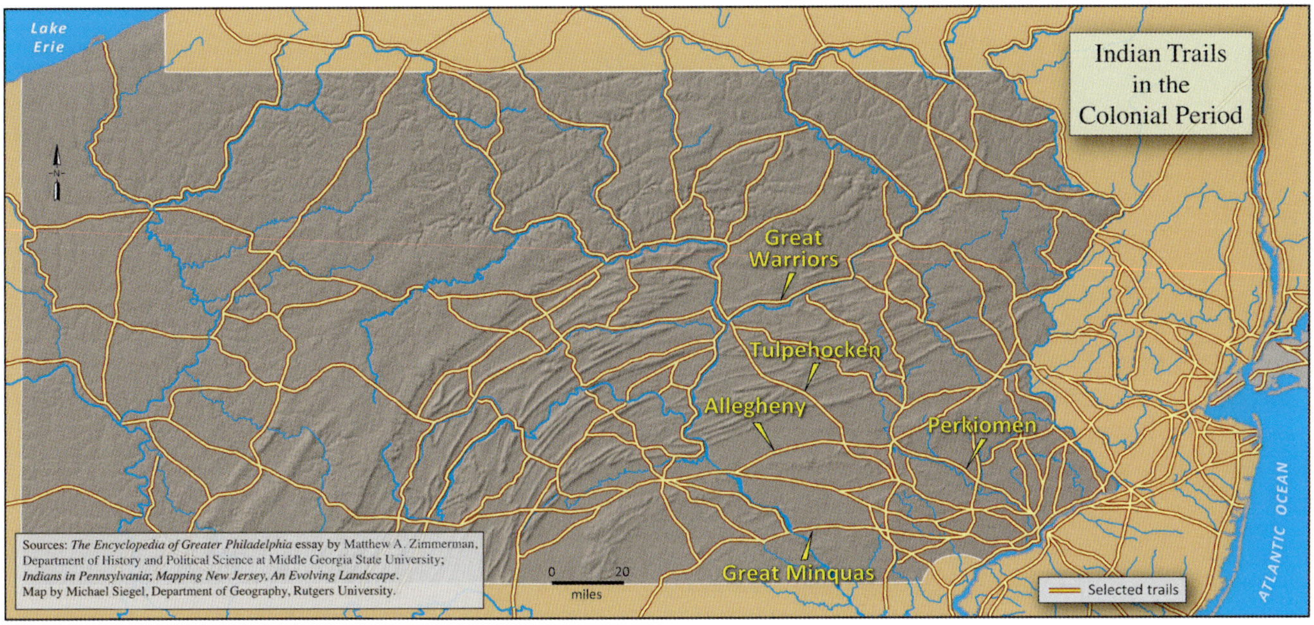

MAP 2. Native trails. By the time Europeans reached North America, the Lenape and other Native people had a complex system of overland paths that crisscrossed the region. Eventually the newcomers used the trails too and gave them names that reflected the original trailblazers. MAP BY MICHAEL SIEGEL.

found at the many Native villages and cabins located along the trails or by hunting the abundant game of the forests. Traveling primarily in the spring or fall, voyagers avoided the icy cold of winter and the heat and harassing insects of summer. As darkness approached, those trekking along well-worn trails could typically find overnight accommodations with fellow travelers in shelters built by those who had spent previous nights in the area.

In an extensive study, historian Paul A.W. Wallace identified 131 distinct Native trails in Pennsylvania. The Allegheny Path, a primary trail leading out of the Delaware Valley, ran from the future location of Allegheny Avenue in Philadelphia, through Paoli to Harrisburg, across the Susquehanna and into Carlisle, where it forked into the Raystown and Frankstown Paths. The Perkiomen Path ran from Philadelphia to Norristown, crossed Perkiomen Creek, and extended into Reading, where it joined the Allegheny Path.

Ironically, the best evidence for Lenape accomplishment in trail making comes from extensive use of the system by Europeans. Individuals and armies ranging from Moravian John Heckewelder to diplomat Conrad Weiser and General John Sullivan used established Native trails. Perhaps most famously, in 1779 Sullivan marched from Easton along the Great Warriors Path to exact revenge on the Iroquois in New York for their attacks the previous year. Less famously, but likely more importantly, Native and European traders journeyed along the Great Minquas Path, from the Susquehanna River to the forks of the Brandywine then to the Philadelphia area, to exchange animal pelts at posts along the Schuylkill and Delaware Rivers. This exchange, and thereby this trail, proved vital in giving early Pennsylvania access to the fur trade.

The Lenapes and other Natives plotted courses that accommodated both the landscape and their needs. These trails were not simply carved by hunters following game but were thoughtfully arrayed routes designed to facilitate travel. Engineered to accommodate people traveling on foot, the trails provided the most efficient routes across difficult terrain. Over time, many evolved into roads and highways, where historical markers recalled the precedents of the Native American trails.

Turnpikes

Charlene Mires

From their earliest introduction in Pennsylvania in the late eighteenth century to their modern incarnations as high-speed highways, turnpikes have expanded Philadelphia's reach to points west and linked the region with other commercial centers and suburbs of the Eastern Seaboard. Beginning with the first turnpike in the United States, which was a sixty-two-mile paved toll road from Philadelphia to Lancaster completed in 1795, private investment authorized by state governments enabled swift and extensive construction of improved roads to meet the needs of changing times. The first generation of turnpikes, completed by the 1820s, gave the Philadelphia region connections reaching as far west as Ohio, north through New Jersey to New York, and south through Delaware to Baltimore. In the automobile age of the twentieth century, when states again embraced toll roads as a way of financing high-speed, limited-access superhighways, the Pennsylvania and New Jersey turnpikes cut through Philadelphia's suburbs and embedded the region in the interstate highway system.

Turnpikes take their name from the pole or pike used to block entrance to a road until a toll is paid. First introduced as a means of road improvement in England in the late seventeenth century, turnpikes emerged in the United States in the decades after the American Revolution. The need to improve the new nation's rudimentary and haphazard dirt roads, many of them created by foot traffic over former Indian trails, far exceeded local capabilities or public finances. Seeking a solution, state legislatures awarded charters of incorporation for turnpike companies and empowered them to sell stock and collect tolls in exchange for improving or creating roads for faster and easier travel. With state economies highly dependent on moving agricultural goods to market and with populations spreading westward, legislatures readily granted charters to hundreds of turnpike companies. Within a few decades, by the 1830s, the nation had almost twelve thousand miles of turnpikes.

Pennsylvania inspired the wave of toll-road construction with the success of the Lancaster Turnpike, which mostly followed the Philadelphia-Lancaster Road that had been in use throughout the eighteenth century. The earlier road, in addition to serving as the link between Philadelphia and Lancaster (founded in 1729), was the "Great Wagon Road" that enabled migrants and freight to move west across southeastern Pennsylvania and from there into the backcountry of Maryland, Virginia, and North Carolina. Discussion of improving the heavily traveled road began among merchants and state legislators shortly after the War for Independence and, with lobbying by Philadelphia elites, came to fruition with a charter of incorporation for a turnpike company in 1792. Residents in and around Lancaster and Philadelphia eagerly bought one thousand shares of stock, valued at $300 each, and the company organized under the leadership of William Bingham, a Federalist political leader and prominent Philadelphia merchant.

By 1795, the completed turnpike to Lancaster required tolls but it had been paved with layers of crushed stone, widened and straightened and engineered for good drainage. Inns and taverns opened along the route—purportedly as many as one per mile—to serve an increasing volume of traffic. A sturdy stone bridge carried the road across Brandywine River in Downingtown; by 1805, a separately chartered toll bridge (the "Permanent Bridge") carried Philadelphia traffic to the turnpike over the Schuylkill River at High (Market) Street. Although some objected to paying to use the road and its bridges, the faster travel time to market made the tolls worthwhile for farmers, and the reliability of the road benefited freight haulers and stagecoach operators. The project produced steady if not spectacular dividends for investors.

The Lancaster Turnpike inspired a nationwide rush of turnpike building and rivalries among cities. As toll roads radiated outward not only from Philadelphia but also from New York, Wilmington, and Baltimore, they knit together a region that later travelers would recognize as the Northeast Corridor. The important connection between the commercial hubs of Philadelphia and New York received attention from turnpike projects extending from both cities. For example, the Frankford and Bristol Turnpike (chartered 1803) carried traffic through Bucks County to the Delaware River at Morrisville, where a ferry crossing allowed connection with turnpikes across New Jersey to New York. (Until the 1850s, most turnpike activity in New Jersey emanated from New York investors eager to bolster New York-Philadelphia commerce or improve connections with agricultural areas in northeast Pennsylvania.) To the south, the Philadelphia, Brandywine, and New London Turnpike Company chartered by Pennsylvania in 1808 and Delaware's Philadelphia Pike, built across the northern neck of the state between 1813 and 1823, enabled travel and trade between Philadelphia and Baltimore.

Toll roads reached out from Philadelphia like spokes of a wheel, connecting the city to the interior of Pennsylvania. Turnpike companies improved the northwesterly Germantown and Ridge Roads through Philadelphia County, and then the Germantown and Perkiomen Turnpike (opened in 1799) extended travel for an additional twenty-six miles to Reading. Turnpikes also strengthened Philadelphia's connections to the Lehigh Valley via Bethlehem Pike (chartered in 1804). Where turnpikes reached into the agricultural countryside of southern Chester County, they met with similar roads extending northward from Wilmington, Delaware. Across the expanse of Pennsylvania, helped by state funding for turnpikes beginning in 1806, a proliferation of short turnpikes between communities created the means for people and products to travel between Philadelphia and any corner of the state, then west into Ohio.

By the 1820s, turnpikes had vastly expanded Philadelphia's regional connections by improved (often paved) roads. Enthusiasm for turnpikes waned, however, with the advent of canals and railroads and the realization that most turnpikes returned meager long-term profits. During the 1850s, South Jersey gained the Black Horse and White Horse Pikes as improvements to earlier roads, and Pennsylvania chartered turnpikes between Philadelphia and West Chester (1848), between Darby and Ridley in Delaware County (1851), and near Philadelphia along the Wissahickon Creek (1856). But most turnpike development at midcentury focused on shorter wooden-plank roads connecting with the railroads and canals. By the end of the nineteenth century, most turnpikes reverted to public use as the charters for turnpike companies ended or as the companies surrendered them for lack of profit. An era of turnpikes ended, but the states gained an extensive network of public roads made possible by private investment. Over time, the nineteenth-century turnpikes became state and U.S. highways.

As a method for financing transformational roadways, turnpikes revived in the twentieth century to meet the demands of the automobile age. The new generation of toll roads in Pennsylvania and New Jersey blazed multilane, limited-access superhighways across long distances, not radiating outward from cities but skirting their suburban fringes. The outlying interchanges for Philadelphia on the Pennsylvania and New Jersey turnpikes still positioned the city within the emerging Northeast Corridor and connected it to the West, but vehicles also could speed by Philadelphia en route to other destinations. Turnpike service plazas, offering gasoline, restaurants, and restrooms, encouraged drivers to stay on the highway.

The Pennsylvania Turnpike, begun during the Great Depression of the 1930s, aimed to produce jobs as well as an improved highway across the state. Its first phase (opened in 1940) ran through central Pennsylvania between Harrisburg and Pittsburgh, a route that allowed its builders to take advantage of a roadbed and mountain tunnels that had been abandoned by a nineteenth-century railroad venture. When the turnpike extended to the Philadelphia area in 1950, its interchange twenty miles west of the city near Valley Forge set the stage for a rush of industrial, commercial, and residential development. The growth of an "edge city" at the former village of King of Prussia gained further impetus from completion of the turnpike's Northeast Extension toward New Jersey and Scranton between 1954 and 1957 and the Schuylkill Expressway connection with Philadelphia in 1958. The turnpike's exits at Plymouth Meeting, Whitemarsh, and Willow Grove also attracted commercial development to Philadelphia's suburbs.

The New Jersey Turnpike, authorized in 1948 and opened in segments during 1951–52, solidified the state's position as a vital East Coast transportation corridor by funneling nonstop traffic on a nearly straight diagonal from rural South Jersey (where the Delaware Memorial Bridge replaced ferry service across the Delaware River in 1951) to the George Washington Bridge into Manhattan. As the interstate highway system developed during the 1950s and 1960s, the turnpike offered an alternative to the partially completed Interstate 95 between that highway's segments in Delaware (the

Delaware Turnpike) and New York, thus speeding trips between Washington, D.C., and Boston. The turnpike's exit closest to Philadelphia, in largely agricultural Mount Laurel Township, Burlington County, spurred plans for development resembling King of Prussia in Pennsylvania—industrial parks, shopping centers, and suburban subdivisions. In Mount Laurel, however, these proposals threatened displacement of longtime African American residents, who viewed the township's development strategy as an attempt to cultivate a more white, middle-class population. Efforts by affordable housing advocates to build low-cost garden apartments for displaced residents led to two far-reaching court decisions (1975 and 1983) banning exclusionary zoning and defining the responsibilities of communities to provide affordable housing.

For the new generation of automobile turnpikes, Pennsylvania and New Jersey created independent agencies with authority to raise revenue, build the roads, and manage the enterprises: the Pennsylvania Turnpike Commission and the New Jersey Turnpike Authority. (In Delaware, the state Department of Transportation held jurisdiction over the tolled segment of Interstate 95.) The Pennsylvania Turnpike, a risky proposition during the Great Depression, began construction with a $29 million grant from the federal Public Works Administration and sold its first $41 million in revenue bonds to the federal Reconstruction Finance Corporation, which in turn sold them to private investors. The New Jersey Turnpike, originating in the boom years following World War II, launched with the largest toll-road bond issue in history up to that time—$250 million in thirty-five-year bonds. The turnpike agencies in Pennsylvania and New Jersey had power, patronage, and unending streams of revenue from toll booths and service plazas operating twenty-four hours a day, every day of the year—circumstances that led to instances of corruption in both states.

For the Philadelphia region, beginning with the Lancaster Turnpike of 1795 and continuing into the twenty-first century, turnpikes achieved transformational change for the movement of people and goods. Private investment and tolls paid for improvements in road surfacing, speed, and safety beyond the capacity of public financing. The resulting turnpikes contributed to forming regional ties between Philadelphia and nearby communities in Pennsylvania, New Jersey, and Delaware while also forging connections to travel and commerce of the nation.

Great Wagon Road

Charlene Mires

Following routes established by Native Americans, the Great Wagon Road enabled eighteenth-century travel from Philadelphia and its hinterlands westward to Lancaster and then south into the backcountry of Maryland, Virginia, and North Carolina. In search of affordable farmland and economic opportunity, thousands of Scots Irish, Germans, and others left the Philadelphia region to establish farms, taverns, villages, and new lives along the rugged road that stretched across southeastern Pennsylvania and eventually continued more than four hundred miles through the Shenandoah Valley of the Appalachian Mountains and beyond. The new population of the backcountry sustained connections with Philadelphia through trade, often facilitated by merchants in market towns such as Lancaster and York in Pennsylvania, Hagerstown in Maryland, and Winchester in northern Virginia.

The Great Wagon Road saw its most intensive activity in the middle decades of the eighteenth century, prior to the American Revolution. During this period, the increasing population of Pennsylvania made land more scarce and costly, not only for new arrivals but for settled farmers seeking to secure livelihoods for future generations. At the same time, governors in Maryland and Virginia were promoting backcountry settlement by Europeans as a means of securing their frontiers. A flow of settlers began by the 1720s, a decade of high immigration of Germans and Scots Irish into Pennsylvania, then increased dramatically after the 1744 Treaty of Lancaster settled Iroquois Nation claims in the Shenandoah Valley. A German immigrant through Philadelphia, Jonathan Hager, bought land in Maryland in 1739 and subsequently founded Hagerstown. The colonial governors of Maryland and Virginia sped settlement by awarding large land grants to individuals on the condition that they recruit specified numbers of migrants. For example, New Jersey speculator Benjamin Borden, born in Monmouth County, moved to the northern Shenandoah Valley by 1734 and received a grant of

100,000 acres on the James River for his pledge to recruit settlers from Ireland. Jost Hite, a German immigrant living on the Perkiomen Creek northwest of Philadelphia, received a grant of 140,000 acres and agreed to recruit 140 families. Their settlement in Virginia, together with Quakers who migrated to a similar grant made to Alexander Ross from Chester County, led to the founding of the new town of Winchester.

In its earliest days, the Great Wagon Road could hardly be termed a "road." The Indian trails that it traced for much of its length originated as pathways for individuals walking in single file. The subsequent road developed from the traffic of more individuals, people on horseback, herds of cattle, carts pulled by animals, and eventually the heavy-duty Conestoga wagons that became the freight haulers of the road. In places, the route consisted of not a single road but of variations created by travelers to avoid hazards or reach new destinations. The journey required fording or ferrying across rivers along the way. The Pennsylvania portion of the Great Wagon Road roughly followed the Great Minquas Trail used by Lenni Lenape, Susquehannocks (Minquas), and European traders. During the middle eighteenth century, travelers on this route between Philadelphia and Lancaster (founded in 1729) found a stump-punctuated dirt road despite its designation as a "King's Road." As the road turned south after Lancaster and York (founded 1741), it approximated the route known to Europeans as the Great Warriors Path, created and still valued by Native Americans for passage through the Shenandoah Valley west of the Blue Ridge. Past the Shenandoah Valley into western Virginia and the Carolinas, additional branches of the road often consisted of little more than tromped grass, mud, and the wagon ruts of previous travelers.

Despite its rugged conditions, "the Great Waggon Road to Philadelphia" appeared designated as such in 1753, on *A Map of the Inhabited Part of Virginia containing the whole Province of Maryland, with Part of Pensilvania, New Jersey and North Carolina*. By that time, the road had enabled a multiethnic ribbon of backcountry settlement reaching from Pennsylvania south to the Yadkin River of North Carolina. In addition to the dominant Germans and Scots Irish, the settlers of the backcountry included Quakers who clustered around Winchester, Virginia (which sheltered exiled Philadelphia Quakers during the American Revolution). German-speaking Moravians from Bethlehem, Pennsylvania, founded the community of Wachovia in western North Carolina in 1753. By 1780, the southern backcountry had an estimated population of about 380,000, including the Pennsylvania migrants as well as English, French Huguenot, German, and Highland Scot settlers who moved inland from coastal Virginia and the Carolinas. The Great Wagon Road also enabled journeys through the region, for example, by socially elite travelers seeking the resort springs of western Virginia.

While most migrants came to establish farms in the broad valley between the backcountry's mountain ranges, towns also developed at intervals along the Great Wagon Road in Maryland, Virginia, and North Carolina. Spaced approximately one day's journey apart, often founded by former Pennsylvanians, and at times with street grids and center squares reminiscent of Philadelphia, towns anchored the backcountry as a market area for Philadelphia trade. They usually developed where the Great Wagon Road intersected with east-west roads from coastal regions. The resulting network of roads made it possible for wheat farmers in the backcountry to take harvests east to market in Alexandria or Richmond, Virginia, but bring back the profits to spend on finished goods imported by local merchants from Philadelphia via the Great Wagon Road. Towns along the Wagon Road served as points of transfer for crops bound for market in Philadelphia, including wheat and flour further exported from Philadelphia to Europe. Peddlers plied their trade along the road, and drovers moved herds of cattle to Philadelphia butchers. Philadelphia merchants and banks extended credit to backcountry businesses and land investors.

The Great Wagon Road became a pathway of settlement deeper into the western frontier after 1769, when Pennsylvania-born Daniel Boone opened the Wilderness Road from North Carolina west into the territory that became Tennessee and Kentucky. Born in the rural reaches of Philadelphia County that later became Berks County, Boone migrated to North Carolina with his Quaker family at the age of fifteen. He gained fame as the trailblazer of the pass through the Cumberland Gap, thereby connecting the Great Wagon Road to points west.

FIGURE 31. Viewed from the West Jersey Ferry Terminal in Camden, New Jersey, the Delaware River in 1876 was a busy passageway demonstrating the centrality of ferries and other vessels linking South Jersey with Philadelphia in the distance. FREE LIBRARY OF PHILADELPHIA.

The Great Wagon Road declined in importance with the development of additional improved roads and then railroads in the early nineteenth century. With some variations in route, it became the Lancaster Turnpike (incorporated 1792) in Pennsylvania and the Valley Turnpike (incorporated 1834) in Virginia. In the twentieth century, U.S. 30 in Pennsylvania and U.S. 11 and Interstate 81 through the Shenandoah Valley approximated the route of the Great Wagon Road. Testaments to connections with the Philadelphia region persisted in the form of surviving eighteenth-century houses, roadside historical markers, Pennsylvania-style bank barns, and towns with Presbyterian and Lutheran churches founded by Scots Irish and German settlers. The old road remained a subject of interest for scholars and a source of heritage tourism, and knowledgeable locals could still point out ruts and trenches believed to be remnants of the original road that linked Philadelphia to the settlement of the backcountry South.

Ferries

Stephen Nepa

Long before bridges, trestles, and elevated expressways, the people and products of Greater Philadelphia required a network of ferries to traverse the region's numerous waterways. Once ubiquitous on the area's rivers, ferries were economic necessities that were phased out over time as industry changed and transportation improved.

Until the advent of steam and internal combustion technologies, ferries required man, horse, or mule power. Swedish colonists operated the region's first ferries in the 1660s along the Christina River in the region that became Delaware. By 1700, several entrepreneurs operated ferries across the Delaware River between growing riverfront settlements in Pennsylvania and New Jersey. As the British consolidated their territorial holdings in the late 1600s, ferries required royal authority to operate. In the Lower Counties (later the state of Delaware), Governor Francis Lovelace chartered the first ferry service on the Christina north of present-day Newport in 1669 with an additional crossing established over Brandywine Creek in 1689; the peninsular land mass between these two ferries eventually became central Wilmington, Delaware (established 1731). In 1724, Governor William Keith granted license to a ferry on the Delaware River between New Castle, Delaware, and Salem, New Jersey, which allowed Salem residents to worship across the river at Old Swedes Church.

Ferry operations also led to the formation of towns and cities. In order to connect a fledgling Philadelphia with the farms of West New Jersey, William Royden received a ferry charter from Gloucester County in 1688. By 1695, the Cooper family, having settled in 1681 at a site that became known as Pyne Point, assumed control of Royden's ferry. William Cooper began additional service from New Jersey to Philadelphia in 1708; by the mid-1760s, his great-grandson Daniel built Parson's Hotel at the landing, which became known as the town of Cooper's Ferry. Nearby Kaighnton and Fettersville (an early Black community) also were served by ferries. In 1828, the three towns merged and were incorporated as the city of Camden.

In Philadelphia, the colonial assembly addressed the need for ferries just after the city's founding; records indicate that Philip England began operating the first, or lower, ferry on the Schuylkill River in 1685 between High Street and newly created roads to Darby and Merion. The upper ferry at Spring Garden Street, operated by William Powel, commenced in 1692, and after 1730, when Lancaster Pike opened, increased traffic prompted a third, or middle, ferry. These crossings, made by pulling ropes, were difficult, and in 1774 the colonial assembly voted to construct a bridge over the river. Yet it was not until 1776, as a military necessity, that a floating bridge was erected. Ferries also spurred travel-related enterprises such as hotels, taverns, and slips. George Gray, who had assumed control of England's ferry in 1744, also operated a floating bridge and popular pleasure garden (Gray's Tavern and Inn) following the American Revolution.

While ferries connected cities to their hinterlands, a growing system of toll roads, pikes, and longer-range boats connected with them, allowing a fluid traversal of the entire area and to distant points such as New York and Baltimore. In his *Autobiography*, Benjamin Franklin recounted his journey from Boston to Philadelphia, much of it by ferry. North of Philadelphia, significant ferry enterprises linked Mercer County, New Jersey, and Bucks County, Pennsylvania. Between 1675 and the outbreak of the American Revolution, Trenton established the Lower, Middle, and Upper Ferry crossings over the Delaware. The Middle Ferry connected with a stagecoach line to New Brunswick and downriver service to Philadelphia.

Ferries between Pennsylvania and New Jersey played key roles in the American Revolution, most famously when George Washington and his army crossed the Delaware on December 25, 1776, at McConkey's Ferry. Earlier that year, tavernkeeper and ferry operator John Coryell denied British soldiers passage on his ferry between Lambertville, New Jersey, and New Hope, Pennsylvania, as General Charles Cornwallis pursued the Continental Army into Pennsylvania. During the conflict, Trenton's Lower Ferry earned the nickname "Continental Ferry" as its proprietor offered active American soldiers reduced rates. While the British occupied Philadelphia (September 1777–June 1778), American spies disguised as farmers used ferries at the Schuylkill River (including Gray's Ferry) to slip in and out of the city.

During the early 1800s, bridges began to replace ferries at narrow crossing points, such as Trenton; Morrisville, Pennsylvania; and Newport, Delaware. Ferries remained important carriers at wider crossings, however, and in the early industrial period they exchanged man, mule, or horsepower for steam. In 1810, James Bispham piloted the first steam ferry on the Delaware from Camden's Cooper Street to Philadelphia's Market Street. By the 1830s several steam ferries, some equipped with passenger cabins, plied the region's crowded waters. In addition to ferries, larger packet boats (carrying goods and people) ran along the Delaware River to the bay with stops at Chester, Wilmington, and New Castle. Safety, however, remained an issue as ferries traversing the Delaware's wider points contended with storms, currents, fog, and, in winter, ice sheets that made crossings treacherous if not impossible.

Overcrowded boats and docks at peak hours as well as the risks of bad weather made the railroad a preferable and more efficient alternative to ferries. Yet because no bridge crossed the width of the Delaware between Philadelphia and Camden until 1926, ferries provided a vital connection for rail passengers bound for New York and points north. Beginning in the 1850s many companies, including the Camden and Atlantic (C&A) Railroad and the Pennsylvania Railroad (PRR), acquired ferries to augment their existing lines. In 1854, the C&A purchased the Cooper family's operations and offered more frequent service between Camden and Philadelphia. Though the region's rail lines expanded throughout the nineteenth century, independent ferry operators, including Philadelphia's Reeves and Knisell; Camden's English, Clements, and Burr; and shipbuilder William Cramp's line for his workers, remained in operation on the Delaware River. Ferries also inspired the imagination. Admiring a sunset from the Camden waterfront in 1882, Walt Whitman described the ferry *Wenonah*, "as pretty an object as you could wish to see, lightly and swiftly skimming along, all trim and white, covered with flags, transparent red and blue, streaming out in the breeze."

By 1900, wooden and/or suspension bridges connected towns along the Delaware River from Bristol, Pennsylvania, north to New Hope. South of Bristol, ferries continued to ply the river, with only the Delair Railroad Bridge (1896) linking Philadelphia and New Jersey. However, the arrival of automobiles in the early 1900s created demand for better crossings. In 1922, construction commenced on the Delaware River Bridge (renamed the Benjamin Franklin Bridge in 1955). When completed four years later, the new span led to the closure of many ferries and demolition of their riverfront facilities. This pattern continued in 1929 with the opening of the Tacony-Palmyra Bridge and in the 1950s with the opening of the Delaware Memorial and Walt Whitman Bridges. The Chester-to-Bridgeport, New Jersey, Ferry operated until the mid-1970s, providing a crucial link between Greater Philadelphia and points along the Jersey Shore. However, when the Commodore Barry Bridge opened in 1974, its days were numbered.

While automobiles, buses, and trains handled the majority of Greater Philadelphia's transportation needs after the 1970s, certain ferries, connecting points inaccessible by bridge, remained in operation into the twenty-first century. These included two lines running from Delaware City, Delaware, to Pea Patch Island and Salem, New Jersey, as well as the Cape May, New Jersey-to-Lewes, Delaware, Ferry, which between 1964 and 2014 carried more than 14 million cars and 43 million passengers across the seventeen-mile mouth of Delaware Bay. In the first two decades of the twenty-first century, with considerable investment and development along the Philadelphia and Camden waterfronts, the Riverlink Ferry provided service between points such as the Adventure Aquarium on the Camden side and Penn's Landing, with its Spruce Street Harbor Park and the Independence Seaport Museum.

Though Greater Philadelphia's mobility once heavily relied on ferries, many factors, including passenger safety, advances in bridge design, the advent of railroads and cars, and increased urbanization, led to their demise. Yet those that survived continued to provide vital links in the region's transportation network.

Bridges

Andrew Slemmon

Bridge crossings in the Delaware River watershed area have been a measure of the connectedness of the inhabitants with each other and surrounding regions. Through the eighteenth century, bridges were of modest size and relatively limited in number. During the nineteenth century the rate of bridge construction rapidly increased, allowing for commerce and travel on an unprecedented scale. It was during this period that bridges were first built across the Schuylkill River, stimulating suburban growth and economic expansion in Philadelphia. This growth continued into the twentieth century, prompting the construction of major bridges across the Delaware River including the Benjamin Franklin Bridge, Walt Whitman Bridge, Commodore Barry Bridge, Betsy Ross Bridge, and Delaware Memorial Bridge. These would serve, and help to create, one of the busiest transportation corridors in the country.

The pace of bridge construction was initially slow compared to that in New England and the South. This was partly because the Delaware and Schuylkill Rivers were themselves useful as highways, and so the need to cross them remained limited throughout the seventeenth and eighteenth centuries. The Lenni Lenape who first lived in the area marked good crossing locations along rivers, particularly the Delaware and Schuylkill. These later became sites of ferry crossings, which would eventually foster bridge spans.

In 1660 King Charles II ordered a road, referred to as the King's Highway, to be built stretching from Boston, Massachusetts, to Charleston, South Carolina. By 1683, however, progress in Pennsylvania had stalled. Consequently, and at the request of William Penn, that same year the Pennsylvania Provincial Assembly passed a law requiring bridges to be built by local inhabitants across all streams and rivers that intersected the highway. Due to technological limitations, which were just starting to be overcome in New England, these first bridges were not able to span major waterways like the Delaware River. Instead, they typically kept to tributaries and smaller rivers. The earliest surviving bridge built along the King's Highway in the Delaware watershed area, the Pennypack Creek Bridge, was just such a structure. Completed in 1697, it was a stone-arch construction and spanned the Pennypack Creek, located north of Philadelphia where it empties into the Delaware River. Due to the way they facilitated travel, these bridges served as early milestones in the delineation of the region.

Bridges spanning the Delaware and Schuylkill Rivers in Philadelphia were first constructed in the early nineteenth century, and, almost invariably, these river crossings originated as ferry points. Swedish colonists operated the earliest ferries in the 1660s and by the 1730s a significant number of modern-day bridge sites had ferries in operation. On the Schuylkill River these included Gray's Ferry, the Middle Ferry at Market Street, and the Upper Ferry at Spring Garden Street (all in Philadelphia). On the Delaware these included ferries at Trenton, New Jersey, and upriver at New Hope–Lambertville and Easton–Phillipsburg.

Several factors drove the conversion of ferries to bridges. As early as 1764 timber rafters using the Delaware for transport proved dangerous to ferry passengers. As late as 1914 there was a collision between a raft and a ferry that caused the deaths of four passengers. Also, ferries had to stop operation during flooding and freezing. The greatest impetus, though, was when a ferry could no longer handle the amount of traffic queuing up to cross. At this point a corporation, typically local residents of the towns on either side of the river, would petition the states for a charter to build a bridge. They would then finance construction by selling stock in the company, and dividends (and repairs) would be paid from collected tolls. Thus, privately owned ferries were converted into privately owned toll bridges.

The most heavily trafficked ferries on the Delaware were at Trenton and Easton, which consequently led to the first bridge construction over the river. The Delaware River Bridge Company commissioned the Easton-Phillipsburg Bridge in 1795. However, the Lower Trenton Bridge, though commissioned later, was completed nine months before the Easton bridge in January 1806. New England had achieved greater technical feats in bridge building at the time, and as a result both of these bridges were designed by men whose earlier works were constructed in New York and Massachusetts: the Trenton bridge by Theodore Burr, designer of the first bridge to span the Hudson River, and the Easton bridge by Timothy Palmer, who designed and built the first timber-truss bridge in the United States over the Merrimack River in Massachusetts. Trenton was an ascending manufacturing center and its bridge helped solidify its importance along the route between New York and Philadelphia. Easton–Phillipsburg was initially a small agricultural area, but, through influences such as its bridge, it would become a transportation hub for the steel industry and funnel large quantities of anthracite coal to Philadelphia.

At the same time that these Delaware River bridges were enhancing the route between Philadelphia and New York, bridge construction across the Schuylkill was laying the potential for the expansion of Philadelphia's suburbs, particularly West Philadelphia. The Schuylkill bridges also generally started as ferry crossings. Technically, the first span across the river was a floating bridge at Gray's Ferry, built shortly after the Revolutionary War. However, the first significant bridge (that did not need to be pulled aside for passing ships) was finished in 1805 and designed by Timothy Palmer (who would then go on to build the Trenton crossing). It was known as Palmer's Permanent Bridge at Market Street. A bridge at Spring Street was completed in 1812 in anticipation of traffic from the growing neighborhood of Mantua. At its completion, this Wernwag Bridge was the longest single-span bridge in the world at 343 feet. The ease of access that these bridges provided to neighborhoods that were initially outside the city would be a justification for their inclusion within the city limits set with the 1854 Act of Consolidation.

The need for railway bridges spurred further bridge construction across the Schuylkill River, both in Philadelphia and further upriver. In 1838 Gray's Ferry finally got a proper bridge. Called the Newkirk Viaduct, this was a railway bridge that provided the first direct rail access from Philadelphia to Baltimore. The Philadelphia & Reading Railroad opened in 1842, and its multiple crossings as it stretched from Philadelphia to Reading and into northwest Pennsylvania's coal region (including a major crossing at Norristown) allowed it to compete with the Schuylkill Navigation Company. Its terminus was at the Philadelphia and Columbia Railroad on the west side of the Schuylkill River from which point cargo would be transported to Philadelphia's Reading Terminal via the Columbia Railway Bridge in Fairmount Park.

The bridges over these two major waterways would become more technologically advanced with time. The Pennypack Bridge was a stone-arch bridge, a design suitable for modest-length bridges over rivers that did not have much downriver traffic. Bridges built in the area, starting with the Permanent and Lower Trenton Bridges, were wooden covered bridges, the Permanent Bridge being the first completely covered bridge in the United States. For wide points in a river these bridges could require many spans (the Lower Trenton Bridge had five), which was a hazard during floods and freshets (spring ice thaws) and for timber rafts. An 1841 flood damaged or destroyed many Delaware River bridges. By some accounts only the Easton and Trenton bridges survived.

Beginning in the 1870s covered bridges were abandoned for steel bridges. These were typically suspension bridges but sometimes truss or cantilever bridges. The last wooden bridge built on the river was the Columbia-Portland bridge (upriver at Knowlton Township, New Jersey) completed in 1869. After a particularly bad Delaware River flood in 1903, most of the covered bridges were damaged or destroyed and their respective companies repaired or replaced them with steel constructions. Steel was typically required for a bridge to be able to handle railroad traffic for any length of time and was consequently used at Trenton (after an initial attempt at modifying the wooden bridge with track). Other bridges farther upriver on the Delaware were also modified to permit rail traffic, which enhanced access to markets in the northeast, including New York City.

Just as development in West Philadelphia required bridges in order to handle the increase in traffic, higher levels of commuter traffic across the Delaware drove plans to connect the city directly to Camden. To this end, the New Jersey and Pennsylvania legislatures created commissions that coalesced as the Delaware River Joint Commission in 1919 (later renamed the Delaware River Port Authority in 1931). Its purpose was the building and maintaining of links between the two states. This initially included a single bridge, which was completed in 1926 and named the Delaware River Bridge (later renamed the Benjamin Franklin Bridge). This would expand to include three more bridges: the Walt Whitman Bridge in 1955, the Commodore Barry Bridge in 1974, and the Betsy Ross Bridge in 1976; the Port Authority Transit Corporation (PATCO) Speedline in 1969, a mass transit rail line running between Philadelphia and Camden over the Benjamin Franklin Bridge; and a ferry. The Benjamin Franklin and Walt Whitman Bridges are steel suspension bridges, the Commodore Barry Bridge a steel cantilever bridge, and the Betsy Ross a steel truss bridge.

The initial reports conducted by the Delaware River Joint Commission in preparation for the Delaware River Bridge showed that most trans-Delaware traffic crossed using the ferry that ran between Market Street, Camden, and Market Street, Philadelphia. Furthermore,

FIGURE 32. Opening day on the Delaware River Bridge (subsequently Benjamin Franklin Bridge), July 4, 1926. Perceived as a special boost to its Camden terminus, the bridge prompted hopes the city would become a "second Brooklyn," generating the growth of the city and its surrounding towns. CAMDEN COUNTY HISTORICAL SOCIETY.

they stressed that nearly two-thirds of this traffic originated locally in Camden, numbering 24.6 million passengers per year. Also, a summary of these reports in 1920 showed that the trend was toward an increasing percentage of traffic across the river that was not local. Therefore, a central conclusion was that, at the time of the construction of the first bridge, it was not economical for the commission to construct an elevated rapid-transit system, but that it would be a plan with "attractive features" as traffic patterns shifted in the following decades to higher numbers of long-distance commuters. The bridge itself would act as a catalyst for these trends.

After the completion of the Benjamin Franklin Bridge, demand grew for a connection across the Delaware River between New Jersey and Delaware. A ferry service started in 1926 to meet this demand almost immediately generated a traffic bottleneck with reported automobile lines of up to four miles long on both sides of the river. Despite this, it was not until 1940 that the Delaware General Assembly studied the possibility of a bridge. The project lagged due to World War II, but in 1947 the Delaware River Crossing Division formed and began construction of the Delaware Memorial Bridge. It was completed in 1951, making it the second bridge across the Delaware in the Greater Philadelphia area.

From the Delaware Memorial Bridge's inception, actual usage far exceeded the estimated projections of traffic. This was due in part to its strategic location on the north-south route between New York and Washington, as well as its connection to major highways running west. While the Benjamin Franklin Bridge had made it possible for automobile travelers to reach New York without having to use a ferry, now it was possible to avoid traveling through Philadelphia altogether. In 1962 the Delaware River and Bay Authority was created to enhance the first span and build a second, making it a twin suspension bridge, which was completed in 1968.

Further development south of Philadelphia was spurred with the opening of the Walt Whitman Bridge in 1957. It was initially conceived by the Delaware River Port Authority as a way to reduce traffic on the Benjamin Franklin Bridge and provide an alternative route to South Jersey shore communities. However, at the thirtieth-anniversary ceremony of the bridge's opening commenters noted that while originally many viewed the bridge as just another route to the shore, its larger consequence was to stimulate growth in southeastern Pennsylvania and southern New Jersey. Migrant workers had easier transport between South Philadelphia and southern New Jersey farms, and many ultimately relocated outside of the Philadelphia area. Furthermore, after its construction, the bridge was connected to the Schuylkill Expressway, opening a major route west of the Delaware. The bridge also helped spur the establishment of the Food Distribution Center, the South Philadelphia sports complex, and the expanded use of Philadelphia International Airport.

The Delaware River Port Authority and the Delaware River Joint Toll Bridge Commission (DRJTBC) assumed responsibility for the majority of bridges crossing the Delaware between Pennsylvania and New Jersey. Launched as the Commission for Elimination of Toll Bridges, the DRJTBC was created for two reasons. It would purchase toll bridges along the Delaware River and convert them to free bridge crossings and use equal annual subsidies from both states to maintain the bridges. From 1920 to 1934 the commission purchased, repaired, and consolidated many bridge crossings on the river. In 1934 it was replaced with the DRJTBC, with responsibility to maintain a total of twelve toll-free bridges out of joint tax subsidies and maintain eight toll bridges including the Easton–Phillipsburg (U.S. Route 22) Bridge and Trenton-Morrisville (U.S. Route 1) Bridge (Lower Trenton Bridge). Although many of these and the Schuylkill's bridges were prompted by a particular need, once completed they had an even greater impact in altering patterns of travel and commerce, thus helping shape the distinct character of the region.

Canals

Christopher F. Jones

Canals transformed the economic and geographic scope of Greater Philadelphia in the first half of the nineteenth century. By providing a cheap and reliable mechanism for shipping goods, these complex technological systems funneled the products of broad hinterland regions to the Quaker City. Although canals delivered a wide variety of goods including farm products, lumber, and manufactured items, one commodity dominated the trade: anthracite coal. Brought to Philadelphia in prodigious quantities, anthracite coal powered much of the city's industrial growth, helping a largely commercial city at the turn of the nineteenth century become the

MAP 3. Canals. For a time, canals laced the region as a primary engine of prosperity. MAP BY MICHAEL SIEGEL.

"Workshop of the World" by 1876. Ultimately eclipsed by railroads, canals were largely abandoned by the early twentieth century, but have been revived in recent decades as sites of tourism and heritage.

Throughout world history, cities have nearly always been established close to rivers to take advantage of their fresh water, ease of transport, and power for mills. Philadelphia was no exception. William Penn founded the city near the meeting of the Delaware and Schuylkill Rivers, thereby positioning Philadelphia to benefit from both waterways. In their natural state, the Delaware and Schuylkill allowed modest levels of lumber and farm products to be floated to Philadelphia when water levels were high (typically during the spring and fall) but only allowed goods to travel downstream above the falls in Trenton. As Philadelphia and its hinterlands expanded in population in the late eighteenth century, a number of politicians, merchants, and farmers sought a more reliable method of intraregional transport that would support larger boats and facilitate two-way traffic.

The incredibly challenging nature of building a canal, however, stymied most early efforts. Canals were not simply large ditches that could be dug and then filled with water. They were complex technological systems requiring locks and dams, underwater cements, storage reservoirs, and regular maintenance. When Benjamin Franklin led an effort in the late eighteenth century to improve the Schuylkill River, for example, his party was only able to remove a few troublesome rocks from the riverbed. Seven attempts to improve the Lehigh River failed before Josiah White created a working system in 1820. Canals were among the most expensive and challenging endeavors of their day, and many of America's first engineers learned their trade while struggling to tame waterways.

The dreams of Philadelphia's canal boosters finally became reality in the 1820s. In 1815—the same time that New Yorkers begin aggressively soliciting funding for the Erie Canal—the Pennsylvania legislature granted a charter to the Schuylkill Navigation Company to build a canal system extending over one hundred miles from Philadelphia to Pottsville. Its directors ambitiously hoped to complete the first sections in a few years at a cost of $500,000, but ultimately ten years would pass before the canal was complete and the final price tag exceeded $2 million. Without being bailed out in 1823 by Philadelphia's richest citizen, Stephen Girard, the project likely would have failed. A more economical option was pursued on the Lehigh River, led by Josiah White, beginning in 1817. Because the enterprise was primarily oriented toward the downriver transport of coal, White set up a one-way transport network that opened in 1820 and cost less than $200,000 to build. Once the level of trade expanded, a full canal system allowing two-way traffic was built between 1827 and 1829 at a cost of approximately $700,000. Other important canals in the Greater Philadelphia region included the Delaware Division (built 1829–32), which complemented the Lehigh Canal in delivering goods to Philadelphia, as well as several competitors that delivered anthracite coal to the New York Harbor, including the Delaware and Hudson (built 1825–28), Morris (built 1824–31), and Delaware and Raritan (built 1830–34) Canals.

Boosters imagined that engineers directed canal construction, but the physical brawn and sweat of thousands of laborers transformed dreams into reality. Canal work was grueling and dangerous. Men taxed their bodies to pull up tree roots, dig trenches, blast stone ledges with dynamite, and reinforce banks. Often this work required them to move in and out of waist-deep water several times a day, thereby exacerbating their exposure to pathogens. As the historian Peter Way argues, the characteristics of canal labor were "strenuous, body-sapping work, crude, deleterious conditions, ubiquitous disease, the lurking spectre of death." This work was performed predominantly by two groups: local farmers, who took short-term contracts to earn money during slow times in the agricultural cycle, and immigrant laborers, often Irish, who could not find other types of work. Canal work was known at the time, as Way observed, as the "roughest of rough work" and therefore was "performed by the lowest of the low." When people had options, they rarely chose the back-breaking labor of digging canals.

Public versus private ownership loomed as a central question in canal construction during the 1820s and 1830s. The immediate financial success of New York's Erie Canal (opened in 1825) led many to argue that Pennsylvania should sponsor canals to facilitate trade, promote the public good, and swell public coffers. Beginning in the late 1820s, Pennsylvania invested

FIGURE 33. Schuylkill Canal, Bridgeport, near Norristown, Montgomery County, ca. 1913. Like many other towns along the canal, Bridgeport utilized the waterway to transport manufactured goods by barge to market. LIBRARY COMPANY OF PHILADELPHIA.

heavily in joint-stock companies authorized to create canals across the state and into the Ohio Valley, hoping the profits of these enterprises would buoy the state's finances. Known collectively as the Main Line of Public Works, in eastern Pennsylvania this included the Delaware Division Canal, parts of the Main Line Canal, and improvements to the Susquehanna River as well as the Philadelphia and Columbia Railroad, which traveled westward and served to connect Philadelphia with the state's main canal network. Unfortunately, state ownership did not yield the dividends its proponents anticipated. Pennsylvania funded so many canal systems in the 1830s that the state acquired more than $30 million of transportation debt by 1841 and ended up defaulting on its loans.

Canals were built in many parts of the nation. The dominant role of anthracite coal as an article of trade—often 75 percent or more of the total traffic—distinguished the canals of Greater Philadelphia from their counterparts elsewhere. Rendered cheap by canals, flows of anthracite increased at an astonishing rate—from thousands of tons in the 1820s to several million tons annually by the Civil War. Due to this high volume of traffic, these canals typically earned higher rates of return than other canals. The Delaware Division, for example, was one of the few profitable lines in the Pennsylvania state canal system. Inexpensive and abundant coal, in turn, helped drive population and industrial growth in the Greater Philadelphia region. Burned to heat homes, power factories, propel steamships, and smelt iron, coal enabled Philadelphia to transform itself from a commercial city of merchants into an industrial powerhouse. By 1838, Philadelphia led the nation in the use of steam engines, and its industrial mix reflected the advantages provided by coal. Whereas New England textile manufacturers focused on activities enabled by waterpower—spinning and weaving textiles—Philadelphia's manufactures focused on processes where cheap heat was an advantage, including bleaching, dyeing, distilling, glassmaking, and metalworking. Canals, coal, and industrial Philadelphia grew together synergistically.

The region's canals also spread the benefits of coal-powered industrialization to a thriving set of towns along their banks. Reading, Phoenixville, Bethlehem, and Allentown are examples of cities that experienced substantial growth due to the fact that canals could deliver raw materials to their factories and then ship manufactured products at low cost to seaboard markets.

Although canal builders were limited by nature's arbitrary distribution of waterways for possible pathways, their choices over which canals to build—and which not to build—reflected human values and self-interests. Canals were competitive weapons, and Philadelphians favored those that connected the city with its hinterland regions. At the same time, they fought alternative projects that might benefit other metropoles. Many farmers in central Pennsylvania, for example, sought the development of a canal along the Susquehanna River that would allow them to easily ship their products to Baltimore. Arguing that central Pennsylvania was part of the "natural" hinterland of Philadelphia, Quaker City merchants worked to block any development that might favor Baltimore merchants at their expense. They were not entirely successful, however. Canals such as the Delaware and Hudson directed coal away from Philadelphia and to New York City. Similarly, the Chesapeake and Delaware Canal (opened in 1829) funneled some of the region's trade to Baltimore. Philadelphia grew its hinterland, therefore, by selective support of canal building.

Beginning in the 1840s, canals faced competition from a new transport system: railroads. Canal and rail interests fought bitterly to gain superiority in the shipment of anthracite coal and other goods, with railroads such as the Reading (built 1833–42), Lehigh Valley (1846–55), and Delaware, Lackawanna, and Western (1849–51) ultimately prevailing by the last third of the nineteenth century. Although this shift in transport technology dramatically altered which organizations profited, its influence on the geography of the Greater Philadelphia region was not necessarily as profound. In many cases, railroads were built right next to canal paths, ensuring a similar geography to the flow of goods.

Canals began a slow decline in the 1870s. However, their eclipse took many decades, and several canal systems maintained operations into the post–World War I era. Even with railroads ascendant, canals often provided price competition that helped lower the cost of all transport services. In many cases, canals offered lower rates to shippers of coal and agricultural goods. Traffic on the Schuylkill Navigation largely dried up by the 1890s, the Delaware and Hudson Canal was drained in 1898, the Manayunk and the Delaware and Raritan Canals ceased operation by the mid-1930s, and the Lehigh Canal followed in the 1940s.

Beginning in the 1950s, several of the region's canals were resuscitated as tourist sites and historical landmarks. Towpaths now serve as bucolic walking trails, and the canal waters and trees along the path provide harbor for many animals. Some old locks have been restored as sites of industrial heritage. For example, the Delaware Division Canal became a state park in the 1950s (now known as the Delaware Canal State Park), several parts of the Delaware and Hudson Canal are now protected by the National Park Service, and some parts of the Lehigh Canal have been preserved starting in the late 1970s, including a section maintained by the National Canal Museum in Easton as part of the Delaware & Lehigh National Heritage Corridor.

Overall, canals played an enormously influential role in shaping the relationships between Philadelphia and its hinterlands during the nineteenth century. Moreover, the legacies of these technologies remain. Even in the modern era of railroad and automobile transport, many of the region's centers of population and industry can still be found in those places initially served by canals.

Main Line of Public Works

Charlene Mires

During the 1820s, seeking to compete with New York and Baltimore in tapping western markets, business and political leaders in Philadelphia pushed for a state-funded canal to link Philadelphia with Pittsburgh. The result, an innovative yet peculiar patchwork of canals and railways known as the Main Line of Public Works, succeeded in moving freight and passengers across the mountainous middle of Pennsylvania. The 395-mile system reduced travel time and spurred growth of towns and market activity along the line, but it proved costly to operate and plunged the state into debt. Within three decades, more powerful locomotives rendered the Main Line of Public Works obsolete.

The impetus for the Pennsylvania canal scheme came largely from the looming threat of New York's state-funded Erie Canal, which began construction in 1817. When completed in 1825, the canal linked the Hudson River to the Great Lakes, thus extending New York City's orbit of trade to all the western interior and vastly increasing that city's competitive edge over Philadelphia. Additional threats to Philadelphia's economic standing lay to the south, where Baltimore benefited from the movement of agricultural products down the Susquehanna River from Pennsylvania's interior. The National Road, a federal east-west road project begun in 1811, also siphoned travel and trade from the southwestern corner of Pennsylvania into Maryland, where it connected with the Baltimore Turnpike.

Facing the loss of economic standing and recognizing the potential for trade as Americans moved west, Philadelphia business and political leaders campaigned for an improved transportation system to span across Pennsylvania. Since the colonial era, Philadelphians had looked west as far as Lancaster—about sixty-five miles away—for trade and travel enabled by the Philadelphia-Lancaster Road (a paved toll road after 1795). They also looked northwest to Reading, established in 1748 along the Schuylkill River. A canal between Reading and the Susquehanna River, discussed since the 1790s, did not come to fruition until 1821. Meanwhile, developments in the early nineteenth century added to Philadelphians' dream of an economic region reaching farther into the interior of Pennsylvania and beyond: the state capital moved from Philadelphia to Lancaster in 1799 and then to Harrisburg in 1812; Pittsburgh grew from the site of a fort into a city; and new western states came into the union (Ohio in 1803, Indiana in 1816, and Illinois in 1818). Whetting appetites for new fortunes, opportunities in the West were growing as steamboats began to ply the Ohio and Mississippi Rivers, reaching the expanding territory of cotton agriculture in the Deep South. What could Philadelphians do to claim a share of the riches to come from the interior? How could they compete with New York and Baltimore, which seemed to be pulling ahead in the race to reach the West?

Matthew Carey, newspaper editor and political economist, launched a vigorous campaign for a state-funded canal between Philadelphia and Pittsburgh. Together with such prominent citizens as Congressman John Sergeant and Nicholas Biddle, then president of the Second Bank of the United States, Carey formed the Pennsylvania Society for Promotion of Internal Improvements. With dues collected from fifty-five members, the society dispatched the architect and engineer William Strickland to England to study the latest in transportation technology. Although Strickland returned with data that included the newest technology, railroads, Carey pushed aggressively for the more time-tested alternative of canals. Petitions, pamphlets, newspaper editorials, and mass meetings added momentum, despite opposition from southern Pennsylvania counties that traded with Baltimore and northeastern counties with economic ties to New York. In 1825, an Internal Improvement Convention in Harrisburg endorsed Carey's preference for a canal, and the next year the Pennsylvania legislature authorized construction of a state-funded Pennsylvania Canal between Philadelphia and Pittsburgh. Adding a note of patriotic nationalism, construction began on the nation's fiftieth birthday, July 4, 1826.

Canal fever faced unavoidable hurdles of geography. Across the breadth of Pennsylvania, the state's major rivers offered good settings for canals, but not continuously and not in a straight line between Philadelphia and Pittsburgh. And how could a canal possibly climb over the Allegheny Mountains? Such barriers did not stop the Main Line of Public Works. After nine years of construction, the system offered a journey that started in Philadelphia, where the new Philadelphia and Columbia Railroad first moved by horsepower from a terminal near Broad and Vine Streets (then the northern city limits) across the Schuylkill via a newly built Columbia Viaduct Bridge. Then, a stationary steam engine pulled the cars by cable up an inclined plane to the top of Belmont Plateau in the area later incorporated into Fairmount Park. Thus

FIGURE 34. Pennsylvania's terrain posed a challenge for the Main Line's engineers, who had to combine canal and railway sections to navigate through the Allegheny Mountains. The Belmont Inclined Plane just west of Philadelphia used a steam-powered winch to haul canal boats up the steep Belmont Plateau, where they were attached to a steam locomotive. John Caspar Wild, ca. 1838. LIBRARY COMPANY OF PHILADELPHIA.

positioned, cars could be joined to a steam locomotive to ride the rails west via Lancaster and down another inclined plane to Columbia on the Susquehanna River.

From Columbia, the journey continued northwest by canal alongside the Susquehanna and Juniata Rivers until the densely forested Allegheny Mountains blocked the way. At this juncture, at the town of Hollidaysburg, the trip required changing from water travel to another system of inclined planes, this one far more extensive than the beginning incline in Philadelphia. The Allegheny Portage Railroad involved hauling cars along a thirty-six-mile sequence of ten inclines and through a tunnel—the nation's first for a railroad—to conquer a 1,400-foot change in elevation. After the trip over the mountains, the Main Line continued by canal from Johnstown to its ultimate destination in Pittsburgh. By the 1840s, the burdens of transferring people and cargo between canals and railways diminished with the introduction of canal boats that could be separated into sections to ride on rail cars when necessary and then reattached to return to the water.

Built at a cost of more than $12 million, the Main Line also extracted human costs as laborers, many of them Irish immigrants, constructed the system's railroads, canals, 174 locks, forty-nine aqueducts, and three tunnels. At a spot in Chester County known as Duffy's Cut, fifty-seven Irish laborers for a contractor building the Philadelphia and Columbia Railroad died during a cholera outbreak during the summer of 1832. Later archaeological investigation revealed blunt-force trauma to some workers and one with a bullet wound.

The Main Line of Public Works succeeded to the extent that it cut travel time between Philadelphia and Pittsburgh from twenty-three days to about four, and it moved both freight and people between Philadelphia and the West. However, it did not restore Philadelphia to its earlier primacy in American trade because it could not compete successfully with the lower costs and easier transit available on the straight-line Erie Canal. Nevertheless, the Main Line brought products such as wheat, flour, whiskey, and lumber into the port of Philadelphia, and it carried manufactured goods from the city to the interior. Along the line, Columbia, Hollidaysburg, and Johnstown became bustling towns. The Main Line's passengers included the English novelist Charles Dickens, the "Swedish Nightingale" singer Jenny Lind, and Jarena Lee, the African American circuit preacher. The system also played a role in the Underground Railroad, as abolitionists including the lumber partners William Whipper and Stephen Smith used their own boats and rail cars to move freedom seekers surreptitiously along the line.

By the 1850s, however, more powerful locomotives made railroads a more feasible option through mountainous terrain as well as a faster alternative to canals. In 1857 the state, deeply in debt from construction of the Main Line and other canals, sold the line to the Pennsylvania Railroad Company. Engineering of the Horseshoe Curve in central Pennsylvania ended the need for the Portage Railroad, which faded, abandoned, into the landscape. The Main Line ceased to exist in its original form, but the name nevertheless survived for the subsequent line of the Pennsylvania Railroad and especially in reference to the elite suburbs that developed along the line west of Philadelphia. Remnants of the system through central Pennsylvania became recreational trails and parks, and tourists could visit the Allegheny Portage Railroad National Historic Site in Southwestern Pennsylvania, some twelve miles from Altoona and managed by the National Park Service.

Although short-lived, the Main Line of Public Works helped to link the Eastern Seaboard to the expanding interior of the United States. At a time when national politicians debated whether the federal government should play a role in "internal improvements," the Main Line tapped state funds for the system sought by boosters of Philadelphia. In the end, though, New York's Erie Canal proved to be more effective—even some merchants in Philadelphia shipped goods to the West via New York rather than bear the cost of multiple transfers on the Main Line.

Omnibuses

John Hepp

One of the earliest forms of public transportation in Philadelphia (and its early suburbs prior to the 1854 consolidation of the city with the county) was the horse-drawn omnibus introduced in 1831. The omnibus, together with the railroad, created the first urban commuters and it effectively became the model for all future street-based public transportation development in Philadelphia.

The omnibus was both a concept and a technology. As a concept, it was simply a short-distance version of the stagecoach that operated on fixed routes, for fixed fares, and without the need for advance reservations. As a technology, the omnibus was a new form of horse-drawn vehicle that allowed for more rapid ingress and egress of passengers. Although the omnibus was "public transit" (in the sense that it was shared), its relatively high fares precluded it from being "mass transit," and the majority of riders in Philadelphia and elsewhere were members of the middle classes and above. Omnibus riders were primarily business owners and senior "clerks" (salaried workers) whose firms were located in the central business district (then centered on Second and Third Streets) and who lived in Southwark, the Northern Liberties, and western Philadelphia. Along with similar people who used the early commuter trains, these were the first Philadelphians who could separate home from work by any appreciable distance.

By 1830, the city and its adjoining suburbs in the county had a population well over 130,000, making it the second largest metropolitan area in the country after New York. As the population expanded northward, westward, and southward from the city's original location along the Delaware River at Market Street, entrepreneurs imported the concept of the omnibus from Paris (where it originated in 1819 and its name was coined in 1828), New York (1827), and London (1829). James Boxall opened the first route in December 1831 on Chestnut Street between Second Street and Schuylkill Seventh Street (modern Sixteenth Street). The service operated hourly and charged a fare of ten cents. From this modest start, omnibus service quickly expanded throughout the city and its immediately adjoining

FIGURE 35. Omnibuses congregated at the Merchant's Exchange at the intersection of Third, Walnut, and Dock Streets, Philadelphia. John Caspar Wild, 1832. LIBRARY COMPANY OF PHILADELPHIA.

suburbs. By the late 1850s over three hundred omnibuses operated over dozens of routes on a regular basis. While fares remained high on many routes (commonly ten or twelve cents), some shorter routes charged lower fares (as little as three cents per trip) and most lines offered annual "subscriptions" (or season tickets) to regular commuters.

Based on evidence primarily drawn from New York, most historians have assumed that the unregulated omnibuses functioned in a rather wildcat manner; the little surviving evidence from Philadelphia in the 1850s, however, indicates a more regular and self-regulated operation with fixed routes on parallel streets. In 1855, the city imposed an annual tax on vehicles used as omnibuses and as this tax nicely coincides with the introduction of street railways in 1858, it allows the tracking of the omnibuses' decline. In 1857, there were 322 omnibuses taxed in the city; by 1859, this had fallen to 59, and reached a mere 1 by 1864. The day of the horse-drawn streetcar had arrived. The rails of the streetcars allowed for smoother and faster transport with fewer horses, and the new technology rapidly replaced the old omnibus as the primary means of transport on most streets.

Streetcars

John Hepp

For more than 150 years streetcars have served the Philadelphia area and helped Center City Philadelphia retain its commercial, retail, and entertainment supremacy in an ever-expanding region. Although the motive power switched from horses to electricity (with

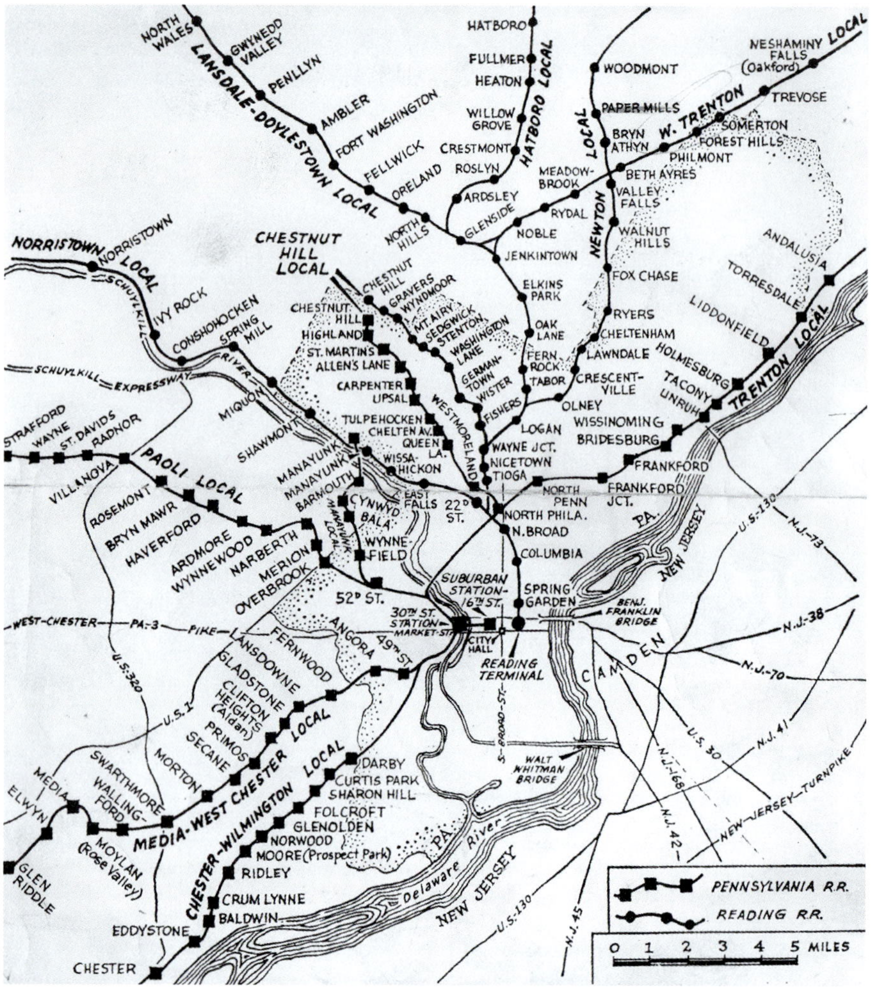

FIGURE 36. Undated commuter map, demonstrating the way rails and roads bound city and suburb. SPECIAL COLLECTIONS RESEARCH CENTER, TEMPLE UNIVERSITY LIBRARIES.

short detours into steam and cable), most change has been evolutionary rather than revolutionary. Perhaps the greatest transformation took place in the early twentieth century when the combination of rising working-class wages and regulated fares allowed streetcars, once a middle-class means of transport, to become a key component of a truly heterogeneous mass transit system. Because of the streetcars' importance to urban life, twice they played key roles in the civil rights movement in Philadelphia.

The first streetcars in the region, running on steel rails and pulled by horses, began operating on the Frankford and Southwark Philadelphia City Passenger Railway on January 20, 1858. Quickly the routes pioneered by the first form of on-street public transportation, the omnibus, became street railways. The steel rails made for a smoother and faster journey for passengers. The result for the operators was an expanded range, and fewer horses and cars were needed to maintain the level of service that the omnibus had provided.

By the early 1860s, streetcars had replaced omnibuses throughout the city. Streetcar fares were lower than those charged by the omnibuses but still remained high enough that most regular riders were middle class or above. Although streetcars were credited with allowing middle-class women to travel freely throughout the city, there were two notable restrictions on patronage in the early years: Black people were not permitted to ride on the cars and there was no

Sunday service. Between 1859 and 1867, after African Americans protested the racial restriction on ridership, a few lines allowed Black passengers (some on segregated cars). Although white passengers in the city voted to continue the racial restrictions, civil rights activists William Still and Octavius Catto moved the debate to Harrisburg and Pennsylvania opened the streetcars to all in March 1867. Also that year, Philadelphia became the last city in the country to institute Sunday streetcar service.

Expansion of Philadelphia's streetcar network allowed middle-class families to move to new residential areas like West Philadelphia east of Fortieth Street and lower North Philadelphia. These developments in areas incorporated into the city by the Consolidation of 1854 became the region's first streetcar "suburbs."

Streetcar service also expanded throughout the region in the 1850s and 1860s. The rails allowed the streetcars to operate in areas where poorly paved or unpaved streets had prevented omnibus service. Trenton, Camden, and Atlantic City in New Jersey had streetcars, as did Norristown and Darby in Pennsylvania.

By the centennial year of 1876, Philadelphia could claim the largest street railway system in the country. Although true, this claim was also a result of the city's many narrow, one-way streets that meant that many streetcars traveled out of the city on one street, then returned on another, thus doubling the length of track in use. But all was not well on the system despite an annual ridership of over one hundred million passengers. In 1872 the Great Epizootic, a fast-moving equine flu, affected most horses throughout the nation. Although many horses recovered, the outbreak caused streetcar operators to consider other means of power. Operators first tried steam engines on the street railways in 1876 and 1877–78, but these were unsuccessful and unpopular.

In 1883 a trio of entrepreneurs, William Kemble, Peter A. B. Widener, and William Lukens Elkins, formed the Philadelphia Traction Company to acquire existing streetcar lines and convert them to cable operation. The higher costs of the cable car infrastructure started the consolidation of the various routes into larger concerns despite restrictions on mergers and cross-ownership (usually avoided by the use of long-term leases and holding companies).

By the mid-1880s, however, the newly invented electric trolley was clearly the technology of the future. Unfortunately, Philadelphia Traction's investment in cable cars and the small size of most other companies contributed to Philadelphia's slow adoption of trolleys (as did safety and aesthetic concerns among the public). Following the conservative Kemble's death in 1891, Widener decided to abandon cable operation for electrification. The first electric line opened in 1892 on Bainbridge and Catharine Streets, and the horse cars made their final runs in Philadelphia just five years later. In 1895 Widener and Elkins formed the Union Traction Company and within three years it controlled nearly all the lines in the city. To help increase off-peak ridership, the company built a large amusement park at Willow Grove in the northern suburbs in 1896. One of the region's other successful amusement parks, Woodside in Fairmount Park, was owned by the Fairmount Park Transportation Company, which operated a popular trolley line through the park from 1897 to 1946.

Starting in the 1890s and continuing for the first two decades of the twentieth century, trolleys expanded throughout Philadelphia's suburbs. Initially from Sixty-Third Street in West Philadelphia (and after 1907 from the Sixty-Ninth Street Terminal in Upper Darby), routes of the Philadelphia and West Chester Traction (later known as the Philadelphia Suburban Transportation Company or Red Arrow Lines) went to West Chester (1899), Ardmore (1902), Media (1913), and Sharon Hill (1917). In Norristown, routes from Berks County and the Lehigh Valley met lines from Philadelphia. Southern New Jersey developed its own intricate systems centered on Camden and Trenton.

The expansion of the lines, combined with the construction of the Market Street Subway-Elevated through West Philadelphia, allowed for streetcar suburbs to become commonplace throughout the region. In the city itself, middle-class development moved steadily in virtually all directions from the core. The Red Arrow Lines allowed for the development of much of Delaware County, and other trolley lines opened up portions of eastern Montgomery and southern Bucks Counties in Pennsylvania. In Camden County, New Jersey, the Public Service Railway owned the bulk of the network that allowed for the development of suburbs like Collingswood and Haddonfield.

In order to build the Market Street Subway-Elevated, the Widener-Elkins interests formed the Philadelphia Rapid Transit Company (PRT) to take over Union Traction in 1902. This new corporation and its financial structure would adversely affect the streetcars. The PRT struggled because of its huge debts and large annual lease payments and, in 1911, following two violent strikes, Thomas Eugene Mitten (with the backing of the banking firm of Drexel, Morgan) took over the company. Mitten began to purchase new cars (known as the "Nearside cars"), modernize the system, and improve both employee and passenger relations. From 1920 onward, however, expansion of the PRT's trolley lines effectively came to a halt as the company switched to using buses and trackless trolleys on new routes.

Although suburban trolley service began to contract in the 1930s as lines closed and were replaced by buses, the PRT system in the city remained largely intact (as did the Red Arrow system in Delaware County). Following Mitten's death in 1929, the PRT struggled again and declared bankruptcy in 1934. Near the end of its existence, the PRT in 1938 placed in service a small number of modern, streamlined streetcars: the PCCs. In 1940 the PRT reorganized as the Philadelphia Transportation Company (PTC) under the control of Albert M. Greenfield, a real estate developer and civic leader, and continued to order PCC cars.

On August 1, 1944, a wildcat strike took place within the PTC to protest the hiring of African Americans in skilled positions (such as motormen and conductors). That protest, the largest U.S. labor action during World War II, lasted for a week and adversely affected war production. The National Association for the Advancement of Colored People moved to end the strike quickly and worked with many community organizations to ensure equal treatment and moderate violence. Because of the strike's impact on war production, President Franklin D. Roosevelt authorized the army to take control of the transit system and five thousand heavily armed soldiers were sent to Philadelphia to end the strike.

After the end of the war, the PTC bought more PCC cars to modernize its existing streetcar system. In 1955, National City Lines (owned by General Motors and oil and rubber companies) acquired control of the PTC and quickly replaced twenty-four trolley routes with buses and abandoned over two hundred miles of track.

Despite National City Lines' efforts, Philadelphia retained a large network of trolleys through the 1970s. In 1968 the Southeastern Pennsylvania Transportation Authority (SEPTA) acquired the PTC and initially made no changes to the existing streetcar network. However, in 1975 a fire at the Woodland car barn destroyed approximately sixty of the PCC cars and this forced SEPTA to shrink its trolley network. Following the purchase of new streetcars for the subway-surface lines in West Philadelphia in the early 1980s, SEPTA retired its PCC cars and abandoned all remaining surface streetcars by 1992. In 2005, SEPTA rebuilt a small fleet of PCC cars and reintroduced streetcar service on its Route 15 between Port Richmond and West Philadelphia via the Philadelphia Zoo.

In the suburbs, very few streetcar lines survived the Great Depression. The notable exception was the Red Arrow system radiating from Sixty-Ninth Street Terminal. Although buses replaced the trolleys to West Chester in 1954 and Ardmore in 1966, the two remaining routes (to Media and Sharon Hill) continued to be operated by SEPTA, which acquired Red Arrow in 1970. Starting in 1981, SEPTA reequipped both lines with a fleet of trolleys similar to the cars used on the subway-surface lines in the city.

Red Arrow Lines

Fallon Samuels Aidoo

The Red Arrow Lines of the Philadelphia Suburban Transportation Company (1936–70) became a national model and local brand of marketable mass transit in the 1950s, when few private companies still built, managed, owned, and operated suburban public transportation services, let alone profited from them. At a time when motor-vehicle commuting forced most transit proprietors into bankruptcy, receivership, or acquisition, the Red Arrow Lines—high-speed railways, trolleys, and electrified and diesel buses operated west and south of Philadelphia by Merritt H. Taylor, Jr. and his family of transit managers—outlasted and outshined most national and local competition.

Paradoxically, the Philadelphia Suburban Transportation Company cultivated loyal ridership of Red

FIGURES 37, 38. Introduced to Delaware County commuters in 1964, Red Arrow's Liberty Liners offered luxury accommodations, including a refreshment lounge and soft music piped into the passenger cars. MONTGOMERY COUNTY HISTORICAL SOCIETY.

Arrow Lines by curtailing services and closing stations it acquired in 1946 from the beleaguered Philadelphia & Western (P&W) railroad and bus company run by A. Merritt Taylor, Merritt H. Taylor, Jr.'s grandfather. Over the next decade, Taylor Jr. reduced train services and servicemen from sparsely populated industrial centers of Chester County, Pennsylvania, like Stafford and West Chester, and added trackless trolleys (powered by overhead wires) and diesel-fueled buses better able to navigate the sprawling towns of Montgomery County such as Ardmore and Haverford. Extensive renovations of Red Arrow–related real estate in Montgomery and Delaware Counties, including the profitable Norristown High-Speed Line's terminals on Sixty-Ninth Street in Upper Darby, Delaware County, and on Main Street in Norristown, made room for back-office operations once assigned to branch offices. The redesign of these art deco structures left them without amenities like restaurants, lunch counters, and barber shops, but postwar residents of Philadelphia suburbs patronized Red Arrow Lines regularly enough to support expansion of the Philadelphia Suburban Transportation Company into New Jersey.

The lean architecture and infrastructure of Red Arrow Lines included a few luxuries that became the Taylor family legacy. Before aerodynamically designed Silverliner trains graced commuter rail lines of the Pennsylvania Railroad Company in 1963, the Red Arrow Lines boasted "bullet trains"—sleek, bullet-shaped rapid transit cars of early modernist style that picked up and discharged passengers every fifteen minutes, every hour of the day, along the 13.7-mile-long Norristown High-Speed Line. These Liberty Liner trains featured vibration dampers and waitstaff, which allowed coffee and tea service during the morning rush hour and beer and wine during the evening rush hour. Less-equipped buses and trolleys earned repeat ridership by traveling in dedicated traffic lanes leading to the Norristown High-Speed Line, express bus stops of the Schuylkill Valley Lines Inc., and rapid transit terminals of the Philadelphia Transportation Company, as well as commuter rail stations of the Pennsylvania Railroad, Reading Railroad, and the Baltimore and Ohio Railroad companies. Together, the styling, synchronized schedules, exclusive rail and road rights, and intermodal connections of the Red Arrow Lines kept the company in business, in the pages of industry periodicals such as *Railway Age*, and in popular television shows like *60 Minutes*.

The financial success of the Red Arrow Lines in the 1950s contributed to Merritt Taylor, Jr.'s decision to abstain from participating in the Southeastern Pennsylvania Transportation Compact (SEPACT) formed by Philadelphia and four surrounding counties in 1961. Taylor, an active member of Delaware County's conservative-leaning political organizations, eschewed public subsidies for replacing rolling stock and denounced public-private partnerships in real estate reinvestment throughout his twenty-four-year tenure as Red Arrow Lines' president. Meanwhile, competitors of the Red Arrow Lines—the Pennsylvania Railroad, Reading Railroad, and the Philadelphia Transportation Company, a local subsidiary of National City Lines Inc.—capitalized on the availability of public funds to cover their ballooning debts and compensate for their reduced ridership. Between 1958 and 1970, Taylor refused to redirect Red Arrow buses and trolleys to commuter rail stations in Media or otherwise participate in projects by SEPACT or SEPTA (the Southeastern Pennsylvania Transportation Authority, formed in 1963) to decrease street traffic and offer discounted direct rail service from the suburbs to Philadelphia's business district.

Taylor's reticence to join government-business compacts of the 1960s preserved his family's political alliances in Delaware County, which also opted out of regional transportation compacts orchestrated by Philadelphia's metropolitan-minded mayors. At the same time, however, the Red Arrow Lines lost revenue to Philadelphia and Montgomery County, which charged the company ever-higher tariffs to use their tunnels, terminals, streets, and bridges. Rather than wait until it could no longer compete against the rail ridership recruitment and retention programs of local, state, and federal transportation authorities, Red Arrow leadership elected in 1970 to sell their stake in P&W to SEPTA at a premium of $13.5 million.

Red Arrow-decorated trains, trolleys, and buses rolled into Upper Darby terminal of the Norristown High-Speed Line for the first time under SEPTA leadership on January 29, 1970. Although authorized by the Taylor family, SEPTA's takeover of Red Arrow Lines sparked a strike lasting more than a month by Red Arrow employees, many of whom had supported the Taylor family's sustained opposition to public management, subsidies, and regulation. SEPTA conceded only temporarily to one of their most expensive demands—retention of the Red Arrow workforce that operated, maintained, cleaned, and stocked the luxurious Liberty Liners. Seven years after SEPTA adopted the Red Arrow legacy and logo, it abandoned them to address pressing problems with service delivery, facilities management, and systems integration throughout southeastern Pennsylvania.

As SEPTA reduced the Red Arrow Lines to essential sites and services, SEPTA's Red Arrow Division grew under its first director, Ronald DeGraw, to include the community-based organizations and anchor institutions that restored or repurposed Red Arrow real estate at SEPTA's behest. Universities, historical societies, and neighborhood and business associations of Montgomery and Delaware Counties such as the Lower Merion Civic Council and Swarthmore College adapted abandoned rail stations to commercial and civic uses. They converted railways to greenways and sponsored transit services such as shuttles to connect new shopping centers with old Red Arrow stations that had survived budget cuts and abandonment in the early 1980s. Now known as "railbanking," such nongovernmental efforts to keep Red Arrow infrastructure and architecture in public use enabled SEPTA, their state sponsor, to retain ownership of land that the Taylor family amassed and reserve the right to reuse or redevelop this real estate at a later date. By the end of the 1980s, SEPTA began to reinstate suburban transit routes and services in sprawling towns that the Philadelphia Suburban Transportation Company once served. With each reactivation of a Red Arrow right-of-way, the landscape of private enterprise once again became integral to public transportation provision in Greater Philadelphia.

Railroads

John Hepp

Although the region's pioneering rail line was built in 1810, it was not until the 1830s that railroads began to play a major role in shaping Greater Philadelphia. At that point, passenger trains began to help define the shape and purposes of the central city and also influenced middle-class residential development in the city's neighborhoods and suburbs. Numerous freight trains linked the region with national markets and helped establish Philadelphia as a "Workshop of the World." The railroad stations in Greater Philadelphia evolved with the industry to serve a wide variety of functions. The vast majority of railroad stations in the Philadelphia region were small and served surrounding local communities, but a few monumental terminals were constructed in Center City Philadelphia and, on a slightly smaller scale, in the region's secondary cities: Atlantic City and Camden, New Jersey, and Wilmington, Delaware.

From the outset, railroads competed with people, horses, and wagons for right-of-way on busy streets in urban areas. Especially after steam locomotives replaced horses as motive power in the mid-1830s, trains running down the center of streets caused a great deal of fear and controversy in Philadelphia and other municipalities. In response to public protests, Philadelphia banned steam locomotives from its streets in 1838. One result of this ban was that railroad passenger stations moved outside the city's pre-1854 boundaries (river to river, between Vine and South Streets) to the then suburbs of West Philadelphia, South Philadelphia, and the Northern Liberties.

The earliest railroad stations in the central city were very small structures that offered minimal services other than ticketing and baggage facilities. Often they combined freight and passenger traffic in one small building. Starting in the 1850s, the newer stations became larger and more architecturally elaborate, but for the most part they offered few additional services. The movement away from these midcentury buildings began in 1876 when the Pennsylvania Railroad (the PRR) built a new passenger station at Thirty-Second and Market Streets in West Philadelphia and the Philadelphia, Wilmington, and Baltimore substantially reconstructed its facility at Prime Street (which later became Washington Avenue) in South Philadelphia to deal with increased traffic generated by the Centennial Exhibition. These two depots were important transitional structures, built largely on the scale of the midcentury termini but with far more complex interiors offering more services, including restaurants. Both these stations fully separated passenger traffic from freight, which typically had not been the case in earlier structures.

FIGURE 39. Postcard depicting the sprawling railroad complex in West Philadelphia, ca. 1910, before the consolidation of tracks and erection of the Thirtieth Street Station in 1933. LIBRARY COMPANY OF PHILADELPHIA.

During the last third of the nineteenth century, railroads assisted in the dramatic physical transformation of the region. By 1900, the region's three dominant carriers—PRR, Philadelphia & Reading (the Reading), and Baltimore and Ohio (B&O)—had built an intricate web of lines that offered passenger and freight service to virtually every community within thirty miles of Philadelphia in Pennsylvania, New Jersey, and Delaware. The busiest lines had frequent and regular passenger service all day long. The railroads also built large freight yards in the major cities and smaller yards in almost every town of any size. The massive Port Richmond terminal of the Reading in Northeast Philadelphia included a freight yard along with coal and grain storage and transfer facilities.

All three systems built impressive passenger terminals in central Philadelphia that served as ceremonial gateways to the city. The main stations of the PRR (Broad Street, which opened in 1881 and was expanded starting in 1892) and the Reading (Reading Terminal, opened in 1893) helped to spur development in Center City and surrounding neighborhoods. These new central stations fully articulated the trends started by the two Centennial depots. Broad Street Station and Reading Terminal were exclusively passenger structures with complex, well-defined interiors offering a multitude of services. Both had large train sheds protecting passengers from weather while they boarded the trains. These train sheds, soaring structures made of glass and steel, were physical manifestations of Americans' love of technology and reflected trends in Victorian architecture and engineering that also characterized the era's world's fairs and new department stores. The elevated approaches to these stations (especially the viaduct to Broad Street Station known as the "Chinese Wall" to generations of Philadelphians) also hindered development in portions of city, as they divided the urban landscape much the way expressways subsequently did.

Because of competition between the PRR and the allied Reading/B&O system in the late-nineteenth and early twentieth centuries, secondary urban centers of the region all had multiple passenger stations that were smaller versions of Philadelphia's grand depots. Cities that had two (or more) stations included Wilmington, Delaware; Atlantic City, Camden, and Trenton, New Jersey; and Chester, Norristown, and Reading, Pennsylvania. Some bedroom communities, like Chestnut Hill and Germantown in Philadelphia, had two stations on competing lines within blocks of each other.

Starting in the 1890s, however, the railroads faced their first real competition for passengers, mail, and freight from the electric streetcars (including suburban lines that connected with the Market Street Subway-Elevated after 1907). Mainline electrification, developed in the first decade of the twentieth century to help railroads compete with these streetcars, became the technology that would eventually define commuter rail service for the Philadelphia region. Initially, the PRR pioneered heavy-rail electrification in southern New Jersey not only because of local needs but as a way to experiment with the technology required for its railroad tunnel to Manhattan under the Hudson River. In 1906, the railroad electrified its underused secondary line between Camden and Atlantic City via Newfield with third-rail technology for both local and through passenger trains. In the next decade, capacity issues at the busy Broad Street Station in Philadelphia helped spur the PRR to electrify its lines to Paoli (in 1915) and Chestnut Hill (in 1918), using what would become the region's standard: overhead catenary. Based on the success of these lines, both the PRR and the Reading electrified other lines in the region through 1933.

The final grand terminal to serve Philadelphia was Pennsylvania Station, opened in 1933 in West Philadelphia. Also known as Thirtieth Street Station, it formed part of a complex that included a new main post office for the city and a distribution center for the Railway Express Agency, a company owned by the railroads that handled high-value express shipments. It was built as part of a PRR scheme known as the "Philadelphia Improvements," a series of projects to improve efficiency by enabling trains to operate more easily through the city. Those projects also included Suburban Station near Sixteenth and Market Streets, so that Broad Street Station could be abandoned and its site and approaches redeveloped as commercial offices. The Great Depression and World War II delayed the full implementation of this part of the plan until 1953.

FIGURE 40. The Baltimore and Ohio Railroad station near Twenty-Fourth and Market Streets, Philadelphia. Completed in 1888, the structure designed by Frank Furness featured special comforts for waiting travelers to make up for the distance from downtown amenities. The railroad ended passenger service to Philadelphia in 1958, and the station was demolished in 1963. FREE LIBRARY OF PHILADELPHIA.

Although the contraction of commuter rail services in the region began in reaction to the trolleys in the 1890s, much of the network remained intact until the Great Depression. Starting in the 1930s, most lines that had not been electrified experienced service cuts. This retrenchment, though delayed by World War II, continued in the 1950s and 1960s as the now struggling railroads sought to slash costs. By the mid-1960s, the only nonelectrified commuter trains operating in the Philadelphia region were those of the Pennsylvania-Reading Seashore Lines, a few PRR branches in southern New Jersey, and the Newtown line of the Reading in Bucks County, Pennsylvania.

In reaction to these service cutbacks, local and state governments became involved in commuter rail traffic starting in the 1950s. In 1960, the City of Philadelphia began subsidizing service and purchasing equipment for use on lines in the city to Chestnut Hill and Manayunk. In 1966, Philadelphia paid for the electrification of the Reading's Newtown line within the city limits to Fox Chase, the first expansion of the electric commuter network in three decades. In 1965, the Southeastern Pennsylvania Transportation Authority (SEPTA) began to coordinate and fund local passenger services in the five counties it served.

In 1968, the PRR merged with its longtime competitor, the New York Central, to form the Penn Central. The company was headquartered in Philadelphia, but just two years later, it declared bankruptcy. One consequence of the Penn Central's insolvency was that many other struggling mid-Atlantic railways were forced to declare bankruptcy (including the Reading). In 1971, the National Railroad Passenger Corporation (Amtrak) took over most intercity passenger trains in the region (except for the Reading's), while in 1976 the Consolidated Rail Corporation (Conrail) acquired the region's freight trains and commuter trains. Conrail was headquartered in Philadelphia and initially Amtrak maintained a key operational hub in the city.

Since the 1970s, government agencies have been responsible for the development of commuter rail service in the Philadelphia region. SEPTA bought new equipment for the lines in Pennsylvania and, in 1983, took over the operation of the former PRR and Reading lines from Conrail. The transition was not an easy one and, after a strike and a period of closure, it took years for SEPTA to recover lost riders. SEPTA opened the Center City Commuter Connection in 1984 that helped create a regional system. It subsequently expanded service on longer-distance routes and opened more park-and-ride stations in the outer suburbs, at the cost of less frequent and more expensive short-distance service. In New Jersey, the rail route to Atlantic City from Philadelphia, closed in 1982, reopened in 1989, with Amtrak initially providing long-distance service and NJ Transit operating local commuter trains that originated in Lindenwold. Since 1995, all service has been operated by NJ Transit. In 2004, NJ Transit opened the River Line between Trenton and Camden. In 2012, DART First State, Delaware's transit provider, purchased its first rail cars ever, for operation with SEPTA coaches on the Philadelphia-Wilmington-Newark line.

Although freight and passenger lines continued to serve the region, Philadelphia declined in importance as a railroad center in 1998 when Conrail was purchased by its two main competitors: CSX (a corporate successor to the B&O) and Norfolk Southern. Although Conrail continued to operate as a jointly owned switching line in the Philadelphia area, for the first time since the 1830s no major railroad company was headquartered in the city.

At the start of the twenty-first century, a wide variety of railroad operations served the Greater Philadelphia region. It remained an important regional transportation hub for passengers and freight trains. The infrastructure of the railroads continued to evolve. Some passenger stations were rebuilt for further passenger use, others became stores, residences, and offices, and still others were preserved for their architectural distinctiveness and their connection to an age when railroads and their stations were the primary mode of transportation in Greater Philadelphia. In 1993, Reading Terminal and its train shed were restored to serve as a gateway to the Pennsylvania Convention Center. Many of the stations in Greater Philadelphia—ranging from small community depots to Pennsylvania (Thirtieth Street) Station and Reading Terminal—have been placed on the National Register of Historic Places for their architectural significance. Throughout the region, abandoned rail lines became trails and bikeways. Remnants of the viaduct that once led to Reading Terminal but was abandoned in 1983 were slowly being converted into a linear urban park in North Philadelphia.

FIGURE 41. On Market Street at Thirty-First Street, West Philadelphia, 1948, elevated trains helped relieve congestion from cars and trolleys between Center City and the Sixty-Ninth Street station, Upper Darby in Delaware County. SPECIAL COLLECTIONS RESEARCH CENTER, TEMPLE UNIVERSITY LIBRARIES.

Subways and Elevated Lines

John Hepp

Philadelphia's subway and elevated network consists of four lines that connect with other transportation options to serve much of the region. Although the network is relatively simple compared with systems in other cities, its history is complex. It took over eight decades to plan and to build, and its construction required a variety of public-private partnerships. Subsequently, public agencies worked to update and to modernize the network.

Agitation for a rapid transit system for Philadelphia began shortly after the Centennial Exhibition of 1876, although a contemporary history of the fair proclaimed that Philadelphia's horse-drawn street railways constituted "the best system of street transportation in the Union." In the 1880s and 1890s, those who wanted better transit often allied themselves with other boosters who sought a "New Philadelphia," and both groups agreed that this should include separating home from work for more Philadelphians by developing rapid transit. Philadelphia and the region experimented with a variety of transportation alternatives at this time, including new steam railway stations in Center City approached by elevated tracks, cable and steam-powered streetcars, and eventually electric trolleys. The extensive electric trolley network provided the city with effective short-distance transportation, and the steam railroad commuter trains gave the region expensive but high-speed, longer-distance service.

Despite all these changes, Philadelphia still faced a rapid transit crisis in 1900. The city was growing fast and lacked adequate high-speed, inexpensive mass transportation to accommodate the growing demands for commuting, shopping, and enjoying parks and other places of recreation. Looking at other cities, Philadelphians could see two possible solutions. London had pioneered the steam-powered subway in 1862 and opened a more practical electrically powered line in 1890. New York City offered the competing vision: it had used steam-powered elevated trains since 1871. Subways were more expensive to construct but less disruptive of the physical environment after they were built, while the cheaper elevated railways were both unsightly and noisy.

After decades of debate, in 1901 Pennsylvania approved a rapid transit ordinance for Philadelphia that allowed for both subway and elevated lines. Franchises were quickly granted, but in the best tradition of machine politics (in this case it was the Matthew Quay machine in Harrisburg), this rapid movement was more about political retribution than urban transit. The William L. Elkins-Peter A. B. Widener syndicate, owners of the near-monopoly trolley company in Philadelphia, had not supported Quay's candidacy in the previous election. The franchises went to political allies of Quay, who eventually transferred them all (at high cost) to the Elkins-Widener group that then raced to complete the lines within five years, as required by the franchises.

Philadelphia Rapid Transit (the final name of the Elkins-Widener property in the city and commonly known as the PRT) promptly started construction on the Market Street line but had trouble raising money because of its large debt from previous transit projects. Eventually in 1907, the PRT and the city negotiated an agreement that gave the city limited oversight of the PRT in exchange for regulatory and subway route changes, including transferring the franchises for the remaining lines to the city. The PRT first began operating the subway-surface cars between Fifteenth Street and the Schuylkill River in 1905. Regular subway-elevated service began on March 4, 1907, between the Fifteenth Street and Sixty-Ninth Street stations, although not all stations on the elevated portion of the route west of the Schuylkill were open initially. This subway service was extended to the Second Street station on August 3, 1908, and a little over a month later the elevated loop that served the ferry termini on Delaware Avenue opened.

This initial line served four important purposes and was a model for future transit development. It dramatically reduced trolley congestion on the streets of Center City. It also allowed the department stores, theaters, and offices of Center City to reach a larger market. It encouraged the residential development of West Philadelphia beyond Fortieth Street and connected with crosstown trolley lines throughout West Philadelphia, opening even more land for development. Finally, it helped establish patterns in suburban development by turning Upper Darby, where the Market Street line interchanged with suburban transportation lines, into a key commercial and transit node.

After the completion of the Market Street line, the city took the lead role in rapid transit planning and funding in the region until the 1960s. It established a Bureau of City Transit in 1912 that created a master transportation plan for Philadelphia. Although most of the proposed lines were never built, this report provided the blueprint for twentieth-century developments.

The city first built an elevated extension of the Market Street line to Frankford in Northeast Philadelphia and began construction at the same time on the city hall station of the proposed Broad Street subway and a Center City subway loop. In 1917, although work continued on the Frankford elevated, it halted on the other lines. The city also purchased the cars necessary to operate the extension and leased both the cars and the line to the PRT, which began operation in 1922. The final two stations in Frankford became transportation hubs that allowed for the development of Northeast Philadelphia. The city next started work on the Broad Street subway. The PRT opened this line between Olney and city hall in 1928 and two years later extended it to South Street. A branch under Ridge Avenue to Eighth and Market Streets opened in 1932.

During the Great Depression subway construction slowed and the only contraction in the system's history occurred. Although the tunnels for the Broad Street line to Snyder Avenue in South Philadelphia were completed in 1933, the line did not open until 1938 because of

FIGURE 42. Traveling on a still-rural portion of Roosevelt Boulevard in about 1926, a No. 206 bus carried passengers toward the Margaret-Orthodox station of the Market-Frankford El. LIBRARY COMPANY OF PHILADELPHIA.

funding issues. The tunnels for the Locust Street line, started in 1917, were completed by 1931, but it did not open until after the war. The Delaware River Joint Commission (now the Delaware River Port Authority [DRPA]) opened a line over what is now the Benjamin Franklin Bridge between Eighth and Market Streets in Philadelphia and Broadway in Camden in 1936, operated by the PRT. In 1939, the PRT abandoned the elevated structure on Delaware Avenue due to declining ridership on ferries that had been relied on to cross the Delaware before the bridge's construction.

Since World War II, only five modifications were made to this system. In 1953, the long-delayed Locust Street subway began operation as part of the Broad Street and Camden systems. The Market Street subway was extended westward under the Schuylkill River to a new portal after the Fortieth Street station and the corresponding section of the elevated was abandoned in 1955. The next year, the Broad Street line was extended one stop northward to a park-and-ride facility at Fern Rock. The most significant change to the system occurred in the 1960s when the underutilized Locust Street line was transferred to the DRPA, which combined it with the Camden line and extended it to Lindenwold, New Jersey (on the route of a lightly used railroad commuter line serving Camden). This Port Authority Transit Corporation (PATCO) line opened in 1969 and featured air-conditioned and computer-operated trains. It helped to further economic development in South Jersey and to maintain Eighth and Market Streets (where it connects with the Market-Frankford subway) as a major transportation and shopping hub in the city. Most of its suburban stations were provided with large parking lots and local bus connections. Finally, in 1973, the Broad Street line was extended southward to Pattison Avenue (later the AT&T station) to serve the sports complex.

Buses

Stephen Nepa

Beginning in the 1920s, the Philadelphia region's independent transit companies added motorized buses (autobuses) to their networks. Superior in comfort to the horse-drawn omnibuses of the nineteenth century and with more range and versatility than electric trolleys, autobuses offered passengers easier means to traverse the metropolitan area.

Prior to the internal combustion engine, mass transit relied on horse-drawn omnibuses (introduced in Philadelphia in 1833) and then streetcars, also called trolleys (introduced in the 1850s and electrified in the 1890s). With the automobile's rising prominence following World War I, many of the private companies then serving the region's commuters purchased gasoline-powered autobuses as a less-expensive alternative to maintaining the costly infrastructure necessary for streetcars. Free from the constraints of rails, motorized autobuses achieved wider geographic scope on the new or expanded roads and highways built for the region's automobiles.

Autobus service within Philadelphia began in 1923, with the first service of the Philadelphia Transportation Company (PTC) running along Northeast Boulevard (later renamed Roosevelt Boulevard). By the late 1930s, buses operated on most major streets of Greater Philadelphia. The Delaware Coach Company (DCC) introduced autobuses in Wilmington in 1925, and the Trenton Transit Company added bus service in 1929. In 1936 the Philadelphia Suburban Transportation Company extended autobus routes between Center City and the Main Line suburbs. The region's school districts instituted their first wood-framed, steel-paneled motorized school buses by the 1930s to improve safety and to phase out "kid hacks" (horse-drawn carriages) from transporting students in rural areas. In 1939, following a recommendation by Columbia University education professor Frank W. Cyr, school buses nationwide adopted the color yellow for safety purposes.

Interstate bus services also came to the region. In 1925, after a series of regional bus line mergers, the Mesaba Transportation Company (renamed the Greyhound Bus Company and incorporated in Wilmington) initiated interstate service in Greater Philadelphia. As a response to Greyhound's growth, National Trailways launched regional interstate service in 1936. To accommodate the transit needs of South Jersey residents commuting to Philadelphia, New York, and other points, Trailways in 1964 initiated service from Mount Laurel, New Jersey; Greyhound commenced service there in the mid-1980s. After the legalization of casino gaming in Atlantic City in 1978, bus companies eager to capture gamblers began daily service, often with discounted fares, from Philadelphia, Wilmington, and Trenton to the resort city.

In the decades after World War II, increased car ownership and suburbanization led many bus companies to consolidate, often under larger public agencies. In 1968, the Southeastern Pennsylvania Transportation Authority (SEPTA) assumed and expanded the autobus lines run by the indebted PTC. The following year, the Delaware General Assembly created the Delaware Authority for Regional Transit (DART) to oversee bus lines formerly operated by the Delaware Coach Company. New Jersey Transit (NJT), created in 1979, acquired bus lines serving Camden, Trenton, and other points in South Jersey.

Buses put an end to many of the region's trolley lines. By the late 1940s, both Camden and Wilmington had replaced nearly all their trolleys in favor of autobuses. Many of Philadelphia's trolley lines were replaced with buses starting in the late 1980s. In 1992, the city's Route 23 trolley, once the world's longest, running from South Philadelphia to Germantown, was suspended and replaced with diesel-powered buses. By 2015, the Route 23 bus ranked as the city's third-busiest transit line, prompting SEPTA to split the route in two. With these mergers and upgrades, autobus lines ultimately provided transportation within and between nearly every area municipality.

With ridership increasing and mounting concerns over fuel costs and emissions, in the early 2000s SEPTA and NJT introduced hybrid autobuses intended to eventually replace their gasoline-powered fleets. Private companies including BoltBus and Megabus began in the 2000s offering low-fare service (with Wi-Fi connectivity) between Philadelphia and other points along the Northeast Corridor. The city's "Chinatown bus," connecting Philadelphia's and New York's Chinese neighborhoods, also offered inexpensive service. Interstate bus companies, such as Greyhound and Trailways, continued to serve the metropolitan area; in 2013, Philadelphia's Greyhound Terminal ranked as the nation's fourth-busiest bus-only terminal, served by regional carriers including Bieber Tourways, Susquehanna Trailways, and Peter Pan Bus Lines.

Though lacking the romance of trolleys and the individual freedoms of the automobile, public and private autobuses provided many in the Greater Philadelphia area with affordable and accessible transportation.

FIGURE 43. At the pump, 1950. SPECIAL COLLECTIONS RESEARCH CENTER, TEMPLE UNIVERSITY LIBRARIES.

Automobiles

Stephen Nepa

Since appearing in the 1890s, automobiles have in many ways shaped Greater Philadelphia's history and geography. Initially a luxury item and later available on a massive scale, cars, while enhancing mobility, required billions of dollars in infrastructure, reordered the landscape of every town and city, and made indelible marks on the region's architecture, culture, and economy.

The automobile, or "horseless carriage," originated in Europe, where in the late 1800s companies such as Daimler-Benz, Peugeot, and Bentley produced limited quantities for niche customers. The first car in Philadelphia, a French import owned by merchant Jules Junker, was registered in 1899. In the early 1900s, brewer Louis J. Bergdoll, Jr., a racing enthusiast, purchased franchises for Philadelphia's first Fiat, Packard, and Benz dealers. Bergdoll and other retailers formed the Automobile Dealers Association of Greater Philadelphia in 1904, the oldest group of its kind in the nation.

By the end of World War I, Philadelphia's "automobile row," anchored by the Albert Kahn–designed Packard Building at Spring Garden Street and stretching along N. Broad Street roughly to Girard Avenue, included carmakers Ford, Cadillac, Studebaker, Hupmobile, and Oldsmobile. Cars also caught on in Wilmington, Delaware, where by 1916, the city's 110,000 residents had fourteen car dealers to choose from. With varied selection and especially following the introduction of Ford's Model T, regional car ownership grew rapidly, prompting journalist Christopher Morley in 1919 to note that Philadelphia's Market Street was "dimmed by the summer haze that is part atmospheric and part gasoline vapor."

For those unable or unwilling to purchase an automobile, auto shows and races allowed people to view cars in terms of style and performance. Philadelphia held its first annual auto show in 1902, the nation's third city (after New York and Chicago) to do so. Wilmington's first show followed in 1916, with more than one hundred thousand attendees viewing cars at the Hotel du Pont. Starting in the early 1900s, auto racing competitions were held throughout the metropolitan area. The Trenton Speedway at Hamilton, one of New Jersey's first, began hosting races in 1900 on its half-mile dirt course. Following enlargement and paving in 1957, the track held NASCAR events until 1972. On an eight-mile, oiled gravel track in Philadelphia's Fairmount Park, the Quaker City Motor Club (whose members included prominent businessmen) ran races from 1908 through 1911. Though popular and drawing spectators from Canada to Paris, the races angered Philadelphia patricians who felt speeding cars disturbed the park's tranquility. Delaware's Wawaset Park hosted New Castle County's first auto races in 1915. Through the 1920s, Wildwood, Cape May Court House, and Longport, New Jersey, held races on the beach during summer months. Other venues included Delaware's Dover Downs (opened 1969) and Long Pond, Pennsylvania's Pocono Raceway (opened 1971), both of which hosted NASCAR races into the twenty-first century.

The advent of the automobile required creative responses from cities formed long before its arrival, including street paving, road building, and traffic-control measures. Paving in Philadelphia commenced in 1894 (Broad Street was the first), yet automobile congestion on the city's narrow blocks led over time to the designation of one-way streets and the installation of kerosene-lit traffic signals (requiring human operation) in the 1910s. Although landscape architect Jacques Gréber's 1917 proposal to alleviate gridlock through an ambitious series of diagonal boulevards across Philadelphia's rectilinear grid never materialized, other built arterials served the purpose, including Northeast (later Roosevelt) Boulevard and Fairmount (later Benjamin Franklin) Parkway. While they may not have alleviated traffic, they increased outlying property values and spurred suburban growth. The 1926 opening of the Delaware River (later Benjamin Franklin) Bridge allowed drivers easy connections between Center City and South Jersey. In Delaware Pierre S. Du Pont, impatient with poor road quality on his daily commute from Longwood, personally financed improvements of the Kennett Pike (State Route 52) to connect central Wilmington with suburban Chester County, Pennsylvania.

Increased car ownership prompted safety concerns. In 1904, due to steam-powered cars' emissions and possible explosion, Philadelphia initiated the Bureau of Boiler Inspection, a forerunner of vehicle inspection. With rising car fatalities in the 1920s, safety campaigns in Pennsylvania, Delaware, and New Jersey led to mandatory vehicle inspection. Penalties for speeding and other violations were addressed in traffic courts. While Philadelphia in the mid-1920s created one of the country's first municipal traffic courts, smaller towns devoted specific days of the week to violations. During Prohibition, Philadelphia's director of public safety, Major General Smedley Darlington Butler, set up military checkpoints to curtail bootlegging and introduced armored squad cars for the city's police force. In Lancaster County, Pennsylvania, the Farmers Anti-Automobile Association, angered by speeding cars, formed in 1910 to set strict rules for drivers using their rural roads.

Greater Philadelphia's motorists required auto-related businesses such as gas stations, repair shops, and parts suppliers. Due to environmental hazards, gas stations were located in urban industrial areas prior to 1920. Yet with roads delivering cars and trucks beyond cities, stations followed. The Lincoln Highway, the nation's first interstate road exclusively for cars, opened in 1925 and passing through Greater Philadelphia, prompted local oil companies such as Sun and Atlantic to open stations along the route. In 1907, Max Paul, an Old City bicycle repairman, opened one of Philadelphia's first car repair shops at 7018 Woodland Avenue; in 1968 Paul's two sons, who inherited the business, opened the city's first Toyota dealership. And in 1921, Pep Auto Supplies opened its first store in Philadelphia. Renamed "Pep Boys" two years later, the company operated forty stores in the region by the mid-1930s.

World War II directly impacted Greater Philadelphians' automobility. Following Japan's invasion of the Dutch East Indies (where the United States procured 90 percent of its rubber supply), local junkyards were scoured for used tires. Additionally, the Office of Price Administration (OPA) stipulated that all "nonessential drivers" could own no more than five car tires. In 1942, the federal government halted all new car manufacturing, established speed limits of thirty-five miles per hour to reduce tire wear, and instituted gasoline rationing. During the war, Philadelphia became notorious for bootlegged fuel. Other measures, such as carpooling and using mass transit, helped conserve valuable resources. Car companies also contributed to the war effort, with Ford's Chester, Pennsylvania, facility assembling tanks and military vehicles and General Motors' West Trenton plant building torpedo bombers.

Greater Philadelphia experienced dramatic automobile-related change after 1945. As suburbanization increased, car manufacturers followed. General Motors and Chrysler opened new factories in Elsmere, Delaware (1947), and Newark, Delaware (1952), respectively. The physical decay of cities such as Philadelphia and Trenton (and their narrow streets) prompted many in the region to move to car-dependent suburbs. At the same time, parking lots and garages were built throughout those cities' downtowns for suburban commuters. Yet not all garage plans materialized. In 1947, the newly created Center City Residents' Association (CCRA) defeated a proposed garage beneath Philadelphia's Rittenhouse Square. In 1950, city council created the Philadelphia Parking Authority to manage lots and garages, but the agency did not oversee on-street parking until 1983.

Driving also led to decreases in mass transit ridership. National City Lines, a shell company created by General Motors, Firestone Tires, and Standard Oil, purchased majority stakes in many U.S. trolley companies, a move intended to phase out the systems in favor of the automobile. Along with National City Lines' acquisitions, inexpensive gas, transit strikes in the late 1940s, and bus lines that provided access to suburbs allowed the automobile to dominate the postwar landscape.

With passage of the 1956 Federal-Aid Highway Act, the area's towns and cities were connected by high-speed expressways, including the Schuylkill Expressway (Interstate 76), the Delaware Expressway (Interstate 95), the Atlantic City Expressway, and the New Jersey Turnpike. New suburbs accessible by highways, such as Levittown, Pennsylvania; Cherry Hill, New Jersey; and Sherwood Park, Delaware, contained slow-speed, curvilinear streets and driveways for homes. Graced further by shopping malls, drive-through restaurants, and drive-in movie theaters, Greater Philadelphia's postwar suburbs reflected the region's continual embrace of the car.

As Greater Philadelphia approached the digital age in the 1980s, highway agencies in New Jersey and Pennsylvania proposed electronic toll collection to reduce bottlenecks. In the early 1990s, the "E-Z Pass" system went into operation on selected highways; by 2015, all area bridges and toll plazas used the system. In the twenty-first century, automobiles, while still the region's preferred method of travel, were challenged by car- and bike-sharing programs in central cities and suburbs, transit-village development, and increased service offered by SEPTA and NJ Transit. As reliance on personal digital devices increased, leading to several fatal accidents, New Jersey and Pennsylvania in the 2010s began issuing penalties for "distracted driving."

While bringing both positive and negative results, automobiles and their many related businesses allowed Greater Philadelphia's residents and visitors personal freedom, faster mobility, and a romantic attachment to the open road.

Gas Stations

Alison Kreitzer

The widespread adoption of the passenger automobile during the twentieth century altered the physical landscape of Greater Philadelphia and the United States. By the late 1910s, gas stations began to serve Philadelphia drivers seeking fuel for occupational and recreational travel. Since consumers could not visually determine the quality of gasoline, petroleum companies distinguished themselves from their competitors by designing gas stations with logos, color schemes, and distinctive architectural styles. These stations proliferated along the region's streets and highways.

FIGURE 44. The Atlantic pyramid gas station with its nighttime lighting as it appeared when new, 1964. Taking advantage of the completion of the Schuylkill Expressway and the subsequent buildup of commercial facilities along City Avenue in Lower Merion Township, Atlantic Refining replaced a boxlike structure with a signature building designed by architect Vincent Kling. Despite community protest, the structure was demolished in 1998. EARL OAKES COLLECTION, ARCHITECTURAL ARCHIVES, UNIVERSITY OF PENNSYLVANIA.

Purchasing gasoline was initially a messy and cumbersome process. Consumers bought gasoline by the bucketful from local garages, hardware stores, or groceries and filled their cars by hand with a measuring can. Sylvanus F. Bowser, an Indiana businessman, invented the self-measuring gasoline storage pump in 1905. Consumers inserted a hose from Bower's contraption into their gas tanks and manually pumped gasoline stored in nearby tanks. Nicknamed "filling stations," gasoline pumps originally lined public streets, but motorists blocked the flow of traffic each time they stopped to refuel.

Off-street service stations with multiple gas pumps allowed petroleum manufacturers to distribute gasoline more safely. Atlantic Refining Company and Gulf Refining Company opened Philadelphia's earliest gasoline stations during the late 1910s. Atlantic hired Pittsburgh architect Joseph F. Kuntz to construct functional yet architecturally sophisticated stations. Kuntz modeled one Atlantic station located at Fortieth and Walnut Streets after a classical Greek temple with columns, white terra cotta tiles, and nighttime lighting.

Easily built and inexpensive prefabricated stations replaced the monumental architecture of the city's initial gas stations during the 1920s. Gasoline manufacturers erected stations that mirrored the cottages and houses located in residential neighborhoods. For example, Gulf Oil opened a brick, Spanish Revival gas station at Twentieth and Arch Streets in 1930. Gas stations expanded their range of services during the Great

Depression by selling tires, batteries, and other automotive products as well as offering repair services to drivers.

Despite the proliferation of gas stations, travel remained a stressful experience for African American motorists, who faced discrimination when they attempted to patronize roadside businesses. This was not the case, however, at gas stations of the Esso brand marketed by Standard Oil of New Jersey (later part of Exxon Corporation) to residents of Pennsylvania, New Jersey, Delaware, and New York during the 1930s. Esso was one of the only gas station chains that openly welcomed African American motorists, who sought out Esso stations for guaranteed service and access to facilities, such as restrooms.

Philadelphia service station owners struggled to supply gas to their customers during World War II. The federal government initiated a national gasoline rationing program in order to conserve gasoline and rubber in December 1942. Philadelphia residents received gasoline coupons based on their driving needs. Priority users, such as doctors, defense workers, and truck drivers, were allotted supplementary gasoline stipends throughout the war. As American men joined the nation's military efforts overseas, female Philadelphians took over key roles as garage attendants at the Atlantic Refining Company's Point Breeze petroleum facility as well as local gas stations.

Following World War II, as Americans purchased automobiles in unprecedented numbers and moved into single-family suburban homes, new service stations provided commuters with convenient places to refuel on the Schuylkill Expressway, at the Pennsylvania Turnpike interchange at King of Prussia (Valley Forge), in the Main Line suburbs, and in downtown Philadelphia. With the expansion of suburban shopping centers, such as Cherry Hill Mall in New Jersey, gas stations multiplied along access roads and highways during the 1960s.

In order to save consumers money, most states moved toward self-service pumps by the 1960s, but not New Jersey, which adhered to its Retail Gasoline Dispensing Safety Act, enacted in 1949. Garden State residents remained opposed to self-service pumps and celebrated full-service gasoline stations as an unusual aspect of New Jersey's automobile culture. As of 2023, New Jersey remained the only state that continued to prohibit self-service pumps.

During persistent gasoline shortages in the 1970s, gas stations became the scene of long lines of motorists waiting to purchase gasoline. After the Organization of the Petroleum Exporting Countries (OPEC) imposed an oil embargo on the United States in 1973 in retaliation for the U.S. decision to aid Israel in the Yom Kippur War, the price of oil per barrel within the United States quadrupled. Left with insufficient supplies of gasoline to meet motorists' needs, stations posted signs to inform customers they were out of fuel.

By the late 1970s, independent and budget-friendly gas stations challenged brand-name gasoline chains throughout the Greater Philadelphia region. Price-conscious motorists increasingly patronized independents, such as Bi-Lo and Skat, because of their lower-priced fuel. Gas stations, including the Kocolene brand, kept prices low by cutting out repair services.

The growing popularity of off-brand and self-service gas stations again altered station design. Gas stations adopted large canopies over their gas pumps to provide customers with quick service and protect them from the weather. Gas stations also constructed rectangular buildings offering grab-and-go food and beverages. Small convenience stores, like Sunoco's APlus chain, became popular gas station staples by the 1980s and 1990s. Along expressways and highways, full-service travel plazas offered motorists brand-named gasoline as well as refreshments from chain eateries, such as Dunkin' Donuts, Burger King, and Dairy Queen. Into the twenty-first century, gas station design and services continued to evolve to meet motorists' changing tastes and needs.

Lincoln Drive

Bradley Flamm

The 4.1 miles of Lincoln Drive that link Philadelphia's northwest neighborhoods to Center City were built in three distinct segments over the course of five decades in the late nineteenth and early twentieth centuries. At its south end, a winding mid-nineteenth-century section along the Wissahickon Creek was originally constructed to provide access to water-powered industrial mills. A middle, City Beautiful–era section, was constructed on top of the channelized and buried Monoshone Creek. And at its north end, a discontinuous section was built to facilitate residential development of the Chestnut Hill neighborhood in the early twentieth century. Lincoln Drive's twisting alignment and complicated character—a single roadway that functions as both a local street and a major arterial—reflect its hydrological origins and gradual evolution from commercial road to parkway to high-volume commuter route.

The first section of Lincoln Drive was a mile-and-a-half-long private toll road known as the Wissahickon Turnpike. Completed in 1856, it ran along the Wissahickon Creek between its confluence with the Schuylkill River, in the East Falls neighborhood, and Rittenhouse Town (also referred to as "Rittenhousetown" in many early sources), a small settlement of mills and residences in the Germantown neighborhood. This earliest section of the road provided access to paper, grist, fulling, saw, and powder mills that contributed to Philadelphia's early industrial development. Inns, such as the Maple Spring Hotel, quickly sprang up along the turnpike to lodge and feed people traveling into and out of the city.

This first incarnation of Lincoln Drive was short-lived, however. Most of the mills along the Wissahickon Turnpike were gone within thirty years of the road's construction. The city's Fairmount Park Commission took title to lands in the Wissahickon River valley in 1869 and 1870 and—to eliminate industrial discharges and protect water quality downstream—razed the mills. Still, the road, renamed Wissahickon Lane in the mid-1880s, remained open to provide access to the city's growing park system and to the southern end of Germantown.

In the late 1890s, Wissahickon Lane was extended one and a half miles from Rittenhouse Town into the Mount Airy neighborhood. The combined length—the newly constructed section and the older mid-nineteenth-century section—was given a new identity by being christened "Lincoln" in honor of the sixteenth U.S. president, though the road was known as Lincoln *Avenue* until an official name change to Lincoln *Drive* in 1931.

This extension of Wissahickon Lane and its renaming resulted from the concurrence of an exceptional opportunity and a growing demand. The opportunity was provided by the construction of a modern sewer system by Philadelphia's Public Works Department. The growing demand was for good roads due to booming sales of the first modern automobiles to wealthy residents of Mount Airy and Chestnut Hill.

Philadelphia's public works department, in just one example of projects occurring across the city in the 1890s, channelized and buried inside sewer pipes much of a small tributary of the Wissahickon called Monoshone Creek (also known as "Paper Mill Run" on some early maps). Then, between 1900 and 1909, the underground sewer was extended into Chestnut Hill and the branch's entire length from Germantown to Chestnut Hill became known as the "Lincoln Avenue Interceptor." This buried stream provided the alignment on which Lincoln Drive was built. (Streams and creeks elsewhere in the city met a similar fate, many of them with names still familiar today because of the roads that were constructed on top of them: Aramingo, Wingohocking, and Tacony, to name a few.) This extension of Lincoln Drive provided a second major roadway connection to Center City. The other was Germantown Avenue, a historic, centuries-old road connecting Philadelphia to Chestnut Hill and to towns and cities to the north and west, including Reading, Allentown, and Bethlehem.

The covering of Monoshone Creek made possible the creation of Lincoln Drive, which provided a route for, and served the functional and social interests of, wealthy northwest neighborhood residents. By the early 1900s Germantown Avenue, still cobblestoned for much of its length, accommodated a busy electric trolley route, making it an inconvenient, uncomfortable, and slow route to use in early cars. Not only did the newly constructed Lincoln Avenue provide a faster route to Center City, it was built to be an aesthetically pleasing parkway in the City Beautiful tradition, an ideal road on which to drive. It complemented the two rail lines already serving the northwestern suburbs.

This conception of Lincoln Avenue in the 1910s and 1920s—as a beautifully designed parkway in keeping with the principles of the City Beautiful movement of the late nineteenth and early twentieth centuries—had a lasting impact on adjacent land uses into the 1940s and 1950s. A few commercial properties were established along Lincoln Avenue/Drive, including gas stations and

FIGURE 45. A postcard, ca. 1910, depicts the s-curve of Lincoln Drive near a pedestrian bridge spanning Paper Mill (Monoshone) Run. LIBRARY COMPANY OF PHILADELPHIA.

automotive garages. But many residents criticized them for being unsightly and out of keeping with the intent of the roadway. Their opposition succeeded in prompting Philadelphia City Council to pass an ordinance in 1930 to prohibit additional filling stations on Lincoln Drive between Mount Airy Avenue and Sedgwick Street. The ordinance was overturned by the Court of Common Pleas the following year, however, because it was deemed an unreasonable and discriminatory prohibition on competition (three gasoline stations already existed nearby). The gas stations remained, but only a few commercial businesses joined them in the following decades and the roadway maintained its primarily residential nature.

Even as the middle section of Lincoln Avenue was being constructed, developers, politicians, and city planners envisioned the extension of the road into Chestnut Hill. There it would connect to Bethlehem Pike and to a proposed bridge over the Wissahickon to link Chestnut Hill to Philadelphia's Roxborough neighborhood and Main Line communities to the west. Pennsylvania state senator George Woodward, son-in-law of Chestnut Hill developer Henry Howard Houston, strongly advocated for the road and bridge investments. The Houston and Woodward families had substantial land holdings in northwest Philadelphia on both sides of the Wissahickon Creek, and faster and easier access to them would have significantly increased their value.

The extension was quickly initiated in the early 1900s, but in an incomplete and discontinuous manner that left a half-mile gap in the road between Allens Lane in Mount Airy and Cresheim Valley Road in Chestnut Hill and saw the road end at Abington Avenue, a half mile short of its envisioned connection to Bethlehem Pike. Although filling in the gaps remained a priority for many in Chestnut Hill, the Great Depression of the

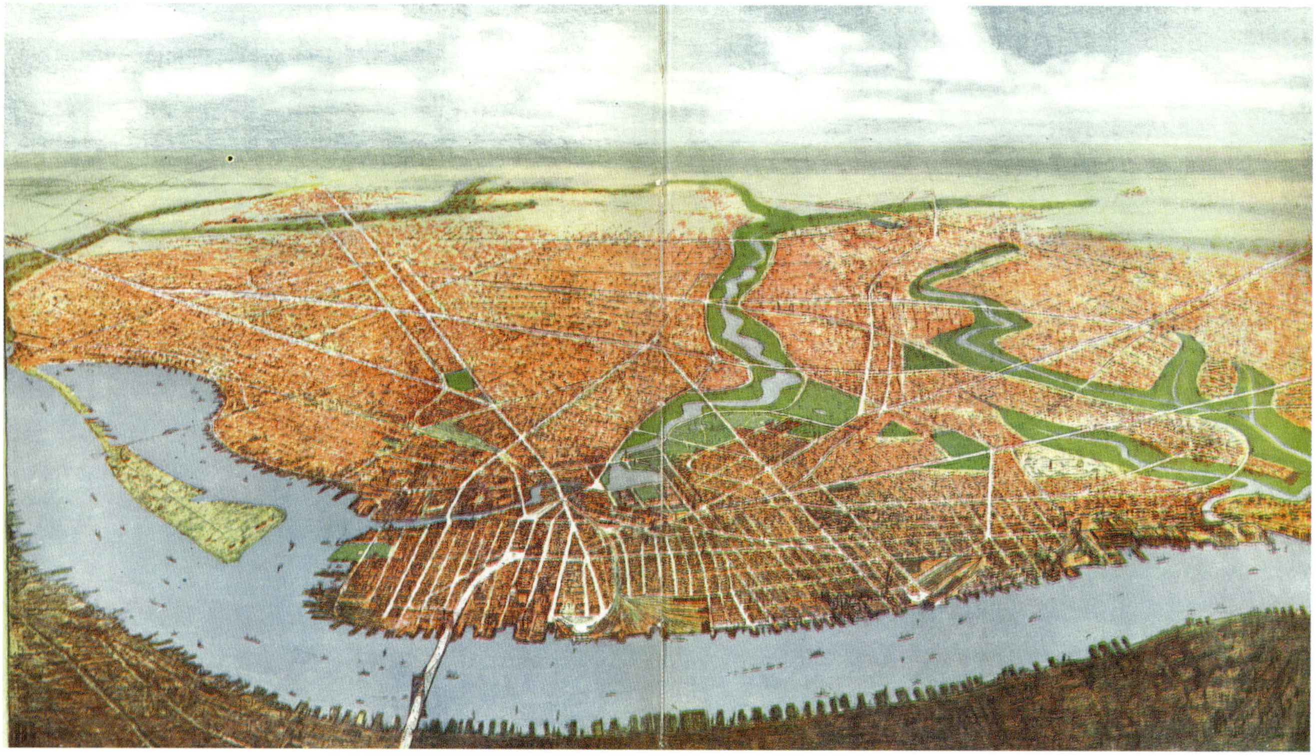

FIGURE 46. Landscape architect and civil engineer Charles Wellford Leavitt's design for a grand approach to the new Delaware River Bridge to Philadelphia, based on the principles of the City Beautiful movement, was envisioned with the hope of creating a "Greater Camden" that would dominate all of South Jersey. *Camden First*, 1924. CAMDEN COUNTY HISTORICAL SOCIETY.

1930s and the war years that followed left the proposals unfunded and unrealized.

In the 1950s, automobile ownership rose quickly and traffic volumes on Lincoln Drive increased rapidly, as they did on roads and highways throughout the city, the region, and the United States. Following public hearings organized by the Philadelphia Board of Surveyors, some roadway modifications to increase vehicle capacity on Lincoln Drive were implemented, such as the widening of the drive from two to four lanes. But eventually, residents and business owners who had come to value the neighborhood's reputation for exclusivity and quiet argued for keeping expansions to travel corridors in Chestnut Hill out of the heart of the neighborhood. In the early 1960s, those arguments won out and city planners dropped proposals for any additional work on Lincoln Drive from official city documents. The northern segment of Lincoln Drive remained a discontinuous and less-traveled section of the road.

By the turn of the twenty-first century, rising car ownership rates and ongoing development in Mount Airy and Chestnut Hill resulted in another change in the character of Lincoln Drive. By 2000, it had become a major route for commuters traveling from the northwestern neighborhoods of Philadelphia to Center City via the drive's southern end, where motorists continued along the Schuylkill River via Interstate 76 (on the west bank) or Kelly Drive (on the east). Traffic volumes rose to a high level: tens of thousands of cars used the southernmost section of Lincoln Drive every day, with volumes tapering down to the low single-digit thousands in the northernmost section in Chestnut Hill. Because of the drive's traffic volumes, narrow lanes, and winding route, buses and large commercial trucks were prohibited from using it.

While Lincoln Drive did not match the traffic volumes or crash counts of Philadelphia's most dangerous roadways, such as Roosevelt Boulevard in the city's Northeast, it developed a reputation for being a risky route. Commuters regularly traveled at double its posted 25 mph speed limit. And serious accidents, some causing major injuries and fatalities, occurred regularly, such as the 1982 crash on Lincoln Drive near Rittenhouse Street that left Philadelphia native and R & B singer Teddy Pendergrass a paraplegic.

None of the 4.1 miles of Lincoln Drive existed before the mid-1850s, nearly two centuries after the founding of the city of Philadelphia by William Penn in 1682, but the eventual road and its alignment became reminders of the economic, infrastructure, and natural histories of the city. The beauty of the southern section's setting along the Wissahickon Creek was impossible to miss, the history preserved in the Rittenhouse Town Historic District evoked the city's industrial past, and the leafy early twentieth-century neighborhoods of Mount Airy and Chestnut Hill illustrated the connection between residential development and investments in transportation infrastructure.

Admiral Wilson Boulevard

Bart Everts

Admiral Wilson Boulevard, a two-and-a-half-mile section of U.S. Route 30 from the Benjamin Franklin Bridge in Camden to the Route 70 overpass in Pennsauken, was the first "auto strip" in the United States. Originally named Bridge Approach Boulevard when it opened in 1926, it was renamed in 1929 to honor Rear Admiral Henry Braid Wilson, a Camden native who served in the Spanish-American and First World Wars. The road had a significant impact on the development of the inner South Jersey suburbs and Camden City in the twentieth century.

When the Benjamin Franklin Bridge (originally named Delaware River Bridge) opened in 1926, the accompanying egress road on the New Jersey side attracted little fanfare. Yet boosters in Camden envisioned Bridge Approach Boulevard as the flagship road in an automotive-centric civic project known as "Greater Camden's Gateway to New Jersey." They hoped the project would elevate Camden's position in the region and make Camden a "second Brooklyn," the hub of southern New Jersey.

To this end, the city hired landscape architect Charles Wellford Leavitt to create an intricate web of highways that would connect Camden to the suburbs all the way to the Atlantic coast. Leavitt was an advocate of the City Beautiful Movement, which advanced the idea that the beautification of cities through parks and monuments would have a positive effect on the morals and behavior of their residents. Leavitt believed the entryway into South Jersey should showcase Camden, and city boosters lobbied for a hotel near the foot of the bridge, as well as a civic center. The remainder of the boulevard, which extended into the suburbs, would feature extensive landscaping and a park with a view of the western tributary of the Cooper River and Camden High School.

It was not long before business interests saw opportunities on the new boulevard that would alter its original civic goals. When it decided to open its first store in Camden, Sears, Roebuck and Company insisted on a location along the boulevard, rather than in downtown Camden. The company and the city struck a deal that modified the original plan for a civic center near the western end of the boulevard, and instead a new Sears with ample parking opened there in 1927. Although the city abandoned the civic center concept, it still influenced the design of the store. Unlike other Sears retail stores it had designed in Boston and Chicago, the architecture firm Nimmons, Carr and Wright adopted the Classical Revival style for the Camden location, influenced by Leavitt and the City Beautiful Movement.

With the opening of Sears, other businesses envisioned opportunities to appeal to the driving consumer on the boulevard. In 1933, Camden native Richard Hollingshead, Jr. opened the world's first drive-in movie theater on the north side of Admiral Wilson. Based on a design he worked out in his driveway, Hollingshead received a patent on the drive-in theater in 1932. The drive-in resonated with an automobile- and Hollywood-crazed public, and Hollingshead's first night showing of *Wives Beware*, in June 1933, was a sellout. In ensuing years, drive-in movie theaters opened all over the country. Unfortunately for Hollingshead, most of the theater owners ignored his patent and he received few royalties from their success. Hollingshead's own theater struggled to make a profit; as an independent theater owner during the studio era he had to pay upward of $400 for each film shown, and many of the pictures had already shown at traditional theaters before he acquired them. Hollingshead sold the theater in 1935 to a Union, New Jersey, theater owner who relocated the screen and equipment to that city.

Other automotive entertainments were attempted on the boulevard, including the "whoopee coaster," a Depression-era attraction in which drivers could take their cars on a series of roller coaster–like tracks. Unlike Hollingshead's drive-in, the whoopee coaster failed to gain national footing.

Businesses continued to grow and expand through the 1950s and 1960s. Several car dealership franchises found success on Admiral Wilson, jointly declaring it "the right route for savings" in a 1952 newspaper advertisement, and motels thrived on both sides of the boulevard. The opening of a bar in 1949 called The Admiral prompted Henry Wilson to unsuccessfully petition the city to remove his name from the boulevard, after which he vowed never to travel on the road again.

In the 1970s a business model that had not been seen before on the boulevard emerged: the go-go club. A Camden City ordinance passed in 1977 restricted businesses related to "prurient interests" to Admiral Wilson Boulevard and banned such businesses from the rest of the city. By the 1980s, adult-themed clubs, hourly rate motels, and other businesses related to sex work dominated the southeastern end of Admiral Wilson. At the same time, Camden's uptick in crime left employees and customers of these businesses vulnerable to robberies, assaults, and other crimes. In addition to the clubs and motels, many sex workers lined the boulevard working outside the sanctioned businesses. As these new businesses thrived, the car dealerships and retail businesses that had been at the heart of the boulevard for much of its existence closed or moved to new suburban locations, following Sears, which left Camden for Moorestown in the early 1970s.

In the 1990s, the State of New Jersey and the Delaware River Port Authority (DRPA) proposed a new plan for the road that would incorporate the original tree-lined design with new development. Called the Gateway Project (later expanded to the Gateway Redevelopment Plan), the proposal called for the destruction of a majority of the businesses on the southeast end of the boulevard, to be replaced by a park along the Cooper River with paths for pedestrians and cyclists.

The plan remained dormant until the national Republican Party announced it would hold its 2000 presidential nominating convention in Philadelphia. Convention planners expected many delegates would stay in hotels in the South Jersey suburbs, using the Benjamin Franklin Bridge and Admiral Wilson Boulevard to commute back and forth to the city. With that prospect in mind, New Jersey's Republican governor, Christie Todd Whitman, seized the opportunity to accelerate the Gateway Project by pledging $45 million to "restore Admiral Wilson Boulevard to the beauty that it enjoyed long ago." Thus, beginning in 1999, demolition of the strip clubs, hourly motels, and other businesses advanced, and by the time the Republican National Convention opened in late July 2000 the south side of Admiral Wilson Boulevard once again resembled the tree-lined road imagined in the original design, with a public park to be completed at a later date. There were exceptions: A new gas station and mini-mart opened on the south side of the road along the Cooper River, and the Sears building remained on the boulevard until it too was demolished in 2013.Throughout the twentieth century, Admiral Wilson Boulevard played a significant role in expanding Camden's retail center from downtown and facilitating the exodus of that center to the suburbs. Originally designed to be a "gateway to Camden," the boulevard became a gateway through the city to both the inner and developing outer suburbs. In the twenty-first century, the boulevard reflects the tree-lined road imagined by Leavitt as well as a new focus on corporate office parks influenced by twentieth-century suburbia. One consistency was Admiral Wilson Boulevard's debt to the driving public. With over one thousand parking spaces, the new office park on the old Sears site would continue the auto-centric nature of the boulevard.

Roosevelt Boulevard

Matthew Smalarz

Snaking its way through parts of North and Northeast Philadelphia, the Roosevelt Boulevard, formally known as the Theodore Roosevelt Memorial Boulevard, has become one of the most heavily traveled thoroughfares in the Philadelphia metropolitan region. Initially

FIGURE 47. The Northeast Boulevard, renamed Roosevelt Boulevard in 1918, spurred construction of single-family homes in lower Northeast Philadelphia. SPECIAL COLLECTIONS RESEARCH CENTER, TEMPLE UNIVERSITY LIBRARIES.

conceived amid political maelstroms during the "corrupt and contented" phase of Progressive Era Philadelphia, "the Boulevard," as it became known, evolved in phases and embodied the complicated planning and political factors, especially following World War II, that went into its convoluted and still unsettled development.

The boulevard's history dates to 1902 when, in a bold effort to continue binding the commercial interests of downtown Philadelphia with the largely untrammeled and unoccupied lands of Northeast Philadelphia following the Act of Consolidation (1854), the mayoral administration of Samuel Ashbridge called for building a modern transportation link to facilitate economic growth and residential opportunities along the proposed corridor. But the incestuous business and political relationships of the Republican Organization, the predominant political machine in Philadelphia, undermined the integrity of the venture from its onset.

Engaging in the sordid practice of "honest graft," the Philadelphia Land Company, which was established in 1902 by well-connected and corrupt organization officials, purchased land extending from downtown Philadelphia to Torresdale through which the modern thoroughfare would be constructed, even though it served no immediate, practical purpose, largely because few inhabitants of the area lived close to the proposed roadway. Because of its close political ties with city officials, the Philadelphia Land Company eventually sold the properties it had acquired from local farmers to the City of Philadelphia for a generous return on its initial investment. Future mayor Rudolph Blankenburg, a highly respected businessmen and civic reformer, criticized the crass process by which the boulevard scheme had been conceived, deeming it the "culmination of Organization effrontery and thievery . . . which is open to curves as crooked as its projectors."

Designated the "Torresdale Boulevard" at its inception—largely because Torresdale would serve as the roadway's northeast terminus—the road developed in phases between 1903 and 1914. To forge the much-sought-after link between downtown Philadelphia and Torresdale, home to many affluent families who might be enticed to patronize the department stores of downtown Philadelphia, the Philadelphia Department of Streets established a right-of-way from Broad and Cayuga Streets to the boulevard, which was renamed the Northeast Boulevard—principally because it did not officially extend to Torresdale upon its initial development—by the time of its official opening in 1914. Over the next four years, real estate interests drove the continued expansion of the boulevard toward Pennypack Creek, largely because they sought to capitalize on the burgeoning, and potentially lucrative, housing market in the lower Northeast. The boulevard underwent one final name change upon the completion of its extension to the Pennypack Creek—making the roadway seven miles long—in 1918, when its principal supporters renamed it the Roosevelt Boulevard, in honor of President Theodore Roosevelt.

As federal and state transportation agencies became more involved in the construction of new highways prior to World War II, the City of Philadelphia gradually relinquished control of the boulevard to federal and state highway authorities. The boulevard therefore slowly grew into part of the nation's transportation infrastructure. With widespread ownership of automobiles and federal oversight of a nationalized highway system following the Federal Highway Act of 1921, the boulevard and its surrounding environment flourished in the 1920s with the construction of new commercial facilities, such as the Sears, Roebuck and Company department store and a mixture of row houses and single-family residences. Formally absorbed into the federal interstate highway system in 1926, the boulevard became part of the newly created U.S. Route 1, a north-south interstate highway stretching from Maine to Florida. Although the boulevard functioned as one of many vital arteries along U.S. Route 1, the federal government ceded control over its local, physical maintenance to the Philadelphia Department of Streets and then, in 1937, to the Pennsylvania Department of Highways (later renamed the Pennsylvania Department of Transportation or PennDOT), which became the primary vehicle for initiating construction projects and obtaining funds from the federal government to finance them.

Following World War II, the Philadelphia City Planning Commission crafted highway policies in collaboration with state authorities that sought to remedy traffic issues and address residential concerns associated with postwar suburbanization and the entrenchment of an automobile culture. In 1947, the planning commission, acknowledging the effects of the automobile on residential decentralization of the surrounding region, announced its plan to build the Roosevelt Expressway to bridge the physical divide between the existing Roosevelt Boulevard and the planned Schuylkill Expressway. As chairman of the commission, Edmund Bacon acted as an intermediary between aggrieved residents and state highway authorities over plans to construct the boulevard extension through densely populated neighborhoods. In 1950, Bacon met stiff resistance from Germantown residents who loathed the extension proposal and lobbied for the construction of a bypass north of the city to keep their neighborhoods free from the possible overflow of traffic congestion on the boulevard. Bacon, however, disagreed with critics of the planning commission's highway program, remarking that such a bypass would only exacerbate, not alleviate, traffic problems inside city neighborhoods.

Although Bacon rejected the residents' overtures for a bypass to divert traffic around their neighborhood, he nevertheless worked behind the scenes to minimize the impact of the extension on local residents. He convinced the Department of Highways to narrow the proposed extension from six to four lanes, which kept five hundred residents from being displaced. The eventual completion of the 3.5-mile Roosevelt Expressway in 1961, however, did little to ease traffic issues on the boulevard, eventually compelling the commission to adopt another plan to relieve traffic snarls besetting the rapidly growing neighborhoods and thoroughfares of Northeast Philadelphia.

The alternative remedy to the traffic quagmires on the boulevard—a proposed Northeast Expressway devised by the Philadelphia City Planning Commission in 1964—met relentless attacks from state officials and Northeast residents. While the boulevard had been expanded into the Far Northeast to accommodate residential expansion and shopping centers in the late 1950s and early 1960s, the Northeast Expressway proposal would have extended 14.9 miles from Hunting

Park in North Philadelphia to Bensalem in Bucks County. An accompanying 9-mile extension of the Broad Street Subway Line also would have expanded public transit options for those living in the Northeast. PennDOT purchased homes along the boulevard during the early 1970s to make way for the expressway, but many residents and activists in the Near Northeast objected, arguing the extension would disrupt residential life and pollute Tacony Creek Park. PennDOT and Philadelphia city officials scrapped the expressway proposal in the early 1980s, daunted by the economic, political, and social hurdles they would have to overcome.

After the demise of the Northeast Expressway proposal, city and state officials worked to improve the quality of transportation and safety along the Roosevelt Boulevard. Attempting to resolve structural problems plaguing the twelve-lane boulevard, in 2003 the Philadelphia City Planning Commission completed the Roosevelt Boulevard Corridor Transportation Investment Study, which explored ways to improve the grading and routing of the boulevard and called for mass transit alternatives to alleviate traffic. In 2008, the Delaware Valley Regional Planning Commission's *Long-Range Vision for Transit* modified some of the ideas in the 2003 study, envisioning, for instance, an extension of the Broad Street Subway and an elevated line along the boulevard to the Bucks County boundary. Far from a settled issue, the ongoing policy debates about the boulevard's development not only remained an outstanding question among city planners and state officials but also reflected the complex forces that brought it into existence over a century earlier.

Vine Street Expressway

Mary Yee

The Vine Street Expressway (Interstate 676), a 1.75-mile depressed limited-access highway traveling east-west across the northern edge of Philadelphia's central business district, resulted from more than sixty years of effort to connect Interstate 95 and Interstate 76 and move traffic more easily between and through the city to surrounding counties in Pennsylvania and New Jersey. Its route through Philadelphia has been important in the imagination of Philadelphia's planners since the days of William Penn, whose surveyor Thomas Holme mapped Vine Street in 1682 as a fifty-foot-wide right-of-way and northern city boundary extending from the Delaware River to the Schuylkill River.

During the eighteenth and nineteenth centuries, Vine Street became lined with a mix of uses ranging from river-related activity at its eastern end, to theaters, saloons, and the Salvation Army near Franklin Square at Eighth Street, to stately town houses farther west. In the 1830s the Philadelphia and Columbia Railroad, running lines west to Lancaster County, operated a rail depot at Broad and Vine. At the Delaware River, the Vine Street Landing was one of the busiest to serve river traffic and a ferry until the 1926 opening of the Delaware River Bridge (later renamed the Benjamin Franklin Bridge). Commercial, warehousing, light industrial, and shipping-related businesses occupied two- and three-story buildings like those still evident in the early twenty-first century along the remains of Vine Street in Old City.

In the twentieth century, public projects and the widespread use of automobiles increased traffic along the Vine Street corridor and its importance as a collector and distributor of traffic. In 1918, the Benjamin Franklin Parkway from city hall to the Philadelphia Museum of Art intersected Vine Street at Twenty-First Street, adding significant traffic. In 1926, the opening of the Delaware River Bridge channeled vehicles onto Vine at Sixth Street. By 1930, the volume forced city officials to consider large-scale traffic improvements. The early proposals for Vine Street included an elevated highway running one-way, with Race Street also elevated and running in the other direction. From 1945 until 1973, plans evolved toward a four- or six-lane depressed highway running west from the Delaware River to the Schuylkill River.

After World War II, national and state priorities that favored interregional connections rather than links within cities delayed the expansion of Vine Street into an expressway. Nonetheless, local government officials and planners continually lobbied for upgrading Vine Street into a limited-access arterial highway. The 1947 "Better Philadelphia" exhibit, created by Edmund Bacon and Oscar Stonorov as a vision for urban renewal, featured a highway system encircling the city with the Vine Street

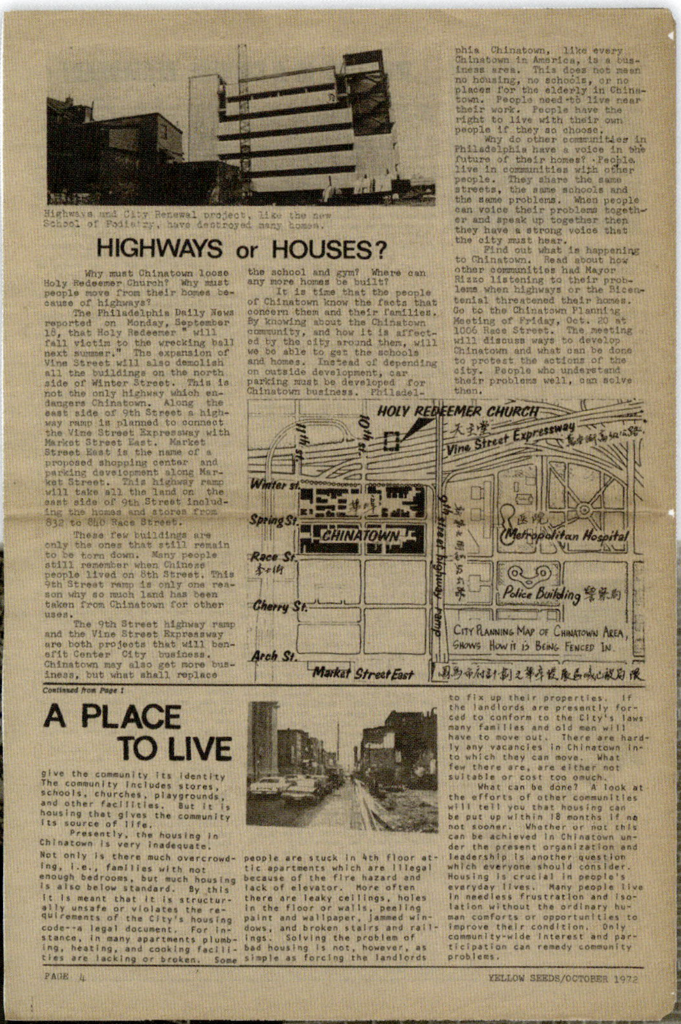

Highways and City Renewal project, like the new School of Podiatry, have destroyed many homes.

HIGHWAYS or HOUSES?

Why must Chinatown loose Holy Redeemer Church? Why must people move from their homes because of highways?

The Philadelphia Daily News reported on Monday, September 18, that Holy Redeemer " will fall victim to the wrecking ball next summer." The expansion of Vine Street will also demolish all the buildings on the north side of Winter Street. This is not the only highway which endangers Chinatown. Along the east side of 9th Street a highway ramp is planned to connect the Vine Street Expressway with Market Street East. Market Street East is the name of a proposed shopping center and parking development along Market Street. This highway ramp will take all the land on the east side of 9th Street including the homes and stores from 832 to 840 Race Street.

These few buildings are only the ones that still remain to be torn down. Many people still remember when Chinese people lived on 8th Street. This 9th Street ramp is only one reason why so much land has been taken from Chinatown for other uses.

The 9th Street highway ramp and the Vine Street Expressway are both projects that will benefit Center City business. Chinatown may also get more business, but what shall replace the school and gym? Where can any more homes be built?

It is time that the people of Chinatown know the facts that concern them and their families. By knowing about the Chinatown community, and how it is affected by the city around them, will we be able to get the schools and homes. Instead of depending on outside development, car parking must be developed for Chinatown business. Philadelphia Chinatown, like every Chinatown in America, is a business area. This does not mean no housing, no schools, or no places for the elderly in Chinatown. People need to live near their work. People have the right to live with their own people if they so choose.

Why do other communities in Philadelphia have a voice in the future of their homes? People live in communities with other people. They share the same streets, the same schools and the same problems. When people can voice their problems together and speak up together then they have a strong voice that the city must hear.

Find out what is happening to Chinatown. Read about how other communities had Mayor Rizzo listening to their problems when highways or the Bicentenial threatened their homes. Go to the Chinatown Planning Meeting of Friday, Oct. 20 at 1006 Race Street. The meeting will discuss ways to develop Chinatown and what can be done to protest the actions of the city. People who understand their problems well, can solve then.

HOLY REDEEMER CHURCH
Vine Street Expressway
11th St.
10th St.
Winter st.
Spring St.
CHINATOWN
Race St.
Cherry St.
Arch St.
Market Street East
9th street highway ramp
Metropolitan Hospital
Police Building
CITY PLANNING MAP OF CHINATOWN AREA, SHOWS HOW IT IS BEING FENCED IN.

Continued from Page 1

A PLACE TO LIVE

give the community its identity The community includes stores, schools, churches, playgrounds, and other facilities. But it is housing that gives the community its source of life.

Presently, the housing in Chinatown is very inadequate. Not only is there much overcrowding, i.e., families with not enough bedrooms, but much housing is also below standard. By this it is meant that it is structurally unsafe or violates the requirements of the City's housing code--a legal document. For instance, in many apartments plumbing, heating, and cooking facilities are lacking or broken. Some people are stuck in 4th floor attic apartments which are illegal because of the fire hazard and lack of elevator. More often there are leaky ceilings, holes in the floor or walls, peeling paint and wallpaper, jammed windows, and broken stairs and railings. Solving the problem of bad housing is not, however, as simple as forcing the landlords to fix up their properties. If the landlords are presently forced to conform to the City's laws many families and old men will have to move out. There are hardly any vacancies in Chinatown into which they can move. What few there are, are either not suitable or cost too omuch.

What can be done? A look at the efforts of other communities will tell you that housing can be put up within 18 months if no not sooner. Whether or not this can be achieved in Chinatown under the present organization and leadership is another question which everyone should consider. Housing is crucial in people's everyday lives. Many people live in needless frustration and isolation without the ordinary human comforts or opportunities to improve their condition. Only community-wide interest and participation can remedy community problems.

PAGE 4 YELLOW SEEDS/OCTOBER 1972

FIGURES 48, 49. Chinatown residents vehemently resisted the Vine Street Expressway, which threatened Holy Redeemer Chinese Catholic Church, shown at its dedication in October 1941. Joining the opposition in circulating this map, *Yellow Seeds* was formed by Mary Yee as a community and political organization to defend Chinatown's integrity, the first of its kind in the area. HISTORICAL SOCIETY OF PENNSYLVANIA.

Expressway as a prominent segment. In anticipation of the expressway, the state widened Vine to ten lanes in 1951. Eight years later, a depressed limited-access section was completed from Twenty-First to Seventeenth Streets as part of construction of the Schuylkill Expressway.

The 1956 Federal-Aid Highway Act, which designated the Vine Street Expressway as an interstate highway (and provided 90 percent federal funding, with the remaining 10 percent funded by the state), also made it feasible to extend the expressway eastward from Seventeenth Street to Interstate 95. This project was strongly supported by the Federal Highway Administration, the Pennsylvania Department of Transportation (PennDOT) and its predecessor agency, and city transportation officials, as well as the Center City business community. However, as the extension came closer to reality in the 1960s, it faced opposition from neighborhood groups. Plans presented in 1966 by PennDOT stressed engineering priorities of providing the most efficient and cost-effective vehicular route. Local residents who attended the plan's unveiling at a public meeting at the Free Library of Philadelphia objected, however, to the ways the highway might damage neighborhoods, citing socioeconomic, cultural, and historic preservation factors.

The Chinatown community adjacent to Vine Street between Ninth and Twelfth Streets faced the most potentially harmful effects. Following release of a draft environmental impact statement in 1977 detailing the effects of the proposed expressway, area residents represented by the Philadelphia Chinatown Development Corporation (PCDC) protested vehemently that the expressway would negatively impact the physical, economic, and cultural character of the neighborhood, compounding the effects of other large-scale projects such as the Gallery at Market East (a mall), the commuter rail tunnel, and "Independence Mall IV," a project that took land by eminent domain in Chinatown along Ninth Street from Arch to Vine. Other unresolved issues included the proposed appropriation of a corner of historic Franklin Square, newly protected by the 1966 federal Historic Preservation Act, and the potential relocation of the Benjamin Franklin Bridge Monument, the subsequent site of Isamu Noguchi's 1984 sculpture at the base of the Benjamin Franklin Bridge. The project also presented complex engineering challenges involving roadways and subway levels at Broad Street and Ridge Avenue and environmental quality problems such as air and noise pollution in the vicinity of schools and residences. These all contributed to the opposition, which stalled the project until 1980.

In 1980, afraid of losing federal funding, Mayor William J. Green III and the secretary of PennDOT, Thomas D. Larson, created a multiagency task force whose objectives were to explore options for the expressway alignment and to develop those which best met transportation, community, and environmental needs. The task force embraced an innovative approach of seeking to balance cost-effectiveness, levels of transportation service, and environmental impacts—in particular, placing a priority on community preservation and cohesion. A public engagement process, which became an exemplar for transportation planners, included efforts to keep the communities along the corridor well informed, to provide ample opportunities for voicing concerns and recommendations, and to assign agency staff with skills in interacting with the public. The process produced revised plans for a scaled-down four-lane expressway, which by this time was all the more necessary because a companion Crosstown Expressway along South Street had been scrapped in the face of community opposition. In 1983, a final environmental impact statement approved by the Federal Highway Administration allowed the Vine Street project to go forward.

When the completed Vine Street Expressway (Interstate 676) opened in 1991, engineers anticipated that thirty-minute peak-hour trips from river to river would be reduced to a few minutes. However, the expressway was adversely affected by conditions at both ends: at its western terminus by the narrow interchange with Interstate 76 and to the east by peak-hour back-ups on Interstate 95 or the Benjamin Franklin Bridge. Extensive delays often resulted. Delays also accompanied necessary repairs and maintenance. In 2009 PennDOT replaced deteriorated concrete along the older segment of Interstate 676, and in April 2015 a four-year project began to replace bridges over the expressway between Eighteenth and Twenty-Second Streets. The Vine Street Expressway continued to be a crucial and integral link in the highway system serving Philadelphia and the region.

Schuylkill Expressway

John F. Bauman

Fully opened for traffic on November 25, 1958, Philadelphia's Schuylkill Expressway was gridlocked from the first day of its operation. Envisioned by city planners as a panacea for economy-suffocating urban traffic congestion, but built on flawed engineering assumptions about traffic flows, the expressway ignored any concern for postwar social and regional realities. Rather than being acclaimed, within years the highway was decried, ignominiously branded the "Surekill Distressway."

Decades before it was built, traffic jammed the narrow streets of 1930s Philadelphia despite the Great Depression, and later the city's World War II–fueled economic revival only exacerbated matters. Postwar pro-growth planners and organizations such as the Greater Philadelphia Movement (GPM) and the Citizens' Committee on the City Plan (CCCP) saw this automobile congestion, together with slums and suburbanization, as draining the city's lifeblood. Well-engineered express highways, they argued, would save the downtown and help restore livable urban neighborhoods.

Highway mania had intensified in 1938 with publication of *Toll Roads and Free Roads*, prepared by the Bureau of Public Roads (BPR). Created in 1918 to free American farmers from the mud, the engineering-oriented BPR in 1938 now advocated a modern urban-oriented highway system that one year later was rendered graphically in General Motors' *Futurama* exhibit at the 1939 New York World's Fair.

After World War II, Philadelphia boosters rallied behind the idea of modern freeways and pressed for a submerged Vine Street Expressway to relieve congestion from traffic flowing into the city from New Jersey via the Benjamin Franklin Bridge. However, Pennsylvania's historically anti-urban state legislature, which controlled both state and federal highway funds, quashed the idea. Instead, momentum built in Harrisburg for an east-west arterial highway in 1947 called the Valley Forge Expressway, connecting Philadelphia with King of Prussia and designed to relieve traffic jams on U.S. Route 30, which served Philadelphia's Main Line suburbs such as Ardmore, Bryn Mawr, and Haverford. Talk of such a highway dated from the 1920s and appeared in the 1931 *Regional Plan of the Tri-State Regional Planning Federation*.

By 1941, the year that President Franklin D. Roosevelt's Interregional Highway Commission proposed a 33,920-mile, federally funded interregional highway system (the Federal-Aid Highway System), the so-called Valley Forge Expressway appeared on Pennsylvania's wish list of modern state highways. Together with the widened and submerged Vine Street and the "Industrial Highway" skirting the Delaware River, the Schuylkill Expressway was featured in planner Edmund Bacon and architect Oscar Stonorov's spectacular Better Philadelphia Exhibit in 1947.

With the Pennsylvania Turnpike nearing completion, Philadelphia's fledgling City Planning Commission in 1947 undertook the Philadelphia-Camden Origin and Destination Survey, whose data officially supported building an express highway following the Schuylkill River from the new Pennsylvania Turnpike exit at Valley Forge into the "heart of Philadelphia."

However, while both the Bureau of Public Roads and Edmund Bacon saw the Schuylkill Expressway relieving traffic congestion regionally, north and south of the proposed multilane highway, as well as east and west, Clarke, Rapuano, Holleran, Hardesty, and Hanover, the engineering firm contracted to design the roadway, interpreted the 1947 origin-and-destination data to alleviate mainly Pennsylvania Turnpike and Philadelphia-generated traffic volumes. They ignored Broad Street traffic and other traffic flowing from Philadelphia's burgeoning northeast where Bacon planned garden-city communities. Nor did Clarke, Rapuano's flawed design grapple any more successfully with the topographical obstacles presented by the rugged, albeit idyllic, Schuylkill Valley terrain as it entered the city limits. Against protest, the historic Schuylkill canal locks and sections of Fairmount Park were sacrificed, and the narrowing of the roadway from six lanes to four as the highway approached Thirtieth Street made a bottleneck inevitable, despite frequent and dangerous turnoffs into Fairmount Park.

Constructed between 1950 and 1959, much of it before the availability of federal funds derived from

FIGURE 50. 1965 aerial view of the Schuylkill Expressway, in the Wynnefield Heights area of West Philadelphia, showing the way the highway followed the path of the river and cut through the adjacent Fairmount Park. FREE LIBRARY OF PHILADELPHIA.

the Federal-Aid Highway Act of 1956, the original Schuylkill Expressway largely predated modern highway standards. By 1962, fatal accidents occurred frequently, and experts identified ten potential deathtraps. In 1970, with federal funds, the state completely redesigned and rebuilt the complex of on- and off-ramps in the vicinity of City Line Avenue and the Roosevelt Boulevard Extension. In the 1980s, the Pennsylvania Department of Transportation added new lanes and rebuilt shoulders along the entire eighteen-mile length of the highway. Long the busiest highway in Pennsylvania, by the twenty-first century the expressway carried 163,000 vehicles daily within Philadelphia County and 109,000 more vehicles daily in adjoining suburban Montgomery County. Its heavy use profoundly impacted the growth of the Philadelphia region. It especially opened the city's western suburbs to intensive residential and industrial development, making Montgomery County, for example, a center of American pharmaceutical industrialism and boosting one of the largest shopping malls in America at King of Prussia. That intense growth, plus the traffic from North Philadelphia and Bucks County flowing from the Roosevelt Boulevard Extension of the expressway, flooded the highway daily with commuter vehicles. Thus, notwithstanding several rebuildings, the Schuylkill Expressway still ranked as one of the most dangerous and congested commuter highways in America in the early twenty-first century, its historic failings attesting to the flawed motivations and assumptions that guided its birth.

Blue Route

James J. Wyatt

Famous for the many protracted conflicts that delayed its full construction for decades, Pennsylvania's Mid-County Expressway, also referred to as the Veterans Memorial Highway and, more commonly, the Blue Route, is the southernmost section of Interstate 476. The expressway stretches through southern Montgomery and Delaware Counties, linking the Pennsylvania Turnpike interchange at Plymouth Meeting with Interstate 95 north of the city of Chester.

Calls for construction of a north-south expressway through Delaware County, southwest of Philadelphia, first emerged during the late 1920s as a new organization created by municipal reformers, the Regional Planning Federation of the Philadelphia Tri-State District, began to work toward a comprehensive plan for the region. Published in 1932, the plan proposed a Delaware County expressway with two route options to alleviate traffic congestion, an outer belt roadway, and a limited access parkway. However, the plans were dropped as the United States became enmeshed in the Great Depression and World War II.

In the immediate postwar years, a large influx of auto-reliant suburbanites further choked Delaware County's roadways and made it increasingly difficult for manufacturers to efficiently transport goods to and from the Chester area. To remedy these problems, the planning commissions of Delaware and Montgomery Counties submitted a joint application in 1955 for a nineteen-mile expressway, which the Southeastern Pennsylvania Regional Planning Association (a public regional planning agency created by the planning commissions of Bucks, Montgomery, and Delaware Counties) quickly approved. Regional planners viewed the project as a core component of a developing highway network that would ease transportation woes, facilitate commerce, help manage sprawl, and keep the Philadelphia region on par with the nation's other major metropolitan areas, most of which constructed similar freeway systems during the era.

The road's prospects seemed to increase with passage of the Federal-Aid Highway Act of 1956, which promised federal funds for up to 90 percent of costs. The highway act transferred responsibility for the expressway to the Pennsylvania Department of Highways (PDH), which then developed three possible routes, labeled Red, Blue, and Green. The Red Route, later redesignated as the Yellow Route, cut through high-population, predominantly working-class communities like Springfield Township in the eastern part of Delaware County. The northern portion of the Blue Route followed the same course but included a separate southern loop that avoided populous areas by cutting westward through the undeveloped Crum Creek Valley and the western edge of Swarthmore College. The Green Route ran farther west than either the Yellow or Blue Routes through mostly undeveloped land.

With most Delaware County residents in favor of a highway but wary of its possible location, the PDH selected the Yellow Route on July 11, 1957, on the grounds that it was the most direct and least expensive course. However, following three months of protests by local residents who feared losing their homes and property tax revenues, the U.S. Bureau of Public Roads rejected the plan and recommended the PDH move the highway's path farther west.

Almost three years later, in June 1960, the PDH chose an alternate Blue Route path that bypassed Swarthmore College. Again the announcement drew protests, as this location threatened newly developed parts of Nether Providence Township and appeared to accommodate Swarthmore College at the expense of nearby homeowners. Swarthmore College president Courtney C. Smith downplayed the accusations and refused to endorse the revised route, but many believed it the result of private negotiations between the college and state officials. Lacking public support, the PDH announced an extended delay for selecting a final expressway route.

In the intervening years, businesses and residents of Delaware County's working-class communities supported the alternate Blue Route plan, believing it would aid Chester's flagging industrial sector. However, many of the county's middle-class and affluent denizens living near the newly proposed path vehemently opposed it. Recalling some of the earlier criticisms leveled at the Yellow Route, anti–Blue Route protesters claimed the expressway would spur declining property values, rising taxes, increasing crime, and the ruination of the Crum

Creek Valley. Angry residents formed civic organizations like the Citizens Council of Delaware County to lead the anti–Blue Route fight and loudly voiced their displeasure at community meetings. Some advocated the PDH revisit the Green Route despite Pennsylvania highway officials' claims that it was located too far from the county's population centers to effectively alleviate traffic congestion.

Despite growing opposition, Pennsylvania governor William Scranton approved a revised Blue Route plan in May 1963. The plan gained federal approval a month later with four contingencies: that the impact on Swarthmore College be reduced as much as possible; that Swarthmore be aided in acquiring land to offset property lost to the highway; that the highway's design preserve the area's natural aesthetic; and that portions of the Crum Creek Valley be made available for public use.

Following final federal approval, the PDH broke ground on the Blue Route in 1966, but acquisition delays and conflicts with local municipalities hindered the project from the start. Several ongoing disputes emerged over locations of the interchanges that would move traffic on and off the highway. Since the expressway's initial plans did not include the interchanges, each required separate negotiations and approvals by the state and affected municipalities. By 1970, less than 10 percent of the expressway had been built, and its estimated cost had skyrocketed from $30 million in 1956 to $173 million.

Anti–Blue Route activists were not alone in protesting an unwanted expressway during the 1960s and 1970s. Grassroots activists successfully prevented the construction of unwanted roadways in Washington, D.C., San Francisco, New York City, and numerous other cities across the nation. In Philadelphia, anti-highway forces successfully prevented the construction of the proposed Crosstown Expressway, a highway project slated to run parallel to the Vine Street Expressway (Interstate 676) near Lombard Street linking Interstate 95, Interstate 76, and Interstate 676, during the 1970s.

As the freeway revolts dragged on, activists increasingly utilized the National Environmental Policy Act of 1969, which required states to file environmental impact statements (EIS) for all federally funded projects, as a tool for combating construction initiatives they opposed. Anti–Blue Route activists adopted these tactics and quickly secured several court decisions that prevented work on most of the approved expressway route during the early seventies. In 1974, Pennsylvania transportation secretary Jacob Kassab ordered the Pennsylvania Department of Transportation (PennDOT) to present an EIS for each section of the Blue Route not already under construction. The decision required additional public hearings and raised the possibility that the project could be abandoned. Delaware County's "Blue Rooters" as well as those opposing the highway turned out en masse for the meetings and ultimately contributed more than 3,900 pages of testimony to PennDOT's final report.

PennDOT submitted the revised Blue Route plan to the Federal Highway Administration (FHWA) in 1978, but a state budget crisis prompted the agency to halt its review a year later. In 1980, Congressman Robert Edgar established a task force to develop a plan for salvaging the project. The subsequent report called for reducing parts of the highway from six to four lanes, shrinking the size of its interchanges, and tying it to mass transit lines. PennDOT adopted the task force's suggestions, and in 1981 the FHWA approved the project. Not to be dissuaded, several local municipalities and citizens groups then filed two lawsuits on the grounds that PennDOT had not adequately investigated less-disruptive routes. The court cases again halted construction and resulted in the completion of a supplemental EIS, which anti–Blue Route activists also contested. Finally, in 1986, the Blue Route's path to completion was cleared by the Supreme Court of the United States, which upheld a Third U.S. Circuit Court of Appeals' decision to allow construction to proceed.

The Blue Route fully opened to traffic on December 19, 1991, thereby completing the network of highways surrounding Philadelphia. At a final cost of $750 million, the Blue Route significantly impacted the western part of the Philadelphia metro area, if not fully in the ways its planners intended. Chester's industrial areas did not experience the economic boost the Blue Route's supporters anticipated, and the nearly thirty years of unpredictable delays prevented Philadelphia-area developers from constructing the sorts of large commercial and retail centers that anchor communities and mitigate sprawl. However, the expressway alleviated traffic congestion on Delaware County's north-south roadways and made it easier for residents to live, work, and shop in the region's western and southwestern suburbs without entering Philadelphia. Several communities located in close proximity to the Blue Route, including Conshohocken and West Conshohocken near the highway's intersection with the Schuylkill Expressway (Interstate 76), experienced rapid development and dramatic economic growth during the 1990s and early twenty-first century. With more than 100,000 motorists using the Blue Route each day in the early decades of the twenty-first century, the highway continued to be a critical factor in the economic and physical evolution of Philadelphia's southwestern suburbs.

Interstate 95

Dylan Gottlieb

Interstate 95—known as the Delaware Expressway in the Philadelphia area—is one of the region's key transportation conduits. Running alongside the western bank of the Delaware River, it links central Philadelphia with Mercer County in New Jersey and Bucks and Delaware Counties in Pennsylvania. Conceived and built in an era when planners promoted automobile traffic above all other considerations, Interstate 95 has played a vital role in Greater Philadelphia's highway network. Yet its history also reveals the costs and benefits of auto-dependent transportation, as individual convenience and economic growth were weighed against neighborhood and environmental destruction.

Planners had been proposing highways through the Philadelphia metropolitan area for decades before construction on Interstate 95 in the Philadelphia region began in 1959. The Philadelphia City Planning Commission issued a design for an expressway along the Delaware River in the late 1930s, but those plans were scrapped due to concerns that it would interfere with the city's shipping industry. After World War II, the Pennsylvania Department of Highways approved similar plans, this time for a toll-funded turnpike. With the passage of the 1956 Federal-Aid Highway Act, the federal government promised to fund 90 percent of the $200 million project, which would be built under direction of local agencies, including the Southeastern Pennsylvania Regional Planning Commission, Pennsylvania's Department of Highways, and Philadelphia's City Planning Commission and Department of Streets.

Designed as part of a planned loop of expressways around central Philadelphia, Interstate 95 was intended to link the city's riverfront with its factories and airport. The City Planning Commission argued that the expressway would "become in effect the conveyor belt of Philadelphia as a producing unit. . . . [I]t will provide access to the piers and the warehouses essential for operation of the port." Planners also hoped that new highways would encourage people to drive downtown from the suburban fringe, helping to revitalize Philadelphia's urban core. Highway planning gave precedence to suburban automobiles—not urban residents or pedestrians. As City Planning Commission executive director Edmund Bacon remarked, "We think it better not to fight with the automobile . . . but rather to treat it as an honored guest and cater to its needs."

When Pennsylvania's Department of Highways unveiled its plans for the expressway in the late 1950s, city residents who lived in its path reacted with outrage. Middle-class residents of Society Hill, a historic area just beginning to undergo revitalization, organized to fight the expressway by forming the Committee to Preserve Philadelphia's Historic Gateway. The committee proposed that Interstate 95 should be built below street grade with a cover to block it from view and preserve pedestrian access to the river. After many years of wrangling, the state agreed to an amended plan in 1969. Instead of a continuous six-block cover, the expressway would be covered in two sections: one from Delancey to Dock Streets and another from Gatzmer to Chestnut Streets.

In Southwark, a working-class neighborhood on the South Philadelphia riverfront, construction of the expressway would prove more destructive. Plans necessitated the demolition of nearly 2,000 row houses and threatened the historic Gloria Dei (Old Swedes') Church. In 1960, Mayor Richardson Dilworth was heckled by 1,500 angry Southwark residents when he attended a neighborhood forum to discuss the highway. The community's protests proved ineffective, however. Unlike the well-connected residents of Society Hill, they were unable to modify the proposed expressway. In 1966, demolition began in Southwark, where Interstate

95 soon became a physical barrier between residents and the riverfront that had once provided jobs for thousands of area longshoremen.

While the city's first section of Interstate 95—a six-mile stretch from Bucks County to Woodhaven Road in Northeast Philadelphia—opened in 1964, delays continued to plague the project. There were contentious battles over where to place entrance and exit ramps in Central and South Philadelphia. Scores of protesters in Philadelphia's Port Richmond neighborhood blockaded the off-ramp at Allegheny Avenue in 1969. The *Philadelphia Inquirer* quipped in 1970 that China's Great Wall had been "built by hand at an average of 31 miles a year" while the Delaware Expressway was "being built by machine at an average of 2.9 miles a year." At that glacial pace, the expressway was finally completed in 1979 (with the exception of a short segment near Philadelphia International Airport, finished in 1985).

Residents of New Jersey's Mercer and Somerset Counties were even more dogged in their resistance to the expressway during the 1970s. Worried that Interstate 95 would bring undesirable development to pastoral Princeton, Hopewell, and Montgomery Townships, wealthy residents banded together to fight the planned highway. In 1983, plans for the final segment of Interstate 95 were scrapped; the expressway, designed to run continuously from Maine to Florida, stopped in central New Jersey. Drivers heading north from Pennsylvania towards New York City were forced to turn onto Interstate 295 south when Interstate 95 ended near Lawrence Township, New Jersey. In 2010, work began on a new link between Interstate 95 and the Pennsylvania Turnpike in Bucks County, which would allow drivers to bypass the interrupted section of Interstate 95 in Mercer County. When completed, the project would finally provide an unbroken highway connection between Philadelphia and New York.

Opposition aside, Interstate 95 ultimately became a vital connection between Philadelphia and its neighboring cities and suburbs. The construction of the highway helped accelerate growth in Bucks County, where the population grew by 30 percent from 1980 to 2012. Developers built sprawling suburbs on former farmland. New business parks sprang up near Interstate 95 exits in Bensalem and Bristol, and by 2009, nearly thirty thousand Philadelphia residents commuted out of the city daily to jobs in the area. Traffic on Interstate 95 grew along with Bucks County. In 1989, 90,000 vehicles per day used the expressway in Pennsylvania. By 2010, the same stretch carried 136,000 cars and 19,000 trucks per day. In the 2000s, Interstate 95 came under criticism again—yet this time its detractors were not neighborhood residents but urbanists concerned with environmental and lifestyle issues. Many Philadelphia planners argued that covering or removing the expressway would restore waterfront access and create acres of new valuable real estate. Inga Saffron, architecture critic for the *Philadelphia Inquirer*, summed up planners' views in 2007 when she wrote that "Interstate 95 must change. Simple as that. . . . Bury it. Narrow it. Put a deck over it. Just get it out of our sight." After a long delay, work finally began in 2023 on an eleven-acre park capping the highway at Penn's Landing. That done, the associated debate over the future of Interstate 95 would continue to expose the growing rift between car-dependent suburbanites and city residents who valued walkability and recreational amenities.

PATCO

John Hepp

The Port Authority Transit Corporation (PATCO) Speedline combined two sets of underutilized transit infrastructure to create a groundbreaking model for regional passenger transportation when it opened in 1969. It was one of Greater Philadelphia's major public transportation successes of the mid-twentieth century. In the early twentieth-first century, however, PATCO struggled to maintain both the infrastructure and relevance of the high-speed rail line from Center City Philadelphia and Camden to Lindenwold in suburban Camden County, New Jersey.

The earliest roots of the PATCO Speedline trace back to the passenger services of the Philadelphia region's two dominant railroads, the Pennsylvania and the Reading. In the late nineteenth century, both systems ran extensive commuter rail operations in southern New Jersey radiating from Camden, with ferry connections to Philadelphia. Many communities, such as Haddonfield, became early railroad suburbs. By the early twentieth century, however, the railroads began

FIGURE 51. The PATCO Speedline in development along a route once used by the Pennsylvania-Reading Seashore Lines looking west toward Collingswood, New Jersey, 1967. SPECIAL COLLECTIONS RESEARCH CENTER, TEMPLE UNIVERSITY LIBRARIES.

to cut back on this service because of competition from streetcars, buses, and automobiles. The completion of what is now known as the Benjamin Franklin Bridge in 1926 sped this decline. The railroads reacted by discontinuing more trains and, eventually in 1933, merging their southern New Jersey systems into one jointly owned company. Despite this combination, commuter train service continued to falter.

The other key portion of what became PATCO was the Bridge Line, a subway that ran between Eighth and Market Streets in Philadelphia and central Camden (crossing over the bridge). Opened in 1936 by a predecessor of the Delaware River Port Authority, the line was owned by the bridge authority but operated initially by Philadelphia Rapid Transit (and later the Philadelphia Transportation Company). In 1951, the long-delayed Locust Street subway in Philadelphia opened and was integrated into the Camden line. Despite numerous adjustments to the schedule, operating hours, and Philadelphia termini, the Bridge Line operated well under capacity for most of its independent existence.

In 1951, Pennsylvania and New Jersey created the Delaware River Port Authority, and among its charges was the creation of an integrated passenger rail system serving Philadelphia and its New Jersey suburbs. Initially the PATCO system was to consist of three lines with a new tunnel under the Delaware River, but by the 1960s the decision was made to construct only one of those lines and incorporate the existing Philadelphia to Camden subway into the system; both were cost-saving measures. The route from Camden to Lindenwold was built on the right-of-way of the railroad to Atlantic City (which had been one of the region's earliest commuter lines).

Opened in 1969, the PATCO Speedline was an immediate success. It was also a model of transit innovation: The trains were among the first to be operated by computer, the line used an innovative advanced fare collection system, and all suburban stations incorporated park-and-ride facilities or coordinated local bus connections. Initially carrying 21,000 riders daily, by the early twenty-first century the number had increased to 38,000. New stations and additional rail cars subsequently allowed ridership to increase. Although most development in southern New Jersey followed the highway system during this period, the PATCO Speedline contributed to the region's economic growth in two key ways. The park-and-ride lots drew suburban commuters from a broad area around the line, and the coordinated rail-bus schedules served both traditional and reverse commuters in the region.

Despite this success and various studies advocating either the extension of the existing line or the construction of one of the other proposed spurs, the PATCO Speedline did not expand, largely due to high construction costs and local opposition. The next addition to local rail transportation in southern New

FIGURE 52. Group bicycling over a canal bridge, Fairmount Park, ca. 1895. LIBRARY COMPANY OF PHILADELPHIA.

Jersey, the River Line, opened in 2004, was not designed to coordinate well with the PATCO system. In the early twenty-first century, PATCO struggled to maintain its equipment and stations and faced decreasing rider satisfaction.

Trails (Recreational)

Silas Chamberlin

An expanding network of recreational paths for walkers, hikers, cyclists, joggers, and commuters serves the Greater Philadelphia region. The first recreational paths date to the mid-nineteenth century, when upper-class residents sought idyllic walking grounds in rural cemeteries and urban parks. In the twentieth century, grassroots hiking clubs built additional footpaths, but by the early twenty-first century governments and large contractors stepped in to create new multiple-use paths with state and federal funding.

Walking, long a necessity of everyday life, also became viewed as a recreational activity in the middle to late nineteenth century. The invention of the telephone, advances in public transportation—first omnibuses, then cable cars and electric trolleys—and the emergence of a middle class that did less physical labor allowed some Americans to reenvision walking as something pleasurable and therapeutic. These potential hikers were also those most likely to be influenced by new ideas about the natural world portrayed in Romantic paintings of pastoral landscapes, Transcendental writings about the spiritual value of nature, and the aesthetics of rural cemeteries such as Philadelphia's Laurel Hill and urban greenways such as Fairmount Park, which contained some of the first designed walking paths. Like many late nineteenth-century Americans, these new walkers formalized their interests by founding clubs.

Hiking clubs—and the trails they built—came relatively late to the Philadelphia region. Early outing clubs, such as the Boston-based Appalachian Mountain Club (1876) and the San Francisco–based Sierra Club (1892), had thousands of members by the time a group of influential newspaper publishers and businessmen founded Pennsylvania's first hiking club, the Pennsylvania Alpine Club, in 1917. Based in Harrisburg, the Alpine Club lobbied the state legislature to enact conservation measures related to outdoor recreation, forestry, and wildlife protection. The club also constructed the Darlington Trail, the state's first modern hiking trail, west of Harrisburg.

During the next several decades, middle-class hikers founded at least a dozen regional clubs throughout Pennsylvania, including the Philadelphia region. In 1928, the Back-to-Nature Club emerged from a series of walks the *Philadelphia Evening Bulletin* organized as part of a "correct posture campaign." The first hikes led groups of more than five hundred people up and down Broad Street before the organizers realized that the hikers would be safer walking along the paths in Fairmount Park, nearby rural roads, and the more distant Appalachian Trail. In 1961, the club constructed the fifty-mile Batona Trail across New Jersey's Pine Barrens.

Other hiking clubs were attracted to trail building even earlier. The New York-New Jersey Trail Conference, originally founded in 1920 as the Palisades Interstate Trail Conference, played an instrumental role in building the early Appalachian Trail from New York City, across New Jersey, and into Pennsylvania. The Philadelphia Trail Club organized regular trips to the Appalachian Trail, some seventy miles to the north, to maintain a section of the rocky, ridgeline path between the Delaware and Lehigh Rivers. In contrast, the Horse Shoe Trail Club, a suburban-based club founded by Henry Woolman in 1934, decided to build its own trail linking Valley Forge to the Appalachian Trail near Harrisburg. In addition to volunteer labor from the region's hiking clubs, Woolman secured assistance from the National Youth Administration for the Depression-era project. As the name suggests, the 140-mile trail was opened to both equestrians and hikers.

In the post–World War II period, the popularity of hiking increased dramatically as new outfitting materials such as nylon and aluminum, dehydrated foods, higher rates of automobile ownership, interstate highway construction, and the expansion of the state and national park systems made hiking more comfortable and convenient. During the late 1960s and early 1970s, the rise of the environmental movement, promoted by grassroots hiking clubs and institutionalized in federal legislation and funding, added new meaning to time spent in the woods. In response to the rising demand, state agencies and volunteer organizations created more and more trails in parks throughout the region.

During the 1980s, a major shift occurred in the region's trail activity, as well-groomed, multiple-use trails appealing to cyclists and walkers of all abilities grew in popularity. In part, the shift resulted from policymakers' evolving understanding of trails' positive benefits for economic development, public health, alternative transportation, and ecological functions such as storm-water management. Greater Philadelphia was well-suited to take advantage of these new ideas. The region's postindustrial infrastructure of abandoned canal towpaths and railroad rights-of-way offered clear, level, and well-engineered corridors for recreational trails.

The Schuylkill River Trail, begun in 1979 by the Schuylkill Greenway Association, followed sections of towpath and railroad beds for 130 miles toward Pottstown, Reading, and beyond. Along the Delaware River, the Commonwealth of Pennsylvania preserved the anthracite-coal canal as a state park in the early 1950s, and, beginning in the 1980s, the towpath was reenvisioned as part of a larger trail system that would follow the Delaware and Lehigh Rivers 165 miles north to Wilkes-Barre. Later studies showed that the two trails combined annually attracted more than one million users and generated at least $25 million for the region's economy. Most trails were shorter in length and relatively local in their impact. In 1978, for example, Montgomery County purchased an abandoned railroad corridor that became the nineteen-mile Perkiomen Trail. It took twenty-five years to complete but quickly became one of the region's most popular trails for walking and biking.

In the early twenty-first century, the trails movement once again experienced a major turning point. A coalition of environmental and bicycle advocacy groups, spearheaded by the Pennsylvania Environmental Council, the Bicycle Coalition of Greater Philadelphia, and the Delaware Valley Regional Planning Commission, successfully advanced a vision for an interconnected, 275-mile network of multiuse trails throughout southeastern Pennsylvania and New Jersey. In 2010, the coalition secured a $23 million grant from the U.S. Department of Transportation to complement nearly $33 million invested by the William Penn Foundation during the previous twenty years. Along with state grants from the Pennsylvania Department of Conservation and Natural Resources, this funding allowed the coalition to fund priority trail projects, brand the emerging network of trails as "The Circuit," and launch a sophisticated fundraising campaign that sought hundreds of millions of dollars to complete more than 450 miles of trails.

EXPLORE MORE

While surviving traces of the trails the Lenape left behind are hard to identify, it is possible to visit one such site in Haddonfield, New Jersey, near the intersection of Kings Highway West and Chews Landing Road. Here, a marker dating from 1906 set in a triangle of land just barely safe from ongoing traffic commemorates a trail that extended from Salem in the south to Perth Amboy in the north.

Traces of early turnpikes and roads remain throughout the region. For a history of the especially important Lancaster Pike, see Charles I. Landis, "History of the Philadelphia and Lancaster Turnpike: The First Long Turnpike in the United States," *Pennsylvania Magazine of History and Biography* 42, no. 1 (1918) and continued in subsequent issues. For a history of the Great Wagon Road, see Parke Rouse, Jr., *The Great Wagon Road: From Philadelphia to the South* (McGraw-Hill, 1973). Much of the original route can still be found in Maryland and Virginia as State Highway 11.

Walk across the Benjamin Franklin Bridge, a suspension bridge across the Delaware River connecting Philadelphia with Camden, New Jersey. The bridge was dedicated at the time of the 1926 Sesquicentennial Exposition celebrating the 150th anniversary of the signing of the United States Declaration of Independence. Pedestrian walkways run along both sides of the bridge, elevated over and separated from the vehicular lanes. In Philadelphia, access to the walkway is located at Fifth and Race Street, across the street from the U.S. Mint. In New Jersey, the walkway can be accessed at Fourth and Pearl Street. The walkway is open daily, weather permitting. Frank T. Dale's *Bridges over the Delaware River: A History of Crossings* (Rutgers University Press, 2003) provides a history of several dozen bridges built during the nineteenth century from the lower Delaware River north into Pennsylvania coal country.

Multiple traces of the effect transportation had on development can be found throughout the region, not the least a drive out Lancaster Avenue from Philadelphia into Chester County, where taverns and mile markers from the turnpike era remain evident amid later business and residential development. One can also trace the many towns and cities boosted by the stimulus canals provided to growth. Although the utility of canals was largely eclipsed by railroads in the early twentieth century, they remain important sites for recreation. In eastern Pennsylvania, one can trace the route of the Schuylkill Navigation Company canal by exploring the Delaware & Lehigh National Heritage Corridor, running from Wilkes-Barre to Bensalem, outside Philadelphia. Within city limits, the canal and its impact can be readily seen in Manayunk. In New Jersey, recreational enthusiasts can follow the path of the Delaware and Raritan Canal along the banks of the Delaware River from Bordentown to Trenton and overland to New Brunswick. The Canal Museum in Easton, Pa., is a good source of information, while the single most authoritative book on the subject is *Routes of Power: Energy and Modern America* (Harvard University Press, 2014) by Christopher F. Jones. See also Robert J. Kapsch, *Over the Alleghenies: Early Canals and Railroads of Pennsylvania* (West Virginia University Press, 2013) and Peter Way, *Common Labour: Workers and the Digging of North American Canals, 1780–1860* (Cambridge University Press, 1993).

For more history of rail development in the region, visit the Railroad Museum of Pennsylvania administered by the Pennsylvania Historical and Museum Commission and located in Strasburg, Pa. The Transit Museum operated by the Southeastern Pennsylvania Transportation Authority at 1234 Market Street, Philadelphia, presents the heritage of the public transportation system that serves both the city and the region. Among its attractions are a 1947 trolley and a transit exhibit chronicling one hundred years of the Market-Frankford Elevated Line known colloquially as "the El." For studies of the two great rivals based in Philadelphia, see Albert J. Churella, *The Pennsylvania Railroad: Building an Empire, 1846–1917* (University of Pennsylvania Press, 2012) and James L. Holton, *The Reading Railroad: History of a Coal Age Empire*, 2 volumes (Garrigues House, 1989 and 1992). George Thomas recounts the aesthetic impact of rail station architecture in city and suburb in *Frank Furness: Architecture in the*

Age of the Great Machines (University of Pennsylvania Press, 2018). For mass transit within Philadelphia, and its effect, see John H. Hepp IV, *The Middle-Class City: Transforming Space and Time in Philadelphia, 1876–1926* (University of Pennsylvania Press, 2003); James Wolfinger, *Running the Rails: Capital and Labor in the Philadelphia Transit Industry* (Cornell University Press, 2016); and Charles W. Cheape, *Moving the Masses: Urban Public Transit in New York, Boston, and Philadelphia, 1880–1912* (Harvard University Press, 1980).

Area residents can still experience a ferry crossing like the one Walt Whitman took many times between his home in Camden and Philadelphia on the Riverlink Ferry, which can be accessed either at Columbus Boulevard and Walnut Street in Philadelphia or 1 Riverside Drive in Camden.

For those interested in the profound effect of the automobile, there is the Simeone Foundation Automotive Museum at 6825 Norwitch Drive, Philadelphia. Among the scholarly articles addressing that subject are chapter 6, "The Planner versus the Automobile," of Gregory Heller's *Ed Bacon: Planning, Politics, and the Building of Modern Philadelphia* (University of Pennsylvania Press, 2013); Raymond A. Mohl, "Stop the Road: Freeway Revolts in American Cities," *Journal of Urban History* (July 2004); and two articles by John F. Bauman: "'The Expressway Motorists Loved to Hate': Philadelphia and the First Era of Highway Planning, 1943–1956," *Pennsylvania Magazine of History and Biography* (October 1991), and "Expressways, Public Housing, and Renewal: A Blueprint for Postwar Philadelphia, 1945–1960," *Pennsylvania History* (January 1990). See also Angus Kress Gillespie and Michael Aaron Rockland, *Looking for America on the New Jersey Turnpike* (Rutgers University Press, 1989). As emblems of automobile culture, gas stations in the modern era are highly standardized, but survivals of a more distinctive approach to these structures can be seen, for instance, in the example of the Pure Oil "Cottage Style" gas station (now closed), at 4431 Lancaster Avenue, Philadelphia, and the Spanish Revival station dating back to 1930, at Twentieth and Arch Streets, Philadelphia, subsequently moved to the Lemon Hill section of Fairmount Park. John A. Jakle and Keith Sculle put such surviving artifacts of an earlier era into context in *The Gas Station in America* (Johns Hopkins University Press, 1994).

Chapter 7

Core and Periphery

Introduction

The modern city coped with competing dynamics. Even as transportation innovation proliferated and settlement extended outward, core investments heightened the central city's hold on its periphery. The construction of Philadelphia City Hall on what was the center square of the city's original plan captured both elements. As the seat of government for an increasingly complex governing structure reaching into ever more lives, the grand building signaled both the symbolic heights of the city's aspirations and the need to abide by its rules ordering the affairs of daily living. Against this centralizing tendency of growing bureaucracy, though, was the growing freedom for residents to live where they wanted, even outside the reach of city government, made possible in large part by the growing transit network that radiated from city hall, among other places.

Before such centrifugal tendencies magnified, and while the growing population still remained largely within the bounds of the consolidated city, critics worried about the health of urban dwellers beset with the difficulties of housing density and limited services. The public squares designated as part of the original city provided some relief, but by the mid-nineteenth century many came to believe that larger park spaces were needed in order that "cities could breathe." In Philadelphia, the conversion of estates along the Schuylkill River to public parkland started as a practical measure to protect the water supply but grew with extended boundaries to provide open space expansive enough to host the 1876 Centennial Exposition as well as many varied social and recreational activities for the general public. By the turn to the twentieth century the Fairmount Park system had become an anchor to the whole region.

Streetcars that could take residents from outlying homes into downtown could also take them to Fairmount Park. But under the influence of grand city building traditions in Europe, notably Baron Haussmann's reconstruction of inner Paris, as well as the City Beautiful movement in the United States, Philadelphians wanted more than a practical connection to the park. A plan to connect city hall to Fairmount Park through a grand ceremonial parkway from the city core would further assert the the structure's historic centrality to the region's identity. Carving such a grand space out of the built environment proved daunting, but with the demolition of hundreds of existing structures, the completed parkway—capped by the new Philadelphia Museum of Art atop Fairmount—established another magnet pulling the whole region toward its core.

The core maintained its centrality well into the twentieth century, not just in recreation and ceremony, but commerce, especially in the evolution of the downtown department store. Epitomized by Wanamaker's, which appropriately affirmed its leading status by constructing its "Grand Depot" at the juncture of two railroads converging in the central city and directly adjacent to the new city hall, such emporiums became sites of sociability as well as of commerce in their daily as well as their annual holiday rituals.

The center could hold only so long against the outward tide. While trains for commuting proved expensive to the working class, middle-class residents took advantage of this service to move outward to live in detached or semidetached homes with porches and yards, a distinctly different environment than the area's urban row houses. As streetcars, with lower fares, added to the suburban mix of housing type and price, suburbs diversified, a process that only accelerated in the 1920s with the advent of wide-scale automobile use. For areas just outside the city where agriculture had persisted into the twentieth century, the automobile spurred the creation of middle- and working-class suburbs. For much of the inner suburban ring, towns grew in population, while retaining their basic character. But the advent of mass housing construction opened the way to a new form of rapid development, epitomized by Levitt and Sons, builders of two Levittown communities, in Bucks County, Pennsylvania, and Willingboro, New Jersey. There, communities formed virtually overnight, accommodating large numbers in similarly fashioned homes and providing clear evidence of the advantages and disadvantages of mass production.

With the dispersion of population came new institutions, not least the auto-dependent shopping center. From the pioneer Cherry Hill Mall designed and developed by the nation's pioneer developers of the new facilities, James Rouse and Victor Gruen, to Philadelphia's Pennsylvania ring suburbs, shopping centers provided the amenities of a bustling downtown street without the nuisance of automobile and pedestrian congestion. Downtown stores tried to compete by opening their own branch stores, but ultimately the new forms of shopping triumphed. The King of Prussia Mall in Pennsylvania took the regional shopping center type to new limits in terms of size and influence as it effectively drew customers off the Schuylkill Expressway and Pennsylvania Turnpike. It was only in the twenty-first century that the town which gave the shopping center its name began to assert its own identity, in the construction of new housing and commercial facilities apart from the mall. Even then, shopping patterns remained fluid in the age of the Internet. Once a mainstay throughout Greater Philadelphia, the last full-service Sears store closed its facility in Willow Grove, Pennsylvania, in 2022. By that time, Amazon was nearing its sixtieth warehouse in the region, promising to bring commodities to customers without requiring them to visit a shopping facility at all.

Regional shopping centers provided focal points within the modern suburban landscape consisting of constantly multiplying housing developments in a pattern that came to be identified as sprawl: the rate of growth in land-use development was outpacing the rate of population growth. While Philadelphia's population remained relatively dense, compared especially with newer cities to the west, its high level of business dispersion added to traffic congestion associated with reverse commuting.

In the final decades of the twentieth century, the real estate boom began to worry observers who had watched developers pave over large swaths of the suburban landscape. A dire warning came in 2001 from a group of regional analysts who observed that in the years between 1969 and 2000, southeastern Pennsylvania lost a worrying 34 percent of its agricultural land to development. Such dramatic losses spurred county activists across the region to seek ways to preserve vanishing farmland, in order to maintain environmental quality and preserve scenic beauty as contributors to their quality of life. Outside Philadelphia, every suburban county established a program to preserve agricultural land by purchasing easements from landowners. Those agreements precluded any future development on the protected farmland, no matter who might become the owner. Across the nine-county region covered by the Delaware Valley Regional Planning Commission from 2011 to 2020, protected private lands (mostly farms) increased by roughly 69,000 acres, while the amount of public open space (mostly parks) increased by about 13,500 acres.

As developers sought ever more opportunities, the implications for the environment became increasingly dire. Urban amenities, such as Philadelphia's park system and grand parkway, retained their appeal throughout the region, especially on special occasions such as Independence Day. But even as planners encouraged residents to recentralize it became increasingly clear that the shape of the modern metropolis no longer was being determined primarily at the core, but was driven as well by social and economic circumstances at the periphery.

Fairmount Park

Elizabeth Milroy

Fairmount Park was developed in the nineteenth century in an effort to protect Philadelphia's public water supply and to preserve extensive green spaces within a rapidly industrializing cityscape. It became one of the largest urban riparian parks in the United States and comprises the largest contiguous components of Philadelphia's public park system as administered by Philadelphia Parks & Recreation Department (PPR): East and West Parks on the Schuylkill and the surface of the Schuylkill River within those parks. From 1867 to 2010, when park management was overseen by the Fairmount Park Commission, the Wissahickon Valley Park (2,042 acres) was also considered part of Fairmount Park.

"Fairmount" is the prominent hill located on the east bank of the Schuylkill River just north of the original boundary of Philadelphia. It was named by William Penn when he claimed it as part of his Springettsbury manor. During the eighteenth century, the Schuylkill district was celebrated for the rural estates and elegant villas that lined the riverbanks west of the evolving city. In 1812, Philadelphia City Council's watering committee purchased Fairmount for a new waterworks facility. Development of the park began in the 1820s, when gardens and walkways were laid out around the waterworks. The park was expanded in 1844, when the city purchased the nearby Lemon Hill estate. The 1854 Consolidation Act directed the development of public parks, and in 1855 Lemon Hill was dedicated as "Fairmount Park." In 1857, the city acquired the adjoining Sedgeley tract. A year later, James C. Sidney and Andrew Adams were hired to relandscape the conjoined estates. Some new roads and plantings were completed, but the project was suspended in the mid-1860s, when park advocates successfully lobbied the state to authorize the development of a much larger park on both sides of the river.

Acts of the assembly in 1867 and 1868 created the Fairmount Park Commission (FPC) with authority to expropriate properties along the Schuylkill and the Wissahickon for recreation and to protect the city's water supply. Although commission members consulted landscape architects Frederick Law Olmsted and Calvert Vaux about viable strategies for reconfiguring the park landscapes, the FPC decided to make minimal changes so as to protect the "scenic contours" of the historic river estates. This plan was also cheaper. The FPC relied on appropriations from the city, and while funds were made available to compensate landowners whose properties were expropriated, the city resisted financing comprehensive landscape improvements.

The rapid acquisition of properties enabled Philadelphia to host the 1876 Centennial Exhibition on a four-hundred-acre exhibition site in West Park. Funding from city, state, and federal governments as well as private sources enabled the FPC to open roads and build drainage systems within the park as well as to build two new cultural facilities: the Horticultural Hall conservatory and Memorial Hall, which subsequently housed the Pennsylvania Museum and School of Industrial Art.

By 1900, the Schuylkill and Wissahickon park areas encompassed some 3,000 acres, and Philadelphians boasted of having created the country's largest urban park. During the twentieth century, more land was added to East and West Parks and the Wissahickon until the three areas comprised roughly 4,500 acres. By acquiring so much acreage so quickly, the FPC assembled disparate landscape spaces that ranged from well-tended gardens to broad greenswards and forests. Some cohesion was provided by the Schuylkill and Wissahickon waterways that bisected these spaces, but the lack of a comprehensive plan for landscaping improvements or management produced some unique features. For example, preexisting railroads and major streets were allowed to remain within the park; at a later date parkways and streetcar lines were added to improve access. Fairmount Park's boundaries varied from the hard edges of city streets to permeable dells along the Wissahickon. The presence of railroads and other thoroughfares left the park areas vulnerable to additional intrusions, most notably Interstate 76, the Schuylkill Expressway, which was cut through the West Park in the 1950s.

BUSHNELL'S
COMPLETE MAP
OF
FAIRMOUNT PARK
PHILADELPHIA.
PUBLISHED BY
ALVAH BUSHNELL COMPANY,
MAP PUBLISHERS, ENGRAVERS AND STATIONERS,
502 MARKET STREET, PHILADELPHIA
WISSAHICKON
VALLEY
FAIRMOUNT
PARK
MANAYUNK
RIVERSIDE
FALLS OF SCHUYLKILL
CHAMOUNIX
NORTH LAURELHILL CEM.
CENTRAL LAURELHILL CEM.
SOUTH LAURELHILL CEM.
MT PEACE CEM.
GREENLAND
WOODSIDE PARK
STRAWBERRY
WOODFORD
RIDGELAND
EDGELEY
BELMONT
ORMISTON
EAST PARK RESERVOIR
ROCKLAND
GEORGES HILL
MOUNT PLEASANT
FOUNTAIN GREEN
LANDSDOWNE
SWEET BRIAR
SCHUYLKILL
RIVER
SEDGELEY
ZOOLOGICAL GARDEN
LEMON HILL
FAIRMOUNT
ROXBOROUGH
MANAYUNK
STATIONS ON
PARK TROLLEY LINE.
1.—Elm Avenue.
2.—52d Street.
3.—George's Hill.
4.—Wynnefield.
5.—Belmont.
6.—Glenside.
7.—Beechwood.
8.—Greenland.
9.—Lilacs.
10.—Chamounix.
11.—Brunnenwald.
12.—Woodside.
13.—Junction.
14.—Strawberry.
15.—Dauphin Street.
PARK TROLLEY NOTES.
Length of Circuit, from Elm Avenue terminus to Chamounix and return, 7 miles; time, 30 minutes.
From Dauphin Street terminus to Junction and return, 5 miles; time, 25 minutes.
Rate of fare over either circuit is 5 cents. Passengers may exchange at Greenland for opposite terminus without extra charge.
PARK STATISTICS.
Area of Park, 3303 Acres.
Length of Drives, 42 Miles.
Boundary around Park, 30 Miles.
Drive from Green Street entrance to upper end of Wissahickon, 12 3-10 Miles.
In calculating distances on this map allow five inches to the mile; except on the Wissahickon Drive, where two and one-half inches equal one mile.
Engraved and Copyrighted by Alvah Bushnell Company 1897.

The creation of Fairmount Park did not introduce recreational areas into Philadelphia's urban landscape because both the Schuylkill and the Wissahickon had been popular recreational destinations since the eighteenth century. Many property owners at the Schuylkill and Wissahickon permitted public access to their lands: in the early nineteenth century Henry Pratt admitted the public to his extensive gardens at Lemon Hill. In the late 1850s, newspapers reported hundreds of residents, "white, yellow, brown and Black," assembled for civic festivals in the newly dedicated Fairmount Park. After 1867, both organized sports and more informal forms of recreation continued throughout park areas. Spectators flocked to the Schuylkill to watch competitive rowing races until baseball supplanted this as a spectator sport. Cyclists first entered the park in the 1880s. Horseback riding was always popular. During the twentieth century, the FPC added more formal recreational facilities such as ball fields and basketball and tennis courts, as well as entertainment venues, including the Lemon Hill band shell, the Robin Hood Dell, and the Mann Music Center.

By the mid-twentieth century, when city government and the FPC had established numerous parks in other areas of the city, the Schuylkill and Wissahickon parks were considered the nucleus of what became known as the "Fairmount Park System," encompassing some ten thousand acres citywide. Following the disestablishment of the FPC in 2010, the term "Fairmount Park System" was retired, the Wissahickon was designated as an independent entity, and "Fairmount Park" was redefined to describe only East and West Parks along the Schuylkill.

FIGURE 53. Bushnell's Map of Fairmount Park, Philadelphia, 1897. Park commissioners preserved the area's original terrain, with the minor additions of carriage roads and walking paths, noting "the diversified character of the grounds, and the abundance of noble trees and groves give us, at many points, a Park made to our hands." FREE LIBRARY OF PHILADELPHIA.

Benjamin Franklin Parkway

Lynn Miller

Created in the first decades of the twentieth century, the Benjamin Franklin Parkway connected the heart of Philadelphia's downtown to its premier park and over time became a district of cultural institutions and a commons for civic celebrations. The broad boulevard and its monumental structures reflected the European-inspired, nationwide City Beautiful movement embraced by the emerging city planning profession.

Before the parkway, Philadelphia's congested downtown lacked any convenient or ceremonial road to give urban dwellers access to Fairmount Park, its bucolic setting beside the Schuylkill River, and the inspiration of the beautiful classical architecture of the Fairmount Water Works. As the park extended to some three thousand acres along both banks of the Schuylkill shortly after the Civil War, suggestions arose for connecting the park directly to Broad Street. In 1871, an anonymously published pamphlet advocated two "grand avenues" extending from north Broad Street, one leading to the east park entrance and the other to a west entrance. Several years later, the construction of city hall at Centre (Penn) Square made that the more obvious terminus for a single boulevard leading to Fairmount. Following a preliminary proposal in 1884, city councils authorized the idea with an ordinance signed into law on April 12, 1892. The planned route was then inscribed on official city maps.

Although immediate execution of the plan faltered, in part due to the financial panic of 1893, it harmonized with trends evident in 1893 at the Columbian Exposition in Chicago, where the temporary "White City" energized planners to embrace a new City Beautiful Movement. The fair's design of clustered civic structures bound by a broad thoroughfare demonstrated an alternative to prevailing urban conditions of dark, unhealthy neighborhoods. In contrast, City Beautiful principles would open built-up portions of the city to sunlight and allow greater ease of movement.

In Philadelphia, such visions inspired the 1902 formation of the Philadelphia Parkway Association, an organization made of the city's most prominent and wealthy residents. They released a new grand plan for

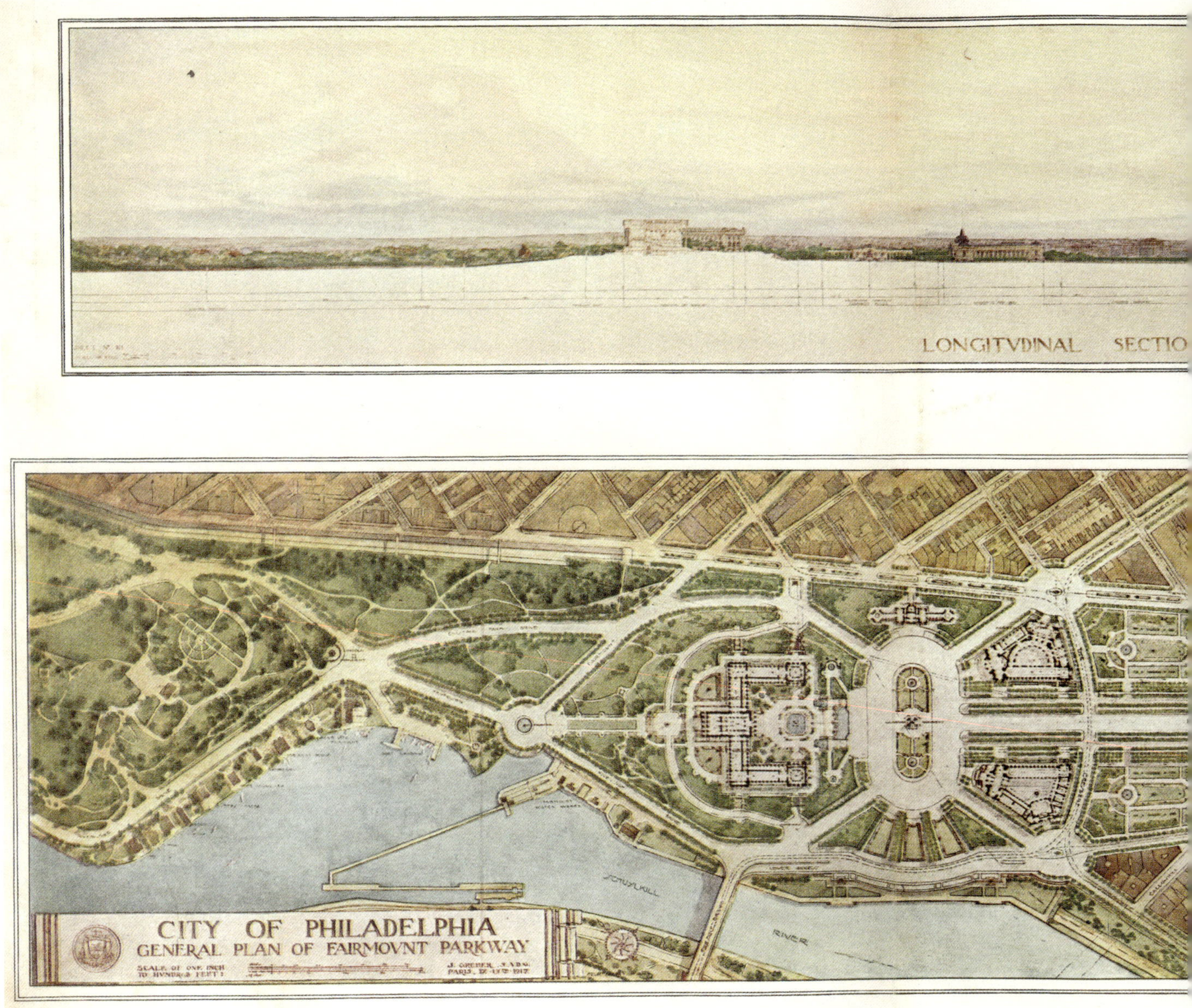

FIGURE 54. Jacques Greber, section and plan of the Parkway from Fairmount to Logan Square, 1919. Conceived and finally executed to provide coherence to a fragmented city, the grand boulevard running from Fairmount Park toward Center City exemplified the design ideals of a "City Beautiful." Eventually it became a focal point for special celebrations by a diverse regional population. FREE LIBRARY OF PHILADELPHIA.

a parkway in March 1903, but debates over location and costs delayed its execution. For the next several years, planners fiddled with the route, some breaking its axis at the Cathedral Basilica of Saints Peter and Paul on Logan Square and continuing the road at a slightly different angle to the Green Street entrance to the park. A more costly option, ultimately adopted, cut straight from the northwest corner of city hall across Logan Square to the foot of Fairmount. With the exact route still unresolved, work began with the demolition of a little row house on north Twenty-First Street on February 22, 1907.

Weeks later, Republican mayor John E. Reyburn took office. Within days, he received an invitation to the mansion of one of the city's most influential Republicans and a leader in the parkway project, the immensely rich

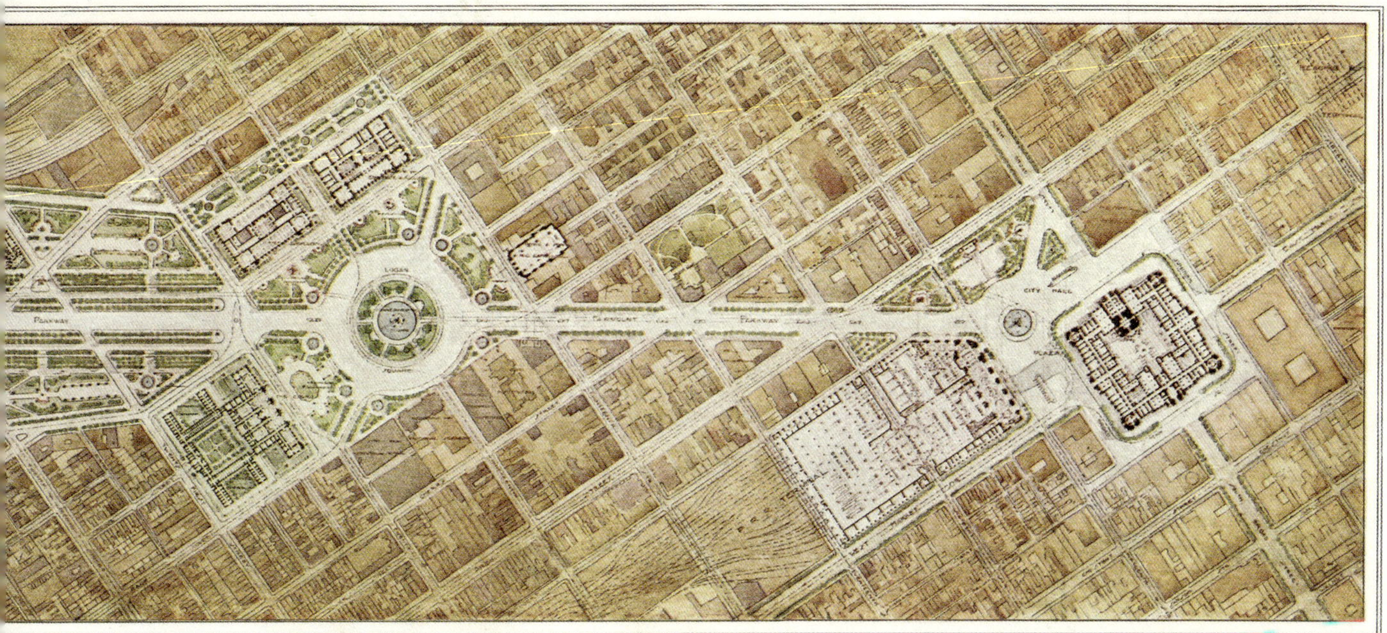

streetcar baron and art collector Peter A. B. Widener. For years, Widener had been arguing for a new art museum to replace the distant and crowded facility at Memorial Hall. He informed Reyburn that he would personally pay construction costs for a new museum if the mayor agreed to build it atop Fairmount, where, both men understood, the Water Works' reservoirs, like the rest of the facility, should soon be closed because of the Schuylkill's pollution. Accepting Widener's offer, Reyburn was persuaded that the new boulevard should terminate at the foot of Fairmount. The Fairmount Park Art Association commissioned a new architectural plan to represent for the first time a vision of a parkway complete with proposed grand new civic buildings. The architects named were the French-born Paul P. Cret, Clarence Zantzinger and his partners, and Horace

Trumbauer. By late summer 1907, Cret produced a bird's-eye view of the plan. It showed a grand rectangular plaza at the foot of Fairmount, a classical art museum at the summit, and a smaller semicircular plaza at the northeast corner of the larger one, where a second avenue would run north parallel to the main parkway before curving toward the river at Boathouse Row.

The project would be very expensive—some $2 million more than if the roadway had been shifted slightly away from the foot of Fairmount. Reyburn campaigned for more than a year to win support for it. In 1908, voters approved a loan for the project, and in June 1909, the updated plan returned to official city maps. By the time Reyburn left office at the end of 1911, he was hailed for his leadership of the parkway project and for making Fairmount the site of the new art museum. High costs and seemingly endless delays postponed completion of the art museum for nearly two decades, however, by which time Widener was long dead and his son had angrily withdrawn his earlier offer to give the family's vast art collection to Philadelphia.

Adding to the delays were disputes between Mayor Rudolph Blankenburg, a reform Republican who succeeded Reyburn in 1912, and the Republican machine that controlled city councils. After the Pennsylvania legislature in 1915 gave Pennsylvania cities the right to control construction within two hundred feet of parkland, city councils voted to annex the parkway to Fairmount Park, which would give control to the Fairmount Park Commission (FPC), then a bastion of Republicanism. Blankenburg vetoed the legislation, only to have the councils override him. The commission waited to exercise its authority until 1916, when Republicans restored their rule over city hall with the election of Mayor Thomas B. Smith. But then things moved quickly. By the time the nation entered World War I in April 1917, the parkway was nearly complete. The Fairmount Parkway, as it was initially named, was declared fully open on October 25, 1918. More than 1,300 properties had been demolished at a cost of $35 million.

Seeking to put its own stamp on the parkway, the Fairmount Park Commission in 1917 hired its own consultant to reexamine the Cret-Zantzinger-Trumbauer plan created nearly a decade earlier. The commission selected French landscape architect Jacques Gréber, the favorite of commission president Edward T. Stotesbury, and early in 1918 approved and published his revised plan. While retaining the basic design of Paul Cret's 1907 plan, Gréber replaced the monumental plaza that Cret had drawn at the foot of Fairmount with a smaller oval and created a green wedge of largely open space extending down into the city. He also created a traffic circle within Logan Square, which was extended to Twentieth Street. He intended that enlarged space, rather than the plaza at Fairmount, to become the main locus of new public buildings, similar to the Place de la Concorde in Paris.

The 1907 plan in which Paul Cret had played such an important role reflected the influence of the Ecole des Beaux-Arts in Paris, where he had trained, and the Avenue des Champs-Elysées and other great Parisian boulevards built during the reign of Napoleon III. Gréber built upon those references, particularly in shifting the allusion to the Place de la Concorde from the foot of Fairmount to Logan Square. Between 1927 and 1941, the Free Library by Julian Abele and municipal court building by John T. Windrim were completed on the square's north side, an obvious homage to comparable buildings at Concorde. Cret, who had been away from Philadelphia serving in the French army during World War I, was at first unhappy when he heard of the changes made by his countryman. But after he returned at the close of the war, he and Gréber reconciled and went on to collaborate on the Rodin Museum in 1929.

During the decades while the parkway was on the drawing boards and under construction, a number of buildings were proposed for it but never constructed. Of those eventually built, most were completed between 1918, when the parkway opened, and December 1941, when the United States entered World War II. These included the Insurance Company of North America (1925) at Sixteenth Street, the Fidelity Mutual Life Insurance Company (1928) at Twenty-Fifth Street and Pennsylvania Avenue, the Philadelphia Council of the Boy Scouts of America (1930) at Twenty-Second and Winter Streets, the School Administration Building (1932) at Twenty-First and Winter, and the Franklin Institute (1934) at Twentieth and the parkway. The Philadelphia Museum of Art, the vast temple crowning the acropolis of Fairmount, officially opened in 1928, although much of its interior remained unfinished.

Outdoor monuments also adorned the parkway. In 1924, the sprawling *Fountain of the Three Rivers* (Swann Memorial Fountain) by Alexander S. Calder was unveiled in the center of Logan Square, the approximate midpoint of the long view from city hall to the Museum of Art. In 1928, the *Washington Monument* designed in 1897 by Rudolf Siemering was moved from its original home at the Green Street entrance of Fairmount Park to the foot of Fairmount and the terminus of the parkway.

The Great Depression, then World War II, brought a halt to new projects for the parkway, which was renamed from the Fairmount to the Benjamin Franklin Parkway in 1937, a year of festivities marking the sesquicentennial of the U.S. Constitution. Little was added during the second half of the twentieth century apart from a juvenile incarceration facility, the Youth Study Center, at Twentieth Street in 1952. But the 1953 demolition of the Pennsylvania Railroad's Broad Street Station, which had long abutted city hall at its northwestern corner, made way for the creation of John F. Kennedy Plaza in the 1960s at the parkway's southeastern terminus in the block bounded by Fifteenth, Sixteenth, and Arch Streets, and JFK Boulevard. That plaza atop a municipal parking garage opened a broader vista from city hall to the art museum than ever before. It later became known as "Love Park" following the installation of the iconic *LOVE* sculpture by Robert Indiana. In 1959, the parkway also gained the Moore Institute of Art (later Moore College of Art) on the south side of Logan Square at Twentieth and Race Streets. Ten years later, between Sixteenth and Seventeenth Streets, the Friends Select School replaced its buildings dating from 1848 with a new school and office building. At the other end of the parkway, also in the 1960s, to accommodate ever-increasing automotive traffic Gréber's small oval at the foot of Fairmount was enlarged into the egg-shaped Eakins Oval, named for artist Thomas Eakins.

By the start of the twenty-first century, new parkway projects came to life with prodding from a 1999 report by the private-sector Central Philadelphia Development Corporation, which laid out proposals for "completing" the parkway in keeping with the visions of Cret and Gréber. New and renovated park space filled the once-empty corners of Logan Square; new benches, sidewalks and crossings created a better experience for pedestrians; a new Dilworth Park replaced the hard-surface Dilworth Plaza on the west side of city hall; and new cafés opened at Sixteenth Street and on Eighteenth Street on Logan Square. Paine's Park for skateboarders arose in the lawn between the roadway and the new Schuylkill Banks park along the riverbank, and Eakins Oval also became a temporary park in the summertime. At Twenty-Fifth Street, the Philadelphia Museum of Art annexed and enlarged the Fidelity Mutual Life building as its Perelman Building with galleries, archives, and office space for the museum. Most importantly, in 2012 the Barnes Foundation opened a new Philadelphia campus on the site of the demolished Youth Study Center on the parkway's north side between Twentieth and Twenty-First Streets. With the renovation of the Rodin Museum next door, this at last realized much of the century-old dream of making the parkway an art-lover's destination.

In the early decades of the twenty-first century, the Benjamin Franklin Parkway remained one of the greatest achievements of city planning in Philadelphia's history. The long process that brought it to fruition marked the start of a century in which professionals united with civic leaders and officials to create a bold vision for the heart of the downtown. The result has been both a prime cultural destination for the region and a distinguished civic space for area residents to gather for holidays and other special occasions.

Department Stores

David Sullivan

As department stores became central to retailing in American cities in the late nineteenth and early twentieth centuries, Philadelphia played a major role. Led by John Wanamaker, whose store was a national model, Market Street became home to the giant stores known as the "Big Six," which were close to rail terminals and subway stations. As the suburbs grew before and after World War II, department stores expanded into developing areas, from the affluent Main Line to working-class Northeast Philadelphia. But while the big stores seemed at their height in the 1950s and 1960s, they were already starting to succumb to new competitors and lifestyle changes, and each decade eliminated one or more of the institutions that once seemed impregnable.

The department store—an emporium selling different kinds of merchandise organized into separate departments with their own accounting—was a Parisian invention of the 1850s that underwent further refinements in the United States. The name "department store" first appeared in the mid-1880s. New technologies, especially mass transportation, made department stores possible as trolleys, elevated rail lines, and later subways brought massive numbers of shoppers to "downtowns"—also a new word. Also important were elevators, fast newspaper presses, and improvements in shipping fashions from London and Paris to foreign shores.

The department stores' preeminence came not just from their size, but from how they influenced culture. In addition to filling immediate wants, the stores created enticing windows, in-store displays, and advertising that fueled shoppers' aspirations. As the United States became a land of immigrants and cities, department stores displayed how Americans lived, or how they might live, while giving them choices about exactly how to do so. Shoppers flocked to Wanamaker's store and its imitators locally and around the nation, drawn by low prices, vast merchandise, and innovations such as charge accounts and tea rooms—the tea cafés among the stores' most fondly remembered elements. Department stores learned to make use of decoration and pageantry, not only lifting shopping out of the mundane but solidifying their roles as community institutions.

Most U.S. department stores grew out of dry-goods stores, which in 1860s Philadelphia centered on two main areas—on Second Street and on Market and Chestnut Streets west from Eighth Street. The development of city hall at Broad and Market Streets and the surrounding railroad stations in the 1870s and 1880s then pulled retailing west, although Eighth and Market remained the eastern anchor of department stores into the late twentieth century.

John Wanamaker, who grew up in Grays Ferry, dreamed of becoming a merchant prince in the manner of Alexander T. Stewart, the New Yorker whose Marble Palace was a Manhattan landmark. In 1861 Wanamaker became a partner in Oak Hall, a manufacturer and retailer of men's clothing at Sixth and Market Streets, and saw success in manufacturing clothing for Civil War soldiers. By 1871 his men's store was the largest in the country. Seeing opportunities in the 1876 Centennial Exhibition, which would draw people to rail depots around city hall, Wanamaker purchased an old freight depot southeast of Centre Square and opened his "Grand Depot." By fair's end, Wanamaker and his store were becoming nationally known.

Wanamaker, a devout Presbyterian, represented many of the conflicts between commerce and piety produced by the new consumer culture. His advertising—he is credited with the first full-page newspaper ad—emphasized the goods on sale but often contained moral aphorisms he wrote, such as his "New Kind of Store . . . came to life at the cry of human need. . . . It rehabilitated the people in their rights by the new deal we instituted."

Wanamaker and others presented their stores as not simply businesses but as community institutions. Nearly all emphasized that their job was not simply to sell but to offer a high level of customer service. Fair treatment of staff was emphasized by cutting work hours and establishing clinics, clubs, and summer camps. The underlying belief was that a happy employee would more pleasantly serve the customer—and that service, as an expression of Christian feeling or as a substitute for it, allowed the newly middle-class shopper to buy a little more without feeling hedonistic.

As Wanamaker set national precedents, other Philadelphia merchants took note. Strawbridge & Clothier was a dry goods house founded in 1868 on the northwest corner of Eighth and Market, where it remained until it closed in 2006. A partnership of two Quaker families, who remained in control until 1996, Strawbridge's emphasized low prices, high quality, and cash sales. It prided itself on fair dealing and its sense of Philadelphia history, as shown by its "Seal of Confidence," evoking William Penn's treaty with the Native Americans, introduced in 1911.

Directly across Market from Strawbridge's was Gimbel Brothers, a firm that began in Vincennes, Indiana, in 1842. The sons of trader Adam Gimbel moved through small towns in Illinois until opening their first big-city store in Milwaukee in 1887. In Philadelphia in 1894 they purchased the large store built by Cooper & Conard at Ninth and Market that had been operated briefly by Granville Haines. Most of the Gimbel family moved to Philadelphia and made it their

FIGURE 55. Located adjacent to Philadelphia's grand City Hall, Wanamaker's long stood as Philadelphia's leading department store, its seven-story grand court the host to the largest functioning organ in the world. CAROL HIGHSMITH, 2007, LIBRARY OF CONGRESS.

base of operations for years, even after opening in New York in 1910.

While Gimbels walked the line between upscale and downscale, the rest of the Big Six went straight for the lower-to-middle market. The third store at Eighth and Market was Lit Brothers, famed for its block of connected five-story buildings and its mottos, "Hats Trimmed Free of Charge" and "A Great Store in a Great City." Lits grew out of a dress store opened on N. Eighth Street in 1891 by Rachel Weddell, who became known for trimming hats free if the materials were bought from her. Two years later, her brothers, Samuel and Jacob Lit, expanded it into a department store.

Completing the Big Six were two stores at Eleventh and Market, N. Snellenburg & Co. and Frank & Seder. Snellenburg's began on South Street in 1873 and moved uptown in 1889. The last store to arrive, in 1915, was Frank & Seder, a branch of a Pittsburgh store that also operated in Detroit. Eventually twelve floors, it was the city's tallest store except for Wanamaker's. In Philadelphia's neighborhoods, meanwhile, Frankford and Kensington also had small local department stores and Germantown was home to George Allen, Inc. and C. A. Rowell.

Wanamaker took steps to stay ahead of the competition. In the early twentieth century, he commissioned Daniel H. Burnham, architect of the Chicago Columbian Exposition, to design a new fourteen-story store on the site of his Grand Depot. Work progressed in three parts, with internal divisions that remained visible in the completed store. The building was opened in 1911 with an address from President William H. Taft, making it the only department store to be dedicated by a sitting president. Also, like the Gimbels, Wanamaker invaded New York, buying the store of his former idol, Stewart.

The giant stores became stages for pageantry that underscored their role in civic life and the culture of downtown. Wanamaker's installed a ten thousand–pipe grand organ from the 1904 Louisiana Purchase Exposition in St. Louis, added eight thousand pipes, and on occasion brought in the Philadelphia Orchestra to

FIGURE 56. Postcard depiction of the Sears-Roebuck distribution plant on Roosevelt Boulevard, ca. 1925. Once a presence throughout the region, the last Sears full-service store closed in 2022. LIBRARY COMPANY OF PHILADELPHIA.

accompany it. At peak shopping seasons, Wanamaker's and other stores re-created the richness of Rome or the Belle Epoque. To balance the frivolity, during each Lent the Wanamaker store exhibited paintings of Jesus before Pilate and on the cross.

For Christmas, store windows drew families to Market Street to see the tableaux of animated dolls skating, opening presents, and writing lists to Santa, who awaited upstairs. Inside, Lits created the Colonial Christmas Village and Strawbridge's offered the Dickens Christmas Village. Wanamaker's Christmas Light Show, introduced in 1955, packed the Grand Court hourly with children and parents watching the antics of Frosty, the Sugar Plum Fairy, and Rudolph the Red-Nosed Reindeer—a character created by the national department store chain Montgomery Ward & Co. in the 1930s.

Although generations of Philadelphians cherished these traditions, as early as the 1920s automobile ownership and suburban housing development signaled a new era in which retailing shifted away from downtowns. In Camden, local stores in the downtown area, such as Munger & Long and Baker-Flick, began to disappear around the time of the opening in 1926 of the Delaware River Bridge (later renamed the Benjamin Franklin Bridge), briefly leaving only a J.C. Penney store downtown. Although Philadelphia's main stores continued to expand in Center City, they also opened branches, at first small and confined to resorts and affluent suburbs. Strawbridge's responded more assertively by opening some of the city's first branch department stores, at Suburban Square in Ardmore in 1930 and just outside Jenkintown on Old York Road in 1931. Frank & Seder also adopted a suburban strategy, opening a store near the Sixty-Ninth Street Terminal in Upper Darby in 1929.

Most of the Big Six remained family owned, but Lits was sold to one of the new chains of department stores being organized in the 1920s, City Stores, an amalgamation of three stores in the South and the Goerke family's operations around Newark, New Jersey. The Depression put City Stores into the hands of Albert Greenfield's Philadelphia-based Bankers Securities Corporation, which broke off Lits as a separate unit.

When suburban growth resumed after the Great Depression and World War II, department stores continued their expansion. Strawbridge's and Wanamaker's opened branches in Wilmington, Delaware, whose own department stores were weakening. Lits bought a store in Trenton, took over from Frank & Seder in Upper Darby, and built new stores in the Northeast and in Camden. Snellenburg's—another part of the Bankers Securities empire since 1951—went to Lawrence Park, Willow Grove, and South Philadelphia and bought the largest store in Atlantic City. Wanamaker's branched out to Jenkintown and Wynnewood, and Strawbridge's also went to Springfield, Delaware County.

The cost of staying competitive was too much for Frank & Seder, which withdrew from Philadelphia in 1953 and went out of business entirely in 1959. Next to fall was Snellenburg's. In 1962, its branches were rebranded as Lits, leaving just the downtown store. One day, the store abruptly closed, with customers being ordered onto the street at two o'clock in the afternoon.

On the other hand, Strawbridge's in 1961 became one of the anchors in the Cherry Hill Mall, the first enclosed mall on the East Coast and the second in the nation. Strawbridge's also responded to the rise of discounters, which were stealing department stores' business, by creating the Clover division, named after the family's estate, Cloverly, in East Falls, as were the widely anticipated Clover Days sales.

While department stores seemed to be booming in the 1960s, they had in fact passed their peak, as discounters, malls, and big-box stores offered wider selections at lower prices and with lower fixed costs, and more new competitors moved in from other cities. Macy's entered the field in 1962 through its Bamberger's division at Cherry Hill Mall. High-fashion New York stores such as Saks Fifth Avenue, Lord & Taylor, and B. Altman & Co. were already on the Main Line, and Bloomingdale's opened local branches.

The national chains of Sears, Roebuck and Company and J.C. Penney Co. had longtime local operations but had never tried to compete in Center City. Sears had one of its national catalog centers in a huge building on Roosevelt Boulevard, and its longtime chairman, Lessing Rosenwald, lived in Montgomery County. Sears's executive staff remained at the company's home base in Chicago, although it opened one of its first retail stores on the Admiral Wilson Boulevard in Camden. Penney's was even less visible, though it had stores in Germantown and on Sixty-Ninth Street (and later in the Gallery in Center City).

For Philadelphia's department stores, decline and transition quickened in the 1970s and 1980s. Lits fell in 1977. The Philadelphia-area Gimbels stores were purchased by the Allied Stores chain and assigned to its Stern's division. By 1989 Stern's was done in Philadelphia, and the Reading-based Boscov's began picking up vacated stores. For a number of years Boscov's sponsored the city's Thanksgiving parade, which had been established by Gimbels in 1920 as the first celebration of its kind in the nation. By the early part of the twenty-first century, Boscov's—whose store footprint now extended from Rhode Island to Ohio—was an anomaly, a successful, nearly full-line, traditional department store down to the candy counters and small appliances, with broad appeal to the growing aged population known as the "silver tsunami." Half of its customers were sixty and older.

Even Wanamaker's was sold, first in 1978 to Carter Hawley Hale Stores from California and then in 1986 to Woodward & Lothrop, a Washington store owned by Detroit mall developer Alfred Taubman. After "Woodies" went bankrupt in 1994, Wanamaker's became part of the Hecht's division of May Department Stores, which then bought Strawbridge & Clothier in 1996.

Finally, in 2005, Federated Department Stores bought May. The firm renamed all of its stores across the nation as Macy's, except for Bloomingdale's stores. Thus, in 2006, Macy's came to Market Street. The Strawbridge location closed and Macy's moved into the store built by John Wanamaker. Macy's pledged to maintain and improve the Christmas Light Show that had delighted generations of children and adults, and it remained a tradition to meet "at the Eagle"—a statue brought back to Philadelphia from the St. Louis World's Fair by Wanamaker, the brickmason's son whose words, still inscribed on a column on the main floor of his store, spoke to a vanished era in retailing:

> *Let those who follow me continue to build with the plumb of honor, the level of truth, and the square of integrity, education, courtesy and mutuality.*

Railroad Suburbs

Charlene Mires and John Hepp

As railroads reached outlying villages and the countryside around Philadelphia during the nineteenth century, railroad companies and other enterprising real estate developers created fashionable residential enclaves, new suburban towns, and vast semirural estates. These developments enabled prosperous Philadelphians to live apart from the city while still enjoying its amenities and maintaining their positions in the urban industries, businesses, and professions that produced their wealth. In the new railroad suburbs, local shopkeepers and service workers also helped sustain semirural living for the upper and middle classes. Although automobiles later changed commuting habits, the railroads and the suburbs that developed around their stations established a geography and social order that in many ways persisted into the twenty-first century.

The region's first railroad suburbs developed along the Philadelphia, Germantown, and Norristown Railroad (the PGN), which introduced commuter trains running northwest from the city in 1832. Using steam locomotives, the PGN operated frequent passenger service along essentially the same routes later served by SEPTA's Chestnut Hill East and Norristown regional rail lines. The commuter trains made Germantown, founded in 1683, a suburb connected with Philadelphia long before its consolidation into the city in 1854. By the late 1850s, in addition to its stock of colonial-era homes Germantown had a cluster of suburban villas in the neighborhood of West Walnut Lane and Greene and West Tulpehocken Streets. Farther northwest, a few commuters from Chestnut Hill connected to the PGN by stagecoach or carriage during the 1830s and 1840s, but after 1854 they could ride the new Chestnut Hill Railroad to Germantown. The construction of a new Episcopal church, St. Paul's (built 1856–61), signaled Chestnut Hill's increasing status as a suburb for the elite.

As railroad commuting expanded during the later decades of the nineteenth century, it produced social and geographic segregation as upper and middle-class families sought distance from the intensifying industrialization and high rates of immigration in Philadelphia and other American cities. The cost of rail fares initially put daily commuting by train out of reach for all but the wealthiest riders, while local streetcars and (later) buses remained the affordable options for others. Because rail fares varied by distance, inner suburbs like Germantown had more middle-class commuters than more distant, semirural idylls of the elite. Steam trains did not appeal to many middle-class commuters to Philadelphia because the locations of terminals on the periphery of the business district required an additional long walk or streetcar ride to get to work. Streetcars running into the central city from closer, newly developing areas of North and West Philadelphia offered more direct access, as did the Delaware River ferries that connected with railroads serving South Jersey. This did not change until late in the nineteenth century, when the two major rail systems serving the city relocated their main facilities to Center City (the Pennsylvania Railroad's Broad Street Station, opened in 1881, and the Reading Terminal, opened in 1893).

The development of railroad suburbs in the Philadelphia region resembled patterns of metropolitan expansion occurring around the same time along railroad lines radiating from other major cities, including New York, Boston, and Chicago. During the 1850s, other Philadelphia-area railroads joined the PGN in offering commuter train services. The Philadelphia, Wilmington and Baltimore Railroad started publishing housing guides for its line through Delaware County, and the West Chester and Philadelphia touted its route for commuters between its namesake communities. In southern New Jersey, the Camden and Atlantic Railroad, which began service in 1854, led to residential growth in Haddonfield, and a group of Philadelphia merchants acquired land and developed Merchantville after the arrival of the Camden & Burlington County Railroad in 1867–68. From these South Jersey suburbs, commuters traveled by rail to Camden and then crossed by ferry to the commercial center of Philadelphia east of Sixth Street.

By the 1870s and 1880s, a period of transition for the railroads, some lines had few commuter trains but on others the service became quite intensive. For example, in 1876, the Chestnut Hill Branch of the Philadelphia & Reading (successor to the PGN) offered thirty daily round trips between Center City and Germantown and encouraged daily commuting by offering special low-fare trains. During the 1870s, the Pennsylvania Railroad created havens for the elite along its Main Line, which extended west of Philadelphia through parts of Montgomery, Delaware, and Chester Counties, and spurred similar suburban development in Chestnut Hill. Developers of new suburbs also sought to appeal to the middle class, and the railroads offered incentives (such as free or discounted tickets) to encourage middle-class families to build houses along their lines. The Pennsylvania Railroad's activity along its Main Line inspired the president of the Philadelphia, Wilmington, and Baltimore Railroad to develop a similar but more affordable planned suburb for the middle class, Ridley Park, simultaneously with the opening of a new line in 1870 through southeast Delaware County between Philadelphia and Chester. In response to the availability of rail service, Sharon Hill and Norwood also developed along the line. A new line of the Pennsylvania Railroad running from Philadelphia to Norristown and Reading, beginning in 1884, enticed real estate developers to buy up farmland to create the middle-class suburb of Cynwyd (formerly known as Academyville). Along the Main Line, during the 1880s the co-owners of the Philadelphia *Public Ledger*, George W. Childs and banker A. J. Drexel, developed the planned suburban community of Wayne. In South Jersey, beginning in 1885 local landholders near the Camden and Atlantic Railroad line sold building lots to create the new suburb of Collingswood. Around the same time, local entrepreneurs began to convert farmland into the new suburb of Haddon Heights and persuaded the Reading Railroad, owner of the Philadelphia and Atlantic City Railroad, to establish a station to serve the community.

In the new railroad suburbs, buyers found large single-family and semidetached homes with expansive porches and yards, a distinctly different environment from Philadelphia's row houses. Making these railroad suburbs attractive to these residents required not only countryside ambiance but also more infrastructure of the type available in the city, such as water systems and paved streets. The Pennsylvania Railroad acknowledged this in a 1916 brochure when it touted "the charm of this suburban life, with its pure air, pure water and healthful surroundings, combined with the educational advantages provided, churches, stores and excellent transit facilities to and from the city, is manifest." Despite developers' appeals to the middle and upper classes, however, the railroad suburbs were never solely the domain of the region's wealthiest residents. Most evolved around or within existing communities with their own people and histories, and even the most luxurious suburban estates required a network of support from local businesses and service workers who lived close to the railroad stations in row houses or other modest homes. Starting in the 1890s, electrified streetcar lines also brought more class diversity to some of the same suburbs that had originated along the rail lines, including Chestnut Hill in Philadelphia and Merchantville and Collingswood in New Jersey. Transit fares held steady while working-class incomes rose, making more distant places affordable to a wider range of residents.

The Pennsylvania Railroad's role in developing Philadelphia's western suburbs originated from its purchase of farmland during the 1860s and 1870s in order to straighten the route of its Main Line between Philadelphia and Pittsburgh. With its expanded holdings within commuting distance of Philadelphia, the railroad developed a corridor of privilege from existing villages and the surrounding countryside. To increase the area's appeal, the company gave Welsh and Scottish place names to towns that did not already have them: Athensville became Ardmore, for example, and Humphreysville became Bryn Mawr. To give prospective buyers an opportunity to become acquainted with the area, the railroad took its cue from the resort ambiance of Cape May, New Jersey, and built the Bryn Mawr Hotel (opened in 1872, rebuilt in 1890 and later home to the Baldwin School). Railroad executives led the way by building estate homes. Alexander Cassatt, later the Pennsylvania Railroad's president, had a city residence on Rittenhouse Square, but in 1872 he began building Cheswold, a mansion set on fifty-four acres in Haverford. Leaders of Philadelphia business and industry followed, including department store partner Isaac Clothier, who built a castle called Ballytore in Wynnewood in 1885. Collectively, the communities and estates that developed around Pennsylvania Railroad stations from Overbrook west to Paoli became "the Main Line," a name that became synonymous with

FIGURE 57. Chestnut Hill station, whose rail service to the city began in 1854, pictured in 1962. SPECIAL COLLECTIONS RESEARCH CENTER, TEMPLE UNIVERSITY LIBRARIES.

upper-class living despite the continuing presence of other local residents as well as the businesses and domestic workers necessary to support a gracious lifestyle. Many of the massive estates later became home to religious orders, schools, or other institutions.

In Northwest Philadelphia, completion of the Pennsylvania Railroad's Chestnut Hill Branch in the early 1880s set off a new wave of suburban development west of Germantown Avenue. Henry Houston, a member of the railroad's board of directors with extensive land holdings in Northwest Philadelphia and adjacent Montgomery County, proposed the new rail line and then followed the pattern of the Main Line by beckoning elite residents to Chestnut Hill with amenities such as the Wissahickon Inn (1883, later the Chestnut Hill Academy), the Philadelphia Cricket Club (1883), and another Protestant Episcopal church, St. Martin-in-the-Fields (1888). In his Wissahickon Heights development (later renamed St. Martin's), he made homes available by lease. Houston's son-in-law George Woodward continued the family tradition and Chestnut Hill's suburban evolution in the early twentieth century with picturesque developments such as French Village (1913), Linden Court (1915), and English Village (1925). Between Chestnut Hill and Germantown, in Mount Airy, the Drexel Company built the planned suburb of Pelham between 1895 and 1910.

In the golden age of railroad suburbs, from the 1880s through the 1910s, more than one thousand daily trains served hundreds of stations in and around Philadelphia. The combination of railroad and streetcar suburbs brought population growth to Philadelphia's suburbs. The population of Montgomery County, Pennsylvania, doubled between 1870 and 1920 while Delaware County, Pennsylvania, and Camden County, New Jersey, quadrupled during the same period. Most early growth took place within about an eight-mile radius of the city, because of both travel time and the distance-based railroad fares. Bedroom communities within this range included Bala Cynwyd, Darby, Jenkintown, Lansdowne, and Narberth in Pennsylvania; and Audubon, Bellmawr, Collingswood, Haddon Heights, Haddonfield,

Magnolia, Runnemede, Westmount, and Westville in New Jersey.

By the 1920s, automobiles and buses came into the suburban transportation mix and railroad suburbs, although still located on train lines, no longer depended on the rails to link them to the city and neighboring communities. In New Jersey, the 1926 opening of the Delaware River Bridge (later renamed the Benjamin Franklin Bridge) also hastened the shift from rail to automobile commuting. As passengers left the trains, the railroads eliminated or cut back service on many lines, although the Pennsylvania and Reading railroads invested in electric trains and often increased services between 1915 and 1933. After World War II, automobile ownership and suburban bus service increased, and by the 1960s, the once-dominant railroads wanted to discontinue their money-losing commuter trains. In Pennsylvania, the City of Philadelphia and then the Southeastern Pennsylvania Transportation Authority (SEPTA) intervened in the 1950s and 1960s, and by 1983 SEPTA had taken over the remaining trains. For the New Jersey suburbs, the Port Authority Transit Corporation (PATCO) between Philadelphia and Lindenwold took the place of earlier rail systems in 1969. New Jersey Transit's River Line began operating between Camden and Trenton in 2004. In the automobile age, some railroad suburbs retained their appeal as fashionable enclaves while others transitioned into neighborhoods of large houses divided into cheap apartments.

In the early twenty-first century, although most people living in Philadelphia's railroad suburbs did not use the train to go to work, the old commuter lines still affected the social geography of the region because the road system largely followed those lines. With the exception of a handful of edge cities like King of Prussia, Pennsylvania, much of Philadelphia's suburban development followed the old railroad lines. In 2017, SEPTA and PATCO trains still carried more than 156,000 daily riders, including not only suburban dwellers but also working-class and lower-middle-class reverse commuters traveling to jobs in the suburbs. Along the tracks, railroad stations and homes built by the enterprising developers of the nineteenth century survived as visible reminders of the origins of the railroad suburbs.

Manufacturing Suburbs

Carolyn T. Adams

Although early industrialization in the eighteenth century took root mainly in urban centers, a substantial share of the Philadelphia region's early manufacturing sprang up in small towns outside the young city. The explanation for that pattern lay in the region's great rivers, the Delaware and Schuylkill. As early as the eighteenth century, enterprising settlers saw that the fast-moving currents in those rivers could drive waterwheels to power gristmills, sawmills, paper mills, and iron foundries, and they built such businesses along the banks. When coal-fired steam engines overtook both waterwheels and hand work, some of those early producers remained on the rivers' edge since waterways provided affordable transportation for raw materials and finished goods. Thus, the map of early suburban manufacturing followed the region's main waterways, a pattern that eventually influenced the paths of subsequent transportation networks of rail lines and highways.

In the first half of the nineteenth century canals enhanced the region's rivers by extending their reach into the hinterlands and overcoming obstructions along particular stretches of river. Canals served especially to transport anthracite coal from the northeastern Pennsylvania coal fields to riverfront manufacturing towns. For example, Bristol Borough in Bucks County began to prosper as a manufacturing center on the Delaware River twenty-three miles northeast of the city after the Lehigh Canal built in 1829 connected Bristol with the state's anthracite coal fields located near Mauch Chunk (later renamed Jim Thorpe) in Carbon County. Bristol's industrial base expanded substantially in 1876 when William Grundy moved his woolen mill from Philadelphia, producing rugs, carpets, hosiery, and cloth. In 1815 the Schuylkill Navigation Company began construction of a canal connecting Philadelphia to Pottstown, making possible the emergence of Manayunk as a mill town on the banks of the river. By 1830 that canal had reached northward into the state's coal region via Port Carbon, Pennsylvania, prompting its textile mills to mechanize to such an extent that Manayunk acquired the unflattering label "the Manchester of America."

A few of the manufacturing clusters outside Philadelphia grew to become small cities. The city of Camden, New Jersey, across the Delaware River from Philadelphia, developed a diversified manufacturing base in the nineteenth century by producing woolens, carriages, writing pens, and, most famously, Campbell Soup. The New York Shipbuilding Corporation began operations in 1899 on 160 acres in Camden, where the company built ships in assembly-line fashion, from barges to passenger liners and battleships. By World War II, it had become a central engine of Camden's economy. Down the Delaware River from Philadelphia, the city of Chester in Delaware County based its prosperity on a diverse manufacturing base that included shipbuilding, textiles, metal products, and paper. Unlike smaller manufacturing suburbs, cities like Camden, Chester, and Wilmington developed beyond their manufacturing base. They gained prominence as hubs of transportation (mainly ports and railroads) and regional business services like banking, finance, and insurance.

By contrast, other early manufacturing villages remained small, focused on one or two industries. On the west side of Philadelphia, ten miles up the Schuylkill River, the town of Conshohocken spawned ironworks on a canal alongside an unnavigable stretch of river. The first foundry was built in 1844. The longest-surviving firm was Alan Wood & Company, which established the Schuylkill Iron Works plant there in 1857. By 1920 Alan Wood Iron and Steel could produce five hundred thousand tons of steel a year. It remained the economic mainstay of Conshohocken until the mid-twentieth century. Many such towns specialized: Phoenixville produced steel; Gloucester City housed DuPont Chemicals; and asbestos plants fueled Ambler's growth. Although they remained small, these nineteenth-century manufacturing towns shared some features in common with cities, including a land-use pattern that mixed together manufacturing, housing, and walkable commercial districts where craftsmen, tradesmen, and merchants clustered. That surviving land-use pattern differentiated early manufacturing communities from twentieth-century suburban towns.

Not every important industry located on a riverbank. Some chose locations near an important source of raw materials. For example, glass manufacturing flourished during the eighteenth and nineteenth centuries on the New Jersey side of the Delaware River, particularly around the town of Glassboro in Gloucester County, named for the distinguished craftsmanship of what came to be known as "South Jersey Glass." The quality of southern New Jersey's sand, a major ingredient in glass manufacture, helped to establish its reputation, while its proximity to Philadelphia provided a large market for the industry.

In the first three decades of the twentieth century, more manufacturers built factories in the suburbs, attracted by cheap land and enabled by cheap energy. In 1916 Sun Oil chose to locate Sun Shipbuilding and Dry Dock Company in Chester in Delaware County eighteen miles downriver from Philadelphia. That plant grew quickly by delivering tanker ships to serve in World War I. In 1906, Baldwin Locomotive expanded its massive Philadelphia operations by building a suburban plant in Eddystone in Delaware County, about twelve miles south of Philadelphia on the Delaware River. In 1925 the Ford Motor Company transferred its regional operations from North Philadelphia to Chester, where it found more space and more efficient transportation for finished cars. Another major auto manufacturer, General Motors, opened a components factory upriver from Philadelphia in 1938 in West Trenton.

The Great Depression dealt a dramatic blow to many of these plants. Markets for their products collapsed in the 1930s, but business revived during World War II. Military contractors in Camden, Chester, and many parts of Delaware, Montgomery, and Bucks Counties employed thousands of defense workers. Sun Shipbuilding once again constructed vital oil tankers for a navy that fought a war on two oceans, while New York Shipbuilding in Camden built aircraft carriers and battleships.

Once the expanded highway network of the 1960s and 1970s increased access to undeveloped parcels of land outside the city, manufacturing spread more widely across the region. Rather than concentrating in towns, many manufacturers chose to build near highway off-ramps to speed transportation in and out of their plants, creating a highly dispersed pattern of industrial development.

To counteract the flight of industrial jobs, the city created its own industrial park in Northeast Philadelphia. In that sparsely populated section of

FIGURE 58. Alan Wood Iron and Steel Plant, built 1910, ca. 1920, Conshohocken, Montgomery County. LIBRARY OF CONGRESS.

the city, the Philadelphia Industrial Development Corporation assembled large parcels of land during the 1960s and equipped them with water, sewer, and other industrial infrastructure. In effect, the city developed its own manufacturing "suburb" within the city limits.

In the space of only a few decades, however, new forces emerged to further challenge both city and suburbs. Obsolete technologies, coupled with competition from low-wage producers around the globe, forced many suburban manufacturers out of business. When diesel technology eclipsed Baldwin's steam engines, the company suspended operations in 1956 and, after several mergers, closed in 1972. Alan Wood Steel closed its Conshohocken plant in 1977, driven out of business by foreign steel. U.S. Steel managed to keep its Fairless Hills Plant in Falls Township, Bucks County open but only until 1991.

Despite a broad regional decline in manufacturing, the Philadelphia metropolitan area remained competitive in various forms of advanced manufacturing that make use of new materials and processes enabled by nanotechnology or other scientific innovations. Those include pharmaceuticals, medical devices and equipment, precision instruments, plastics, chemicals, aircraft, and other defense industries.

As factory after factory fell victim to overseas competition and outsourcing, the loss of that industrial base brought a host of fiscal and social problems to manufacturing suburbs, including distressed schools, brownfields, deteriorating housing stocks, and stagnating tax bases. Populations aged in some of these suburban towns because the housing stock turned over so slowly that homeowners could not find buyers for their houses. Even in towns that were able to attract new populations, including African American and immigrant families, often the newcomers' incomes and property values could not provide an adequate tax base for services.

Yet manufacturing suburbs also offered significant opportunities for redevelopment. Towns built before the automobile resembled the city's industrial neighborhoods, densely developed with worker housing built within walking distance of manufacturing plants. They remained walkable communities usually with a Main Street commercial district. Planners and developers recognized a preference among some homebuyers for higher-density housing in communities with historic character that allowed residents to rely less on automobiles and more on walking, bicycling, and passenger rail lines serving many older river towns. The market potential was especially high for manufacturing

FIGURE 59. 900 S. Sixtieth Street, West Philadelphia, ca. 1905. Much of West Philadelphia's housing stock was built on speculation during the streetcar boom of the late nineteenth century. Streetcars made it easy to commute from West Philadelphia and other outlying neighborhoods to Center City. LIBRARY COMPANY OF PHILADELPHIA.

suburbs built along rivers because of the premium that real estate markets place on waterfront locations. In places like Conshohocken and Bristol, developers repurposed mills, lofts, and other industrial buildings to house offices and commercial businesses. The success of such projects led regional planners to recognize that old manufacturing towns could help concentrate future commercial and residential development and lessen sprawl.

Streetcar Suburbs

Dylan Gottlieb

Beginning in the middle of the nineteenth century, Philadelphia's growing streetcar network facilitated the movement of upper- and middle-class Philadelphians to residential districts outside of the urban core. New streetcar-centric suburban developments combined the allure of pastoral living with fast access to work and commerce in central Philadelphia. In this way, streetcar suburbs represented a paradox: While their chief attraction was their seemingly natural setting, their existence depended on Philadelphia's industrialization, which expanded the ranks of the city's middle class while also making central Philadelphia a less desirable place to live.

Previously, most of Philadelphia's elites had lived in the center of the city, with poorer residents inhabiting the periphery. The mid-nineteenth-century influx of working-class immigrants, however, forced well-heeled Philadelphians to rethink that arrangement. The arrival of Irish and German immigrants led to overcrowding, crime, disease, and social unrest; the city was wracked by anti-Catholic riots during the 1840s. For the middle classes, moving to the city's fringes provided a buffer from such disorder—a comfortable distance from what they believed were undesirable nonnative populations.

The era of industrialization also changed the middle classes' perception of the city. As the industrializing city grew increasingly packed and polluted, there arose a newfound appreciation for picturesque natural landscapes. For those who worked in the commercial heart of the city, the rural fringe promised a refuge—a private residential sphere for the bourgeois family. In the

1840s, influential landscape architect and author Andrew Jackson Downing popularized the connection between country houses and moral behavior among his middle-class readership. While elites had long built manors in Philadelphia's rural hinterland, after the Civil War the middle class—factory managers and businessmen who worked in finance or retail and their families—now aspired to spacious pastoral housing of their own.

That said, the suburban lifestyle would have been impossible without the advent of an efficient means to transport middle-class suburbanites to and from the central city. While horse-drawn omnibuses operated since the 1830s, they were slow and inefficient. At mid-century, Philadelphia remained a walking city. In 1850, the average worker lived within six-tenths of a mile of his or her job. By the late 1850s, however, the advent of faster horse-powered streetcars running on rails greatly increased the distance commuters were able to travel. Too expensive for the working classes to afford, streetcar ridership was restricted to the growing ranks of middle-class commuters. As they extended their tendrils outward, streetcar lines made possible the creation of class-segregated residential districts at the urban fringe.

In the 1850s, speculators began to erect suburban-style housing for middle-class buyers in West Philadelphia—which, as of 1854, had been consolidated into Philadelphia proper. Early developers sought to emulate the style of the elite country houses that already dotted the area. Hamilton Terrace, a row of Gothic Revival and Italianate twin houses on S. Forty-First Street between Baltimore and Chester Avenues, was one of the first developments. Architect Samuel Sloan gave Hamilton Terrace features that evoked upper-class country homes: front and rear lawns, porches, and ample tree cover. Sloan also designed nearby Woodland Terrace, a development of semidetached houses built in 1861. Woodland Terrace's charter protected its character as a residential refuge, mandating that "no slaughterhouse, skin dressing house or engine house, blacksmith shop or carpenter shop, glue, soap, candle or starch manufactory or any other offensive occupation be erected" in the area.

Development accelerated as streetcar operators joined in the speculative real estate market. In the 1880s, investors Peter A. B. Widener and William Lukens Elkins joined forces to consolidate control over the city's street-railway franchises. Their Philadelphia Traction Company ran new lines along the path of their property holdings, enabling them to capitalize by building new suburban-style developments. In the 1890s, they laid trolley lines on Springfield and Chester Avenues, sparking new construction in the Squirrel Hill and Kingsessing neighborhoods in Southwest Philadelphia.

West Philadelphia grew denser as builders synthesized the country-house style with the density of urban row houses. While they retained front porches and lawns, they began to build attached rows of Queen Anne and Colonial Revival-style houses in neighborhoods like Cedar Park. Developers advertised their communities' urban-style amenities—sewers, gas lines, and, later, electricity—along with their pastoral setting. As housing became denser and more affordable, the population of West Philadelphia swelled from under twenty-four thousand in 1860 to about two hundred thousand in 1910. By the 1890s, development pushed past Forty-Second Street. Commercial corridors sprang up to serve these farther-flung suburban areas. Shops soon dotted stretches of Lancaster Avenue, Fifty-Second, and Sixtieth Streets in West Philadelphia. Streetcar ridership flourished as more people moved farther from the city center: ninety-nine million passengers rode the Philadelphia streetcars annually by 1880.

As the areas around Philadelphia and Camden developed, streetcar-led construction extended farther from their city centers. Streetcars linked growing communities in Delaware County—Lansdowne, Media, Collingdale, Glenolden, and Sharon Hill—to the urban streetcar network via a hub in Darby. Montgomery County's expanding network of suburban streetcar lines converged in Norristown, northwest of Philadelphia along the Schuylkill River. In southern New Jersey, streetcar routes radiated out from Camden's industrializing core. By the early 1900s, new lines eased travel between Camden and the nearby suburbs of Merchantville, Collingswood, and Haddonfield, complementing their existing railroad links to Philadelphia. Well-heeled buyers moved out to suburban Chestnut Hill in Philadelphia's northwest, commuting downtown via the Germantown Avenue streetcar (and multiple railroad lines). To ensure that Chestnut Hill would remain uniformly white and middle class, area developers employed restrictive covenants that barred industrial or commercial uses, along with Black and Jewish residents. Residents included the renowned father of scientific management, Frederick W. Taylor, who conducted his time-efficiency studies at North Philadelphia's Midvale Steel plant.

At the start of the twentieth century, non-elites began to move out to suburban districts within (and eventually outside of) city limits. Electrification of the city's streetcars in 1892 and completion of the Market-Frankford Elevated Line in 1907 lowered transit costs, making it possible for some workers and upwardly mobile immigrants to afford a daily commute. In West Philadelphia, the demand for housing led to the construction of four- and five-story apartment buildings in areas formerly devoted to single-family homes; it also sparked development in the outlying neighborhoods of Wynnewood and Overbrook. In North Philadelphia, developers built homes in Olney and Oak Lane to accommodate the growing ranks of successful Germans and Irish (and later Jews) who sought refuge from central Philadelphia's industrial neighborhoods. Across the river in southern New Jersey, streetcar electrification lowered the costs of commuting into Camden, allowing shopkeepers and clerical workers to move to nearby towns like Haddon Heights. Developers' advertisements enticed former immigrants to move to neighborhoods like Strawberry Mansion, an enclave on the edge of Fairmount Park. One broker's 1913 Yiddish-language ad for the neighborhood promised residents "fresh air" and a "beautiful country landscape"—the same sort of pastoral features that had originally drawn the middle class to West Philadelphia's first streetcar suburbs.

With the advent of the automobile after World War I, suburban construction no longer needed to follow transit routes. In West Philadelphia, developers began to target areas not serviced by streetcar lines. The Garden Court district, built during the 1920s, was among the first to incorporate rear garages on homes' basement levels. In the following decades—particularly in the years after World War II—auto-centric suburban development exploded in areas outside of Philadelphia's city limits.

Government policies that helped to underwrite automobile suburbs also accelerated the transformation of older streetcar suburbs into lower-class neighborhoods. Middle-class residents of inner suburbs took advantage of favorable government-backed mortgages to buy new houses outside the city. Meanwhile, African Americans migrating to Philadelphia were subject to residential restrictions that pushed them into neighborhoods—Mantua, Parkside, Strawberry Mansion—that the white middle class was abandoning. Landlords took advantage of the situation by dividing historic single-family homes into multiple apartments. Owners failed to invest in upkeep, and many early suburban-style houses began to deteriorate. Federal agencies like the Home Owners' Loan Corporation hastened disinvestment when they deemed aging and racially transitioning streetcar suburbs unworthy of mortgage financing.

In the final decades of the twentieth century, however, streetcar suburbs began to experience a limited resurgence. New immigrants flocked to areas like Cedar Park and Upper Darby for their affordable housing and access to jobs downtown. Middle-class returnees were also attracted by the supply of inexpensive historic houses. Streetcar suburbs offered amenities that automobile suburbs lacked: density, walkability, defined commercial corridors, and, most importantly, easy access to public transit. By the beginning of the twenty-first century, middle-class residents filled many of Philadelphia's earliest streetcar suburbs, and the most architecturally distinctive area of West Philadelphia received designation as a historic district. Once again, streetcar suburbs came to embody the ideal intersection of urban convenience and bucolic refuge.

Inner Suburbs

Suzanne Lashner Dayanim

Presenting a varied and complicated patchwork of both thriving and distressed communities, Philadelphia's inner suburbs developed during different eras to serve different purposes and populations. European influence predated the Revolutionary War, with English, Swedish, Dutch, and Welsh settlers establishing tight-knit farming communities in what were then outlying areas of William Penn's Philadelphia. During the eighteenth and nineteenth centuries of slow but steady population increase, stately mansions were built in many of these well-positioned borderland communities as summer homes for wealthy Philadelphians, while other communities were setting the foundation to become vibrant industrial towns. Beyond a common penchant toward small-town life and local allegiance, during the twentieth century these communities acquired identities ranging from upscale hamlets with storied histories of housing wealthy families for more than a century, to working-class towns rooted in manufacturing, to post–World War II suburbs whose middle-class housing began to lose value by the end of the century. These early suburban communities represented a critical juncture in metropolitan dynamics. As the first places outside of the city limits to experience rapid population growth during the twentieth century, their residents were still essentially connected to the urban core while adopting new localized daily routines that began to disconnect them functionally from an urban sensibility.

Clustered around the city boundaries, the inner suburbs formed a contiguous ring of older jurisdictions within which most housing dated to 1970 or before. This buffer, extending out approximately eight miles from Philadelphia's city limits, corresponded roughly to the service area of the region's popular commuter rail system along which early suburban development coalesced. As such, the region's inner suburbs could be considered to include the townships, boroughs, and a few cities within eight miles of Philadelphia's border in Pennsylvania's Delaware, Chester, Montgomery, and Bucks Counties as well as New Jersey's Burlington, Camden, and Gloucester Counties. U.S. census population figures attested to an enduring attraction of inner suburbs to the region's residents. During the post–World War II era of mass suburbanization, migration flowed mainly to the inner suburbs, which grew to be almost equal to the population of Philadelphia by 1970. At the close of the twentieth century, population in the inner suburbs well exceeded that in either the city or the outer suburbs.

During the nineteenth century, many towns along waterways developed as centers of manufacturing in the era of industrialization and became working-class suburbs. Waterpower and transportation influenced development in places such as Upper Darby, Pennsylvania, where the abundance of creeks and streams allowed for the development of mill towns. Along the Delaware River, Chester, Pennsylvania, became known for its shipyards and factory work in the early 1900s. Paulsboro, New Jersey, home to the Port of Paulsboro, developed its capacity for petroleum transfer and manufacturing. Industrial parks were situated in Pennsauken, on the New Jersey side of the Delaware River. The boroughs of Conshohocken and West Conshohocken, Pennsylvania, along the Schuylkill River, became centers for steel and iron production.

Although places that formed this suburban inner ring had unique longstanding histories, the introduction of rail lines in the mid-1800s shaped modern municipal demarcations. One string of affluent inner suburban communities, encompassing parts of Lower Merion and Radnor, Pennsylvania, acquired its moniker "the Main Line" because the Main Line of the Pennsylvania Railroad ran through these towns. These "bourgeois utopias" with their ample supply of sprawling estates remained prosperous and prestigious areas. In Camden County, New Jersey, a pair of high-income suburbs with lengthy histories similarly retained their appeal for wealthy residents. Haddonfield and Haddon Heights were built as classically laid-out towns with large homes that drew affluent professionals. Railroad connections were integral to the plans of both communities, initially to the Camden and Atlantic Railroad and by 1969 to the PATCO High Speed Line.

The region's suburban footprint changed dramatically with the mass suburbanization that defined the post–World War II period. Tract-housing subdivisions transformed many of Greater Philadelphia's inner-ring agricultural areas into middle- and working-class bedroom suburbs to mirror the nationwide trend. Levitt and Sons builders chose Greater Philadelphia's inner suburbs for two of its iconic Levittown communities, one spanning four jurisdictions in Pennsylvania's Lower Bucks County and the other in Willingboro, New Jersey. Population in the inner suburbs mushroomed. For example, in Lower Moreland, Pennsylvania, a 1940 resident count of 1,451 grew to 11,665 by 1970. In Deptford, New Jersey, a 1940 resident count of 4,738 grew to 24,232 by 1970. With the construction of an extensive network of highways and roads, inner suburbs drew middle- and working-class households seeking the quintessential American dream of owning a single-family home in a neighborhood with good schools, a safe and community-oriented environment, and easy automobile access to anywhere in the metropolitan region. White flight from city neighborhoods fueled the dramatic population increases in the inner suburbs between 1945 and 1970.

After 1970, African Americans began moving into suburbs where a pattern of disinvestment in aging homes had lowered prices enough to make them affordable. Typically, declining housing conditions preceded the arrival of minority buyers, yet many white residents assumed the reverse—namely, that the arrival of minority residents caused housing conditions to deteriorate. In an effort to stem the racial animosity that such transitions prompted, citizens in some racially changing suburbs like Pennsauken, New Jersey, as well as Lansdowne and Upper Darby, Pennsylvania, formed organizations to support minority homebuyers and combat racial discrimination in housing. After 1970, however, some inner suburbs experienced population decline, especially losing white households to outer suburbs and, starting around 2000, to Philadelphia's downtown. The racial makeup of inner suburbs grew more varied than in outer suburbs whose residents continued to identify predominantly as "white alone" in U.S. census figures. In a few of the region's distressed inner suburbs such as Chester and Yeadon, Pennsylvania, racial integration could not be maintained and a process of resegregation into predominantly minority communities ensued by the end of the twentieth century.

Inner suburbs increasingly became a destination of choice for immigrants to the region. By the twenty-first century, immigrant settlement in the inner suburbs followed class divisions as educated professionals chose upper-class enclaves and working-class immigrants gravitated to the more affordable working-class areas with easily accessible public transit. Inner suburbs recorded disproportionate shares of elderly residents, although the trajectory was decidedly upward for both inner and outer suburbs. And poverty began to rise in the inner suburbs, mirroring national trends as well as the trajectory of Philadelphia's inner-city neighborhoods. Public schools in distressed suburbs came to be counted among the worst performing in the region. In underfunded Pennsylvania school districts like the William Penn School District, Southeast Delco School District, Norristown Area School District, and Bristol Borough School District, over 90 percent of fifth graders tested "Not Proficient" on the state's standardized tests for math and English in 2021.

A number of factors explained these trends of population decline, demographic change, and increased poverty in Greater Philadelphia's inner suburbs as well as underperforming schools in certain places. Outdated post–World War II housing stocks and aging infrastructure made many older suburbs less appealing to homebuyers. The regional tide of deindustrialization undermined working-class manufacturing suburbs. In addition, the region's governmental fragmentation, assigning each suburb responsibility for taxation and service delivery within its boundaries, played a role as small suburban jurisdictions struggled to fund services with a stagnating tax base. The most threatened were bedroom communities that lacked commercial property to bolster tax revenues. For example, the William Penn School District was created in 1972 to serve six small boroughs clustered together near Delaware County's border with Philadelphia. All were residential communities with little commercial tax base, so the full weight of paying for local services and schools fell on homeowners. Thus, inequalities widened among inner suburbs as prosperous communities strategized effectively to strengthen their amenities and advantages with a focus on commercial and office park development as well as educational and medical infrastructure, leaving more vulnerable places to decline. Struggling inner suburbs were thus caught in a "policy blind spot," overlooked in policy debates that contrasted flourishing outer suburbs with declining cities.

Even as some inner suburbs declined, however, others possessed qualities that positioned them to prosper. Many smaller boroughs offered the charm, walkability, sense of community, and Main Street orientation that the Delaware Valley Regional Planning Commission touted in its promotional campaign for the region's treasured "Classic Towns." Boroughs such as Narberth and Media in Pennsylvania, and Collingswood in New Jersey, began drawing people to their independently owned Main Street shops and restaurants as well as their robust community life centered on festivals and public events. Conshohocken successfully capitalized upon its traditional town layout to reinvent itself as a major hub of the region's knowledge economy. The ample inventory of older housing built before 1939 offered stately and unique architectural features increasingly of interest to homebuyers.

FIGURES 60, 61. Levittown, Pennsylvania, 1977. Located in Lower Bucks County northeast of Philadelphia, the new inner suburb emerged in the post–World War II period to offer affordable homes within reach of the central city and a growing range of assets spurred by exurban development. SPECIAL COLLECTIONS RESEARCH CENTER, TEMPLE UNIVERSITY LIBRARIES.

FIGURE 62. The George School, ca. 1922. Founded in 1893 in Middletown Township, Bucks County, to educate Hicksite members of the Religious Society of Friends, the formal school buildings contrasted with the countryside around them, even as the county populated. By contrast, parts of densely developed Levittown materialized in the same township in the 1950s. LIBRARY COMPANY OF PHILADELPHIA.

The Philadelphia region's densely settled inner suburbs exhibited far greater variation than its outer suburbs. In this complicated metropolitan mosaic, pockets of distressed places developed side by side with prospering ones. But all shared the continuing geographic advantage of easy access to central Philadelphia in an era when sprawled development patterns shifted growing numbers of suburban residents farther away from, and less able to sustain connections with, the region's core.

Public Education: Suburbs

William W. Cutler III
and Catherine D'Ignazio

In the second half of the twentieth century, many parents moved their families out of Philadelphia, Camden, or Wilmington so that their children could enroll in suburban public schools because they perceived them to be better than their urban counterparts. Before then, many believed that the best public schools were urban and that rural schools were inadequate. But as many rural communities became suburban, they created comprehensive public school districts with programs and facilities that matched or exceeded those found in the region's cities.

More often than not, the rural districts that upgraded their public schools were in communities that began to suburbanize as early as the 1870s with the advent of commuter railroads and, later, electric trolley lines. The residents of these communities wanted urban benefits and services—paved roads, sewer lines, and, above all, comprehensive systems of public education. Audubon, Collingswood, and Haddonfield, in Camden County, New Jersey, and Abington, Cheltenham, and Lower Merion, in Montgomery County, Pennsylvania, acted on such expectations. So, too, did those who lived in the several small but thriving centers of commerce and industry outside the region's big cities, in places like Norristown, Pottstown, and Conshohocken in Pennsylvania and Gloucester City in New Jersey.

Between 1895 and 1920 many rural school districts in Montgomery County became suburban. In 1897 there were 498 public schools and fifty-five public school districts in the county; forty-four of these operated only one-room schools. By 1916 the number of districts operating just one-room schools had been reduced to ten; the total number of public schools had been reduced by more than two hundred; and the number of districts operating high schools had risen from a handful to twenty-one. Not surprisingly, these included Norristown (with 474 students in high school), Pottstown (380), and Conshohocken (101), along with Abington (205 students), Cheltenham (273), and Lower Merion (336). Jenkintown and Narberth did not have separate high school buildings in 1916; instead, they set aside rooms for high school classes in their elementary school. But the suburban die was cast, and by 1930 there were high schools in thirty-six of the county's sixty-six public school districts.

The fifty years that followed the end of World War I might be called the era of suburbanization in Greater Philadelphia. Population grew substantially in the four Pennsylvania and three New Jersey suburban counties between 1920 and 1940, and the pace accelerated after World War II. In South Jersey, for example, the population in Burlington, Camden, and Gloucester Counties grew more than twice as fast in the twenty years after 1940 (+77 percent) as it did in the twenty years before (+33 percent). Some of this demographic growth resulted from the baby boom that began in 1946. But some of it came about because many young families relocated, and they often settled far from the city, renting or buying housing in newly developed communities. In 1960, for example, more than one-third of Burlington County residents had been living in their present house for no more than two years. Levitt and Sons persuaded many white-collar and even some blue-collar families to uproot by building planned communities for them in both Bucks (1951) and Burlington (1958) Counties.

Most public school systems were unprepared for this demographic shift. Those in Pennsylvania had some time to adjust because the effect was modest at first; between 1954 and 1958 public school enrollment in the four Pennsylvania counties surrounding Philadelphia grew by just 18 percent. Over the next twelve years, however, it increased by more than two-thirds, climbing from 228,551 to 384,200 students. The comparable numbers for the three New Jersey counties across the Delaware River from Philadelphia are staggering. Public school enrollment in Burlington, Camden, and Gloucester Counties nearly tripled between 1950 and 1970, soaring from just over 78,000 to just under 211,000 students. The lion's share of this growth (60 percent) took place in Burlington and Gloucester Counties where the population before 1945 had been small and scattered.

These numbers alarmed educators and reformers not only because none of the school districts in these suburban counties had enough teachers or classrooms but also because many districts still functioned as they always had. In 1945 more than a few in both New Jersey and Pennsylvania relied on supervising principals rather than superintendents. Several did not operate their own high schools, paying for their students to go elsewhere. But by far the most vexing problem was the persistence of small school districts. When Harvard University's former president James Bryant Conant loudly complained in 1959 that far too many communities in the United States had public high schools that were too small to offer sufficiently rigorous academic programs, his words described the Greater Philadelphia suburbs. Most of their residents still believed that smaller was better in public education or at least not bad enough to justify consolidation through reorganization of small school districts. New Jersey codified this expectation by requiring local school boards to submit their annual budgets to the voters for approval by referenda.

Reorganization was not a new idea in 1950. As early as the turn of the twentieth century many school reformers advocated it. They wanted to eliminate the one-room, one-teacher school and form high schools that offered a modern curriculum including contemporary foreign languages, social studies, physical science, bookkeeping, and stenography. They wanted schools capable of housing a varied extra curriculum, including interscholastic athletics for boys and in most cases girls. Small rural districts could not provide these amenities; their tax base was too small, their unit costs too high. Between 1910 and 1940 reformers made considerable progress in achieving reorganization, especially in New England and the South Atlantic states. But progress came more slowly to the mid-Atlantic region where local loyalists resisted.

Delaware is a case in point. The crucial variable there was not the economic disparity between Wilmington, its biggest city, and the rest of the state but the political gap between Dover, its capital, and its rural school districts. The idea to reorganize came from the state's first commissioner of education, Charles A. Wagner; his boss, Governor John G. Townsend, ran with it. At Townsend's behest the legislature authorized the governor to appoint a school reform commission in 1917. It devised a new school code that put considerable power in the hands of county school boards. One of the most powerful men in the state, industrialist and philanthropist Pierre S. Du Pont, endorsed this reform, but in the face of fierce opposition from local school districts the legislature reversed itself in 1921, dismantling the county school board system. Once again, public education would be overseen by local authorities working with the state Board of Education. But the unintended consequence of this reform was to increase the power of the state board and the state commissioner of education.

The state board hoped to modernize public education through reorganization. At the time there were 395 incorporated school boards and unincorporated school committees in Delaware. Many supervised just one school. The state's first consolidated rural district (Caesar Rodney) had been formed south of Dover in 1916. By 1921 there were thirteen such districts, and the reformers hoped that consolidation would make it possible for more rural students to get a high school education. Not including Wilmington, there were only 116 students in the state poised to graduate from a four-year public high school in 1918. Over the next twenty years the state commissioner convinced some rural districts to accept consolidation in exchange for help from Dover with teacher salaries and pupil transportation. In 1953 the state board drafted legislation to reduce the number of school districts from 105 to 15, but rural school consolidation did not really come to pass until the Delaware General Assembly adopted the Educational Advancement Act in 1968. It cut the number of school districts in the state from 60 to 26. Meanwhile, reorganization barely touched the lives of Delaware's African American children before the 1970s because until then the state maintained a dual system of public education. Only Howard High School in Wilmington was available to Black students while school segregation remained widespread. In 1965 the state board of education ordered the closure of 25 "Negro" districts, but most of them were in rural communities.

In New Jersey reorganization reshaped the map of public education following World War II, but the state's tradition of local control affected the way this occurred. Perhaps because New Jersey lacked a major metropolis, most people had no experience with anything other than "neighborhood" schools. Not surprisingly, new school districts formed when the population grew. Between 1900 and 1970 the number of school districts in the state rose from 395 to 576. In the three-county region the number of school districts with a high school almost doubled between 1950 and 1976 (from 21 to 41) with Burlington (7) and Gloucester (8) Counties registering the largest increases. Twelve of these were regional high schools operated by regional high school districts. For many years families living in a rural district without a high school sent their children to one in a nearby suburban district. In Camden County, for example, they sent them to Merchantville, Haddon Heights, or Haddonfield. But now rural and suburban families could send their children to one of twelve high schools operated by a regional high school district (RHSD). The first two of these, Rancocas Valley RHSD in Burlington County and Lower Camden County RHSD were formed in the 1930s; the rest came to life after World War II. The reason for them, according to the New Jersey State Department of Education, was that they "bring together a sufficient number of pupils and financial resources to offer a broad and comprehensive educational program." Collaboration, not consolidation, was New Jersey's response to the people's demand for public secondary education.

Pennsylvania took a different approach, committing itself to school reorganization after World War II. Larger than New Jersey and Delaware combined, it had 2,544 school districts in 1945, nearly 10 percent of which (240) were in Bucks, Chester, Delaware, and Montgomery Counties. Thirty years later the number of school districts in Pennsylvania had been drastically reduced to fewer than 600. In Bucks, Chester, Delaware, and Montgomery Counties there were 61 (as before, about 10 percent), but they were now educating more than twice as many students. The justification for reorganization was partly financial. Even in Montgomery County the tax base in some suburban communities was not large enough to pay for an educational program with all the essentials, much less any extras. The state could have used its equalization subsidy program to compensate for the differences, but it chose to help less affluent communities by achieving economies of scale.

Lawmakers knew that Pennsylvania had too many small school districts as early as 1854 when they first made provision for collaboration among them. At the beginning of the twentieth century the commonwealth adopted a new school code that authorized the use of state aid for student transportation in districts that collaborated or consolidated. But it was not until the late 1940s, when many Americans realized that public education had been neglected for far too long, that the Pennsylvania legislature mustered the political will to attack the problem. In 1947 it passed a law that gave the county boards of school directors, created in 1937, the "power and duty" to prepare long-range plans for eliminating districts with no or only a few students. It also set aside money to give school districts an incentive to collaborate. Such financial incentives proved ineffective so in 1961 the legislature acted again, only to find that the problem continued as too many communities were granted exceptions.

Perhaps the most outspoken opponents of school district reorganization came from the Philadelphia suburbs. Jenkintown's Wilmot E. Fleming believed that the best small districts should remain independent. Others argued that consolidation would lead to higher taxes or decline of community spirit and loss of local control. In 1966 state senator Clarence Bell, a Republican from Delaware County, warned that reorganization would eventually lead to the formation of a metropolitan school district, an idea that Richardson Dilworth floated while he was the president of the Philadelphia School Board. If such a district had been created, it would have brought a wave of African Americans from the city to the suburbs, a prospect certain to upset many of the whites living there. They did not see the minority children already in their midst, perhaps because they lived in neighborhoods and patronized schools that were mostly segregated. This discrimination led to civil rights protests in places like Mount Holly, New Jersey, and Abington, Pennsylvania. It even convinced the Lower Merion School District to close the Ardmore Avenue Elementary School in 1963 because it was segregated. But it also led to a long and bitter fight against school reorganization—in Delaware County especially.

Just beyond West Philadelphia, southeastern Delaware County began to suburbanize at the beginning of the twentieth century. Public transportation allowed many of its white-collar and blue-collar residents to commute to jobs in Chester or Philadelphia. Some of the area's public school districts took on suburban characteristics. In 1908, for example, the Darby Borough district replaced its supervising principal with a superintendent. It also opened a four-year high school, as did the Lansdowne Borough School District in 1914. The population of southeastern Delaware County, which rose rapidly at the beginning of the twentieth century, leveled off during the Great Depression but started growing again once prosperity returned. Folcroft's mostly white population increased by 26 percent in the 1950s. Public school enrollment did not increase as fast, in part because many young families chose the leafier suburbs of Bucks and Montgomery Counties instead.

Between 1900 and 1960 the African American proportion of the population in Delaware Country shrank from 10 percent to 7 percent. But in places like Darby Township and Yeadon Borough there were already enough Black families to deter prospective partners in any reorganization effort. In 1964 the county's plan for reorganization faced opposition because it proposed to combine three school districts that were almost exclusively white—Collingdale (99.7 percent), Folcroft (100 percent), and Sharon Hill (98.5 percent)—with two that were significantly Black, Darby Colwyn (22.1 percent) and Darby Township (68.2 percent). Responding to an appeal from the white districts, the State Board of Education placed Darby Colwyn in another reorganized district. The Delaware County Board of School Directors approved the consolidation of the Folcroft, Sharon Hill, Collingdale, and Darby Township school districts in 1968, and subsequent appeals that eventually went all the way to U.S. District Court failed to prevent the formation of the Southeast Delco School District. But discrimination persisted because minority students living in the southern portion of Darby Township were bused past all-white schools in nearby Folcroft and Sharon Hill to schools in the northern part of Darby Township that already had many Black students.

The elaborate appeals procedure set up by the state in 1968 (Act 150) slowed but did not prevent reorganization from being implemented. In 1975 there were thirteen local and forty-eight regional school districts in Bucks, Chester, Delaware, and Montgomery Counties; many of the latter emerged out of cooperative arrangements, known as "jointures," which had been in place for years. For example, the eight districts in Montgomery County that had participated in the North Penn Jointure for grades seven through twelve stayed together as the North Penn School District. Its 11,402 students in 1973 made it one of the largest in Greater Philadelphia. But some small districts avoided reorganization, especially in Montgomery County, because they met the state's requirements for independence. Despite never enrolling more than 828 students, the Jenkintown School District was not forced to merge with either Abington or Cheltenham because its leadership convinced county and state officials that it had the economic resources and the educational standards to remain self-governing.

By the early 1980s segregation had become a regional problem in Greater Philadelphia because the public schools in Philadelphia, Wilmington, and Camden now had such a high proportion of Black students. There were simply not enough whites enrolled in these urban school systems to achieve racial balance. Aware of this disparity, most educators and politicians ignored it. Change did occur in Delaware when the U.S. Supreme Court affirmed a District Court decision (*Buchanan v. Evans*, 1975) that led to the consolidation of all the public schools in New Castle County, where Wilmington is located. Formed in 1981, the Brandywine, Colonial, Christina, and Red Clay Consolidated school districts brought the Black children of the city together with white children living in its suburbs. But such sweeping changes may have helped convince at least some people that public education was failing not just in the region's cities but everywhere. Whether urban or suburban, public schools increasingly found themselves being compared unfavorably with private schools, charter schools, and even homeschooling.

The crisis of confidence in public education that began in the 1980s stemmed in part from the fact that suburban public schools were not able to escape the problems of their urban counterparts. Given a choice, suburban educators would immunize their schools against violence and substance abuse. All their students would excel on standardized tests and be admitted to college. None would be victimized by the ravages of poverty or the sting of racism. But this is not how public education works, even in the most affluent suburbs.

Public schools are open and free to all—by definition. Those in charge cannot ignore at-risk students, no matter what the problem. Children with special academic needs or debilitating personal problems are not geographically bounded, and their right to a "thorough and efficient" public education is legally protected. But some previously all-white suburbs had to contend with more equity issues than others at the end of the twentieth century because by then they had absorbed enough nonwhite residents to make race a significant issue in their public school systems. Consider, for example, the Cheltenham School District in Montgomery County, whose minority population had become big enough by the mid-1990s to attract attention. In 1996 the Cheltenham School Board decided to achieve better racial balance by busing some elementary students. This decision was denounced—not by white, but rather by some Black parents, who accused the board of racism because its busing program increased one school's proportion of white students. The board members who made this decision did not anticipate such opposition, but they stuck by it because they believed it would make the Cheltenham public schools better for everyone.

Over the course of the twentieth century the relationship between suburban and urban public schools in Greater Philadelphia flipped. Suburban schools at first emulated their urban counterparts and hoped to be compared favorably with them. When urban public education fell on hard times, suburban schools ran away from such comparisons. But suburban and urban public schools could not run away from each other, not only because they shared the same fundamental characteristics but also because they served a region that was itself becoming increasingly diverse and interdependent.

Automobile Suburbs

Carolyn T. Adams

In the twentieth century the internal combustion engine brought massive change to the region, as households and industrial producers increasingly relied on automobiles and trucks to conduct daily business. Philadelphia and Camden factory owners moved their plants to cheaper locations in nearby suburbs, especially those near highways. Assisted by the Federal Housing Administration and the Veterans Administration, residents of Philadelphia and Camden also moved to the suburbs, where the family car expanded housing choices beyond the towns served by streetcars and rail lines. While the advantages conferred by the new suburban lifestyle were obvious, few people fully appreciated the social challenges that the automobile would create.

Early twentieth-century developers built one of the first auto-centered residential neighborhoods just inside the Philadelphia city limit. Later designated on the National Register of Historic Places as the "Cobbs Creek Automobile Suburb District," this community sat adjacent to the newly created automobile parkway along Cobbs Creek, which formed part of Philadelphia's western boundary. The neighborhood's rows of two- and three-story houses, constructed mostly in the first quarter of the twentieth century, accommodated the family automobile with rear alleys and rear basement garages. Car ownership increased dramatically during the 1920s, accelerating middle-class suburbanization in both Pennsylvania and New Jersey. The Delaware River Bridge, which opened in 1926 (later known as the Benjamin Franklin Bridge), forged an easy connection between the two states.

Manufacturing firms as well left older urban industrial districts for the green fields beyond the city limits. The owners of industrial plants in Philadelphia, Camden, and Chester played an early role in shaping twentieth-century suburbs. The federally funded interstate highway system launched in the 1950s made it convenient for them to move their plants out of nineteenth-century industrial districts to cheap land at the edge of the city. There they replaced their multistory operations with one-story plants that accommodated continuous-flow production processes. They favored locations near highway on-ramps, where they could dramatically reduce the time it took truck drivers to deliver raw materials and pick up finished goods. Since suburban plants were typically more automated than older urban factories, owners could also save money on labor. For example, RCA, long a mainstay of Camden's industrial economy, moved a significant part of its offices and laboratories to Cherry Hill in 1964. Camden's combined losses of retail and manufacturing employment to Cherry Hill were so significant that by 1965 Cherry Hill's assessed property value surpassed that of Camden, deepening the economic challenge facing that aging city.

Federal funds for building highways in metropolitan areas constituted only part of the national government's spur to suburban growth following World War II. In addition, the GI Bill of 1944 provided low-interest loans to veterans for buying single-family homes, fueling the exodus from older residential neighborhoods in Philadelphia, Camden, Wilmington, and Chester. In 1940 the city of Philadelphia contained 57 percent of the total population living in nine counties that the Delaware Valley Regional Planning Commission (DVRPC) defined as the Greater Philadelphia region. By the year 2000 that figure had plummeted to 28 percent.

The suburbs built beyond the city limits at mid-twentieth century featured one-story or split-level houses, each home surrounded on all sides by its own grassy yard. Typically, builders offered a limited number of house plans and architectural styles, most of which offered either a side garage or a carport, building the automobile into the culture of the families who bought them. Surrounding the residential enclaves, shopping malls, drive-through restaurants, and drive-in movie theaters lined suburban highways to serve the car-owning population. By the late 1950s these services began to cluster in early shopping centers surrounded by massive parking lots. Satisfying so many household needs, these and numerous other shopping centers gave suburban homeowners fewer reasons to drive into Philadelphia, Camden, or Wilmington.

Growing segments of the suburban workforce both lived and worked outside the city limits. The automobile enabled businesses to disperse along major auto routes, rather than cluster in a handful of edge cities. That dispersed pattern of employment produced increasing

FIGURE 63. Once farmland and subsequently a summer retreat for Philadelphians which only accelerated in the 1890s when trolleys connected the city to the Willow Grove Amusement Park, Willow Grove, Montgomery County took a turn to suburban living with the advent of the automobile, as this 1926 photograph testifies. Subsequent development overwhelmed the residential quality of the township, as commercial investment, capped by the Willow Grove Mall, opened on the site of the amusement park after it closed in 1975. LIBRARY COMPANY OF PHILADELPHIA.

traffic flows from suburb to suburb, breaking the spoke-and-wheel pattern that had marked earlier commuting by streetcar and rail.

Rather than locating most services, entertainment, and employment in town centers where they could be reached on foot, the automobile encouraged real estate developers to spread out those everyday destinations. Admittedly, some stores, restaurants, and services were clustered in strip malls or enclosed shopping malls, but almost all accommodated the automobile. Both commercial and residential developers sought large tracts of suburban land on which to build—a practice that worked against a consistent pattern of outward expansion. Builders constantly leapfrogged over already-developed areas in order to acquire cheaper land that was not near already-developed territory. The resulting pattern created broadly scattered subdivisions and commercial and industrial development. That scattering reinforced the necessity of car travel as a requirement of life in the suburbs.

The one consistent element in all suburban plans was parking space for autos and trucks. Not just shopping centers, but also schools, hospitals, medical centers, and office complexes provided free parking as a matter of course. Often zoning boards required developers to assure at least one space per employee, and the easy availability of free parking led commuters to drive alone to work. The absence of sidewalks in many suburban commercial and office districts, along with the prospect of crossing massive asphalt parking lots, discouraged both walking and transit use in the suburbs.

The spread of massive suburban parking lots especially affected water quantity and quality. Paving over land that could otherwise filter rainwater reduced the amount of water recharging suburban aquifers, which often serve as primary sources of drinking water. Stormwater that drained off paved areas heightened the potential for flooding. And the proliferation of impervious parking surfaces in suburban locations increased the quantity of contaminants being washed into local streams, rivers, and lakes by stormwater runoff.

Even more threatening than the automobile's impact on water quality was the air pollution generated by auto exhaust. Philadelphia's embrace of the automobile in the 1950s and 1960s blinded some civic leaders to this threat. A 1969 DVRPC transportation analysis (projecting the region's needs and conditions in 1985) drew blistering criticism from the U.S. Environmental Protection Agency (EPA) for its heavy emphasis on accommodating automobiles at the expense of public transportation and environmental quality. Specifically, the federal agency criticized DVRPC for planning to spend three times as much money on limited-access roads as on mass transit.

Subsequent trends confirmed the EPA's fears about the impacts of auto transportation on the region's air quality. From 1990 to 2019, the amount of greenhouse gas emissions produced by autos and trucks in the Philadelphia metropolitan area increased faster than the population grew, according to Boston University's Database of Road Transportation Emissions. Among the neighborhoods burdened with the most auto-related pollution were Old City, Northern Liberties, Callowhill, and Chinatown—all areas adjacent to the Vine Street Expressway, which community leaders in Chinatown had fought bitterly. Suspecting the massive expressway project would damage their district, they had demanded unsuccessfully that the submerged road be capped, at least in their vicinity.

Not only inside the city, but also in the suburbs, dependence on the automobile endangered air quality at the turn of the twenty-first century. The single largest contributor to ozone was automobiles on congested roads. Lower Bucks County consistently recorded some of the highest smog levels in Pennsylvania, increasing the risk of cardiovascular disease and strokes. In some years, the two Bristol census tracts bordered by Interstate 95, the Pennsylvania Turnpike, and Route 3 recorded the highest asthma rates in the United States, exceeding 10 percent of adults. Advocates for cleaner air proposed that employers in Lower Bucks County allow employees to work from home on days with poor air quality, or organize ride-sharing, and reduce the company's use of motor vehicles.

Among the most important long-term effects of the automobile culture was to enable social separation of residents by income and race in the Philadelphia suburbs. As the suburban job base ranged across long distances (instead of concentrating in industrial districts like those within the central city), commuters needed daily access to an automobile. That requirement prevented many lower-income Philadelphians from living in the suburbs.

In some suburbs, trends toward income, racial, and ethnic separation were reinforced by restrictive covenants, sales, rental or financing opportunities, and real estate agents who steered African American buyers away from all-white neighborhoods. The resulting pattern separated the suburban population into homogeneous enclaves. By the 1970s, the social mixing of residents that had been common in earlier streetcar suburbs had become distinctly uncommon in suburbs.

As the twenty-first century opened, suburban planners faced changing consumer preferences that affected suburban planning. The dominance of shopping malls as retailing centers had begun to erode in competition with online shopping. Several of the region's largest malls suffered serious declines. At the same time, young adults appeared less committed to auto ownership than their parents' generation and more inclined to favor walkable environments for recreation, shopping, and entertainment. To accommodate the growing interest in walkable communities, the U.S. Environmental Protection Agency in 2014 began publishing a "National Walkability Index" because walkability had emerged as an important factor in real estate markets across the nation.

The Delaware Valley Regional Planning Commission encouraged redevelopment of walkable suburban centers with its Classic Towns initiative pursued between 2008 and 2018. That program encouraged and publicized a group of suburbs working to encourage pedestrian traffic by investing in walkable commercial districts. Typical Main Street improvements included historic preservation of stores, office buildings, restaurants, bars, and movie theaters, plus the addition of street trees and other greenery, historic lighting fixtures, and benches for sitting.

Some of those walkable suburbs served as county seats (for example, Doylestown and West Chester), while others developed lively town centers around regional rail stops (for example, Ambler and Collingswood). Such town-based initiatives, while they certainly could not eliminate the place of the automobile, could at least signal the end of its overwhelming dominance in suburban life.

Shopping Centers

Matthew Smalarz

Shopping centers, which bound retailers together into one physically convenient and accessible commercial venue for suburban consumers, profoundly altered Greater Philadelphia, redefining the region's socioeconomic dimensions and destabilizing the city's old, commercial core, the central business district. Commercial retailing also underwent significant changes, as the location, planning, and physical proportions of shopping facilities dramatically transformed the identity of the modern metropolis.

In the decade immediately following World War I, commercial real estate developers and department store owners devised new strategies to make retail shopping accessible to the area's growing suburban communities. Some developers, along with Sears, Roebuck and Company, a national retail chain, designed nascent strip malls in lower Northeast Philadelphia, Camden, and Upper Darby's Sixty-Ninth Street shopping district, directly appealing to working-class consumers in these urban communities. Other developers targeted affluent streetcar suburbs, especially along the Main Line. The Suburban Company, which designed Suburban Square in Ardmore, constructed an automobile-friendly shopping district that appealed to area shoppers' commercial tastes and interests.

Fearing escalating prices for downtown real estate and competition from suburban commercial centers, Philadelphia's department stores gradually embraced the decentralized retailing formula unfolding around the metropolitan area in the 1920s. In 1930, Strawbridge & Clothier, in shifting its retail strategy to focus on emerging upscale suburban communities, built its first branch store in a planned suburban shopping facility in Ardmore on the Main Line, followed the next year with a branch in Jenkintown. It thus became the first of the "Big Six" Philadelphia department stores to join the trend toward suburban shopping centers.

Although the Great Depression presented investment and financial hurdles to further suburban retail expansion, both Philadelphia department store owners and suburban developers laid plans for expansion outward during the downturn. Real estate developer John McClatchy, for instance, approached Lit Brothers executives to open a branch store at Sixty-Ninth Street in the late 1930s, but delayed the project until 1949 because of lingering financial fears stemming from the Great Depression. As World War II drew to its conclusion, other "Big Six" stores, namely Gimbels and Wanamaker's, entertained the possibility of building branch stores in anticipation of further shopping center development in the suburbs.

Accelerated residential decentralization after the war hastened the central business district's decline and inspired Philadelphia-area retailers and developers to expand their commercial footprint outside the city's borders. Together retailers and developers collaborated to carve out auto-friendly commercial marketplaces, with department stores functioning as anchor facilities. To attract middle-class consumers, they constructed outdoor pedestrian and strip malls, which often included ample parking, various specialty stores aimed especially at women, supermarkets, banks, and restaurants, creating sumptuous commercial conditions to meet emerging consumer demand.

Philadelphia's major department store chain and shopping center developers built or planned for fourteen branch stores between 1947 and 1955 in what they deemed competitive retail locations in Pennsylvania, New Jersey, and Delaware. In 1953, for instance, real estate developers planned to build a $15 million shopping center in Cheltenham, Pennsylvania, reaching agreement with Gimbels to construct a 240,000-square-foot facility to anchor the site. Gimbels constructed two additional branch facilities, in the Sixty-Ninth Street Upper Darby commercial district and Northeast Philadelphia's Bustleton-Cottman shopping center.

FIGURE 64. Artist's conception of the Cherry Hill shopping center, Camden County, New Jersey, 1956. Once opened, the mall helped transform once-rural Delaware Township into Camden County's wealthiest community by property assessment. SPECIAL COLLECTIONS RESEARCH CENTER, TEMPLE UNIVERSITY LIBRARIES.

Wanamaker's, on the other hand, targeted more affluent suburban communities with its branch initiative, building stores in the Wynnewood shopping center in 1954 and the Jenkintown shopping center in 1958. Lit Brothers, meanwhile, principally focused on Northeast Philadelphia and Lower Bucks County, opening branch stores in the Castor-Cottman shopping complex in 1954 and the Morrisville shopping center in 1957. In Philadelphia's western suburbs, the Kravitz Company undertook a $20 million open-air shopping center project in King of Prussia, which partnered with national retail chains (J.C. Penney and F.W. Woolworth) and local department stores (Wanamaker's and Gimbels).

Aside from strip mall development, prominent commercial developers designed and erected enclosed shopping malls, which served as regional commercial hubs. In the mid- to late 1950s and early 1960s, the aesthetic of shopping centers underwent a dramatic change, as mall architects and developers envisioned consumption spaces intended to mitigate the negative implications associated with suburban sprawl. They constructed enclosed malls, which incorporated garden courts, fountains, and air-conditioning to enhance the social and aesthetic features of mass consumption. Opened in 1956, Southdale Center, located in Edina, Minnesota, served as the archetype for enclosed malls around the nation, especially the Cherry Hill Mall.

Victor Gruen, the esteemed shopping center architect who conceived Southdale, was hired to plan what would become the Cherry Hill Mall, which opened in 1961, in Delaware Township, New Jersey. He sought to recreate the atmosphere of a town square, which would promote social order in an age of sprawling suburban development. Embracing Gruen's design, the mall's developer, James Rouse, collaborated with Strawbridge & Clothier president G. Stockton Strawbridge to forge an idyllic shopping complex for middle-class consumers.

Civic-oriented events also legitimized the communal stature of newly erected shopping complexes, as they employed marketing tactics, constructed large parking lots, and excluded "unsavory" social constituencies—namely racial minorities, vagrants, and the impoverished—to entice potential shoppers. In 1955 Gimbels executives, for instance, celebrated the opening of their branch store in the Cheltenham Square Mall by calling upon Montgomery County civic and business leaders to attend their facility's opening ceremonies in an effort to equate civic participation with commercial progress.

Shopping centers made special efforts to appeal to female shoppers, who became the primary target audience of suburban mass consumption. To enhance their shopping experiences, local developers built spacious, well-lighted parking lots and established carefully monitored "public" spaces and activities, such as baby-sitting services and fashion shows, to attract female shoppers and their children. Consumer questionnaires, often sent to suburban households in the 1950s to gauge shopping sentiments and preferences, also found that white, middle-class women preferred to shop in suburban malls and department stores, especially Strawbridge & Clothier's in Jenkintown, Lits Northeast, and Snellenburg's in Willow Grove, instead of venturing downtown to Philadelphia's central business district.

By the 1970s and 1980s, the commercial landscape of metropolitan Philadelphia had undergone a radical transformation. The development of major regional shopping centers, such as Cherry Hill and King of Prussia—which would become an enclosed shopping facility over multiple development phases during the 1970s and early 1980s—in the 1960s, spurred further commercial real estate expansion in Plymouth Meeting, Pennsylvania, and Deptford and Moorestown, New Jersey, during the 1970s.

Although suburban shopping centers continued to flourish, James Rouse, the well-regarded shopping center developer, collaborated with Philadelphia's Urban Redevelopment Authority to resuscitate Market Street's long-suffering central business district during the 1970s. Under his direction, he designed the Gallery at Market East, which marked a critical turning point in downtown Philadelphia's commercial fortunes. Upon its opening in 1977, it became the first regional shopping facility constructed in a major American downtown after World War II, reviving the city's commercial stature and serving as a major regional shopping destination.

In the 1990s, however, shopping centers in the Philadelphia region and around the nation confronted new commercial rivals and made economic and spatial modifications to remain competitive. As discount retail chains, specialty shops, and "big box" stores appeared in proximity to traditional shopping centers, established shopping centers responded by undergoing structural upgrades. Cherry Hill Mall officials, for instance, installed "retail neighborhoods," which catered to specific social lifestyles and economic niches and a social services' station, which addressed family-related concerns and medical emergencies. The Willingboro Plaza in New Jersey, which had been mired in economic decline since the 1970s, also became a target for redevelopment in the late 1980s. Developers reconfigured the plaza's physical dimensions to create a refurbished "town center," which included a public library, town houses, and community college classrooms. In making such adjustments, Philadelphia's shopping centers adapted to the evolving commercial model unfolding around them, redefining their commercial spaces to ensure continued social and economic relevance in the twenty-first century.

King of Prussia, Pennsylvania

Carolyn T. Adams

Twenty miles northwest of downtown Philadelphia, where the Pennsylvania Turnpike converges with the Schuylkill Expressway, a sleepy rural town clustered around a colonial-era tavern expanded massively in the twentieth century to become the region's largest employment center outside of Center City Philadelphia. Its suburban location in fast-growing Montgomery County proved irresistible to real estate developers in the 1950s when highway builders added the turnpike-expressway interchange to the area's already-existing connections to two national routes slated for significant upgrades: U.S. Route 202 running north-south and U.S. Route 422 stretching west into Ohio. Although built as an auto-dependent suburb, King of Prussia in the twenty-first century fell increasingly under the influence of new urbanist preferences for a higher-density grid pattern and transportation options that accommodated pedestrians, bicyclists, and transit users.

King of Prussia's name comes from an inn and tavern opened in 1769 in a converted farmhouse originally built by Welsh Quakers in 1719. The owner named his tavern to honor King Frederick II of Prussia, an eighteenth-century monarch who opposed Britain's imperial ambitions. The business prospered because its location stood at a crossroads exactly one day's travel from Philadelphia by horse, a favored position further boosted with the arrival of a rail connection to the Pennsylvania and Reading Railroads. By 1850, both the inn and the place were called King of Prussia. By the twentieth century, its size warranted its own zip code (19406) and post office, but King of Prussia existed as an incorporated governmental jurisdiction in Upper Merion Township, not a separate town. In this edge city, so-called because of its replication of historically central city functions in a previously rural area, the King of Prussia Business Improvement District established in 2010 became the closest thing to a governing framework through its work to enhance the commercial environment and to influence township policies on zoning, planning, taxes, and transportation issues.

Highway construction in the mid-twentieth century set the stage for King of Prussia's rapid development into an edge city. The Pennsylvania Turnpike, constructed from west to east across the state, arrived at Valley Forge in 1950, and by 1954 it extended eastward to the Delaware River. Almost at the same time Philadelphia was building its Schuylkill Expressway, which fully opened in 1958. That same year, spurred by the turnpike's arrival near King of Prussia, Boston developer Cabot, Cabot & Forbes acquired rights to 710 acres north of the turnpike interchange and began signing up companies like Western Electric; Smith, Kline & French Laboratories; Merck Sharp & Dohme; and Pennwalt Chemicals Corporation to occupy warehouses, office buildings, and factories. Since the highway interchange made it a reasonable commute from many other suburban communities, jobs quickly multiplied in what was then called the King of Prussia Industrial Park (later known as the Business Park). While some companies came from outside the region, others moved from Philadelphia to this convenient suburban location. For example, General Electric in 1962 relocated a major division from West Philadelphia to King of Prussia.

Subsequently the business park hosted software, biotech, pharmaceuticals, medical devices, finance, and insurance firms. From the beginning it welcomed defense contractors, one of which became the target of a famous antiwar protest by the Plowshares Eight. In September 1980 antiwar activists Daniel and Philip Berrigan with a half dozen other protesters illegally entered the General Electric plant in King of Prussia, vandalized the nose cones of several nuclear warheads being assembled there, and poured blood on company documents. Their arrest and trial sparked the Plowshares Movement, which grew into an international Christian peace movement. The business park continued to house numerous defense-related firms, most notably Lockheed Martin Space System Company, which took over the General Electric facility through corporate mergers.

To the average resident of the Philadelphia region, King of Prussia became known even more for its retailing than for its industrial production. The Kravitz Company began building its first-generation mall near the highway interchange in 1963. That early outdoor mall consisted of a strip of anchor stores (Korvettes 1962, J.C. Penney 1963, Wanamaker's 1965, Gimbels 1966) around an Acme supermarket, along with a cluster of smaller specialty shops. Starting from that mid-market retail cluster intended to serve middle-income households, the mall gradually shifted toward luxury goods for higher-income shoppers. This evolving business strategy reflected the mall's location in a favored part of the region where high-paying jobs abounded.

As early as 1970 the mall added an enclosed arcade to provide some indoor shopping at what came to be known as "The Plaza." Then, in 1981, a second complex called "The Court" opened, adding upscale stores including Bloomingdale's and Abraham & Straus. The Court signaled the developers' effort to rebrand King of Prussia as a higher-end shopping location for the increasingly affluent population living in the area. In a subsequent upgrade during the 1990s, the owner added nearly a million square feet to the older Plaza to make it the second-largest mall in the United States, behind only the Mall of America in Minnesota. The renovations of the 1990s made room to add increasingly pricey shops to the existing retail mix, leading locals to distinguish between the "poor mall and the rich mall" because different sections of King of Prussia attracted different customers.

In 2003 a major retail developer based in Indianapolis, the Simon Property Group, bought a controlling interest in the King of Prussia Mall. It continued upgrading the property to provide the largest collection of luxury retailers in the region (for example, Neiman-Marcus, Nordstrom, Tiffany and Company, and Hermès). Additional renovations done in 2016 included an indoor heated connector between the two main shopping centers—The Plaza and The Court—to tie them into a single complex while simultaneously adding fifty new stores and restaurants. The resulting

FIGURE 65. Undated aerial view of early construction at the King of Prussia Mall, a prime example within the region of an "edge city." SPECIAL COLLECTIONS RESEARCH CENTER, TEMPLE UNIVERSITY LIBRARIES.

three million square feet of mall space was projected to serve twenty-six million visitors a year, about one-fifth of them tourists in the region. Interestingly, that renovation sacrificed four hundred parking spaces, signaling a shifting vision for the edge city as a place that would also be reached by public transportation.

King of Prussia's history of reliance on the automobile made congestion on local roads a major problem for daily commuters, shoppers, and even tourists visiting nearby Valley Forge National Historical Park. Regional transportation planners and township zoning officials took steps to reduce dependence on automobiles and encourage people to live near their workplaces. With the closest rail station located two miles away from the mall, bus service on congested roads offered the only transit option, especially frustrating to the large number of transit-dependent riders commuting daily from Philadelphia to jobs in King of Prussia. To address this problem, SEPTA reviewed proposals for a five-mile rail extension to bring the Norristown High Speed Line into the core of King of Prussia, winding through the high-end stores, chain restaurants, and offices, with stops in both the shopping mall and business park. Planners hoped to start construction in 2020, but after multiple delays the plan was scrapped when the federal government declined to provide support for the multi-billion-dollar project.

Nevertheless, developers continued to pursue efforts to create a more traditional urban environment. Upper Merion Township rezoned the Business Park in 2014 to foster mixed uses and more compact development, to reduce parking requirements, and to promote pedestrian-friendly designs. The new guidelines authorized multifamily residential developers to build as many as thirty units per acre. Over time, plans called for replacing existing buildings with multipurpose structures to house people as well as businesses, restaurants, and shops, allowing residents to live near their work.

That trend continued in plans to develop the last major open parcel, a former golf course west of the mall, as the Village at Valley Forge, centered on a "lifestyle shopping mecca" with streets laid out in a walkable grid pattern, sidewalk cafés, living spaces built above stores and restaurants, and a town square area for programming public events like yoga sessions and movie nights for families. Beyond that core, additional elements of the new Village at Valley Forge were to include hotels and a conference center along with a new surgery center for Children's Hospital of Philadelphia. This ambitious plan prompted some critics to question whether the area really needed more shopping, restaurants, and services. Wouldn't that simply worsen congestion?

Despite spirited debate, it should not have surprised critics to see township officials approve the plans. Ever since the highway cloverleaf triggered new development in the late 1950s, Upper Merion Township's government mostly maintained a pro-development stance, largely because new investment generated enough tax revenue to allow the township to keep its residents' property taxes among the lowest in the region.

Sprawl

Robert J. Mason

Despite Philadelphia's twenty-first century-resurgence as the urban center of a vital multistate region, the city's revival did not stem the tide of outward expansion in a largely uncontrolled pattern known popularly as "sprawl." The steepest population growth in the region continued to occur in the newer suburbs and rural locales, in a low-density and heavily auto-dependent form. Regional and community leaders took important steps to slow the pace of that outward growth, but comparatively low energy prices and ongoing preferences for suburban living challenged their efforts to curb the land-consuming development, traffic congestion, and social inequalities that are the hallmarks of regional sprawl.

Philadelphia was designed as a compact city, constrained by the Schuylkill River to the west and the Delaware to the east. Commuting did not begin to become widespread until electric rail and paved roads became more common. But it was widespread automobile ownership, beginning in the 1920s, that fully facilitated "middle-class sprawl" and led to rapidly rising rates of per capita land consumption. Fears about neighborhood change, loss of property value, and safety in the wake of the 1960s race-based riots accelerated outmigration as whites fled from many parts of the urban core, not only in Philadelphia, but in other cities in the region, including Trenton and Camden, New Jersey. Widespread auto ownership was a critical enabling factor, but so too were federal policies that provided home mortgage subsidies; offered tax deductions for property tax and mortgage interest payments; supported redlining and associated disinvestment in specific core urban areas, particularly minority neighborhoods; and created the interstate highway system, which enabled long-distance commuting by car.

Between 1930 and 2010, the Philadelphia region's population increased by 70 percent, yet land consumption more than tripled. That sprawl was distributed unevenly, consisting of large expanses of low-density residential and commercial development punctuated by more dense suburban centers, including the "edge cities" of King of Prussia and Cherry Hill, each home to a regional mega-mall; pharmaceutical clusters in Mercer County, New Jersey, New Castle County, Delaware, and Montgomery County, Pennsylvania; and office parks in Great Valley, to Philadelphia's west, and along U.S. Route 1 in Mercer County, New Jersey. These concentrations of commercial and industrial activity helped drive and shape new residential development, leading to dramatic increases in intersuburban commuting. Sprawl has been deliberately limited to a significant extent only in the region's far eastern reaches, by the federal/state regulatory program that protects ecological resources and manages development in New Jersey's Pinelands National Reserve.

In 2014, the national coalition Smart Growth America listed the Philadelphia Metropolitan Statistical Area (MSA) as thirty-third in its ranking of least sprawled out MSAs of 221 metropolitan areas analyzed. This assessment reflected the city of Philadelphia's denser-than-average pattern of residential development and several centuries of settlement that produced dozens of small towns outside the city, built at fairly high density on old-fashioned street grids. At the same time, Philadelphia's greater-than-average dispersal of employment contributed to growth in traffic congestion associated with reverse and intersuburban commuting.

Philadelphia, along with four other core cities of the region—Camden and Trenton, New Jersey; Chester, Pennsylvania; and Wilmington, Delaware—all had reached their population peaks in 1950 and mostly have experienced declines since then. By contrast, the general trend for the counties in the metropolitan statistical area (Philadelphia excepted) was one of mostly robust postwar growth, with more modest growth toward the turn of the millennium and beyond. Much of that growth came in the form of single-family homes and sprawled commercial development.

The Delaware Valley Regional Planning Commission (DVRPC), formed in 1965 and subsequently federally designated as the planning agency for the nine-county Greater Philadelphia area, creates regional plans, conducts research, and has some control over regional disbursement of federal transportation funds. Yet it does not have direct regulatory power over land use, which limits its capacity to guide regional development. New Jersey has a comprehensive state plan, in effect in various incarnations since 1992, that seeks to guide and control development and protect valued natural, agricultural, aesthetic, historic, and recreational resources. But the plan is more aspirational than enforceable and regulatory. It provides a blueprint for directing state investments and incentives toward supporting its objectives, but it does not dictate to local governments how they should develop the land within their borders. New Jersey's Pinelands region, proving the exception, is subject to more direct, enforceable regulation.

The Greater Philadelphia region, as defined by the Delaware Valley Regional Planning Commission, contains over 350 municipalities, each of which is preeminently concerned with its own fiscal health rather than regional economic and environmental sustainability. Regional planning efforts are further challenged by the fact that the municipalities are governed by the differing constitutional and political frameworks of three states: Pennsylvania, New Jersey, and Delaware. To the extent that municipalities have coordinated regionally, they have opted for less regulatory, more collaborative programs dealing more often with the consequences of sprawl—such as traffic congestion, lack of affordable housing, and loss of open space—than the root causes of sprawl.

Notwithstanding continued outward development, establishing protected status for open space has proved somewhat successful in preventing sprawl from consuming valued landscapes. Protected lands have been preserved in such areas as state and local parks, forests, and wildlife areas; preserved farmlands; and conservation easements that limit future development of privately owned lands. In addition to its Pinelands National Reserve, New Jersey has had a long history of land preservation pursued through its Green Acres program, established in 1961 to acquire lands and support agencies' and nonprofit organizations' land-protection activities.

Pennsylvania's Growing Greener program initiated in 1999 has distributed several billion dollars among state agencies, to support farmland and open-space protection, state park maintenance, watershed restoration, local land-use planning assistance, and other environmental projects. Local government ballot measures in the early twenty-first century also provided significant funding for land protection. Between 2008 and 2014, voters approved $141 million of funding for land conservation in Pennsylvania; nearly $2.5 billion in New Jersey (excluding Green Acres statewide ballot questions); and $4.25 million in Delaware (entirely in Newark, which is within the Philadelphia Metropolitan Statistical Area). Nonprofit organizations also became active in protecting lands, through direct purchase as well as acquisition of conservation easements. In this respect, Chester County—one of America's wealthiest—has had a very active nonprofit land-trust sector that has been quite effective in protecting its valued pastoral and equine landscapes.

Twentieth-century master plans and ordinances in many of the region's suburbs failed to support "smart growth," that is, the building of communities with dense mixed development in order to concentrate residential construction and protect common areas of open space and critical ecological resources. Post-1990, however, a majority of municipalities in the DVRPC region began to adopt one or more smart growth measures, such as multi-municipal comprehensive plans, ordinances that support denser suburban development, and transportation plans that encourage alternatives to automobile travel. A limited amount of new, greenfield development adopted conservation design principles. For example, the Hankin Group garnered considerable acclaim for its Eagleview development in Chester County. In 2003, the regionally headquartered megadeveloper Toll Brothers created a "Toll Brothers City Living" division, devoted to building suburban communities with something of a townlike feel. Smart growth and related measures are politically palatable alternatives to straightforward imposition of stringent land-use regulations, since they accept and promote economic, residential, and commercial growth, while at the same time seeking to direct it in ways that protect open space, preserve farmland, reduce traffic congestion, and improve regional "livability" generally.

In addition, twenty-first-century transportation planning transitioned toward managing and limiting sprawl, rather than promoting it. The "post-interstate" era was represented by such projects as the long overdue interchange linking Interstate 95 with the Pennsylvania Turnpike and the widening of portions of several existing expressways. Many of the post-interstate projects were accompanied by walkways, bicycle paths, and "traffic-calming" design features.

Transit-oriented development (TOD), encouraged and incentivized by state governments, aimed at countering sprawl by concentrating development around transit stations and promoting commuting by public transportation. DVRPC listed, in 2015, 154 "development near transit" projects, the vast majority of them in the city of Philadelphia, at a wide range of scales and in various states of proposal or completion. One of the city's success stories was Paseo Verde, a development completed in late 2013 that provided affordable LEED-certified housing, a mix of retail and community-service enterprises, and access to all SEPTA regional rail trains at the Temple University rail station.

Public transit ridership increased regionally after the turn of the millennium, but it could not be presumed that would automatically reduce sprawl. Ironically, easier access to outer parts of the region could in some cases foster further sprawl, depending on regional and local planning efforts, economic conditions, and general demographic trends. Nor have smart growth strategies necessarily provided solutions to social and spatial inequalities. Even though the smart growth agenda supports urban redevelopment and regional equity, suburban locales frequently employ smart growth and other growth management rhetoric to preclude most new developments, especially higher-density development that could provide affordable housing. Even when higher-density developments are built, they usually offer little in the way of low-income housing options, and most residents do not hold jobs within these communities.

Many factors—difficult to predict—help determine how a growing population gets distributed across the region's land base. These include energy markets and prices, concentrations of employment opportunities, the extent to which young people continue to favor urban living, and immigration trends. Another trend that pushed sprawl even beyond the traditional boundaries of the region was the development of second homes in the Poconos region and along the New Jersey shore, driven in considerable part by people with first homes in the Philadelphia area. Moreover, Philadelphia has attracted residents moving from New York City to both Philadelphia and to Bucks and Mercer Counties. And there is increased commuting into the region, notably from Lancaster County, to Philadelphia's west, where the additional demand for housing has exacerbated the already extreme pressure on the area's rich agricultural lands.

National, state, and local studies have blamed urban sprawl for a laundry list of maladies, among them wasteful government spending, inefficient energy consumption, high per capita greenhouse gas emissions, traffic congestion, loss of prime farmland and open space, air and water pollution, excessive water demands, declining social capital, obesity, shortened life expectancy, and a host of social and environmental injustices. Yet at the same time, sprawled development patterns have provided desirable residential choices to people able to make such choices. That makes managing sprawl an immense challenge, especially given the reluctance to consider carbon taxes, higher gasoline taxes or vehicle-miles-traveled charges, congestion charges, adjustments to the tax deductibility of home mortgages and property taxes, or stringent land-use regulatory measures. Greater Philadelphians—like many Americans—are conflicted about sprawl and what to do about it, leading some frustrated planners to declare that while Americans hate sprawl, they also hate density.

EXPLORE MORE

The Fairmount Park system at the city's core is one of the largest and most impressive urban open spaces of its kind in the country. Laced through with attractions for entertainment, education, and repose as well as recreation, the park is home to the Philadelphia Zoo, the Sofuso Japanese House and Garden, and the Mann Center for the Performing Arts as well as historic houses and industrial sites such as Mount Pleasant, Woodford, and Strawberry Mansion, and the Fairmount Water Works. The Please Touch children's museum occupies the last major building remaining from the 1876 Centennial Exhibition in the park. For the park's history and effect, see Elizabeth Milroy, *The Grid and the River: Philadelphia's Green Places, 1682–1876* (Pennsylvania State University Press, 2016). For the larger context of the park's role in Philadelphia, see David Contosta and Carol Franklin, *Metropolitan Paradise: The Struggle for Nature in the City: Philadelphia's Wissahickon Valley, 1620–2020* (Saint Joseph's University Press, 2010).

James McClelland and Lynn Miller make the connection between park and parkway in *City in a Park: A History of Philadelphia's Fairmount Park System* (Temple University Press, 2015). The classic study of the parkway is David Brownlee, *Building the City Beautiful: The Benjamin Franklin Parkway and the Philadelphia Museum of Art* (Philadelphia Museum of Art, 1989). In addition to serving as a primary gathering spot for special events and holidays, the parkway became over the years a primary cultural spine for the city and the region. Along the parkway below the imposing Philadelphia Museum of Art atop the Fairmount plateau lie the Rodin and Barnes Foundation museums, the Franklin Institute, and the Philadelphia Free Library, among other institutions. Taken together the classical architecture lining the broad avenue provides a stunning example of the City Beautiful planning ideals that swept the country at the start of the twentieth century.

John Hepp recounts the ways the city retained its hold on the middle class, even as transportation innovation opened new possibilities for their residential location in *The Middle-Class City: Transforming Space and Time in Philadelphia, 1876–1926* (University of Pennsylvania Press, 2003). He describes Wanamaker's as a haven for the middle class, offering amenities long since lost in such institutions. Wanamaker's "Grand Depot" remains in operation, but as a Macy's. The store still offers organ concerts to enthusiastic audiences. Lit Brothers is long gone, but its distinctive façade remains on Market Street at Seventh Street as part of the Market Street East development instituted by James Rouse in the 1970s. Herbert Ershkowitz's *John Wanamaker: Philadelphia Merchant* (Combined Publishing, 1999) provides a thorough history of the man and his creation. Richard Longstreth, *The American Department Store Transformed, 1920–1960* (Yale University Press, 2010), provides a larger context for the rise and fall of downtown department stores. Stephanie Dyer tells the story of commercial decentralization in "Markets in the Meadows: Department Stores and Shopping Centers in the Decentralization of Philadelphia, 1920–1980," *Enterprise & Society* (December 2002). An early Sears store, classical in design and widely popular with South Jersey residents at its location on the Admiral Wilson Boulevard near the entrance to the Benjamin Franklin Bridge in Camden, was torn down in 2013 to make way for the U.S. headquarters of Subaru.

The larger context for greater Philadelphia's shifting metropolitan landscape can be found in Carolyn Adams, David Bartelt, David Elesh, and Ira Goldstein's *Restructuring the Philadelphia Region: Metropolitan Divisions and Inequality* (Temple University Press, 2008). See also Ann Marie T. Cammarota, *Pavements in the Garden: The Suburbanization of Southern New Jersey Adjacent to the City of Philadelphia, 1769 to the Present* (Fairleigh Dickinson University Press, 2001).

Carolyn Adams recounts the history of manufacturing suburbs in chapter 6 of *Nature's Entrepôt: Philadelphia's Urban Sphere and Its Environmental Thresholds* (University of Pittsburgh Press, 2012), edited by Brian C. Black and Michael J. Chiarappa. Robert Mason recounts the evolution of Philadelphia-area sprawl in chapter 9 of the same volume. The region's two Levitt communities, in Bucks County, Pa., and Willingboro, N.J., are worth visiting for what they say about the ideas and practices behind mass-produced housing, and how such communities have adapted over the years. Sociologist Herbert J. Gans provided the classic evaluation of such communities in his 1967 study of the New Jersey site, *The Levittowners: Ways of Life and Politics in a New Suburban Community* (Pantheon Books, 1967). An edited book by Dianne Harris, *Second Suburb: Levittown, Pennsylvania* (University of Pittsburgh Press, 2010), draws on both the reflections of those who lived and worked in Levittown and scholars who bring their critical insights to the time and place. Of particular interest is Christopher Sellers's essay describing how the intensive development of Lower Bucks County, where Levittown is located, prompted efforts in the 1950s and 1960s in the more affluent central and upper parts of the county to preserve open space.

For a review of the changing suburban environment after World War II, see Campbell F. Scribner, *The Fight for Local Control: Schools, Suburbs, and American Democracy* (Cornell University Press, 2016). The growing racial and ethnic diversity of suburbs has drawn attention over time. A 2009 film documentary on the inner New Jersey suburb of Pennsauken, *The New Neighbors* (Torrice Media, 2009), charts the challenges of maintaining stable integration even as a town shifts its racial makeup. *The Goldbergs* (2013–23), a television situation comedy set in 1980s Jenkintown, Pennsylvania, portrays a slice of life in middle-class suburbia built during the postwar era of mass suburbanization. Myron Orfield includes Philadelphia in his assessment of suburban diversification in his 2002 book issued by the Brookings Institution, *American Metro Politics: The New Suburban Reality*.

Chapter 8

COUNTIES

Introduction

Like many Americans, residents living within the Greater Philadelphia region affiliate more strongly with their hometowns (whether city, township, or borough) than with the county in which they reside. That is perhaps surprising since county governments play a critical role in the daily lives of residents. Never was that more apparent than during the COVID-19 epidemic that gripped the region in the early 2020s. Tasked with protecting the public health, county governments mustered resources to fight the epidemic, publish health information, and establish vaccination sites. In addition to their role in protecting public health, counties shoulder responsibility for assessing property values for the purpose of levying taxes on residents, planning for development and land use, operating courts and jails to keep communities safe, and administering free and fair elections. They provide crucial—and sometimes highly contested—public services. Still, counties remain among the least visible tiers of government to many citizens.

Pennsylvania's model of county government descended from the proprietor William Penn, who was following long-established precedent when he divided his province into counties. In 1682 he laid out Pennsylvania's three original counties—Philadelphia, Bucks, and Chester. And by deed, Penn gained the three lower Delaware counties: New Castle, Kent, and Sussex. Penn instructed his agents to subdivide each county into small towns, which he expected to be ruled by direct democracy. So wedded was the proprietor to the model of small-town democracy that his agents allowed townships to be formally recognized even if their starting population totaled as few as ten families.

Expecting small towns to meet everyday needs of settlers who lived nearby, Penn established county governments as administrative arms of his provincial government, performing such necessary duties as collecting taxes and overseeing the justice system, including courts and jails. Early county governments built roads, provided for the poor, and preserved the public peace. In doing so they served, and still serve, as administrative arms of higher-level (provincial, and later state) government, while partnering with local townships. In colonial Delaware, too, county structure was imported from England and put in place as early as 1664.

William Penn also strongly influenced the colony of West New Jersey, where county courts were established in Burlington, Salem, and Gloucester to try criminals, adjudicate disputes, and collect taxes for roads and bridges. Even though its settlements were sparse and scattered, some of New Jersey's roadways were the best in the colonies due to the area's central location between New York and Philadelphia and between the northern and southern colonies.

The term "county seat" arose because only one town within each county housed its seat of justice, meaning its court of law. Overland travel was cumbersome in the

MAP 4. Greater Philadelphia. MAP BY MICHAEL SIEGEL.

seventeenth and eighteenth centuries, so settlers took a keen interest in the geographic location where courts resolved their disagreements about property boundaries, water rights, tax delinquencies, and many other issues affecting citizens. Inevitably, conflicts arose about the location of the county seat. For example, at the founding of Bucks County in 1682, Falls Township on the Delaware River was designated as the county seat. Then in 1705 the county seat shifted to Bristol on the Delaware River, but as the population spread farther northward through Bucks County, Bristol was considered too far to travel for some. So the county built a new courthouse in Newtown in 1726. Ultimately, residents of Central and Upper Bucks pushed again to move the county seat from Newtown because it was too hard to reach by primitive roads, and in 1810 Doylestown became the compromise choice, both because of its location and because it offered stagecoach service and inns where lawyers and others could stay during court sessions.

County seats were located in communities designated as "boroughs," which were typically small towns containing commercial buildings along with court houses and borough offices. Before the American Revolution, one such borough had been established in each of Philadelphia, Chester, and Bucks Counties. In those early boroughs, one could find general stores and could hire the services of blacksmiths, iron mongers, shoemakers, gunsmiths, wheelwrights, and other tradesmen. Although most farmers operated independently, producing many of the tools and agricultural products they needed, landowners nevertheless relied on those market towns for the services of specialized craftsmen and traders. Boroughs also provided useful public facilities like landing docks and weighing stations. Outside of boroughs, the counties were subdivided into rural townships that typically covered broad expanses of territory dotted with farmsteads.

Across the centuries, the thriving ports located on two sides of the Delaware River spurred the growth of Philadelphia County and Camden County. On the New Jersey side, Camden's commercial advantage prompted it to assert its independence from Gloucester County, causing a split from that early county in 1844. Within Pennsylvania, none of the region's other county seats could compete commercially against the port of Philadelphia. Even Norristown (seat of Montgomery County) did not attain the status of municipality until 1986, although it had become an industrial, retail, banking, and government hub. In the state of Delaware, it was not until the twentieth century that Wilmington emerged as an international seaport.

Rather than concentrating in county seats and other town centers, early European settlers spread broadly across the land, establishing farmsteads and building water-powered mills for processing grains and lumber and docks for shipping agricultural products to Philadelphia and then onward to the Caribbean and Europe. Early roads connected outlying farms and mills to Philadelphia, the region's main marketplace and port connecting the colony to distant markets. The coming of railroads in the nineteenth century multiplied connections within the region, making it convenient for Philadelphians employed in office jobs to live in nearby suburbs and travel downtown each day, and connecting South Jersey and shore towns with Philadelphia via Camden. The most dramatic opening of outlying areas came with mid-twentieth- century highways that made a daily commute possible for thousands more households. Many white and middle-class Philadelphians benefited from federal housing subsidies that made it possible to move outward to newly built developments. Those new homeowners found the most affordable developments at distances beyond the railroad suburbs that had been settled earlier in the twentieth century. Even on twenty-first-century maps of the region, one observes the historic continuity of that pattern; a number of the region's most affluent communities are still located in mid-distance suburbs, while more affordable housing is available farther out at the edge of the metropolis. Clearly, upper-income households remained willing to pay high housing prices in order to enjoy convenient access to Center City Philadelphia, and to Wilmington for residents of Chester and New Castle Counties. In the latter decades of the twentieth century, the traditional hub-and-spoke commuting pattern was augmented by new patterns of daily trips connecting suburbs with one another. In particular, the Pennsylvania Turnpike built across Montgomery County from west to east generated a daily stream of workers and shoppers that began to rival the earlier pattern of suburb to city.

In the final decades of the twentieth century, the real estate boom began to worry observers who had watched developers pave over large swaths of the suburban landscape. A dire warning came in 2001 from a group of regional analysts who observed that in the years between 1969 and 2000, southeastern Pennsylvania had lost a worrying one-third of its agricultural land to development. Such dramatic losses spurred county activists across the region to seek ways to preserve vanishing farmland in order to maintain environmental quality and preserve scenic beauty as contributors to their quality of life. Outside Philadelphia, every suburban county established a program to preserve agricultural land by purchasing easements from landowners. Those agreements precluded any future development on the protected farmland, no matter who might become the future owner. Across the nine-county region covered by the Delaware Valley Regional Planning Commission from 2011 to 2020, activists working to protect private lands (mostly farms) achieved an increase of roughly 69,000 acres, while the amount of public open space (mostly parks) increased by about 13,500 acres.

Within a legal framework handed down by colonial-era proprietors, the region's residents have built a physical landscape whose fields, farms, roads, rails, neighborhoods, and commercial centers reflect the cumulative imprint of many generations. That legal framework assigns many important aspects of suburban life to county governments (for example, highways, public health, welfare, courts, and jails). Yet because counties function mainly as administrative arms of the state government, they may not inspire the emotional attachment that so many citizens display for their hometowns, where residents can exert more direct control. The high degree of citizen attachment to small towns led one national authority on local government to describe the Philadelphia suburbs as a landscape of "little boxes" whose fragmentation makes it challenging to forge regional solutions to shared problems. The final chapter of this volume examines the work of many citizens who have met that challenge by forming voluntary regional institutions and alliances.

Philadelphia County, Pennsylvania

Andrew Heath

Dating to 1682, Philadelphia County's founding coincided with the origin of the city. Although the county faded from view after its consolidation with the city in 1854, it remained important for understanding Philadelphia's urban development, local government, and long battles for political reform.

When founding Pennsylvania, William Penn followed long-established precedent by dividing his province into counties. As an ancient jurisdiction, the county had roots in the shires of England's Saxon earls. After the Norman Conquest of 1066, the shires became known as counties. Over the following centuries they became the primary administrative subdivisions for a growing state, including in the American colonies beginning in Virginia in the 1630s. Penn followed suit, creating Philadelphia, Bucks, and Chester Counties in 1682.

Over the course of the eighteenth century the Pennsylvania Provincial Assembly and then General Assembly altered Philadelphia County's borders as the colony expanded. As colonists who had migrated westward petitioned for local governments of their own, portions of Philadelphia were sliced off to form

FIGURE 66. Philadelphia County map, 1819.
FREE LIBRARY OF PHILADELPHIA.

Berks (1752) and Montgomery (1784) Counties. By 1800 Philadelphia County's boundaries had been fixed in a manner that roughly corresponded to the future city limits, running along the Delaware River from southwest to northeast and stretching over the Schuylkill River to the west.

Local government in early Philadelphia County took place at three levels. Incorporated municipalities enjoyed rights granted by the proprietor, much in the manner of self-governing English towns. Within the county, the two-square-mile city of Philadelphia (1691) as well as the separate settlement of Germantown (1691) each benefited from these privileges, although Germantown lost its charter in 1707 after devout Quakers and Pietists proved reluctant to hold local offices on religious grounds. Between that point and the Revolution, only Southwark (1762), which stood just to the south of the city proper, secured incorporation. Beyond these self-governing municipalities, county government held sway, with Philadelphia city serving as the seat. As the county covered a large rural area, it was subdivided into townships—twelve in all by 1718—that took on administrative roles. In Blockley, Bristol, and Byberry, for instance, township constables performed many of the same duties as Philadelphia's sheriff.

COUNTY POLITICS

County government played an important role in the lives of the colonists. Together with its townships, it built and maintained highways, provided for the poor, preserved the public peace, prosecuted and punished offenders, and impounded stray animals. Like a chartered corporation, Philadelphia County could hold property and could sue and be sued. As the most visible form of local government, moreover, it became a political battleground. Despite holding Pennsylvania as a feudal estate, Penn and his heirs soon had to grant the province a measure of self-rule, which extended to counties and townships. Thus while a few county officers were directly appointed, voters usually had at least some say. The proprietor, for instance, chose the county sheriff, but only from the two leading candidates at the polls. Because a far higher proportion of Philadelphia County's rural men than their urban counterparts met the property qualification for voting, rural areas were over-represented by elected officials like property assessors and tax collectors.

Colonial patterns persisted long after the proprietorship of the Penns. In the decades after American independence, growing parts of Philadelphia County sought incorporation as self-governing municipalities, a process that gathered pace in the Jacksonian era. Many of these municipalities, like Moyamensing and Kensington, stood on the edge of Philadelphia proper, separated from the city only by lines on the county map that were more imaginary than real. Others, notably Manayunk (1840) and a rechartered Germantown (1844), burgeoned as villages, miles from the growing metropolis. The vast majority of Philadelphia County remained rural, and in these areas county and township government appeared perfectly adequate, especially as more positions—including sheriff from 1838—opened to direct election. County jurisdiction also extended into the incorporated municipalities. Residents of the city, districts, and boroughs voted for county officers and paid the county tax, which went toward the upkeep of highways, courts, bridges, and prisons; some of the biggest building schemes proposed around midcentury—including early plans for public buildings at the Broad and Market intersection—were county projects. Among such designs was Moyamensing's imposing jail—designed by Thomas U. Walter, fourth architect of the U.S. Capitol building—which stood from 1835 until 1968.

Philadelphia's "turbulent era," however, exposed the limits of county government. Between 1828 and 1849 the city was wracked by riot after riot, including the anti-Catholic violence of 1844. Much of the trouble took place in the newly incorporated suburbs. Neither city nor suburbs maintained a modern police force prior to 1845, and when crowd action got out of hand, it usually fell on the sheriff, as traditional conservator of the peace, to restore control by raising a posse comitatus ("power of the county"). Although the sheriff's powers were broad in theory (a judge in 1844 compared them to those of a dictator in the Roman Republic), they proved weak in practice. One Kensington strike in 1843 concluded with weavers turning on the sheriff, and a year later, after the posse proved unable to stop two major mobs, the county was placed under martial law. Attempts to improve the county's response to rioting—notably an 1841 statute that made taxpayers liable for losses incurred during riots—had little impact, and instead citizens began to look to either the creation of a professional police force or the consolidation of the city and built-up districts into one municipal government.

As if to step into the vacuum created by the want of strong municipal authorities, the county became more assertive. In 1853, the county commissioners tried to borrow $2 million to help fund a railroad to Lake Erie. Such actions, along with the money made in fees by county and township officers, drew censure from prominent citizens; one labeled the purchase of stock "the most flagrant act of injustice ever attempted." Frustration with spendthrift officials swelled support for a consolidation, which, when it finally came in 1854, swallowed the entire county into the city.

That extension of the city's boundaries to embrace the county's vast rural environs went far beyond the designs of most consolidators. Opposition to consolidation came largely from rural townships, where the routine work of maintaining highways and providing for the poor seemed a world away from the complex administration of a big city. In the years leading up to the Civil War residents in the remote northeast petitioned the state legislature to break away from the city and either form a new county or merge with neighboring Bucks; such secessionist sentiment in Philadelphia's northeast persisted late into the twentieth century. But in 1854 consolidators promised county landowners spectacular returns on their property, lower rates of taxation, and the maintenance of separate poor boards. The mixture of incentives and concessions tempered hostility to annexation.

With the 1854 charter, Philadelphians were not quite sure whether city and county had become one and the same—even the architect of the Consolidation Act expressed his doubts, and the city commissioners retained a degree of independence from councils and the mayor—but the new charter seemed to have done its work. The county board disappeared, as did the townships, except for the purpose of providing poor relief. County officials came under the city's control, including the county commissioners, who oversaw elections and tax collection. The county continued to play a role in the justice system, but the cost of maintaining courthouses and prisons fell on the city. A single municipal treasury had authority to raise taxes and disburse funds for both city and county purposes.

Yet in the late nineteenth century divisions between city and county began to reappear. The state constitution of 1874 made several offices—including commissioner and treasurer—county positions. Courts subsequently confirmed that these city officers under the Consolidation Act were constitutionally protected county officials. To municipal reformers, such a seemingly academic distinction had serious political consequences. First, county officials could spend money of their own accord and then leave the bill with city government. This "mandamus evil," as Progressive reformers called it, reminded residents of post–Civil War commissions that had similar powers to burden the municipal treasury. Second, elected county officials had access to a rich patronage pot and considerable income in the form of state-mandated fees. A new city charter in 1919 established a merit system for city employees, but as the county lay beyond its jurisdiction, jobs there could still be used as political rewards. By the middle of the twentieth century, about a thousand county employees were excluded from Philadelphia's civil service requirements. Long before then, however, county offices had become a boon to Republican bosses like Simon Cameron and James McManes.

The task of completing what one early twentieth-century critic called the city and county's "half-hearted" consolidation preoccupied reformers from the Progressive Era (ca. 1890–1920) onward. The independent Bureau of Municipal Research, which acknowledged the "complicated and technical" relationship between the two governments, nonetheless argued in 1923 that the matter was "of sufficient importance to engage the attention of every citizen." The bureau led the drive for "home rule": a measure adopted in other states that gave cities the freedom to draw up their own charters without legislative interference. Calls for the consolidation of city and county offices accompanied the campaign. Given that the 1874 state constitution safeguarded county offices, this required amending the state constitution, and a measure enabling such a reform failed in a 1937 statewide referendum despite being approved by a large majority of voters in Philadelphia.

In the post–World War II era reformers found friendlier terrain for consolidation. Democrats Joseph S. Clark and Richardson Dilworth exposed swindling in the Republican city machine, and for once "corrupt and contented" Philadelphians responded. Civic organizations called for home rule and the merger of city and county functions. In 1951, they secured a home rule charter, and state voters approved an amendment allowing cities and counties to merge. By 1952, under the reform charter, the work of bringing county offices under city control was well underway.

Philadelphia's first consolidation in 1854 had merged the territory of city and county; its second, almost a century later, brought their separate institutions together under unified control. Yet though it was conceived in part as an efficiency measure, city-county consolidation did not always have the desired effects. The Home Rule Charter coincided with white flight to suburbs beyond the city-county border. Unlike in many other urban centers, where the cost of county institutions like courts and prisons was shared between city and

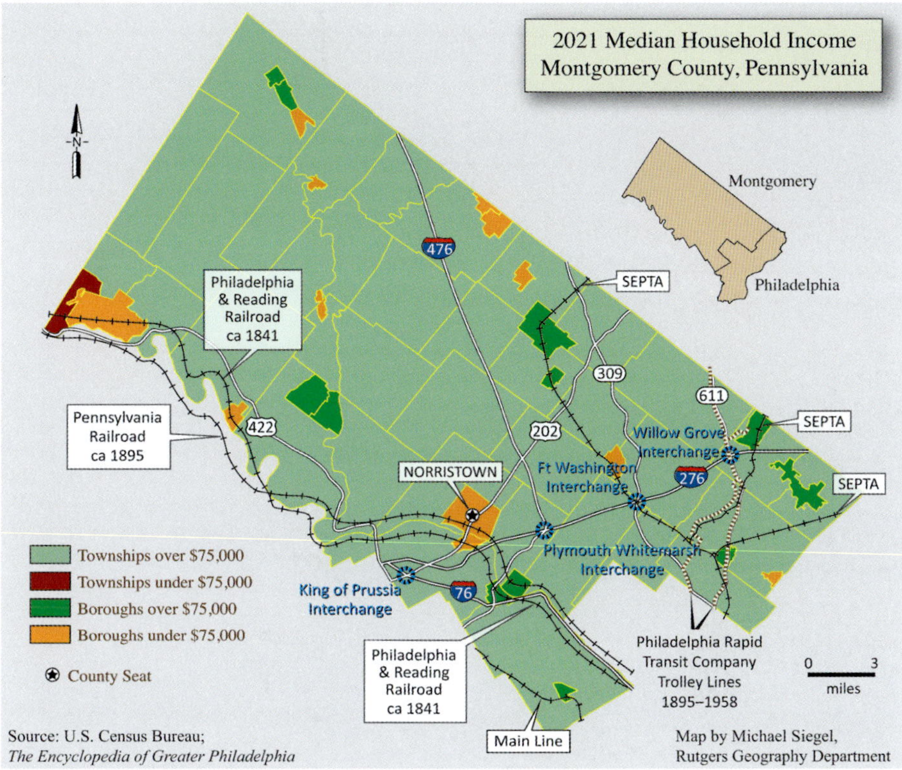

MAP 5. 2021 Median Household Income Montgomery County, Pennsylvania. MAP BY MICHAEL SIEGEL.

suburbs, Philadelphia's residents footed the bill alone. And with post-1945 regional growth concentrated in the suburbs and exurbs of neighboring counties, and the city itself going through a period of demographic decline that diminished property tax revenues, local politicians increasingly turned to a wage tax—first introduced in 1939 but increased regularly in the 1960s and 1970s—to compel commuters to pay their share toward the running of the metropolis. Critics accused the tax of placing a drag on economic growth, but its defenders insisted it was right and proper for suburbanites to contribute to the city in which they worked. Nor did the Philadelphia County "row offices" disappear entirely with home rule. In 2017, the sheriff, the city commissioners, the clerk of quarter sessions, and the register of wills remained a part of city government. Reformers saw them as expensive anachronisms. The register of wills, for instance, was just about the only part of the municipal apparatus exempt from Philadelphia's civil service rules. Philadelphia County died as a unit of local government, but in pockets of city hall its legacy lived on.

Montgomery County, Pennsylvania

Carolyn T. Adams

The early Europeans who settled in what would become Montgomery County in the eighteenth century tended prosperous farms, forges, and mills. They depended on the Philadelphia market to sell their products and on its port to connect them to the wider colonial world. Subsequent generations built a dense transportation network that linked county laborers, suppliers, and consumers with each other and with the city, fueling the county's prosperity across the nineteenth and early twentieth centuries. Beginning in the 1950s, however, county residents depended less on Philadelphia for employment, entertainment, shopping, and other daily activities. By the close of the twentieth century, Montgomery County had become an economic engine in its own right, boasting the largest population and by far the largest job base among the counties surrounding Philadelphia.

Lenape people, along with some Dutch and Swedes, inhabited this land before William Penn acquired it in

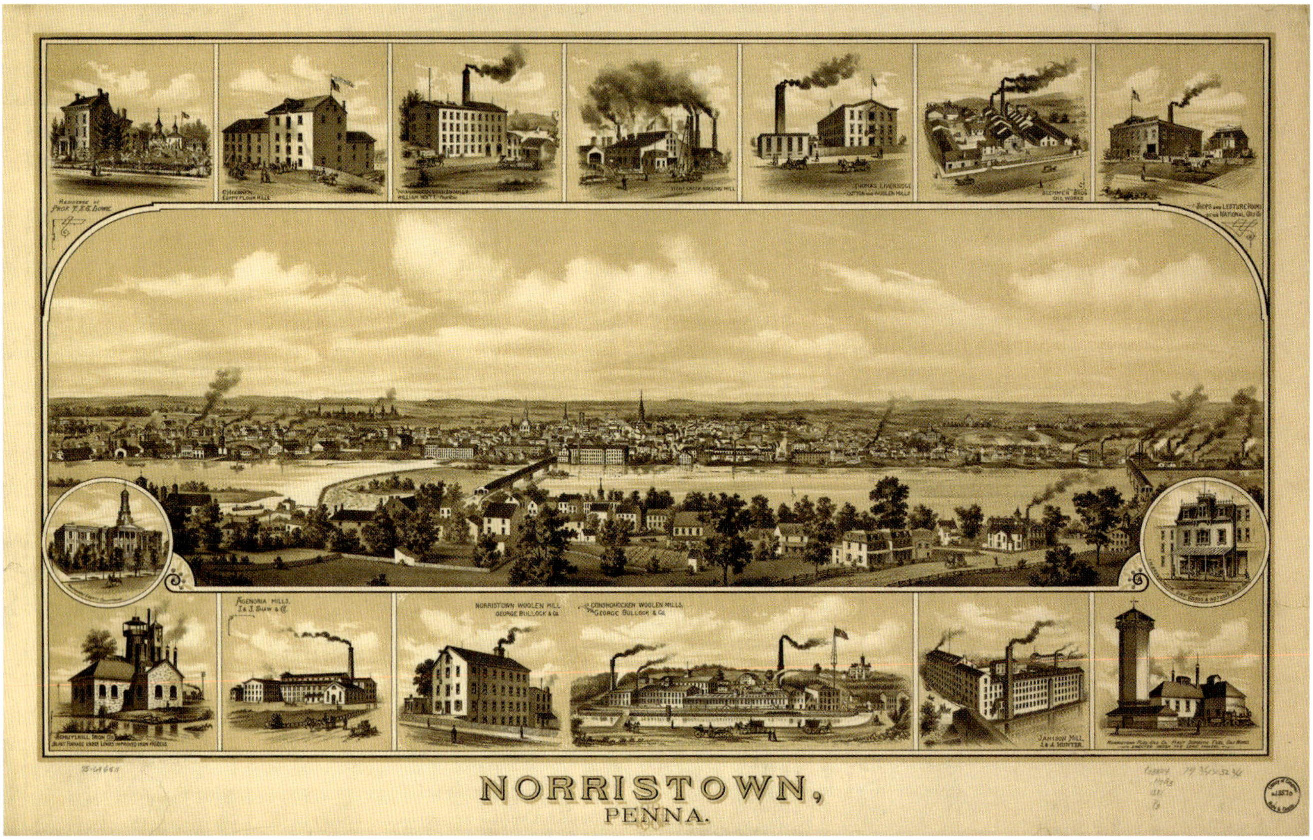

FIGURE 67. Norristown panoramic map, 1881. The Schuylkill Navigation Company's system of canals helped boost Norristown's position on the Schuylkill River as a center for industry. LIBRARY OF CONGRESS.

1681 and sold what he called the Welsh Tract to Quakers fleeing from persecution in Wales. The newcomers gave Welsh names like Gwynedd and Bala Cynwyd to their communities. English Quakers also acquired land in the area that eventually became lower Montgomery County. Many Germans arrived during the eighteenth century, including Schwenkfelders who settled there as a group.

Penn encouraged early settlers to form townships and practice self-government. Among the earliest to incorporate were areas located nearest to the port of Philadelphia. They included Cheltenham Township, incorporated in 1683, Plymouth in 1701, Abington in 1702, Whitemarsh in 1704, and Lower Merion in 1714, all communities that had been included within Philadelphia County. After the American Revolution people in the upper part of Philadelphia County petitioned the state assembly for a separate county, complaining about the inconvenience of traveling all the way to Philadelphia to conduct business at the county seat.

In 1784, state authorities carved Montgomery County out of the original Philadelphia County and placed the new county seat in Norristown. That small town grew over the nineteenth century into an important industrial center, attracting mills, foundries, and factories. By mid-twentieth century, Norristown ranked as the most populous borough in Pennsylvania, but shopping malls soon challenged its commercial district, increasing the town's dependence on governmental functions to support its economy and population.

From the county's earliest days, farmers participated in long-distance commodity trading through the Philadelphia port. They sent much of their wheat crop to

Philadelphia to be milled into flour for export to Europe. Later the railroad system opened broader domestic markets to county farmers, but at the same time brought greater competition from elsewhere. Local farmers eventually reduced their grain crops in the 1880s when cheap midwestern grain flooded East Coast markets. Montgomery County farmers shifted more heavily toward dairy production, because rail lines could quickly carry perishables to broader markets.

BUILDING A DENSE TRANSPORTATION NETWORK

Beginning in the early 1800s, the county embarked on an era of turnpike construction. Companies built hard-surface, all-weather roads to serve forges and mills and the freight hauling necessary to operate them. They maintained those roads by selling stock and collecting tolls. Across the nineteenth century, turnpike companies built at least two hundred miles of such roads in Montgomery County.

Germantown Pike had served from 1687 as a simple cart road from Philadelphia through Germantown, and northward to Plymouth Meeting. Between 1801 and 1804, investors lengthened and improved it, transforming the road into the Germantown and Perkiomen Turnpike. Eventually investors extended the road as a turnpike all the way to Reading, completing that project in 1815. Another major north-south route originated as a road connecting Philadelphia to Bethlehem during the 1700s; in 1804 it became a toll road, the Bethlehem Turnpike.

Starting in the 1830s county residents could travel by rail as well. Residents of Lower Merion Township gained easy access to Philadelphia when the Philadelphia and Columbia Railroad's Main Line passenger service crossed through the lower corner of Montgomery County on its way outward to Chester County. Taken over by the Pennsylvania Railroad during the period of rail consolidation, it eventually became one of the busiest commuter rail lines on the East Coast.

The Philadelphia, Germantown, and Norristown Railroad (PGN) began operating within Philadelphia County in 1832, and by the spring of 1835 it had made its way outward to Norristown. (PGN became part of the Reading Railroad system in 1869.) In 1841, when the Philadelphia & Reading Railroad opened its line along the Schuylkill River to the coal fields in northeastern Pennsylvania, it began hauling anthracite to power factories in Pottstown and Norristown as well as Philadelphia.

Rail lines pushed development northward beyond the well-traveled southern portion of the county. The North Pennsylvania Railroad line (which later became the Lansdale regional rail line) made Cheltenham Township the city's gateway to the northern suburbs and gained importance as a local carrier of passengers along Bethlehem Pike, with branch lines from Lansdale to Doylestown (1856), from Glenside to Hatboro (1872), and on its Jenkintown–Beth Ayres–Langhorne–Bound Brook line (1874–76).

To attract passengers, rail investors promoted leisure travel. Shortly after the Civil War, the Perkiomen Railroad Company started running a passenger line from Valley Forge north along the Perkiomen Creek up to Pennsburg Borough. In the 1920s the Perkiomen Valley became a favored vacation spot served by rail. The Reading Company bought the line in 1944, but the advent of the automobile forced passenger trains on this route to cease operations by 1955.

With leisure travelers in mind, investors in the Pennsylvania Railroad guided real estate development in Humphreysville, a town that straddled the border between Montgomery and Delaware Counties. The railroad company acquired large tracts of land in the area and built a posh hotel for summer visitors, creating by the 1880s a booming summer resort business. To burnish the reputation of the new development, the railroad rebranded Humphreysville in 1871, giving it the Welsh name of Bryn Mawr. With a similar intent to develop Main Line suburbs as affluent enclaves, the railroad company also renamed Athensville in 1873, preferring the Scottish name of Ardmore.

In the 1880s trolley companies began serving passengers for short trips. The first horse car lines ran on DeKalb Street in Norristown in 1884, and Pottstown soon got streetcars as well. Like the railroads, some trolley companies lured new customers by offering leisure travel. Willow Grove Park operated for eighty years as an amusement park from 1896 until 1975. The Philadelphia Rapid Transit Company conceived the park as a way to encourage weekend customers to patronize the trolley lines. One of the biggest attractions was the music pavilion, where John Philip Sousa and his band played annually from 1901 to 1926, along with other important bands and orchestras.

Another trolley company, the Philadelphia Transportation Company, ran lines from Germantown Avenue to Bethlehem Pike. In 1898 they opened the Chestnut Hill Amusement Park (also known as White City) at the corner of Bethlehem Pike and Paper Mill Road. They intended to provide a park for Philadelphia's working classes by charging a trolley fare of only a nickel, far less than their competitor's thirty-cent fare to Willow Grove Park. Nearby residents complained that the new park lowered the tone of the area, however, and by 1912 it closed. A handful of wealthy Chestnut Hill families living near the amusement park had pooled their money, bought the park for about $500,000, and immediately shut it down. The trolley companies prospered for only a half century. By the 1950s, all these routes had closed and the tracks had disappeared to make way for automobiles.

MILLS, MINES, AND MANUFACTURING

Many streams flowed into the Schuylkill River, including the Wissahickon, Plymouth, Sandy Run, Skippack, Pennypack, and Perkiomen Creeks. Early settlers erected dams and built mills to produce grain, lumber, oil, paper, and powder. In 1795 the county boasted ninety-six gristmills, sixty-one sawmills, six fulling mills, and ten paper mills. The Langstroth paper mill opened on the Pennypack in Moreland Township in 1794. Riverside Paper Mills in Whitemarsh Township began in 1856 to produce a fine grade of book, card, and envelope paper. Lower Merion Township was especially noted for its mills, including plaster, grist, and saw mills.

Water power also enabled early settlers to exploit the area's rich iron ore deposits. Valley Forge was named for the Mount Joy iron forge built on Valley Creek in 1742. Those ironworks on Valley Creek devoted a large part of their production to the Revolutionary War effort, which prompted British forces to target that location in September 1777, burning the forge and carrying off supplies. Not long afterward, General George Washington arrived at Valley Forge in December 1777 to winter his troops there.

Pottstown on the Schuylkill River initially relied on grain mills for local livelihoods. Local mills transported their flour to both Philadelphia and Reading markets. However, by the 1850s the iron and steel industry had surpassed grain mills in economic importance. A bridge-building company founded in 1877 as Cofrode and Saylor was acquired by Bethlehem Steel in 1931, providing thousands of jobs. Pottstown-made iron and steel contributed to major national and international projects like the Panama Canal and Golden Gate Bridge.

Conshohocken, another important industrial town on the Schuylkill River, initially produced spades, saws, iron pipe, and machinery in the 1840s. Alan Wood Company built the Schuylkill Iron Works there in 1857, and the plant became a mainstay of the borough's economy. So successful was that enterprise that the company built its own railway in 1907—the Upper Merion and Plymouth Railroad Company—a wholly owned subsidiary operating on both sides of the Schuylkill River. Lee Tire & Rubber Company, founded in 1912, made automobile tires and accessories there until 1980.

The borough of Ambler depended on grain milling to power its early economy, but it suffered losses when the coming of the railroads made it possible for Philadelphia merchants to buy cheap midwestern grain and grind it themselves. In 1896 Henry Keasbey and Richard Mattison built an asbestos plant in Ambler and launched the industry that powered the town for almost a century. They used asbestos mined in Quebec to manufacture asbestos-treated fabric used for wrapping steam pipes as well as asbestos fireproof roof shingles. In the late twentieth century, public health officials publicized the health dangers of asbestos and that industry collapsed, leaving Ambler to renew itself once again.

The dense rail network that emerged in the latter half of the nineteenth century allowed individual towns to specialize in manufacturing and fostered a resilient economy whose diversity of products and services kept the area strong across the economic upturns and reversals of the decades. The variety of products included automobile works in Ardmore, worsted and felt textiles in Bridgeport, shovels and spades in Cheltenham, flags and banners in Collegeville, men's clothing in Lansdale, and cigars in Schwenksville.

FIGURE 68. Recruitment print depicting members of an African American regiment posed with their white commander at Camp William Penn, the first Pennsylvania camp for volunteer Black regiments, Cheltenham Township, Montgomery County, 1863. LIBRARY COMPANY OF PHILADELPHIA.

SOCIAL DISPARITIES

Even with its diverse and productive economic base, Montgomery County always included residents who did not share in its prosperity. The early European settlers who worked modest-size farms owned some African-descended enslaved people, though in small numbers. The first U.S. census in 1790 reported a total of 118 enslaved people in the county. By the 1810 census, that number had dropped to three. Many of the county's Quaker, Mennonite, and Schwenkfelder landowners opposed slavery, and some actively undermined that system.

Starting in the 1830s, thousands of Black escapees traveled through Montgomery County by the Underground Railroad. Abolitionists would conceal them in homes and barns until the evening hours when they could take night trains on the Norristown railroad to Philadelphia, where a well-organized network could set them on the path to Canada. One resident in Plymouth Township, George Corson, hid escaping African Americans on his property and also built Abolition Hall as a meeting place for the antislavery movement on Butler Pike, near its intersection with Bethlehem Pike. Frederick Douglass and other famous abolitionists visited there.

Farm workers came mainly from Germany, Britain, and Ireland through an indenture system. Known as "redemptioners," they bargained with ship captains to give them free passage across the Atlantic; in exchange, the ship captains sold their labor to buyers who came to the Philadelphia docks. The purchaser would buy an immigrant's labor contract for a specified number of years of service. After working off that contract, the immigrants were free to pursue their livelihoods as independent citizens. Not all succeeded in supporting themselves in farming or trades, and some ended up in the county's poorhouse.

Religion exercised significant influence on daily life, including on education. So strongly did residents prize faith-based education that proponents of universal public education met considerable opposition in Montgomery County. When Pennsylvania passed the Common School Law of 1834, the state allowed residents of local school districts to decide whether to adopt the state requirements and become part of the state system. A majority of local school districts in Montgomery County initially opposed joining the state system, not because they refused to support public education but because they did not want their schools secularized. German Lutherans as well as the Amish, Catholics, Episcopalians, and Quakers preferred faith-based schools. Not until 1853 did the last district in the county join the state system.

The county's diversity stemmed not only from differences *between* towns, but even *within* towns, one of the best examples being Cheltenham Township immediately across the county border from Philadelphia. One prominent nineteenth-century resident, railroad tycoon and financier Jay Cooke, contributed significantly to that town's social mix. Cooke had helped finance the Civil War by selling government war bonds. Having been involved in both the abolitionist movement and the Underground Railroad, Cooke along with fellow businessman Edward M. Davis leased land for the U.S. government to operate Camp William Penn, a thirteen-acre training compound for African American soldiers. Frederick Douglass helped recruit volunteers to form "colored regiments," and in 1865 Harriet Tubman, the legendary Underground Railroad operator, gave a stirring speech to one of the last detachments of soldiers trained there. The camp opened in the summer of 1863, and by the time it closed in 1865 it had trained about eleven thousand soldiers. Cheltenham Township subsequently drew African American residents who regarded it as hospitable.

After the Civil War, Jay Cooke and Edward Davis turned to land development that served their own social class. They promoted Cheltenham Township as a place where rich industrialists and merchant families could build mansions befitting their newfound wealth. While Philadelphia families with inherited wealth generally preferred the Main Line or Chestnut Hill, self-made millionaires built estates in Cheltenham, including a number designed by the noted architect Horace Trumbauer. Subsequent generations often converted Trumbauer's monumental estates into schools, colleges, seminaries, and other religious institutions.

Even while Gilded Age industrialists chose Cheltenham for their lavish estates, the township gained significant numbers of lower-income Italians who came to work in quarries in the township's Edgehill section (later known as Glenside). Also in the twentieth century, Koreans established themselves in large enough numbers that Cheltenham became the Korean epicenter of the metropolitan region. Other Asian immigrants arrived, along with many African American residents, so that by the end of the twentieth century Cheltenham was one of the two most diverse municipalities in Montgomery County.

The other markedly diverse municipality was the county seat of Norristown. In the mid-nineteenth century, its mills and factories had drawn large numbers of Irish immigrants, followed by Italians. The Great Migration from the American South to northern cities during and after World War I brought many African American residents to work in Norristown. During the second half of the twentieth century, Latino immigration, especially from Mexico, became the overwhelming source of the increase in Norristown's foreign-born population. By 2000, Montgomery County had attracted a percentage of foreign-born residents (9 percent) that was smaller than the 11 percent foreign born in Philadelphia, yet higher than the three other suburban counties in Pennsylvania.

DEVELOPMENT PATTERNS

In the 1950s, the construction of the Pennsylvania Turnpike played a significant role in shaping the county's development. Philadelphia's business leaders saw the turnpike as an opportunity to link the city to the national highway network, and they vigorously supported construction of the Schuylkill Expressway in 1958 to connect downtown Philadelphia with the turnpike at Valley Forge. What they did not anticipate, however, was the turnpike's impact in creating a major route across Montgomery County that bypassed Philadelphia entirely, creating new employment and shopping centers along its path and enabling a pattern of daily trips from suburb to suburb that eventually surpassed the suburb-to-city travel pattern established during the rail era.

The turnpike exit serving Valley Forge/King of Prussia turned a small village in the 1950s into the most significant job center in Montgomery County. Located at the confluence of the turnpike with Route 202, Route 422, and the Schuylkill Expressway, King of Prussia drew companies in aerospace, defense, and security industries like General Electric and Lockheed Martin, along with many pharmaceutical companies. This prime location also gave rise to the King of Prussia Mall. In 1963 the Kravitz Company began building a strip of anchor stores (Korvettes, J.C. Penney, Wanamaker's, Gimbel's) around a supermarket. Starting from that midmarket retail cluster, the mall gradually expanded into one of the nation's largest shopping centers and shifted toward luxury goods for higher-income shoppers.

The 1980s witnessed the completion of the Route 422 expressway stretching through the county's quiet west end. Completed in 1985, it connected Pottstown in the north and Collegeville in midcounty with the King of Prussia megaplex. That made the Route 422 corridor attractive to developers. Businesses, most notably pharmaceutical companies, built facilities employing hundreds along Route 422 near Collegeville. Pfizer and Dow Chemical shared a global research and development campus. GlaxoSmithKline located a research and development facility nearby. Wyeth also came to Collegeville. So many pharmaceutical jobs located there that one GlaxoSmithKline vice president referred to the Collegeville area as "the legal drug capital of northeastern America."

An important path connecting other towns to King of Prussia was Route 202, an east-west route that experienced an increase in population along its path during the 1980s, when low mortgage interest rates spurred residential construction. Route 202 was a convenient path across the mid-county suburbs carrying local traffic to workplaces, shopping centers, and other destinations inside the county, giving them less incentive to travel into Philadelphia.

By the opening of the twenty-first century, Montgomery County received more daily commuters traveling into its employment hubs than it sent outward. It epitomized the pattern of suburb-to-suburb commuting. It even enjoyed a positive commuting balance with Philadelphia, receiving more daily workers from Philadelphia than it sent into the city. As in earlier eras, the diversity of the county's modern economic base remained an important strength. The county developed advanced manufacturing specialties like precision instruments, business machines and electronics, along with industrial chemicals and pharmaceuticals. It added high tech jobs in the fields of computer science, information technology, and telecommunications. Service jobs were also abundant in education, health care, retail, financial and professional services.

COPING WITH ECONOMIC SUCCESS

The county's enviable economic growth created winners and losers among its towns. Highways made it convenient to locate production near off-ramps instead of in older population centers. Many companies operating in the county's older manufacturing centers moved to new facilities. Newer retail developments lured customers away from older shopping districts, causing their deterioration. Over time, the shift of employment and retailing into job centers defined by highway interchanges generated marked differences in taxable resources available to different local jurisdictions.

Not only did older industrial towns lose jobs and employers, they also faced environmental costs left behind when manufacturing plants closed. However, some real estate investors saw opportunities in brownfield sites. After an industrial landmark, the Lee Tire factory, closed in Conshohocken in 1980, developer Brian O'Neill transformed the vacant factory into an office and light industrial complex called Spring Mill Corporate Center. His brother Michael O'Neill transformed a 1929 chemical plant, adding an office extension for the Quaker Chemical corporate headquarters. These projects triggered an office and condominium boom in Conshohocken, helped by the town's advantageous location at the intersection of the Schuylkill Expressway and the Blue Route.

In Ambler, the closing of the former Keasbey & Mattison asbestos company in the 1970s also left behind a major brownfield site. After nearly ten years of environmental remediation and financial problems, the Ambler Boiler House rose from the neglected site as a multitenant office building that provided a new workplace within a two-minute walk of a regional rail station. Shortly after that, a nonprofit organization bought the historic downtown Ambler Theater and spent millions restoring its original character. That project anchored additional Main Street development.

Even the U.S. government left environmental contamination in its wake when it decommissioned the Willow Grove Naval Air Station, leaving the groundwater in and around the base tainted from years of chemical dumping. When the township of Horsham launched plans in 2015 to develop a multimillion-dollar residential-retail-office complex to replace the military base, its first challenge became environmental remediation.

The twentieth century transformed a county that had once boasted a sizable rail network into a suburban landscape shaped largely by highways. Travel from suburb to suburb increased, creating a pattern that was ill-served by rail lines constructed to carry passengers back and forth to Philadelphia. According to the 2000 census,70 percent of Montgomery County workers got to work by driving alone.

Facing this reality of auto dominance in the early twenty-first century, municipalities adopted different development strategies. Some towns sought to take advantage of highway-based transportation patterns. For example, planners in the county seat of Norristown saw their town's resurgence tied to the very turnpike that had earlier undermined their commercial vitality. For decades, the King of Prussia and Plymouth Meeting Malls and suburban industrial parks arrayed along the turnpike had drawn commerce away from Norristown. At the turn of the twenty-first century, Norristown boosters lobbied the state to build a new exit off the turnpike at Norristown in order to spur redevelopment. The Pennsylvania Turnpike Commission committed to build that interchange, projected for completion by 2027.

Other towns tried to limit auto dependence by creating walkable environments within town centers. Pottstown, for example, worked to reinvent itself as a walkable Main Street community, restoring its disused train station as a bank and transforming a long-vacant shirt factory into a mixed-use arts center along with affordable housing. By promoting their sidewalks, historic architecture, street trees, and storefronts, Pottstown leaders hoped to attract young adults to an urban-style setting.

Despite the successes of some plans adopted by individual municipalities, the county failed to address the broader issue of the massive daily commute caused by so many workers living at significant distance from their workplace, unable to find affordable housing near the job centers where land and housing prices were high. Some communities had adopted zoning laws making it impossible for entry-level workers to find housing near their jobs. In 2006, the Montgomery County Planning Commission began urging municipalities to increase the housing stock accessible to moderate-income workers. However, planners could do little more than urge local officials to promote what they labeled "workforce housing," since municipalities carried responsibility for land use and zoning under Pennsylvania law. As a result, housing choices remained limited in many towns and progress toward diversification was slow at best.

The history of Montgomery County more than justified the early settlers' confidence that they need not depend entirely on Philadelphia markets, wealth, and employers to achieve prosperity. By the opening of the twenty-first century, they had built an economic base and quality of life in many communities that ranked among the highest in the metropolitan region.

Delaware County, Pennsylvania

Jodine Mayberry
and Carolyn T. Adams

Carved out of Chester County in 1789 (with the remainder of that county lying to its southwest), Delaware County long served as a distinct but close neighbor to the city of Philadelphia. Linked to the Philadelphia port from the eighteenth century onward, the eastern part of the county, including Chester and its neighboring municipalities along the Delaware River, was almost indistinguishable from nearby Philadelphia neighborhoods, while much of the rest of the county remained agricultural into the late twentieth century. In the mid-nineteenth century, the introduction of regional railways fostered new town centers at commuter stations. The westernmost section remained predominantly rural until the late twentieth century, when the county began to experience the effects of large-scale development. That mixed settlement pattern created some of the widest social disparities observable in any suburban county in the Philadelphia metropolitan area.

Lenni Lenape were the original inhabitants of the area that became Delaware County. In the early seventeenth century, Swedish farmers settled in the area, while Dutch trappers came to trade pelts. Later in that century, William Penn gained control of the area as part of a land grant from the English king. Arriving in the new territory in 1682, Penn initially made the existing Swedish settlement of Upland his "shire town," renaming it Chester after a county in England. Only when an established landowner there refused to sell him enough property for the town to expand did Penn turn north to locate his provincial capital, Philadelphia, twelve miles up the Delaware River.

Although no longer the provincial capital, Chester remained a county seat and continued to serve that role after Delaware County separated from Chester County in 1789. During its early history it remained a small market town, hemmed in by farms and the river. In 1850, when the county courthouse and jail became dilapidated and too costly to fix, residents established a new county seat in midcounty and named it Media. That prompted many prominent county citizens to relocate from Chester to Media, where they built fine brick homes and offices surrounding the new courthouse.

William Penn encouraged the formation of self-governing communities in his new territory. The earliest towns became incorporated well before Delaware County separated from Chester County, some even before 1700. Penn's followers named their settlements after the places in England that they left behind or adopted biblical or descriptive names. In Delaware County, these included Darby, Ridley, and Lansdowne as well as Middletown and Concord. Quakers from Wales settled along the "Welsh tract" on the county's northern border, where they founded several villages, including Haverford, Radnor, and Tredyffrin, all named for places in Wales.

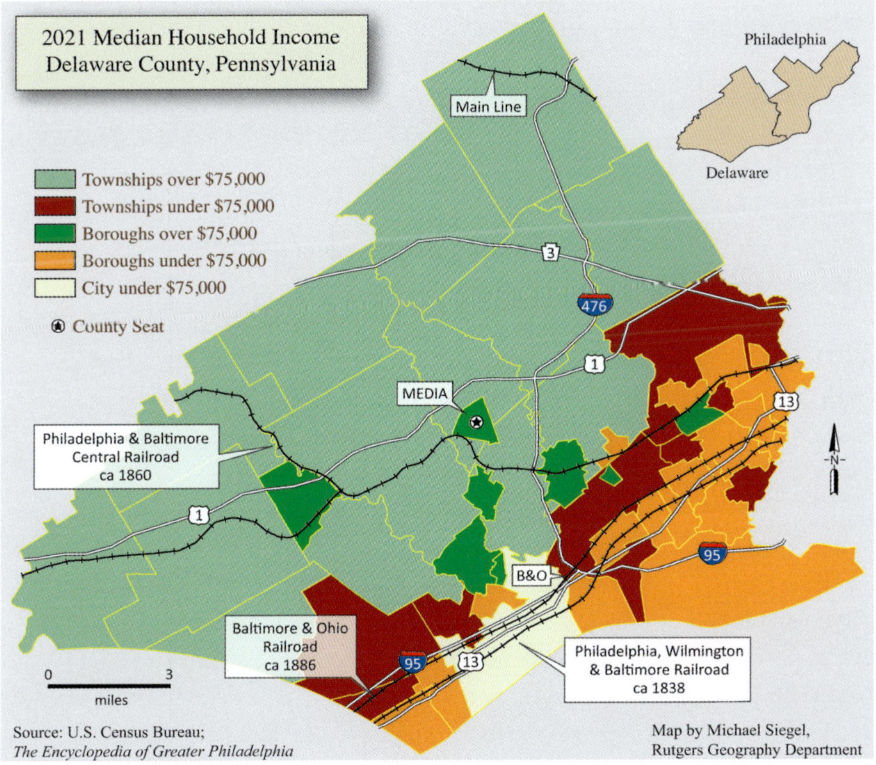

MAP 6. 2021 Median Household Income Delaware County, Pennsylvania.
MAP BY MICHAEL SIEGEL.

Some settlers clustered in market towns and manufacturing centers that prospered largely due to their connections to Philadelphia. Living at increasing densities, residents wanted reliable water supplies, well-maintained roads, docks, other transportation and commercial facilities, and peacekeeping by hired constables. They secured those services by carving out small self-governing boroughs from large townships. Most such population centers sat near the border with Philadelphia, with housing stock and population mix very much like adjacent areas of the city. By the 1880s and 1890s, a number of them had seceded from large eastern townships like Darby, Upper Darby, and Ridley and successfully established themselves as independent boroughs. Over time this historic pattern of intense fragmentation in southeastern Delaware County brought disadvantages to the smallest jurisdictions.

TRANSPORTATION ROUTES AND SETTLEMENT PATTERNS

The county's earliest east-west transportation routes made a lasting impact on development, spawning settlements and boosting their populations over time. One of the most important routes ran along the Delaware River connecting Philadelphia with Wilmington, Delaware. Well before the American Revolution, travelers used a roadway that crossed the southern border of the county between those two cities. In 1851 the state chartered a privately owned company to maintain a section of that roadway as the Darby and Ridley Turnpike (also known as the Chester Pike) and collected tolls to support its upkeep. Eventually, with the creation of the U.S. highway system in 1926, this route became U.S. Route 13.

Railroads boosted settlements along the Delaware River when, in the first half of the nineteenth century, the Philadelphia, Wilmington, and Baltimore Railroad (PW&B) ran a line along the river. Construction began between Baltimore and Philadelphia in 1837, and by 1850 the extended route connected Delaware County to Washington, D.C., in the south and New York City to the north. In 1870 the PW&B built a line north of the river called the Darby Improvement, aimed at skirting areas prone to flooding and serving growth in this largely undeveloped southeast corner of Delaware County. Around rail stations on that line, developers built new towns such as Ridley Park, Sharon Hill, and Norwood.

The Baltimore and Ohio Railroad (B&O) reinforced development along the Delaware River by starting its own service from Philadelphia to Baltimore in 1838 on tracks owned by PW&B. When the Pennsylvania Railroad bought control of PW&B in 1884, the new owner barred its competitor from using its right-of-way. That forced the B&O to build another rail line only a few miles north of the PW&B, completed in only two years. In 1887 the B&O also came into possession of an important north-south rail route when its subsidiary, the Baltimore and Philadelphia Railroad, acquired a rail spur originally built by the Thomas Leiper family to haul quarried stone from their property on the Crum Creek. The B&O network boosted industrial development by providing direct passenger and freight service to the massive Baldwin Locomotive Works in Eddystone on the Delaware River.

Halfway up the county from the Delaware River, settlers in the early eighteenth century began constructing an east-west route known as the Baltimore Pike, making it among the earliest public roads in the English colonies. Later known as U.S. Route 1, this road spurred growth in towns along its path, including Media, Swarthmore, Wallingford, and Lansdowne.

In the northern tier of the county, a major east-west route was created in 1848 when private investors built a toll road called the Philadelphia and West Chester Turnpike. During the 1850s, private enterprisers added a horse-drawn rail line along part of the turnpike, and by the 1890s they had introduced trolley service that ran all the way from West Chester to Upper Darby down the middle of the road that became known as West Chester Pike, later Pennsylvania Route 3. These east-west routes of roads and rails made commuting to Philadelphia possible. Developers built communities for the new professional classes to inhabit Victorian-style homes. Almost overnight, builders gobbled up any farmland within walking distance of commuter railroad stations. In 1850, when Media was established, the population of Delaware County was 24,679, according to that year's census. By 1910 it had grown to 117,000.

In the late twentieth century, planners added an important new north-south route to the county's already-dense transportation network. The southernmost section of Interstate 476, known as the "Blue Route" because of its color designation on planning maps, extended through the middle of the county to link the Pennsylvania Turnpike north of Delaware County to Interstate 95 at the county's southern border. The protracted, thirty-year negotiation over the route, caused mainly by vigorous opposition from residents living in its path, meant that suburban development had already overtaken most of the land adjacent to the highway by the time it opened in 1991. While the Blue Route did not change the settlement patterns much in midcounty, it did increase traffic and commerce at interchanges with the major east-west routes. Some observers credited the Blue Route with spurring redevelopment near the southern end of the highway on the Chester waterfront, including a professional soccer stadium, a Harrah's casino, and a race track.

MANUFACTURING AND COMMERCIAL CENTERS

Although farming dominated Delaware County throughout the eighteenth century, many paper, cotton, woolen, lumber, and grain mills proliferated along four creeks: Darby, Crum, Ridley, and Chester. Along the Delaware River, early investments in shipping, shipbuilding, brickworks, and iron foundries prompted further industrial development after the Civil War, especially shipbuilding in and around Chester. Delaware River Iron Ship Building and Engine Works, founded in 1864, ranked as the largest shipbuilding company in the United States during the 1870s. By 1900, a third of the county's population lived in Chester, and the waterfront industrial complex contributed significantly to the country's defense during both world wars, particularly Sun Shipbuilding and Dry Dock Company, founded in 1916 by Joseph N. Pew.

The Baldwin Locomotive Works moved from Philadelphia to the borough of Eddystone on the Delaware River in 1906, and by 1916 it was building army tanks for use on the battlefields of Europe during World War I. Sun Oil, also owned by the Pew Family, built an oil refinery in 1901 in Marcus Hook at the southern tip of the county. There the convergence of rail, roads, a deep water port, and the nation's growing thirst for petroleum gave rise to the refineries that became the borough's dominant industry. Other manufacturers located on the Delaware River included Scott Paper Company, which produced paper and foam products, and American Viscose Corporation, which made rayon and other synthetic fibers. Ford Motor Company, Boeing Helicopters, and Westinghouse Electric & Manufacturing Company also flourished along the river, drawing workers from all over the country.

From the 1950s onward, Delaware County manufacturers fell victim to the same forces that had already begun to dismantle Philadelphia's industrial base. From 1970 to 2000, Delaware County lost 54 percent of its manufacturing jobs. Of the manufacturing employment that remained, over a third (38 percent) was in aerospace manufacturing, largely due to Boeing's continuing presence.

Unlike manufacturing jobs, the service jobs that replaced them were scattered more broadly throughout the county. Retailers, restaurants, and services followed the spread of population into communities that offered desirable housing styles and schools. Health care provided another important source of employment, dominated by general medical and surgical hospitals, but also including physicians' practices, residential facilities treating intellectual disabilities, community care services for the elderly, and nursing homes.

In some cases, shopping malls served as focal points for development. For example, the Springfield Mall, a 590,000-square-foot, two-level facility, opened in 1974 along Baltimore Pike, near its busy intersection with Pennsylvania Route 320. Its original anchors included a John Wanamaker department store. Although the mall declined during the 1980s, it recovered strongly after the Blue Route opened in 1991, helping to spawn a nearby development of age-restricted townhomes, condominiums, and a golf course, as well as the Springfield Healthplex and hospital. Shopping centers and retirement communities like these brought increased traffic and commerce to the county's major east-west corridors like U.S. Route 1 and West Chester Pike.

Beginning as early as the 1830s and continuing through World War II, early industrial opportunities along the Delaware River drew thousands of Irish Catholic workers to mill and factory jobs in Upper Darby and Clifton Heights across the border from West Philadelphia. Polish and Italian workers came in the twentieth century to work in factories or to run small businesses. Irish, Polish, and Italian immigrants built churches and parochial schools that flourished until the 2000s, when they started to decline along with the county's aging Catholic population.

Some companies erected housing for their workers. The Simpson Print Works built Eddystone Village, named for a lighthouse in England. The village, just north of Chester, subsequently became the borough of Eddystone. Flooring manufacturer Congoleum- Nairn, Inc. built housing for its workers in Trainer on the Delaware River west of Chester City. In other instances, independent developers constructed housing for workers in the county's older settlements, ranging from apartment buildings to row houses to small cottages, in Chester, Clifton Heights, Eddystone, Ridley, and Nether Providence before and during both world wars.

When manufacturing declined, housing values in many blue- collar neighborhoods also declined. As these neighborhoods became more affordable, they drew growing numbers of minority and immigrant residents, especially in the last few decades of the twentieth century. By the 1990s, African Americans comprised 80 percent of the population of the city of Chester and some of the inner suburbs along the border with Philadelphia, such as Yeadon, Colwyn, and Darby Borough. Because of its transportation system and large rental housing stock, Upper Darby—the county's largest municipality in both area and population—became a major catchment area for immigrants from eastern Europe, Asia, and Latin America. Asians from the Indian subcontinent constituted the majority in tiny Millbourne, the county's smallest municipality at just .07 of a square mile, nestled between Philadelphia and Upper Darby Township.

At the turn of the twenty-first century, many municipalities remained more than 90 percent white. They included townships in the northern and western suburbs like Newtown, Edgmont, Chadds Ford, and Bethel. Perhaps more surprisingly, some boroughs in southeastern Delaware County with homes priced affordably for a broad range of both white and nonwhite buyers remained over 90 percent white in 2000 (for example, Eddystone, Norwood, Prospect Park, and Ridley Park). The result was a pattern of racial and ethnic separation into predominantly white or Black towns, through a combination of zoning ordinances and informal real estate practices that materialized despite objections from fair housing activists as early as the 1970s.

SOCIAL DISPARITIES

The final decades of the twentieth century witnessed dramatic population shifts in Delaware County, with some older communities losing population while newer suburbs to the west and north gained. Those population shifts mirrored the widening income gaps between communities. By 2014, fast-growing Bethel Township boasted a median household income of $123,349, while the shrinking number of residents in Chester City survived on a median household income of only $28,607.

These contrasting development patterns created differences in tax resources and therefore in municipal services. Compared to area townships, boroughs were especially disadvantaged because their very small landmasses (in some cases only one square mile or less) were entirely developed, leaving little room to create new taxable property. Their municipal budgets were too small to fund first-rate services. To support the schools and other services that residents expect from local government, the older boroughs were forced to levy substantial taxes on property owners, often at rates higher than the tax rates in more affluent townships. For example, the older boroughs of Yeadon and Sharon Hill in 2022 imposed school tax rates, respectively, of $28.18 and $30.09 per $1,000 of home value. In that same year, property owners in affluent townships like Marple, Newtown, and Radnor were assessed school taxes at only $10.97 and $13.92 per $1,000 of home value. Because of the high property values in the latter townships, their schools received enough revenue to provide some of the most desirable learning environments in the region.

According to the U.S. Census Bureau, in 2021 the county population was roughly 64 percent white and 23 percent African American, with Asians, Hispanics and mixed-race residents comprising the rest. The growing diversity appeared to have an impact on political attitudes and behavior. Historically the Republican Party dominated county politics starting before the Civil War and continuing through most of the twentieth century. Republican-dominated municipal governments were able to keep many communities virtually all white

FIGURE 69. The bustle of Sixty-Ninth Street, Upper Darby, near the Sixty-Ninth Street rail terminal, 1978. Upper Darby thrived as a commercial and transit node after the Philadelphia Rapid Transit terminal opened in 1907. SPECIAL COLLECTIONS RESEARCH CENTER, TEMPLE UNIVERSITY LIBRARIES.

for decades but, as in Upper Darby and Millbourne, the racial makeup of some communities started to change at the end of the twentieth century. The political makeup of some municipal governments such as Media and Swarthmore also slowly changed, while gerrymandering of state and congressional election districts helped the Republican Party maintain its grip on the county as a whole. In national elections, the voters shifted in the 1990s toward Democratic candidates. County voters who had given majorities to Republicans Ronald Reagan and George H. W. Bush, favored Bill Clinton in the 1990s and continued supporting Democratic presidential candidates in subsequent elections.

TWENTY-FIRST-CENTURY DEVELOPMENT PATTERNS

While the populations of many communities in eastern Delaware County remained stable or declined over time, at the end of the twentieth century the western suburbs experienced growth and sprawl. The county's last valuable unprotected wetlands, woodlands, and farms were located in the western and northern municipalities where new development rapidly replaced open land. As the population in that area continued to grow, so did the need for open space. To preserve farms and woodlands, the county government published a plan in 2013 for economic development and land use that encouraged infill development to preserve and rehabilitate existing infrastructure and housing stock wherever possible while also protecting green spaces.

Key to that strategy was revitalizing the Delaware riverfront. Nearly twenty-five million people lived within a two-hour drive from the heart of Delaware County's waterfront industrial area, making that location potentially attractive to businesses that relied on quick access to markets up and down the East Coast. Moreover, the nearby Philadelphia International Airport provided passenger and cargo service to waterfront producers.

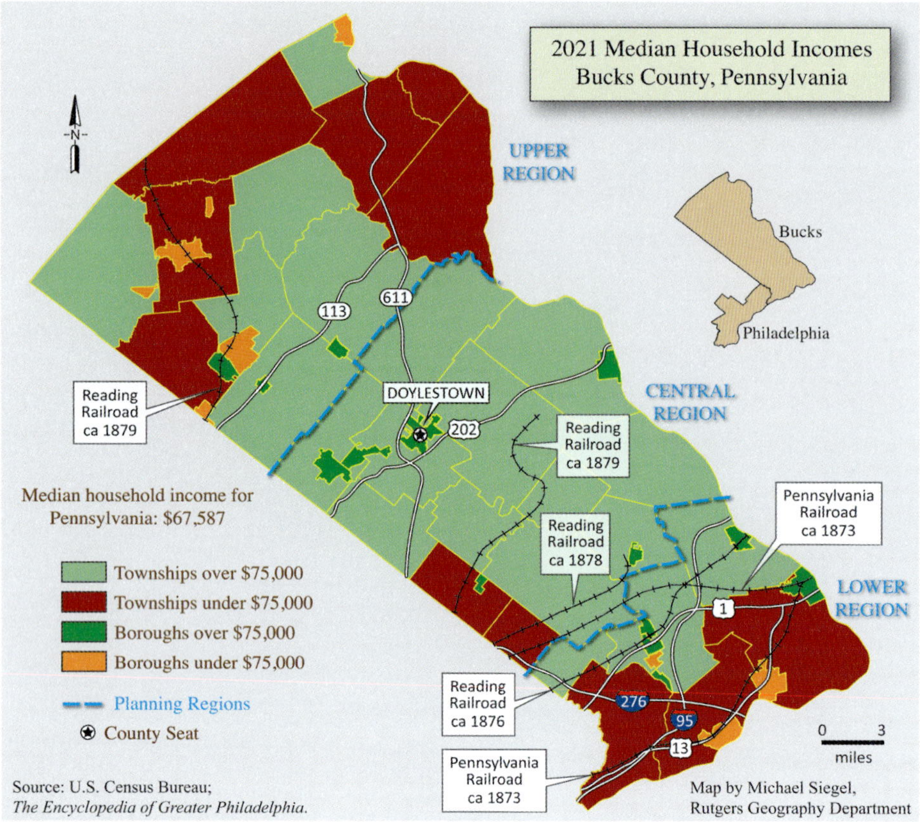

MAP 7. 2021 Median Household Income Bucks County, Pennsylvania. MAP BY MICHAEL SIEGEL.

County planners favored guiding residential investments on the eastern side of the county into transit-oriented developments around regional rail lines and bus ways, for example at Sixty-Ninth Street (Upper Darby/Millbourne), in Darby, Lansdowne, Media, Parkside, Ridley Park, and Swarthmore. For the western and northern suburbs, planners advised a shift in development patterns away from the sprawling single-family homes popular in the 1990s and 2000s, to more dense housing patterns such as townhomes.

No matter how carefully the county government documented the need for, and potential benefits of, such development strategies, the structure of local government in Pennsylvania gave primary responsibility for regulating land use to local governments, which controlled zoning. County governments played only a limited role, mainly advising and supporting local planning efforts. Not surprisingly, affluent townships like Radnor and Middletown devoted the most open space for both recreational and passive uses. Local governments in those communities, along with other affluent townships like Concord, Nether Providence, and Upper Providence persuaded citizens to approve bond issues for millions of dollars to purchase and preserve open space. In contrast, leaders in the older suburbs, especially the small boroughs, faced greater obstacles. These small, densely populated communities possessed few undeveloped parcels. Moreover, local leaders felt pressed to develop any available spaces in order to bolster their precarious tax bases.

One large-scale example of the trend to direct new investment into already-developed locations involved repurposing Granite Run Mall in Middletown Township, near the center of the county. That mall, opened in 1974 as a middle-class shopping venue, failed to compete against e-commerce and the higher-end retailers occupying Springfield Mall. By summer 2015, an investment partnership that included longtime developer Bruce Toll demolished the retail spaces located between two large anchor stores in order to replace them with high-end retailers and restaurants. The plan would transform the site into a mixed-use town center called "The Promenade at Granite Run." This new incarnation included not only retail but also hundreds of residential apartments, a renovated movie theater, bowling alley, and seven thousand square feet of pediatric offices operated by Children's Hospital of Philadelphia.

Delaware County's long arc of development created dramatic contrasts: from a gritty industrial belt along the Delaware River, to Victorian towns built around rail stations, to pastoral landscapes painted by Andrew Wyeth in Chadds Ford on the county's western edge. These stark differences created both challenges and opportunities for county leaders. The broad variation in the age, character, and social composition of different communities, while making coordinated planning difficult, also ensured that Delaware County offered living choices for newcomers of almost all backgrounds and means. The combination of abundant rail transportation, high-density town centers, and surviving open spaces made the county a prime candidate to adopt a "smart growth" plan aimed at concentrating future development in existing settlements in order to preserve natural landscapes.

Bucks County, Pennsylvania

Carolyn T. Adams

Bucks County, one of three counties established in 1682 by William Penn, originally stretched northward along the Delaware River all the way to the Delaware Water Gap and westward past Allentown. Even after shrinking dramatically when Northampton and Lehigh Counties were carved from its territory in 1752, the county still encompassed multiple regions that developed along different historical trajectories. A largely bucolic Upper Bucks County remained distinct from the areas that became blue-collar Lower Bucks County and the white-collar townships of Central Bucks County. This tripartite division shaped many institutional patterns, from colonial-era disputes about where to locate the county seat to twentieth-century decisions to create three chambers of commerce and divide the county's community college into three campuses.

Lenni Lenape people resided in the area before Europeans arrived. In 1640 Swedes purchased parts of Lower Bucks County from the Lenape, and a handful of Swedish settlers began building log houses in the region. In July 1682, William Penn's agent purchased other lands from the Lenape, which eventually became the townships of Bristol, Falls, Middletown, Lower and Upper Makefield, Newtown, and some of Wrightstown. When Penn arrived in Pennsylvania later in 1682, he chose to build his family's manor house, which he called Pennsbury, in Falls Township.

English newcomers first settled the lower portion of Bucks County along the Delaware River, but soon the abundant and fertile land available farther north drew them upward to Newtown, Wrightstown, and Buckingham Townships. Other religious reformers unwelcome in Europe followed the English Quakers, including German Mennonites and Lutherans, Dutch Reformed, Welsh Quakers, and Baptists.

The town of Bristol, which afforded the county's only port with access to the Atlantic Ocean via the Delaware River, served as the first county seat from 1705 to 1726. But early sectional differences arose when residents living in Central and Upper Bucks complained about the long distances they traveled to do business. So officials moved the county seat northward to Newtown in 1726. Even Newtown, however, proved too distant for settlers in Upper Bucks, who grumbled that they had "long labored under the great disadvantage of having the courts of justice held in a place very un-central in Bucks County." That forced the legislature in 1810 to authorize three commissioners to select a new county seat, instructing them to choose a location within three miles of the exact geographical center of the county. They picked Doylestown, which remained the county seat across the centuries.

Bucks County played a significant role in the Revolutionary War. In 1776, the army of George Washington camped in Central Bucks, using it as a base for the Trenton campaign. On the night of December 25–26, Washington famously crossed from Bucks County into New Jersey to win the battle of Trenton. After securing that victory, Washington returned to Pennsylvania and quartered his men at Newtown. August 1777 found Washington's army camped in Bucks County, this time in Warwickshire, on its way to the Battle of Brandywine. Again in 1778, his army camped at Doylestown.

MAP
OF
BUCKS COUNTY
Pennsylvania
FROM SURVEYS
Under the direction of
W. E. MORRIS. C. E.
1850
Published by R. P. Smith No. 15 Minor St.
PHILADELPHIA.
PLAN
OF
DOYLESTOWN
Mill Pond
Cemetery
St. Paul's Episcopal Church
BUCKINGHAM TURNPIKE
COUNTY BUILDINGS.
SCALE.

Although Upper Bucks was more sparsely populated than other sections of the county during the Revolutionary period, a group of German farmers there attracted national attention by fomenting the so-called Fries Rebellion in 1798–99. Having just overthrown British taxation without representation, residents in the northwest corner of the county balked at paying a new federal property tax that President John Adams invented to fund another war that the United States expected to face with France. (As it happened, that war never broke out.) Federal troops quickly quelled the rebellion.

PREINDUSTRIAL TRAVEL PATTERNS

As early as 1700, farmers began producing substantial surpluses and found they needed roads that extended all the way to the markets of Philadelphia. To construct those long routes, early road builders often linked together a series of shorter spans. They strung these routes across the county from northeast to southwest so that farmers and craftsmen in different sections of Bucks County could move their goods southwesterly toward Philadelphia.

Early dirt roads were unreliable enough to suffer a strong challenge from canals in the early 1800s. Canals proved especially important in transporting coal and iron from the Lehigh Valley to Bucks County communities. In 1827 the Pennsylvania legislature authorized construction of a canal from Easton, Pennsylvania, south to Bristol in Bucks County. The first section of that canal ran between New Hope and Bristol in 1830, and the rest of the waterway up to Easton opened two years later.

Supplementing the canals, investors upgraded roads to become "turnpikes." Even before the advent of canals, private companies had applied to the provincial government for permission to reinforce dirt roads with crushed stone to make them sturdy enough to support heavy wagonloads. The turnpike companies then required travelers to pay tolls at intervals along the route to cover the costs of improving and maintaining the road.

FIGURE 70. Detail, Doylestown, Bucks County map, 1850. The county seat's original courthouse and jail are depicted in the lower right. LIBRARY OF CONGRESS.

One of the early turnpikes ran along the banks of the Delaware River, connecting Philadelphia to New York. Called the King's Highway (later U.S. Route 13), it followed an existing Native American trail. The road was laid out in 1686 by order of William Penn. After critics deplored "ye unevenness of ye road from Philadelphia to ye falls of Delaware," its maintenance was assigned to the Frankford & Bristol Turnpike Company, incorporated in 1803.

About halfway up the county, U.S. Route 202 emerged out of a string of shorter roads, many of which were already in place by 1800. The national government brought those individual stretches into the national highway system in 1927. When connected together, they crossed the county, linking New Hope on the eastern boundary of the county to Doylestown and Chalfont on the western side. In Upper Bucks, residents of Bedminster Township could travel southwest on Bedminster Road (later Pennsylvania Route 113) as far as the border with Montgomery County, and there pick up the Bethlehem Pike that would take them all the way south to Philadelphia. The diagonal orientation of roadways (running from northeast to southwest) reinforced the county's historical separation into three regions.

In 1833 the Philadelphia and Trenton Railroad Company built the county's first rail line. It ran between Philadelphia and Trenton via Bristol. That line was acquired in 1873 by the Pennsylvania Railroad, which also operated a second east-west line across Bucks County farther north to link other Bucks County towns with Trenton. Other lines operated by the North Pennsylvania Railroad also spanned the county from west to east. For example, in 1856 the North Pennsylvania Railroad Company built an offshoot from its north-south route that carried passengers and freight east to Doylestown. In 1855 that same company also built a line across Lower Bucks through Yardley to Trenton, an expansion that continued to operate after the Reading Railroad leased routes from the North Pennsylvania Railroad Company in 1879 and operated them as part of the Reading system. In 1891 Reading also chose to significantly expand a short line running from Warminster to Hartsville, all the way across the county to New Hope on the Delaware River.

At the close of the nineteenth century, trolleys became the "poor man's railroad." Doylestown occupied the center of a countywide network of street railways. Initially the Bucks County Electric Railway Company and later the Philadelphia Rapid Transit Company ran a trolley line between Doylestown and Willow Grove, later adding lines to Newtown and Easton. By 1902 a twenty-six-mile network connected Doylestown to many other county places, including Bristol, Hulmeville, Penndel, and Langhorne.

SHIFTING PATTERNS OF PRODUCTION

Agriculture furnished livelihoods for the early Europeans, who favored growing wheat, partly because it required a few periods of intensive labor, while leaving farmers free at other times to tend other crops like flax and potatoes. When the adoption of fertilizer allowed farmers to feed more livestock, they began to shift toward dairy cows that produced enough milk to make butter and cheese in large enough quantities to sell.

Along the Delaware River, builders constructed mills producing textiles and paper. The river port of Bristol attracted ship building in the early decades of the eighteenth century. In 1727 a group of Philadelphia investors built the county's first iron furnace at Durham in the far northeast corner of the county. The Durham iron works forged cannonballs and other munitions for Washington's colonial troops.

After a canal built in 1830 had connected Lower Bucks with Easton and other upriver towns, mills in Bristol relied on Pennsylvania coal to drive their machines. In 1876 William Hulme Grundy moved his Grundy Brothers and Campion woolen mill from Philadelphia to Bristol, partly to escape from union organizing by the Knights of Labor. There it became Bucks County's largest industrial employer and made Bristol the county's manufacturing center.

In both Lower and Upper Bucks County, the cigar industry proved to be a major economic force. In both places, many farmers raised tobacco. Government records in 1871 reported 470 manufactories of cigars in Bucks County as well as one snuff mill at Bristol. Even in the largely agricultural spaces of Upper Bucks, cigar factories served as important employers during the first half of the nineteenth century. When the North Pennsylvania Railroad opened through Quakertown in 1856, it connected those cigar makers with new suppliers and markets, spurring new factories in several towns where the railroad stopped, including Quakertown, Sellersville, and Perkasie. The collapse of Cuban tobacco plantations during the Spanish-American War helped the Pennsylvania producers, but ultimately the mechanization of the industry during the 1890s undercut their profits and drove many out of business by the 1920s.

The early decades of the twentieth century brought heavy industrial development to Lower Bucks, particularly in shipyards along the Delaware River, where land was cheaper than in the city and the river afforded easy access to Philadelphia and other Atlantic ports. When Averell Harriman built the Bristol shipyards in 1917, that enterprise spawned not only shipbuilding but also related business. At about the same time, Rohm and Haas Company built a chemical plant that remained a major force in the town's economy for decades. During World War II, shipyards were converted to build airplanes. But by the 1960s, these factories stood empty, victims of a combination of obsolete technology and higher costs than competitors were facing in the American Sunbelt and overseas.

The rise and fall of heavy industry in Lower Bucks County involved multiple industries and companies, but is best captured in the history of United States Steel Corporation. In 1952 that company built its Fairless Works in Falls Township. Within a year, the facility employed nearly eight thousand workers in the main plant and adjacent shops. That plant became a symbol of post–World War II prosperity. Yet the Fairless Works could not withstand relentless competition from overseas steel manufacturers. By 2001, the company had shut down virtually the entire massive plant except for a small galvanizing facility.

CREATIVE ARTS AND THE KNOWLEDGE ECONOMY

Compared with other parts of the county, Central Bucks distinguished itself in the nineteenth and early twentieth centuries in the production of arts and literature. As early as 1815, Quaker artist Edward Hicks worked there, painting the image of *The Peaceable Kingdom* that would make him a celebrated folk artist. However, the real influx of artists into Central Bucks began when the painters William L. Lathrop and Edward Willis Redfield each moved there in 1898, attracting other painters and sculptors to the area around New Hope. The work they and their followers produced would ultimately be dubbed "Pennsylvania Impressionism."

The Arts and Crafts tile maker Henry Mercer built his Doylestown home Fonthill as a castle where he designed tiles, gathered an extensive collection of tiles, prints, and tools, and built an equally fanciful castle-like museum for the collection of the Bucks County Historical Society (renamed the Mercer Museum after his death).

During the 1930s Bucks County also gained a reputation as a haven for novelists, playwrights, actors, and songwriters. New Yorkers bought properties in the small stretch between Doylestown and New Hope and along the Delaware River, including Margaret Mead, Pearl S. Buck, Oscar Hammerstein, Stephen Sondheim, Charlie Parker, Moss Hart, George S. Kaufman, James Michener, Dorothy Parker, and S. J. Perelman. Their numbers and notoriety led the novelist Michener to dub this part of his native Bucks County "the genius belt."

Despite the demise of heavy industries in the late twentieth century, Bucks County retained some manufacturing, although not the kind that could provide employment for workers operating milling machines and assembly lines. By the turn of the twenty-first century, knowledge-based enterprises like finance and other business services, along with biotechnology and pharmaceuticals, required college-educated workers.

An early turn toward high technology took place at the Naval Air Warfare Center in Warminster. Originally in the 1930s a private company built an aircraft assembly plant there. However, by 1942 the U.S. Navy had become so frustrated by the firm's inability to deliver on contracts that it bought the plant to operate as a government facility. Over the decades, the navy built one of the most important research and development facilities in the United States, developing early prototypes of global positioning systems (GPS) and constructing a centrifuge that trained NASA astronauts for space. The Naval Air Warfare Center closed in 1996 in a wave of military cutbacks, and the land was converted to a park and residential and commercial developments.

In Lower Bucks as well, the economy began shifting in the late twentieth century toward high technology companies. After U.S. Steel shut down Fairless Hills in Falls Township, the Commonwealth of Pennsylvania designated over a thousand acres at the site as a Keystone Opportunity Improvement Zone (KOIZ). That created tax benefits to persuade companies to locate there. An early arrival was Gamesa Corporation, a Spanish wind energy company that located a manufacturing facility in Fairless Hills. In 2010 Gamesa and Bucks County Community College started the Green Jobs Academy in Bristol to train workers for the green economy. Another milestone of the site was the launch in 2014 of a company called Keystone NAP (short for Network Access Point) to take over the part of the abandoned steel mill containing the electric motors that had run the mill. They converted that electrical heart of Fairless Hills into an advanced data center serving the Northeast Corridor of the United States. It offered cloud computing and other services to hospitals and insurance, telecommunications, financial services, and other data-intensive businesses.

POSTWAR POPULATION GROWTH

Bucks County experienced its highest percentage growth during the 1950s. The county's population more than doubled during that decade. That growth concentrated in Lower Bucks County, spurred by the state's decision to extend the Pennsylvania Turnpike from Philadelphia eastward to connect with the New Jersey Turnpike. By far the largest and best known of the new housing developments was Levittown, the massive assembly-line suburb built by William Levitt. Levittown was so large that it encompassed land in the townships of Bristol, Middletown, and Falls, as well as the borough of Tullytown. Buyers snapped up Levitt's affordable houses priced from $9,000 to $17,500 as soon as they came on the market and began moving into their homes in June 1952. Eventually, Levittown brought tens of thousands of new residents into Lower Bucks.

By 1980 population growth had shifted upward to Central Bucks. That growth was most pronounced for townships sitting in the path of U.S. Route 202. As a very old route crossing the county on a diagonal path, Route 202 enabled suburb-to-suburb commuting that had become popular by the 1970s. The combined population of five townships arrayed along Route 202 in Central Bucks (Solebury, Buckingham, Doylestown,

New Britain, and Warrington) grew by 60 percent in just two decades between 1980 and 2000.

As new subdivisions multiplied in Central Bucks, Upper Bucks remained far less developed. Its rolling hills and farmlands continued to appeal not only to farmers who tended its fields, but also to others who enjoyed its unspoiled beauty. During the 1940s, well-to-do families from Philadelphia and New York had bought land and hired managers to operate their farms, which they dubbed "country estates." During the 1980s, a new generation of wealthy New Yorkers started buying land and old stone houses to serve as retreats from life in Manhattan. They paid local residents to stock their refrigerators and clean their swimming pools before weekend visits. They had little reason to change the unspoiled landscapes that had drawn them there. The comparatively modest growth in Upper Bucks around the turn of the twenty-first century concentrated mainly around Quakertown in the northwest corner of the county.

As different as they remained, the three sections of Bucks County shared a common demographic pattern: population growth concentrated in the townships, while the boroughs' share of the county population declined. Early residents in the county had established boroughs as small, dense settlements carved out of larger townships, often where travelers stopped overnight at inns or taverns. They became the county's market towns. Since many boroughs were entirely built out by the mid-twentieth century, their housing styles and floor plans did not appeal to suburban buyers in the late twentieth century. Many boroughs had limited space to build large new developments. Whereas in 1970 the boroughs taken together had housed 17 percent of Bucks County's population, by 2010 they accommodated less than 13 percent. Bristol Borough, which had played such an important role in the county's history, lost 20 percent of its population from 1970 to 2010. Not all boroughs declined at comparable rates, but overall the boroughs gained a much smaller share of the county's population growth compared to the townships.

SOCIAL DISPARITIES

The early Quakers' belief in the equality of all people in God's eyes did not prevent social disparities from emerging. Most significant was the plight of the enslaved in the county. Although early settlers mostly depended upon family members to work their farms, some owned enslaved workers, including William Penn. After the Pennsylvania legislature adopted the Act for the Gradual Abolition of Slavery in 1780, slaveholding declined rapidly. The federal census of 1790 counted 261 enslaved persons in Bucks County; by 1810 those records showed only 11 African people remained enslaved in the county.

In 1837 the Bucks County Anti-Slavery Society held its first meeting, focused mainly on eliminating slavery beyond the county borders. Quakers in all three sections of the county took part in the Underground Railroad. Activists transported runaways to farmlands in Lower Bucks owned by the Philadelphia abolitionist Robert Purvis and his brother Joseph Purvis. From there, the escaping Africans rode northward by wagon or stagecoach, sometimes stopping at the Mount Gilead African Methodist Episcopal Church in Central Bucks halfway between Doylestown and New Hope. Other times, they rode all the way to Upper Bucks to the safe house in Quakertown owned by Richard Moore, who in turn sent them up the valley of the Lehigh or the Susquehanna River.

At the opposite end of the social scale were merchants who made fortunes in Philadelphia and built lavish Bucks County estates along the Delaware River. Abraham Bickley III, the descendant of a wealthy Quaker shipping merchant, at age eighteen inherited the family fortune and in 1754 built Pen Ryn, a spacious and dignified mansion in Bensalem, flanked by formal gardens, stables, and barns. Another example was Andalusia, built in the 1790s by Philadelphia merchant John Craig, who engaged the noted architect Benjamin Latrobe to design an elegant mansion in Bensalem Township across the border from Philadelphia, naming the estate to reflect Craig's business as an importer of commercial goods from Spain. The Grundy mansion, another overlooking the Delaware River, was originally built to a modest scale in 1818. But William Hulme Grundy, who moved his woolen mill from Philadelphia to Bristol, bought the property in 1884. He spent a year transforming it into a Queen Anne mansion. The property remained in the hands of that prosperous family for more than seventy years until 1961, when it became a house museum for visitors.

During the first half of the twentieth century, as working-class families moved into Lower Bucks County

FIGURE 71. Andalusia, the Bucks County estate on the Delaware River originally purchased in 1795 by Philadelphia merchant John Craig and procured around 1814 by his son-in-law Nicholas Biddle. William Russell Birch, ca. 1808. LIBRARY COMPANY OF PHILADELPHIA.

for jobs in shipbuilding and other industries along the Delaware River, the population of the area remained overwhelmingly white. After World War II, when the developer William Levitt began building his massive Levittown development for workers at the Fairless Hills steel plant, he deliberately and openly restricted sales to white buyers.

The obvious racial imbalance inspired two important efforts in the early twentieth century to open the housing market to people of color. In the 1920s a white farmer, Frank K. Brown, set aside eighty acres near U.S. Route 1 that he named Linconia and invited African American families to build homes there. Another racial pioneer, builder Morris Milgram, acquired fifty acres near Linconia and in 1954 opened a housing development called Concord Park to attract both Black and white buyers. Over time, the two interracial developments in Bensalem Township blended together to become Lin-Park.

Immigrants also contributed to the county's diversity in the late twentieth century, especially in Lower Bucks. In Bristol, Ukrainian and Russian immigrants arrived in the 1990s. Bensalem and Warminster also took in many new arrivals between 1990 and 2010, including Russians and eastern Europeans. In those two townships, the large number of immigrant arrivals not only replaced the households who had moved out, but also accounted for *all* of the population gains registered during those two decades. The 2010 census counted fifty-one thousand foreign born across Bucks County, with Asians and Hispanics providing the largest numbers of newcomers in the county as a whole.

Despite some active efforts to promote racial inclusion and the noticeable expansion of immigrant communities, in the early twenty-first century Bucks remained the whitest among the Pennsylvania suburban counties outside Philadelphia. In 2010 only 3.6 percent of Bucks County residents were Black in a state with more than 10 percent African Americans. Foreign-born residents made up about 8 percent of the population, the lowest among the suburban counties outside Philadelphia.

SECTIONAL DIFFERENCES IN RESPONSE TO GROWTH

In the late twentieth century, Upper Bucks remained less developed and more rural than other parts of the county. In addition to farms, several parks—the largest being Nockamixon State Park—provided large areas of protected open space. Longtime residents watched the development boom in Central Bucks and dreaded the prospect of tract housing, office complexes, shopping centers, and sprawling parking lots advancing northward, swallowing horse farms, woodlands, and wetlands. When pressure increased from developers wanting to build on open parcels, residents mobilized during the 1980s to preserve the green spaces that defined the character of their landscapes.

Starting in 1989, Bucks County began participating in a statewide program to protect agricultural land by acquiring agricultural conservation easements. Together, the county and state governments paid landowners in order to obtain the development rights on specific parcels. While landowners could subsequently sell that land, the restrictions against development remained in force, guaranteeing that the land would remain in agricultural production. Although the program covered the entire county, it was most active in Upper Bucks.

While Upper Bucks townships mobilized to slow development, communities in Lower Bucks worked to repurpose industrial lands abandoned by manufacturers that had moved away. Brownfield remediation became an important priority for communities trying to convert abandoned industrial areas to new uses. For example, Falls Township promoted industrial reuses that emphasized green technology, particularly at the abandoned U.S. Steel plant. In Bristol, local officials sought to repurpose an abandoned airplane plant that later served as a soap factory but completely shut down in the late 1980s. They welcomed an experienced redeveloper of brownfields who bought the 43-acre site in 2003 and converted it into offices. In 2015 Bensalem's leaders launched an ambitious plan to redevelop 675 acres of waterfront property, whose first element was a riverside "urban village" called Waterside constructed on a 40-acre brownfield site. In addition to commercial and industrial reuses, builders also proposed new residential developments in several communities of Lower Bucks, including Bensalem, Lower Makefield, and Middletown Townships, as infill development or redevelopment of abandoned or underutilized sites.

The townships in Central Bucks, meanwhile, experienced by far the most intense development pressure. Many residents resisted by opposing proposals for infrastructure—especially highways, sewers, and trash disposal facilities—that would support larger populations. In the mid-1990s when state highway planners proposed converting U.S. Route 202 into a four-lane, limited-access expressway between Doylestown and Montgomeryville, Buckingham Township sued in federal court. The lawsuit stalled the project long enough that state planners offered a lower-impact alternative of a two-lane "parkway" intersected by crossroads at grade level. When that alternative Route 202 Parkway finally opened in 2012, flanked by attractive bicycle and jogging trails, local residents hailed it as a project that met their needs but was unlikely to generate massive levels of new traffic.

Some older boroughs in Central Bucks reacted to the population influx by encouraging developers to build new homes on vacant lots in established neighborhoods—a strategy known as infill development. Doylestown, for example, began working with infill developers in the 1990s to bolster the borough's tax base and to discourage sprawl by keeping development in areas where infrastructure and services already existed. Noticing that younger homebuyers favored smaller homes and walkable communities, planners for Newtown, Yardley, and other older Central Bucks communities worked to revitalize their town centers.

As some townships worked to preserve open space, others encouraged new development to reclaim brownfields, while still others tried to steer population and commerce into historic town centers where infrastructure already existed to serve them. Those differing strategies reflected the contrasting sectional identities that marked Bucks County across more than three centuries.

Chester County, Pennsylvania

Carolyn T. Adams

As one of the original counties established by William Penn, Chester County was only modestly influenced by Philadelphia in its early development because after 1789 it shared no border with the city. Although the Pennsylvania Railroad linked the county's central valley to Philadelphia in the mid-nineteenth century, it remained a largely rural landscape whose farms, mills, and forges operated within a mostly self-sufficient economy while sending surpluses to the Philadelphia market. Not until the second half of the twentieth century did dramatic changes come to its pastoral landscapes and small towns. Starting in the 1970s the arrival of financial services firms along with biomedical research and development companies drew thousands of new residents, turning it into a county of farms plus pharma.

Lenni Lenape (also known as Delaware), along with some Dutch and Swedes, already lived in the area before Penn laid out the county boundaries stretching more than one hundred miles from the Delaware River to the Susquehanna River. That initial county structure proved too large to serve its inhabitants well. In 1729, provincial authorities carved out Lancaster County, then in 1752 shifted a small part to Berks County as well. Not long after the American Revolution, the residents in the western portion of the remaining county objected to traveling so far to conduct business in the county seat at Chester City on the Delaware River. They wanted a county seat located farther west. They got their wish when West Chester became the county seat, and three years later, in 1789, Delaware County was carved out. From that time, Chester County no longer shared a border with Philadelphia.

Penn had encouraged the early formation of townships throughout the entire territory as a way to promote self-government. Many boroughs and townships had incorporated by the early eighteenth century, for example Caln in 1686, Coatesville in 1687, Kennett in 1704, Uwchlan in 1712, and numerous others. But the Quakers who predominated in much of Chester County shunned town living, preferring life on their farms. Based on religious scruples, Quakers

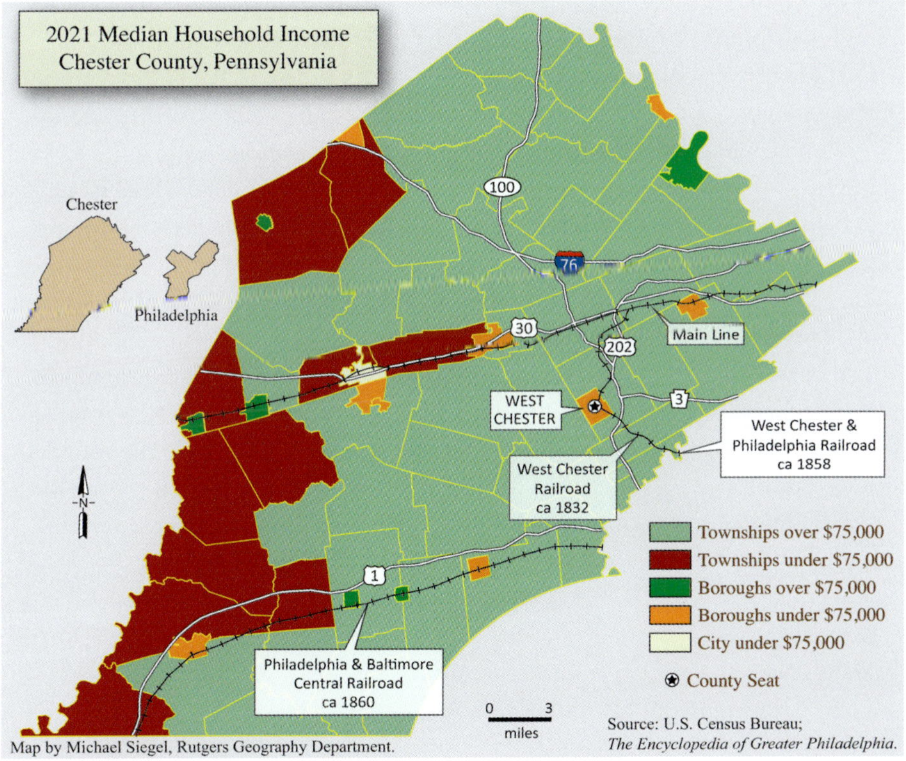

MAP 8. 2021 Median Household Income Chester County, Pennsylvania. MAP BY MICHAEL SIEGEL.

showed little interest in formal governance of their territory. Except for the county seat, early towns carried few public responsibilities beyond providing small local marketplaces and serving as units for assessing taxes. Rural families produced a large share of the goods for home consumption, and craftsmen lived among the farmers, trading their products for food.

TRANSPORTATION ROUTES SHAPED SETTLEMENTS

The land formation known as the "Great Valley," stretching from the Schuylkill River in Montgomery County to the southwest through Chester and Lancaster Counties, provided early travelers with a natural route. The first major east-west road following the Great Valley westward was the Lancaster Road or the Great Road, which became the most traveled route of its time. Benjamin Rush in 1789 remarked of German farmers that it was "no uncommon thing, on the Lancaster and Reading roads, to meet in one day fifty to a hundred of these [Conestoga] wagons on their way to Philadelphia, most of which belong to German farmers."

Largely following that same route, the Philadelphia and Lancaster Turnpike Road Company constructed in 1795 the first long-distance paved route in the United States stretching sixty-two miles between Philadelphia and the city of Lancaster. The improved road bed allowed farmers and craftsmen to haul heavy freight and drive stage coaches from Lancaster to Philadelphia. It brought travelers to dozens of inns, taverns, saddleries, and shops of every variety and helped build Downingtown and a few other commercial centers along its route.

To serve the southern part of the county, the state chartered the Philadelphia, Brandywine and New London Turnpike Company in 1808 to build a stagecoach road from Philadelphia to Baltimore. That route, known as the Baltimore Pike (designated U.S. Route 1 in 1926), entered Chester County from Delaware County at Chadds Ford and ran through the Brandywine Valley—a mix of farms and woodland, as well as commercial towns and villages like Kennett Square. Farmers in the Brandywine Valley hauled their grain to mills powered by the Brandywine River, which also powered paper mills that supplied Philadelphia printers.

Railroads exerted less impact on early settlement patterns in Chester County than in other suburban counties around Philadelphia because the rail network was less densely built on the western edge of the region. The great exception was the Main Line, a railroad designed as one component of a larger network of canals and rails that the state government sponsored in order to help Pennsylvania compete commercially against New York State. Construction started in 1829, carried on largely by Irish immigrants. In 1857 the Pennsylvania Railroad purchased the line since known as the Main Line.

Across the middle of the county, investors built the Philadelphia and Baltimore Central Railroad (P&BC) just before the Civil War. They broke ground in 1855 in Concord Township in Delaware County, where the celebrants tossed one shovelful of dirt toward Philadelphia and another toward Baltimore to signify the goal of connecting the two cities.

As those two major lines crossed the county from east to west, they helped spur the economies of some towns along the way, including Downingtown and Coatesville on the Main Line and Oxford Borough on the P&BC near the county's southern border with Maryland. But their main function was to link Philadelphia to the distant cities of Lancaster to the west and Baltimore to the south. One of the few places within the county that did purposely build rail lines to spur its own development was the county seat of West Chester, where business leaders formed a railroad company to connect their town to the Main Line running some miles to the north. They opened the West Chester Rail Road (WCRR) in 1832 to carry both passengers and freight. In the 1850s a second group of investors built West Chester and Philadelphia Railroad (WC&P) to offer an alternative connecting West Chester to the Philadelphia and Baltimore Central line running through southern Delaware and Chester Counties. During the period of railroad consolidations around the turn of the twentieth century, the Pennsylvania Railroad gained control over both West Chester railroads, as well as the Main Line and the Philadelphia and Baltimore Central.

FIGURE 72. Rolling mill, Phoenix Iron Company, showing equipment left over from pipe and tube making in the 1970s and 1980s, Phoenixville, Chester County, 1999. LIBRARY OF CONGRESS.

AGRICULTURE AND INDUSTRY

Abundant sources of water power made milling the county's first industry. Farmers grew corn, wheat, barley, oats, rye, buckwheat, and flax, and most settlements had a grist mill, which could also be used as a sawmill. However, as improved transportation networks made long-distance shipping easier, farmers shifted away from diversified crops to produce more livestock. The growth of Philadelphia and increasing purchasing power of the population persuaded farmers to supply more meat. By mid-nineteenth century, agriculture in Chester County focused most heavily on grazing and dairying. The 1860 agricultural census showed that of Chester County's roughly fifty thousand cattle, half were for dairy and the other half for beef purposes.

Waterpower enabled the county's residents to exploit the area's rich iron ore deposits. Early iron manufactories established a basis for nationally known ironworks. In 1790 on the banks of French Creek, the French Creek Nail Works opened the first nail factory in the United States, later renamed the Phoenix Iron Company. It grew into an extensive ironworks consisting of furnace, foundry, rolling mill, and nail factory. During the Civil War, Phoenix Iron produced the Griffen Gun and became a major supplier of the Union army. As railroads multiplied, the company focused on structural steel for bridge building, a crucial requirement for railroad expansion.

Lukens Steel in Coatesville was born in 1810 when Isaac Pennock began the Brandywine Iron Works and Nail Factory on the banks of the Brandywine River. All the raw materials needed—iron ore, limestone, and hardwood forests for charcoal—were available in the Coatesville area. In 1813 Pennock's daughter Rebecca married Charles Lukens, who oversaw the operation of his father-in-law's business. When Lukens died in 1825, Rebecca took over operation of the steel mill. She managed the business until 1849 and turned it into the top producer of boilerplate in the country.

Agriculture continued to operate profitably throughout the nineteenth and twentieth centuries, aided by the rail lines that crossed the county. By the 1890s, the Pennsylvania Railroad trains that ran all the way to Lancaster gave farmers in western Chester County a way to ship fresh milk and produce daily to Philadelphia. In 1906 Abbott's Dairy opened in Oxford on the far west side of the county yet still transported its products to the Philadelphia market.

Plant cultivation contributed significantly to the county's economy. In the borough of West Grove in 1868 the Dingee & Conard Company began growing and selling fruit trees, roses, and other nursery products. They pioneered the use of mail- order catalogs, and by the late 1880s shipping of their nursery products made West Grove the second-largest post office in Chester County. The company became nationally known for its roses, most notably the Peace Rose. In 1945, the company provided one of this specially bred flower to every international delegate meeting in San Francisco to establish the United Nations.

Undoubtedly mushrooms became Chester County's best-known food crop. In the 1890s William Swayne, a florist in Kennett Square, began growing mushrooms in the unused space underneath his greenhouse benches. Because he required precise regulation of the temperature, humidity, and air quality, Swayne erected the first building to be used exclusively for mushroom growing, and Kennett Square eventually became the national center of mushroom cultivation. Ironically, old-fashioned mushroom cultivation helped build Chester County's twenty-first-century specialization in bio/life sciences. Starting in the 1920s chemist G. Raymond Rettew began providing testing services to area mushroom growers. He devised a process for growing penicillin that made mass production of the drug possible. He sold the idea to Reichel Laboratories of Phoenixville, which was acquired by Wyeth Laboratories in 1943. The penicillin case demonstrated the important process of turning research into production that became a hallmark of Chester County's high- tech economy.

SOCIAL DISPARITIES

From the start, Chester County's population contained both rich and poor. In 1800, the wealthiest 10 percent of the county's households paid 38 percent of the taxes, and the poorest 30 percent of the citizenry paid only 4 percent, largely because taxes were based on land ownership. To house the poor and unemployed, county leaders in 1798 built a poorhouse about eight miles from West Chester on the banks of the Brandywine Creek. On 325 acres, they built a large brick building and a barn to house a working farm. This county almshouse system replaced the aid provided by individual townships. The intent was to provide a more consistent level of care and a more efficient use of funds. Reflecting their shared belief in the value of work, they required every able body to work, even the children. Residents of the poorh ouse sold homespun cloth, brooms, smoked meats, and even quarried limestone.

Early European settlers held enslaved Africans, though in relatively small numbers. In Chester County the number of slave owners reached 4 percent of taxpayers in 1759. The strong Quaker influence in the affairs of the county discouraged slavery as did economic factors. At the start of the Civil War, African American residents represented about 8 percent of Chester County's population; although a modest share, that was the highest percentage of African Americans in the counties of southeast Pennsylvania. Those free African Americans worked for hire or owned their own small businesses.

Chester County residents included people who actively embraced the social reform movements of the mid-nineteenth century such as antislavery, women's rights, and temperance. Local European American, primarily Quaker, and African American abolitionists concealed runaway enslaved people who traveled from the South through the mid-Atlantic and north to safety in Canada. Antislavery sentiment was particularly strong in Kennett Square, a center of abolitionism. Disagreement over the authority of Quaker meetings and how best to address the issue of slavery led to the establishment of the Pennsylvania Yearly Meeting of Progressive Friends in 1853 (Longwood Yearly Meeting). The Longwood meetinghouse opened in 1855. Its annual meetings hosted radicals and reformers such as Sojourner Truth and William Lloyd Garrison. County residents also hosted the first Pennsylvania Woman's Rights Convention in June 1852 in West Chester, advocating for equal legal, social, economic, and political rights, including suffrage.

The African American population grew after the Civil War, when iron companies in Phoenixville and Coatesville recruited Black workers in the South as a way of discouraging European immigrants from striking for higher wages. Animosity between working-class white and Black people came to a head in Coatesville in 1911 with the horrifying death of Zachariah Walker, a Black man who was literally burned alive by a white mob after his conviction for killing a white guard at a local steel plant.

In part to address social inequality, the Society of Friends supported education for all children. As early as 1787 the Kennett Monthly Meeting began raising funds to support "schooling the children of such poor people, whether Friends or others, as live within the verge of the Monthly Meeting." For the offspring of more affluent families, the county was dotted by dozens of single-sex boarding schools, for example West Chester Academy, a private, state-aided school opened in 1813. It went through a series of transformations across the years that resulted in it becoming West Chester University. In 1854 the Pennsylvania legislature incorporated another of Chester County's prominent educational institutions as Ashmun Institute for the education of young men of color, a name that changed in 1866 to Lincoln University.

Despite important efforts to promote broad social advancement, the county entered the twentieth century with wide disparities among its residents. Wealthy families built rural retreats on large estates, many of them designed in the Victorian style popular among early twentieth -century architects. West Whiteland Township, served by the Pennsylvania Railroad running along the Main Line, boasted an impressive collection of such homes. Important Philadelphia architects built many of them, for example the Francis W. Kennedy House designed by Frank Miles Day in 1889 for a vice president of the Wilkes-Barre and Western Railway; the Joseph Price House, an older structure that was extensively altered in 1894 for a wealthy Philadelphia surgeon; and Meadowcourt (sometimes called Autun), which was designed by Edmund Gilchrist in the French style in 1928 for insurance executive Benjamin Rush, Jr. Owners of these large properties pursued diversions like foxhunting, for which a group of well-to-do families established the Whitelands Hunt.

In the Brandywine Valley in 1906 Pierre S. Du Pont of the wealthy Delaware Du Pont family bought the Peirce farm in Kennett Township and created an estate of incomparable beauty. He repaired and expanded the original Peirce farmhouse, connecting new and old wings with a conservatory whose courtyard was planted with exotic foliage and a marble fountain. In 1923, he added an elegant music room with walnut paneling, damask-covered walls, teak floors, and a molded plaster ceiling, opening onto the central axis of the main greenhouse. Du Pont named his estate Longwood Gardens for the nearby Longwood meetinghouse. built by Quakers.

At the other end of the social spectrum, in nearby communities of southern Chester County, immigrants lived in deplorable conditions. Around the turn of the twentieth century, southern Europeans came to the county. One of the county's most successful plant nurseries, Hoopes, Bro. & Thomas in West Chester, began hiring Italian immigrants in 1906 because they could not find enough local labor. By 1908, newspapers were criticizing these immigrant workers for drying their laundry on the outside of their shanties. Despite the social stigma the Italians stayed, and a century later 11 percent of West Chester residents still claimed Italian ancestry. In industrial towns like Coatesville and Phoenixville, eastern Europeans, notably Hungarians and Poles, served as a significant source for factory labor.

Puerto Ricans initially arrived in Chester County after World War II, while Mexicans arrived in the 1960s. Recruiters brought them to Pennsylvania to farm labor-intensive crops like vegetables, fruits, and mushrooms. Kennett Square, the center of mushroom production, attracted a substantial Spanish-speaking population, as did the smaller community of Toughkenamon a mile west of Kennett Square.

Limited by their very low wages and undocumented status, many immigrants settled for dilapidated, overcrowded houses, apartments, or mobile homes. In 1994 the Alliance for Better Housing composed of clergy, mushroom growers, and local officials began working to improve housing conditions for farm workers and other low-income residents in southern Chester

County. Additional help came from local organizations like United Way, La Comunidad Hispana, PathStone, Mission Santa Maria, local food cupboards, and local churches.

Newcomers from South and East Asia lived a completely different immigrant experience from the mushroom workers in southern Chester County. Hired into knowledge- economy jobs, they clustered in affluent townships along U.S. Route 202 or Pennsylvania Route 30—for example, East Whiteland, West Whiteland, East Caln, and Upper Uwchlan—in the northeast section of the county, where they worked in technology and finance companies.

The county's rapid economic ascent after 1980 attracted a workforce equipped to prosper in the knowledge, finance, and service economy. The 2017–2021 American Community Survey showed that 55 percent of county residents had college degrees, the highest percentage among suburban counties surrounding Philadelphia. Of the population twenty-five years or older, 95 percent were high school graduates.

Not all towns shared that success. Because of its reliance on the steel industry, the city of Coatesville suffered the most visible and dramatic setbacks in the county. Lukens Steel had flourished there since the early 1800s, building major national projects from the Verrazano-Narrows Bridge to the battleship, the USS *New Jersey*. But faced with competition from foreign steel producers, in 1982 the company reduced its workforce by 22 percent between January and September 1982 and cut the pay of salaried employees by 10 percent. After 187 years of continuous operation, Lukens Steel Company sold its Coatesville operation to Bethlehem Steel Company, which in turn sold the plant to new international owners. Each new owner reduced the workforce, so that by the end of the twentieth century the steel plant that had employed over six thousand workers at midcentury provided jobs for fewer than one thousand.

DEVELOPMENT PATTERNS

The Pennsylvania Turnpike (Interstate 76) dramatically altered development in the northeast section of the county. Builders completed the Chester County section of the turnpike in 1950. Designed as a limited-access route to allow fast travel across Pennsylvania, the Pennsylvania Turnpike initially provided just two exits located within Chester County (Downingtown and Malvern/Phoenixville). Those two exits became focal points for growth, as did the Valley Forge/King of Prussia exit located in Montgomery County right at the border with Chester County.

Another example of an expressway influencing development was U.S. Route 202, a highway dating back to 1926. In 1964, the Pennsylvania Department of Highways designed a continuous four-lane expressway along the Route 202 corridor, opening the section of that new expressway south from King of Prussia toward West Chester in 1967. Over the next several decades that stretch of Route 202 attracted hundreds of computer-related companies, biomedical concerns, and other service- and information- based firms.

Suburbanizing relatively late, Chester County in the 1970s offered developers a chance to acquire huge open parcels on which to build a series of high profile and often controversial industrial parks. Some occupied more than a square mile of ground, making them larger than some boroughs in Chester County. Businessman Raymond Carr built Chester County's first industrial park on what had previously been cornfields. Carr and his partner, David Knauer, recognized the value of farmland sitting near the Downingtown exit off the Pennsylvania Turnpike, which was the only connection to the national superhighway system in Chester County. In 1965 the partners bought 180 acres for sale in Lionville and turned them into Pickering Creek Industrial Park, a collection of more than a dozen multipurpose buildings that housed companies specializing in product testing, manufacturing, and eventually biotechnology and life sciences.

In 1969 not far from the turnpike's Valley Forge exit, developer Richard Fox bought Chesterbrook Farm, located between the turnpike on its northern border and Route 202 on its southern border. His plan, unusual for combining residential neighborhoods with a corporate complex, faced stiff public opposition when unveiled in 1971. Opponents feared that the traffic it generated would negatively impact Valley Forge State (later National Historical) Park. The ensuing legal battle went all the way to the Supreme Court of Pennsylvania. Hundreds of residents attended meetings and signed petitions against construction, but eventually Fox prevailed and began to build housing in 1977, gradually adding a shopping center, restaurants, corporate offices, and a hotel, along with open spaces.

The business complex that launched Route 202's reputation as Tech Alley was the Great Valley Corporate Center, started in 1974 on pasture land located between a landfill and a quarry. Philadelphia-based developer Willard Rouse convinced young companies to locate in his new development by building facilities to their specifications and helping them finance the move to Chester County. Biotechnology companies valued a location that put them close to Philadelphia universities and medical centers and at the same time close to pharmaceutical companies like SmithKline Beecham, Merck Sharp & Dohme, and Rhône-Poulenc Rorer.

Also in the mid-1970s, Willard Rouse's uncle, James W. Rouse, built the Exton Square Mall. The Maryland developer acquired a tract of land at the intersection of Route 30 and Pennsylvania Route 100 that held little more than a few gas stations, a drive-in movie theater, a diner, and a motel and built his mall there in 1972. Exton Square remained a major retail center well into the twenty-first century. Its size and scope attracted additional services, including a public library, the Exton Transportation Center with connections to the King of Prussia Mall, and medical facilities.

Watching such large-scale, master-planned developments multiply during the 1970s and 1980s, Chester County residents feared the loss of open land and the road congestion that such developments brought with them. Those apprehensions brought an end to one of the most ambitious proposals ever considered in the county. In 1987 Willard Rouse announced plans to build Churchill, a 1,500-acre mixed-use development on Church Farm School property on Route 30 in Exton. That unspoiled expanse of cornfields was so massive that it spanned parts of four townships, forcing Rouse to negotiate for years with multiple local governments to secure permission to build. In the end the sheer scale of development proved too much for local residents. Both East Whiteland and West Whiteland denied Rouse permission to build.

TAKING CONTROL OF DEVELOPMENT PATTERNS

From 1969 to 2000, Chester County lost 26 percent of its farmland to development. If that pace had been allowed to continue, all of the county's farmland would have been paved over within forty years. To stave off such a future, the county government adopted a dramatic and far-reaching plan titled *Landscapes: Managing Change in Chester County* to shape its growth until 2020. The plan prescribed preserving open space while directing future development into already-existing towns, to ensure Chester County would remain attractive as a place for knowledge industries to locate. Although the county government could do little more than offer technical assistance for implementing the plan to local governments that retained control of land use under Pennsylvania law, nonetheless by 2015 about one- quarter of the land area in the county had been permanently preserved.

Some private developers fell in line with county plans by making investments that reduced the number of auto trips workers needed to make each day. For example, the owners of Great Valley Corporate Center redesigned their auto-dependent complex to incorporate everyday services like day care, fitness centers, stores, and restaurants within a walkable mixed-use development. Other developers saw opportunities in older boroughs like Phoenixville and West Chester to reinvest in Victorian structures and community character that would attract residents.

In one important respect, Chester County's late suburbanization proved a blessing. It gave county leaders a greater chance to preserve farms, wooded areas, and historic landscapes than in other counties in the Philadelphia region. Yet the negative consequence of delayed development was that Chester County possessed even less public transit than neighboring counties. Chester County entered the twenty-first century with little hope of convincing motorists to abandon their cars. The county's heavy auto dependence, combined with a pattern of erecting massive job centers along major highways, virtually ensured that traffic congestion would continue to be its residents' unceasing complaint.

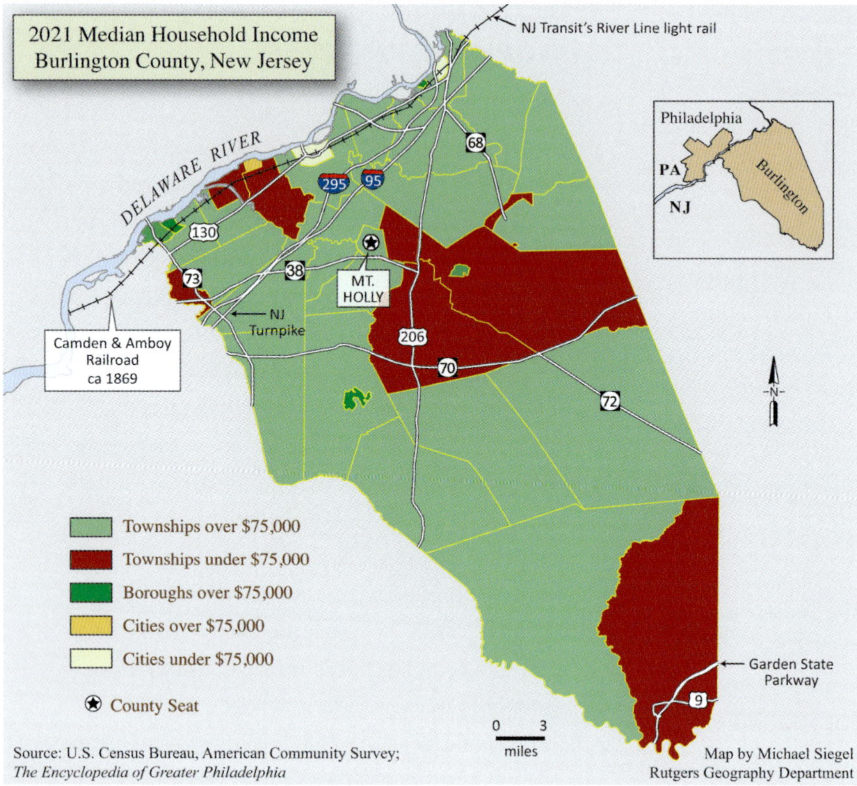

MAP 9. 2021 Median Household Income Burlington County, New Jersey.
MAP BY MICHAEL SIEGEL.

Burlington County, New Jersey

Howard Gillette, Jr.

Settled primarily by Quakers in the seventeenth century, Burlington County occupied a strategic location between the Delaware River and the Atlantic coast that made it a site for commercial and agricultural development as well as spiritual refuge. Marginalized over time as money and power shifted elsewhere, the area diversified in the formation of forty communities spread over 819 square miles stretching from the Delaware River to the Pine Barrens near New Jersey's eastern shore.

Originally occupied by the Lenape, the area became an important crossing point of the Delaware River with the arrival of the first Dutch settlers in the mid-seventeenth century. In 1676 a group of Quakers, including William Penn, obtained title to West Jersey. The following year proprietors adopted the West Jersey Concessions, a liberal system of government and basic laws granting religious freedom, trial by jury, and security from arbitrary arrest, prompting further migration from England. Quakers from Yorkshire landed near Raccoon Creek, where they encountered a few Swedish households, then proceeded to Chygoes (Burlington) Island to negotiate terms with the Indians. Choosing land from the Assunpink Creek to the Rancocas Creek, known as the First Tenth, they were soon joined by a second ship's cargo of London Friends, who purchased the land between the Rancocas and Timber Creeks, known as the Second Tenth. For mutual protection, the two settler groups jointly agreed to build a town, known first as New Beverly, then Bridlington, and finally Burlington, after a village in Yorkshire. In 1681 it became the capital of West Jersey.

Soon after its founding, Burlington City became a major colonial port maintaining a brisk trade with Ireland, Great Britain, Europe, and the West Indies. The city's first shipyard was established in 1698, and shipbuilding quickly became an important economic activity. With the establishment of other towns, the assembly formed Burlington County in 1694. Unable to exercise central control over the sprawling settlements in West Jersey, however, the proprietors in 1702 surrendered their title to the Crown, which then reunited West with East Jersey and named Burlington and Perth Amboy, the capital of East Jersey, co-capitals.

With its stake in maintaining trade with England, Burlington City remained favorable to the Crown during the years leading to the American Revolution. Resistance to British authority concentrated instead in Mount Holly—also founded by Quakers, in 1676—at a location farther inland along the Rancocas Creek, where grist and sawmills emerged to support the predominantly farm community. When war came to New Jersey in 1776, both communities had to defend themselves, but when British troops threatened Trenton, the capital shifted temporarily to Mount Holly. In 1796 the county seat shifted there from Burlington.

While the greatest portion of the county remained agricultural in the early years of the new republic, industry did emerge in several locations. Shipbuilding declined in Burlington City as Philadelphia's dominance of the industry grew, but shoemaking emerged as a major industry in the early nineteenth century. Other products followed, including patent medicine, hats, iron stoves and pipe, terra cotta, carriages, and canned fruits and vegetables, which were shipped by water and rail to markets throughout the United States.

By 1790 Burlington County had the largest Black population and largest number of free Black people among the state's five southern counties, the result of Quaker opposition to slavery. During the 1820s free Black people who had originally lived in scattered areas on or near farms or in the woods began to form settlements of their own. These included Cross Roads in later Medford Township, Ingletown in later Shamong Township, and several in Evesham Township, a Quaker community dating back to 1688. The oldest of these was Colemantown, along Elbow Lane in a part of Evesham that became part of Mount Laurel after its incorporation in 1872. Named for Charles Coleman, the area's first Black homeowner, a modest edifice that served as meeting house for different denominations and a school for Black children was soon accompanied by a cemetery designated for Black people. Shortly after the Civil War, congregants built a new home of worship, known as Jacob's Chapel after Jacob Mitchell, an African Methodist Episcopal minister noted for his success in building other congregations in the area. The chapel subsequently became a stop on the Underground Railroad running from Delaware through Woodbury in Gloucester County and on to Mercer County. Another Black community formed in Mount Holly. Known as Timbuctoo, it first formed in 1826 when four African American men, all believed to have escaped slavery in Maryland, purchased parcels of land from a Quaker businessman. In addition to farming, residents found employment in two brickyards north of the settlement owned by Quakers. Reaching its peak in the nineteenth century with some 125 residents, the area supported a school, Zion Wesleyan Methodist Episcopal African church, and a cemetery.

NEW TRANSIT AIDS GROWTH

Burlington City's growth, and that of towns emerging along the Delaware River between Philadelphia and New York, was aided by transportation advances, starting with steamboat service to Philadelphia inaugurated in 1788. The advent of the Camden and Amboy Railroad and its related entity, the Delaware and Raritan Canal Company, both chartered in 1830, further spurred development. When the forty-four-mile-long canal opened in 1834, passengers moved by rail and freight by canalboat. Protected from competition by the state legislature through a partial merger producing what was referred to as the Joint Entities, together the canal and railroad assured profits over a heavily traveled route across New Jersey. Among the many products shipped north were Pennsylvania's anthracite coal and such agricultural goods as flour, cornmeal, grain, and feed. By 1839, as it absorbed other rail lines, including the Pennsylvania-chartered Philadelphia and Trenton Railroad, the Camden and Amboy controlled all rail service between Camden and New York City.

Communities along the Joint Entities route thrived. These included, in addition to Burlington, nearby Florence, initially known as High Banks. Its riverfront location a short boat ride from Philadelphia made the area a popular recreation destination. In 1849 investors from New York, recognizing the area's residential potential, purchased six hundred acres to form the Florence City Company. Despite providing amenities to attract buyers, including a wharf, hotel, landscaped

FIGURE 73. Roebling, 1924. The planned industrial village on the Delaware River, subsequently part of Florence Township, was designed and built in 1905 by the Roebling family, notable Trenton industrialists. HAGLEY MUSEUM AND LIBRARY.

streets, and brick houses, the venture faltered and was sold in 1854. It was up to manufacturers, then, to restore the area's prospects with the formation of the Florence Iron Works in 1858. Sold nine years later to R.D. Wood & Company (based in Millville, Cumberland County), the iron works expanded after inducing the Camden and Amboy to build a spur to its plant. The company built modest homes for its workers, a library, and other amenities. It fabricated water and gas pipes, fire hydrants, valves, and other cast iron products. Sold to Griffin Pipe Products in 1962, the facility subsequently became part of a larger manufacturing corporation, Amsted Industries, whose plant in Florence produced ductile iron pressure pipe used by the construction industry until 2009.

Immediately adjacent to Florence emerged the town of Roebling, named for the company founded by John Roebling that designed and built the Brooklyn Bridge, among other structures. Based in Trenton for a number of years, the family enterprise, seeking cheaper land to build a new wire rope plant and its own steel mill, bought a 115-acre farm fronting the Delaware River in 1904 in the small village of Kinkora. There it laid out a model company town consisting of 750 homes for its workers as well as a hospital, school, post office, and other facilities for their use. The company sold the mill to Colorado Fuel and Iron Company in 1953, which ran the plant until it closed in 1974. Although the mill was declared a federal Superfund site in 1983, the community of some eight thousand residents remained in place as part of Florence Township.

CHANGING IDENTITY

Closer to Philadelphia, at the confluence of the Delaware River and Rancocas Creek, steamboat and rail connections spurred development over time. A scattered group of squatter farms in the mid-nineteenth century, the area known originally as Goat Town, attracted the interest of Philadelphia investors who conceived a resort area at the location. When new rail connections diverted vacationers to the Jersey Shore instead, manufacturing took over with the introduction of woolen and worsted textiles, led by the German American William F. Taubel whose company ultimately extended to thirty-three locations in the eastern United States. The area was absorbed first into Cinnaminson, then Delran Township, before emerging as independent Riverside Township in 1895. Two years later the area gained a new identity when the Swiss German immigrant Theophilus Zurbrugg moved his Keystone Watch Case Company from Philadelphia to Riverside, where he set up his factory in the town's first resort hotel. The company soon added a metalwork facility, and the construction of low-cost housing further put the company's mark on the town. In 1908 the company relocated to the Watch Case building, which remained a local landmark. In contrast, the township of Riverton, which also split from Cinnaminson, became the location of prime Victorian homes constructed by wealthy Philadelphians, whose settlement there as early as the 1850s fostered one of the nation's first yacht clubs, known for its stunning Victorian clubhouse.

Farther inland along the Rancocas emerged another company town under the direction of Hezekiah B. Smith, whose walled compound included factory buildings and worker housing as well as Smith's mansion. Originally a cotton and textile plant, the facility known as the H.B. Smith Machine Company was converted to a woodworking plant in the 1860s. Located within what became Eastampton Township, the Smith factory was connected to Mount Holly by a one-mile wooden rail line. Following the factory's closure during the Depression, Smithville was incorporated into the Burlington County park system.

Quite a different industry emerged in the southeastern section of the county within the Pine Barrens in what was to become Washington Township. Drawing on an abundance of bog ore in area streams and rivers and charcoal for smelting, Charles Read, a Philadelphia merchant who had moved to Burlington City in search of a political career, established the Batsto Iron Works along the Batsto River in 1766. When Read fell into financial difficulty, he sold the plant to area investors, who oversaw iron production at more than thirty forges and furnaces throughout the Pine Barrens. The Batsto plant prospered for nearly a century under the direction of the Richards family, who bought the works in 1784. When demand for iron ore slackened, the company tried unsuccessfully to shift to glassmaking and fell into receivership. In 1876 Philadelphia businessman and founder of Bethlehem Steel Joseph Wharton purchased the plant and a number of related properties. Managed after Wharton's death until 1954 by the Girard Trust Company in Philadelphia, the historic Batsto Village and associated museum subsequently became a prime visitor destination in South Jersey.

INDUSTRIES RISE AND FALL

The same year Charles Read launched the Batsto works, he constructed another facility, the Aetna Furnace, on nine thousand acres at the edge of the Pine Barrens in an area known as Upper Evesham, but later incorporated in 1847 as Medford. In 1766, Read followed with a second facility, the Taunton furnace and forge, which produced among other products cannon balls for the American Revolution. The collapse of Read's iron empire forced the furnace's closure in 1773 after which the area lay fallow until its sale in 1926 to a developer who converted it to a resort-like community of log cabin cottages in the Pines known as Medford Lakes. Although Read's venture collapsed, other industry emerged, including glassmaking. Dating to 1825 with the formation of a farmers' co-op that made window panes, glass remained in production in the township for ninety years.

Benefiting from its location as the port closest to the Pine Barrens and Philadelphia in the era before the Delaware and Raritan Canal opened, the village of Lumberton diversified its agricultural base to incorporate textile mills and a steel furnace, which remained profitable for the first decades of the nineteenth century. In anticipation of its prospects, the town authorized the layout of a city-style grid geared for residential development, but growth did not follow. Established as a township in 1860 when the population was just over 1,800, the community lacked growth until the 1950s, when its farmland began to give way to suburban development. A town of just 1,325 in 1950, Lumberton's population climbed to 2,833 in 1960 and to 12,228 in 2020.

Much of the county inland from the Delaware River remained largely agricultural and rural into the twentieth century. A staging and training center for World War I established in 1917 in New Hanover Township, Fort Dix, as it was formally named in 1939, served as a base for the New Deal's Civilian Conservation Corps in the 1930s. Its construction boosted area employment in Mount Holly some ten miles distant, ultimately providing consumers for town products and homes. The buildup of personnel during World War II further boosted area homebuilding.

Growth came not just from the expansion of Fort Dix, which merged with McGuire Air Force Base and the Lakehurst Naval Air Engineering Station in 2009. The completion of the New Jersey Turnpike in 1952 further boosted development, nowhere more directly than at Exit 4, in Mount Laurel. A town of only several thousand people in 1940 despite its sprawling territory over twenty-two square miles, Mount Laurel's population grew modestly during World War II to 2,800 before witnessing accelerated growth in the 1950s and 1960s after the turnpike opened. In 1970 the population reached 11,000. With so much empty land, the township attracted not just tract housing but whole new communities through a new procedure for planned unit development, which allowed building on tracts of ten acres or more using a single unified ground plan. When Larchmont opened in 1970, it was only the second such development to be built in New Jersey. Spurred by construction of nearly three thousand new housing units, many of them in planned unit developments, the population climbed to 17,000 by 1980 and 30,000 in 1990. To this were added three industrial parks and a host of businesses taking advantage of easy access to the turnpike and Interstate 295, which ran parallel to and only a mile distant from the turnpike. By 2000 Mount Laurel's population had climbed to 40,000, transforming the once agricultural landscape into a prototypical exurban landscape tied intimately to the automobile.

RAPID GROWTH IGNITES SOCIAL TENSION

Growth brought unwanted change to longtime residents of Mount Laurel, including many Black households. Faced with the rising cost of single-family homes, they sought a change in local zoning to allow multiunit housing, only to be told that if they could not afford to stay in Mount Laurel, they could move to Camden. Ultimately the New Jersey Supreme Court supported their cause by ruling in 1975 and 1983 that every community in the state would be responsible for providing its "fair share" of affordable housing. One result of that Mount Laurel doctrine, as it came to be called, was the construction of the Ethel Lawrence Homes, so named for a chief plaintiff in the lawsuit, a model of affordable development in Mount Laurel practically indistinguishable in quality and form from the many gated communities nearby.

The expansion of Willingboro, a community founded by Quakers dating back to 1688, from an agricultural community of less than one thousand in 1950, raised racial issues of another kind. By introducing eleven thousand homes on some 4,900 acres of open land, developer William Levitt transformed the township between 1958 and 1972 to a community of forty-seven thousand people, renaming it Levittown. Levitt barred African Americans from purchasing the new homes, a position that held until a Black soldier from Fort Dix successfully sued the town, challenging its right to receive federal subsidies while discriminating against Black buyers. Following the decision by the New Jersey Supreme Court, Levitt adopted an active integration program, and by 1970 Willingboro's Black population had reached 11 percent. As the numbers continued to grow, panic selling by whites ensued, so that by 2020, though the population had fallen to thirty-one thousand, whites represented only 13 percent of that total. By referendum in 1963, the township reverted to its original name of Willingboro.

The growth of automobile registrations in the early years of the twentieth century increased demand for river crossings between Pennsylvania and New Jersey. In 1922 businessmen in Palmyra, a borough located along the rail line and about halfway between Trenton and Philadelphia, initiated car ferry service to the growing neighborhood of Tacony in Philadelphia. Demand for ferry service grew so quickly, company directors decided to build a bridge to supplement the service to be provided by the Delaware River (later Benjamin Franklin) Bridge planned to open seven miles to the south in 1926. Soon after opening in 1929, the Tacony-Palmyra span attracted so much traffic that it quickly fell behind in its ability to meet demand from the growing population in the surrounding area. The bridge was privately owned and operated until 1948, when it was purchased by the Burlington Bridge Commission.

NEW DIRECTIONS

As in practically every metropolitan region that expanded after World War II, shopping malls proliferated in Burlington County. The Moorestown Mall, opened in 1963 in Moorestown Township, was overshadowed from the start by South Jersey's first mall, in Cherry Hill, built two years earlier and only three miles away. Although the Moorestown Mall counted among its early tenants the Sears, Roebuck store that left Camden for the new facility, it encountered increasing difficulties over the years. Parts of the mall were renovated in 1986 to meet competition and completely remodeled in 1993 and 1994 after a serious fire damaged the northeast quarter. As bricks-and-mortar retail sales tumbled in the second decade of the twenty-first century, major stores closed or departed, including Macy's, Lord & Taylor, and Sears. To stem losses, the Pennsylvania Real Estate Investment Trust (PREIT), after purchasing the mall from the Rouse Company, planned alternative uses on portions of the property, including three apartment buildings and a hotel.

Developers took a similar tack in Burlington Township, the fourteen-square-mile area that separated from Burlington City in 1894. Once the home of six hundred thousand square feet of retail space, the ninety-seven-acre Burlington Mall was earmarked after its closure in 2018 for mixed use, including as many as five hundred townhomes and multiple restaurants. Other redevelopment in the area benefited from an aggressive state program, New Jersey Grow, aimed at retaining business. When Burlington Coat Factory threatened to move its national headquarters from Burlington Township to Pennsylvania, a $40 million state subsidy issued in 2012 enabled the company to move a few miles up U.S. Route 130 to build a new facility in Florence. In Moorestown, Lockheed Martin, the county's largest business, with some 3,400 workers, took advantage of a $40 million state subsidy to obtain a $100 million government contract for missile research, enabling the company to retain many workers considered otherwise vulnerable to layoffs.

In Burlington City, closure of the United States Pipe and Foundry Company facility in 2008 left a prime site for redevelopment, but grand plans for restoring the former company headquarters and the surrounding facilities floundered until Amazon opened a million-square- foot fulfillment center on the 177-acre property in 2019. Among the possibilities for the remaining 26 acres was an indoor waterfront park and resort hotel. Both initiatives illuminated the shifting role of prime locations in the twenty-first century.

Changing regional demographics affected several county communities in a complex fashion. On the western side, the once- thriving industrial township of Riverside, as it stagnated, attracted a wave of Brazilian immigrants looking for affordable housing. Their presence brought a host of new small businesses, but also clashes with established residents as their numbers reached as many as five thousand people in the town of only eight thousand. Farther east, the decline of conditions in subsidized housing in Mount Holly prompted a redevelopment initiative that spurred displacement of tenants of color from their affordable homes and a prolonged court contest over the future of the site. The dispute was ultimately resolved, but not without highlighting the mixed response to redevelopment.

Other towns benefited from a different kind of investment: public transportation. The completion of NJ Transit's River Line light rail connection between Camden and Trenton in 2004 did not make a profit, but it lifted the fortunes of towns along its route. Constructed on the former Camden-Bordentown section and Bordentown-Trenton branch of the Camden and Amboy Railroad, the line boosted population and new investment at stops along the line: Riverside, Delanco, Beverly, Burlington, Florence, and Bordentown. The county also pursued a companion reinvestment strategy to enhance commercial outlets along the parallel Route 130 corridor to attract new housing and boost population along the line even as it declined in the exurban areas to the east. Although Bordentown's population growth lagged behind that of other towns along the corridor, its easy access to the New Jersey Turnpike prompted a boom in warehouse development.

As of 2020, the Burlington County population was 462,269—72 percent white, 18.7 percent Black, and 9.2 percent Hispanic—and the median household income was $90,329. Land use from west to east became less dense as older suburban areas gave way to larger developments built where farms once dominated, to smaller older towns like Medford, which retained their early roots, to more scattered housing and facilities in communities within the Pine Barrens.

Camden County, New Jersey

Howard Gillette, Jr.

Formed in 1844 from parts of what had been Gloucester County since 1686, Camden County maintained throughout its history a prominent role in the Greater Philadelphia region, sustaining its close association with the city of Philadelphia and serving a central role in the social and economic life of South Jersey. Always a diversified area, the county's more rural areas to the east of Philadelphia suburbanized in the mid-twentieth century even as the county seat and historic county keystone, Camden City, fell in influence and power. By the early twenty-first century, despite considerable effort to reverse the trend, the county reflected every element of the modern balkanized metropolitan area: an impoverished urban core, fraying older suburban areas fringing Camden, and more affluent outer suburbs.

Early settlement in the area that became Camden County stemmed from European competition to exploit the material resources of the region then designated as West Jersey. Although Swedes and the Dutch settled there first, the desire to be competitive spurred West Jersey's British trustees, including William Penn, to sign a Concessions and Agreements document in 1677 granting assurances of religious freedom, equitable taxation, and representative government. Aimed at Quakers seeking refuge from persecution, the document induced the settlement of a contingent of migrants from Ireland, in an area known as the Irish Tenth, whose boundaries were contiguous with modern Camden County. Initially coexisting peacefully with Native inhabitants, the Lenni Lenape, the European settlers over time displaced Native inhabitants as trade and settlement grew in close association with the city of Philadelphia after its establishment in 1682.

A ferry operating as early as 1688 provided the earliest means of communication and transportation between the two colonies on the Delaware River. Operated in its early years by members of the Cooper family, the area of modest settlement on the New Jersey side was known for nearly a century as Cooper's Ferry. Under Jacob Cooper's direction, an area of some one hundred acres was built up with the intent of making the area Philadelphia's most prominent suburb. Cooper named his project Camden Town, after Charles Pratt, First Earl of Camden, a British judge known for his defense of the American cause. The effort faltered but did not collapse during the American Revolution, when British troops occupying Philadelphia foraged the area for food and supplies.

Settlement took a big step forward when ambitious entrepreneurs based in Gloucester City laid out city streets in 1820, leading to the incorporation of Camden City in 1828. Early manufacturing plants along the Delaware River boosted the city's standing and put it in competition with the Gloucester County seat at Woodbury for influence in the region. After rural interests succeeded in carving a new Atlantic County out of the eastern portions of Gloucester County in 1837, Camden enthusiasts pressed their own case for a new county. Divisions hardened, however, as political partisans fought for state as well as local control, and the creation of the new Camden County, finally, in 1844, was bitterly contested. A new courthouse designed by the noted Philadelphia architect Samuel Sloan in 1853 signified the city's stature, but it was Camden's emergence as the heart of improved transportation networks, not politics, that explained its rise from a mere hamlet at the time of the Revolution to a city of 9,479, more than a third of the county's population, at midcentury.

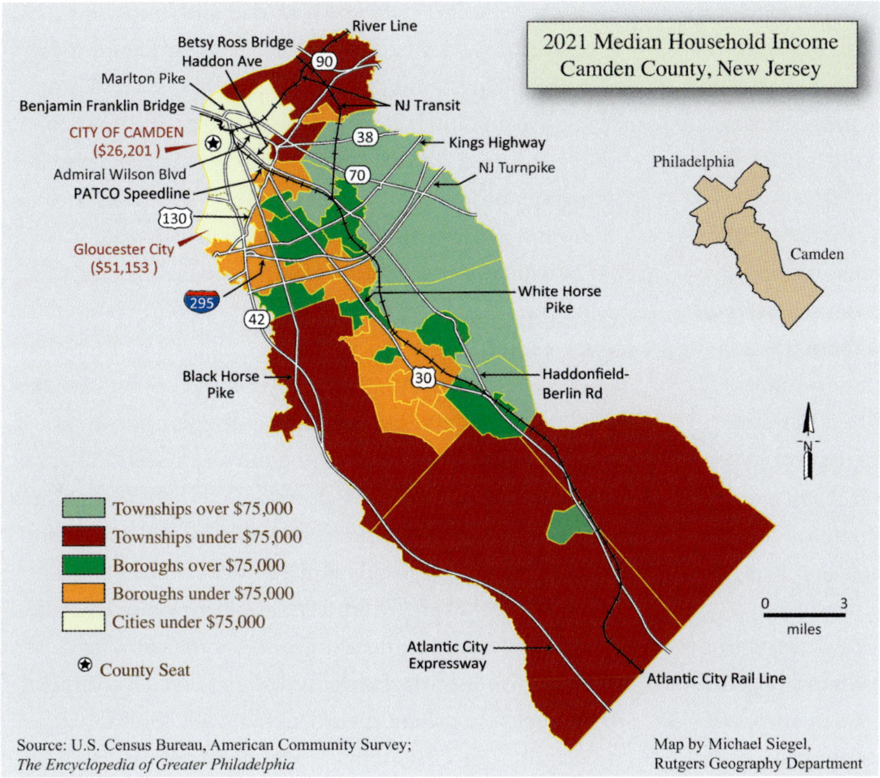

MAP 10. 2021 Median Household Income, Camden County, New Jersey. MAP BY MICHAEL SIEGEL

TRANSPORTATION NETWORKS

A number of entrepreneurs sought to build up rivals to Camden through development expected to follow from the establishment of turnpikes and railways. A number of these enterprises failed, including the Moorestown & Camden Turnpike, chartered in 1849 with the intent of boosting suburban development on the northeastern bank of Cooper's Creek. More successful was the advent, in 1834, of the Camden and Amboy Railroad with connections to New York City, not just from southern New Jersey but also from southeast Pennsylvania, for those traveling by ferry to Camden and then north. A second railroad, the Camden and Atlantic, organized in 1852, further enhanced the city as a transportation center, as area residents made their way to the Jersey Shore.

As transportation corridors extended out from Camden at the core, trade picked up in older communities. Originally settled by Quakers seeking religious freedom in 1682, Gloucestertown rose from a tiny fishing village to become the center of local political and military organization in the years immediately before the American Revolution. Early manufacturing activity there was promising, but lack of rail connections to Camden, until 1873, retarded growth, despite the area's incorporation as Gloucester City in 1868. With that rail connection in place, the city grew by nearly 50 percent in the ensuing decade to 5,347 people. The area north of Camden also flourished with gristmills and sawmills established along Pennsauken Creek in an area designated as Delaware Township. In 1854 a group of investors, seeking to capitalize on a proposed rail line passing through a cluster of country estates owned by Philadelphia dry goods merchants and known locally as Merchantville, laid out additional lots intended to spur growth. With the arrival of the Camden and Amboy in 1869 they realized returns on their investments, and in 1874 the tiny hamlet—at seven-tenths of a square mile—officially formed as Merchantville Borough, separating itself from Stockton Township, which had itself formed out of the north portion of Delaware Township in 1859. In 1892 another portion of Stockton, which had fostered its own industries, withdrew to form Pennsauken Township. Finally, in 1899 the city of Camden annexed the remaining part of what had once been Stockton Township.

Camden County grew steadily throughout the second half of the nineteenth century, rising fourfold from a population of 25,422 in 1850 to 107,643 in 1900. Even as rail connections prompted town growth along the Delaware River, railroads boosted suburban development to the east. The Camden and Atlantic line's decision to locate a stop and telegraph station on Collings Farm Road in 1871 prompted local residents six years later to incorporate as Collingswood. Spurred by investments, including the creation of the sixty-one-acre Knight Park, by Philadelphia import-export merchant and sugar refiner Edward Collings Knight and other Collings family members, the area realized its aspirations to form a desirable residential enclave. Describing itself as supporting "the clean, pure life essential to social advancement," Collingswood was one of the first communities in New Jersey to elect to go dry under 1873 legislation that provided the local option to do so. Just to the east, Haddonfield, whose incorporation stretched back to 1701 and whose early history included the New Jersey legislature's adoption of the state seal at the Indian King Tavern in 1777, also grew as a result of the arrival of the rail connection between Camden and Atlantic City that materialized in 1853. After investors with connections both to turnpikes and rail lines formed the Haddonfield Improvement Company to market building lots in the area, Haddonfield grew sufficiently to break away from Haddon Township to form its own borough, in 1875. Farther along the Camden and Atlantic City line, rail officials opened a station at Long-A-Coming, derived from the name used by Native Americans who used the Lonaconing Trail to describe the route that connected the Jersey Shore to the Delaware River. As the area grew, it assumed the new name of Berlin, not because it drew settlers from Germany, although Germans were among the railroad's directors, but as a community specifically created for Philadelphia Germans seeking to escape nativist attacks.

The opening of the Delaware River (subsequently named Benjamin Franklin) Bridge in 1926 scrambled established transportation patterns for the region, forcing the Reading and Pennsylvania Railroads to consolidate their once highly competitive rail connections between Camden and the Jersey Shore and spurring greater reliance on automobiles for travel. A grand boulevard connecting to the bridge, designed in the City Beautiful style and named in 1929 to honor Rear Admiral Henry Braid Wilson, a Camden native who served in the Spanish-American and First World Wars, was intended to bind Camden City to surrounding towns, even prompting the idea of consolidating city and suburbs.

Camden never formally annexed its suburbs, but boosted by war production incentives, the city, dominated by its big three industries—New York Shipbuilding, RCA- Victor Company, and Campbell Soup—thrived into the 1950s, when the bottom began to fall out of its economy. Loss of jobs, outmigration, and growing racial turmoil undercut Camden's preeminence, and the city ceded much of its human and monetary assets to other parts of the county. Nowhere was Camden's relative decline highlighted more than in nearby Delaware Township, until the 1950s, mostly farmland with the exceptions of Garden State Park racetrack opened during World War II and a grouping of fine brick homes in the town's Colwick section with generously proportioned lots and streets named for elite suburbs on Philadelphia's legendary Main Line. That changed after the war as developers laced new tract housing throughout much of the twenty-four-square-mile township. The location of a new RCA electronics plant on a ridge known as Cherry Hill brought newcomers to the area, many of them engineers from New York, even as it marked a shift of resources out of Camden. Even more important, the first enclosed regional mall on the East Coast opened on October 11, 1961. Designed by shopping center pioneer Victor Gruen and developed by James Rouse, the Cherry Hill Mall was not responsible for the choice of the new name given the township the same year, but it helped establish Cherry Hill as a central destination for all county residents. By 1965, Cherry Hill's assessed property value, up from $9.5 million in 1950 to $156.2 million, exceeded that of Camden, making it the richest community in the county and all of South Jersey.

EMPLOYMENT EXPANDS TO THE SUBURBS

Even as employment opportunities declined in Camden, they grew in Pennsauken, which boasted the region's busiest airport during the 1930s, until larger planes required longer runways and air travel shifted

FIGURE 74. Yorkship Village, 1926, subsequently the Fairview section of Camden, the planned community for ship workers constructed near work facilities during World War I.
CAMDEN COUNTY HISTORICAL SOCIETY.

to Philadelphia. Both before and after World War II, Pennsauken attracted companies like Kieckhefer Container Company, which established its business at what had once been a yacht club on the Delaware River, employing some six hundred workers throughout the 1930s, and Randall Manufacturing Company, the makers of plumbers' enamelware, which hired another five hundred. Nearby, Cities Service Company established refining facilities covering most of Petty's Island. After the war, Pennsauken attracted a host of midsize companies to a newly established industrial park on the Delaware waterfront. Between 1958 and 1970 manufacturing jobs in Camden County outside the city increased from 6,184 to 21,316, a number on a par with Camden itself. Even as the city lost close to half its manufacturing base in the 1960s, suburban manufacturing employment increased at a rate of 85 percent.

Blessed with an array of housing options and employment opportunities, the suburbs boomed in the mid-1960s and afterward. With a population of 255,727 in 1940, Camden County climbed to 392,035 twenty years later. It added another 64,000 people over the next decade, when growth slowed considerably. As Irish, Italian, and other white ethnic families made the transition from factory work to white-collar occupations in Philadelphia and Camden, they moved to new homes aimed at a burgeoning suburban middle class. In a conscious effort to protect the newly acquired benefits of suburban life, these towns introduced building restrictions, through practices that came to be called exclusionary zoning. In Delaware Township, Mayor Christian Weber and his colleagues altered the township's zoning code to require larger lots. As Weber asserted, "there will be no row houses, twin houses or prefabricated homes in the township." Similarly, Collingswood placed controls on garden apartments with the clear intention of keeping out renters who might prove a tax burden to the township.

Due to its proximity to shipbuilding facilities on both sides of the Delaware River, Camden County became home to several distinctive planned communities during World Wars I and II. Seeking to alleviate a severe shortage of housing options for ship workers employed at Camden's New York Shipbuilding facility, the U.S. Shipping Board's Emergency Fleet Corporation designated 225 acres of farmland at the eastern edge of Camden to accommodate 1,400 new housing units. Laid out according to "Garden City" principles established by Ebenezer Howard in England in the early twentieth

FIGURE 75. Lawnside's existence and reputation as a distinctive Black community grew in the 1930s with a thriving jazz and barbecue scene in the wake of Prohibition, including the High Hat Club, pictured here. Such establishments attracted patrons from all over the Northeast to hear and rub shoulders with top African American performers. NEW JERSEY STATE ARCHIVES.

century, the new community allocated generous amounts of open space, including a central town square lined with shops, to support modest homes sited close to public ways with the intent of enhancing sociability among workers. Known originally as Yorkship Village, the area was annexed into Camden after World War I and subsequently became known as Fairview.

Several decades later, as another war approached, area planners utilized a new version of a planned community for war workers by laying out Audubon Park. Composed of some five hundred prefabricated units and supported by Camden #1, the Industrial Union of Marine and Shipbuilding Workers of America, Audubon Park operated according to a pioneer "mutual plan" under which residents bought shares in the mutual benefit company that owned the land. Designed by the prominent Philadelphia-based architect Oscar Stonorov, who had been codesigner of Yorkship Village, Audubon Park combined elements of city density with easy access to the amenities of suburban life. Such could also be said of the second mutual home development in Camden County, Bellmawr Park, some five hundred units carved out of an estate dating back to the seventeenth century. Both projects were meant to house war workers with construction costs being provided by the federal government's Works Progress Administration.

Historically, African Americans had lived throughout the county: in pockets of Camden, in an area of Cherry Hill known as Batesville separated from other settlements by a country road, in Haddonfield just off the Haddonfield-Berlin Road, in Chesilhurst, and most visibly in the historically Black town of Lawnside (originally known as Free Haven, then Snowhill when it was closely associated with Underground Railroad activity). Laid out initially in 1840 by Haddonfield Quaker and abolitionist Ralph Smith, the area offered small lots to free Black people at low cost. Incorporated in 1926, Lawnside became widely known as a rich source of Black entertainment for the region as well as a thriving community of upwardly mobile residents.

Elsewhere, zoning restrictions, often combined with overt hostility, blocked Camden City's African American population, which reached a majority in the decade following civil disturbances that erupted in the city in 1971, from accessing homes in the suburbs. Housing choices in the 1970s and beyond thus became racially skewed in spite of the national fair housing legislation adopted in 1968. Spurred by discrimination in housing in Mount Laurel, just across the Camden County line in Burlington County, lawyers for plaintiffs seeking a zoning change to allow multiple-unit construction achieved a state supreme court ruling that every community should make available its "fair share" of affordable housing. While the ruling anticipated opening the suburbs to a broader class of residents, executing it proved difficult. Forty years after the first Mount Laurel ruling, Camden still had four times its share of affordable housing, while nearby communities Cherry Hill, Pennsauken, and Haddonfield fell well short of fulfilling their obligations to house residents with modest incomes.

Over time, suburban development shifted even farther east and away from Camden, a pattern evidenced especially in Voorhees, which came to be perceived as more exclusive than the once-premier destination of Cherry Hill. A town of just some six thousand in 1970, Voorhees boomed following the 1970 opening of the Echelon Mall, doubling its population in the next decade and reaching a population of twenty-eight thousand by 2000, after which growth slowed considerably. Some former white Camden residents who had settled along bus lines in nearby Pennsauken or the western portion of Cherry Hill in the 1960s chose to move farther out. As one sign of such decisions, the Beth El synagogue, which traced its origins as Camden's first conservative congregation to 1920, moved first to Cherry Hill in 1967 and subsequently to Voorhees in 2009.

To the far east, Winslow Township, the largest jurisdiction in the county at fifty-eight square miles remained largely farm country for its eleven thousand residents as late as 1970. Nestled at the edge of the Pine Barrens, where environmental restrictions circumscribed growth, the township exploded in the 1980s as developers cleared land for larger, exurban homes that had come into demand. The area added another ten thousand residents in the 1970s and again in the 1980s, achieving a population of just under forty thousand in 2010. Connected both to the shore communities by the Atlantic City Expressway and other population centers to the north through U.S. Route 30 and New Jersey Route 73, Winslow offered a rare combination of easy access to employment as well as premier recreational and entertainment facilities.

SOCIAL DISPARITIES

Outward movement from Camden continued in the late twentieth and early twenty-first centuries as Black and Hispanic families followed the pattern of earlier outmigration, to the west sides of Cherry Hill and Collingswood and especially to Pennsauken. As the minority population grew there, and with it the number of children eligible for free school lunches, local residents seeking to incorporate newcomers while still hoping to moderate the pace of racial turnover persuaded town officials to establish a Stable Integration Review Board. Formed in the mid-1990s with the purpose of encouraging white residents to buy homes and stay put, the initiative drew support of both Black and white residents. The effort, which lasted more than a decade, had limited effect, as by 2020 the white population had fallen from 55 percent in 2000 to 26 percent. Meanwhile, the African American population increased to 29 percent and Hispanic to 35 percent.

As Camden County made the transition into the twenty-first century, it witnessed a number of initiatives aimed at achieving more balanced growth. When New Jersey took the extraordinary step of assuming day-to-day control of the city of Camden for seven years starting in 2002, it required the formation of a regional impact council intended to stem the spread of problems such as crime and blight out of Camden while offering hope that the difficult issues of affordable housing might be taken up on a regional basis. Local officials only reluctantly formed a council composed of the mayors of nearby jurisdictions two years after it was mandated, and they failed to pursue its stated goals with any rigor. As a result, efforts to diversify the housing stock of communities outside Camden proceeded largely as a result of the threat, if not actual exercise, of court actions. More hopefully, Collingswood invested in multiunit developments near the PATCO Speedline to Philadelphia, thereby fulfilling the smart growth goals behind such transit planning. An effort to convert the deserted race track in Cherry Hill into a compact town center linking homes and apartments to shopping proved less successful, as resulting development created largely big box retail well beyond walking distance of residences.

As of 2021 Camden County's relatively diverse population had reached 523,771: 54.5 percent white, 22 percent African American, 18.5 percent Hispanic, and 5 percent Asian. The city of Camden remained the county's largest entity, at 77,344, with Cherry Hill not far behind at 71,045. Eighty-eight percent of county residents had completed high school, while more than 30 percent held a bachelor's degree or higher.

In its modern form, Camden County proved reliably Democratic, as evidenced by the party's complete control of its governing body, the Board of Chosen Freeholders (subsequently known as the Board of Commissioners). A holdover from the colonial era, the Freeholders advanced some modern concepts, taking over the function of policing Camden in 2012 and advancing an ambitious building program through the Camden County Improvement Authority, including hospital and university construction projects and highway improvements. Public figures associated with county politics, most notably South Jersey's most prominent political broker, George Norcross, and his brother, Donald, a state senator and subsequently Camden County's congressional representative, parlayed a generous state incentives program to relocate businesses from different parts of South Jersey into Camden. Facilitated by Republican governor Chris Christie, the reinvestment program did not immediately alter the high level of poverty in Camden, but it nonetheless altered Camden's image as well as its skyline as a city rising. With affordable housing still largely concentrated in Camden, so too was poverty, leaving Camden County still racially and socially divided.

Gloucester County, New Jersey

Howard Gillette, Jr.

Strategically located along the Delaware River opposite the southern portion of Philadelphia, Gloucester County played an important role in the region as a location for waves of settlement, industry, and recreation, and even defense during the American Revolution. Formed in 1686 with the intention of establishing townships and jurisdictional courts and named for Gloucestershire, England, the county originally stretched from the Delaware to the ocean, encompassing what later became Camden and Atlantic Counties. With a combination of farms, suburban settlement, and industry, the county represents a complex mix of historic practices and modern adaptations.

The 337-square-mile territory was first inhabited by the Lenape, who formed villages along the county's many creeks. Dutch traders arrived in 1623, seeking to trade with the Lenape for furs. Establishing a base at the Big Timber Creek, a tributary entering the Delaware across from Philadelphia, they built Fort Nassau for defense, only to abandon it in 1651 for a location on the other side of the river. The decision was prompted in part by the arrival in 1642 of Swedes, who were themselves anxious both to trade with Natives and to establish a New World outpost, which they christened New Gothenburg. Instructed to treat the Indians fairly and to buy any land that they would sell, settlers purchased land from the Mantua Creek to the Raccoon Creek, tributaries running from the area's interior to the Delaware. There they formed the settlement of Raccoon (from the Lenape word "narraticon"). Under a land lease system, unique to New Jersey, the settlement developed south from Raccoon Creek to the present center of Swedesboro, as it came to be known in 1765. It was incorporated in 1903.

In 1664, England, after being stymied by years of internal division, joined the race for settlement in the area when King Charles granted the land between the Connecticut River and the Delaware Bay to his brother, James, Duke of York, who in turn sold it to Sir John Berkeley and Sir George Carteret. In 1674, the proprietorship of New Jersey was divided in half, with Berkeley taking West New Jersey, which he promptly sold to John Fenwick in trust for the wealthy London brewer Edward Byllynge. When the English Quakers Fenwick and Byllynge quarreled over settlement rights, three Quaker trustees, including William Penn, mediated the dispute. Byllynge was awarded the land between Oldman's Creek and Timber Creek to the river, narrowly avoiding the area's incorporation into territory subsequently designated as Penn's Philadelphia. Two hundred and thirty settlers who came with Penn and

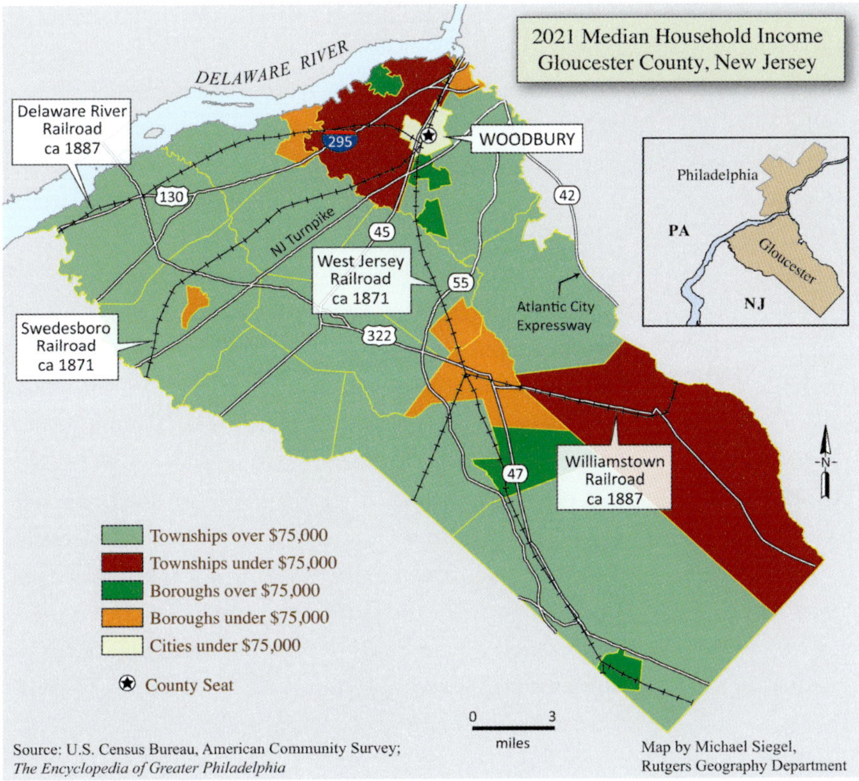

MAP 11. 2021 Median Household Income Gloucester County, New Jersey. MAP BY MICHAEL SIEGEL.

Byllynge bought land for one penny an acre. The place was named Byllings Port, now Billingsport.

With the resolution of his claim, Byllynge became part of a group of prosperous landowning families who dominated the area through their prime locations along the tidal creeks and tributary streams that granted them control over the remaining undeveloped land. Damming streams to make millponds for their sawmills and securing legislation to bank the creeks that nourished their fields in order to prevent erosion, they brought prosperity to themselves and the area. As Philadelphia emerged across the river, they marketed land for sale, stressing its salubrious qualities as a salve to city dwellers.

DEVELOPMENT YIELDS PROSPERITY

Settlement increased gradually, with farms dominating most of the occupied land and mills scattered along area creeks. Dating back to the settlement of the first Quaker family in the area in 1683, Woodbury, a part of Deptford Township and located along the creek that gave the village its name, became the county seat in 1786 after fire destroyed the courthouse and jail in Gloucester City, at the mouth of Big Timber Creek, where the county seat had been previously located. A Quaker community from its onset, the village constructed its Friends meetinghouse in 1715.

As revolution captured the country, Quakers in the area struggled. While they opposed taxation by the British Parliament, their pacifism prevented them from taking up arms. Some chose to pay taxes only on that portion unrelated to the war effort, risking fines and even imprisonment, which proved the fate of some who refused to serve. When American troops requisitioned a large part of the four hundred–acre Red Bank farm of the prominent Whitall family in Woodbury, the military inflicted extensive damage to the property where they constructed fortifications—named Fort Mercer—immediately north of the house in an effort to prevent British ships from ascending the Delaware to Philadelphia. Paired with another fortification, Pennsylvania's Fort Mifflin on Mud Island coordinated with Billingsport on the New Jersey side of the river, to install chains of large iron-tipped logs known as *chevaux-de-frise* spread across the river channels to prevent British warships from coming upriver. American troops successfully repelled a land assault by Hessian troops at the Woodbury Creek in October 1777 and turned back a naval attack the following day. Known as the Battle of Red Bank, the fighting focused on the fort at the Whitall farm, which was turned into a military hospital. Success was short-lived, however, as both forts in the county were abandoned by November. Starting in 1895, the Red Bank battlefield area was commercially developed as National Park on the Delaware, a religious resort and retreat for members of the Methodist Episcopal Church, eventually becoming the borough of National Park.

Given the area's early Quaker influence, it could not be too surprising that Gloucester County played an active role in the Underground Railroad. In the years before the Civil War several thousand runaway slaves from the upper South traveled through Woodbury north to Mount Laurel or through Greenwich to Swedesboro to Mount Holly in Burlington County. One of the most important stops on the way was Mount Zion African Methodist Episcopal Church in what was known then as Small Gloucester, now Woolwich Township. Constructed in 1834, the one-story frame building had a secret, three-by-four-foot trapdoor in the floor of the church's vestibule, affording refuge in the crawlspace under the floor.

QUAKER DOMINANCE SLIPS

Peace brought new challenges to Quaker domination, as national pride advanced military measures anathema to the Friends and aggressive settlement by other denominations reduced their dominance. Further settlement extended along the area's many creeks, including Big Timber, which powered a number of mills into the 1950s, and Mantua Creek, which enabled transportation, supported saw and grist mills, and encouraged floodplain development for agriculture. Settlement remained limited, however, as evidenced by the modest beginnings of Paulsboro (originally Crown Point), which despite its prime location at the confluence of Mantua Creek with the Delaware, had attracted only a handful of households by the mid-nineteenth century. As new counties formed out of Gloucester—Atlantic in 1837 and Camden in 1844—the county remained thinly settled, with a high of 28,431 residents in 1830, dropping to only 14,655 in 1850, and rising again to 28,649 by 1890.

Early growth was constrained by the limits of overland travel. During the colonial period it took place largely along the Indian trail that ran from Salem to Burlington, a pathway that ultimately became the route of the "Salem Road." Authorized in 1681 by the "General Free Assembly" held at Burlington, the highway that later became the Kings Road or Highway, was fairly well laid out but not complete by 1688. Its crossing at Big Timber Creek spawned a town since few fords of large streams existed at the time. Thomas West built a tavern a few hundred yards away from the creek that became a favorite stopping place for travelers going to or coming from the lower counties. Originally given the name Buck Tavern, the settlement was renamed Westville in 1840 and gained the reputation as serving as the "Gateway to South Jersey." As a sign of how limited travel was in the county's early days, the area's first turnpike, the Gloucester Turnpike, did not open until 1851.

Stagecoaches ultimately gave way to railways, following the advent, in 1838, of the area's first rail service, offered by the Camden and Amboy Railroad between Camden and Woodbury. Stronger and sturdier bridges made the railroads possible. The line operated three trains each way daily excepting Sundays. Other lines followed, albeit sporadically and with limited effect. The Millville and Glassboro Railroad incorporated in 1859; the 10.8-mile Swedesboro Railroad extended to Woodbury in 1869; and the Delaware-Shore Line entered Paulsboro in 1876.

It took a pair of regional recreational destinations to spur robust rail traffic to the area. Trolleys from Camden brought picnickers from Philadelphia and points between to the beach in Westville and to Washington Park, complete with Ferris wheel and toboggan slide. Although Washington Park succumbed to fire in 1913, never to reopen, area vacationers continued to summer in Westville. Farther south along the Delaware River, at the twenty-eight--acre Lincoln Park amusement center, opened in 1890 in Paulsboro, visitors could enjoy concerts and fireworks that were offered every two weeks. Sixteen trains a day brought visitors from the Philadelphia-Camden area. Two ferries and five steamboats made the trip across the river daily. Trains terminated in the historic Quaker settlement of Billingsport located within Greenwich, the county's first incorporated township. Billingsport joined with Crown Point to become the independent borough of Paulsboro in 1904. The advent of the automobile forced Lincoln Park's closure, but Philadelphians continued to use the area as they built their own small resort homes along the shore.

THE EMERGENCE OF GLASS WORKS

Although agriculture continued to dominate the area, the presence of fine sand encouraged the production of glass as it did in other parts of South Jersey. As early as 1799, Solomon Stranger established the second major glassworks in New Jersey. Known initially only as "Glass Works in the Woods," the town eventually came to be known, appropriately enough, as Glassboro. Among the survivals of the era is the handsome Victorian Hollybush /Whitney Mansion, built in 1849 by Thomas and Samuel Whitney, owners of the Whitney Glass Works. Designed by John Notman and constructed of native Jersey sandstone obtained from the Chestnut Branch quarry, it later became part of the Rowan University campus. It gained international attention when President Lyndon Johnson and Russian premier Alexei Kosygin met there for their famed summit meetings in June 1967. Nearby, Jacob Fisler, the son of a Swedish immigrant, and his business partner, Benjamin Beckett, began glass manufacturing in 1850 in a central part of the county known as Fislerville. The Fislerville Glass Works spurred the growth of the community to the point that in 1858 the area was incorporated as Clayton. Fisler's fortunes suffered, however, and two brothers, John M. and David W. Moore, assumed ownership of the plant where workers continued successfully blowing glass until 1911, when the shift to mass-production machinery directed business elsewhere. Despite the loss, William Henry Clevenger, who had come to work for the Moore brothers in 1890, opened a new facility. Describing himself as a "master glass shearer" or a "window glass blower," his company passed through several generations until it finally closed in 1964. Taken over once again, and the old forms of reproduction rekindled, the Clevenger plant continued the craft to critical acclaim into the twenty-first century.

The county's industrial base diversified in the latter part of the nineteenth century. The DuPont Company Repauno Works opened in 1880 in Greenwich, also known as Gibbstown, after Ethan Gibbs, a blacksmith and major landowner, to distinguish the town from Greenwich, Warren County. Repauno was the first of the major chemical and petroleum refiners that would come to dominate the county's riverfront from West Deptford to Paulsboro. Incorporated for the purpose of manufacturing the new high explosive dynamite at a remote site on the Delaware River near Gibbstown and taking its name from nearby Repaupo Creek, the plant was the site of a number of explosions, including one that claimed the life of cofounder Lammot Du Pont. In 1917 Vacuum Oil opened a refinery to support its export business, also in Gibbstown, though it was popularly known as the Paulsboro plant. Subsequently a part of what became ExxonMobil, the site added a research laboratory to its production facility to generate lubricating oil.

Paulsboro itself attracted its share of industry, including an oil storage and fueling terminal that first came into use during World War I. Purchased by Patterson Oil in 1929, the terminal expanded under the new ownership of Eastern Gas and Fuel in 1954, eventually operating under the ownership of British Petroleum until its closure in 1996. Nearby, West Deptford, another town dating back to early settlement, witnessed the transformation of its agricultural roots as industries streamed in. These included Coe and Richman, the largest phosphate works in the country, in 1880, Vacuum Oil in 1917, and Hangsterfer's Laboratories, a producer of metalworking lubricants and compounds, in 1935, among others.

HIGHWAYS SOLIDIFY LINKS TO PHILADELPHIA

The introduction of a modern system of state highways in the twentieth century brought Gloucester County further into the orbit of greater Philadelphia's employment market, spurring suburban growth and development, especially in the towns most easily within reach of the city. In the northeast section of the county, Deptford, which took its name from the English seaport and dated its origins to 1695, remained largely

FIGURE 76. The DuPont explosives department at Repauno Works, Gibbstown, Gloucester County, 1929. HAGLEY MUSEUM AND LIBRARY.

agricultural until the suburban boom that followed World War II. From a population of 7,304 in 1950, the town jumped to 17,878 in 1960 and 24,232 in 1970. With the opening of the Deptford Mall in 1975, it became a regional shopping destination. At Deptford's southern border, Washington Township, having remained overwhelmingly agricultural since its incorporation in 1836, boomed in the late twentieth century, becoming the county's most populated jurisdiction with 48,559 people in 2010. Its easy connection to employment centers to the north by New Jersey Routes 42 (Black Horse Pike) and 168 spurred its growth in the twenty-first century as a premier bedroom community. Directly across the county, the smaller jurisdiction of Woolwich also boomed, in the first decade of the twenty-first century growing to 10,200 in 2010, a 236 percent increase from 2000.

Such growth prompted county officials to actively seek the preservation of farmland. Starting in the mid-1990s, the county issued bonds, and, after 2011, drew on state funds, to put farmland under covenants to preserve its character. By 2018, the county had preserved more than fifteen thousand acres, the eighth highest total in the state, at a cost of $118.4 million. Targeted especially were the three communities along the Delaware River, Logan, Woolwich, and South Harrison, where development pressures were especially intense.

The importance of the effort was confirmed in the history of Pureland in Logan Township, which formed through the 1970 consolidation of fifty-five farms under the ownership of the State Mutual Life Assurance Company of America and opened for construction in 1975. Praised from its inception as the nation's first ecologically planned industrial complex, Pureland not only converted farm use, it became the largest industrial complex in New Jersey, hosting 180 companies employing over 8,500 people by 2015, mostly in the area of warehousing and distribution. Much later, Amazon located its first warehouse in South Jersey in Logan, following shortly thereafter in 2018 with an additional warehouse—this one the equivalent of thirty football fields—in West Deptford. Together the facilities employed about 5,000 people.

Overall, Gloucester County was largely white over the course of its history. Although pockets of African American settlement remained from the pre–Civil War settlement associated with the Underground Railroad—Jericho in Woodbury Heights, for instance—in 2020 county population was still 76.5 percent white, 11.8 percent Black, and 9 percent Latino.

Industry did not come without serious problems of pollution, and in 1979 British Petroleum began a long process of remediation under state supervision at its Paulsboro facility. The company ultimately abandoned the terminal; its demolition began in 1996. Even as remediation continued, public officials debated how best to reuse the site until reaching a decision in 2002 to build the river's first deep-water general cargo port in fifty years. The 2008 recession delayed the project, but it finally launched in 2014 when shipping company Holt Logistics agreed to give up a sliver of land in Camden to facilitate construction of Holtec International's new headquarters at the former New York Shipbuilding facility in return for the right to operate the new terminal. Shortly afterward, Holt secured a steel company as its first tenant. The terminal processed more than four million tons of imported steel slabs in the first three years after its opening in 2017.

Not all such reclamation projects worked out as well. ExxonMobil Oil's operation in Paulsboro and East Greenwich also proved devastating to the environment as the disposal of drums containing petroleum products and other hazardous materials polluted soil, surface and ground waters, wetlands, and fish, according to the state. Although the oil company conducted some cleanup efforts, many contaminants remained, prompting a lawsuit against the company. Governor Chris Christie's settlement, for $225 million, ended litigation but brought charges that the amount was much lower than it should have been. When Greenwich Township sold the 1,800-acre former DuPont Repauno plant to private investors in 2019, they expected to create a port-related industrial park for imports and exports. Not expected was the new owners' decision, cleared by the Delaware River Basin Commission, to use the facility to store and export large volumes of liquid fuels produced from fracking Pennsylvania shale gas wells. Under the plan, objected to by state environmentalists, liquefied natural gas would be shipped from a facility in Wyalusing, Pennsylvania, by road or by rail to Gibbstown where it would be loaded directly onto ships for sale overseas or barged to domestic customers.

The reconfiguration of work and living arrangements inevitably set jurisdictions on the path of seeking further revenue sources to keep their tax rates down. As the shopping mall in West Deptford faltered, the township encouraged its renovation. In Paulsboro, city officials hoped to use the opening of its new port facility to attract investment to rehabilitate the two hundred abandoned properties within its jurisdiction.

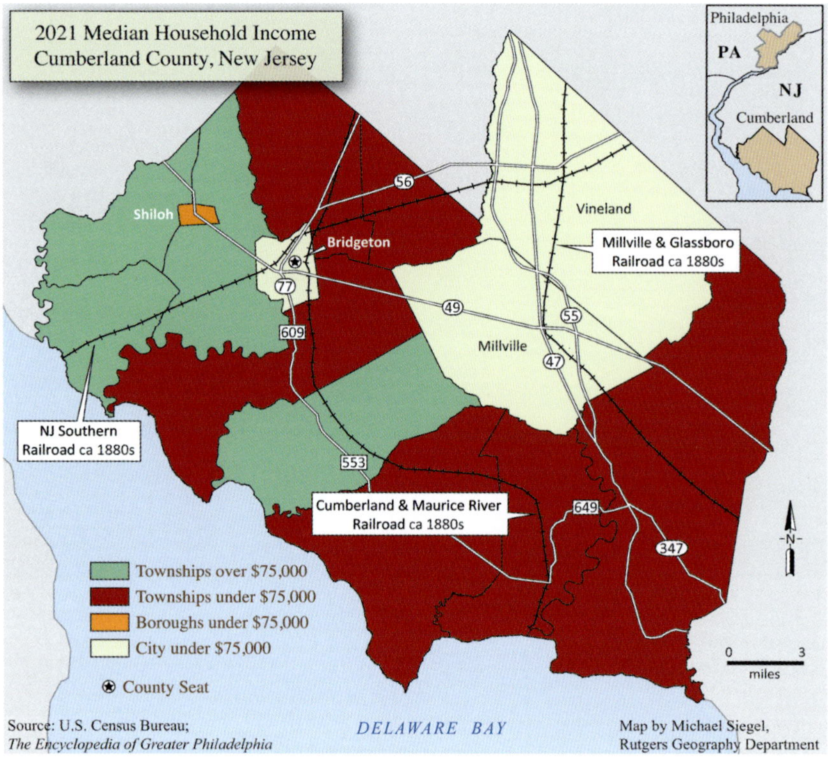

MAP 12. 2021 Median Household Income Cumberland County, New Jersey. MAP BY MICHAEL SIEGEL.

In a particularly distinct set of circumstances, Woolwich sought buyers to redevelop a thirty-three-acre Nike missile base that had been closed since 1974 for mixed commercial use and a park, two years after consummation of the SALT I treaty eliminating the nation's antiballistic systems. Change as it might, the county was destined to retain a central position both in South Jersey and in the Greater Philadelphia region.

Cumberland County, New Jersey

Penelope S. Watson

Cumberland County, New Jersey, located on the Delaware Bay about thirty-five miles south of Philadelphia, was formed from the southeastern part of Salem County in 1748. Its location and natural attributes led to a three-faceted economy that bridged centuries: rich farmland supported agriculture, two tidal rivers and the Delaware Bay provided a maritime economy, and deposits of silica sand fostered a glass industry. A diversity of immigrants, from Quakers, Presbyterians, and Baptists seeking religious freedom in the seventeenth century, to German glassblowers in the eighteenth, and Mexican and Central American agricultural workers in the twenty-first, generated three primary population centers: Bridgeton, Millville, and Vineland, separated by farmland interspersed with smaller settlements. As several industries declined in the second half of the twentieth century, they were only partially replaced economically, making Cumberland the poorest county in New Jersey.

Ancient geological forces combined to give Cumberland a thriving agricultural economy from the beginning. A large river system, often referred to as the "proto-Hudson," flowed in from the north, followed what became the Delaware River valley from Trenton, New Jersey, then curved back across southern New Jersey's interior. Waterways cut into the earlier marine sands of the local Cohansey Formation to lay down the fluvial deposits known as the Bridgeton Formation, thus building the county's surface deposits. During the Ice Age windblown silt known as "loess" enriched the sandy-gravelly deposits of the Bridgeton Formation, which accounted for the high productivity of soils found in the western part of the county.

The area that became Cumberland County was first inhabited by the Lenni Lenape, whose settlements clustered along the rivers. Archaeological studies have revealed evidence of ten thousand years of continuous occupation at the Indian Head Site in Deerfield Township. The Lenni Lenape population plummeted after settlement by the Dutch and Swedes, and Natives claimed two of their people died for every Christian who arrived. About nine thousand people with ancestral links to the Lenni Lenape lived in Cumberland in the twenty-first century, and in 2018 New Jersey formally recognized the existence of the Nanticoke Lenni Lenape Tribal Nation.

John Fenwick established Salem in 1675, the first English settlement in West Jersey, but Swedes and Dutch had already been living in the area for forty years. The nucleus of the Swedish settlement was northwest of what became Cumberland County, but Swedes hunted and cut lumber along the Maurice River without obtaining title to the land. Swedish family names remained common in the area.

From the beginning, Fenwick planned to found a second town on the Cohansey River, fifteen miles southeast of Salem. He intended for it to be called Cohansey, but settlers renamed it Greenwich, probably after Greenwich, Connecticut. It was not until three years after Fenwick died in 1683 that his executors laid out the town and began selling sixteen-acre lots.

Early colonists included Quakers, Presbyterians, and Baptists, attracted by the religious tolerance of Fenwick's colony. The first settlers in Greenwich were Quakers from Salem, beginning in 1686. Sometime between 1680 and 1685, Presbyterians from Fairfield, Connecticut, and Long Island established New England Town on the east side of the Cohansey. About the same time, Baptists from Rhode Island and from Ireland also settled on the east side of the Cohansey, and Welsh Baptists came to Bowentown, between Greenwich and Bridgeton, by way of Swansea, Massachusetts.

PHILADELPHIA CONNECTIONS

Commercial connections with Philadelphia were extensive from the beginning. By the turn of the eighteenth century, Greenwich had become one of three official ports of entry in New Jersey. From 1695 until 1765, the West Jersey General Assembly authorized Greenwich to hold semiannual fairs, in April and October, where anyone could peddle wares. Each fair attracted as many as twenty goods-laden ships from Philadelphia.

Cumberland County came into existence when the New Jersey General Assembly (after the unification of East and West Jersey in 1702) passed an act forming a new county from the southern part of Salem County on January 19, 1748. The act responded to citizens' petitions, which objected to the inconvenience of all official business being carried out in Salem, at the extreme western edge of the county. The new county was named for the Duke of Cumberland, a contemporary hero credited with defeating Charles Edward Stuart (Bonnie Prince Charlie) at the battle of Culloden in 1746.

Greenwich was the primary settlement at the time, and its citizens were so confident it would become the county seat they neglected to vote in a referendum to locate a new courthouse. The handful of residents of Bridgeton (then Cohansey Bridge) outvoted them, claiming the courthouse site and, by default, designation as the county seat, to the consternation of the Greenwich inhabitants.

The rest of the area remained largely unpopulated in 1748 except for farms scattered along the two main rivers, the Cohansey and the Maurice, and a tavern located where Port Elizabeth was eventually laid out, on the Maurice in the southeastern section of the county. Of the 677 square miles that comprised the county, 484 were land and the rest water. The tidal Cohansey and the Maurice (pronounced Morris) Rivers drained toward the Delaware River, while the Tuckahoe River, a rare northern blackwater river, flowed toward the Atlantic Ocean. The high point in the county, 140 feet above sea level, was located in what became Upper Deerfield Township. At sea level, salt marshes bordered the Delaware River and the tidal reaches of the Cohansey and Maurice.

Slavery existed in Cumberland County, though not to the extent found farther north in the state. The estimate for 1790 was 120 slaves, decreasing to 75 by 1800; by 1830, only 2 people remained in slavery. Cumberland County was a destination for enslaved people escaping from the Eastern Shore of Maryland and Virginia since it was accessible by boat across the Delaware Bay. The presence of abolitionist Quakers and free Black people created a haven. As the Underground Railroad evolved, one of the three main routes north through New Jersey became known as the Greenwich Line, named for its southern terminus. While many escapees continued north, some settled in Cumberland County, especially in the village of Springtown, in Greenwich Township, populated by five or six hundred Black people, both freeborn and self-manumitted. The settlement was operated as an armed camp, allowing in no unknown whites and subjecting all unknown Black people to questioning by a tribunal. According to Rev. Thomas C. Oliver, an Underground Railroad agent, "the strongest settlement among the colored people that I knew of was Greenwich. None were ever taken out of that place. The fugitives were as safe there as if they were in Canada."

QUAKERS SET THE COUNTY TONE

The Quakers set an egalitarian tone for the county. In 1843, when Philadelphia historian John Fanning Watson visited Greenwich, his ancestral village, he noted that farmers ate at a common table with hired hands, both Black and white. It may have been the tolerant atmosphere promulgated by the Quakers that made possible the founding of Gouldtown, a historically prosperous settlement of free, mixed-race people—primarily African American and white—that was established east of Bridgeton between 1755 and 1774, when Benjamin Gould purchased a 249-acre tract. According to oral tradition, free Black men from the West Indies settled there and married women of Dutch and Finnish descent. Their descendants continued to inhabit the settlement, which survived as an unincorporated village in Fairfield Township, into the twenty-first century, when Philip Roth made Gouldtown the hometown of his protagonist Coleman Silk in his 2000 novel *The Human Stain*.

The presence of Quakers and free Black people probably accounted for the county's strong support of the Union during the Civil War. Many companies formed over the course of the war, and none was ever short of volunteers, some of whom were encouraged to join by the bounties offered by various towns and townships. Those in the minority who sided with the Confederacy were sometimes treated harshly by the Unionists. Although New Jersey as a whole voted in 1860 and 1864 for Lincoln's opponents, Cumberland County overwhelmingly supported him in both elections.

Immigrants also were attracted to the county. The failure of the 1848 democratic revolution in Germany instigated a massive migration of Germans, a sizable number of whom settled in Cumberland County. Some worked in the glass factories and some started businesses. Italian farmers were recruited by Charles Landis when he founded Vineland in 1861 to realize his vision of a grape industry, and Italian migration continued well into the twentieth century. Many Italian families remained active in agriculture in the county.

The 1881 pogroms against Jews in Russia initiated a worldwide relocation effort funded by Jewish philanthropists. Expanses of vacant land were purchased in South Jersey, funded by the Hebrew Immigrant Aid Society of New York. Settlements were clustered on the Salem-Cumberland border, west of Vineland, with Rosenhayn (1883) and Carmel (1882) located in Cumberland County. Farming was a struggle, as many of the settlers came from urban backgrounds. Many turned to clothing manufacturing, first under contract with manufacturers in Philadelphia and New York and eventually with their own factories in Bridgeton, Millville, and Vineland.

Farm labor in the first half of the twentieth century was provided by African Americans who moved north each year from Florida as crops were ready for harvest, and by Philadelphians of Italian descent whom labor brokers transported down for the season; members of both groups settled permanently in the county. Midcentury saw a rise in migrant laborers coming to the county from Puerto Rico, many of whom remained, particularly in Vineland. In the twenty-first century, farm laborers immigrated from Mexico and Central America. Bridgeton became a residential center for Hispanic immigrants, whose proportion of the population approached 60 percent. Some of the migrants commuted from as much as an hour away for work in the fields.

Other significant immigrant groups included Ukrainians, Russians, and Greeks. To deal with a World War II labor shortage, Seabrook Farms, three miles north of Bridgeton, recruited interned Japanese Americans and Latin Americans of Japanese descent, eventually relocating a population of three thousand. After the war, the corporation brought Europeans, primarily Estonians, from displaced persons camps. Eventually, five thousand workers and their families, from twenty-five countries, speaking thirty languages, formed the cohesive community of Seabrook, a rural global village.

INDUSTRY AND COMMERCE

Shipbuilding began in 1780 when the schooner *Governor Livingston* was constructed at Bridgeton. Unfortunately, on her first homeward voyage, she was captured by a British frigate, discouraging further shipbuilding for another fifteen years, until John Lee established a shipyard in 1795 in what became Leesburg. Prior to a decline around World War II, 583 ships were built in Cumberland County, with Bridgeton (153 ships), Dorchester (100), and Leesburg (71) dominating the industry.

In another facet of maritime commerce, in the nineteenth century, schooners from the Maurice River plied the coastal trade, transporting goods up and down the East Coast from Nova Scotia to the West Indies and South America, and even to Europe. Mauricetown served as the home port for most of the captains, and their homes remained in what subsequently became the Mauricetown National Register Historic District.

Fishing and oystering made up the third aspect of maritime business. The Cumberland County shore and river mouths were the ideal oyster habitat, which thrived in a mix of fresh and salty waters. The Lenape harvested oysters at low tide, and they became a food source for settlers in the seventeenth century. In the eighteenth century, oysters became the nation's fast food and in Philadelphia were sold by dozens and hundreds up to ten o'clock at night in the streets. In the last quarter of the nineteenth century, the national oyster harvest became centered on the Delaware Bay, and in particular the Maurice and Cohansey Rivers. By 1874, 372 oyster boats were listed in Cumberland County. Some of the oysters shipped by boat, but a direct railroad line to Bridgeton offered an alternative form of transporting the oysters to market. At the height of the industry in the 1920s, seven thousand boxcars left Bivalve on the Maurice River alone, with 58,800 tons of oysters shipped in shell during 1923.

The tiny settlement of Caviar on the Delaware Bay in Greenwich Township briefly became the center of the world's caviar production in the 1880s, after the sturgeon of Russia and Germany were fished almost to extinction. The industry was so profitable that a new rail line, the New Jersey Southern Railroad, was built between Caviar and New York City. At the height of the fishing season, fifteen railcars full of caviar left daily for the city, where most was sent on to Europe, including Russia. Overfishing decimated the Delaware Bay sturgeon population, which declined in the 1890s and crashed to almost nothing in 1900.

The county's land-based economy transformed around the turn of the nineteenth century, when local entrepreneurs implemented developing hydropower technology by damming both the Cohansey and the Maurice Rivers. Earlier saw and grist mills had used more primitive forms of waterpower, but the new dams were intended to drive emergent industries. In Millville, Philadelphians Henry Drinker and Joseph Smith formed the Union Company in 1790 to purchase twenty-four thousand acres in the eastern part of the county. Drinker and Smith built a dam and mills. Five years later, they sold out to Joseph Buck and partners, and Buck laid out the town of Millville, producing a plan that reserved the land bordering the river for mills, with residential areas on higher land away from the river.

R.D. Wood & Company descended from an iron foundry and furnace established in Millville in 1814. An expansion of waterpower allowed the company a diversification of industries that included a cotton mill, a bleach and dye works, and a glass factory, all of which were eventually managed in Philadelphia. In 1890 a Wood family member moved to Delaware County, Pennsylvania, and started a dairy farm as a hobby. The hobby grew into Wawa Dairy Farms, which began selling milk from its own stores in 1964. In 1968 the two businesses merged as Wawa Inc. From 1971 until 2009, its regional headquarters was located in the Wood family's 1814 homestead in Millville.

Bridgeton's industrial development began in 1815, when brothers Benjamin and David Reeves of Deptford Township purchased waterpower to operate the Cumberland Nail & Iron Works, which became Bridgeton's major industry for the rest of the century. Steam power had replaced waterpower

FIGURE 77. Night scene in the Cumberland Glass Works, Bridgeton, New Jersey. Lewis Hine, 1909. LIBRARY OF CONGRESS.

by the time Oberlin Smith founded the Ferracute Machine Company in Bridgeton in 1863. By the end of the century, Ferracute was shipping presses around the world, including an entire mint to China. The automobile industry became the mainstay of the company, and Ford Motor Company was the major client until Ferracute closed in 1968.

The nineteenth century also saw the development of the glass industry. Cumberland was an ideal location because of the presence of weathered quartz sands of the Cohansey Formation, used in making glass, and molding sands, aggregates of sand and clay used for making cast-iron molds for the glass. The industry began as early as 1799, when James Lee built a factory in Port Elizabeth. Lee moved his operation to Millville in 1806, and the business evolved into Whitall Tatum Company, specializing in bottles, jars, and vials, many custom made for Philadelphia pharmacies until it closed in 1999.

The first glass factory in Bridgeton, Stratton, Buck and Company, began operations in 1836. Eventually, the town supported twenty glass operations. Cumberland Glass Manufacturing, formed in 1880, evolved into Owens-Illinois, Inc., one of the largest glass manufactories in the country and Bridgeton's major employer until it ceased operations in 1984. Owens-Illinois closed the plant because the equipment was outdated and the decreased need for glass containers in the era of plastic did not warrant the expense of modernization.

A PROCESSING AND TRANSPORTATION CENTER

While Cumberland County as a whole prospered in the nineteenth century, and Bridgeton became the processing and transportation center for the agricultural products of the western side of the county, the poorer soil toward the northeast was left fallow and appropriated for open cattle range. Before the Civil War, the population in that area amounted to only about two hundred people. Charles K. Landis, born in Philadelphia and educated as a lawyer, had already participated in the founding of Hammonton, Atlantic County, New Jersey, when he purchased twenty thousand acres from Richard D. Wood in 1860; further acquisitions brought the total to about fifty-three thousand acres.

Landis, a liberal thinker who supported abolition and women's suffrage, planned a utopian agrarian community and hoped that Vineland would attract progressive thinkers as well as farmers and grape growers. He banned alcoholic beverages, which appealed to suffragists, many of whom also promoted prohibition. He advertised nationally starting in 1861, and though some called him a charlatan for selling unproductive farmland, he had many buyers. Advances in agriculture meant that with much effort and investment, the poor soil could be made productive. In 1866 alone, over twelve hundred buildings were constructed, and by the decade's end, there were over seven thousand residents.

To encourage the agricultural aspect of his community, Landis reached out to Italian grape growers, offering a twenty-acre property in exchange for building a house within a year and clearing and cultivating the land for vineyards. In the 1860s and 1870s northern Italians moved to Vineland; in the 1870s and 1880s newcomers shifted to emigrants from southern Italy. Vineland continued to attract Italian immigrants up to the 1920s. The vineyards, orchards, and berry patches flourished, contributing to Vineland's prosperity and Cumberland County's agricultural economy.

In the last quarter of the nineteenth century, the Cumberland County bay shore became a vacation destination. A forty-room hotel, the Warner House, was built in 1877 at Sea Breeze, south of the mouth of the Cohansey, to accommodate Philadelphians leaving the Chestnut Street wharf on the steamer *John A. Warner.* The resort boasted a pier, a toboggan slide, a boardwalk a bowling alley, and an occasional clam bake and yacht regatta. Attractions at East Point, near Heislerville, included a hotel and a tavern, and the Fortescue Hotel offered lodgings in Fortescue, a fishing resort along the bay shore. Railroad access from Philadelphia to the ocean resorts diminished the appeal of the bay destinations by the time of World War I, and Sea Breeze and Fortescue catered mainly to county residents after that.

THE MODERN ECONOMY

In the twentieth century and into the twenty-first, Cumberland's economy continued to depend in large part on the three components of agriculture, maritime activities, and glass manufacturing. Agriculture, and the related industries of processing and distribution, were still the mainstay of the county's economy. Founded near Bridgeton in 1933, Seabrook Farms was a national

FIGURE 78. *Pushing for Rail* by Thomas Eakins, 1874. Reaching the small game birds that populated marshes was possible only at high tide, when the "pusher" could propel the flat-bottomed boat through the thick reeds. The artist enjoyed hunting waterfowl with his father and friends in the tidal marshes of New Jersey's Delaware River. METROPOLITAN MUSEUM OF ART.

leader in the development of frozen foods, and in 1955 *Life* magazine called it "the greatest vegetable factory on Earth." The tomato and asparagus fields in western Cumberland County in the mid-twentieth century gave way to corn and soybeans. The original Seabrook Farms closed in 1976, but in 1978 grandsons of the founder, Charles F. Seabrook, built a new frozen vegetable processing plant in Upper Deerfield. In the twenty-first century, much of the farmland was bought or leased by nurseries, as rising land values in central New Jersey forced growers to seek less expensive acreage. Around Vineland, farmers specialized in growing vegetables and herbs, particularly for ethnic cuisines.

Parasites devastated the oyster industry at midcentury. Research into management of the parasites, conducted, in part, at Rutgers University's Haskin Shellfish Laboratory in Bivalve, led to the industry's slow revival in the twenty-first century. The Bayshore Center, home of restored oyster schooner *A.J. Meerwald*, New Jersey's official tall ship, celebrated and interpreted the industry.

In the late twentieth century, the glass industry declined as plastic supplanted glass for many uses. The loss of the major glass manufacturers—Owens-Illinois in Bridgeton and Whitall Tatum and the major operations of Wheaton Glass in Millville—eliminated glassmaking as the county's major industry but did not end it altogether. In the second decade of the twenty-first century, the glass industry employed close to three thousand people, with eight companies in operation. Most concentrated on specialized products for medicinal and laboratory needs, but the largest, Durand Glass, produced a variety of hollowware.

Tourism continued to be a major supporting industry. The five-hundred-acre New Jersey Motorsports Park opened in Millville in 2008, featuring two road courses, a go-karting complex and other amenities. In 2010 the surviving World War II buildings at the still-active Millville Airport became the Millville Army Air Field Historic District and were home to the Millville Army Air Field Museum.

Nonprofit arts and cultural organizations generated significant revenue, over $16 million in 2015 alone. In 1994 Millville developed the downtown Glasstown Arts District, a public art center with galleries and studios. Also in Millville, Wheaton Arts and the Creative Glass Center of America featured a museum with a major collection of early American glass and working glass artists in a re-created nineteenth-century glass factory. In the twenty-first century, the restored Landis Theater in Vineland and the reconstructed Levoy Theater in Millville provided live musical performances, and the Off Broad Street Players Theater Company and the Cumberland Players contributed live theater.

As the twenty-first century progressed, the county faced a serious threat to its continuing existence. The proximity to the Delaware Bay with its rising sea level, exacerbated by sinking land (known as glacial forebulge subsidence), endangered the survival of the bay-shore communities. Thompsons Beach, Moores Beach, Money Island, Seabreeze, and parts of Fortescue, once thriving villages along the bay shore, were bought out by the state's Blue Acres program (a fund for buying property subject to increased flooding to discourage further habitation) and the buildings bulldozed. With sea level rise predicted to reach as much as six feet by the end of the century and threatening to inundate up to a third of the county, the continued long-term existence of large portions of the area was uncertain.

The county maintained many historic connections and patterns in the twenty-first century, as development evolved at a slower rate than in other parts of the region. With a county per capita income of $28,311 according to the 2020 census, the search continued for new, compatible industry. Growing cultural diversity made Cumberland a majority-minority county (in which no racial group makes up more than half the population), the only one in the southern part of the state. Cumberland County kept its historic connection to agriculture by purchasing preservation easements on twenty-two thousand acres of farmland, one-third of the remaining total. It grew 20 percent of New Jersey's produce and 28 percent of the state's horticultural product, making it by far the most productive agricultural economy in the Garden State. Agriculture and related industries provided more than four thousand jobs. Glassmaking endured as a viable industry. Commercial oystering, fishing, and crabbing continued at a diminished level, as the rivers and bay were used primarily for recreation. The lack of explosive economic development was a trade-off that many residents were willing to accept in return for a less congested and more community-oriented quality of life.

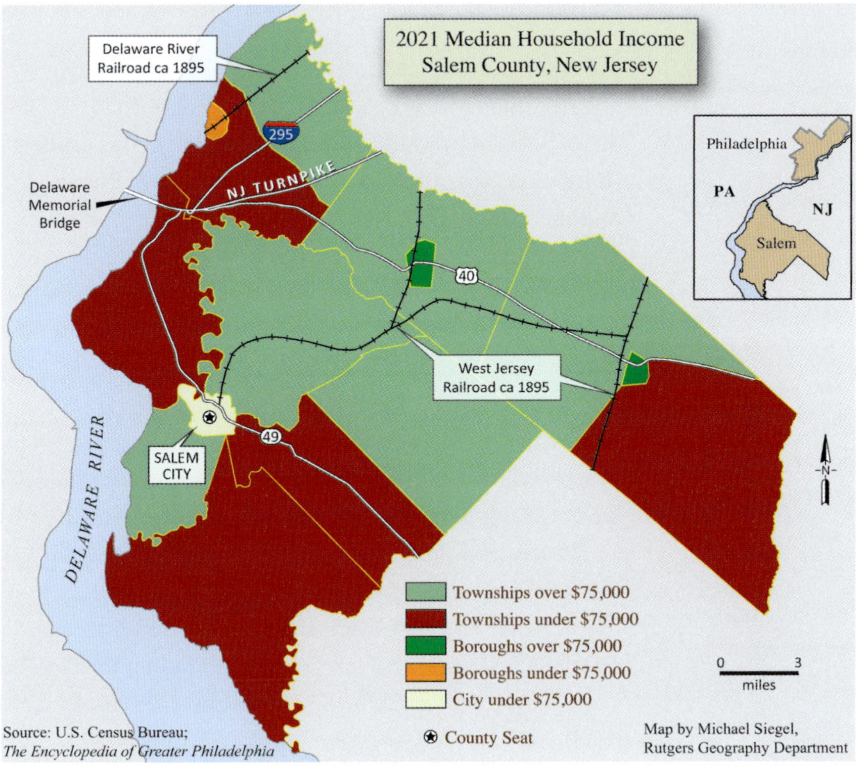

MAP 13. 2021 Median Household Income Salem County, New Jersey. MAP BY MICHAEL SIEGEL.

Salem County, New Jersey

Bonny Beth Elwell

Before Philadelphia, Salem, New Jersey, was the first English Quaker colony along the Delaware River. Established in 1675, the city of Salem had early prominence and served as a port of entry, but it was soon overshadowed by Philadelphia. Although the eighteenth-century settlement consisted primarily of farmers and craftsmen, the proximity of the Philadelphia market by ship, steamboat, and railroad spurred additional industry during the nineteenth century. With the advent of World War I, DuPont's Powder Works at Carneys Point and Chemours Chambers Works in Deepwater permanently changed the county, bringing an influx of new residents and immigrants and establishing the precedence of industry over agriculture. The Delaware Memorial Bridge and the modern highway system further increased growth. By the twenty-first century, Salem County remained a rural region of farm fields and small towns, still close to the urban hub of Philadelphia, yet the decline of former manufactories created a pressing need to increase jobs, industry, and tourism.

The area that became Salem County was first settled by the Lenape, followed by Swedes who arrived in the Delaware Valley in 1638 and purchased the New Jersey side of the Delaware River from Cape May to Raccoon Creek. To curb English settlement and establish their precedence over the Dutch, the Swedes built Fort Elfsborg at what was later called Elsinboro to guard the Delaware River. By 1655, when the Dutch took control, the Swedes had settled at Finns Point and other locations on the neck of land between the Delaware and the Salem River.

The first permanent English settlement in the county was established by John Fenwick, who arrived with Quakers and other Englishmen on the *Griffin* in 1675. Prior to his departure, Fenwick had purchased the West Jersey holdings of Lord John Berkeley—a transaction of disputed validity. After negotiations with William Penn and others, Fenwick was granted one-tenth proprietorship of West Jersey. Shortly after Fenwick arrived to plant his colony, he affirmed his claim by purchasing from the resident Lenape three tracts of land stretching along the Delaware River from Oldman's Creek to the Maurice River, known as the Salem Tenth. At the mouth of the Salem River, Fenwick founded the city of Salem, which became a port of entry in 1682. Although the Swedes still lived on the land along the Delaware River, Fenwick brought them under English rule, and they were eventually absorbed by the English colony. Due to ongoing controversy regarding his ownership of the land, Fenwick had to relinquish all but 150,000 acres of his colony to William Penn in March 1682, just months before Fenwick died. The Salem Tenth officially organized as Salem County in 1695 with Salem City as the county seat; it was one of the two original West Jersey counties and included the area that later separated to form Cumberland County.

The first major road laid out in Salem County was the Kings Highway, commissioned by the West Jersey General Assembly in 1681 to connect Salem with Burlington, at that time the other principal town of West Jersey. The next major roads, beginning in 1707, connected Salem with Greenwich in the area that later became Cumberland County. Settlements formed around three principal bridges across Alloways Creek: Hancock's Bridge, Quinton's Bridge, and Thompson's Bridge (later Alloway). By the early 1700s, settlements had also formed inland at mills in Woodstown and Daretown along the Salem River and at Centerton along Muddy Run, feeding into the Maurice River. At the northern border, Pedricktown and Sculltown (later Auburn) formed along Oldman's Creek. After Cumberland County separated from Salem County in 1748, Stow Creek became the southern border of Salem County. Roads continued to be laid out to connect these early settlements, which generally centered on mills or taverns.

During the late seventeenth and early eighteenth centuries, additional English colonists arrived from Great Britain and New England, and French Huguenots and Dutch migrated south from New York. The county's strong Quaker presence and religious tolerance attracted Quakers and Baptists. Less nobly, wealthy Salem County residents purchased enslaved persons from the West Indies and Africa for housework and farm labor. By 1737, Salem County's population had reached 5,884, with 184 enslaved people forming roughly 3 percent of the population. Initially residing in log houses, many colonists built pattern-brick houses during the early eighteenth century; a few dozen examples of this unique architectural style survived as private residences or tourist attractions into the twenty-first century.

FARMS AND MANUFACTORIES

From the port of Salem, the early settlers exported grains (wheat, corn, rye, and oats), animal products (beef, pork, tallow, and pelts), and timber (cedar posts, shingles, staves, and cordwood) to New York, Boston, and the West Indies. As Philadelphia emerged as a rival in foreign trade, Salem shifted focus to supplying the Philadelphia market. In addition to mills, farming, tanning, woodworking, and masonry, the first major industry was glassmaking, which Caspar Wistar of Philadelphia established in 1738 with a glassworks at Wistarburg in Alloway Township. The Wistarburg Glass Works, which operated until the Revolutionary War, attracted many German immigrants to the county.

The Revolutionary War figures strongly in Salem County lore, although no major battles occurred there. Salem County provided militiamen for the Continental army, provided cattle and fodder for George Washington's troops at Valley Forge, and fiercely fought the British and Loyalists during skirmishes. With rich farm fields, the area tempted both the American and British troops, whose foraging in Salem in 1778 prompted the Battle of Quinton's Bridge and the Hancock's Bridge Massacre.

By the late eighteenth and early nineteenth centuries, the rich soil of Salem County had been exhausted of nutrients, farms yielded poor harvests, and many farmers migrated to the Midwest. In 1826, however, the discovery of marl, an excellent fertilizer, in Pilesgrove, led to revitalized soil and solidified the agricultural presence. Farmers raised cattle, potatoes, fruits, vegetables, poultry, and dairy products to supply the Philadelphia markets, and fishing for shad, herring, and sturgeon became important industries along the Delaware River. As the need for shipping increased, shipbuilders in Salem and Alloway responded by producing schooners, canal boats, brigs, and later steamboats. By the 1830s, steamboats ran regularly from Salem and Penns Grove to Philadelphia and Wilmington, transporting crops to market and goods for export.

Salem County's population rose by 1800 to 11,371, including 85 enslaved and 607 free Black residents. The oldest African Methodist Episcopal (AME) church in New Jersey, established in Salem City in 1800, predated the founding conference of the AME denomination in Philadelphia in 1816. The Quaker influence significantly reduced slavery, and by 1830 only one slave remained, with approximately 1,400 free Black persons among the total population of 14,155 residents. The significant increase of free Black people resulted partially from the Underground Railroad and an influx of escaped slaves. Because of its proximity to Philadelphia and its strong Quaker presence, Salem County became a haven for many fugitives, who settled in free Black communities in Mannington, Pilesgrove, and other townships.

When the Civil War began, Salem men quickly enlisted in the Union army. Local women also contributed to the cause, most notably Cornelia Hancock, who served as a nurse after the Battle of Gettysburg. Although no battles occurred on Salem County soil, Fort Delaware in the Delaware River housed Confederate prisoners in overcrowded and unhealthy conditions; 2,436 prisoners died and were buried at Finns Point Cemetery, across the river from Fort Delaware.

IMPACTS OF THE RAILROAD

In 1863, the West Jersey Railroad connected Salem to Camden and Philadelphia, passing through Salem County's small towns along the way. The Delaware Shore Railroad crossed the northern region of the county to Penns Grove in 1876. These railroads offered daily passenger trains between the county and Philadelphia, allowing residents to commute to work in the city. In addition, railroads offered a new way to transport goods and produce to the metropolitan area. Taking advantage of the shipping opportunities, industry expanded. Glass factories formed in Salem and Quinton in 1863. The Quinton Glass Works supplied glass for the Centennial Exhibition buildings in Philadelphia in 1876. A variety of other factories (spindles, shoes, cigars, and others) also emerged near these railroad lines. The American Oil Cloth Company started in Salem in 1868. Later, Mannington Mills became a significant flooring manufacturer.

The railroad also allowed farmers to ship tomatoes, potatoes, asparagus, and other vegetables and fruit to Philadelphia to be sold or to South Jersey canneries such as Campbell Soup in the late 1800s and early 1900s. Small local canneries emerged in several Salem County communities, and a Heinz food processing plant operated in Salem City from 1905 to 1977. The increased need for agricultural workers attracted immigrants from Europe (especially Italy), and some canneries built housing for immigrant workers. In addition to produce, caviar harvested from sturgeon became a key export from Penns Grove during the 1880s. Dairy farms shipped milk to Philadelphia, and local creameries created ice cream and other dairy products for export. Abbott's Alderney Dairies, founded in Mannington, shipped milk by train to the Centennial Exhibition in Philadelphia in 1876; the creamery moved to Philadelphia the following year. By the 1920s, roads and trucks had surpassed railroads as the preferred shipping method, allowing farmers to drive produce to Camden and Philadelphia.

In addition to facilitating commerce, railroads and steamboats brought tourists, vacationers, and immigrants to Salem County. The New Jersey Southern Railroad brought Russian Jewish immigrants from New York City to Pittsgrove Township, where in 1882 they established the Alliance Colony, subdividing the land into fifteen-acre parcels with the intent of forming an agricultural utopia. With limited agricultural experience, however, the settlers had to supplement their crops with clothing factories and other industry, later adding poultry and egg businesses. The community expanded during the early 1900s, but by 1959 the Jewish presence had waned, and a new wave of migrants—primarily African Americans and Hispanics—moved into the houses.

During the late nineteenth and early twentieth centuries, vacationers from New York, Philadelphia, and other cities rode the railroad to parks at lakes such as Rainbow Lake, Centerton Lake, Palatine Lake, and Parvin State Park, while steamboats traveling daily from Philadelphia to Salem brought vacationers to groves along the Delaware River such as French's Grove at Penns Grove and Silver Grove in Pennsville (later known as Riverview Beach Park). These parks and groves featured swimming, boating, rides, and pavilions for skating and dancing. The Wilson Line provided regular transportation from Philadelphia, Camden, and Wilmington to Penns Grove and Salem along the Delaware River, which became popular vacation spots for city residents.

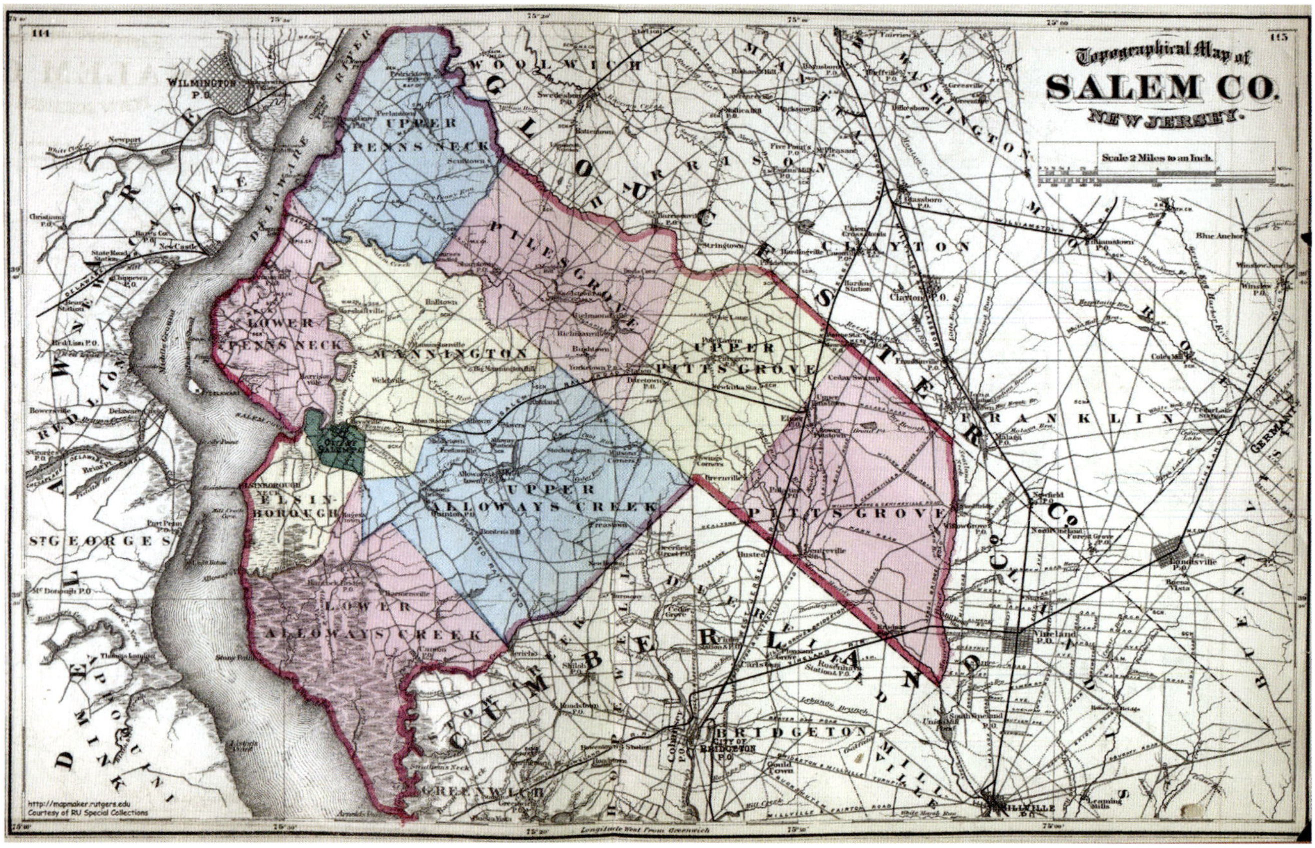

FIGURE 79. Topographical map, Salem County, New Jersey, 1872.

As automobiles took over from railroads, the ferries crossing between Delaware and Salem County could not adequately handle the surge of vehicles, and the Delaware State Highway Department constructed the Delaware Memorial Bridge between Wilmington and Deepwater (the first span opened in 1951, and the second in 1968). Along with the bridges in Gloucester and Camden Counties, highways linked Salem County to Philadelphia, Delaware, and the rest of the country. Commuters traveled on the New Jersey Turnpike (completed 1951) and Interstate 295, vacationers headed through the county to the shore, and trucks exported and delivered goods.

POPULATION GROWTH AND CHANGE

Industry boomed at DuPont's Powder Works once World War I broke out, and Salem County changed forever. DuPont had opened the Powder Works at Carneys Point just south of Penns Grove in 1893 to create smokeless gunpowder for the Spanish-American War, but World War I dramatically increased the need for munitions. Workers from around the United States, as well as immigrants from Italy, Russia, Poland, Ireland, Germany, and other countries, flooded into Carneys Point, Penns Grove, and Pennsville to work at DuPont. Between 1910 and 1920, Salem County's population increased by about ten thousand, compared to a typical increase of one thousand in prior decades. Carneys Point's population jumped from 744 to 6,259, while neighboring Penns Grove's population increased from 2,118 to 6,060. During World War I, the plant employed a high of over twenty thousand people. To accommodate the influx of workers, DuPont built temporary housing, barracks, and bungalows, and even put up tents to house the workers.

In 1917, DuPont started the Dye Works (renamed Chambers Works in 1945) at Deepwater in Pennsville

Township, initially focusing on creating dyes, an industry previously dominated by war-torn Germany. The Chambers Works became a worldwide leader in organic chemicals by discovering and creating materials such as Teflon, nylon, and Freon. DuPont remained a major employer for the rest of the century, with high wages that continued to draw both locals and new residents to Salem County. By 1964, approximately 25 percent of county households included a DuPont employee. Although Carneys Point's population dropped after World War I, it increased again from 1930 to 1960. From 1930 to 1970, Pennsville dramatically increased in population, rising from 2,933 to 13,296, making it the most populous municipality of the county. A once-rural area had become densely populated, lining the industrial belt along the Delaware River between Salem City and Penns Grove.

In the latter half of the twentieth century, Salem County's industrial towns slumped, especially Salem City and the borough of Penns Grove. Both places experienced decreases in jobs and industry as factories and small businesses closed, prompting a rise in poverty and abandoned housing. Because Salem and Penns Grove also had high minority populations, racial tensions aggravated the situation. At the time schools integrated in 1947, most Salem County elementary schools were segregated while high schools were integrated. It took several years before all the schools integrated, due to local resistance as well as the need for additional facilities to accommodate extra students. An NBC television special in 1964, which calculated that Salem City most embodied "Average Town USA," also revealed local prejudice. Racial tensions continued to escalate during the following decade with a few cross burnings that were soon halted. At the time, African Americans comprised 29 percent of Salem City's population.

By 2020, minorities had become the majority in Salem and Penns Grove; Salem City was 63 percent African American, and Penns Grove was 40 percent African American and 28 percent Hispanic. These regions, along with Carneys Point and Pennsville, also had the highest numbers of foreign-born residents and Hispanics. Puerto Rican migrant workers began arriving after World War II to pick vegetables between spring and fall and later settled permanently. The Puerto Rican Action Committee (PRAC) of Southern Jersey, formed in 1971 by Salem County agricultural workers to rally the Hispanic community and advance opportunities, remained active into the twenty-first century.

Blighted by poverty, over 20 percent of the households in Salem City and Penns Grove received public assistance in 2010, and the unemployment rate was 27 percent in Penns Grove and 18 percent in Salem. Over 60 percent of houses in these cities were rentals, with high percentages of multiple unit dwellings and several hundred vacant homes, 22 percent vacant in Salem City in 2010. Volunteers from organizations such as Stand Up for Salem (established in 1988) attempted to revitalize the county seat through restoring neglected buildings, developing downtown businesses, fund-raising, and promoting events with modest results.

SMALL TOWN SURVIVAL IN THE SUBURBAN ERA

In contrast to the declining urban populations, Salem County's rural areas gained residents as suburban housing and commuting became popular in the second half of the twentieth century. Rural townships experienced growth in the 1950s or gradually increased throughout the century. Pittsgrove Township received the most new residents, increasing from a population of 2,808 in 1950 to 8,121 in 1990. Developments such as Palatine Lake Village and trailer parks attracted new residents, many of whom longed to live in a rural setting. The completion of New Jersey Route 55 in 1989 and the ease of access to Interstate 295 and the New Jersey Turnpike made living in rural Salem County while commuting to jobs outside the county feasible. According to the 2010 census, although 14,002 Salem County residents worked within the county, 10,730 residents commuted to work in other South Jersey counties or out of state, with the top work locations being Cumberland County (30 percent), Delaware (24 percent), Pennsylvania (16 percent), and Camden County (11 percent).

Public Service Electric and Gas Company's (PSE&G) Salem Generating Station, built between 1968 and 1981, became Salem County's largest employer. Consisting of three nuclear power plants on Artificial Island off the coast of Lower Alloways Creek, the facility supplied New Jersey, Philadelphia, and the Delmarva Peninsula. DuPont's Chambers Works, Mannington Mills, and hospitals in Mannington and Elmer continued to be significant employers. Although Salem's glass factory closed in 2014, Salem Community College (founded in 1972) continued the glass tradition by offering Glass Art and the only Scientific Glass Technology degree in the country. The Salem County government attempted to expand use of the railroad between Salem and Swedesboro, repairing it to connect with the port of Salem, another underused asset in the twenty-first century. New businesses in Salem County included distribution centers and warehouses at the Gateway Business Park in Oldmans Township. Still, the need for more jobs and businesses to counteract high property taxes remained.

Despite its industrial enterprises, Salem County remained primarily agricultural with small towns, and many residents resisted further development. In response to the community's desire to preserve farmland, the county freeholders established the Salem County Agriculture Development Board and the Agricultural Land Preservation Program (1990) and the Farmland Preservation Plan (2006). At both the county and municipal levels, voters approved taxes dedicated to support farmland preservation, resulting in over three hundred farms preserved after 1990. By 2023, Salem County had the most preserved farmland in the state, with 52,361 acres under protection. Salem County farms still produced corn, hay, soybeans, vegetables, and fruits for market; horse farms, nurseries, sod farms, and wineries also were on the rise. The biggest tourist attraction in Salem County remained the Cowtown Rodeo, founded in 1929, which is the longest running weekly rodeo in the United States. Other cultural attractions bringing tourists from urban areas included the Salem County Fair, the Appel Farm Arts & Music Center, the Nanticoke Lenni-Lenape Pow Wow, the Arts in Bloom tour, historic house tours, wine trails, and other festivals, as well as a multitude of outdoor activities at local state parks and nature preserves. Whether marketing rural charm, exporting goods and produce, or seeking employment at a commutable distance, Salem County continued to benefit from both the opportunities and the needs of Philadelphia and its suburban area.

New Castle County, Delaware

W. Barksdale Maynard

Of the eleven counties in the Philadelphia metropolitan statistical area, New Castle County is perhaps the most varied geographically. Stretching from the Piedmont to the Coastal Plain, it is marked by rolling hills and fast-flowing crystalline streams to the north and sluggish brown tidal creeks meandering toward Delaware Bay to the south. Its northernmost neighborhood at Claymont is virtually an outer suburb of Philadelphia; to the south, the county extends down to the latitude of Baltimore, where southern culture begins to be detectable. The great majority of the county lies south of the Mason-Dixon Line (drawn between 1763 and 1768). Of all the counties around Philadelphia, it may be the most culturally heterogeneous, for no other touches three states, with distinctive influences flowing in. Southern New Castle County shares the Delmarva Peninsula with Maryland and partly drains into Chesapeake Bay; Wilmington is a stone's throw across the river from New Jersey; scenic Brandywine Creek knits New Castle County together with Pennsylvania.

Not only is New Castle County diverse, its early settlement history is unusual among the American colonies for the multitude of European nations that claimed it. Sweden, the Netherlands, and England all jockeyed for control throughout the seventeenth century, each establishing settlements that indicated serious claims to the fur trade and other bounties of the New World. Pushed aside were the Native peoples who belonged to the Delaware or Lenni Lenape tribe.

Arriving on the ship *Kalmar Nyckel*, the Swedes built Fort Christina near the later site of Wilmington in 1638. The fort comprised the first Swedish settlement in the Western Hemisphere. In 1651 Dutch director-general Peter Stuyvesant established Fort Casimir, later called New Castle, just south on the Delaware River. By 1682 Quakers were starting to flood the region, quickly diluting whatever remained of the culture of New Sweden. Upon arrival in America—at the wharf in New Castle in 1682—William Penn moved quickly to give representative government to the Three Lower Counties, including New Castle County, which had officially been founded in 1673, with its courthouse at New

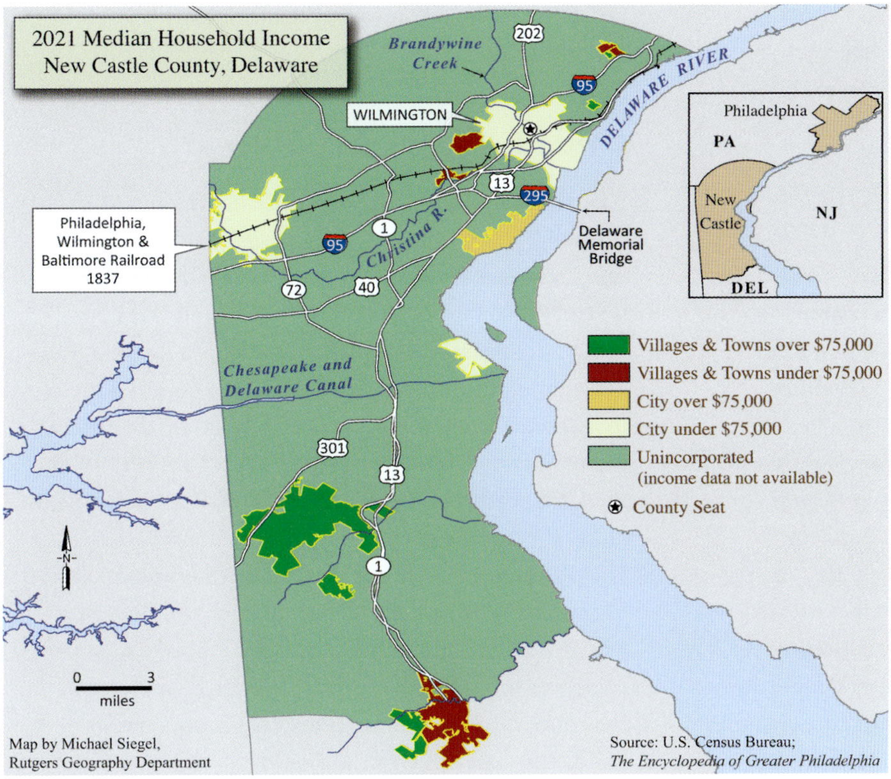

MAP 14. 2021 Median Household Income, New Castle County, Delaware. MAP BY MICHAEL SIEGEL.

Castle. Otherwise, he feared that these counties could be wrested from his control by Lord Baltimore, who dreamed of annexing them to Maryland. The matter was hotly contested: Lawsuits raged in London until 1750, finally determining that the Delaware counties belonged to Pennsylvania. Not that the marriage was always amicable. Anglican Delawareans often clashed with their pacifist Quaker neighbors to the north, finding them dilatory in appropriating funds for military necessities, in particular the protection of Delaware Bay against enemy ships and pirates.

The early history of New Castle County was inextricable from that of Philadelphia. It was one of Pennsylvania's "Three Lower Counties," providing crucial access to the sea. The town of New Castle thrived as an overnight stop for travelers coming and going from Philadelphia, and to the south of there, Port Penn attempted to compete with Philadelphia's shipping trade.

Philadelphia's influence on Wilmington (chartered in 1739) was extensive. Along streets that bore the familiar Philadelphia names (Walnut, Spruce, and Pine) rose sturdy brick Georgian houses as fireproof as those recommended by William Penn in the Quaker City, and the handsome Old Town Hall (1798) virtually copied Philadelphia's Congress Hall. Even Wilmington's Old Swedes Church was built in 1698–99 by a Philadelphia mason of English descent in an English architectural style. The sophisticated colonial houses of Odessa in southern New Castle County showed how closely the leading families there were tied to Philadelphia by the grain trade around 1770.

The Philadelphia campaign of the American Revolution brought war to the quiet agricultural landscapes of New Castle County. George Washington's September 1777 efforts to protect Philadelphia from British attack centered on Delaware before shifting just north to the banks of the Brandywine at Chadds Ford, Pennsylvania, where the second-largest land battle of the Revolutionary War was fought, the Battle of the Brandywine. The opening skirmish of that campaign happened in New Castle County, the Battle of Cooch's Bridge, on a site preserved in the twentieth century by the State of Delaware and, according to much-debated legend, the place where the Stars and Stripes may have first flown in battle. Later Washington's army marched rapidly to Chadds Ford along the river, through what later became First State National Historical Park (founded 2013), Delaware's first and only federal park.

TRANSPORTATION SHAPES THE GROWTH OF THE COUNTY

New Castle County's early history was thoroughly shaped by rivers and boats, the only practicable means of getting products to market, and a galaxy of little towns sprang up along waterways, only to dwindle and fade once the railroad passed them by. The town of New Castle is perhaps the best example, filled with stylish houses of the Federal period, clustered near the once-thriving riverfront. Several blocks from the wharfs stands the courthouse (begun ca. 1730), one of the nation's oldest surviving government facilities, scene of heated trials regarding slavery and abolitionism—a reminder that slavery was legal in more southern-leaning New Castle County for eighty years after Pennsylvania first took steps in 1780 to abolish it. The courthouse was also, according to legend, the point from which Delaware's distinctive circular border with Pennsylvania was measured in colonial times (1701 and again in 1750, actually from multiple center points). But New Castle's economy sputtered once railroads eclipsed water transportation. The gradual nineteenth-century decline of the town was measured by the fact that the county seat eventually shifted to flourishing Wilmington in 1881, leaving New Castle as a time capsule of early American architecture.

At New Castle, the full impact of successive changes in transportation is evident. The historic road that linked to Wilmington crossed the top of an ancient dike, one of several built by the Dutch and English starting in the 1650s to improve transport and reclaim marshland for agriculture. Remarkably, these still protect the low-lying town from flooding, and some were rehabilitated as barriers against sea level rise as recently as 2014. Later, travelers both famous and obscure got off boats to and from Philadelphia, then trudged up narrow Packet Alley in New Castle to catch overland transport to the Chesapeake Bay. In 1832, New Castle briefly became the terminus for one of America's first railroads, the New-Castle and Frenchtown, and the nation's second-oldest train station still stands there, though exhibiting a typically modest Delawarean scale, hardly bigger than a broom closet.

CANALS, RAILROADS, HIGHWAYS

The 1820s brought a nationwide canal mania. A canal through New Castle County linking the Chesapeake and Delaware Bays had been proposed as early as the seventeenth century. As Philadelphia and Baltimore grew, a fourteen-mile canal emerged as a favored way of reducing the four-hundred-mile trip between them to less than one hundred. Partly funded by the federal government and constructed between 1824 and 1829, the Chesapeake and Delaware (C&D) Canal extended along the middle of the Delmarva Peninsula. The Deep Cut at Summit Bridge (east of Chesapeake City, Maryland) was one of the most arduous engineering feats of the age. The C&D Canal cost nearly nine times more per mile than the slightly earlier Erie Canal as the route through soft Coastal Plain sediments was constantly plagued by mudslides.

The ambitiously titled Delaware City was established at the east end of the canal in anticipation of a boom. It was backed by two brothers, originally from New Jersey, who hoped it would steal much of Philadelphia's shipping. The canal did see steady increases in tonnage through 1872 and played a critical role in Union troop movements during the Civil War. Thereafter, competition from railroads was stiff, and Delaware City largely fizzled. Much enlarged in the twentieth century, the C&D Canal grew to one of the busiest waterways in the nation, carrying 40 percent of the maritime freight of the Port of Baltimore and much of Philadelphia's as well. Culturally, the canal formed an unofficial divide between north and south, "Below the Canal" being a Delaware byword for a more rural and relaxed lifestyle in the so-called "Slower Lower" part of the state—a distinction that blurred with rapid suburbanization.

The advent of the railroad completely refigured the patterns of travel and commerce in New Castle County. Wilmington mushroomed due to its location on the main line between New York and Washington, D.C. The routing of the Philadelphia, Wilmington, and Baltimore (1837) through northern New Castle County triggered an explosion of industry, including tanneries, carriage factories, and textile and flour mills. Starting in the 1830s, Lobdell Car Wheel Company mastered the difficult art of forging metal wheels tough enough to withstand high-speed railroad use. Nearby, Jackson & Sharp dominated American production of railroad coaches after the Civil War. Another historic railroad line cut through the county (and the outer suburbs of Wilmington) in the 1880s, the Baltimore and Ohio, with picturesque stations on the northwestern edge of Wilmington and at Newark designed by renowned Philadelphia architect Frank Furness, both subsequently demolished in the automobile age.

But the most historic railroad story in New Castle County was the first-ever attempt to cross the Delmarva Peninsula by rail: the New-Castle and Frenchtown Railroad. It came extremely early, with surveying begun in spring 1830, the year the Baltimore and Ohio opened for business in Maryland as America's very first railroad. A private company undertook the project, with Philadelphia investors playing a key role and Philadelphia architect and engineer William Strickland working as a consultant. The reach of this enterprise was remarkable. Trains ran on granite blocks hauled from Maryland and Pennsylvania, on which were stretched timbers from Georgia, topped with iron straps from Liverpool, England, nailed in with spikes forged at Troy Nail Works in New York. Notably, two locomotives were imported from England in 1832, duplicates of the lightest locomotives in use on the famous Liverpool and Manchester Railway (opened 1830), designed by the esteemed Robert Stephenson. Locomotives were named Delaware and Maryland; Pennsylvania was ordered a year later, in 1832.

Another hundred years later New Castle County again saw a transportation innovation of importance, not just nationally but internationally. Delaware's fertile farms lay tantalizingly close to the giant urban market of Philadelphia, but poor roads meant that highway transport was slow, causing fruits and vegetables to perish. Industrialist T. Coleman Du Pont proposed a concrete highway to stretch the entire length of the state, hoping for a multilane thoroughfare with swift cars separated from slower trolleys, trucks, and horses, a suggestion only partially acted upon. He personally funded the DuPont Highway, later U.S. Routes 13 and 113, which was completed in 1923 and served as a key proving ground for highway-improvement campaigners nationwide. The smooth, white concrete invited high speeds, but problems were soon identified. Curves were frighteningly tight, headlight glare dazzled drivers, and head-on collisions were frequent. An experiment followed in 1929–33, when the forty-five miles from Wilmington to Dover were reconfigured as a divided highway, Delaware Dual Road, said to be the first in the world to adopt the dual roadway technique (well before the German autobahns opened in 1935–36, or the Merritt Parkway, Connecticut, in 1938–40, or the Pennsylvania Turnpike in 1940). Closely involved with the DuPont Highway was Coleman's son, Francis V. Du Pont, later a leading figure in the creation of the U.S. interstate highway system under President Dwight Eisenhower.

For most of its history, New Castle County was heavily agricultural, in common with the entire state. As late as the 1920s, Delaware was first in the country for its percentage of land under cultivation. But at the same time, New Castle County's Brandywine Creek had been a key center of the Industrial Revolution in the United States, with scores of mills springing up along it. Here about 1790 occurred the historic American debut of the mechanized production of flour and, in 1817, machine-made paper for newsprint and books, helping spur the nineteenth-century explosion in publishing. Well before that, in 1794, Scottish immigrant William Young had opened the Rockland Paper Mills, providing paper for his shop and printing press on Chestnut Street in Philadelphia, so that Brandywine paper from New Castle County became the watermarked standard for U.S. government documents.

In 1802 the Du Ponts arrived as part of the larger wave of refugees from the French Revolution to found their famous gunpower manufacturing complex along Brandywine Creek and subsequently dominate the state economy. By the early twentieth century, the DuPont company was the nation's top producer of gunpower and dynamite and increasingly dominated the chemical industry as well, with products woven into the daily life of every American, from toothpaste to nylon hosiery to automotive paints. Later still came Tyvek for building insulation, Kevlar for bulletproof vests, Teflon for nonstick pans. The wealth of the family became legendary. The corporation brought high salaries and an influx of talent, making Wilmington the wealthiest

FIGURE 80. Rolling Mill, DuPont Powder Works, Brandywine River, 1868. HAGLEY MUSEUM AND LIBRARY.

city per capita in the United States following World War I. The family was ardently philanthropic, founding schools and churches for the company's early Irish and Italian workforce. Pierre S. Du Pont, great-grandson of E. I. Du Pont who immigrated from France, proved one of the most generous contributors to charity in the nation's history. Concerned about the poor quality of schools throughout Delaware, he began to finance them himself, including the sumptuous P.S. duPont Middle School in Wilmington (1935), one of the most beautiful public schools in the country, a brick-and-limestone masterpiece in Delaware's signature Colonial Revival style. He also paid for eighty-nine mostly rural schools for African Americans (built 1919–28), one of which, School House #112C, remains preserved as Iron Hill Museum near Newark after it was shuttered, like virtually all of the Black schools, following the court-ordered desegregation of all Delaware schools in 1965.

Another legacy of the Du Pont family was the preservation of scenic land in Piedmont New Castle County and the creation of house museums that enjoy a national reputation as "Chateau Country," a major driver of tourism to the region. Countless workers were employed on these estates, from housekeepers to chauffeurs and gardeners, many of them recent immigrants from Europe. When not engaged in his legendary feud with certain Du Pont cousins, Alfred I. Du Pont—proud of his direct line of descent via "oldest sons" from the family in France—built a state-of-the-art children's hospital on the grounds of his French-style estate, later called Nemours Mansion & Gardens. Hagley Museum and Library preserves the first Du Pont home in America, Eleutherian Mills, and the nearby gunpowder manufactory. Winterthur was the dream of Henry Francis Du Pont, another cousin of A. I.'s. Starting in 1927, Henry built a gigantic addition to showcase his growing collections of classic American interiors and antiques. The existing thirty-two-room mansion was supplemented by a wing with more than a hundred "period rooms" housing the largest collection of American antiques in the world.

FARM FIELDS AND CROSSROADS TOWNS

Long overwhelmingly rural outside of Wilmington, New Castle County developed slowly, with farmers cultivating grain that was ground at mills along local streams, then shipped by the Delaware River to distant markets. At crossroads that sometimes dated back to Indian times, settlements sprang up with taverns to serve travelers who were just passing through Delaware on their way to somewhere more populous. Often these were millers transporting grain. At the hamlet of Christiana, near Christiana Mall, the crossroads settlement pattern remains intact. The main north-south colonial highway ran directly through town, as did an important east-west county road, so that a Connecticut visitor of 1749 was surprised to find, after countless mid-Atlantic log houses, "a Clump of very fine brick houses a Dozen or more & Several Taverns," this being "a place . . . of much Business." A wharf on the Christiana River provided a small but prosperous port for this well-inland settlement. George Washington slept regularly in Christiana taverns during his frequent travels between Virginia and the North.

Milling flourished on many of New Castle County's streams, as at the John England Mill east of Newark, founded by an immigrant from Staffordshire in the 1720s, two decades before he built the sturdy brick colonial house that survives amid modern suburban development. This miller was English, but many of his

FIGURE 81. DuPont Company metal keg mill workers, 1885. HAGLEY MUSEUM AND LIBRARY.

neighbors were Scots Irish, the most populous minority in the county, and not far west were a group of Welsh settlers at Iron Hill. Newark itself was, in the eighteenth century, yet another crossroads town, although strung along a considerable straightaway, later named Main Street. Just outside of town, the Curtis Paper Company operated on White Clay Creek from 1789 until 1997, the longest-running paper mill in America. Home to the University of Delaware, Newark was a sleepy place for generations, but after World War II, with the expansion of the school and construction of two DuPont facilities and a Chrysler plant, it grew to be Delaware's third-largest town (population thirty-one thousand), nearly as large as Dover.

Unusual in Delaware for having been founded away from any navigable river, Middletown in southern New Castle County coalesced at another early crossroads. The place experienced rapid growth after the railroad came through in 1855. Demographically, the lower county was southern, with slaves working in the peach orchards. Freedom was not far away in Pennsylvania, however, making Middletown a vital link in the Underground Railroad that extended straight through New Castle County, up to the dreaded Market Street Bridge over the Brandywine in Wilmington—a covered span watched closely for runaways. In a celebrated 1845 case, a Quaker farmer and abolitionist of Middletown, John Hunn, assisted a group of escaped slaves who arrived in the night from Maryland's Eastern Shore, part of a regular flow from the South seeking freedom. Neighbors called the local constable, who arrested the runaways and delivered them to the jail in New Castle.

MODERN SUBURBANIZATION

The familiar agricultural ethos of New Castle County persisted for centuries until finally succumbing to implacable economic forces in the mid-twentieth century. A 1992 memoir by elderly Emma Mariane about farm life in Brandywine Hundred, north of Wilmington, recounts the swift disappearance of a rural way of life, long organized around haymaking, cutting corn with knives, and bottling milk. She tells how small-scale dairies, once thriving, were finally regulated out of existence by modernizing state health authorities. With the coming of supermarkets after 1945, the King Street farmers market downtown—where curbs were lined with hundreds of horse wagons bearing eggs, broiler chickens, and an array of vegetables—was ruled unsanitary and closed, meaning locals had nowhere to sell their products. With big business ascendant, once self-sufficient farms failed. Mariane's little farm converted into a nursery serving the front-yard needs of suburban homeowners; all the neighboring farms were paved over for housing developments.

Along with the rest of the Philadelphia region, New Castle County was utterly transformed by suburbanization and the automobile after World War II. Growth in industry, stimulated in part by the war effort, reshaped the county. Companies relocated to the area to take advantage of cheap land and proximity to major markets, the area lying about midway between New York and Washington. Wilmington had long been ringed by trolley suburbs, but now the automobile allowed neighborhoods to spring up in odd corners largely untethered from the city—for example, seven hundred boxy housing units by developer Alfred J. Vilone sprouted in a cow pasture at Fairfax in 1950.

Like many of his customers, Vilone was of Italian descent. New Castle County long had relatively little ethnic diversity, other than African Americans and the many Irish who had built antebellum canals and railroads and later worked in cotton mills. But a huge influx starting in the 1880s changed the picture dramatically. German immigrants became bakers, butchers, and cabinetmakers; Poles excelled in leather tanning and ironworking. After 1900 they were joined by Italians whose many enterprises included boot- and shoemaking, tailoring, and masonry. Compared to other ethnic groups, Italians grouped tightly together rather than dispersing, with concentrations at Wilmington's Little Italy around landmark St. Anthony's Church (1926) as well as at Hockessin and Claymont. By midcentury their descendants had mastered the English language and spread throughout the county, producing a dominant cultural strain marked by intermarriage between Irish and Italians. The postwar suburbanization of northern New Castle County owed much to these ethnic groups abandoning Wilmington row houses, joined by many others who sought to escape crowded city conditions in South Philadelphia.

For generations, practically everybody had gone to Market and King Streets in downtown Wilmington to go shopping—old photographs show the sidewalks thronged at Christmastime. The focus shifted dramatically after World War II when the Philadelphia firm of John Wanamaker proposed to build a state-of-the-art department store on sixteen acres along the edge of a forest far outside of town (1948–50). Seemingly audacious, this marked the beginning of a whole new era of land use in the county, as the company broke free from Wilmington taxes and zoning and felled trees to build an enormous parking lot of the kind one never found in crowded downtown. The elegant marble architecture in "conservative-modern" style by local architect Alfred V. Du Pont, son of A. I. who owned Nemours, was meant to suggest a country club, with an Ivy Tea Room overlooking the Brandywine River, an aspirational design for upscale Wilmingtonians moving to the suburbs. The idea was to lure out-of-state shoppers as well, a model later taken up by the Christiana Mall, which opened east of Newark (Delaware Route 1 at Interstate 95) in 1978. Its name, borrowed from the nearby village, recalled Queen Christina of Sweden and Delaware's earliest permanent European settlement. It became one of the most successful regional malls in the country, with an appraised value of a billion dollars. New Castle County's convenient location, low property taxes, and lack of sales tax kept Christiana Mall thriving, although the Brandywine Wanamaker's succumbed by the end of the twentieth century to a plethora of new malls and retail outlets in the booming region.

The Wanamaker store had been planned to coincide with the opening of the Delaware Memorial Bridge (1948–51), which finally linked northern Delaware to the New Jersey Turnpike and allowed an influx of commerce, fully linking New Castle County to the surging economy of the larger megalopolis. A plan for the bridge was conceived in earnest during the last months of World War II, as a war memorial, with Francis V. Du Pont a key proponent. This suspension bridge represented an extraordinary engineering achievement, its 2,150-foot span over the busy shipping lanes of the Delaware River claiming for a time the title of sixth-longest bridge ever built.

New highways and automobiles shook old-fashioned Wilmington to the core. The city had long dominated

New Castle County and as recently as 1920, 74 percent of county residents had been Wilmingtonians. But during the 1950s, Wilmington's stature swiftly collapsed as riverfront industries shut down and the population of its suburbs nearly doubled, and it ignominiously fell out of the list of American cities of one hundred thousand for the first time in fifty years. By 1960, only 31 percent of county residents lived in Wilmington, the suburban population of the county having doubled since 1930. Although urban depopulation was a national trend, the DuPont company remained, and as a result, the Wilmington urban area in 1955 ranked the sixth wealthiest in the United States in terms of average family income ($6,900). By 1960, DuPont was one of the largest industrial concerns in the nation. Money was available for a vast rebuilding of downtown, revolving around a key question broached as early as a Wilmington Chamber of Commerce publication in 1926: "'*Where shall we park the car?*'—that is the burning question before the shoppers." Wanamaker's had shown that suburbanites would skip downtown altogether, so long as parking was easy outside of town. As an answer, in the 1960s twenty-two vast blocks downtown were leveled for urban renewal—mostly replaced by parking lots, along with a few governmental buildings, as commercial development seldom materialized. Increasingly, drivers found little to lure them into Wilmington, then palpably in decline, with stores closing and aging Victorian neighborhoods looking decrepit.

As with Philadelphia, Interstate 95 had a powerful and ultimately deleterious effect on urban planning in Wilmington. New Castle County had long been a place that one traveled through to get somewhere else, going back to the Kings Highway of colonial times. Now the greatest of America's north-south interstate highways would run directly through the county, traversing twenty-three miles. Interstate 95 could have bypassed Wilmington through wealthy suburbs to the west, but this was overruled in favor of annihilating several blocks through the residential sections adjoining downtown, starting in 1959.

The damage that Interstate 95 did to Wilmington has been emphasized to the point, perhaps, of overstatement; the centuries-old city might have declined in any case. The highway did contribute to economic growth outside of the town, allowing a rapid commute to Newark in the 1960s and then, in the 1980s, to sprawling new developments in Pike Creek and Hockessin. Thanks in part to that often-maligned interstate, New Castle County thrived in subsequent decades. Delaware became the business-incorporation capital of the world, incorporating more than a million businesses (including two-thirds of the Fortune 500), with thousands of local jobs the result, from bankruptcy lawyers to corporate-service specialists. Powerful New Castle County politicians have long nurtured relationships with corporations. A disproportionate number of governors, congressmen, and senators have lived in this one corner of a small state, including a charismatic senator who became president of the United States, Joseph R. Biden. Like many residents of New Castle County, Biden was born someplace farther north—in Scranton, Pennsylvania, a fading town that his father soon fled, seeking economic opportunity as a used-car salesman in Delaware and buying a house in a new development near Claymont. The 1981 Financial Center Development Act capitalized on Delaware's business-friendly reputation by giving special breaks to the credit card industry. An influx of highly educated outsiders came to the area from New Jersey and elsewhere, tipping the political scales firmly toward the Democratic Party in a state long considered southern-leaning and conservative. Many banks built headquarters in New Castle County, and residents engaged in financial careers at nearly twice the national average. Service-sector jobs supplanted manufacturing. For example, the post–World War II Chrysler automotive plant at Newark and the General Motors plant at Newport were replaced, respectively, by a high-tech "innovation community" associated with the University of Delaware (2010) and a colossal Amazon fulfillment center (2019)—both symbolic of the constantly changing economic and demographic picture in an ever-evolving New Castle County.

EXPLORE MORE

A starting point for examining the role of counties in Pennsylvania is James T. Lemon, *The Best Poor Man's Country: A Geographical Study of Early Southeastern Pennsylvania* (Johns Hopkins University Press, 1972). A dated but still useful source is E. R. L. Gould, "Local Self Government in Pennsylvania," *Pennsylvania Magazine of History and Biography* 6, no. 2 (1882). A number of older histories of individual counties survive, including some that have been made accessible digitally, but for more modern accounts, see Jean Barth Toll and Michael Schwager, eds., *Montgomery County: The Second Hundred Years* (Montgomery County Federation of Historical Societies, 1983) and Jeffery M. Dorwart, *Camden County, New Jersey: The Making of a Modern Metropolis, 1626–2000* (Rutgers University Press, 2001). For an example of a county history linking people and place in a series of vignettes, see Mark E. Dixon, *The Hidden History of Delaware County: Untold Tales from Cobb's Creek to the Brandywine* (History Press, 2010).

The classic book on New Jersey governance is Alan J. Karcher, *New Jersey's Municipal Madness* (Rutgers University Press, 1998). *The Encyclopedia of New Jersey* (Rutgers University Press, 2004), edited by Maxine L. Laurie and Marc Mappen, provides profiles of every New Jersey county. Wendel White's stunning black-and-white photographs and associated commentary about predominantly Black communities in New Jersey are collected in his 2003 book, *Small Towns, Black Lives: African American Communities in Southern New Jersey* (Noyes Museum of Art, 2003).

Every county in the Greater Philadelphia region has its own historical society, some of them in or associated with historic properties. The Burlington Historical Society, for instance, is steward to, among other buildings, the James Fenimore Cooper House at 457 High Street, Burlington, which includes displays of Cooper artifacts, implements, and furnishings, along with objects from the estate of Joseph Bonaparte, Napoleon's brother who settled not far from Burlington after the battle of Waterloo. Such organizations can be helpful in pointing visitors not just to the peoples who settled in the area but also to important historic sites, such as battlefields or individual buildings. Other, more localized societies are also great sources of information about regional ties. Among these are the Lower Merion Historical Society in Bala Cynwyd, Pa., and the Haddonfield Historical Society in New Jersey. The South Jersey Culture & History Center, located at Stockton University, publishes a twice-yearly journal, *SoJourn*, as well as other publications related to the area.

Courthouses have played central roles in the history of the counties, and a number of historic buildings survive as sites for visitation, including the New Castle Court House Museum. Built in 1732, it served as Delaware's first court and state capitol after New Castle, Kent, and Sussex Counties declared their independence from Pennsylvania and England in 1776, creating the state of Delaware. For Pennsylvania, see Oliver P. Williams, *County Courthouses of Pennsylvania: A Guide* (Stackpole Books, 2001).

The Valley Forge National Historical Park represents a major commitment to preserving the history of the American Revolution. Other sites in the region include Red Bank Battlefield Park in Gloucester County, New Jersey, the site of Fort Mercer. Jeffery Dorwart provides a regional assessment of the war and its effect in his 2008 book with the University of Delaware Press, *Invasion and Insurrection: Security, Defense, and War in the Delaware Valley, 1621–1815*. Other forts maintained as historic sites include Fort Mifflin, 6400 Hog Island Road, Philadelphia, and Fort Mott State Park, 454 Fort Mott Road, Pennsville, Salem County, N.J.

To explore the region's rich industrial history, visit the Roebling Museum at 102 Second Avenue, Roebling, which offers exhibits and programs about the Roebling Company's history. In addition to maintaining a number of structures on the site, Historic Batsto Village in the Pinelands area of Burlington County offers museum exhibits on area industry history as well as trails for walking and biking. WheatonArts, encompassing eighteen buildings spread over forty-five acres, celebrates the ongoing tradition of glasswork in South Jersey. Located at 1501 Glasstown Road, Millville, Cumberland County, the complex includes the Museum of American Glass, a folklife center, artist studios, and museum stores. In Pennsylvania, the National Iron & Steel Heritage Museum, 50 South First Street, Coatesville, is devoted to promoting an understanding of the iron and steel history of Coatesville, Chester County, and southeastern Pennsylvania. The Hagley Museum and Library, located at 200 Hagley Creek Road on the banks of the Brandywine River in Wilmington, is a major source of information about business and technology, not just in the region but the nation. By contrast, the Mercer Museum, at 84 South Pine Street, Doylestown, Bucks County, displays some thirty thousand everyday objects largely discarded with the advent of the Industrial Revolution collected and preserved by archaeologist Henry Mercer.

Another important regional story local buildings convey is that of the Underground Railroad, which offered pathways to freedom for those fleeing slavery in the nineteenth century. In New Jersey, the Burlington County Underground Railroad Museum, at 803 Smithfield Road, Eastampton, provides information on area sites extending through the southern part of the state. Among the extant sites is the Mount Zion AME Church at 172 Garwin Road, Woolwich Township, Gloucester County. Dating to 1834, the small structure is still in service to worship. The Greenwich Line extended twenty-five miles north to Mount Holly, Burlington, and Jersey City. The restored Peter Mott House, 26 Kings Court, in the predominantly Black town of Lawnside, Camden County, serves as a museum of the Underground Railroad as well as Lawnside history. In Pennsylvania the Plymouth Friends Meetinghouse, built in 1708, served as a stop on the Underground Railroad in conjunction with Abolition Hall on the opposite side of Germantown Pike, a property spared in 2022 from almost certain demolition. Bucks County maintains a roster of Underground Railroad sites, including the Harriet Tubman statue at 150 Basin Street in Bristol. In Wilmington, the Quaker Hill Historic Preservation Society maintains the records and stories attached to them of the area's active involvement in the Underground Railroad. Another site open to the public is the New Castle County courthouse, 211 Delaware Street, New Castle, Del. Much of what historians know about the Underground Railroad in the region comes from William Still's meticulous records and 1872 book, *The Underground Railroad*, now preserved at the Historical Society of Pennsylvania. His contribution is detailed in Andrew K. Diemer's book, *Vigilance: The Life of William Still, Father of the Underground Railroad* (Knopf, 2022).

To further pursue county diversity over time, visit the Seabrook Educational and Cultural Center, 1325 Highway 77, Seabrook, N.J. It recounts the stories of relocated Japanese Americans and Japanese Peruvians from United States incarceration camps; wartime refugees from Europe; and migrant laborers from Appalachia, the Deep South, and the Caribbean. Rutgers University hosts an online exhibit of the history of Jewish farming in the Garden State. Gertrude Dubrovsky recounts that history in her book *The Land Was Theirs: Jewish Farmers in the Garden State* (University of Alabama Press, 1992).

At the other end of the social spectrum, visitors can garner a sense of high living outside the city through the history of a number of grand estates, some of which have become house museums. Not the least is Andalusia, initially a summer retreat and eventually the Biddle family ancestral home, at 1237 State Road, Bensalem, in Bucks County. Dating to 1795, the property expanded quickly under the direction of America's most prominent architects, first Benjamin Latrobe, then Thomas U. Walter. Other estates have attracted considerable attention over the years, notably Ardrossan, 807 Newtown Road, Villanova, Montgomery County, completed in 1913, a thirty-three-thousand-square-foot baronial brick Georgian Revival structure designed by Horace Trumbauer. The property is most closely identified with Hope Scott, the daughter of the first owner, who served as the inspiration for two great films about the area, *The Philadelphia Story* (1940) and *High Society* (1956). David Nelson Wren provides a thorough account of the property and its inhabitants in *Ardrossan: The Last Great Estate on the Philadelphia Main Line* (Bauer and Dean, 2017). Point Breeze, the home of the exiled Joseph Bonaparte near Bordentown, N.J., no longer stands, but its rich history is recounted by Patricia Tyson Stroud in two books: *The Emperor of Nature: Charles-Lucien Bonaparte and His World* (University of Pennsylvania Press, 2000) and *The Man Who Had Been King: The American Exile of Napoleon's Brother Joseph* (University of Pennsylvania Press, 2005).

Chapter 9

Regional Governance and Stewardship

Introduction

OUTSIDE OF A HANDFUL OF URBAN centers like Philadelphia, Camden, Wilmington, and Norristown, the region has retained the pattern of hundreds of small-town governments established by the proprietor William Penn as his way of encouraging citizens to participate in the democratic process. That pattern of mostly small governments has persisted into the twenty-first century, posing a challenge to civic and political leaders trying to address large-scale shared problems. Adding to the sheer number of municipalities is the constant pressure facing small-town officials to raise enough revenue from their local tax base to pay for schools and municipal services. That fiscal pressure sometimes drives neighboring communities to compete with each other to attract commercial development that can enhance their local tax base.

An important source of friction putting Philadelphia at odds with its suburbs has been the wage tax that Philadelphia imposes on its own residents and also on suburbanites who work inside the city limits of Philadelphia. That tax dates back to 1932, when Pennsylvania's legislature passed the Sterling Act granting Philadelphia the right to impose a tax on employees of Philadelphia firms, regardless of where in the region those workers lived. In 1939, when the city started exercising that newly acquired right, the so-called commuter tax rankled suburban officials and residents who resented paying taxes to both their home community and their place of work.

Despite this fragmented pattern of government, local leaders at times succeeded in forging connections across the region, the most important example being the 1854 consolidation of many small localities into a dramatically expanded city of Philadelphia. Later politicians, however, never attempted further annexations on that scale. One reason was that the region spread across multiple states governed by separate constitutions and legislatures. A further obstacle to municipal consolidation was the stringent requirement under Pennsylvania law that a majority of voters in both the affected suburbs and the city would have to vote in favor of consolidating—a highly improbable outcome, given the strong attachment that many suburban residents display for their small towns and their fears about having to assume the costs and problems of the big city.

Within this fragmented picture, the region always had its share of "connecters"—individuals and groups of citizens determined to forge alliances and address shared challenges. As the essays in this section illustrate, regional connecters typically operated outside of traditional government boundaries. Nineteenth-century abolitionists created clandestine networks to help escaping slaves move safely through the region. Commercial investors built transportation and communication companies. Other social entrepreneurs established nonprofit organizations or quasi-public authorities for the purpose of building and operating facilities that serve the broad public. Still others were volunteers who stepped forward to preserve historical and natural assets for future generations to enjoy.

As far back as social historians have been able to trace, the region benefited from the efforts of individual entrepreneurs and networks of volunteers to connect, coordinate, and sometimes mediate among the interests of different parts of the region. Among the earliest successes were communication networks built by Lenni Lenape inhabitants whose settlements ranged broadly across the territory nourished by the Delaware, Hudson, and Susquehanna Rivers. Indigenous communities within those vast networks dealt with Europeans through trusted individuals who acted as go-betweens to carry messages and interpret cultural differences. European settlers found it useful to meet periodically with Lenni Lenape leaders to exchange gifts, share food, and, through translators, negotiate land and water rights as well as trade agreements. In effect, such treaty councils represented early efforts at regional coordination.

In the absence of strong governmental institutions, European colonists recognized that building regional connections afforded profit-making opportunities. Although roads connecting colonial towns to one another were often built by community residents, waggoners had few clear routes all the way into Philadelphia or to other regional centers. So private entrepreneurs stepped in to construct and maintain turnpikes for which they charged waggoners a toll. That pattern persisted into the nineteenth and early twentieth centuries, as railroads, followed by streetcar companies, built networks connecting disparate parts of the region, sometimes directly linking transportation routes to real estate development financed by the same investors who held stock in the transit companies. As private entrepreneurs shaped development patterns throughout the region from the nineteenth century onward, their plans were not always well coordinated, and sometimes they deliberately competed against each other.

In 1909, a group of reform-minded businessmen established Philadelphia's Bureau of Municipal Research to provide the citizenry with nonpartisan, well-researched information about public issues, with a specific focus on best practices for managing public services and infrastructure. That was the forerunner of the Economy League, whose leaders took an active role in the Philadelphia charter reform movement of the 1950s. In the 1960s the Economy League backed the consolidation of the region's rail lines into a single, centrally managed service. But by the early twenty-first century the organization was shifting a large part of its research and advocacy to human capital, with initiatives to bolster education from preschool to college in order to create the strong regional workforce considered crucial to prosperity in the information economy.

Governmental leaders spurred efforts to build and manage major infrastructure serving multiple jurisdictions, like rail systems, bridges, and ports. Interestingly, legislative bodies often created quasi-governmental authorities to pursue such projects, preferring to shift responsibility out of the hands of politicians who might be tempted to exploit large contracts and revenues to advance their own careers. In addition, creating independent entities to build and manage major infrastructure projects made it easier to borrow the sums needed for construction. Unlike cash-strapped local governments, these separate operating authorities could confidently promise lenders that the tolls collected from motorists would provide a constant stream of revenue to pay back the loans.

To harmonize the investments going into public infrastructure, twentieth-century reformers adopted new models of intercounty and even interstate regional cooperation. As early as 1919, the New Jersey and Pennsylvania legislatures collaborated to establish the Delaware River Joint Toll Bridge Commission chaired by Pennsylvania governor William C. Sproul, which in turn formed the Delaware River Port Authority (DRPA). By 1926 that authority had opened the Delaware River Bridge (later known as the Benjamin Franklin Bridge). In 1951 President Harry Truman recognized the Delaware River Port Authority as a formal interstate compact to operate bridges and transit lines crossing the river between Philadelphia and Camden. DRPA earned a constant revenue stream by collecting bridge tolls and transit fares. The assurance of those constant revenues allowed DRPA to borrow funds from private lenders to maintain what eventually grew to encompass four bridges along with a high-speed rail line. The interstate authority subsequently built the Walt Whitman Bridge (1955), the Commodore Barry Bridge (1974), and the Betsy Ross Bridge (1976), as well as the PATCO

Speedline (1969)—a mass transit rail line connecting Philadelphia with Camden.

An early attempt at regional planning in the Delaware Valley was that of the "Regional Planning Federation of the Philadelphia Tri-State District" formed in 1928, which issued the first regional plan in 1932. The agency was the forerunner of what would eventually become the Delaware Valley Regional Planning Commission (DVRPC), the metropolitan planning organization for the Delaware Valley created in 1965 by an interstate compact. DVRPC assumed responsibility for transportation and regional planning in the Greater Philadelphia area.

In another regional initiative, in 1961 Philadelphia leaders joined with the leaders in three suburban counties to form the Southeastern Pennsylvania Transportation Compact (SEPACT). Delaware County initially declined to join that compact because its largest provider of transportation was a private company that did not desire subsidies. But only two years later in 1963 the Pennsylvania legislature created SEPTA (Southeastern Pennsylvania Transportation Authority), led by a SEPTA board enlarged to include representatives from Delaware County.

While twentieth-century civic and political leaders established new quasi-governmental institutions to manage shared infrastructure like bridges, ports, and transit services, other activists built nonprofit organizations to counteract the negative side effects of growth, including threats to the region's shared environmental resources. In 1953, a Philadelphia bird-watcher named Allston Jenkins discovered that Gulf Oil Company intended to dredge the Schuylkill River and dump the spoils into the Tinicum Marsh near the Philadelphia International Airport. He recruited other birders and environmentalists to form the Philadelphia Conservationists (which eventually became Natural Lands, a nonprofit land conservation organization). Jenkins's group of citizen activists successfully fought the destruction of Tinicum Marsh, and in 1955 the Gulf Oil Corporation donated 145 acres that became the John Heinz National Wildlife Refuge at Tinicum.

Subsequently, additional voluntary citizen organizations sprang up across the region to serve as stewards for creeks and streams threatened by ever-increasing development. They worked across formal boundary lines between towns and counties, as did citizen efforts to preserve threatened elements of the historic built environment. For example, the nonprofit Preservation Alliance for Greater Philadelphia was established to inform real estate developers, community organizations, and individuals throughout the region about the value of preserving historic structures and to protect historically important properties from demolition.

As stewards of some of the area's most important shared assets, the civic activists who built these nongovernmental organizations worked to knit together the hundreds of separate communities comprising the Greater Philadelphia region.

Treaty Negotiations with Native Americans

Stephanie Gamble

From the arrival of Europeans in the seventeenth century through the era of the early republic, treaties were an important tool in diplomacy between Native nations and colonial Pennsylvania and later the nascent federal government. Treaties followed Indigenous modes of diplomacy, into which colonists introduced, and imposed, the signing of treaty documents. However, treaty councils did not always culminate in a signed document. Indeed, throughout the colonial period the term "treaty" described the process of negotiation and diplomacy, regardless of what such meetings produced.

Most famous in Pennsylvania was the legendary treaty of Shackamaxon negotiated by William Penn and Tamanend, which produced no written record. In the colonial period, treaty councils took place in Philadelphia as well as Native and colonial towns within and beyond the growing colony like Shamokin, Conestoga, and Lancaster. Treaties that secured large swaths of land for Pennsylvania at times occurred outside the colony, as with the Albany Purchase of 1754 and the New Purchase (1768) and Last Purchase (1784), both of which occurred at Fort Stanwix in New York. In 1758, at Crosswicks, Lenapes ceded rights to most of their lands in New Jersey to that colony's government.

Councils were formal affairs steeped in Native diplomacy, particularly Iroquoian ceremonies. As

FIGURE 82. *Penn's Treaty with the Indians*, by Benjamin West, 1771–72, depicting the traditional story of William Penn's peaceful treaty with the Lenape. PENNSYLVANIA ACADEMY OF THE FINE ARTS.

negotiators came together, they participated in the Wood's Edge Ceremony, which acknowledged and ritually cleansed the arriving party of the perils of their journey and opened the lines of communication.

Over the ensuing days, or often weeks, Pennsylvania officials and Native leaders exchanged speeches, gifts, and strings of wampum. While chiefs and colonial officials were key players, more often than not it was skilled orators who conducted negotiations, aided by interpreters. Metaphorical language, compelling voice and gestures, and command of an audience were all key to being a skilled Native orator. Interpreters and intermediaries, or go-betweens, who relied on their trustworthiness, excelled when they could translate not only the languages but also the cultural nuances that inflected negotiations. Colonial scribes recorded speeches from the interpreters and created minutes for treaty councils that offer historians a glimpse of the process and rhetoric of negotiation.

In the early decades of colonial settlement, treaties were often small local gatherings consisting of a few dozen participants. As the eighteenth century progressed, councils grew in size so that several hundred attendees would swarm the treaty grounds. At the Treaty of Fort Stanwix in 1768, commissioner Sir William Johnson recorded 2,200 Native participants as the council opened. The vast concourse of spectators at treaties was important to the process itself, for Native diplomacy relied on a notion of consensus. Indigenous onlookers became participants as they signaled their assent or discontent at the speeches that made up formal negotiations. The struggle for consensus also played out away from the formal and public arena as Native leaders, officials, and intermediaries deliberated and worked out their differences in private. The search for common ground could protract the process, and treaty councils sometimes lasted for weeks.

While diplomats and intermediaries worked toward agreement on the issues at hand—land and boundaries were common concerns, but trade and, most importantly, war and peace spurred negotiations—colonial and Native spectators busied themselves as well. Councils attracted traders of victuals, cloth, tools, munitions, and accessories. There were times for feasting, singing, dancing, and playing games.

By all accounts, Native diplomats seemed impressed with their interactions with the Quakers, likely attributable to the Friends' professions of peace and fraternal harmony in a period when Indian-colonist violence was foremost in the minds of Native ambassadors. Quaker authority declined in the province during the eighteenth century, however, as did their formal role in Indian-colonist negotiations. Indeed, following the Paxton Boys' war to drive all Indians from the Susquehanna region, the belief that Quakers elevated Native interests above those of backcountry colonists helped oust the "Quaker party" from the colonial assembly. Nevertheless, treaties of colonial officials with local Indian nations and Iroquoian nations dominated the colonial period, even as relations between Natives and the Pennsylvania government deteriorated—at times due to treaties themselves. Pennsylvanians' crafty dealings in the 1737 Walking Purchase displaced and alienated their Lenape neighbors.

By the time the federal government ensconced itself at Philadelphia in the waning days of 1790, treaty negotiations in the city became more diverse and less conclusive. From their new seat, President George Washington and Secretary of War Henry Knox were deeply concerned with Indian relations in Iroquoia, the Ohio country, and the Southeast, rather than in Pennsylvania, where relatively few Native people remained. Indeed, delegations to Philadelphia in the early 1790s primarily concerned the developing war in the West, where confederated nations of the Ohio country defeated the American army in 1790 and again in 1791.

During the capital's tenure in Philadelphia, two dozen delegations arrived in the city to negotiate and fortify their ties to the federal government. While only the Cherokees signed a treaty in Philadelphia in these years, negotiations at the capital preceded or followed treaties elsewhere in the country. Visiting diplomats hailed from many nations, including Creeks, Choctaws, Chickasaws, and Cherokees from the south; Wyandots, Delawares (newly residing in the Ohio country), Ottawas, Chippewas, Potawatomies, Eel River, Weas, Kickapoos, Piankashaws, Kaskaskias, Miamis, and Shawnees from the west; and Mohawks, Senecas, Oneidas, and Onondagas from the north.

As in earlier treaty councils, formal speeches, or talks, formed the core of negotiation between delegates and the federal government. The Seneca Red Jacket was among the most famous orators (Native or white) in the early republic, and his speeches from treaty councils were recorded and published in newspapers around the country. However, negotiations in the capital were much smaller than those from earlier decades. The largest visit in the 1790s consisted of forty-nine Iroquois who attended Philadelphia in 1792, though no treaty was signed at the conclusion of negotiations. However, the average delegation numbered fewer than a dozen. Deliberations with the president and secretary of war were protracted, with days sometimes intervening between the exchanges of talks, prolonging negotiations, as in the past, over weeks and sometimes months.

During that time, Native negotiators toured many cultural and civic sites, such as theaters, museums, churches, and the new waterworks. Several of the iconic prints of William Birch captured Native visitors moving about the city. As they negotiated the urban landscape, diplomats engaged with Philadelphians informally in streets and taverns and in more formal meetings with members of the Quaker Indian Committee and local and foreign dignitaries. Through these meetings, long-standing relationships were solidified and new ones forged between the Friends and distant nations like the Creeks and Cherokees.

Gifts and hospitality remained crucial to the treaty negotiations, as reflected in President Washington's 1792 address to Iroquois diplomats "that during your residence here you should be well fed, well lodged and well cloathed, and that presents should be furnished."

Gifts varied but almost always included clothing and other textiles, and guns and ammunition were common. Cast in large lots at the mint in Philadelphia, medals were a ubiquitous gift to Indigenous diplomats. Rank determined the size of medals that the diplomats received, as the most prominent leaders received the largest medallions.

With the transfer of the federal capital to Washington in 1800, Philadelphia's role in treaty negotiations diminished. Nevertheless, Native people continued to come through the city on their way to and from Washington, often to exchange talks with Quaker allies and to take in the sights of one of the nation's most vibrant cities.

Native and Colonial Go-Betweens

Stephen T. Staggs

During the colonial period, the diversity of the region that became southeastern Pennsylvania, southern New Jersey, and northern Delaware made trade and diplomacy difficult. The many cultural, especially linguistic, barriers between various Native American and European groups required go-betweens, or intermediaries. The intermediaries who were called upon to interpret across cultures and help maintain the fragile peace were as diverse as the region from which they came. They included, among others, a Swedish fur trader, an English-speaking Susquehannock, an Unami-speaking Quaker, an Onyota'a:ka (Oneida) living in a multiethnic town, a German farmer, a French-Onyota'a:ka-Algonkin guide, and a Prussian Moravian missionary.

Trying to maintain peace from the early seventeenth century to 1763 was demanding work. Intermediaries spent much time on the road carrying letters and wampum belts across treacherous terrain. Once they reached their destination, they translated the letters and belts as well as swapped and gathered information. At the great councils, which followed Native American customs, intermediaries translated the speeches given by Indigenous and colonial leaders. Following Indigenous protocols enabled Native American leaders to select go-betweens based on kinship connections and their standing within the community, while colonial leaders identified individuals with an intimate knowledge of a particular Indigenous culture and language, which were extremely difficult to learn.

The earliest colonial intermediaries in the region were Dutch fur traders. Two of the first were Simon Root, who lived in a home at Wigquakoing (now Wicacoa in South Philadelphia), and Jan Andriessen, who lived near Fort Casimir (present-day New Castle, Delaware). On July 13, 1647, for example, Root and Andriessen, who claimed to understand the Susquehannock language, testified to New Netherland director-general Petrus Stuyvesant that Aquariochquo and Quadickho, two Susquehannock leaders, wanted to continue mutual trade with the Dutch even though New Sweden governor Johan Printz had asked for permission to set up a trading post among them. Printz claimed that he, not the impoverished Dutch, could sell them plenty of powder, lead, and guns.

Root and Andriessen were soon joined by a number of other Dutch and Swedish intermediaries, including Jacob Svensson who acted as a go-between for the Swedes and Dutch with the Susquehannocks and Lunaapeew (Lenapes). However, the most important intermediary in the second half of the seventeenth century was one of Root's neighbors, the Swedish fur trader Lars Petersson Cock. Prior to the arrival in 1682 of the new proprietor of Pennsylvania, William Penn, Cock arranged, in his own home, land sales between Lunaapeew leaders and the proprietor's representatives.

When Cock died in 1699, finding a replacement proved to be quite difficult. Although Pennsylvania officials employed a number of Native American go-betweens, including a Conoy named Ouseywayteichks who reportedly knew four Indigenous languages, and the English-speaking Susquehannock Shawydoohungh, provincial officials were loath to rely solely on Indians no matter how effective they might be. Thus, officials also turned to French fur traders such as the Huguenot Jacques Le Tort and his son James Le Tort, who married a Shawnee woman; the brothers Pierre Bizaillon and Michel Bizaillon; and Martin Chartier, who married a Shawnee woman named Sewatha Straight Tail. Provincial leaders also relied on the Quaker fur traders John Cartlidge and Edmond Cartlidge who spoke Unami, the language of the Lunaapeew groups who occupied the southern part of Lenapehoking, which included present-day southern New Jersey and a small portion of eastern Pennsylvania and northeastern Delaware. By 1722 Native American and colonial leaders had plenty of intermediaries to call on when trade and land crises arose.

In 1728 rumors of war swept across the region. The Lunaapeew proposed war against the European settlers while Susquehannocks threatened war against the Shawnees. Meanwhile, a skirmish between eleven Shawnees and twenty colonists in the Tool-pay hanna (Schuylkill River) valley led to the murder of three Lunaapeew. Governor Patrick Gordon immediately dispatched several fur traders, including James Le Tort, to gather information about the circulating rumors, offer condolences to the Delawares, and reprimand the Shawnees. The go-betweens were also instructed to remind as many Indians as possible of William Penn's friendship. To renew that friendship, intermediaries brought the parties together at a series of treaty councils in 1728, in May at Conestoga, in June at the Quaker meetinghouse in Philadelphia, and in October at the Philadelphia courthouse. As a result, a frontier war was averted.

Following the councils of 1728, a new group of intermediaries emerged. The most prominent of these men were Shickellamy, an Onyota'a:ka leader living in the multiethnic town of Shamokin (present-day Sunbury and Shamokin Dam), and the German farmer Conrad Weiser of Tulpehocken. They helped orchestrate a series of major treaties between the leaders of the Haudenosaunee (Iroquois) and the province of Pennsylvania in 1732, 1736, and 1742, which promoted trade and asserted control over the peoples living between Onondaga and Philadelphia. The population increased steadily between the two capitals, however, leading to more frequent disputes between Native Americans and their colonial neighbors.

Competing claims to the lands of the Ohio country led to the outbreak of the Seven Years' War (1756–63) between the English and French and their various Native American allies. After the French defeated a British expedition sent to capture Fort Duquesne on July 9, 1755, a group of Delawares began raiding provincial settlements from the Juniata River to Shamokin. Following the raid on the settlement at Penns Creek (October 16, 1755), the intermediaries hit the road once

FIGURE 83. In 1764 intermediaries of the Shawnee, Delaware, and Ohio tribes met in Ohio to negotiate with British Colonel Henry Bouquet for the return of captives taken by Native Americans on the Pennsylvania border. Engraving, Benjamin West, 1776. LIBRARY OF CONGRESS.

again. Scarouyady, an Onyota'a:ka leader, and Andrew Montour, a French-Onyota'a:ka-Algonkin guide, headed for Onondaga. In 1756 Kos Showweyha, an Onöndowa'ga (Seneca); Sata Karoyiз, a Kanien'kehá:ka (Mohawk); and William Lacquis, a Jersey Delaware, trod the paths multiple times between Philadelphia and the Delaware villages on the North Branch of the Susquehanna. Then, in 1758, the English-speaking Delaware Pisquetomen and the Moravian missionary Christian Frederick Post set out for the Allegheny Valley with the offer of Governor William Denny to renew the peace with the Ohio Indians provided they remained neutral. Remarkably, in the midst of the Seven Years' War, this new group of intermediaries was able to ensure the loyalty of the Haudenosaunee, appease the Delawares, and neutralize the Ohio Indians.

Hearts, however, were hardening. Many Native Americans had become disillusioned with the colonists' apparent intent on achieving their end of acquiring land at any cost, which included the use by colonial intermediaries of presents, bribes, liquor, fake maps, and vague treaty statements. On the other hand, the majority of colonists, incensed by Indian attacks, believed the time for Indian councils had passed. Although intermediaries such as the Irish fur trader turned deputy Indian agent, George Croghan, continued to negotiate treaties, the government of Pennsylvania called upon them less and less frequently.

Over the course of the seventeenth and much of the eighteenth century, Indigenous and European go-betweens had often interpreted the kaleidoscope of cultures that existed in the region that became southeastern Pennsylvania, southern New Jersey, and northern Delaware. For many years they helped maintain a tenuous peace, but, with questionable methods such as fake maps and vague treaty statements, some intermediaries collaborated with the government of Pennsylvania and land speculators. This triggered resentment among many Native Americans, which played a role in the outbreak of violence and the Seven Years' War.

Philadelphia Maritime Exchange

Terry L. Potter

In 1875, a group of influential maritime and business leaders, who recognized the importance of the port of Philadelphia's standing with respect to other North American ports, formed the Philadelphia Maritime Exchange. The goal of the exchange was to position Philadelphia as a premier port in North America by increasing the city's direct trade with foreign countries and ensuring that the Delaware River ports would offer quick turnaround and better ship handling. From these beginnings, the exchange played an active role in the port's growth and served the Delaware River maritime community into the twenty-first century.

By the time of the exchange's founding, the port of Philadelphia had long been a key aspect of the region's economic life. By 1750 Philadelphia had surpassed Boston as the largest city and busiest port in North America and held that position until it was eclipsed by New York in 1825. During the post–Civil War era, as Philadelphia became an industrial giant and a key hub for commercial trade, demands on the port reached new levels with the rise of iron, steel, coal, and oil production, along with the increasing use of the railroad to transport these materials. To improve efficiency, the exchange built reporting stations along the Delaware to track ship arrivals. The observation stations reported to a central point in the city and from there the information was distributed to any party concerned with the ship while it was in port.

The exchange took an increasingly active role in proposing and instituting rules and regulations governing local shipping after April 29, 1882, when the Commonwealth of Pennsylvania granted it a perpetual charter to "acquire, preserve, and disseminate all maritime and other business information, and do such other and lawful acts as will tend to promote and encourage trade and commerce of the Port of Philadelphia." In 1887, the exchange issued its first eighteen Maritime Rules, covering points on which disputes tended to arise, such as ways of determining the readiness of ships or methods for handling hazardous cargo. These and other regulatory actions became the model for many U.S. ports as well as the foundation of international shipping governance.

At the time the exchange was formed, the port of Philadelphia consistently handled three principal commodities: grain, sugar, and petroleum. The exchange formulated and approved standard practice for the carriage of these goods and became one of the first to adopt forms of charters for specific commodities or trades. These charters defined issues such as the loading, unloading, and discharge of vessels; how many days a ship was allowed in port (lay days) and the port charges resulting from overstay (demurrage); and rules regulating the delivery and receipt of special cargoes. In most ports these were matters decided by boards of trade, chambers of commerce, merchants, or combinations of the respective groups. In Philadelphia the advent of the Maritime Exchange streamlined the process.

To assure that the port of Philadelphia would remain competitive, the exchange also played a role in the development of the Delaware River, the Schuylkill River, and the harbor. Over time, advances in ship design, construction, and operation created the need for the port to accommodate deeper drafts and longer ships. From 1885 through 1938 the exchange promoted actions such as the removal of Smith's and Windmill Islands from the Delaware River between Philadelphia and Camden and projects to widen and deepen the channel. Similarly, the exchange maintained and improved the Schuylkill River, the main tributary to the Delaware River and a key channel for moving commodities from the interior of the country to the port.

The interests and actions of the Philadelphia Maritime Exchange always reached beyond the water to related issues such as the railroad transportation of commodities, quarantine of goods and immigrants on land, immigration, outbreaks of yellow fever, and civic affairs. The exchange actively promoted technological advancements such as electricity and telephones that required cables across the river and it became a key advocate for establishing bridges across the Delaware River in response to population growth in New Jersey and Pennsylvania. Over the years, it supported humanitarian aid to foreign countries, endorsed state legislation such as the 1937 Clean Streams Law to assure water quality, and opposed the sale or charter of government-owned vessels to foreign countries.

By the late 1980s, the exchange became the primary advocate for all segments of the tristate port industry after a sister organization, the Joint Executive Committee for the Improvement of the Harbor of Philadelphia and the Delaware and Schuylkill Rivers, closed its doors. In keeping with its broadened geographic scope, the activities of the exchange expanded to more extensive connections to legislators, regulators, policymakers, and other industry members concerned with international transportation matters including trade and quota issues, maritime security, automation, safety, environment, and dredging.

The increase in scope of the exchange led to a name change in the 1990s to the Maritime Exchange for the Delaware River and Bay. The exchange's mission, however, remained focused on promoting and encouraging commerce and international trade while working closely with public port organizations on issues with impact on the port and related businesses. Maintained by membership dues collected from merchants, importers, shipowners, tug and lighter operators, suppliers, and others connected with the maritime trade of the lower Delaware River, by 2016 the exchange had a membership of more than 275 and remained the voice of safe, efficient, and cost-effective commerce on the Delaware River and Bay.

Fairmount Park Commission

Elizabeth Milroy

The Fairmount Park Commission (FPC), constituted by the Pennsylvania state legislature in the Park Acts of 1867 and 1868, administered the city's public park system from 1867 to 2010. Consisting of six municipal officials or their delegates and ten private citizens appointed by the courts to five-year terms, the FPC had authority to expropriate land throughout the city for recreational use and to protect the municipal watersheds. The commission was semiautonomous, with its own territories, budget, and (until 1972) police force. The commissioners hired park staff, wrote and enforced regulations, and supervised park improvements and maintenance, including the opening of roads, trails, and streetcar lines and the licensing of public transit through park areas.

Appointing commissions to implement public works projects was a longstanding practice in England that William Penn and his associates brought to the colony of Pennsylvania by the beginning of the eighteenth century. Other commissions created in Philadelphia opened streets, managed markets and wharves, ran the gasworks, and supervised the construction of city hall. Over the course of its existence, the FPC developed a citywide system of parks and recreation sites, including a network of parks along sections of the Schuylkill and Delaware River watersheds. It also built major roads and parkways, including the Benjamin Franklin Parkway, Roosevelt Boulevard, and Cobbs Creek Parkway, and took an active role in administering historic sites and cultural institutions such as the Philadelphia Museum of Art, the Philadelphia Zoo, and the Fairmount Water Works. At the time of its disestablishment in 2010, the FPC managed more than sixty-three parks covering 10 percent of Philadelphia's area or roughly ten thousand acres.

As a result of the FPC's considerable, albeit ostensibly nonpartisan, authority, appointment to the commission

FIGURE 84. Frank H. Caven and E. T. Stotesbury, members of the Fairmount Park Commission, with Captain Joseph A. Koch, of the Park Guards, inspected the guards at Twentieth Street and the Parkway, June 1936. SPECIAL COLLECTIONS RESEARCH CENTER, TEMPLE UNIVERSITY LIBRARIES.

was highly desirable. Although officially appointed to five-year terms, many of the commissioners served for life. Influential civic and business leaders who served on the FPC included publisher Morton McMichael, military commander George Gordon Meade, attorney John G. Johnson, investment banker Edward Stotesbury, radio personality Mary Mason, and attorney Robert N. C. Nix III. Multiple generations of the Price and Widener families served on the FPC, including Eli Kirk Price, a founding commissioner, and his grandson Eli Kirk Price, Jr. Industrialist P. A. B. Widener served on the commission from 1889 to his death; his great-grandson Fitz Eugene Dixon was president of the commission from 1983 to 2002.

The FPC's financial history is complex. It had executive power but no authority to collect taxes. Most revenue from park operations went to the city's general fund. On the one hand, the FPC was able to obtain loans as well as gifts of land to pursue an expansionist strategy of park development, adding hundreds of acres to create the citywide system by the mid-twentieth century in an effort to realize William Penn's vision of a "greene Country Towne" and to protect watersheds. On the other hand, unlike many American cities where a percentage of tax income is earmarked for park development and maintenance, the FPC had to request maintenance appropriations annually from city administrations that typically resisted providing more funds to improve or upgrade park landscapes and facilities. In contrast to park administrations in other American cities that operated more transparently as municipal departments, the FPC's operations became increasingly opaque. Between 1876 and 1899, for example, the FPC issued only one annual report.

Growing concerns among city and state legislators about the FPC's finances led to a 1937 legislative report that recommended the FPC be abolished. Investigators noted that none of the commissioners was trained in parks management and that important decisions often were made without a quorum because many commissioners failed to attend meetings. As a result, the FPC frequently overpaid for unnecessary land purchases and made questionable policy decisions. The report also criticized the FPC for focusing too much on land acquisition and for failing to establish recreational facilities on a par with other American cities. In response, the FPC created a committee on recreation and began to add more recreational facilities, though the outbreak of World War II delayed these upgrades. This effort also created some conflict with the city's Bureau of Recreation, which managed historic properties and small parks as well as playgrounds and recreation centers.

The FPC affirmed its resilience when it emerged without change under the new Home Rule Charter enacted in 1951. Although nominally assigned to the reorganized Department of Recreation, the commission continued to operate independently, though its effectiveness had started to weaken. Among notable setbacks was the FPC's failure to prevent construction of the Schuylkill Expressway through West Fairmount Park. Railroads already traversed many sections of the city's parklands, and an alternate route farther to the west would have been more expansive and politically difficult because it entailed demolishing residential properties. However, there were some notable successes. During the 1960s, the FPC effectively defeated attempts to build an industrial facility in Fernhill Park and a plan to convert East River (now Kelly) Drive to a limited-access highway. In the 1970s, the FPC secured the cancellation of the Pulaski Expressway (Pennsylvania Route 90) project that threatened the Tacony and Pennypack Creek watersheds. During the 1980s, it commissioned comprehensive master plans for the conservation of natural features of the park system, funded by a grant from the William Penn Foundation.

Further efforts by such commissioners as John B. Kelly and Fredric R. Mann to improve maintenance and recreational programming and Ernesta Drinker Ballard, who championed natural lands conservation and historic preservation, extended the commission's legacy. Throughout the FPC's existence, most commissioners endeavored to fulfill the founding mandate to provide adequate green space and to protect Philadelphia's water supply. But because the criteria for appointment to the FPC and the actual workings of the commission were unclear, many residents assumed that the city's parks were adequately managed by well-intentioned stewards who nonetheless were unaccountable to voters. As the city's tax base diminished with the decline of industry, park appropriations dwindled.

The diminishing effectiveness of the commission was most clearly demonstrated in 2007 when city council attempted to grant the Fox Chase Cancer Center a long-term lease on a section of Burholme Park in Northeast Philadelphia donated to the city in 1896 by Robert Ryerss. The majority of commissioners supported the lease because it promised much-needed funding, but this was later nullified when the courts determined that any lease of parkland to a private, commercial entity for nonrecreational use abrogated the public trust doctrine. The Commonwealth Court of Pennsylvania upheld this decision, reiterating that the municipal government has a duty to hold the property "in trust for its originally intended use as parkland." The decision cost the FPC what remained of its credibility, and in a 2008 referendum Philadelphians voted to disestablish the commission and therefore to amend the Home Rule Charter. In the commission's place, city parks fell under the administration of Philadelphia Parks & Recreation (PPR), led by a commissioner appointed by the mayor, charged with working with an advisory Parks and Recreation Commission appointed by city council to draft and implement policies and standards governing the use of Philadelphia's parks and recreational facilities.

Delaware River Port Authority

Peter Hendee Brown

The Delaware River Port Authority (DRPA) was created over one hundred years ago as a bistate commission for the purpose of building a single toll bridge. By the 1930s regional leaders had begun to envision a larger maritime role for their new agency, but efforts to broaden its powers to include port operations were repeatedly thwarted. The DRPA continued to grow into a major regional transportation agency, making major investments in infrastructure and gaining significant expertise in bridge and commuter rail operations. A 1992 compact amendment gave the DRPA two important new mandates—port unification and economic development—but despite the best intentions of policymakers, the implementation of both mandates proved to be difficult. The agency plunged confidently into economic development with mixed and sometimes controversial results, while the goal of a unified port proved to be a reach too far.

Regional leaders in the Delaware Valley began discussing the idea of building a bridge that would span the Delaware River and connect Philadelphia and Camden as far back as the early 1800s. Their vision took nearly a century to realize, but finally, in 1912 and 1917, the New Jersey and Pennsylvania legislatures created a pair of commissions for the purpose of jointly building, operating, and owning a single toll bridge. Construction on what would briefly become the world's longest suspension bridge started in 1922, and in 1926 the Delaware River Bridge—renamed the Benjamin Franklin Bridge in 1956—was opened to traffic.

The 1931 creation of the Delaware River Joint Commission formalized the agreement between the two states while expanding the scope of operations of their new agency. The commission would now be responsible for planning and providing future bridges and passenger rail service across the river and for promoting passenger and freight commerce on the Delaware River, as "a highway of commerce between Philadelphia and Camden and the sea." With this last duty, legislators intended to give their new bistate agency the responsibility for unifying the region's fragmented system of ports.

Five times between 1931 and 1952 legislators amended the commission's enabling act in efforts to expand its duties to include port operations. The draft legislation for each amendment granted the commission the power to acquire, build, own, and operate maritime cargo facilities, but every time powerful private interests successfully lobbied to curtail these powers and weaken the final legislation. In 1935 the United States government, through an act of Congress, recognized the agreement between the states as a federal "compact," and the 1952 compact amendment optimistically rechristened the organization the "Delaware River Port Authority." As with previous amendments, however, the power to acquire port facilities was stripped from the final legislation.

Following the 1952 compact amendment, planning for bridges and commuter rail continued, and in 1955 the Walt Whitman Bridge opened to the south of the Ben Franklin Bridge. The Port Authority Transit Corporation or "PATCO Speedline" trains began to operate in 1969, providing a commuter rail line running from the southern New Jersey suburbs across the Benjamin Franklin Bridge and into Center City Philadelphia. The Commodore Barry Bridge opened in 1974, south of the Walt Whitman Bridge, and a final bridge, the Betsy Ross, opened in 1976, to the north of the Benjamin Franklin Bridge.

In 1992, the compact was amended one more time, finally making port unification a true mandate of the DRPA by granting it the power to acquire the two state-chartered port agencies on the Delaware River—the Philadelphia Regional Port Authority and the South Jersey Port Corporation. But over the next several years, entrenched interests at the two public port authorities succeeded in blocking the DRPA's acquisition plans, and by 1998 port reunification was dead. The 1992 amendment, however, also granted the DRPA the power to engage in "economic development," broadly defined. After the failure of port reunification, this power—which was added as an afterthought—became central to the DRPA's mission.

By 2013, nearly a century after its creation, the DRPA was still a port authority in name only. Maritime operations included a seasonal cruise terminal, a small multimodal cargo yard, and a ferry service, but otherwise the DRPA remained almost entirely a bridge and commuter rail operation. Together, the four toll bridges and the PATCO Speedline served as an integrated transportation system that brought workers from the New Jersey suburbs to their jobs in Philadelphia in the morning and back to their homes at night.

In 2010, the DRPA earned $275 million in operating income and incurred expenses of $202 million for a net operating income of $73 million. More important, a full 90 percent of operating income came from bridge tolls. An additional 9 percent came from PATCO fares, while maritime operations accounted for a scant one-tenth of 1 percent of operating income.

Like most governments, the DRPA effectively operates as a monopoly, so its bridge tolls are both a large and dependable revenue source and its bonds are a low-risk investment, together giving the agency enormous borrowing power. In 2010 the DRPA had about $1.4 billion in outstanding debt, backed primarily by future toll revenues. More important, periodic toll increases had a big effect on the agency's borrowing capacity, and the unique institutional character of the DRPA as a bistate public authority influenced the allocation of funds that flowed from these increases.

Unlike a municipality that provides a wide variety of tax-funded services and facilities, the DRPA has operated as a "public authority," a specific type of government created by legislators to provide a single service or facility, such as a highway, airport, maritime cargo port, or bridge. Authorities typically pay for these facilities with proceeds from the sale of "revenue bonds" that are backed by future rents, tolls, or other charges that will be paid by the people who use the facility. Because authorities typically do not rely on tax revenues, they can skirt public review of their projects, unlike municipalities that must seek voter approval of bonding bills to avoid claims of taxation without representation. Authorities are governed by appointed boards or commissions rather than by elected officials so their leadership typically is less sensitive to political pressures. Together, appointed leadership and the lack of a need to seek voter approval for projects makes authorities more politically insulated than other units of government.

But the DRPA is not just any authority; rather, in 2013 it was one of only four in the United States that enjoyed a "bistate" jurisdiction, with a service area of 5,840 square miles that included five counties in southeastern Pennsylvania and eight counties in southern New Jersey. A commission of sixteen leads the DRPA, eight commissioners from each state. In Pennsylvania, all but two commissioners are appointed by the governor, while in New Jersey, all eight are appointed by the governor. This division of the commission into two equal delegations ensures an unusual level of internal stability but it also virtually guarantees ongoing stress between the two delegations that stems from their different views of the DRPA's purpose and duties. These differences of opinion reflect the contrasting geographies and constituencies that the two delegations represent: suburban New Jersey bedroom communities filled with workers interested in a cheap commute to the city and densely developed Philadelphia, whose politicians have long thought that low tolls and fares promote the flight of businesses and residents to the suburbs.

Prior to commission meetings, the two delegations meet separately, in closed "executive" sessions, where they conduct most of their business out of the public's eye. Thus the public meetings of the full commission usually lack controversy or meaningful debate and serve instead as perfunctory events where agreements hashed out in private are merely finalized in public. The same process has typically been used to make spending decisions.

Because the governors of the two states are term-limited and gubernatorial politics are central to raising tolls and fares, the DRPA usually announces increases only every eight years, although the agency broke the pattern in 2011 when it increased tolls after only three years. But this puts stress on the agency's operating budget because revenues remain flat year-to-year, while annual operating costs continue to increase because of inflation. More important, new debt cannot be issued until there is a new source of future revenues to back it. When tolls do go up, however, the impact on borrowing can be huge. Each of the four times between 1992 and 2012 that the DRPA raised tolls on its four bridges by one dollar, the agency's bonding capacity—the amount it could borrow—rose by about a half billion dollars.

That meant that the commission's next job was to decide how and where to spend about $500 million dollars on economic development projects. The method was simple. The two delegations agreed to split the funds equally, half going to each side of the river. Then each delegation proposed a list of projects and values that added up to half the total amount of funds and the commission voted and approved all of the projects.

Between 1992 and 2001 alone the DRPA's debt grew by five times, from $250 million to $1.4 billion. During this period approximately $443 million in toll-backed proceeds from the sale of "Port Project Development Bonds" (PPDBs) were invested in economic development projects worth a total of $4.4 billion. Some of these funds were spent on job creation projects, including location subsidies to lure private shipbuilder Kværner to the Philadelphia Naval Shipyard after it closed in 1995, as well as patents for "FastShip" technology, support for a charter school, and expansion projects for several private manufacturing companies in Camden. Other funds were spent on waterfront redevelopment projects on both sides of the river including a ballpark, aquarium expansion, and a new DRPA headquarters building on the New Jersey riverfront; a new performing arts center, a new museum devoted to the U.S. Constitution, improvements to a science museum, and an aborted riverfront entertainment center on the Philadelphia side; and an aerial tram connecting the two cities across the river that was eventually canceled over a decade after its foundations had been poured in 2000 at a cost of $10 million.

A particularly interesting example is the DRPA's $50 million contribution—and one of its largest grants—to the nearly half billion dollars in government subsidies to Kværner. Despite being politically popular with Democrats and labor unions in Philadelphia, Kvaerner was used as an example in a 1998 *Time* magazine cover story about corporate welfare, in which the authors calculated that each new job at the Philadelphia Naval Shipyard cost $323,000 in subsidies to create. In a 2000 performance audit, Democratic state auditor general Robert Casey found that the location subsidies provided to Kvaerner by the state and other agencies grossly over-subsidized Kvaerner, which made only a relatively modest investment in the facility and bore very little risk.

The DRPA's challenges with economic development projects stem from a simple but important disconnect: Because the bridges generate substantial surpluses, the DRPA has been able to provide financial support in the form of loans, forgivable loans, and grants to projects that did not need to perform economically because their debt was backed by bridge tolls rather than by project income. This presented a two-edge sword, because while it allowed for the subsidization of worthy projects and initiatives, it also made it easier for commissioners to allocate money to questionable projects such as the tram and Kvaerner because the funds would be repaid whether or not the project was economically successful. At the policy level, the DRPA's spending decisions raised a recurring equity question, as the commuters who were required to pay higher and higher tolls and fares saw their money spent on facilities and programs that they might never use or benefit from and that were completely unrelated to the bridges. The lack of due diligence and controls to assure sound economic performance left the door open for poorly vetted pet projects that could and sometimes did embarrass the agency, cause needless distraction, and waste money that could have been spent on more worthwhile endeavors.

Infusions of huge amounts of cash every four or eight years, the lack of a connection between project funding and economic performance, and the perception of increased political insulation on the part of commissioners have also led to instances of inside dealing, cronyism, graft, and corruption. A remarkable case was that of DRPA commissioner and Pennsylvania state senator Vincent Fumo, who created a $40 million economic development fund fueled by toll revenues and directed at initiatives on the Pennsylvania side of the Delaware River. The supposed purpose of the fund was to offset disparities in spending between the two states resulting from cheap fares and tolls that benefited New Jersey. Instead, Fumo and a handful of close associates quietly spent all of the funds with little oversight and on projects of direct personal interest to the senator. In 2009, Fumo was convicted in federal court of 137 charges of corruption and sentenced to fifty-five months in prison for the illicit spending of public funds, including those of the DRPA.

By the twenty-first century, the DRPA had become a large and mature regional transportation agency successfully serving a densely populated region, but the divisions between its constituencies, governance structure, and bistate jurisdiction promoted conflicting ideas about its purposes. With its future as a port authority out of the question, the DRPA's dependable stream of toll revenues continued to support the new economic development powers that it was still learning to wield. Together, these unique tensions, powers, and limits continued to influence the operations, investment decisions, and evolution of the DRPA a hundred years after its creation.

Delaware Valley Regional Planning Commission

Dylan Gottlieb

The Delaware Valley Regional Planning Commission (DVRPC) was founded in 1965 to coordinate planning activities within a nine-county area, which included Philadelphia, Bucks, Montgomery, Chester, and

Delaware Counties in Pennsylvania and Camden, Burlington, Gloucester, and Mercer Counties in New Jersey. In the decades since its founding, DVRPC has worked to foster economic development, direct transportation projects, protect the natural environment, and study land use and housing conditions within the Greater Philadelphia metropolitan area. Throughout its history, DVRPC has tried to balance the needs of its urban centers with the growing power of its car-dependent suburbs.

In the early twentieth century, Philadelphia's regional planners advocated for an intentionally decentralized vision for metropolitan growth. Taking advantage of the expanding range and popularity of the automobile, they sought to alleviate the overcrowding of central cities by directing growth into the rural hinterland. In 1928, a coterie of Philadelphia-area power brokers—municipal reformers, corporations, planners, and real estate developers—created the region's first formal planning organization, the Regional Planning Federation of the Philadelphia Tri-State District. The federation's director, Russell Van Nest Black, drew up a utopian plan for the area. His proposal suggested the construction of newly built garden cities—planned, dense, self-contained communities—surrounded by parks and open space, to be connected to Philadelphia via rail and automobile. But these plans proved quixotic, hamstrung by a lack of funds and coordination between local, state, and federal governments.

All of that changed in the 1950s as the federal government made massive investments in the nation's highway system. The 1956 Federal-Aid Highway Act, which provided $25 billion toward the construction of new interstates, required the close synchronization of federal and state planners. As automobile use skyrocketed and government subsidies helped underwrite the construction of new suburbs, the need to harmonize the planning decisions of cities and surrounding counties became acute.

In 1959, the Penn Jersey Transportation Study brought together experts from nine area counties and local universities, under executive director Henry Fagin, to coordinate the region's implementation of the highway act's transportation initiatives. They sought answers to several key questions: Where would Pennsylvania and New Jersey build their interstate highways? How could the region optimize land use while maximizing economic development? What path might growth take, given different governmental policies, transportation decisions, corporate behavior, and market forces? The study also explored the possibility of creating a permanent organization to manage ongoing land use and transportation planning.

The direct impetus for the creation of the DVRPC was the 1962 Federal-Aid Highway Act. It mandated that all urbanized areas with populations over fifty thousand establish a metropolitan planning organization to direct the local expenditure of federal transportation and housing funds by means of a "continuing, comprehensive and cooperative" planning process. In response, the counties and cities that had participated in the Penn Jersey Transportation Study formed DVRPC by means of the Delaware Valley Urban Area Compact, which Pennsylvania's Governor Raymond Shafer signed into law on June 30, 1965. New Jersey officially joined the commission by ratifying companion legislation in 1967. The new commission included appointed representatives from each of the member states and counties and the cities of Camden, Philadelphia, Trenton, and Chester, along with New Jersey's commissioner of transportation and commissioner of community affairs, and Pennsylvania's secretary of highways and executive director of its State Planning Board.

DVRPC began work on its first regional long-range plan with an extensive series of aerial photographs. Beginning in 1959 and repeated every five years thereafter, flyovers were conducted across the 3,833-square-mile DVRPC region. These aerial photographs were used to document the chronological progression of area land use and economic growth. Survey by survey, photographs documented the spread of suburban development into the rural areas surrounding the region's urban centers. Aerial photography also had a powerful effect on planners' imaginations. Traditional political maps had encouraged parochialism by reinforcing the importance of municipal boundaries. But overhead photography demonstrated the region's interconnectedness. Roads, rail, and rivers seamlessly connected cities to suburbs, farms to factories, and ports to the sea. Viewing the Delaware Valley through these photographs, planners began to acquire a sense of the region as a coherent whole.

In the years to follow, that holistic vision fostered a newfound awareness of the environmental impact of urban development. After the passage of the National Environmental Policy Act in 1970, DVRPC began research on the region's air and water quality. It also assumed responsibility for water supply, natural resource, greenway, and solid waste planning. Later in the decade, DVRPC issued a region-wide watershed management plan to protect the area's surface and groundwater resources in accordance with the Clean Water Act of 1972.

DVRPC's scope extended beyond environmental, land use, and transportation planning. In the late 1960s, it turned its attention to historic preservation, which thereafter became a key factor in its comprehensive planning mission. DVRPC's 1969 report on historic preservation compiled the first master list of sites worthy of protection in its open space plans. DVRPC promoted historic designation for numerous historic structures—ones like the birthplace of James Fenimore Cooper in Burlington, New Jersey, and Frank Lloyd Wright's multifamily homes in Ardmore, Pennsylvania. DVRPC also emphasized the importance of historic sites to the tourism industry, which was expected to explode as visitors flocked to the region in 1976 for bicentennial celebrations.

In the 1980s, DVRPC issued sweeping reports that forecast future transportation needs. Using predictive modeling, these reports demonstrated the economic importance of expanded public transit and highway facilities. Long-term projections were instrumental in the construction of new roads—Interstate 476, Interstate 95, U.S. Route 422, New Jersey Route 55—which helped to accelerate growth in the region's suburbs. It also called for new rail lines, including the Center City Commuter Connection, which finally linked all of Philadelphia's major railroad stations when it was completed in 1984. DVRPC also began to encourage greater public participation, soliciting input from area citizens on its long-range plans. To formalize this process, it created the Regional Citizens Committee, which became an important—if sometimes contentious—forum for residents to comment on the DVRPC planning process.

During the 1990s, DVRPC's planning scope expanded considerably with passage of the 1991 Intermodal Surface Transportation Efficiency Act (ISTEA). It provided expanded federal funding for metropolitan planning organizations to establish more seamless connections between transportation modes—pedestrian, bicycle, transit, air, marine—not directly targeted by earlier highway-focused legislation. DVRPC incorporated these recommendations into their federally mandated Transportation Investment Program reports, which ranked hundreds of local transportation projects in order of priority. During the 1990s, DVRPC also issued reports on the region's housing supply, recommending that municipalities promote multifamily and rental construction to increase the availability of affordable housing. And DVRPC redoubled its environmental efforts, initiating a new air quality program and providing commuters with subsidies to encourage public transit ridership.

After the appointment of executive director Barry Seymour in 2006, DVRPC tried to balance auto-centric development with more progressive planning goals, including a focus on public transit and regional equity. As in previous years, suburban governments and developers resisted this shift toward urban-focused planning. Still, DVRPC's efforts included a regional food-system plan—the first by a metropolitan planning organization—that encouraged local stakeholders to improve foodsupply equity. It also invested in recreational facilities, including improved trail infrastructure for bicyclists and pedestrians. In 2011, DVRPC faced an internal controversy: it disbanded the long-standing Regional Citizens Committee (RCC) because of fierce infighting among its members. While it was replaced by the Public Participation Task Force, ex-members of the RCC lamented the commission's alleged unwillingness to consider public input.

In 2013, DVRPC issued a long-range plan for the region, *Connections 2040*, calling for continued investment in transportation infrastructure despite funding shortfalls. As DVRPC approached its fiftieth anniversary, its long-range plan echoed the same goals it had set forth at its founding: "creating livable communities, managing growth and protecting the environment, building the economy, and establishing a modern multimodal transportation system."

FIGURE 85. *The Delaware Water Gap,* by Thomas Doughty, 1827. PHILADELPHIA MUSEUM OF ART.

Delaware River Basin Commission

Gail Friedman

The four-state compact that established the Delaware River Basin Commission (DRBC) was a breakthrough innovation in addressing the impacts on both land and water resources when development spreads across multiple political jurisdictions. For the first time, the federal government and several states joined as equal partners in a single agency to regulate and develop the watershed of an entire river basin. Following its inception in 1961, the DRBC made significant progress toward meeting the environmental and political challenges that led to its founding, even as it grappled with emerging issues created by population growth, new technologies, and ecological change. In the process, it straddled the long-standing polarity between resource conservation, which allowed measured use, and preservation of natural resources in an untouched state.

The Delaware River is a key regional water resource spanning the boundaries of four states in the northeastern United States: Delaware, New Jersey, New York, and Pennsylvania. Established October 27, 1961, through concurrent legislation ratified by the four basin states and the federal government, the DRBC was formed to address the often-contentious planning, development, regulatory, and allocation issues posed by the expanse of the Delaware watershed (the area drained by the river). Among the issues prompting its founding were water supply shortages, pollution of the tidal Delaware in the urbanized stretch below Trenton, New

Jersey, and flooding spawned by the hurricanes of 1955. The first such federal-state partnership in the United States, the DRBC subsequently served as a national and international model.

The DRBC oversees the longest undammed river in the United States east of the Mississippi; the Delaware flows 330 miles from Hancock, in upstate New York, to the mouth of the Delaware Bay. As of 2016, more than fifteen million people (about 5 percent of the nation's population) relied on the waters of the Delaware River Basin for drinking, agricultural, commercial, and industrial use, although the river drains only 0.4 percent of the nation's continental land mass. A powerhouse of the regional economy, the basin supported the largest freshwater port in the world along with six hundred thousand jobs generating $10 billion in annual wages, according to a 2011 study.

Interstate wrangling over Delaware River water rights began in earnest as early as the 1920s, driven in large part by the water needs of the region's two largest cities, New York and Philadelphia. New York City, situated just outside the Delaware River Basin, sought to tap Delaware tributaries within New York State to fill its reservoirs, while Philadelphia, within the basin, was counting on the river's waters to meet its present and future needs. Efforts to reconcile competing demands for water, beginning as early as the 1920s, resulted in multiple failed attempts at an interstate compact, as well as litigation before the U.S. Supreme Court, as the three downstream states opposed New York City's efforts to divert water from the Delaware. Representatives of both New York City and Philadelphia took part in the negotiations that led to the creation of the DRBC.

At the same time, efforts by the federal government to establish national or regional water planning agencies had been rebuffed by states concerned that their water rights might be abridged. During the New Deal, the administration of Franklin D. Roosevelt created a National Resources Planning Board, but Congress quashed it in 1943 for fear of excessive centralization of power. Legislation establishing the DRBC compact was forged during the administration of President John F. Kennedy after months of fine-tuning to craft an agreement that would allow coordinated federal and state action in the river basin while addressing federal concerns about constitutionality and potential threats to jurisdiction and protecting state prerogatives in managing water and related land resources within their borders.

The pioneering interjurisdictional compact that replaced a patchwork of forty-three state agencies, fourteen interstate agencies, and nineteen federal agencies was termed by an article in the magazine of the American Water Resources Association "a regional body with the force of law to oversee a unified approach to managing a river system without regard to political boundaries." Under the water law doctrine of equitable apportionment, states have the right to a share of river water that originates within or flows through their terrain. Recognizing the need to manage resources throughout the entire Delaware watershed, the compact empowered the DRBC to allocate water supply, protect water quality, regulate water withdrawals and discharges, develop water conservation initiatives, create flow management policy, plan for water needs and recreation, and finance capital projects, programs, and operations through bond issuance and cost sharing.

Headquartered in West Trenton, New Jersey, the commission was one of the few basin management agencies to have regulatory, as well as planning and monitoring responsibilities. Key successes included improved water quality, implementation of an effective drought management policy, and comprehensive watershed planning. Much of the river was afforded special protection status, to preserve water quality, and was enrolled in the National Wild and Scenic River System to maintain its scenic nature.

The commission's membership, as defined by the compact, consisted of the governor of each of the basin states, plus a presidentially appointed federal representative (as of 2023, the U.S. Army Corps of Engineers' North Atlantic Division commander). Decisions were to be made by majority vote except for drought declarations or member funding quotas, which required unanimity. The initial term of the compact was one hundred years, renewable for a second century, unless any of the partners gave advance notice of intention to leave.

Along with interstate water rights litigation, a second prime impetus for creation of the DRBC was the planned implementation of the multimillion-dollar Tocks Island Dam project. The dam would have been built on the main stem of the river six miles upstream from New Jersey's Delaware Water Gap, on the northern tip of an island owned by the State of New Jersey, creating a lake forty miles long and up to 140 feet deep. It was ultimately rendered unbuildable by its scope and cost.

The multistate impacts of flooding spawned by two hurricanes in 1955 had cleared the way for federal involvement in Delaware River water affairs. The Senate directed the Army Corps of Engineers to prepare a comprehensive basin-wide resource management plan, which was funded by Congress as part of a massive public works bill, the Flood Control Act of 1962 (Pub. L. No. 87–874). The plan included the Tocks Island Dam as the centerpiece of a multipurpose reservoir project that had flood control, recreation, and hydropower generating components, initially estimated at a cost of $122.4 million. Almost 250 billion gallons of water were to be stored behind the dam. Another ten dams would have been built on Delaware River tributaries. A recreation area, later enlarged and known as the Delaware Water Gap National Recreation Area, was proposed to develop the recreation opportunities promised by the project.

Project costs began escalating almost as soon as the dam was approved, due to inflation, land acquisition prices, and construction issues. The DRBC was intended to serve as the local sponsor of the project on behalf of the four river states and would have owned most of the water behind the dam. Construction was supposed to start in 1967, with project completion scheduled for 1975, but the schedule was delayed by litigation and design problems.

The dam drew resistance first from residents whose property was taken by eminent domain and then from an environmental movement that steadily gathered force after the first Earth Day in April 1970. The plan foundered amid concerns about stagnant reservoir water, unstable geology, cost overruns, budget cuts due to spending on the Vietnam War, and the enactment of new, more stringent environmental regulations. The DRBC, long a proponent of the dam, in July 1975 voted three to one against starting construction, with Pennsylvania the only vote in favor. The federal government representative abstained.

But the dam remained nominally viable as a component of the DRBC Comprehensive Plan and for complex reasons related to land earmarked for the national recreation area, as well as the water supply and flood control issues the dam was supposed to address. Federal legislation to remove the project from the books failed several times during the mid- to late 1970s. It was not until 1992 that Congress formally deauthorized the Tocks Island project.

The DRBC's regulatory responsibilities again placed it in a key regional role in the early twenty-first-century controversy surrounding the practice of hydraulic fracturing, commonly known as fracking, the process of drilling into rock and injecting a pressurized liquid to extract gas or oil. About one-third of the Delaware River Basin, in Pennsylvania and New York, overlies the Marcellus Shale formation, which contains rich deposits of natural gas. Concentrated in southwestern and northeastern Pennsylvania, the state's fracking industry mushroomed, bringing with it revenue and jobs, but also environmental impacts that included noise, concrete well pads, pipelines, wastewater disposal, and deforestation. Faced with the looming expansion of fracking into the Delaware River watershed, the potential construction of a gas transport pipeline under the river, and opposition to fracking by compact member states Delaware and New York (the New Jersey legislature and the state's governor were at odds on the issue), the DRBC in 2010 issued a temporary stay on fracking, pending its enactment of regulations for gas production activities. In 2016, a federal lawsuit filed against the DRBC by landowners in Wayne County, Pennsylvania, who held fracking leases, claimed the agency lacked the power to regulate gas drilling. The suit was joined by three Republican Pennsylvania state senators, who claimed the DRBC had usurped authority already addressed under state regulations. That lawsuit ultimately failed, so the ban remained in place. In 2022, DRBC imposed further limitations by prohibiting the open discharge of wastewater remaining from the fracking process.

Born in litigation and political horse-trading, the DRBC more than a half century after its creation continued to struggle with its mandate of managing an essential natural resource transcending multiple state boundaries. Often a source of technical expertise and mediation in the ongoing process of maintaining adequate water quality and supply throughout the watershed, the DRBC's interjurisdictional regulatory and administrative powers nevertheless thrust it into the foreground in high-profile regional controversies with multiple constituencies, such as those surrounding Tocks Island and fracking. Despite the goal of those who intended the DRBC as a strong advocate and mediator for the river and its resources, the agency found its powers constrained by the complexity of the environmental regulatory system in which it operated, the often-conflicting interests of the many public and private stakeholders in the Delaware River Basin, and financial constraints stemming from the reluctance of its membership to fully fund its work.

SEPTA

John Hepp

The Southeastern Pennsylvania Transportation Authority (better known by its acronym SEPTA) is a state authority charged with funding and operating public transportation in the city of Philadelphia and surrounding counties of Bucks, Chester, Delaware, and Montgomery in Pennsylvania. From its creation in 1963, SEPTA often struggled with management issues, employee morale, strikes, aging equipment, inadequate funding, and poor public relations. Despite such challenges, at the close of the twentieth century SEPTA ranked as the sixth-largest transit agency in the United States in terms of weekly ridership of its complex system of subways, buses, trolleys, and commuter rail lines.

SEPTA is an example of the regional authorities formed to stem declines in urban public transportation nationwide after World War II. The need for a regional approach for Philadelphia and its suburbs developed in the 1950s as the area's largest provider of public transportation, the Philadelphia Transportation Company (PTC), declined financially and the two largest commuter rail providers (the Pennsylvania and Reading Railroads) threatened service cuts and fare increases. Philadelphia initially led the response in 1960 by subsidizing service and purchasing equipment for use on commuter rail lines in the city through a state-created but city-funded agency, the Passenger Service Improvement Corporation (PSIC). Philadelphia then joined with three of its four suburban counties to form the Southeastern Pennsylvania Transportation Compact (SEPACT) in 1961 to explore regional funding. Delaware County did not join the compact because the largest provider of transportation in the county was a private company that did not desire subsidies. Finally, Pennsylvania created SEPTA as a regional authority in 1963, and the SEPTA board (the existing SEPACT board plus representatives from Delaware County) held its first meeting on February 18, 1964.

Inherent in the way Pennsylvania founded SEPTA were two serious structural flaws that have caused political and operating issues for the authority. The SEPTA board has equal representation for each county, so although Philadelphia has the bulk of service and ridership, it has the same vote as each suburban county. This has created political friction between the suburban counties, which tend to emphasize regional rail, and the city, which seeks higher levels of service and lower fares across the board. As a creation of the State of Pennsylvania, SEPTA also has struggled to deal with the reality of operating in a tristate region. The agency offers few interline fares with transportation authorities in Delaware and New Jersey, and only Delaware has contributed to the costs of operating the regional rail system.

SEPTA took over the functions of SEPACT and PSIC in 1965 and the next year entered into comprehensive subsidy arrangements with the Pennsylvania and Reading Railroads. In 1968, it acquired the PTC and began operating public transportation services in the city and inner suburbs. Purchases of two private suburban companies in 1970 (Philadelphia Suburban Transportation, centered in Delaware County) and 1976 (Schuylkill Valley Lines with a hub in Norristown) completed SEPTA's first phase of acquisitions. This phase established SEPTA's initial structure: the bus, trolley, and subway lines operated by the authority with the commuter rail lines funded by SEPTA but operated by others (first the Pennsylvania and the Reading and, after 1976, Conrail).

In 1983, SEPTA was forced to take over the direct operation of the region's commuter rail lines by a federal law that allowed Conrail to withdraw from the operation of commuter trains. Because of poor planning by SEPTA, the transfer was extremely difficult and commuters suffered disruptions in service. Initially

FIGURE 86. Rerouted train commuters coming from SEPTA's Red Arrow Lines jam turnstile area at the Sixty-ninth Street terminal in Upper Darby as they head toward the Market-Frankford Elevated on their way to Center City, December 1970. SPECIAL COLLECTIONS RESEARCH CENTER, TEMPLE UNIVERSITY LIBRARIES.

SEPTA ceased all commuter trains in the region and then, under court order, restored limited service. Shortly thereafter, a three-month strike by the rail unions caused all service to be suspended again. With exceptions of the completion of the Center City Commuter Tunnel (linking the old Reading and Pennsylvania rail lines) in 1984 and the rail line to the airport in 1986, SEPTA's operation of commuter rail service became a story of service cutbacks, line abandonments, and fare increases.

It was not until the early twenty-first century that service and fares on the rail lines stabilized. As the second decade of the twenty-first century unfolded, SEPTA succeeded in increasing ridership, having replaced all its older railcars between 1973 and 2013, and improving its on-time performance. In fiscal 2013, total ridership was at 337.3 million trips, with an average weekday ridership of about 1 million trips. Despite this positive news, an increased operating deficit raised the possibility the system might have to shrink.

From its founding, SEPTA struggled with structural, funding, and management issues. In addition, as a creation of Pennsylvania, it has had difficulty serving a region that does not end at state lines. These issues, along with the growth of reverse commuting and labor strife, continued to challenge SEPTA and its riders in the early twenty-first century.

Philadelphia Regional Port Authority

Elizabeth M. Marcello

The Philadelphia Regional Port Authority, or PhilaPort, is an independent agency of the Commonwealth of Pennsylvania whose mandate is to govern port facilities and activities on the Pennsylvania side of the Delaware River. The river serves as a busy commercial highway and has supported the growth and development of Philadelphia since the early eighteenth century, well before the city and port were incorporated. While port governance has changed over the years, the port remains a significant economic engine for Philadelphia and its environs.

Since the founding of the city in 1682, Philadelphia's port has been a center of international commerce, enabling trade with distant markets in Europe and the Caribbean. William Penn incorporated the port at the same time as the city of Philadelphia in the charter of 1701. From the decades following its establishment through the first part of the twentieth century, the port operated under city supervision. The Department of Wharves, Docks, and Ferries, a division of the Philadelphia Department of Commerce, oversaw the construction and maintenance of piers and port facilities. The department's director was authorized to make surveys and soundings; prepare plans; regulate, fix, and establish bulkhead and pierhead lines and distances between piers; and set rules and regulations for wharves, piers, and bulkheads.

The building and maintenance of port facilities, however, was costly and a financial burden for the city. In 1965, Philadelphia separated the port from the annual city budget by creating the Philadelphia Port Corporation with authority to issue municipal bonds for the purpose of improving and expanding the port. The corporation serviced its debt by leasing the port facilities to private shipping and cargo companies. In addition to managing port facilities, the city's Port Corporation marketed the port.

By the late 1980s, the Port Corporation was not adequately managing its facilities. The city-run agency posted a $7 million operating deficit in 1988 and could not afford to repair existing facilities, much less invest in new ones. Aware of the city's inability to effectively manage the port, Mayor W. Wilson Goode Sr. asked the state to assume control.

In 1989, the Pennsylvania state legislature passed, and the governor signed, legislation creating the Philadelphia Regional Port Authority (PRPA). The new state-run authority freed Philadelphia from a multimillion-dollar drain on its annual budget, including port operating costs and debt service on bonds, while also making state funds available for capital and marketing projects at the port.

Enabled by the Philadelphia Regional Port Authority Act (Pub. L. 291, No. 50, Cl. 53) of 1989, PRPA was empowered to manage, lease, acquire, and own port facilities, port-related projects, and equipment within the port zone. The agency's jurisdiction ran along the Delaware River beginning with Pennsylvania's border with the state of Delaware in Delaware County, through Philadelphia County, ending in Upper Bucks County and encompassing up to a mile inland from the river. As with other port authorities, PRPA was authorized to borrow money, make and issue negotiable notes, bonds, and other evidences of indebtedness or obligations of the authority, and secure the payment of such bonds. PRPA also acquired the power of eminent domain and zoning supersession, which it can exercise when necessary to locate port facilities. The authority was granted such powers by the state legislature to ensure that Philadelphia's port could compete with other ports and provide economic-development benefits statewide. Its task was to enhancing trade and commerce along the Delaware River while also contributing to economic development and job creation.

In November 2016 Governor Tom Wolf unveiled a $300 million state investment to fix ship berths, buy new cranes, update and relocate warehouses, and double cargo-handling space. The investment, made possible by a bond, was expected to create two thousand waterfront jobs and nearly seven thousand jobs for truckers, rail workers, suppliers, and port-related businesses, as well as jobs for construction workers. The investment came at a time when competition among East Coast ports was particularly fierce in light of the Panama Canal expansion, completed in June 2016, that allowed larger ships to bring goods from Asia. The investment spearheaded a development plan and signaled the commonwealth's commitment to creating and maintaining a robust and efficient port.

The authority rebranded itself as PhilaPort in 2017. The port board of directors and staff felt that the authority needed a new, more memorable and recognizable name, particularly to distinguish it from the neighboring Delaware River and Bay Authority (DRBA) and the Delaware River Port Authority (DRPA). On the heels of the $300 million state investment, the name change was part of an aggressive effort to market Philadelphia to shippers around the world.

Its approach to economic development has been three-tiered. First, it has encouraged the use, growth, and development of its own terminal and port facilities. Second, it promotes ports within Pennsylvania. Third, it encourages the extensive use of the Delaware River. The port is responsible for thousands of direct jobs, such as those held by workers on docks, and indirect jobs that include warehouse employees in the Philadelphia area and throughout Pennsylvania. PhilaPort manages fifteen facilities: Tioga Marine Terminal, Tioga Liquid Bulk Terminal, 3200 E. Tioga, Piers 78 & 80, Pier 82, Pier 84, Piers 96, 98, & 100, Packer Avenue Marine Terminal, Pier 98 Annex, Pier 122, Pier 124, Southport Auto Terminal, PhilaPort Distribution Center, Philadelphia Wholesale Produce Market, and Citizens Bank Regional Maritime Training Center. PhilaPort is a "landlord port," meaning that it leases its facilities to private operators. In 2020, PhilaPort was the fourteenth-largest port in the country when measured by TEUs (twenty-foot equivalent units) handled, with 388,749 TEUs.

PhilaPort is governed by an eleven-person board of directors. Four board members are appointed by Pennsylvania's governor for a term of four years. One member is appointed by the president of the state senate for a term concurrent with the term of the appointing authority. One member is appointed by the speaker of the house of representatives, and another is appointed by the minority leader of the house of representatives, each for a term concurrent with the term of the appointing authority. Finally, the governor appoints three members, one from each of two lists prepared by (1) the mayor of Philadelphia and (2) the governing bodies of the counties within the port zone.

Investment in PhilaPort, in addition to the rebranding, was driven in large part by the dredging of the Delaware River. The decades-long plan to deepen 103 miles of the river along the Pennsylvania, New Jersey, and Delaware shoreline from forty to forty-five feet was completed in February 2020. Led by the United States Army Corps of Engineers, the project was devised to allow bigger ships, which were expected to be traveling from the expanded Panama Canal, to navigate the river more easily. Further, the deeper channel allowed for more efficient transportation of containerized, dry and liquid bulk, roll-on/roll-off, and project cargoes to and from Delaware River ports.

Officials at PhilaPort maintain relationships with other agencies and departments at various governmental levels. To market the Delaware River, PhilaPort coordinates with the port of Camden across the Delaware River; the Diamond State Port Corporation, which operates the port of Wilmington; and the Maritime Exchange for the Delaware River and Bay, which is a nonprofit trade association advocating for port and port-related business in the Delaware River region. To ensure that port operations run smoothly, the port also works with federal agencies including the United States Department of Transportation, United States Coast Guard, United States Army Corps of Engineers, United States Department of Homeland Security, and United States Customs and Border Protection.

EXPLORE MORE

Long before Europeans populated the region, it was home to a vast network of Lenni Lenape communities. Penn Treaty Park at 1301 N. Beach Street in the Fishtown section of North Philadelphia is the site of Lenape formal negotiations with Europeans. According to a long-standing legend, that is the spot where William Penn is said to have entered into a treaty of peace with a sachem (trusted spokesperson) of the Lenape Turtle Clan named Tamanend. For a deep dive into that famous meeting, see Albert Cook Myers, ed., *William Penn's Own Account of the Lenni Lenape or Delaware Indians* (Middle Atlantic Press, 1970). To learn about the Philadelphia park that commemorates the famed meeting, consult Kenneth W. Milano's book, *The History of Penn Treaty Park* (History Press, 2009). See Benjamin West's famous painting depicting Lenni Lenape leaders meeting with William Penn at the Pennsylvania Academy of the Fine Arts at 118–128 N. Broad Street, Philadelphia. Those who are willing to go further afield for evidence of Tamanend's legacy in the region can visit Southampton Township in Upper Bucks County to see the Tribute Rocks in Tamanend Park, where a cluster of weathered river boulders honors the Lenape leader and other members of his family.

Much can be learned about the role that the region's waterways played in the development of the region by visiting the Independence Seaport Museum at 211 S. Columbus Boulevard, which provides family-friendly exhibits about the Delaware River and the history of shipbuilding. It gives visitors a chance to visit a working boatbuilding shop. For scholars, the museum's J. Welles Henderson Research Center contains holdings covering the Delaware River watershed, the major commercial ports of Philadelphia, Camden, and Wilmington, and the maritime culture of the region. Peter Hendee Brown's *America's Waterfront Revival: Port Authorities and Urban Redevelopment* (University of Pennsylvania Press, 2009) puts the Camden and Philadelphia port authorities in a national context.

Philadelphia's most important shipbuilding was done at the Navy Yard located at the southern tip of the city, where both military and commercial vessels were produced starting in 1801. Throughout the nineteenth century the Navy Yard employed thousands of workers, operating as a U.S. naval base until 1996 when the federal government shut down its installation. Thomas Heinrich's *Ships for the Seven Seas: Philadelphia Shipbuilding in the Age of Industrial Capitalism* (Johns Hopkins University Press, 1997) describes the complex industry including the subcontracting networks spread out across the region. See also Jeffery M. Dorwart, with Jean K. Wolf, *The Philadelphia Navy Yard: From the Birth of the U.S. Navy to the Nuclear Age* (University of Pennsylvania Press, 2001). The city government opted to convert the navy installation to a corporate campus including offices, high-tech manufacturing, and homes and restaurants.

In Philadelphia and surrounding counties, the Delaware Valley Regional Planning Commission began in 2012 to assist a coalition of nonprofit organizations, foundations, and government to create a massive circuit of multiuse trails covering nine counties in Pennsylvania and New Jersey, and connecting people to jobs, communities, parks, and waterways. By 2023 the coalition had completed over 300 miles of the planned 750-mile regional network. Find a map and description that allows visitors to access this regional trail network at https://www.dvrpc.org/webmaps/thecircuit/.

Those who are interested in how regional coalitions and organizations pursue their work may want a first-hand view. Citizens can learn about—and sometimes influence—important nongovernmental organizations and authorities through public meetings. For example, members of the public are welcome at meetings of the Delaware Valley Regional Planning Commission. They can learn when DVRPC meetings are scheduled at https://www.dvrpc.org/calendar/. The Southeastern Pennsylvania Transportation Authority (SEPTA) Citizens Advisory Committee, established in 1967, serves as an advocate on behalf of the customers who use public transportation. Citizens who are interested in attending SEPTA's full board meetings can obtain information on SEPTA's website, https://www5.septa.org/about/boards/cac/. In 2010 the Delaware River Port Authority established its own Citizens Advisory Committee of twenty-four members, twelve each from

Pennsylvania and New Jersey, to hear from citizens who have a stake in the authority's day-to-day operations. That committee's monthly meetings are open to the public, and information is available at https://www.drpa.org/cac/. Hearings and business meetings of the Delaware River Basin Commission are also open to the public; dates for those public hearings and business meetings, as well as location information, are at https://www.nj.gov/drbc/meetings/upcoming/annual_dates.html. Many other nongovernmental organizations also offer information on their websites about when and how interested members of the public may participate.

Several of the essays in the Counties section of this volume emphasize the historical fragmentation of Greater Philadelphia into hundreds of small communities. That marked fragmentation has sometimes created frictions and inefficiencies hampering broad efforts to improve the lives of individuals and communities. But as the essays in this final section of the volume have shown, activists have often overcome that governmental fragmentation by building institutions capable of crossing local and county boundary lines. Such broad-based regional coalitions will become increasingly important in the twenty-first century, as the trend toward globalization elevates the importance of high-functioning metropolitan regions (not just central cities) as the geographical units that count most in global economic competition.

Contributors

Carolyn T. Adams, Emerita Professor and Dean of Liberal Arts at Temple University, has published a half-dozen books, including four focused on the Philadelphia region.

Fallon Samuels Aidoo, Ph.D., a preservation planner and architectural historian, researches, teaches, and advises urban design and development in places of Black, Indigenous, and immigrant settlement.

David Amott received his Ph.D. in architectural history at the University of Delaware. Currently, he serves as Executive Director of Preservation Utah, the oldest statewide nonprofit organization in the western United States.

John F. Bauman is Professor Emeritus at California University of Pennsylvania. He also taught at the University of Pittsburgh and the University of Southern Maine and has authored or co-authored several books, including *Public Housing, Race, and Renewal* (1987) and *Before Renaissance: Urban Planning in Pittsburgh, 1889–1943* (2006).

Jake Blumgart is a reporter for the *Philadelphia Inquirer.*

Peter Hendee Brown, FAIA, FAICP, PHD, is a Minneapolis-based development consultant, teacher, and the author of *How Real Estate Developers Think* (2015) and *America's Waterfront Revival* (2009).

Silas Chamberlin holds a doctorate in environmental history from Lehigh University and is author of *On the Trail: A History of American Hiking* (2016).

Michael J. Chiarappa is Research Professor of Chesapeake Regional Studies and Director of Cultural and Natural Resource Initiatives at Washington College's Center for Environment and Society.

William W. Cutler III is Professor of History Emeritus, at Temple University. His publications include *Parents and Schools: The 150-Year Struggle for Control in American Education* (2000).

Suzanne Lashner Dayanim holds a Ph.D. in geography and urban studies from Temple University and is currently on the faculty at West Chester University. Her research measures the value of community facilities to inner-ring suburban resilience.

Lu Ann De Cunzo, Ph.D. in American civilization and historical archaeology, is Professor of Anthropology at the University of Delaware. She researches lower Delaware Valley history and cultures.

Catherine D'Ignazio holds a Ph.D. in urban education from Temple University. She is an adjunct professor in gender studies at Rutgers University–Camden.

Bonny Beth Elwell is a Salem County historian and genealogist, serving on the board of several historical organizations and as editor of local history publications.

Bart Everts is a librarian at Rutgers University–Camden. His articles and reviews have appeared in *Library Journal, Pennsylvania History,* and other publications.

Jordan AP Fansler is a professor at Great Bay Community College in Portsmouth, N.H., where he studies the Atlantic world at its local levels through history and archaeology.

Bradley Flamm, Ph.D., is Director of the Office of Sustainability at West Chester University, a researcher and academic, and a resident of Northwest Philadelphia.

Gail Friedman is a public historian and retired city planner. She worked for sixteen years as a community planner in Bucks County, Pa. She now lives in North Carolina.

Stephanie Gamble received her Ph.D. from Johns Hopkins University in 2014 for her dissertation, "Capital Negotiations: Native Diplomats in the American Capital, 1789–1837." She is a librarian at Sidwell Friends School.

Howard Gillette, Jr. is Professor of History Emeritus at Rutgers University–Camden and co-editor of the Encyclopedia of Greater Philadelphia. He is the author of *Camden After the Fall* (2005) and *The Paradox of Urban Revitalization* (2022), among other works.

Dylan Gottlieb is an assistant professor at Bentley University. He works on the history of cities and capitalism in the twentieth-century United States.

Skylar Harris is Digitization and Metadata Coordinator for the Hagley Library. Her publications include contributions to *Pennsylvania History* and various reference works.

Tim Hayburn earned his Ph.D. in colonial American history from Lehigh University and currently serves as an evaluator at Western Governors University.

Andrew Heath teaches history at Sheffield University. He is the author of *In Union There Is Strength: Philadelphia in the Age of Urban Consolidation* (2019).

John Hepp is Emeritus Professor of History at Wilkes University, and he writes on social, economic, and technological change in urban settings since 1700.

Laura Turner Igoe, Ph.D., is Chief Curator at the James A. Michener Art Museum in Doylestown, Pa. She specializes in nineteenth-century American art and material culture and its engagement with environmental conditions and change.

Christopher F. Jones is Associate Professor of History at Arizona State University. He is author of *Routes of Power* (2014).

Alison Kreitzer, Ph.D., is a historian and an independent researcher. Her work focuses on twentieth-century American recreation and technology-centered hobbies, such as automobile racing.

Anne E. Krulikowski, Ph.D., teaches the American city and material culture studies at West Chester University. She has published on these topics and a history of West Chester University.

Elizabeth M. Marcello is based in New York City. Her scholarship concerns how public authorities fit into transparent and democratic planning and policy processes.

Robert J. Mason was a long-tenured professor of geography and environmental studies at Temple University, with interests in land use, environmental policy, and hazards in North America and East Asia.

Jodine Mayberry is a retired journalist. She was a legal writer and editor for West Publications, a division of Thomson Reuters, for eighteen years.

W. Barksdale Maynard is a lecturer at the University of Delaware and author of seven university press books on history, art, and architecture.

Lynn Miller is Professor Emeritus of Political Science at Temple University. In addition to his scholarly publications, he is the author of a novel and a memoir. He also exhibits his work as a painter.

Elizabeth Milroy is Professor Emerita of Art & Art History, Drexel University. She is the author of *The Grid and the River: Philadelphia's Green Places, 1682–1876* (2016).

Charlene Mires is Professor of History at Rutgers University–Camden and Editor-in-Chief of The Encyclopedia of Greater Philadelphia.

Michael Nairn is a landscape architect and faculty member of the Urban Studies Program at the University of Pennsylvania.

Stephen Nepa teaches history at Temple University and Moore College of Art and Design. A contributor to numerous books and journals, he lives in Philadelphia.

Abigail Perkiss is Associate Professor of History at Kean University, specializing in oral history, public humanities, and the recent past.

Terry L. Potter was Director of the J. Welles Henderson Research Center at the Independence Seaport Museum. She held a master's degree in American History from Rutgers University–Camden.

Mary Rizzo is Associate Professor of History at Rutgers University–Newark, where she specializes in twentieth-century U.S. cultural and urban history and public history.

Catharine Dann Roeber, Ph.D., is Interim Director of Academic Programs and Brock W. Jobe Associate Professor of Decorative Arts and Material Culture at Winterthur Museum, Garden & Library.

Andrew Slemmon is a graduate student in the Department of History at the University of Arizona.

Matthew Smalarz is Professor of History and Chair of General Education at Manor College. *Manor College* (2022), which is his first book, was published through Arcadia Publishing.

Robert F. Smith is Provost at Valley Forge Military College and author of the book *Manufacturing Independence: Industrial Innovation in the American Revolution* (2016).

Jean R. Soderlund is Professor of History Emeritus at Lehigh University and author of *Separate Paths: Lenapes and Colonists in West New Jersey* (2022).

Stephen T. Staggs, Ph.D., is a historian of early North America and author of *Calvinists and Indians in the Northeastern Woodlands* (2023).

Austin Stewart is currently serving as Visiting Professor of History and Native American Studies at Northland College in Ashland, Wis.

Cameron B. Strang is Associate Professor of History at the University of Nevada, Reno.

David Sullivan is a retired assistant managing editor at the *Philadelphia Inquirer.*

Mark L. Thompson is the author of *The Contest for the Delaware Valley: Allegiance, Identity, and Empire in the Seventeenth Century* (2013). He teaches at the University of Groningen.

Penelope S. Watson is an architect with Watson & Henry Associates in Greenwich, N.J., specializing in historic preservation.

Stephanie Grauman Wolf, a retired professor of history at the University of Delaware, was Director of the Winterthur Program and the McNeil Center for Early American Studies.

James J. Wyatt is Assistant Director at the National Archives and Records Administration's Center for Legislative Archives and a past president of the Association of Centers for the Study of Congress.

Mary Yee, Ed.D., is an urban planner and educational researcher who has worked extensively to ensure the rights of immigrant and refugee communities in education and neighborhood development.

Matthew A. Zimmerman earned his Ph.D. in history at Lehigh University and is currently Chair of the Department of History at Middle Georgia State University.

Subject Index

A

B

C

D

E

F

G

H

I

J

K

L

M

N

O

P

Q

R

S

T

U

V

W

Y

Z

Place Index

A

B

C

D

E

F

M

N

O

P

Q

R

S

T

U

V

W

Y

Biographical Index

D

E

F

G

H

I

J

K

L

Y

Z

Acknowledgments

This book would not be possible without the many years of effort by individuals, associations, and funders associated with *The Encyclopedia of Greater Philadelphia* project. Preliminary plans for an encyclopedia of Philadelphia were discussed at the University of Pennsylvania Press as early as 2000. Then conceived as a print volume, the idea revived during 2007 among individuals involved in commemorating the twenty-fifth anniversary of *Philadelphia: A 300-Year History* with a special issue of the *Pennsylvania Magazine of History and Biography* (October 2007) and an event at the Historical Society of Pennsylvania (HSP). *PMHB* editor Tamara Gaskell and the special issue guest editor, Charlene Mires, worked together to initiate these projects, with the cooperation of the Barra Foundation and HSP. Mires encouraged historian Gary Nash to mention the prospect of an encyclopedia as a new initiative for Philadelphia history in his historiographical essay in the special issue, a call he amplified in his featured address at the HSP event.

The University of Pennsylvania Press subsequently enlisted three Philadelphia-area scholars to serve as general editors and leaders of the project: Charlene Mires, then of Villanova University; Howard Gillette of Rutgers University–Camden, then the director of thwe Mid-Atlantic Regional Center for the Humanities (MARCH); and Randall Miller of Saint Joseph's University. Gillette's influence broadened the project's focus from the city of Philadelphia to the region at large. The project began in earnest in April 2009 with a two-day Civic Partnership and Planning Workshop, and public engagement continued through a series of Greater Philadelphia Roundtable discussion programs, thematic essays copublished with WHYY and the *Philadelphia Inquirer*, teachers' workshops in collaboration with public history partners, and an online invitation for nomination of topics.

In 2010, the Mid-Atlantic Regional Center for the Humanities at Rutgers–Camden became the project's home after Mires succeeded Gillette as the center's director. Guided by public input and advice from potential funders, the project evolved from the concept of a book with companion website (the model of *The Encyclopedia of Chicago*, 2004) to a digital platform envisioned as aggregating and disseminating knowledge in a variety of ways. The project grew topic by topic online, making possible the set of thematic books now published with the University of Pennsylvania Press. Readers are encouraged to visit the digital encyclopedia, https://philadelphiaencyclopedia.org/, to explore topics beyond the scope of the present volume and to read new topics as they appear.

The Encyclopedia of Greater Philadelphia TEAM, 2009–23 (CUMULATIVE LIST)

EDITOR-IN-CHIEF: Charlene Mires.

CO-EDITORS:
Howard Gillette, Randall Miller, Tamara Gaskell.

CONSULTING EDITORS:
Gary Nash, Emma Lapsansky-Werner.

ASSOCIATE EDITORS:
Carolyn Adams, William W. Cutler III, Andrew Heath, Tyler Hoffman, Hillary Kativa, Cyril Reade, Nancy Rosoff, Philip Scranton, Jean R. Soderlund, Domenic Vitiello, Stephanie Grauman Wolf.

EDITORIAL, TECHNICAL, AND EDUCATIONAL ADVISERS:
Eugenie Birch, Vibiana Bowman Cvetkovic, Richardson Dilworth, Travis DuBose, Charles Hardy, Amy Hillier, Ken Hohing, Guian McKee, Alexis Moore, Elizabeth Nash, Richard Newman, Daniel Richter, Mary Rizzo, Lori Shorr, George Thomas, Zara Wilkinson, Kathryn Wilson, Rebecca Yamin.

MANAGING EDITORS:
Donald D. Groff, Hillary Kativa (books).

PRODUCTION EDITORS:
Lucy Davis, Luther Hoheisel.

EDITORIAL ASSISTANTS:
Tia Antonelli, Lucy Davis, Joshua DiPrima, Luther Hoheisel, Hannah Lee, Mikaela Maria, Gina Torres.

COPY EDITORS:
Donald D. Groff, Lauren Cooper, Lucy Davis.

MAPPING:
Michael Siegel, Department of Geography, Rutgers University.

DIGITAL MEDIA COORDINATORS:
Sharece Blakney, McKenna Britton, Audrey Johnson, Scott AlHearn, Jennifer Long Levy, Amy Osterhout.

ADMINISTRATIVE COORDINATOR: Sharon Smith.

RESEARCH, DIGITAL PUBLISHING, AND FACT-CHECKING ASSISTANTS:
Tia Antonelli, Kelly Banks, William Bartleson, Sharece Blakney, Brandon Borrelli, McKenna Britton, Melissa Bryson, Melissa Callahan, Vincent Cammarota, Kimberly Coulter, Amanda Cross, Lucy Davis, Joshua DiPrima, Elizabeth Eimer, Olivia Errico, Sabrina Gonzalez-Morabito, Scott Hearn, Luther Hoheisel, Fatima Ijaz, Audrey Johnson, William Krakower, Sebastian LaVergne, Hannah Lee, Joshua Lisowski, Mandi Magnuson-Hung, Mikaela Maria, Daniel Marren, Thomas McPherson, Maggie Montalto, Arthur Murphy, Andin Ncho, Darragh Nolan, Alaina Noland, Miriam Parrotto, Victoria Scannella, Nicole Skalenko, Benjamin Thompson, Gina Torres, Kevin Wakefield, Quincy Wansel, Mariam Williams, Emily Winters, Victoria Wroblewski, and additional students in publishing and editing seminars taught by Carol Singley at Rutgers–Camden.

WEBSITE DEVELOPMENT:
Azavea (Brian T. Jacobs), Roy Rosenzweig Center for History and New Media (Ken Albers), Rutgers Web Consulting Services (Ivanok Tavarez, Bart Grebowiec).

CIVIC AND ARCHIVAL PARTNERS:
African American Museum in Philadelphia, American Philosophical Society, Association of Philadelphia Tour Guides, Athenaeum of Philadelphia, Avenging the Ancestors Coalition, Camden County Historical Society, City of Philadelphia Department of Records, City of Philadelphia Mural Arts Program, Eastern State Penitentiary Historic Site, Economy League of Greater Philadelphia, Fels Institute of Government, Foundations of the Union League, Free Library of Philadelphia, Friends of Laurel Hill Cemetery, Global Philadelphia Association, Greater Philadelphia Tourism Marketing Corporation (Visit Philadelphia), Historic Germantown, Historical Society of Pennsylvania, Independence Hall Association, Independence National Historical Park, Independence Seaport Museum, International Visitors Council, Library Company of Philadelphia, National Archives–Mid-Atlantic Region, National Constitution Center, National Museum of American Jewish History, Philadelphia Consortium of Special Collections Libraries, Philadelphia History Museum, Philadelphia Museum of Art, Preservation Alliance for Greater Philadelphia, Temple University Libraries, WHYY, Young Involved Philadelphia.

FUNDERS:
Barra Foundation, Mayor's Fund for Philadelphia, Mid-Atlantic Regional Center for the Humanities, National Endowment for the Humanities, Pennsylvania Humanities Council, Pew Center for Arts and Heritage, Poor Richard's Charitable Trust, Rutgers–Camden Dean of Arts and Sciences, Rutgers–Camden Digital Studies Center, Rutgers Research Council, William Penn Foundation, University of Pennsylvania Press, and generous individual donors.